JUDITH FLANDERS

The Invention of Murder

How the Victorians Revelled in Death and
Detection and Created Modern Crime

Harper
Press

Harper*Press*
An imprint of HarperCollins*Publishers*
77–85 Fulham Palace Road,
Hammersmith, London W6 8JB
www.harpercollins.co.uk

Visit our authors' blog: www.fifthestate.co.uk
Love this book? www.bookarmy.com

First published in Great Britain by Harper*Press* in 2011

A catalogue record for this book
is available from the British Library

ISBN 978-0-00-724888-9

Typeset in Minion by G&M Designs Limited,
Raunds, Northamptonshire
Printed and bound in Great Britain by
Clays Ltd, St Ives plc

Mixed Sources
Product group from well-managed
forests and other controlled sources
www.fsc.org Cert no. SW-COC-001806
© 1996 Forest Stewardship Council
FSC

FSC is a non-profit international organisation established to promote the
responsible management of the world's forests. Products carrying the FSC
label are independently certified to assure consumers that they come
from forests that are managed to meet the social, economic and
ecological needs of present or future generations.

Find out more about HarperCollins and the environment at
www.harpercollins.co.uk/green

For Susan and Ellen
without whom …

CONTENTS

TEXT ILLUSTRATIONS

of Bonny Black Bess. (Theatre & Performance Collection, Victoria and Albert Museum, London/© V&A Images)

'"Parties" for the gallows', *Punch* cartoon, 1845.

'Interior of the court-house, during the trial of Rush – examination of Eliza Chestney', from the *Illustrated London News*, 7 April 1849. *(Mary Evans Picture Library)*

'See, dear, what a sweet doll Ma-a has made for me', *Punch* cartoon, 1850.

'Madame Tussaud her wax werkes: ye Chamber of Horrors!!', *Punch* cartoon, 1849.

'Execution of the Mannings', broadside of 1849. *(Bodleian Library, University of Oxford: John Johnson Collection/JJ Crime 2[5])*

'The Telegraph Office', from *The Progress of Crime: or, Authentic Memoirs of Marie Manning* by Robert Huish, 1849. *(© The British Library Board. All rights reserved 2011)*

'Awful Murder of Lord William Russell, MP', broadside of 1840. *(Bodleian Library, University of Oxford: John Johnson Collection/JJ Broadsides: Murder & Executions Folder 10[29])*

Advertisement for Dr. Mackenzie's Arsenical Toilet Soap, 1898.

'Sarah Chesham's Lamentation', broadside of c.1851. *(Bodleian Library, University of Oxford: Firth c.17[261])*

'Fatal facility; or, Poisons for the asking', *Punch* cartoon, 1849.

Thomas Griffiths Wainewright, self-portrait, from *Janus Weathercock* by Jonathan Curling, 1938.

'Drs. Taylor and Rees performing their analysis', from *Illustrated and unabridged edition of the Times report of the trial of W. Palmer for poisoning J.P. Cook*, 1856. *(© The British Library Board. All rights reserved 2011)*

'The Life, Confession and Execution of Mrs. Burdock', broadside of 1835. *(© The British Library Board. All rights reserved 2011)*

'Copy of Verses on the Awful Murder of Sara Hart', broadside of 1845. *(© The British Library Board. All rights reserved 2011)*

Execution of Henry Wainwright, from *Supplement to the Illustrated Police News*, 21 December 1875. *(Guildhall Library, City of London/The Bridgeman Art Library)*

William Terriss and W.L. Abingdon in *The Fatal Card*, 1894. *(Theatre & Performance Collection, Victoria & Albert Museum, London/© V&A Images)*

'Murder and mutilation of the body', from *The Alton Murder! The Police News edition of the life and examination of Frederick Baker*, 1867. *(© The British Library Board. All rights reserved 2011)*

'"Scott", alias E. Sweeney, of Ardlamont mystery fame', from the *Graphic*, 14 April 1849. *(Mary Evans Picture Library)*

Portrait of Mary Eleanor Wheeler (alias Pearcey), pencil, pen and ink drawing by Sir Leslie Ward, 1890. *(© National Portrait Gallery, London)*

'Removing Lipski from under the bed', from the *Illustrated Police News*, 9 July 1887.

'Horrible London; or, The pandemonium of posters', *Punch* cartoon, 1888.

'With the Vigilance Committee in the East End', from the *Illustrated London News*, 13 October 1888. *(Mary Evans Picture Library)*

Advertisement for 'The Great Surprise Watch' from M.J. Haynes & Co.'s Specialities,1889. *(© The British Library Board. All rights reserved 2011)*

PLATES

'The Red Barn', Staffordshire Potteries model c.1828. *(Courtesy of Bonhams 1793 Ltd)*

'W. Corder and M. Marten', Staffordshire Potteries model c.1828. *(Courtesy of Bonhams 1793 Ltd)*

'W. Corder before the judge', Staffordshire Potteries model c.1828. *(Courtesy of Bonhams 1793 Ltd)*

Plate from *Wretch's Illustrations of Shakespeare* by R.H. Nimmo, 1829. *(© The British Library Board. All rights reserved 2011)*

'The Lancett Club at a Thurtell Feast', ink and watercolour over pencil by Thomas Rowlandson, c.1824. *(Clements C. Fry Collection, Harvey Cushing/John Hay Whitney Medical Library, Yale University, New Haven, CT)*

Profile of John Thurtell, pen and ink drawing by William Mulready, 1824. *(Victoria and Albert Museum, London/© V&A Images)*

Portrait of Joseph Hunt, pencil drawing by William Mulready, 1824. *(Victoria and Albert Museum, London/© V&A Images)*

Stage set for the 1833 Surrey Theatre production of *Jonathan Bradford! or, The Murder at the Roadside Inn. (Theatre & Performance Collection, Victoria and Albert Museum, London/© V&A Images)*

Mixed playbill for the Royal Pavilion Theatre, March 1844, including *Jonathan Bradford!. (Theatre & Performance Collection, Victoria and Albert Museum, London/© V&A Images)*

Past and Present (triptych), oil on canvas by Augustus Leopold Egg, 1858. *(© The Tate Gallery, London 2011)*

Toy theatre characters from *Oliver Twist*, published by Benjamin Pollock. *(Bodleian Library, University of Oxford: John Johnson Collection/JJ Miniature Theatre 3[7a])*

Toy theatre characters from *Oliver Twist*, published by Benjamin Pollock. *(Bodleian Library, University of Oxford: John Johnson Collection/JJ Miniature Theatre 3[14])*

Toy theatre characters from *The Maid and the Magpye*, published by Benjamin Pollock. *(Bodleian Library, University of Oxford: John Johnson Collection/JJ Miniature Theatre 2[49])*

Scene from the 1873 Lyceum Theatre production of *Eugene Aram*. *(Theatre & Performance Collection, Victoria and Albert Museum, London/© V&A Images)*

Sir Henry Irving as Mathias in *The Bells* by Leopold Lewis, Lyceum Theatre 1871. *(London Stereoscopic Company/Getty Images)*

Title page for the sheet music for *The Colleen Bawn Galop*, c.1861. *(Special Collections, Templeman Library, University of Kent, Canterbury)*

Title page for Purkess's Penny Pictorial Play, *The Colleen Bawn, or, The Collegian's Wife. (Special Collections, Templeman Library, University of Kent, Canterbury)*

Medal struck to commemorate the hanging of James Blomfield Rush, 1849. *(Ashmolean Museum, Oxford)*

Mixed playbill for the Pavilion Theatre, September 1854, including *Eliza Fenning, The Persecuted Servant Girl!. (Theatre & Performance Collection, Victoria and Albert Museum, London/© V&A Images)*

Waxwork model of Maria Manning. *(© Madame Tussauds Attractions)*

Maria Manning, pen and ink drawing by William Mulready, September 1849. *(Victoria and Albert Museum, London/© V&A Images)*

Waxwork model of Frederick Manning. *(© Madame Tussauds Attractions)*

Frederick Manning, pen and ink drawing by William Mulready, September 1849. *(Victoria and Albert Museum, London/© V&A Images)*

William Palmer's poisons box. *(© Madame Tussauds Attractions)*

Mourning card for John Parsons Cook. *(© Madame Tussauds Attractions)*

Madeleine Smith, 1859. *(Courtesy of the Mitchell Library, Glasgow)*

Adelaide Bartlett, 1886. *(Russell & Sons/Getty Images)*

Constance Kent, 1860. *(Mary Evans Picture Library)*

Madame Tussaud's set for Mrs Pearcey from the 1970s. *(© Madame Tussauds Attractions)*

The restored Hogg baby bassinette. *(© Madame Tussauds Attractions)*

Richard Mansfield as Dr Jekyll and Mr Hyde, 1888. *(Pach Brothers/ Library of Congress)*

Shocking Murders in Whitechapel, broadside of 1888. *(Bodleian Library, University of Oxford: Harding b.20[196])*

A NOTE ON CURRENCY

Pounds, shillings and pence were the divisions of British currency in the nineteenth century. One shilling was made up of twelve pence; one pound of twenty shillings, i.e. 240 pence. Pounds were represented by the £ symbol, shillings as 's.', and pence as 'd.' (from the Latin *denarius*). 'One pound, one shilling and one penny' was written as £1.1.1. 'One shilling and sixpence', referred to in speech as 'One and six', was written as 1s.6d., or '1/6'.

A guinea was a coin to the value of £1.1.0 (the coin was not circulated after 1813, although the term remained and tended to be reserved for luxury goods). A sovereign was a twenty-shilling coin, a half-sovereign a ten-shilling coin. A crown was five shillings, half a crown 2/6, and the remaining coins were a florin (two shillings), sixpence, a groat (four pence), a threepenny bit (pronounced 'thrup'ny'), twopence (pronounced 'tuppence'), a penny, a halfpenny (pronounced hayp'ny), a farthing (a quarter of a penny) and a half a farthing (an eighth of a penny).

Relative values have altered so substantially that attempts to convert nineteenth-century prices into contemporary ones are usually futile. However, the website http://www.ex.ac.uk/~RDavies/arian/current/howmuch.html is a gateway to this complicated subject.

'We are a trading community – a commercial people. Murder is, doubtless, a very shocking offence; nevertheless, as what is done is not to be undone, let us make our money out of it.'

'Blood', *Punch*, 1842

ONE

Imagining Murder

'Pleasant it is, no doubt, to drink tea with your sweetheart, but most disagreeable to find her bubbling in the tea-urn.' So wrote Thomas de Quincey in 1826, and indeed, it is hard to argue with him. But even more pleasant, he thought, was to read about someone else's sweetheart bubbling in the tea urn, and that, too, is hard to argue with, for crime, especially murder, is very pleasant to think about in the abstract: it is like hearing blustery rain on the windowpane when sitting indoors. It reinforces a sense of safety, even of pleasure, to know that murder is possible, just not here. At the start of the nineteenth century, it was easy to think of murder that way. Capital convictions in the London area, including all the outlying villages, were running at a rate of one a year. In all of England and Wales in 1810, just fifteen people were convicted of murder out of a population of nearly ten million: 0.15 per 100,000 people. (For comparison purposes, in Canada in 2007–08 the homicide rate was 0.5 per 100,000 people, in the EU, 1.8 per 100,000, in the USA 2.79, while Moscow averaged 9.6 and Cape Town 62 per 100,000.)

Thus, when on the night of 7 December 1811 a twenty-four-year-old hosier named Timothy Marr, his wife, their baby and a fourteen-year-old apprentice were all found brutally murdered in their shop on the Ratcliffe Highway in the East End of London, the cosy feeling evaporated rapidly. The year 1811 had not been kind to the working classes. The French wars had been running endlessly, and with Waterloo four years in the future, there was no sense that peace – and with it prosperity – would ever return. Instead hunger was

1

ever-present: the wars and bad harvests had savagely driven up the price of bread. In the early 1790s wheat had cost between 48*s*. and 58*s*. a quarter; in 1800 it was 113*s*.

The murder of the Marrs, however, was more dramatic than the slow deaths of so many from hunger, or the faraway deaths of soldiers and sailors in unending war, and the story was soon everywhere. The Ratcliffe Highway was a busy, populous working-class street in a busy, populous working-class area near the docks. At around midnight on the evening of his death, Marr was ready to shut up shop. (Working-class shops regularly stayed open until after ten, to serve their clientele on their way home after their fourteen-hour workdays. On Saturdays, pay day, many shops closed after midnight.) The hosier sent his servant, Margaret Jewell, to pay an outstanding bill at the baker's, and to buy the family supper. After paying the bill she looked for an oyster stall. Oysters were a common supper food, being cheap, on sale at street stalls and needing no cooking. The first stall she came to had shut up for the night, and looking for another she lost her bearings – before gas lighting streets had only the occasional oil lamp in a window to guide passers-by – and was away for longer than expected, returning around 1 a.m.* She knocked; knocked again. She heard scuffling, someone breathing on the other side of the door, but no one opened it. She stopped the parish watchman on his rounds, telling him she knew the Marrs were in, she had even heard them, but no one was answering the door. He had passed by earlier, he said, and had tapped on the window to tell Marr that one of his shutters was loose. A man had called out, 'We know it!' Now he wondered who had spoken.

Their talking attracted the attention of Marr's next-door neighbour, a pawnbroker. From his window he could see that the Marrs'

---

* Even a decade later, after the arrival of some gas lighting, the streets were still darker and more confusing than can be imagined today. In 1822 Daniel Forrester, a detective for the City of London, became involved in a street fracas. It was only when he got the man who rescued him under a street lamp that he realized it was his own brother. With streets as dark as that, it is not surprising that 'One gas light is as good as two policemen' was a common maxim.

back door was open. With the encouragement of the neighbours and the watchman, he climbed the fence between the houses and entered (some reports say it was the watchman who entered). Whichever man it was, once inside he found a scene from a horror film. Marr and his apprentice were lying in the shop, battered to death. The apprentice had been attacked so ferociously that fragments of his brains were later found on the ceiling. Blood was everywhere. Mrs Marr was lying dead halfway to the door leading downstairs. The pawnbroker staggered to the front door, shouting, 'Murder – murder has been done!' and the watchman swung his rattle to summon help. Soon an officer from the Thames Division Police Office appeared. Meanwhile Margaret Jewell rushed in with a group of excited bystanders, looking for the baby. They found him lying in his cradle in the kitchen, his throat cut. Some money was scattered on the shop counter, but £150 Marr had tucked away was untouched. On the counter lay an iron ripping chisel, which seemed not to have been used; in the kitchen, covered with blood and hair, was a ship's carpenter's peen maul – a hammer with sharpened ends. A razor or knife must have been used on the baby, but none was found. Outside the back door were two sets of bloody footprints, and a babble of voices reported that a couple of men, maybe more, no one was quite sure, had been seen running away from the general direction of the Marrs' house at more or less the right time.

In the morning, a magistrate from the Thames Division Police Office took over the case. An officer from the Thames Division Police Office had responded the night before, and therefore the magistrates at the Thames Office were now in charge. A magistrate ordered the printing of handbills offering a reward, and visited the site of the murder, where the bodies lay where they had fallen the night before.

He was not the only one. What might be termed murder-sightseeing was a popular pastime, and many went 'from curiosity to examine the premises', where they entered 'and saw the dead bodies'. Inquests were held as quickly as possible after the event, usually at a public house or tavern near the scene of the crime. The bodies were left *in situ* for the jury to view. Until they had been, visitors traipsed through the gore-spattered rooms, peering not only at the blood splashes and other grisly reminders of the atrocity, but also at the bodies themselves.

For those who wanted a tangible souvenir, there were always broadsides, which were swiftly on sale on street corners. Broadsides had been around since the sixteenth century, but modern technology made their production easier, cheaper and quicker, and their distribution more widespread. A typical broadside was a single sheet, printed on one side, which was sold on the street for ½*d*. or 1*d*. Broadsides had their heyday before the 1850s, when newspapers were expensive. Most commonly, sheets were produced sequentially for each crime that caught the public's imagination: the first report of the crime, with further details as they were revealed; the magistrates' court hearing after an arrest; then the trial; and finally, and most profitably, a 'sorrowful lamentation' and 'last confession', usually combined with a description of the execution. These 'lamentations' and execution details were almost always entirely fabricated for commercial reasons: they found their readiest sale at the gallows, while the body was still swaying. For those who could not find a penny, pubs and coffee houses pinned up broadsides of popular crimes, to be read by customers as they drank. Other broadsides appeared in shop windows, frequently attracting crowds of bloodthirsty children.

One broadside, published before the Marrs' inquest, which opened three days after the murders, reported that 'the perpetrators are foreigners', which could have done little to reassure readers in this dockyard area of town, filled with sailors from across the world. Another spent less time on the possible murderer, and more on the gory details and the rumours that were prevalent: that Mrs Marr had, several months before, discharged a servant for theft. 'Words arose, when the accused girl is said to have held out a threat of murder. Mrs. Marr … gently rebuked her for using such language'; later Mrs Marr 'remonstrated with her on her loose character and hasty temper'. Anyone with a penny to spare would get a fair idea of the crime and the latest news of the search for the murderer.

Those with a few more pennies could buy a pamphlet on the subject. These were available nearly as swiftly as the broadsides. One covered all the details of the inquest, so it was probably on sale within five days of the deaths. While the pamphlets looked more substantial at eight pages, much of their information was identical to that in the broadsides. In some, such similar wording is used that either they must have shared an author, or one was copied from the other. Mrs Marr again sacks her servant, who 'is said to have held out a threat of murder. Mrs. Marr ... gently rebuked her for using such language'; later she again 'remonstrated with her on her loose character and hasty temper'. Now, however, we get the additional detail that the servant was leading a 'prostituted life'. This is reinforced by a description of her clothes: 'a white gown, black velvet spencer [jacket], cottage bonnet with a small feather, and shoes with Grecian ties'. No servant could afford such fashionable items: they were signs that her money was earned immorally.

Another way to savour the thrill of murder was to attend the funerals of the victims. Many people did so out of respect, as friends or as members of the same community. But far more did so out of curiosity. Still more read about them afterwards. Even four hundred miles away the *Caledonian Mercury* gave a detailed account of the funeral of the murdered apprentice: its readers were able to follow the precise path of the cortège as it travelled 'from Ratcliffe-highway, through Well-close-square, up Well-street, to Mill-yard'. In Hull too newspaper readers followed the crowds that turned out for the Marrs' triple funeral: 'The people formed a complete phalanx from the [Marrs'] house to the doors of St. George's church.' The church itself was so crowded that the funeral procession could only enter 'with some difficulty'. Then the paper gave the order of the procession, as was normally done for royal weddings and funerals, or the Lord Mayor's parade:

> The body of Mr. Marr;
> The bodies of Mrs. Marr and infant;
> The father and mother of Mr. Marr;

The mother of Mrs. Marr;

The four sisters of Mrs. Marr;

The only brother of Mr. Marr …

The friends of Mr. and Mrs. Marr.

Newspapers churned out stories, handbills circulated, witnesses were questioned. But none of this got any closer to finding the murderer or murderers. Then, like a recurring nightmare, twelve days after the Marrs' deaths it all happened again. On 19 December a watchman found John Turner, half-dressed and gibbering with fear, scrambling down New Gravel Lane, a few hundred yards from the Ratcliffe Highway. He had gone to bed early at his lodgings above a public house. After closing time he heard screaming and he went part-way down the stairs, where he saw a stranger bending over a body on the floor. After a panicky attempt to leave via the skylight (he was so frightened he couldn't find it), Turner tied his bedsheets together and

The funeral of the murdered Marr family as it processed through the East End. The funeral mutes with their staffs and the coffins topped by plumes were watched by residents lined all the way along the route, which had been publicized by the newspapers.

THE FUNERAL OF THE MURDERD MR. AND MRS. MARR AND INFANT SON

6

slid out of the window into the yard, shouting, 'They are murdering the people in the house!' The watchman was quickly joined by neighbours, and they broke in through the cellar door to find, yet again, bodies lying with their heads beaten in and their throats cut. The body of John Williamson, the publican, was in the cellar; his wife Elizabeth had been in the kitchen with their servant Bridget. Only the Williamsons' granddaughter, asleep upstairs, had escaped. Once more, money was scattered about, but little of value had been taken; once more, the escape was via the back door and over the yard fence.

The newspapers covered the story widely, but the information they gave was not terribly helpful. The *Edinburgh Annual Register* described John Turner as being 'about six feet in height', while *The Times* said he was 'a short man' with 'a lame leg'. The *Morning Chronicle* described his 'large red whiskers', but thought he was 'about five feet nine inches' and 'not lame'. Turner, therefore, was either tall, short, or in-between; he was lame, or possibly not; and he had large red whiskers, unless he didn't. This was the description of a man who had stood in front of journalists at an inquest. Imagine how reliably the papers described the man briefly seen by Turner, or those who had been glimpsed running away from the Marrs' house.

The police had no more idea where to look for the perpetrators of this new outrage than they had had after the deaths of the Marrs. They arrested plenty of people: people who were violent; people who looked in some way suspicious; people against whom a grudge was held. But one by one they were questioned and released.* In small communities criminals were usually revealed fairly swiftly; in areas with larger populations, handbills with descriptions of the wanted person and offers of rewards generally brought in information,

---

* The stages of prosecution for felonies and serious crimes were as follows: first, the accused appeared before a justice of the peace or a magistrate, where it was decided whether there was a sufficiently strong case; if so, the prisoner was committed for trial; a bill of indictment was drawn up, setting out the charge; a Grand Jury then considered the written depositions of the witnesses and, if they found a 'true bill' that there was a case to answer, the prisoner was tried by a jury. For murder cases, the early hearings often coincided with the inquest on the body, which was held separately. For concision's sake I have omitted the repetition of evidence from one stage to the next.

frequently from fellow criminals who found this a convenient way of earning a bit of cash and removing a competitor at the same time. With no response to the initial reward offered after the murder of the Marrs, the only thing the magistrates could think to do was increase the sum. To the initial £50 reward, another £100 was added by the Treasury, and that was increased two days later to an astonishing £700 – a very comfortable middle-class annual income, the sign of increasing government anxiety, verging on panic. After the Williamsons were murdered, another 120 guineas was offered: twenty guineas to anyone who could identify the owner of the weapons, and 100 guineas more if that person were to be convicted of the murders.

One man, arrested on suspicion, attempted to turn king's evidence, identifying eight men as his fellow murderers. Unable to come up with a motive, the newspapers attributed a love of wholesale slaughter to this mysterious gang. The gang theory was widely popular. A magistrate from the Thames Police Office wrote to his colleague at the Lambeth Street Office that the crime 'gives an appearance of a gang acting on a system', but to what end was not clear. Many were caught up: at one point seven men were held for questioning because 'In the possession of one of them were found two shirts stained with marks very much resembling blood, and a waistcoat carrying also similar marks ...' The men turned out to be hop-pickers, and the stains were vine sap.

The first clue that led towards an arrest was noticed only on the day of the Williamsons' murder, twelve days after the death of the Marrs, when it finally registered that the peen maul found in the kitchen had the initials 'JP' scratched on it. A handbill advertised this, and Mrs Vermiloe, the landlady of the Pear Tree Tavern, reported that her lodger, a Danish sailor named John Petersen, had left his tools in her care on his last shore leave. Petersen was at sea at the time of the murders, but his fellow lodger, John Williams, was said to have shaved off his whiskers the following day; furthermore, he had been seen washing his own stockings at the pump in the yard; and both he and another lodger, John Ritchen, knew Petersen. This was enough for an arrest. On 27 December the magistrates' court was packed with eager spectators when the news came that Williams had committed suicide in his cell.

The immediate reaction was that the suicide was an outright confession. Anything that contradicted this comforting notion was pushed to one side. On reflection, the questions greatly outweighed the certainties. It was not even clear that John Williams' name was John Williams – he had told the Vermiloes it was Murphy. Mr Vermiloe, the landlord, had been in prison for debt when his wife directed the police to Williams. The twenty-guinea reward for identifying the maul would pay off at least some of his debts, possibly all of them; how much weight could be given to her evidence? And two men at least had been at the Marrs': the footprints of two men were found, and at least two men had been seen running down the road. Who were they? Vermiloe had used the maul to chop wood, and both it and the ripping chisel that was also found in the Marrs' kitchen had been used as toys by his children in the yard – anyone could have taken them.

None of these questions was asked. Instead everyone agreed that they had long suspected Williams. One witness swore that, three weeks before the Williamsons were murdered, he had seen Williams with 'a long French knife with an ivory handle'. No one else had ever seen that knife and Williams together, but the *Gentleman's Magazine* reported that on 14 January 1812, miraculously, a lodger at the Pear Tree had found a blue jacket which he said had belonged to Williams, and it was reported that the inside pocket was marked, 'as if a blood-stained hand had been thrust into it'. But bloodstains could not definitely be identified until the twentieth century – what the witness meant was that the stain was brown. Furthermore, no one else had seen Williams wear this jacket, nor was there any discussion about who might have had access to it during the period of the murders, or in the following month. Mrs Vermiloe turned it over to the police, at which point they returned to the Pear Tree, searched the house once more and found a clasp knife, 'apparently dyed with blood', hidden behind a wall. The *Edinburgh Annual Register* added that a pair of trousers had been found shoved down under the 'soil' in the privy in the Pear Tree yard, which 'are spoken to very confidently by Williams' fellow-lodgers'.

Half a century later, magazines were still reprinting these rumours, and creating new ones: 'Williams was so notorious an infamous man, for all his oily and snaky duplicity, that the captain of his vessel, the Roxburgh Castle, had always predicted that ... he would mount the gibbet.' This comes from *All the Year Round*, Charles Dickens' magazine, and Dickens was evidently fascinated by Williams, and in no doubt about his guilt. As well as commissioning this article, he owned an illustration of 'the horrible creature', and had also touched lightly on the subject in *Dombey and Son* (1847–48): when Captain Cuttle, who lives down by the docks, keeps his shutters closed one day, the neighbours speculate 'that he lay murdered with a hammer, on the stairs'.

Meanwhile, the authorities had to decide how to respond to Williams' death. Most immediately, they needed to show the local residents that he would not escape justice by his suicide. It would be another century before a British judge decreed that it is 'of fundamental importance that justice should not only be done, but should manifestly and undoubtedly be seen to be done', but the idea was already well understood. So on the last day of 1811, an inclined wooden platform was placed atop a high cart. Williams' body was laid out on this, dressed in a clean white shirt (frilled, say some sources), blue trousers and brown stockings: in other words, in the neat, clean dress of a labouring man, although without a neck-handkerchief or hat, marks of decency and respectability. His right leg was manacled, as it would have been when he was in gaol. The maul was placed on one side of his head, the ripping chisel on the other.

At ten o'clock, a macabre and unprecedented procession set off at a stately walking pace. The head constable led the way, followed by

> Several hundred constables, with their staves ...
> The newly-formed Patrole [sic], with drawn cutlasses.
> Another body of Constables.

Parish Officers of St. George's and St. Paul's, and Shadwell, on
   horseback.
Peace Officers, on horseback,
Constables.
The High Constable of the county of Middlesex, on horseback
THE BODY OF WILLIAMS ...
A strong body of Constables brought up the rear.

Crowds lined the route; more watched from windows and even the
rooftops. Shops were shut, blinds drawn as a mark of respect to the
Marrs and the Williamsons. The cart travelled first to the Ratcliffe
Highway, where it stood for a quarter of an hour outside the Marrs'
house. An enraged member of the public climbed onto the cart and
forcibly turned Williams' head towards the house, to ensure that the
murderer was brought face to face with the scene of his crime. Then
the procession travelled on to New Gravel Lane, where again the cart
rested outside the death site. Finally it processed to Cannon Street, on
the edge of the City, and paused again. Then a stake was driven
through Williams' heart (some reports say hammered home by the
fatal maul), and his body was tumbled into a grave – some sources say
a large one, so he could be tossed in; others that it was purposely
made too small and shallow. Either way, the intention was to show
deliberate disrespect. The crowd, which had so far watched in almost
total silence, howled to see the last of the man who had killed seven
people – half as many as had been murdered in the entire previous
year throughout England and Wales.

   This was not the last the world was to see of John Williams. Bodily,
he reappeared in 1886, when workmen laying a gas pipe in what was
now the heart of the City dug up a skeleton with a stake through its
heart. Rumour later had it that at some point Williams' skull
appeared in the keeping of the publican 'at the corner of Cable Street
and Cannon Street Road'. In 1886 the *Pall Mall Gazette* further
reported that Madame Tussaud's waxworks had a 'beautifully
executed' portrait of Williams, drawn from life by Sir Thomas
Lawrence. But when precisely had Lawrence seen Williams? In the

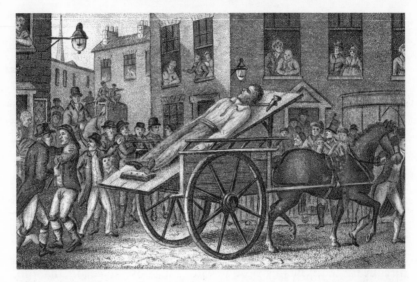

After John Williams' suicide, the authorities wanted to show that death would not permit the supposed murderer to escape justice. His body was placed on a cart with the murder weapons and brought to stand in front of his victims' houses, watched by the local community.

two days between his arrest and suicide? Or perhaps in his final, cart-top appearance?

Williams was to cast a longer shadow on the mental attitudes to crime and crime prevention in the nineteenth century than his skeletal remains could do physically. His ghost made several appearances in Parliament in the months that followed his death. The government was slower than the public to embrace the solution of Williams as the sole murderer. In a debate, the radical MP William Smith simply assumed that the crimes had been committed by 'a gang of villains, of whom few or no traces had yet been discovered'. The Prime Minister, Spencer Perceval, agreed with him.* The case 'was still wrapped up in mystery. It undoubtedly seemed strange that a single individual could commit such accumulated violence.'

---

* Perceval would himself be murdered four months later, the only British Prime Minister ever to be assassinated, but for some reason the crime barely captured the imagination of the public, and will feature no further in this book. Similarly, I will not be discussing the seven attempts to assassinate Queen Victoria.

It was not the mystery that troubled the politicians; it was that policing throughout London was now seen to be completely inadequate. The city was still eighteen years away from establishing a centralized police force, and relied on a patchwork of overlapping organizations that had developed independently. By 1780 there were 800,000 inhabitants living in London's two hundred parishes, which were responsible for the watch and policing, and also for lighting, waste disposal, street maintenance and care of the poor. But nothing was straightforward: Lambeth parish had nine trusts responsible for street lighting, St Pancras eighteen for paving; by 1800 there were fifty London trusts charged with maintaining the turnpike roads alone. In 1790, a thousand parish watchmen and constables were employed by seventy separate trusts. And even twenty years before that, in a city that was then much smaller, Sir John Fielding, the famous Bow Street magistrate, had warned Parliament that 'the Watch ... is in every Parish under the Direction of a separate Commission', which left 'the Frontiers of each Parish in a confused State, for that where one side of a street lies in one Parish, the Watchmen of one Side cannot lend any Assistance to [a] Person on the other Side, other than as a private Person, except in cases of Felony'.

In 1792, in a preliminary attempt to rationalize this motley collection of responsibilities, the Middlesex Justice Bill was passed, creating seven metropolitan police offices, each to be staffed by three magistrates and six constables, with at least one magistrate in each of the offices having legal qualifications (previously magistrates had simply been men of a certain status and level of wealth). In 1798 a privately funded force was set up to police the river and docks, paid for by the local West Indies merchants. In 1800 this force was taken over by the magistrates, and named the Thames River Police, with its own magistrate, Patrick Colquhoun.

By the end of the eighteenth century, with the population of London approaching a million, crime prevention was the responsibility of fifty constables and eight Runners at Bow Street magistrates' court and the seven police offices, plus a thousand additional constables and two night-time Bow Street patrols of 122 men. There were also 2,000 parish watchmen, who covered the 8,000 streets of London after dark. Some indication of the attitudes towards these two groups of men can be seen from their pay. The Bow Street patrols were paid between 17s.6d. and 28s. a week; by contrast, many watchmen received a beggarly 4s.11d. Colquhoun commented on the contempt that was shown these forces: 'It is an honourable profession to repel by force the enemies of the state. Why should it not be equally so to resist and to conquer these domestic invaders of property, and destroyers of lives who are constantly in a state of criminal warfare?'

The answer was that this 'honourable profession' was shrouded in mystery, and what people did know of it, they despised, the prevailing mental image being not a law-enforcer, but more a law-breaker: the eighteenth-century thief-taker, the criminal turncoat. That was about to change, partly through the publication of the memoirs of the French detective Eugène Vidocq (1775–1857). Vidocq had started his career as a not terribly successful criminal. After a number of convictions, he became a police spy, or informer, working secretly for the government while still in prison. In 1811 he was one of four ex-convicts to be made a detective, and in 1812 he became the head of the newly created Brigade de Sûreté, with thirty men under his command. None of this would have been of more than passing interest in Britain, had it not been for his *Mémoires*, which in translation swiftly became a best-seller.

It is almost certain that Vidocq did not write his own *Memoirs*. Nor can they truly be called biography. The last two volumes borrow wildly from a variety of sources, including a short story previously published by one of his ghost writers, while entire passages are blatantly lifted from *The Police of London*, a work of policy reform by Patrick Colquhoun, with French place names substituted for Colquhoun's original English ones. Nonetheless, the *Memoirs* were brilliant PR, with Vidocq transformed from an old-style thief-taker to a sympathetic outlaw, and then to a new thing altogether – both in literature and in life – a detective, although what he described barely resembled what was later to be known as detection (and it would be another twenty years before the word itself was invented). For the moment, Vidocq merely intensified the spy system of the Revolution, keeping extensive records on known criminals and paying inform-ants. Mostly in the *Memoirs* he disguises himself and hangs about in low haunts in order to overhear criminals plotting, or just bribes someone to tell him about a planned crime, which he then foils.

Vidocq's *Memoirs* found a ready audience, and, more importantly for popular recognition, in 1829 they were adapted in two theatrical versions: at the Coburg Theatre, as *Vidocq, the French Police Spy*, by J.B. Buckstone; and, just down the road from the Coburg, at the Surrey, in Douglas Jerrold's rival version, with only an exclamation point's difference: *Vidocq! the French Police Spy*. That year the words 'police spy' had particular resonance, as Home Secretary Sir Robert Peel finally managed to finesse through Parliament the Act that created the Metropolitan Police, replacing the old parish watch system and creating what has been called the first professional police force.*

Three decades earlier, Colquhoun had written, 'Police in this coun-try may be considered as a new science, the properties of which consist not in the Judicial Powers which lead to Punishment, and which belong to the magistrates alone, but in the Prevention and Detection of crimes ...' This, today so routine, was groundbreaking, in a single sentence setting policing on an entirely new track: that it was a professional job; that it and the legal system were two different arenas; and that it should be preventative, acting prior to the commis-sion of criminal acts. John Fielding, a remarkable magistrate, had, it is true, begun to move towards detection when he set up a 'Register of Robberies, Informations, Examinations, Convictions, suspicious Book [sic], and Newgate Calendars' – that is, not a register of crimes only, but of potential criminals and potential crime. But for the most part, prosecution after the commission of a crime was all that was expected. This had been fairly efficient in rural communities and

---

* Colquhoun and the River Police were among the first to use the word 'police' in English. There had been a London Police Bill in 1785, and the magistrate John Fielding used the word that same year, but it was not yet common. In 1814 the Irish police (Sir Robert Peel's first attempt to form a centralized force) were called the 'Peace Preservation Force' and manned by 'constables' not 'policemen'.

towns, where populations were small and people all knew each other. In rapidly urbanizing areas, however, crime detection was more difficult, and the number of cases that came before the magistrates put them under enormous pressure.

Frequently the system functioned well: there were six House of Commons select committee reports in the decade leading up to 1822, and many parish watch schemes were commended as 'exemplary and meritorious'. But others were unimaginably venal and corrupt. When Sir John Fielding was on the bench, Bow Street magistrates' court had been a model of what might be achieved under the old methods. For example, a Runner named John Clarke, previously a silversmith, used his knowledge of metalworking to track down counterfeiters, testifying at nearly half of the Old Bailey coining trials between 1771 and 1798. When he gave evidence, the conviction rate was 82 per cent; when he was absent, it dropped to 40 per cent. But by the time William Mainwaring took over in 1781 as Chairman of both the Middlesex and the Westminster Sessions, corruption was endemic. Mainwaring persuaded the government to pay him a secret extra salary, while institutionalizing cronyism and nepotism.

The lack of success following the Marr murders ensured that changes were swiftly made at local level. The watchmen in Shadwell were relieved of their duty and replaced by two companies of eighteen men patrolling nightly, each equipped with a rattle, a lantern, a cutlass and a pistol. At Wapping, sixteen extra men were drafted in, and the Thames Police Office arranged for further street policing over Christmas. Several neighbouring parishes also drew up volunteer patrols to augment the watch. Even so, a letter to the Home Office on 28 December 1811 warned that 'the frequency of the late horrible Outrages must induce a Belief that the wicked Part of the Community is becoming too strong for the law'. The *Morning Post* concurred: 'Either respectable householders must determine to be their own guardians, or we must have a regularly enlisted armed police under the orders of proper officers.' Many frightened citizens wrote to the Home Secretary with their own ideas, nearly all of which involved increasing the size and frequency of rewards: in effect buying improved detection from criminals and their cohorts. Many believed that these cohorts included the watch themselves, who seemed to spend far too much time with criminals. William Smith harrumphed that 'it was extremely scandalous that the Police Officers should be upon such terms of intimacy with the most notorious offenders'.

To deal with the crisis of confidence, a parliamentary select committee was set up to study the question, and it reported in March 1812. The effects of this report still matter today, because it advocated taking crime prevention away from the local authorities, and putting a single centralized authority in overall control of policing throughout London. Robert Southey, who would be named Poet Laureate the following year, and was now as ardent an opponent of political reform as he had once been a promoter of Thomas Paine and the French Revolution, agreed: 'I have very long felt the necessity of an improved police, and these dreadful events, I hope and trust, will lead to the establishment of one as vigilant as that of Paris used to be. The police laws cannot be too rigorous; and the usual objection that a rigorous police is inconsistent with English liberty might easily be shown to be absurd.' True, there was a dissident voice in the Earl of Dudley, who said that he 'would rather half a dozen people's throats should be cut in Ratcliffe Highway every three or four years than to be subject to domiciliary visits, spies, and all the rest of Fouché's contrivances'.* But then, Dudley's socio-economic position made him safer than most.

Thomas de Quincey might at first appear to have taken the affair more lightly, as he mockingly reported on his neighbour, who after the murders 'never rested until she had placed eighteen doors … each secured by ponderous bolts, and bars, and chains, between her own bedroom and any intruder of human build. To reach her, even in her drawing room, was like going … into a beleaguered fortress.' This

---

* Joseph Fouché (1759–1820) was Napoleon's Minister for Police. He had been an ardent Jacobin in the early part of the French Revolution, eventually being dubbed the 'Executioner of Lyons', as he oversaw so many executions that the victims' blood blocked the city's gutters. Under Napoleon, he exerted an iron grip on state security, and the British considered – rightly – that his police force consisted almost entirely of spies and *agents provocateurs*, hence Dudley's comment.

seemed at first simply a comic coda, but de Quincey's contribution was greater than anyone at the time could have imagined, as the Ratcliffe Highway murders spurred him to one of literature's greatest flights of fancy, in the satirical essays referred to collectively under the title *On Murder Considered as One of the Fine Arts*. In the first essay, de Quincey's narrator introduces himself and his subject at a meeting of connoisseurs of murder: 'GENTLEMEN, – I have had the honour to be appointed by your committee to the trying task of reading the Williams' Lecture on Murder considered as one of the Fine Arts' – a task, he goes on to explain, which is increasingly difficult, as excellence in the field raises the bar for more aesthetic murders: 'People begin to see that something more goes to the composition of a fine murder than two blockheads ... a knife – a purse – and a dark lane ... Mr. Williams has exalted the ideal of murder to all of us ... he has carried his art to a point of colossal sublimity.' De Quincey is making a serious point: in *Macbeth*, we are interested not in the victim, Duncan, but in the thoughts of the murderer, Macbeth, just as we are more interested in murderers than we are in their victims. De Quincey's narrator suggests that murder is an art, that murder is theatre, and that Williams was an artist who had written a sensational play that hundreds of thousands wanted to see.

De Quincey then takes the story of the Marr and Williamson murders and himself turns them into art. The main figures are given psychological depth, and a motive is imagined. Most importantly, Williams is turned, as one literary critic observes, into 'a sort of Miltonic, ruined God', with a glamorized physical description to match his inward corruption of spirit. A sandy, undistinguished-looking man in life, in art Williams has a 'bloodless, ghastly pallor', and hair of 'the most extraordinary and vivid colour ... something between an orange and a lemon colour'. His clothes, too, undergo a metamorphosis. He no longer wears the rough dress of a sailor. Instead de Quincey imagines a dandified being, dressing for an evening's slaughter in black silk stockings and pumps and with a long blue coat of 'the very finest cloth ... richly lined in silk'. The murderer is now more vampire than cash-strapped sailor, more great actor than street thug.

In reality, there were few of de Quincey's type of murderer. Yet, as his imaginary lecturer knows, 'the world in general … are very bloody-minded; and all they want in a murder is a copious effusion of blood'. How this desire was transformed over the nineteenth century, and how it, in turn, transformed that century, is my subject.

TWO

Trial by Newspaper

'A copious effusion of blood' was something that John Thurtell certainly provided. His crime has been said to have founded newspaper fortunes, for his was the first 'trial by newspaper', his actions read and judged by people across the country long before he was brought to trial. That it should have been Thurtell who caught the imagination of the public in this way is extraordinary, for his was a sordid, brutal and remarkably unsuccessful crime. John Thurtell, failed cloth merchant, failed publican and failed gambler, was also a failed murderer.

On 28 October 1823, one Charles Nicholls, of Aldenham in Hertfordshire, arrived in Watford, anxious to notify the magistrates of 'some singular circumstances pointing to foul play'. He had been passing through Gill's Hill Lane (then countryside, now in the small town of Radlett) when he saw some road-menders combing the bushes. They told him that that morning they had met a stranger searching the verge. He explained that his gig had overturned the previous night, and he was trying to find his missing penknife and handkerchief. After he left, the road-menders continued his search, hoping that valuables might also have fallen from the gig. Instead they found a knife and a pistol, both of which had dried, caked, brownish deposits on them, looking suspiciously like blood; the pistol, furthermore, had hair and what might even be brains sticking to its butt. Charles Nicholls consequently hot-footed it to Watford.

One of the magistrates immediately went to Gill's Hill – with no police, magistrates did their own investigation. He learned enough there to lead him to arrest a man named William Probert, who rented a cottage nearby. Two men, John Thurtell and Joseph Hunt, were reported to have spent the night at Probert's cottage, but they had returned to London that morning. The next day, therefore, the magistrate sent for the Bow Street Runners.

The Runners had no formal status, and were not linked to the metropolitan police offices, which were under the aegis of the Home Office. The Bow Street magistrates were, for historical reasons, paid from a secret-service account, while the Runners were in turn Bow Street's own, privately paid detective force. The Runners' salary was small, 25s. a week plus 14s. expenses, their main income coming from hiring themselves out to other police offices or to private individuals across the country. Now two Runners were hired to locate the suspicious Thurtell and Hunt. After a brief visit to Gill's Hill the senior Runner, George Ruthven, returned to London, where:

> I found [Thurtell] at the Coach and Horses, Conduit Street … I said: John, my boy, I want you … Thurtell had been anticipating serious proceedings against him for setting his house on fire in the city [see p. 24] … It was highly probable that he supposed that I wanted him on that charge … My horse and chaise were at the door. He got in and I handcuffed him to one side of the rail of my trap … On the road nothing could be more chatty and free than the conversation on the part of Thurtell. If he did suspect where I was going to take him, he played an innocent part very well, and artfully pretended total ignorance … I drove up to the inn, where Probert and Hunt were in charge of the local constables. Let us have some brandy and water, George, said Thurtell … I went out of the room to order it. Give us a song said Thurtell, and Hunt, who was a beautiful singer, struck up 'Mary, list awake'. I paused with the door in my hand and said to myself – 'Is it possible that these men are murderers?'

The newspapers had no such doubts, even though no charges had yet been laid and there was as yet no body. One week after the crime took place, six days after the weapons were found in the bushes, two days after the arrest of Thurtell, the *Morning Chronicle* ran its first piece on the 'Most Horrible Murder Near Watford'.

Thurtell and his friends had the disadvantage of poor reputations. Thurtell himself had been born into relative gentility: his father was a prosperous Norwich merchant, later an alderman and in 1828 mayor. Thurtell had been commissioned as a second lieutenant in the Marines in 1809, when he was fifteen or sixteen. Despite the French wars, he saw action only once, and in 1814 he retired on half-pay and returned to Norwich. His father set up him as a bombazine (woollen cloth) manufacturer, but Thurtell became enamoured of 'the fancy', the world of Regency prize-fighters, gamblers and their followers.

This was his first downward step. Prize-fighting was illegal, and fights were held in fields, for preference near county boundaries, so that in case of trouble the crowds could disperse across more than one jurisdiction. Thurtell became what in modern parlance would be called a fight promoter, or manager, although the role was then much more informal. The first fight that we know he was involved in was between Ned 'Flatnose' Painter, a Norwich fighter, and Tom Oliver, in July 1820. This meeting was later immortalized by George Borrow, in *Lavengro* in 1851 ('Lavengro' is Romany for 'philologist', supposedly the name given to Borrow himself by the Rom he befriended). Much of *Lavengro* is fictionalized, but the description of Thurtell is based on reality:

> a man somewhat under thirty, and nearly six feet in height ... he wore neither whiskers nor moustaches, and appeared not to delight in hair, that of his head, which was of light brown, being closely cropped ... the eyes were grey, with an expression in which there was sternness blended with something approaching to feline; his complexion was exceedingly pale, relieved, however, by certain pockmarks, which here and there studded his countenance; his form was athletic, but lean; his arms long ... You might have supposed him a bruiser; his dress was that of one ... something was wanting, however, in his manner – the quietness of the professional man; he rather looked like one performing the part – well – very well – but still performing the part.

Borrow recounted how one day Thurtell and Ned Painter called on a local landowner, asking for the use of a small field in which to stage a fight. They were refused, the man explaining that, as a magistrate, he could not become involved. 'Magistrate!' says Thurtell, 'then fare ye well, for a green-coated buffer and a Harmanbeck.'* The magistrate was wiser than he knew, as Thurtell had a reputation for being 'on the cross' – involved in match-fixing. When in September 1820 Jack Martin, 'the Master of the Rolls' (he was a baker), fought Jack Randall, 'the Nonpareil', the match was thought by many to have been a cross arranged by a gambler named William Weare to allow Thurtell to recoup some of the money Weare had won off him. Thurtell, ultimately, would be the death of Weare – and vice-versa.

Borrow, although obviously impressed by Thurtell, had no illusions about him: 'The terrible Thurtell was present ... grim and pale as usual, with his bruisers around. He it was, indeed, who *got up* the fight, as he had previously done twenty others; it being his frequent boast that he had first introduced bruising and bloodshed amidst rural scenes and transformed a quiet slumbering town into a den of Jews and metropolitan thieves.'

Thurtell by now had a thorough knowledge of metropolitan thieves and Jews. (All moneylenders were regarded as Jewish, whether they were or not.) He had failed as a cloth merchant in Norwich, after defrauding his creditors by claiming to have been robbed of the money he owed them. Few believed in these convenient thieves, and Thurtell was declared bankrupt in February 1821. Shifting his base of operations to London, where his reputation might not have preceded him, he set up as the landlord of the Black Boy, in Long Acre, but the pub became a byword for illegal gambling, and soon lost its licence. Thurtell moved from job to job, from money-making scheme to money-making scheme. At the Army and Navy pub he met Joseph

* A harmanbeck is a constable. A buffer might, as in our current use of the word, mean a doddery old man, or it might be one of two slang words in use at the time: a dog, or 'A Rogue that kills good sound Horses only for their Skins'. Either way, Thurtell was not happy. I have been unable to discover why a green coat is a term of contempt. Perhaps they were old-fashioned, reinforcing the 'old man' element of the insult?

Hunt, briefly its manager, a gambler who had already been to prison once; he met William Weare and his friends at yet another pub. Weare claimed to be a solicitor, and lived at Lyon's Inn, formerly an Inn of Chancery and now lodgings frequented by legal professionals. In fact he had been a waiter, then a billiard-marker, and had finally joined a gang 'who lived by blind hooky [a card game], hazard [dice], billiards, and the promotion of crooked fights'. He was a legendary figure in the gambling underworld, and it was reported that he always carried his entire savings, said to be £2,000, with him.

Thurtell's brother Thomas was the landlord of the Cock Tavern, in the Haymarket, and there they became acquainted with Probert, a spirit merchant who helped them to raise money on dubious lines of credit. Thurtell was operating once more as a cloth merchant, but just as his credit ran out, by an amazing coincidence his warehouse, insured to the hilt, was destroyed by fire. The insurance company refused to pay, and in 1823 Thurtell sued. Despite witnesses testifying that he had earlier discussed arson with them; despite information that he had bought fabric on credit and resold it for less than he had paid; despite evidence that he had blocked up the single window that would have permitted the nightwatchman to see the flames as they started – despite all this, the jury found for Thurtell, with £1,900 damages.* The insurers appealed, withholding the insurance money, while the money from the damages went to Thurtell's creditors. The Thurtell brothers' financial situation continued parlous. They were by now reduced to selling off the drink from the pub they managed in order to eat, while they couldn't leave the building in case the insurance company had them arrested for conspiracy to defraud; they would have been unable to post bail.

Weare, meanwhile, was doing splendidly, alternating between trips to the races and days spent in billiard saloons. Then one day he said he was off to Hertfordshire for the weekend to go shooting with

---

* One legal historian has suggested that this verdict had more to do with a private feud between the insurance company's lawyer and the judge than with the merits of the case.

Thurtell. There would be shooting, it is true, but it was not Weare who held the gun.

On 24 October, two men who very strongly resembled Thurtell and Hunt bought a pair of pistols from a pawnbroker in Marylebone. The same day, Hunt hired a gig and horse, and asked at the stable where he could buy a rope and sack; at a public house in Conduit Street, he was overheard to ask Probert if he wanted to be 'in it'. In the late afternoon, Thurtell drove Weare down to Probert's cottage at Gill's Hill in the gig, leaving Probert to follow on with Hunt. Their horse was a grey with unusual markings: a white face and white socks. Probert dropped Hunt at an inn near Gill's Hill, to wait for Thurtell as arranged, and drove on to his cottage on his own. As he neared home, he found Thurtell in the lane. Thurtell asked him where Hunt was, and grumbled – or boasted – that he had 'done the business without his help'. Probert returned to the inn to collect Hunt, and on his return Hunt and Thurtell reproached each other for missing the appointment. It didn't matter, said Thurtell off-handedly, he had killed Weare on his own: the pistol had misfired, so he had bludgeoned him to death, 'turning [the pistol] through his brains', and then slitting his throat.

Hunt poured all of this out at the magistrates' hearing. When more than one suspect was arrested for a crime, only one could be given immunity from prosecution by turning king's evidence. This frequently produced an unseemly scramble to be the first person to 'peach'. Hunt's 'natural pusillanimity' encouraged his pragmatism, and he revealed all. After the three men met up at the cottage, he said, they ate the pork chops Hunt had brought with him for supper. (At the trial, Probert's servant was asked, 'Was the supper postponed?' 'No,' she replied innocently, 'it was pork.')* Telling Mrs Probert that they had to visit a neighbour after supper, they collected Weare's body from where Thurtell had stashed it, took what valuables he had on

---

* This example of servant humour provided the middle classes with much merriment. Even forty years later, Dickens knew his readers would recognize the reference in *Our Mutual Friend* when he suggests that a Fat Lady at a fair kept up her weight 'sustained upon postponed pork'.

THE INVENTION OF MURDER

him, and put the corpse in a sack. Back at the cottage, Thurtell presented Mrs Probert with a gold chain. Mrs Probert, greatly wondering, later watched from a window as Thurtell and Hunt, who said they would sleep in the sitting room, instead took a horse from the stable. When they returned, having dumped Weare's body in a nearby pond, she overheard them dividing the money they had found on Weare's body, which was a wretched £15, instead of the legendary £2,000. The next day Thurtell and Hunt took the gig back to London, together with some of Weare's clothing. They returned the following day, Hunt bringing a newly purchased spade. Probert was anxious about the proximity of the body to his cottage, so soon Weare was on the move once more, this time to a pond near Elstree.

As soon as the authorities located the body, Thurtell was committed for trial, with the other two remanded as accessories. Things were not looking good for them – some of Weare's belongings had been found in Hunt's lodgings, and a shirt marked 'W' in the stable near Probert's cottage. The gig and the unusual horse were identified at various pubs along the route between Gill's Hill and London, as were its passengers. At the inquest Hunt claimed that he had no connection with Thurtell and Probert, that he had only been hired to sing (he was a modestly successful tavern performer; his more famous brother sang at Covent Garden). He agreed that he had bought a sack and rope before he left London, but said they were for the game that Probert and Weare planned to shoot. Probert too tried to claim that Thurtell acted alone, but the jury found that Weare had been murdered by Thurtell, while Probert 'counselled, procured, incited, and abetted the said John Thurtell the said murder and felony to do and commit'. Thomas Thurtell meanwhile was arrested for conspiracy to defraud the County Fire Office.

In November, Probert's wife, sister-in-law and brother were all arrested. Mrs Probert's brother Thomas Noyes had played cards with the men after the murder, and she herself had received what was now identified as Weare's watch-chain. Noyes and his sister were soon released, but Mrs Probert remained under arrest, while the authorities approached Probert to turn king's evidence. Hunt had proved an

The journeyings of the body of William Weare fascinated the reading public, and there were many images of his murderers either putting his body in the pond or, later, removing it.

unreliable witness, clearly terrified, happy to agree with anything anyone suggested. The main reason to use Probert, however, was that if he were indicted, Mrs Probert's evidence of what had passed at the cottage could not be heard – a wife could not testify against her husband.

In the run-up to the trial the newspapers whipped themselves into a frenzy. At the end of the French wars, a 4*d*. tax had been added to the price of a newspaper, ensuring a hefty cover price – at the time of Thurtell's trial, the *Morning Chronicle*, *The Times*, the *Morning Herald* and the *Observer* each cost 7*d*. Yet their prosperous, middle-class readers were avid for crime stories.On a random day in the month of Weare's murder, the four pages of *The Times* consisted of two pages of advertisements, two columns of news, a few letters, some birth and death announcements; and the rest of the paper was entirely given over to police, trial and magistrates' court reports. The *Morning Chronicle* similarly gave the majority of its editorial space to crime on a regular basis, continuing a long tradition of prurient upper-middle-class love of crime: the *Gentleman's Magazine* had, between 1731 and

1818, reported on 1,172 murders – over one a month for nearly a century.

Pierce Egan, one of the most famous journalists of the day, claimed to have interviewed Thurtell as he awaited trial. Egan had started as a sporting journalist, writing *Boxiana, or, Sketches of ancient and modern pugilism* in 1812. In 1821 his *Life in London, or, The day and night scenes of Jerry Hawthorn, esq., and his elegant friend, Corinthian Tom*, illustrated by the Cruikshank brothers, a comic story of two young swells on the razzle, was wildly popular. Imitations and even outright plagiarisms quickly appeared, as well as several stage versions. As a member – albeit a more respectable one – of the fancy, Egan dealt with Thurtell's story as sympathetically as possible, while still maintaining an appropriately shocked tone.* His piece was very much for slightly raffish men about town, presenting Thurtell as a 'foolish young [man] from the country' whom the professional gamblers had 'picked up as a *good flat* [an easy dupe]; and the rolls of country *flimseys* [banknotes] which he brought with him to town, were soon reduced … The *Swell Yokel* as he was first termed … was hailed as a rare customer; and numbers were on the look out to have a *slice* of his *blunt* [piece of his money]…Mr. Weare was one of this number: (he was what is termed in the sporting world a dead nail [a crook]), a complete sharper [swindler] …'

Thurtell in this version is not only naïve, but even cowardly. Egan gives a history of incidents where Thurtell had issued challenges, or pretended to, but was not actually willing to fight. This is all done very delicately, by imputation rather than outright statement. After telling the history of the fire and the arson trial, Egan concludes, 'It is decidedly the opinion of Thurtell's most intimate friends, that his conduct for the last two years, had been more like that of a madman than of a rational being.'

This seems kind when compared to the newspapers. Long before the trial began, *The Times* printed a stream of vitriolic – and

---

* This meeting has been much disputed, and Egan may simply have worked from press reports and information supplied by sporting friends.

completely unsubstantiated – stories. On 6 November it told its readers that 'Thurtell is reported to have been with Wellington's troops at the siege of San Sebastián, where he lurked behind the lines to murder and rob a fallen officer,' and he was reported as saying of this victim, 'I thought by the look of him that he was a nob, and must have some blunt about him; so I just tucked my sword in his ribs, and settled him; and I found a hundred and forty doubloons in his pocket!' This was one of the few stories that was denied in print, as commentators noted that 140 doubloons would be so heavy the possessor would not have been able to walk. Nothing daunted, that same day there was another story about Thurtell, saying that in his lodgings the police had found an air-gun in the shape of a walking stick, cunningly painted to look like wood, although nothing more was ever heard of it. Four days later, a story appeared about one James Wood, Thurtell's supposed rival for the supposed charms of Miss Caroline Noyes, Mrs Probert's sister. Wood was said to have been decoyed into an ambush in a tenement, where he was attacked by Thurtell with a pair of dumbbells. *The Times* added, as proof of this remarkable story, that a search of the building had produced a set of dumbbells. And on the same day the paper reported that Probert had testified that Thurtell had 'picked out 17 persons of substance that he intended to rob and murder, and that [Weare] was one of them'. The journalist had no doubt that the remaining sixteen had had lucky 'escapes from the late horrid conspiracy', and added a story of a man named Sparks, who declined to go into business with Thurtell, thus escaping a 'horrible doom, which otherwise, in all probability, awaited him'. A week later the daily update, otherwise relatively low-key, referred to Thurtell, Hunt and Probert – still awaiting trial – as 'the guilty culprits'.

The *Morning Chronicle*, too, referred to the three as 'the murderers'. The *Hampshire Telegraph* claimed that Probert had 'debauched' both the unnamed wife and daughter of his unnamed landlord, and 'Indeed ... no woman, whom he wished to possess, could escape him; for if he could not get her by fair means, he would not scruple to assail her by foul.' The *Derby Mercury* reported that an unnamed 'person who was known to be acquainted with the Thurtells ... [had] suddenly disappeared, and has not since been heard of'. The *Caledonian Mercury* liked the death-by-dumbbells story, and threw in an additional report of 'an offensive smell' emanating from Probert's cottage, similar to 'that which proceeds from a corpse in a state of decomposition'. The *Examiner* reported that yet another unnamed man had been murdered, this time 'cast into the Thames from Battersea Bridge'. For good measure it added that Thurtell and his gang had also attempted to murder Mr Barber Beaumont, the director of the County Fire Office, and had only been foiled because, contrary to habit, on the night of the attempt Mr Beaumont had failed to take his usual seat by a window. Many of the papers featured this story, apparently never pausing to ask themselves why such a dastardly gang had not summoned the energy to make a second attempt on Mr Beaumont's life. The *Bristol Mercury* reported yet another 'mysterious disappearance', this time an unnamed pregnant woman, said to be a clergyman's daughter, who had been ravished by one of the gang. 'The worst is surmised,' it added hopefully.

The hysteria infected everyone. A thirteen-year-old schoolboy wrote to his mother that Thurtell had 'positively' plotted to murder 'a long catalogue of rich persons': his schoolmaster had assured him that 'the bodies of 6 persons have been found in the Thames, 2 of them are women. Two clergymen are engaged in this scandalous affair. Two clergymen of the Established Church!'

In this febrile atmosphere, a fortnight before the trial was scheduled to begin, plays were advertised at two London theatres, the Surrey and the Coburg.* Since 1737, a Licensing Act had severely restricted the number of theatres that were permitted to stage spoken drama or comedy; these were referred to as 'legitimate' theatres. The Act had not, however, included musical theatre, which could legally

* The Coburg changed its name to the Royal Victoria (the Vic) in 1833. Later in the century it became known first colloquially, then formally, as the Old Vic, which it remains today.

be performed in theatres licensed by local magistrates and known in London as 'the minors'.*

Throughout the century working-class theatre audiences were an increasingly powerful economic force, particularly in industrial areas. In the East End of London the rapid development of the docks along the Thames created a vast, and almost entirely working-class, community: from 125,000 people in 1780, the population grew to just under a million in 1888, and nearly two million by the end of the century, when it became perhaps the largest working-class community in the world. To serve its needs, theatres, taverns, saloons and other places of entertainment sprang up: ten new theatres in the quarter-century after 1825. These were not small places, either: at mid-century the Standard held 3,400 people, the Pavilion 3,500, the Royal Victoria gallery alone nearly 2,000. (The Vic was not in the East End but south of the river, but the audiences for the 'transpontine theatres', as they were known, came mainly from the river-workers and other East End residents.) Other new industrial cities had equally large spaces: in Birmingham in 1840, a single theatre gallery held 1,200 people. Working-class audiences far outnumbered middle-class ones: in 1866 there were 51,363 nightly seats in twenty-five London theatres; of these, 32,395 were located in the East End or south of the river in the transpontine theatres – the Coburg, the Surrey and Astley's Amphitheatre being the most famous. When the cheap seats in the West End, and the sort of places that were too rough or too small even to be considered theatres, are added in, it is clear why working-class tastes predominated.

In 1840, a writer on theatre noted that at the Pavilion Theatre in Stepney, 'the Newgate calendar [a multi-volume true-crime

---

* All plays were subject to governmental oversight, and all theatres had to submit their scripts to the office of the Lord Chamberlain before performances could be licensed. Historians have cause to be grateful for this censorship. The Lord Chamberlain's office kept the scripts, and they are frequently the only surviving copies, particularly for plays produced at the minor theatres. Much of the material that follows relies heavily on the Lord Chamberlain's Plays, now held in the British Library, and only slightly the worse for wear after being kept for a century or so in a coal cellar in St James's Palace.

compendium] and tales of terror stand in the same place as Homer did to the ancient dramatists'. *Punch* parodied this taste, describing a leading man at the minor theatres as one 'who is murdered at least twice a week, commits parricide several times in the course of the year, and is torn by remorse every night at about nine o'clock'.

Playwrights were thus always on the lookout for new murderous material, and with two plays called *The Gamblers*, a stimulated public immediately made the connection to the story that had been monopolizing the newspapers. *The Gamblers* opened at the Surrey on 17 November 1823, *The Gamblers, or, The Murderers at the Desolate Cottage* at the Coburg the following day.*

The Surrey and the Coburg were two of the homes of melodrama, the century's predominant dramatic form. Melodrama simplified an increasingly complex world. It depicted brutal crime and violent death, which were familiar enough in the world its audiences inhabited; but unlike real life, in the world of melodrama justice always triumphed in the last act. What realism rejects as ludicrous coincidence is, to a melodrama audience, the workings of providence: the greater the coincidence, the greater the sense of meaning. The subjects tended to be those audiences could identify with: the rustic adrift in the big city, or working men oppressed by evil masters; the 'pride of the village' seduced by a villain. The villains were authority figures (squires, landlords, judges) or those who served them (stewards, lawyers, beadles). Melodrama characters have preordained parts: a villain is a villain, and will not become a hero. Costume was as much an indicator of character as occupation. The heroine wore white; heroes, even those with no connection to the sea, were frequently dressed as sailors (the dockyards were the major employers around

---

* The author of the Surrey's play is always listed as 'unknown', but a seemingly hitherto unnoticed letter from the journalist Leman Blanchard, dated 23 April 1883, has survived in the British Library: 'The piece called *The Gamblers* [was] hashed up by Milner if I remember rightly.' Blanchard cannot actually have 'remembered' the production at all, as he was born only in 1820, but he was a professional playwright by 1839, and his father, William Blanchard, was a comic actor before him, so he may well have heard the play spoken of. Certainly its notoriety long outlived its run at the Surrey.

many minor theatres); while villains wore the guise of men about town, usually with the addition of a dashing pair of boots.

This typing permitted stock companies to function: the rustic, the 'heavy', the heroine, the comic servant, were all a standard type, with standard make-up and a standard costume. Each week, therefore, a new drama could draw in the same audiences to watch similar characters in different situations, which were also standard: the last-minute reprieve from the gallows, the overheard conversation, the long-lost foundling child, the secret marriage. Melodrama also relied on highly stylized speech, in which thoughts were articulated – in *Tom Bowling*, a well-loved 1830 melodrama, Dare-Devil Bill, the smuggler, shouts that his enemy: 'shall hang! hang! hang! and on the same gibbet as myself! And how I will exult, and how my eyeballs, starting from their sockets, will glare upon him in their convulsive brilliancy! And I will laugh, too … ha, ha, ha!' – regularly interspersed with comedy, mime, spectacle, song and dance, all no more realistic than the dialogue. Nor were they intended to be. In an 1829 adaptation of Walter Scott's *Guy Mannering*, a character is lost on a storm-racked Scottish heath, when suddenly: 'Ha! What do I see on this lonely heath? A Piano? Who could be lonely with that? The moon will shortly rise and light me from this unhallowed place; so, to console myself, I will sing one of Julia's favourite melodies.' And he does.

The surviving playbill for *The Gamblers* gives some indication of the furore that the Surrey expected. Unusually, the standard description of the evening's entertainment is prefaced by a notice 'To the public ☞', claiming, implausibly, that the play had been written before 'the recent SANGUINARY MURDER'. After the news broke, it continued, the managers had considered withdrawing the play, but as the newspapers had printed 'columns filled with the *most trivial* particulars of the Murder, [and] have also given *illustrations* of every Scene attached to the fatal deed', they felt that 'in denying to our Audience a Drama' they would be failing 'a duty unquestionably due both to them and to ourselves'. Having set out their virtuous credentials, only now do they come to the play's great selling point: sets '*illustrated by CORRECT VIEWS taken on the SPOT*', and 'THE IDENTICAL

HORSE AND GIG *Alluded to by the Daily Press*', which, in a moment of commercial genius, the theatre had purchased.

The play itself was a standard melodrama, telling the tale of a country innocent taking a bloody revenge after being fleeced by big-city gamblers. The highlight was the horse and gig; this, said the *Observer* the next day, 'formed the strongest feature of interest in the eyes of the audience, if we could safely collect that expression from the applause that followed their appearance'. *The Times* tsk-tsk-ed at the very idea of showing William Weare's murder onstage, but its reviewer the next night was nonetheless disappointed to discover that the Coburg's *The Gamblers, or, The Murderers at the Desolate Cottage* had no connection to the murder of William Weare at all, 'except we could fancy the cabriolet in which the ghost travels to be Probert's gig ... and a French hut being Gill's-hill-cottage, and a pool of fire to be his pond'.

The horse and gig were easy for the Surrey to get hold of: they had only been hired by the murderers. Other, more personal, items were also available. Probert had owed rent on the cottage, and an auction quickly sold off most ordinary household goods at ordinary household prices.* While purchasers were not plentiful, many came for a day out as murder tourists, wandering through the grounds and, for a shilling, even the cottage itself. One publication claimed that five hundred people had paid the entrance fee. Soon a little sightseeing route was worked out: 'At Elstree the curious made their first halt. Here the grave of Mr. Weare, in Elstree Church-yard, was visited, and the pond, about a quarter of a mile out of the village ... The Artichoke Inn, to which the corpse was carried, and where the Coroner's Inquest was held ... Mr. Field, the landlord, being one of the Jury, was therefore fully competent to the task of answering the numerous questions put to him by his customers. Here the sack, in which the remains of the victim had been carried from Probert's cottage, was shown. The marks of blood which it bears gave it peculiar interest ...'

* Some of these items retained a posthumous glamour. In the twentieth century Norwich Public Record Office was the proud owner of a pair of scissors said to have been Thurtell's in his cloth-merchant days, and of his original certificate in bankruptcy.

Just as with a sightseeing trip today, the circuit could be finished off with a souvenir: a lucky few managed to buy a bit of the sack; for others, a Staffordshire pottery figure was soon available; those with less money could buy a book at the cottage, complete with a map of Weare's posthumous journeys. Those with no money at all could still take away a memento: the *Caledonian Mercury* reported that by mid-November the hedge outside the cottage was vanishing, filched 'by those curious people, who consider a twig from the hedge, through which the remains of a murdered man had been dragged, must furnish a treat to their equally curious friends'.

Murder tourists came from all walks of life. As late as 1828, Walter Scott recorded in his journal that he and his companions travelled out of their way to visit Gill's Hill Lane and do the circuit. After taking in the lane and the ponds, they went on to the cottage itself, now partially dismantled, and were shown around by a 'truculent looking hag' for 2*s*.6*d*. Five years after the event, the 'hag' could ask, and receive, nearly a week's pay for a workman.

Private entrepreneurship was one thing. Theatre was another. After the Surrey's first night, the Lord Chamberlain stepped in and ordered the play to be withdrawn. Furthermore, Thurtell's solicitor swore out an affidavit for an attempt to pervert the course of justice by showing Thurtell and Hunt committing murder onstage before they were tried, much less convicted. The management attempted to claim that there was no resemblance at all between the play and the murder of William Weare, but the purchase of the gig and the white-faced horse made this impossible to sustain.

When the Hertfordshire Assizes, at which Thurtell and Hunt were to be tried, opened on 4 December, Thurtell's lawyer immediately applied for a postponement because of pre-trial prejudice, claiming that the press had caused 'the grossest injustice towards his client'. As if to prove his case, his affidavit was immediately reprinted in *The Times*, despite a judicial ban on its publication, as it contained a compilation of all the worst articles that had appeared. The papers followed every twist and turn of these legal arguments. The *Morning Chronicle* gave thirteen of its daily twenty columns to the subject, and it also produced snappy summaries: the judge, for example, 'loves the Press, but wishes it had fewer readers'. The crusading liberal paper the *Examiner*, which had been founded in 1808 by Leigh Hunt and his brother as a Radical voice to counter both the Tory government and the (then) Prince Regent's Whig cronies, agreed: the judge 'has been guided throughout by that keen and constant hatred of the press which is the mainspring of two-thirds of the political sentiments of his party ... And why is all this? Because the press is the great organ of knowledge ... To keep the body of the people in the dark, is the dear and leading aim of many ...' The leader-writer added that the law as it stood did not permit the accused to know what the prosecution's case would be: 'A pretty law, then, truly!' which forbids a man to know what he will have to refute. The newspapers' job, as he saw it, was to supply that lack.

The trial was postponed for a month, to January 1824, although the press excitement then was no less. The *Chronicle* printed a supplementary sheet after the first day, and also doubled its normal four pages to eight for a full report; on the second day it returned to four pages, but devoted three of them, plus a leader, to the trial. *Bell's Life in London and Sporting Chronicle* devoted five of its six pages to the trial. The *Chronicle* calculated that over the two days of the trial there were a hundred horses reserved to carry the reports from Hertford by express, to feed the insatiable demand. Even local papers had expresses: the *Ipswich Journal* finished its report of the opening of the assizes with a triumphant, 'BY EXPRESS. HERTFORD. FRIDAY, ONE O'CLOCK'.

The *Observer* printed five pictures in its report – a great novelty, as technology was just beginning to permit the use of engravings in newspapers, instead of the clumsier, and slower-to-produce, woodblocks. Another paper included illustrations of the court, maps of Gill's Hill, and views of Probert's cottage. Pictures could also be purchased separately. A journalist returned to London after the adjournment in company with 'a tradesman from Oxford-street, who had been frightened out of his wits ... by hearing that pictures of Gill's Hill Cottage were actionable, for he had brought "some very good likenesses of the Pond to sell", and had been obliged to take them out of the window of [his shop], almost the very moment they were placed there!'

The trial itself almost reads as an anti-climax. At this period, prisoners accused of a felony could have legal counsel, but only for advice and to deal with points of law. How rigorously this was applied varied from circuit to circuit, but the theory was that it was up to the prosecution to prove its case so well that no defence could be mounted. And in this particular case there was no defence: publicans and stablemen between London and Gill's Hill all testified to seeing Thurtell with Weare in the gig. Then Weare vanished, while the pistol with human remains on it was found just where Thurtell had been seen searching. Items belonging to Weare were in the possession of the three men, and Hunt knew where the body was to be found. Thurtell spoke in his own defence, as the law permitted. He read out a list he had compiled of wrongful convictions throughout history, but one journalist thought it was so long that it was counterproductive: everyone stopped listening.* He blamed everybody except himself for his misfortunes: his creditors, his solicitor, fellow merchants, the insurance office – all had betrayed him. As to the murder itself, Hunt and Probert had done it, he said. Hunt tried to read his defence, but was so overcome he managed to read only a bit of it 'in a poor dejected voice, and then leant his wretched head upon his hand' while someone else read the rest.

The law required that trials were held continuously, unless the jury demanded a break. Thurtell and Hunt's trial began at eight o'clock on the morning of 6 January, and ran without pause until after nine o'clock that night, when the jury called a halt. The two defence speeches and the summing-up were heard the next day, after which the jury may not even have retired to consider their verdict: the journals merely say the members 'conferred' for twenty minutes. Hunt

---

* Almost every report agrees that Thurtell read his defence, and read it well. Yet a contemporary scholar thinks that Thurtell's letters 'show him to have been semi-literate' at best, and suggests that Egan may have had a hand in his defence speech. Perhaps Thurtell, a lover of theatre, had memorized it.

was convicted as an accessory and sentenced to transportation; Thurtell was found guilty of murder, and the only sentence for that was death.*

Immediately, the horse expresses set off for the printers. For some, even that wasn't fast enough. The artist William Mulready, having attended the trial, quickly sent a long account to his patron in Northumberland – the trial finished on a Wednesday, and this way he would receive the news long before the Sunday newspapers' account.† By then, the execution would have taken place – forty-eight hours from verdict to gallows was the rule, unless a Sunday intervened.

This compression was a godsend to the newspapers, the weeklies in particular: they could print the trial, verdict and execution, all in one. The *Observer* advertised that its execution special would be double its usual length (which was only two pages), and would cost 14*d.*, instead of 7*d. Bell's* advertised the same: a double issue, at double the price, and, for its sporting readership, 'The same publication will contain an account of the Great Fight for Six Hundred Sovereigns between SPRING and LANGAN, for the rival Champions of England and Ireland ... written by the celebrated PIERCE EGAN.' Thurtell's supporters loved a good fight, and 'among the sporting circles bets are still offered on the result of the trial, and in many cases these are connected with the fight between Spring and Langan', noted the *Chronicle.*§ The connection continued to be made. An anti-capital-punishment essay from the 1860s reported on Thurtell's execution: 'It is said that the championship of England was to be decided ... on the

---

* Probert's escape via immunity was short-lived. In 1825 he was convicted of stealing a horse and hanged at Newgate. A broadside claimed that so many people attended his execution that 'a boy actually walked from one side of the street to the other, on the heads of the people'.

† Mulready also sketched both Hunt and Probert. The drawings are now in the Victoria and Albert Museum.

§ Thurtell lived on among the sporting set. In 1868, at a dog show, a 'champion stud' included the pups Palmer, Probert and Williams. For Palmer, the Rugeley poisoner, see below, pp.258ff. Williams may either be the Ratcliffe Highway murderer, or one of a trio of murderers in the Burke and Hare style, who was executed for the murder of an Italian beggar-boy in 1831.

morning of the day on which Thurtell was executed, and that, when he came out on the scaffold, he inquired privily of the executioner if the result had yet become known. Jack Ketch* was not aware, and Thurtell expressed his regret that the ceremony in which he was chief actor should take place so inconveniently early in the day.'

For those who could not afford newspapers, Thurtell broadsides had been pouring out over the past months. Many provided updates and trial reports, while others had songs and poetic effusions. One had an 'action' picture, with Thurtell dragging Weare's body into the bushes (this cost double the normal price, 2*d*.). 'The Hertfordshire Tragedy; or, the Fatal Effects of Gambling. Exemplified in the Murder of Mr. Weare and the Execution of John Thurtell', a particularly long example, can stand here for many. It opened with a description of Thurtell's idyllic childhood, and his poor, loving mother. But then he sets off for that fatal city, London, and

> Like many a gay young man,
> He mix'd with thoughtless company,
> Which thousands has trepan'd [sic].
> He soon forgot his mother dear,
> And all his friends behind ...
>
> From bad to worse he did proceed,
> 'mid scenes of guilt and vice,
> Until he learn'd the cursed art,
> To play with cards and dice.
>
> And from that fatal, fatal day,
> His ruin we may date,
> Nor were his eyes e'er open'd,
> Until it was too late.

---

* Jack Ketch was a seventeenth-century hangman, and his name was used colloquially to mean any executioner.

The story of his being fleeced by Weare is rehearsed, and then the unsuspecting gambler heads for Hertfordshire.

> When they had reached Gill's Hill Lane,
> That dark and dismal place,
> Thurtell drew a pistol forth,
> And fir'd it in Weare's face.
>
> The helpless man sprung from the gig,
> And strove the road to gain,
> But Thurtell pounc'd on him, and dash'd
> His pistol through his brains.
>
> Then pulling out his murderous knife,
> As over him he stood,
> He cut his throat, and, tiger-like,
> Did drink his reeking blood.

This was accompanied by what were claimed to be portraits of Thurtell and Hunt, and eight illustrations.

Yet after the verdict was handed down, strangely, Thurtell the monster, Thurtell the drinker of blood, began to disappear, to be replaced by Thurtell the gallant, Thurtell the debonair. One broadside respectfully reported his considerate behaviour on the day of his execution, when he stood under the scaffold: 'he looked at the crowd, and made a slight bow, instantly every head was uncovered, and many muttered "what a Gentleman". His appearance at that moment was affecting beyond description.' In the 1920s the historian G.M. Trevelyan claimed that, a hundred years before, children wrote the sentence 'Thurtell was a murdered man' as an exercise in penmanship.

In 1857 George Borrow drew for his middle-class audience a picture entirely in keeping with this debonair post-trial image. In his novel *The Romany Rye*, the narrator is in money difficulties. 'A person I had occasionally met at sporting-dinners' comes to hear of his trouble and lends him £200.

I begged him to tell me how I could requite him for his kindness, whereupon, with the most dreadful oath I ever heard, he bade me come and see him hanged when his time was come. I wrung his hand, and told him I would, and I kept my word. The night before the day he was hanged at H—, I harnessed a Suffolk *Punch* to my light gig ... and ... in eleven hours I drove that *Punch* one hundred and ten miles. I arrived at H— just in the nick of time. There was the ugly jail – the scaffold – and there upon it stood the only friend I ever had in the world. Driving my *Punch*, which was all in a foam, into the midst of the crowd, which made way for me as if it knew what I came for, I stood up in my gig, took off my hat, and shouted, 'God Almighty bless you, Jack!' The dying man turned his pale grim face towards me – for his face was always somewhat grim, do you see – nodded and said, or I thought I heard him say, 'All right, old chap.' The next moment – my eyes water.

He concludes philosophically, 'Well, some are born to be hanged, and some are not; and many of those who are not hanged are much worse than those who are.'

It was said that 40,000 people attended Thurtell's execution, and afterwards his body was sent to St Bartholomew's Hospital for dissection by the faculty of medicine and its students, as was standard for felons. In theory, the anatomization process was a matter for the faculty alone, but on the day crowds of people descended on the anatomy theatre. For those who couldn't be there, *The Times* reported on the appearance of the body in the dissecting room, and Pierce Egan's *Account of the Trial of John Thurtell and Joseph Hunt* carried a notice from the publisher: 'SPECIAL PERMISSION having been given to the Editor of the MEDICAL ADVISER to examine the body of Thurtell after the execution, a full account of the PECULIAR CRANIOLOGICAL Appearances, with illustrative engravings, will appear in the next Number.' Rowlandson produced a watercolour of the scene, 'The Lancett Club at a Thurtell Feast'. (The surgeon doing the dissection is grotesquely caricatured, while the corpse of Thurtell is entirely realistic.)

Despite the finality of death, some found it hard to let go of such a money-spinner. 'Light be the stones on Thurtell's bones,' Thackeray wrote satirically; 'he was the best friend the penny-a-line men had for many a day ... and when he was turned off [hanged], their lamentation was sincere. There are few windfalls like him.' It was later claimed that James Catnach, the most successful broadside printer of the day, had sold 250,000 Thurtell broadsides, and after his execution he produced yet another, headlined 'WE ARE ALIVE', with the space between 'we' and 'are' so reduced that the unwary read 'WEARE ALIVE'. Another was less tricksy, and simply lied. 'The Hoax Discovered; or, Mr. Weare Alive' claimed that Thurtell had bet Weare that he could be arrested, tried and then, 'at the very crisis of their fate, the supposed murdered man should appear, stagger the belief of the world, and make *John Bull* confess his being hoaxed'.

The theatres returned to this profitable subject. At the Coburg, *The Hertfordshire Tragedy, or, The Victims of Gaming* was back onstage the day after the execution. The Surrey re-offered *The Gamblers* three days later, and as well as the 'identical Horse and Gig', it also promised an eager public that the set now contained the 'TABLE AT WHICH THE PARTY SUPPED, The SOFA as DESCRIBED to having been SLEPT on, with Other Household Furniture, AS PURCHASED AT THE LATE AUCTION'. In January, the theatre combined two items of popular interest by adding a 'new scene of Jackson's Rooms [Jackson was a prize-fighter who taught the gentry], for the purpose of introducing the celebrated Irish Champion', Langan himself.

The selling of Thurtell went on. A novel, *The Gamblers; or, The Treacherous Friend: A Moral Tale, Founded on Recent Facts*, by Hannah Maria Jones, appeared, borrowing elements from the play (both have characters named Woodville). The novel also acquiesced in the growing legend of Thurtell's nobility of spirit. Here Arthur Townley is purely 'a victim to his own lawless passions', a noble dupe brought down by 'hardened villains'. The novel, by one of only two women known to have successfully produced penny-bloods (her speciality was gypsies and gothic subjects), is unimportant except insofar as it may have influenced Edward Bulwer-Lytton.* Bulwer has been called one of the forefathers of the detective novel, and he popularized the outlaw-as-hero in *Paul Clifford* (1830), a novel with a good-hearted highwayman, and *Eugene Aram* (1832), this time with a self-sacrificing scholar-murderer (see pp.99–123). In *Pelham* (1828) his hero is Lord Pelham, who steps in to save a friend from a false accusation of murder. Thornton, the real murderer, is a fairly straightforward portrait of Thurtell. Unlike the prevailing attitudes to Thurtell, Thornton here is not a good-hearted naïf, but has coldly murdered his victim in a botched robbery.

Everything to do with Thurtell had a commercial value. In February 1824 an advertisement in *The Times* offered for sale the model of the cottage and outbuildings that had been used in court to explain the details of the crime to the jury. The advertisement appeared only once, so presumably the model sold quite quickly. This would hardly be surprising, for the Thurtell legend was growing with every day that separated him from his brutal crime. The most unlikely people were fascinated. The Radical journalist William Cobbett claimed that his son Richard had learned to read 'to find out what was said about THURTELL, when all the world was talking and reading about THURTELL'. Richard was born in 1804, and was therefore nineteen or twenty when Thurtell came to notoriety, yet the legend made it worth building stories around him. The philosopher Thomas Carlyle also followed the case closely, complaining that, 'Thurtell being hanged last week, we grew duller than ever.' He soon cheered himself up, however, with one of his longest-running jokes. An (erroneous) trial report claimed that a witness had considered Thurtell to be respectable 'because he kept a gig'. Carlyle found this immensely comic, and coined the words 'Gigmania' and 'Gigmanity' to describe

* Bulwer-Lytton (1803–73) was born Edward George Earle Lytton Bulwer, and until 1838 he was known as Edward Lytton Bulwer. On his father's death he became Sir Edward Bulwer, and in 1843 he added his mother's maiden name, Lytton, to become Sir Edward Bulwer-Lytton. Ultimately he became 1st Baron Lytton of Knebworth. For simplicity, I refer to him as Bulwer throughout. Unlike Bulwer, Hannah Jones's success was one of scale, not finance or renown: she wrote and sold widely, but was, according to *The Times*, given a pauper's burial. For more on penny-bloods, see pp.58–60.

those who judged character by the value of a person's possessions. George Eliot later expanded this, writing of 'conventional worldly notions and habits without instruction and without polish … proud respectability in a gig of unfashionable build'. And in 1848, towards the end of his novel *Vanity Fair*, Thackeray gave the dangerous Becky Sharpe a law firm named Burke, Thurtell and Hayes – the reader is entirely expected to recognize the three murderers' names.* And the joke ran and ran. In 1867, in *Miss Jane, the Bishop's Daughter*, a novel that used elements of the Constance Kent case (see pp.362–79), the Bishop is advised to put his case 'into the hands of Bedloe [a seventeenth-century fraudster], Wade and Weare of Thurtell's Inn … Very respectable solicitors in, ahem! their own line.'

In 1862, this kind of post-mortem approval made Thurtell, Probert and Hunt names to give authority pause. The Marylebone Theatre, a melodrama house, applied for a licence for a play to be called *The Gipsey* [sic] *of Edgware*. On the manuscript submitted for approval, in handwriting that appears to be that of the Lord Chamberlain's Examiner of Plays himself, notations marking the resemblances between the play and the murders appear in red ink throughout. At the end of the script 'Turtle's' half-sister dies, crying out, 'You are innocent, I know it …' Next to this, the censor simply added a large red exclamation point, and the licence was refused.

Another quarter of a century later, the poet Robert Browning remembered a bit of doggerel he had learned as a child:

> His throat they cut from ear to ear,
> His brains they battered in,
> His name was Mr William Weare,
> Wot lived in Lyons Inn.*

* * *

* Catherine Hayes (1690–1726) murdered her coal-merchant husband by beating him to death with the help of two men, then dismembering the body. She was the last woman in England to be burned alive for petty treason.

† It perhaps suits the theatricality of Thurtell's legend that Lyon's Inn was later pulled down to build the New Globe Theatre.

When the next great murder to capture the public's imagination rolled around only four years later, Thurtell was the reference point to which people naturally returned. Maria Marten was the daughter of a mole-catcher in Polstead, a small Suffolk village. She was no better than she should be, having had two illegitimate children by two different men. A third man, a farmer named William Corder, was her current companion, by whom she had a third child. This time she was pressing for marriage. She was last seen in May 1827, heading to meet Corder at his barn on her way to Ipswich to be married. Corder returned to Polstead several times that year, telling her father and stepmother that he and 'Mrs Corder' had settled in the Isle of Wight. At first he said she had hurt her hand, and so couldn't write; then that she had written and her letters must have gone astray. After the harvest, he left Polstead for good. Eleven months after the supposed marriage, her father found his daughter's remains buried in a shallow grave in the Red Barn (barns in the area were traditionally painted red, but this one quickly became *the* Red Barn). The local magistrates sent for a Runner to trace Corder, and he was soon arrested in the London suburb of Ealing, where he was now married and the proud co-proprietor of a girls' school.

Seducer-murders were not unknown, but the details of this one were a newspaper's dream. First Miss Marten was tidied up, while opprobrium was spread over Corder. From a modestly prosperous tenant farmer, he was transformed into the rich squire of melodrama, preying on the innocent village maiden: one broadside called him the 'son of an opulent farmer', 'living in great splendour'. Miss Marten, by contrast, was 'a fine young woman' who had merely formed an 'imprudent connexion'. George IV, the erstwhile Prince Regent whose numerous affairs had been daily fodder for prints and satire, had come to the throne in 1820; Victorian mores were some time in the future, and the broadsides do not deny her two illegitimate children, they just don't think they mattered. In one, Miss Marten was 'of docile disposition', inculcated with 'moral precepts', and her behaviour aroused 'the esteem and admiration of all'; her little missteps (the children) were caused entirely by a 'playful and vivacious disposition';

although 'her conduct cannot be justified, much might be said in palliation'. *The Times* even commended the father of her second child, for sending financial support; and his letters to his discarded mistress 'express the goodness of his heart … his conduct throughout has been that of a man and a Christian'.

Corder was condemned untried. He was 'unfeeling and wretched', said *The Times*, adding that he had also attempted to kill his mistress's second child. The *Observer* picked up this story, which it elaborated. Corder had offered the child a fig, but – 'as if by Divine interference' – it was refused. Miss Marten's stepmother, the story went on, cut open the fig, to find 'something in the shape of a pill … in it'. Oddly enough, Mrs Marten did not trouble to question Corder about this, and he next gave the child a pear. Mrs Marten, fruit-examiner-extraordinary, again found a pill in it, and again did nothing – from which we may safely conclude, unlike the newspapers at the time, that the incident never took place. But the newspapers were in full cry: Corder had murdered his child by Miss Marten, they reported; Corder had been involved in forgery; Corder had been engaged with 'the convict Smith' in 'transactions of a felonious nature … such as pig and horse-stealing'. Another report stated that Miss Marten's first child was by Corder's own brother.

But the real excitement for the readers was the facts of the murder and its discovery. Corder had persuaded Miss Marten to wear men's clothes for her trip to the barn: he claimed, falsely, that the village constable was going to arrest her for having no visible support for her surviving child. (A later broadside gives an alternative explanation, that she was dressed this way to throw his disapproving relatives off the track.) Then there was the legend of the discovery of the body. Broadsides and even sermons recounted how Miss Marten's stepmother had had a dream, three nights running, as in a fairy tale, in which she saw Miss Marten dead and buried in the barn. At these supernatural promptings, she persuaded her husband to go and search the Red Barn. The story of the dream was put in evidence at the inquest, although it is noticeable by its absence at the trial itself, being replaced with a more pragmatic explanation: as Miss Marten's continuing silence became more worrying, a neighbour remembered that Corder had borrowed a spade on the day of her disappearance, and another person had seen him leaving the barn with a pickaxe. More cynically, the *Observer* suggested that the Martens had not worried unduly until Corder stopped sending money; then 'the old people ... began to dream about the murder of their child'. Most print outlets, however, were happy to give credence to the dream: 'For many a long month or more, her mind being sorely oppress'd ... she dream'd three nights o'er, Her daughter she lay murdered, under the Red Barn floor.' Theatres loved it too: W.T. Moncrieff, in an 1842 version of the Red Barn story, *The Red Farm, or, The Well of St Marie*, noted in his foreword to the printed edition that 'The extraordinary *discovery of a murder* ... through the *agency of a dream*, might reasonably be doubted, did not the Judicial Records of our own Criminal History place it beyond all reach of scepticism.' As late as 1865–66, the dream in particular continued to be a perennial favourite.

Another piquant detail was found in Corder's life after he left Polstead, for he had met his wife by placing advertisements in the *Morning Herald* and the *Sunday Times*:

MATRIMONY. – A Private Gentleman, aged 24, entirely independent, whose disposition is not to be exceeded ... To any female of respectability ... and willing to confide her future happiness in one every way qualified to render the marriage state desirable, as the advertiser is in affluence; the lady must have the power of some property, which may remain in her own possession ... should this meet the eye of any agreeable lady, who feels desirous of meeting with a sociable, tender, kind and sympathising companion, they will find this advertisement worthy of notice. Honour and secrecy may be relied on.

Scandalized and thrilled, readers learned that Corder had received more than forty replies from the *Herald* alone; there had been another fifty-three from the *Sunday Times*, but by then he was fixed up, so he never bothered to collect them. After the murder the owner of the accommodation address where the replies to the newspaper advertisement had been sent published them in a pamphlet, to the delight of all. In Douglas Jerrold's play *Wives by Advertisement*, a send-up of Corder's love life, the Hon. Jenkins Cigar advertises: 'To the fair sex possessed of ten thousand a-year! A desirable opportunity! The advertiser is a gentleman aged five-and-twenty ... has been inoculated and had the measles ... he wears his own hair, and his moustachios, though in the stubble at present, promise to be forward in the spring ... The advertiser wishes to meet with an agreeable partner ... No letters received unless brought in a carriage and four ...'*

After a number of fairly standard farcical scenes, Cigar, 'alias Tomkins, alias Winks, alias Puppylove', is arrested, and the remaining characters, having learned their lesson, sing:

> ... oh, ye youths, the dame for ever scorn
> That's advertised with horses, pigs, and corn! ...
>
> And, oh, ye maids, from husbands turn away,
> If advertized with razors, dogs, and hay! ...

Jerrold's farce was at least staged after the trial. The same could not be said for many others. A dramatic version of the murder was reported to have been presented at the Stoke-by-Nayland Fair in May 1828; in July, while Corder was still awaiting trial, two 'theatrical representations' of 'The Late Murder of Maria Marten' were staged at the Cherry Fair in Polstead itself, one of which included a scene in

---

* Jerrold (1803–57) was a prolific playwright, with over seventy plays to his name, including the smash hit *Black-Ey'd Susan*. He wrote for *Punch*, and from 1852 he was the editor of *Lloyd's Weekly Newspaper*. His son Blanchard Jerrold (1826–84) was also a journalist, and became editor of *Lloyd's* on his father's death. He was named for his father's great friend, the journalist Laman Blanchard (1803–45), not to be confused with the playwright Leman [sic] Blanchard (1820–1889), who was no relation, but who also turns up in this book.

the Red Barn, 'where the mutilated body was [seen] lying on ... the floor, surrounded by the Coroner and the gentlemen of the jury as they appeared ... after the fatal discovery'. Ballad-singers also cried their wares, selling broadsides that stated outright that Corder was a murderer.

The prosperous were as much absorbed as the masses. Staffordshire pottery figures were produced of Corder and Miss Marten, and, even more importantly, of the Red Barn, impossibly bucolic, and frequently with Maria Marten looking winsome in the doorway. These were big, expensive pieces, not for the working classes. There were further options for those who wanted to disguise their interest under the cover of morality: long before the trial began the Revd Mr Young preached an entire sermon on Corder's evil deed, to a congregation said to number 5,000.

When Corder finally came to trial in August, the court spent some time on these affronts to justice.

> DEFENCE: Pray had you not got a person preaching about this murder in the very barn itself?
>
> THE LORD CHIEF BARON: What! what d'ye mean by preaching? – Is it a sermon?
>
> DEFENCE: Yes, my Lord, and to a congregation of several thousand persons, specially brought together after regular notice in the parish, to hear this man described as the murderer of this unfortunate girl.
>
> THE LORD CHIEF BARON: Scandalous! ...
>
> [Mr. W. Chaplin, the churchwarden is asked by the defence]: Did you hear the parson preach in the barn?
>
> MR CHAPLIN: No, certainly not; but I heard of the occurrence.
>
> DEFENCE: And you never interfered to prevent it?
>
> MR CHAPLIN: I did not.
>
> DEFENCE: Are there not exhibitions going round the neighbourhood, representing Corder as the murderer ... And you've not interfered to prevent them? Is there not a camera obscura near this very hall at this moment, exhibiting him as the murderer?

MR CHAPLIN: There is a camera obscura, I believe about the streets, but I do not know the nature of the exhibition, neither am I aware that I have any power to prevent them in my own parish, much less in this town.

Technically, a camera obscura is a box with a lens, which projects an image of a place or a person onto a flat surface. They were frequently used by artists at the time for sketching from nature. It may be that here the term is used to describe some form of peepshow using projections. George Sanger, later the proprietor of one of Europe's largest circuses (self-ennobled as 'Lord' George Sanger), as a boy in the late 1820s and 1830s toured fairgrounds with his father. Their peepshow 'Murder in the Red Barn' had pictures 'pulled up and down by strings', lit at night by candles.

I stood outside and asked the folks to 'Walk up and see the only correct views of the terrible murder of Maria Martin. They are historically accurate and true to life ... see how the ghost of Maria appeared to her mother on three successive nights at the bedside ...'

When we had our row of spectators getting their pennyworths from the peep-holes I would describe the various pictures as they were pulled up into view. The arrest of Corder was always given special prominence, as follows: 'The arrest of the murderer Corder as he was at breakfast ... Observe the horrified faces, and note also, so true to life are these pictures, that even the saucepan is shown upon the fire and the minute glass upon the table timing the boiling of the eggs.'

None of this publicity was enough to halt the trial, any more than the irregularities of the inquest had been. Corder had been barred from attending by the coroner, who claimed that 'he did not believe that the accused had any right to be present [at an inquest]; he never knew an instance of the kind'. It was explained to the coroner at the trial that, on the contrary, it was an obligation of the court that the accused should hear the depositions against him. Yet his abrogation of

Corder's rights did not appear to be any bar to him taking part in the trial itself, in which he acted as a prosecuting counsel.*

It probably made no difference. James Lee, the Bow Street Runner, had found Miss Marten's reticule in Corder's study, together with a pair of pistols and a sword, which was proved to have been sharpened at Corder's request just before the murder. Furthermore, letters from Corder to Miss Marten's parents, claiming his 'wife' was with him in 'our lodgings, in the Isle of Wight', were read out, in which he told them how they had married in Ipswich and that she 'unites with me for your wellfare [sic]', together with an ominous 'P.S. I think you had better burn all my letters.' Corder put up a miserable defence.† He claimed that Miss Marten had left Polstead to hide a new pregnancy from her family. (Why? She had already had three bastard children.) Then he asserted that she had had some unspecified relationship with an unnamed man in London, and that when she reached the barn, 'she flew into a passion, upbraided me with not having so much regard for her as the gentleman before alluded to', and shot herself. Terrified to find himself with a body on his hands, he buried her. The stab wounds noted at the autopsy must have been made by a spade when the body was exhumed, he claimed.

This last is not as implausible as it sounds today. Post-mortems were still rudimentary (the first use of the term had only appeared a

---

* In very simplified form, until the 1880s, prosecutions in England and Wales were brought privately, by the victims or (in cases of murder) representatives of the victims. (Scottish law had slightly different procedures.) The most important cases were frequently taken over by the Home Office, with the Treasury Solicitor overseeing the case for the prosecution. In 1879 the creation of the Department of Public Prosecutions gave the Attorney General an enhanced role, and improved coordination. The police, as hunters of criminals, gradually took over the preparation of the prosecutions through the century.

While the government was not necessarily involved in any prosecution, for much of the century there was a marked lack of separation of function. As late as 1877, in the case of a woman accused of murdering a child, the Chief Constable sat on the bench during the magistrates' hearing, and a policeman who gave evidence at the same hearing served as a juror at the inquest on the child.

† Many newspapers claimed that Corder was planning to use Thurtell's defence speech. He may have been planning it, although given the different circumstances of the two cases it would be hard to understand how, much less why. Ultimately he did not, and the story is probably more likely to be newspaper hype, a way of alluding to the previous exciting murder.

decade before). An initial post-mortem had decided that the 'chief cause of death' was 'a [bullet] wound in the orbit [eye-socket]', but after the remains had been re-interred, 'It has been regretted that for the ends of justice, more time was not given for the inspection of the body, or that the inspection had not been minutely made,' as on reflection a bullet through the eye was 'little likely to be chosen for the perpetration of a murder of this deliberate character'. The body was therefore re-exhumed, and two stab wounds were now found, one between the ribs and one in the heart, both entirely unnoticed at the first PM. By the time the trial was under way, yet further thought had suggested that the silk kerchief Miss Marten had worn had been pulled 'so tight upon the neck as to have produced death by strangulation'.

Corder was found guilty and sentenced to death. *The Times* was not sure which was more important, the verdict itself, or the speed with which the newspaper had reported it. 'We yesterday morning, by extraordinary exertion, published the proceedings of the court up to the adjournment on the previous day, – or, in other words, gave in six closely printed columns the report of a trial which took place on the previous day at a distance of 72 miles from London, and which was not adjourned till eight o'clock in the evening,' it boasted.

More sermons were immediately preached. On 17 August, the Revd Charles Hyatt of the Ebenezer Chapel, Shadwell, travelled to the Red Barn to deliver a sermon to 'about 2,000 persons', taking his text from Numbers 32:23: 'Be sure your sin will find you out', and using it to recycle the type of newspaper rumour familiar from the Thurtell case. When Corder was at school, Mr Hyatt told his congregation, 'the depravity of [his] nature often displayed itself, by his constant habit of telling falsehoods, and by the depredations he committed upon his companions'; he had later formed 'an acquaintance with a girl of very loose character' and, as 'the wages of her iniquity', had supplied her with 'peas and other articles from his father's farm'. The sermon ended by warning 'the peasantry' against poaching, which Mr Hyatt stressed would lead to greater vices (presumably murdering women and burying them in barns).

That same evening, the Revd J. Pilkington preached from the same text at the Baptists' Meeting House in Rayleigh, Essex, and at Bury St Edmunds the Revd George Hughes took a different text, but also preached on Corder. 'A Suffolk Clergyman' published *An Address to My Parishioners and Neighbours on the Subject of the Murder lately committed at Polstead, in Suffolk*, in which a certain amount of space was given to how the wages of sin lead only to death, while a great deal more was devoted to the details of Miss Marten's murder. Furthermore, the clergyman had attended Corder's final church service in gaol before his execution, a regular stop on the route to the gallows. The condemned was placed in a special, black-painted pew, while the coffin that he or she was shortly to fill stood in the centre of the chapel. The Suffolk clergyman evidently paid little attention to divine service that day, for he was able to describe Corder's every gesture for his readers.

A novel, published together with a transcript of the trial, quickly appeared. This was 'founded on fact', the reader is assured, although it is an absolutely standard melodrama: there is the pure maiden, with her virtuous father, a model of 'industry and frugality'; a gypsy fortune-teller; some smugglers; a gambler who in a Thurtell-ish moment 'plucks', or cheats, the Corder character; and a rejected suitor who returns having made a fortune in India. The author was probably the penny-blood writer Robert Huish (possibly together with the journalist William Maginn), who later wrote similar 'true' crime novels about James Greenacre and Maria and Frederick Manning (see pp.92–8, 157–82).*

The Times reported that by nine o'clock on the morning of the execution a thousand people had gathered at the scaffold in Bury St Edmunds. Three hours later this had swelled to 7,000. Unlike Thurtell's, Corder's death could not be mythologized. At the scaffold, claimed one broadside, he was 'so weak as to be unable to stand without support', and 'he looked somewhat wildly around' while he waited

---

* It is probably safe to say that Huish was the only penny-blood author who was also an expert on beekeeping. For many years he was a columnist for the *Gardener, Florist and Agriculturalist*, and he was the author of *A Treatise on the Nature, Economy, and Practical Management of Bees*.

for the rope to be adjusted. In 1824, technical changes had been made to the scaffold, allowing adjustable chains which reduced delays while the hangman corrected the length of the rope. Even so, prisoners were still assessed only by height, not by weight, and some, in the phrase of the day, 'died hard'. Corder was one of them. The hangman had to perform the 'disgusting but necessary task, of suspending his own weight around the body of the prisoner, to accelerate his death'. Even then, it took another eight minutes for him to die.

Not everyone was disturbed. Physical remains were treated with a pragmatism that has since vanished. During the trial, the surgeon had 'produced the skull of the deceased', which was handed round to the jury members so they could see the fracture for themselves. A broadside commemorated this moment: 'They brought her heart, her scull [sic], and ribs,/And showed before his face …' Mr Marten, testifying to the finding of his daughter's body, merely said he had 'put down a mole spike into the floor … and brought up something black, which I smelt and thought it smelt like decayed flesh'. For those who may

The execution of William Corder was watched by perhaps 7,000 people. This type of illustration of the death was common, and shows how many of the prosperous middle classes, male and female, attended. One of the many food-sellers who supplied the crowd's needs is in the centre foreground.

have missed these details in the newspapers and broadsides, Corder's body itself was soon on display. After the execution it was transported to the town's Shire Hall, where 'Two incisions were made in the breast, the skin taken of [sic], and the muscles exposed to view.' Then the body was displayed on a table in the middle of the Court, 'quite naked, with the exception of the trowsers, shoes, and stockings'.* 'Many thousands' were admitted. For those who couldn't be there, 'two eminent artists, Mr. Mizotti of Cambridge and Mr. Child of Bungay', made plaster casts. The following day the body was taken to the County Hospital and wired up to a battery to make it twitch in a demonstration of galvanic power, while the phrenologists, quack scientists who read character from the shape, or bumps, in the skull, competed for a cast of the head. Only after that did dissection proceed, for the benefit of the medical students. The bones 'having been cleared of the flesh', they were 're-united by Mr S. Dalton, and the skeleton is now placed in the Suffolk General Hospital' (one visitor was reported to be Mr Marten himself). 'A great portion of the skin has been tanned, and a gentleman connected with the hospital intends to have the Trial and Memoirs of Corder bound in it. The heart has been preserved in spirits.' Many years later the pickled scalp was displayed by a leather-seller in Oxford Street.†

Other souvenirs, slightly less macabre, were also available. The executioner, as a matter of right, got the clothes Corder died in, and also the rope. Such was the excitement over this case that it was reported that he had sold off the rope sections at a guinea an inch, including among his purchasers, it was rumoured, a gentleman from Cambridge who came especially to add this trophy to the university collection. For the artistic, a miniature of Corder was on display at the

---

* John Williams' body, too, had been described as 'naked', and it too was dressed in shirt, trousers and stockings. For much of the century 'naked' meant dressed only in under-clothes, but in these cases it seems to mean without jacket, hat, kerchief or neck-cloth – that is, without any outdoor clothes.

† In 1943 *The Times* reported that the town clerk in Bury St Edmunds had turned up the prosecution brief for the trial. It was given to the Bury St Edmunds museum, which was already the proud possessor of the book bound in Corder's skin, and his preserved scalp.

following Royal Academy Summer Exhibition. (The journals claimed to be appalled that respectable people were interested: 'we looked, paused, reconsulted our catalogue, looked again, rubbed our eyes ... No, it is impossible!' But they reported it all the same.) For those with less cash and more enterprise, there was the barn itself, which was taken apart and 'sold in tooth-picks, tobacco-stoppers, and snuff-boxes'.

Kaleidoscope magazine mocked the entire circus, with a picture of Corder lying on a dissecting table under which are sacks labelled 'Mr Corder's clothes' and 'Relics for sale'. Standing on the table over the body is an auctioneer, who is calling out, 'Now then, Ladies & Gentlemen – the Halter is going at a Guinea an inch,' while a person in the crowd responds, 'I want some of it for the University,' and another cries, 'Oh! how delightfully Horrible!' To one side, a man is saying to another, 'The Officer says, Mr Sheriff, that the Pistols belong to him,' while the other replies, 'Why I would not part with them man for 100 Guineas!' A second picture shows Corder's body twitching, naked, on the dissecting table. A man at the door says, 'I came to take a cast of his head,' only to be told, 'You must wait till the galvanic operations are over.' Outside, the crowd gathers around a sign advertising 'Camera obscura of the murder'.

From the outset fairs loved the story of the doomed Maria Marten. The journalist Henry Mayhew interviewed a strolling player who performed the Red Barn murder at a fair 'in cavalier costume'. Reality was not the key: excitement was. The whole country was getting younger: at the end of the eighteenth century, 17 per cent of the population was between five and fourteen years old; by the 1820s, it was 25 per cent, and almost half the population was under twenty. This was an audience worth catering to: even if, individually, they had almost no money, collectively they could create riches. For many children, however, even minor theatre was out of reach. A place in the gallery of somewhere like the Britannia Theatre in Hoxton appeared cheap to the middle classes, but it cost between 3 and 4*d*., a significant sum to the less fortunate. Instead many boys and girls frequented illegal, unlicensed penny-gaffs, housed in disused shops and turned into theatres by erecting a rough stage at one end, with the remaining space filled with benches.

In 1838 it was estimated that there were about a hundred gaffs in London, each with a capacity of one hundred to 150 per sitting, with up to nine daily sittings. Thus attendance in any twenty-four hours was, at the least, and in London alone, 50,000 people. The audiences, almost entirely under the age of sixteen, were given, for their penny, three-quarters of an hour of some abbreviated play, two further pieces of about twenty minutes each, and a song. Much of the material was a debased version of what the regular theatres showed, and a great deal of it was obscene.* There were no playbills, only a board with details of the evening's entertainment outside. One example was:

On Thursday next will be performed

at

Smith's Grand Theatre,

THE RED-NOSED MONSTER,

or,

THE TYRANT OF THE MOUNTAINS ...

To conclude with

the BLOOD-STAINED HANDKERCHIEF,

or,

THE MURDER IN THE COTTAGE

Marionettes were frequently on the bill at the gaffs, and at fairs across the country. By the 1870s some marionette companies were substantial outfits, having five or six wagons touring in annual circuits, performing on stages set up at each stop for up to seven hundred people nightly. Thomas Holden, a later Victorian puppeteer, had a stage that was eight feet deep, and a proscenium arch fourteen feet across. Maria Marten was one of the touring staples, in the repertory

---

* Almost everything we know about penny theatres comes from middle-class journalists, who wrote for equally middle-class readers who expected to be horrified and perhaps titillated by their reports. Class biases are a given, even from the most sympathetic reporters.

of companies in the Midlands, Yorkshire, Wales and even into Europe. *The Times* report of a police raid on a penny-gaff in 1844 noted that the play being performed by 'automaton figures ... made to move with wires' was *Maria Martin, or, The Red Barn Murder*. The police took into custody not only eighty-three audience members, but also 'the wretch Corder, and his victim, Maria Martin; also the figure of death'.* Later Clunn Lewis, the proprietor of a long-lasting marionette company, claimed that Corder's son came to see his family perform; Charles Middleton, another proprietor, countered by saying that in the 1860s his company had from delicacy refrained from performing in Colchester, where a surviving Corder lived.

The youth audience was avid, and penny-bloods quickly appeared. 'Penny-bloods' was the original name for what, in the 1860s, were renamed penny-dreadfuls. Each booklet, or 'number', consisted of eight (sometimes sixteen) pages, with a single black-and-white illustration on the top half of the front page. Double columns of text filled the remainder, breaking off wherever the final page finished, even in the middle of a sentence. The numbers appeared weekly, and could be bought as they were issued, or in monthly parts of four numbers bound together in a coloured wrapper. Bloods developed out of late-eighteenth-century gothic tales. G.A. Sala, in his youth a blood-writer, later a renowned journalist, described the bloods as 'a world of dormant peerages, of murderous baronets, and ladies of title addicted to the study of toxicology, of gipsies and brigand-chiefs, men with masks and women with daggers, of stolen children, withered hags, heartless gamesters, nefarious roués, foreign princesses, Jesuit fathers, gravediggers, resurrection-men, lunatics and ghosts'.

The bloods' astonishing success created a vast new readership for cheap fiction. Between 1830 and 1850 there were probably as many as

---

* Some puppets from the Tiller-Clowes company have survived and are now in the Victoria and Albert Museum. The museum has filmed a tiny clip of the marionettes in action in the Red Barn, which was at one point viewable on its website. It has recently vanished, and can now be seen only by appointment at their Hammersmith archive. This is a great pity, for it is well worth watching for the red handkerchief that flowers on Maria's bosom as she is knifed, and the dastardly Corder's final 'heh-heh-heh' and hop for joy after her death.

a hundred publishers of penny fiction – ten for every one publisher of 'respectable' fiction. Many magazines, previously seen as improving reading for the working classes, now wholeheartedly gave themselves over to this type of tale. The first ever penny-blood, in 1836, was *The Lives of the Most Notorious Highwaymen, Footpads, &c.*, in sixty numbers. *Gentleman Jack* followed, running for 205 parts over four years, without too much worry for historical accuracy or continuity. (The historical highwaymen Claude Duval, Dick Turpin and Jack Rann all appear as coevals, even though their lives actually spanned a century; Jack Rann is, rather carelessly, killed twice.) The main characteristics of the highwaymen conformed to melodrama type: they were upper-class, usually switched at birth, and yet despite being reared among thieves, they were noble and protected the poor and virtuous. The illustrations, crude to modern eyes, were an essential element. One publisher's standing instruction to his illustrators was, 'more blood – much more blood!' The most successful penny-blood, and what might be the most successful series the world has ever seen, first appeared in 1844, written by G.W.M. Reynolds, politically a Radical, who two years later founded the journal *Reynolds's Miscellany*. His *Mysteries of London* was based on a French series, *Mysteries of Paris*, by Eugène Sue, but it took on a life of its own, spanning twelve years, 624 numbers, nearly 4.5 million words and a title change to *Mysteries of the Courts of London*.

Henry Mayhew interviewed thousands of the working class in the 1840s and 1850s for his monumental study of street life, *London Labour and the London Poor*. These people were Reynolds' prime market, and Mayhew reported that an 'intelligent costermonger', who regularly read bloods aloud to his less literate friends, told him: 'You see's an engraving of a man hung up, burning over a fire, and some costers would go mad if they couldn't learn what he'd been doing, who he was, and all about him.' The illiteracy of the auditors did not mean they had little vocabulary or understanding, however. The costermonger told Mayhew of 'one of the passages that took their fancy wonderfully': 'With glowing cheeks, flashing eyes, and palpitating bosom, Venetia Trelawney rushed back into the refreshment-room, where she

59

threw herself into one of the arm-chairs ... scarcely had she thus sunk down upon the flocculent cushion, when a sharp click ... met her ears; and ... her wrists were caught in manacles which sprang out of the arms of the treacherous chair ...' Anyone who was happy to hear about flocculent cushions and palpitating bosoms could take most things in their stride.

In the1860s, after highwaymen and evil aristocrats, the next penny development was the remorseless policeman hunting down criminals. A Corder blood merged the two genres. The evil William Corder, hoping to marry 'lady Amelia', has first to 'dispose' of his illegitimate child by Maria, who stands between 'Amelia, happiness and myself!' Maria threatens to tell Amelia of her situation, and, 'yelling in demoniac rage and ungovernable passion, the sinful man' drives his knife 'into her throbbing breast, from which the fell demon had torn the covering', shoots her for good measure and buries her in the barn. Now Captain Dash, a notorious highwayman, appears at Corder's 'grand masked ball' and reveals all, before taking up a siege position in the Red Barn. Dash turns out to be Maria's rejected suitor, who loved her truly and became a highwayman from grief. There is no date on this publication, but it must be post-1860, as a detective appears to tidy away everything at the end, and a further title is advertised on the back cover: 'Lightning Dick, the Young Detective' – boy detectives first appeared in the 1860s.

Melodrama, too, took Maria Marten to its heart. The earliest stage version of the story was announced at the Pavilion Theatre, Mile End, shortly after the trial, and there is a brief outline of the scenes in the playbill. In Act I, Corder promises to marry Maria, but is already planning her betrayal: 'The deed were bloody, sure, but I will do't ...' After Maria's murder, her mother wakes from a nightmare: 'Help, help! My child! I saw her, sure, lifeless, smeared with blood! 'Twas in the Red Barn! – and there stood Corder with a pickaxe digging out her grave ...' When Mr Marten discovers the body, there is an 'affecting scene': 'she was the darling of my age, the prop of my existence'. In the final scene in Bury Gaol, Maria appears to Corder as a ghost. His last words are 'Guilt, guilt ... I am, I am her murderer!'

This story remained a favourite: a version in Cheltenham in 1828 had Miss Marten shot in front of the audience's eyes; a production in Weymouth introduced gypsies into the plot (this element swiftly infiltrated most productions, usually in the guise of Pharos Lee, the renamed Runner); there was a Welsh version in 1829, in Monmouth and later in Cardiff; an undated production in Swansea; a production in Hull advertised 'Maria Marlin [sic], the Pride of the Village', who after death conducts her mother to her resting place 'IN A FLAME OF FIRE'. In an early 1860s version, James Lee, the Bow Street Runner who had arrested Corder, now aged seventy-six, recreated his arrest onstage for a benefit performance.* All of these productions conformed to the standard melodrama casting, with Corder played by the 'heavy'; Mr Marten the 'second heavy', or 'heavy father'; Tim Bobbin, the comic servant, by the 'first low comedian'; Mrs Marten the 'character old woman'; and Maria herself, the 'leading lady'.

Despite the multiplicity of productions, only two Red Barn scripts survive from the nineteenth century, one from what may be the Swansea production, the second from an 1890s northern touring company. The Swansea production conforms to all the standard melodrama requirements: it has the aged father blessing his child's forthcoming marriage, the comic servants, the villain resolved on murder, the beautiful heroine pleading for her life 'For my aged parents' sake', 'the voice of Heaven conveying to a mother's heart the murder of her darling child', and finally, forgiveness for the sinner, amidst scenic effects in the condemned cell: '*Ghost music. Blue fire. The spirit of Maria Marten appears.*' Corder confesses, '*Bell tolls. Characters form picture* [that is, stand frozen in a tableau]. *Blue fire.*'

By the 1890s, melodrama was no longer treated entirely seriously. A Manchester revival had music-hall turns interpolated into the story:

---

* Benefits were performances for which the box-office receipts were given to a particular actor, playwright, or some other person connected with the theatre. At many East End theatres, all actors and writers – even the stage manager – expected to have a benefit every season. The theatres also had benefits for local causes, or for famous people in need of financial support, like Lee.

'Sometimes the actor brings in a sly sentence in a burlesque of a line in *Hamlet*, and sometimes the house is made to roar over an allusion to a great cabbage which is brought on the stage.' There was also a role for the 'intelligent donkey, Jerry', who would 'prove that all men are descended from donkeys', not to mention an unexplained 'statue song' and some dancing.

Long before the intelligent donkey took over, more frightening murderers were to stalk the stage. These were two Irishmen living in Edinburgh: William Burke and William Hare. Burke and Hare were, if you will, pioneers of capitalism, meeting rising demand with a more efficient supply. Medical schools officially used only the corpses of executed criminals for dissection, but by the late 1820s demand far outstripped the number of criminals executed – in Surgeons' Square, Edinburgh, alone there were six lecturers on anatomy, all of whom required bodies on which to demonstrate. Thus, most medical schools quietly dealt with resurrection men, men who stole recently buried corpses from cemeteries. This was semi-illegal ('semi' because dead bodies in law belonged to no one; resurrectionists could be charged only with stealing grave clothes), but for the most part the trade was winked at.

The resurrection market was, however, tightly controlled, and two good-for-nothings like Burke and Hare had no hope of entering this macabre profession. These two men, whose names became synonyms for brutal murder, stumbled into their occupation by chance. Burke had been a navvy on the Union Canal, and then a cobbler; Hare kept a poor man's lodging house in Tanner's Close, where a third-share in a bed could be purchased for 3*d*. a night. Sometime in 1827, Burke and his common-law wife Helen McDougal moved in with Hare and his wife Margaret, after their own lodgings had burned down. Together they drank and got through life as best they could until a pensioner named Dougal died owing Hare rent. Burke and Hare recouped the debt by selling his body to Dr Knox, who ran one of Edinburgh's three anatomy schools. To their astonishment, they received £7.10*s*. for the body – easily six months' pay for an unskilled labourer. They lived off this windfall for the entire winter, and it was only in the new year that they realized that even £7.10s. would not keep them for ever. But old, frail people with no family ties don't die on command. Then they had their brainwave – old, frail people with no family ties died every day among Edinburgh's underclass, and no one questioned the death of one pauper more or less. So Burke, the more personable character, lured the unwary to Hare's lodgings, where the two men gave them a drink and, when they were pleasantly fuddled, asphyxiated them. Then there was another fresh corpse for Dr Knox, and another few months' income for the Burke and Hare families. In February 1828 an old woman, name unknown, vanished from their lodgings; sometime later that winter so did 'Joseph the miller'. There were possibly more before Mary Paterson, a local prostitute, was disposed of the same way in April. But the pair were getting reckless. Mary Paterson's friend Janet Brown had accompanied her when Burke enticed them to his lodgings, offering to keep them in fine style. Mary became stupefied with drink, but Janet left before she reached that stage. There was now a witness to the fact that at least one person had visited the Tanner's Close lodging house and then vanished. Mary Paterson had been dead only five or six hours when her body was purchased by Dr Knox's attendant. Yet no questions were asked about her obviously recent death, nor the lack of any indication that she had ever been buried. In his confession, Burke said no questions ever were asked. The assistant who bought Mary Paterson's corpse was one William Fergusson – later Sir William Fergusson Bart, FRS, Serjeant-Surgeon to Queen Victoria and President of the Royal College of Surgeons.

Fergusson and his associates regularly paid Burke and Hare between £8 and £10 per corpse, and things went on smoothly until October 1828, when hubris was followed by nemesis. James Wilson, or 'Daft Jamie', was their next victim. Daft Jamie was a well-known Edinburgh street character who lived by begging and petty trading. He was about twenty years old at the time of his murder, physically large, but simple-minded and with a physical handicap, possibly club feet. It appears that Jamie refused the offers of alcohol, and thus, unlike all the other victims, was young, strong and sober, and able to fight back. Burke and Hare finally overpowered him, but it was impossible that his body showed no signs of violent death. It was even more impossible that no one would recognize his corpse. Some of the students did, but this simply hastened the dissection. Daft Jamie's head and feet, which would have been familiar to many, were kept separate, again contrary to practice, as if Dr Knox and his assistants wanted to get rid of the recognizable bits first.

Even then, Burke and Hare continued unchecked. Their final victim was an elderly Irishwoman named Docherty. The Burkes had lodgers sharing their room, an ex-soldier named Gray and his wife. They were asked to move to Burke's brother's room for the night so

Broadsides gave the details of murders in prose and verse. Frequently the illustrations were stock images – an execution, or even a landscape or pastoral view. Others were more relevant, but this one is unusual in its brutally comic verdict on the victim's end.

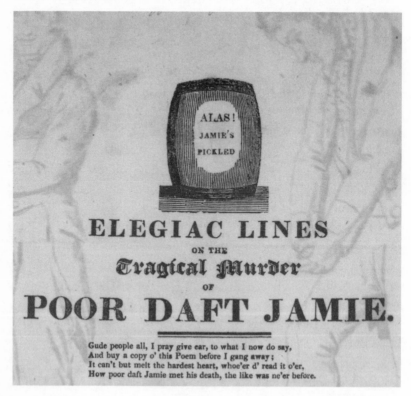

ALAS!
JAMIE'S
PICKLED

ELEGIAC LINES
ON THE
Tragical Murder
OF
POOR DAFT JAMIE.

Gude people all, I pray give ear, to what I now do say,
And buy a copy o' this Poem before I gang away;
It can't but melt the hardest heart, whoe'er d' read it o'er,
How poor daft Jamie met his death, the like was ne'er before.

the Burkes could entertain their 'kinswoman'. The next morning, the Grays were told that she had become drunk and quarrelsome, so they had sent her on her way, Burke adding, 'She's quiet enough now.' They also told Mrs Gray to stay away from a pile of straw in the corner. She had never been forbidden any area of their room before, so when the Burkes went out she investigated, and uncovered the corpse of an old woman. The couple, shocked, told Mrs Hare, who blandly offered them £10 to keep quiet. They left and notified the police.

By the time the police arrived, there was no body, but it was soon located in Dr Knox's rooms, and the story unfolded. The Burkes and the Hares were all arrested, yet a successful prosecution was uncertain. The medical evidence for death by asphyxiation without violence on an old and frail woman like Mrs Docherty would be minimal, and apart from this one body, all the previous 'sales' had already been disposed of through the dissecting room. Hare was therefore chosen to turn king's evidence, particularly as, if he had been charged, Margaret Hare would not have been able to testify against her husband.* It was Hare's evidence that enabled indictments to be laid against Burke and his wife, Helen McDougal, on 8 December, for the murders of Mrs Docherty, Mary Paterson and Daft Jamie, and it was these three murders that formed the basis of the prosecution's case.

Huge crowds surrounded the court for the trial, with three hundred special constables drafted in to hold people back, and the cavalry and infantry on standby. The trial lasted two days – 24 and 25 December – and it took the jury only fifty minutes to find Burke guilty, and the case against McDougal 'not proven'.† Burke was sentenced to be hanged, dissected and anatomized. Helen McDougal was officially

---

* There is no evidence that Hare or Burke ever married the women they lived with, but under Scottish law, living together made them legally man and wife.

† 'Not proven' is a verdict in Scottish law, indicating that the prosecution has failed to make its case sufficiently strongly to secure a conviction, yet neither has the jury been persuaded that the accused had no involvement in the crime. A 'not proven' verdict means that the prisoner is released.

released, but was kept in custody to protect her from the mob, who felt that she too should be 'burked'. The Hares were kept in prison while the courts heard a suit by Daft Jamie's mother to bring a private prosecution for his death; when that failed, another civil action, for 'assythment', or compensation, kept them imprisoned until after Burke's execution.

All three ultimately skulked out of town, trying to escape their notoriety. Hare was recognized in Dumfries, and a crowd estimated at 8,000 gathered, hoping to lynch him. It took a hundred special constables to rescue him, and he was kept in prison overnight for his own protection before being set on the road to Carlisle. McDougal, according to one broadside, was recognized as she was attempting to get passage to Ireland, and at a cry of 'Hare's wife! Burke her!' a mob gathered. Legends of the afterlife of all three abounded, particularly for Hare – he was said to have been tossed in a lime kiln and blinded, or to have ended as a beggar on London's Oxford Street – but nothing more is known of any of them.

Public interest in the case was all-consuming. In 1815, in his novel *Guy Mannering*, Walter Scott had briefly mentioned the earlier case of Helen Torrence and Jean Waldie, 'resurrection women', as he styled them. They had promised to procure a child's body for a surgeon and, no child having conveniently died, they murdered one. Now Scott, sorry to be away during Burke's trial, was amused to receive that same month 'a very polite card from the Medical Society inviting me to dine with them. It sounded like a card from Mr Thurtell inviting one to a share of his gig.' At the same time an enterprising citizen had rented Hare's cellar, and was showing it 'for a trifle' to visitors who queued twenty deep to have a look, and Scott was a wry observer of the 'well dress'd females' who visited it: 'I did not go ... although the newspapers reported me one of the visitors.'*

---

* He may not have gone, but he remained fascinated: two years later he wrote to the publisher of one of the trial reports, saying he had compared Burke's and Hare's confessions, and listing over twenty instances where they conflicted.

Everything to do with the case was enthusiastically retailed in the newspapers. The *Aberdeen Journal* gave four of its five columns to the trial transcript, plus an editorial, and then ended with the rather naked hope that a local woman, one 'Abigail Simpson, a miserable old woman, a pauper', who had vanished some time before, might also have been one of the victims. The *Courant*'s circulation increased by 8,000 copies on the day it reported the trial. Nothing was too minor to be repeated, and, in default of other news, repeated several times. Many newspapers, rather than sending their own journalists, simply copied other papers' reports, creating an echo chamber of innuendo and rumour. This applied to the London dailies as well as the smaller provincial weeklies or bi-weeklies. *The Times* had no non-Scottish-sourced article on Burke and Hare until after Burke's conviction, and even then it was only an editorial. That same day, an article on Burke's confession stressed that 'The information from which the following article is drawn up we have received from a most respectable quarter' – but that 'we' is somewhat fudged, as the entire article, 'we' included, is an unacknowledged reprint from the *Caledonian Mercury*.

The crowd at Burke's execution – perhaps 20,000 people – cheered as the scaffold was built. For most executions, the labourers who constructed the scaffold drew lots to decide which of them would perform the hateful task. This time there were volunteers. Not for this crowd the respect frequently given to a gallant outlaw, or the pity for a pathetic victim only too closely resembling themselves. When Burke appeared, the crowd screamed its hatred: 'The murderer! burke him! choke him!' A journalist reported one spectator 'hallooing and encouraging the mob to persevere in these manifestations of their feelings', raising a roar each time the dying Burke was convulsed, conducting the crowd's response until the body was cut down. *The Times*, normally quick to condemn not only the behaviour of the crowds at an execution, but their very presence, praised these outbursts as 'ebullitions of virtuous and honest resentment … we honour them for it'.

As Burke's body was removed from the scaffold, souvenir-hunters descended, grabbing at shavings from the coffin, or pieces of the rope.

As usual, these relic-gatherers were condemned by the middle-class press. Yet middle-class scavengers were every bit as avid: a wallet made from Burke's scalp is in the History of Surgery Museum in Edinburgh's Royal College of Surgeons. Meanwhile Burke's corpse took the same trip to an anatomy theatre as had many of those he had accompanied. This time, though, it was to the rooms of Professor Monro, a competitor of Knox, who was keeping a very low profile. First the grandees got a private viewing – the surgeon Robert Liston; the phrenologist George Combe; his follower, the sculptor Samuel Joseph, who took a cast of Burke's head; and Sir William Hamilton, the philosopher, and Combe's enemy, as a debunker of phrenology. Then Monro performed a public dissection, initially delayed by a riot staged by the vast number of students refused entry. The police restored order only when they promised that all would get a turn, fifty at a time. The next day, there was a display of the now-anatomized corpse for non-medical visitors. Visitors filed past Burke's body between ten in the morning and dusk – perhaps as many as 30,000 came through the anatomy theatre. One man recorded in his diary: 'Burke's body was lying stretched out on a table in a large sort of lumber or dissecting room, quite naked. The upper part of the skull had been sawn off and the brain extracted, but in other respects he was untouched, except, indeed, that the hair had been all shaven off his body.'

All of these episodes were repeatedly recounted, not only in the newspapers, but in broadsides and ballads. The distinction between these forms of news was less rigid than it seems retrospectively. 'The Confession of Burk' [sic] is a broadside, but the content is in fact a reprint of news that had appeared in the *Edinburgh Evening Courant* the previous Saturday, while some of the newspapers elaborated an already extraordinary story with fictional devices: the *Aberdeen Journal* evidently saw no crossing of boundaries when it described, as though by an eye-witness, the death of one of the elderly victims.

This type of true-crime fiction was spreading. *The Murderers of the Close* was what today would be called a novelization, with 'conversations put into the mouths of the different persons, as well as a few of the events, trifling in themselves, [that] are indeed fictitious'. The story sticks pretty closely to fact, with additional dialogue tacked on for drama or pathos. The book ends with Burke's execution, and his religious meditations and remorse, and Hare's escape, rounded off with pious thoughts for all. The illustrations were provided by Robert Seymour, whose fame was otherwise for comic imagery. (Seven years later he was to suggest to his publisher creating a series of comic illustrations, with text to be provided by a young journalist. Mr Charles Dickens duly agreed, and what became *The Pickwick Papers* was born.)

Actual Burke and Hare comedy was supplied by 'Mansie Wauch's Dream' in the *Aberdeen Journal* the month after Burke's execution. 'Mansie Wauch' was a fictional creation of David Macbeth Moir, a Scottish doctor, whose *Life of Mansie Wauch, Tailor* had appeared in *Blackwood's* magazine and then in book form the previous year. Now, in his dream, Mansie is assaulted and boxed up for Dr Knox. First he is sanguine: 'I had once dined with Dr Knox, and had some hope that, if I were beside him, I had a fair chance for my life.' But when he is unpacked in the dissecting room, he hears Knox saying, '[T]his is indeed a prize; you have heard of Mansie Wauch, that's him. I'd get five guineas for his skull from Mr —, the Phrenological Lecturer.' '[M]y hopes in his mercy vanished like the morning dew,' despairs Mansie, but fortunately the phrenologist is unwilling to buy a burked corpse. And so Mansie takes heart and shouts: 'Murder – murder! I am Burked, but I winna be Knoxed.'

Unlike their practice with Maria Marten, the theatres in Britain at first held off from transforming this ugly story into melodrama. Not so in France, where the father of melodrama, René-Charles Guilbert de Pixérécourt (1773–1844), adapted it immediately as *Alice, ou, Les Fossoyeurs écossais* ('Alice, or, The Scottish Grave-diggers'). Alice, a poor orphan, works for her aunt, a French innkeeper, and is in love with their lodger Edouard, a Scottish medical student. When he is wounded in a duel, Alice absents herself on mysterious trips, which the audience understands are to raise money for his medical care by in some way selling her body to be anatomized while she is alive – she daily 'bares her arm to the unskilled knife of a young surgeon', we are told vaguely. Edouard, recovered, goes home to Scotland to see his dying mother, and never returns. The abandoned Alice travels to Inverness, where Edouard confesses that he now has a rich fiancée. Alice then mysteriously vanishes, and in the last scene three resurrection men, Burke, Mac-Dougall and Rosbiff, arrive to sell Edouard a corpse, which is of course Alice. A very similar if much less elaborate British short story on the theme appeared two years later, when 'The Victim. A True Story. By a Medical Student' was published in the *New Monthly Magazine*. Again, a medical student's fiancée vanishes, he buys a corpse from 'an exhumator', and it again turns out to be the missing fiancée, at which point the student goes mad.

Apart from these two forays, Burke and Hare provided little immediately in the way of popular entertainment that we know of. Generally the story was transformed into urban legend and scandalized word of mouth – in the early 1830s a friend of the poet John Clare was warned that trapdoors on London's streets were left open deliberately, for the unwary to fall into underground lairs where they were robbed, killed and sold to the doctors. However, one newspaper reference to a fairground exhibition might indicate that there were ephemeral shows that were never recorded. The *Examiner* recorded that at Barnet, then a town outside London, an exhibition of some form of painted display, possibly a long, panoramic illustration on rolled canvas, showed the murderous pair at work, 'certified to be correct to the minutest particular'. It had apparently also been shown in Edinburgh, and was to tour further.

There were a few other scattered references. Madame Tussaud, the founder of the waxworks dynasty and creator of the 'Chamber of Horrors' (at this date more sedately known as the 'Separate Room'), had arrived in England in 1802, with models of the heads of executed French revolutionary heroes and villains. She spent the next thirty years touring the country, and in 1829, sixteen days after Burke's execution, the *Liverpool Mercury* reported that she had on display 'a likeness of the Monster Burke said to be taken from a mask of his face ... we have no doubt that it will cause her exhibition to be crowded by persons anxious to see the features of a wretch whose crimes have hardly any parallels'. Two years later an advertisement for her show in Bristol promised that 'THE BAND WILL PLAY EVERY EVENING' while visitors examined both Burke and Hare's features.

There appear to be no surviving plays about Burke and Hare in the Lord Chamberlain's files, although there almost certainly were some productions at the minor theatres, never submitted for a licence. H. Chance Newton, a theatre critic born in 1854, said that among the earliest crime dramas he ever saw was one called *Hawke the Burker*. Leman Blanchard, in 1877, remembered that a theatre called the Shakespeare in Curtain Road, London, had at some time in the past produced 'a piece founded on the murder of the Italian boy by Burke and Hare'. Whatever Blanchard was remembering had now become hopelessly confused: the murder of 'the Italian boy' took place in London in 1831, when two thugs named Bishop and Williams killed Carlo Ferrari, a street beggar, and tried to sell his body; Burke and Hare had no connection to this crime. Cecil Pitt's *Carlo Ferrari, or, The Murder of the Italian Boy* played at the Britannia in 1869, but it seems unlikely that Blanchard would be so confused about a play that had been staged only eight years previously. Furthermore, the most comprehensive listing of London minor theatres gives only two named the Shakespeare, but neither was in Curtain Road.

By the 1860s, however, there was renewed interest in the Burkers. In 1859 the journalist G.A. Sala published 'How I went to Sea', a reminiscence of his schooldays, in which the boys were served up 'a dreadful pie for dinner every Monday; a meat pie with … horrible lumps of gristle inside, and such strings of sinew (alternated by lumps of flabby fat) … We called it kitten pie – resurrection pie – rag pie – dead man's pie …' More soberly, Alexander Leighton, who otherwise specialized in tales of Scottish folklore, brought out *The Courts of Cacus* in 1861. (In Greek myth, Cacus was one of the sons of Vulcan, an eater of human flesh.) This was a highly romanticized novelization, beginning: 'When the gloaming was setting in of an evening in the autumn of 1827, and when the young students of Dr Knox's class had covered up those remains of their own kind from which they had been trying to extract nature's secrets, one was looking listlessly from the window into the Square ...' and continuing with seventy-five pages of colour-ful tales of resurrection men, before finally getting around to the story of Burke and Hare.

Soon after came *Mary Paterson, or, The Fatal Error*, a serial in twenty-eight parts, by David Pae, a respected Scottish novelist, and pioneer of newspaper serial-fiction. Mary Paterson, the prostitute murdered by Burke and Hare, is here transformed, like Maria Marten, into the most beautiful girl in the village, the daughter of a respected village elder. She is loved by an honest farmer, but, 'vain, giddy, and thoughtless', she has 'given her heart to one who moved in a higher station', who has 'wooed her clandestinely for the basest of all purposes'. This is Duncan Grahame, an Edinburgh medical student who is already engaged to his heiress cousin. He makes Mary pregnant and secretes her in a lodging run by Helen McDougal. Mary gives birth, finds out that Grahame is married, and returns home in remorse, only to discover that her aged father has died of grief and the wicked lawyer has managed to gain possession of the family farm – and that's all in the first fifty pages. We skip over two years, and Mary is now walking the streets, Burke and Hare murder her, and when her corpse inevitably shows up on Grahame's dissecting table, he is filled with 'remorseful memories', as well he might be. There is a particularly nasty section where the farmer, now the guardian of Mary's child, watches Burke's execution, 'clap[ping] his hands with frantic vehe-mence'. Meanwhile Helen McDougal dies of exposure in a snowstorm, to be found the following spring with her face eaten away by rats; Margaret Hare is washed overboard as she travels back to Ireland; and Hare is set on the road to Carlisle, where we lose sight of him. After a lot of picaresque adventures, finally a murdered hermit is revealed to be Hare, the murderer-in-chief turns out to be Hare's unknown son, who goes mad, runs amok and kills the alcoholic village doctor, who is – Mary's Edinburgh student love, Duncan Grahame!

An advertisement for a penny-dreadful on the same subject followed the next year, but no copy of it seems to have survived, so it is unclear if this is Pae's story repackaged, or whether his serial trig-gered a revival of interest. Now plays began to be staged. Again, no scripts appear to have survived, or even playbills. But the *Era*, a journal for theatre professionals, has an advertisement in 1867 offering: 'BURKE and HARE … Manuscripts of this Startling Drama – terrific Situations, and Incidents Unparalleled in History of Fiction – now Ready. Terms moderate'. Over the next forty years, further Burke and Hare advertisements appear, never that many, but regularly: plays for sale, advertisements for a Burke and Hare 'amusement' (type unspecified), or a request for employment by a 'Scotch Actor, accustomed to [play] daft Jemmy'. These plays were probably of the type known as 'fit-up', staged by travelling troupes in barns or saloons. One version toured Scotland for decades: the actors knew the outlines of their parts and nightly created their own dialogue, modified to suit the number of actors – if a second low-comedy player was available, an organ grinder was inserted into the action (another conflation with the Italian boy). Local children were always welcome additions as the burkers' victims.

Only in the 1880s did Burke and Hare begin to appear in literature by writers of quality, and even then it tended to be among their weaker works. Conan Doyle, in his pre-Sherlock Holmes days, produced 'My Friend the Murderer', about a New Zealand bushranger who in seven months 'hocussed and made away with' twenty or thirty people. When the story begins, he is on the run after turning informer. As with Hare, he is constantly recognized and barely escapes lynching, before he is killed in a brawl. Conan Doyle was piling on effects: the bushranger is called Wolf Tone Maloney, the name echoing that of Theobald Wolfe Tone, the founder of Irish republican separatism. The choice probably reflects Doyle's deep dislike of such politics (the story was written shortly after the Phoenix Park murders) and is at least an unsubtle reminder of Hare's Irish origins. Robert Louis Stevenson, two years later, also chose the short-story form for a treatment of Burke and Hare's crimes. His narrator is Fettes, an alcoholic village doctor, who studied in his youth under 'a certain extramural teacher of anatomy, whom I shall here designate by the letter K'. Fettes' job was to deal with 'the unclean and desperate interlopers who supplied the table … It was the policy of Mr K— to ask no questions … "They bring the body, and we pay the price." ' But when Fettes recognizes the body of 'Jane Galbraith' [Mary Paterson], whom he had seen only the previous night, he knows that the crime is not simply grave robbery. He consults with a more senior student, who tells him to shut his eyes: 'Do you know what this life is? There are two squads of us – the lions and the lambs. If you're a lamb, you'll come to lie upon these tables like … Jane Galbraith; if you're a lion, you'll live and drive a horse like me, like K—, like all the world with any wit or courage.'* Then the plot veers off and the two turn resurrection men themselves. One dark night they set out to disinter a newly buried farmer's wife. On the way home they become more and more uneasy about their gruesome burden, until finally they open the sack. 'A wild yell rang up into the night': instead of the farmer's wife, inside is the body of one of K—'s long-dissected corpses.

The *Pall Mall Gazette*, which published the story in its 1884 Christmas issue, ran an advertising campaign that was long acknowledged as being uniquely macabre: one man remembered 'posters so horrific that they were suppressed', another that it had included a procession of sandwich-board men dressed as corpses, carrying their own coffins. While the advertising was unusual, the story was less so. Stevenson had initially set out with a fictionalized version of the facts, only to turn gruesome reality into nothing more than a standard ghost story.

Genre fiction was embracing Burke and Hare. James McGovan, the pseudonym of William Crawford Honeyman (1845–1919), an early writer of detective stories set in Edinburgh, returned frequently to the subject. In 'The Missing Bookbinder' a woman consults a detective: 'If this is no another Burke and Hare business I'll eat my ain bannet.' Her sister has vanished from her lodgings at a cobbler's, and 'they would get something for her body; and ye ken Burke was a cobbler too, but he found that bodies paid better'. The all-knowing professional is patronizingly dismissive: 'Nothing could dissuade this big,

---

* It seems impossible that Stevenson could be thinking of anyone except Sir William Fergusson here (see p.63).

warm-hearted woman from the idea that doctors were still eager and willing to buy bodies from the first offerer, asking no questions as to how the goods came to be bodies; or from believing that her sister's delicate frame had been utilised in that manner after the brutal fashion introduced by Burke and Hare.' (The sister, it turns out, died naturally, but the cobbler registered her death under his wife's name to get some insurance money.)

The detective's superior tone was now the prevailing attitude to these anatomization fears. As early as 1844, the comic sporting writer R.S. Surtees had treated the common people's fascination with Burke and Hare in precisely this manner: when the grand Duke of Donkeyton recommends a speech by the MP and political theorist Edmund Burke: 'Fine speech of Burke's; monstrous fine speech,' but the lower-middle-class Mr Jorrocks knows better: ' "He was 'ung for all that," observed Mr. Jorrocks to himself, with a knowing shake of the head.'

Finally, Burke and Hare, those thuggish, vicious men, like Thurtell ended up as a children's jingle:

> Up the close and doun the stair,
> But and ben* wi' Burke and Hare.
> Burke's the butcher, Hare's the thief,
> Knox the boy that buys the beef.

* * *

The crimes of Burke and Hare had convulsed the entire country. Other stories were more local, but in retrospect may have had more importance. Such a one was the killing of John Peacock Wood in 1833.

For decades, policing had been endlessly discussed. Originally, the term 'police' had merely meant the administration of a city, and the civic well-being that followed (the word derives from the same source as 'policy'); but during the French Revolution 'police' in France began to mean the men who were charged with maintaining 'public

---

* 'But and ben' is given variously as dialect for 'in and out' or the two rooms of a two-room cottage.

order, liberty, property, individual safety'; in Britain, nothing like it existed. Even a century earlier, a French visitor had been amazed: 'Good Lord!' he cried, 'how can one expect order among these people, who have no such word as Police in their Language.' The government regularly called out the army to control mobs and quell uprisings, but there was no civil force whose job included the prevention and detection of crime. This lack was considered a virtue: Fouché's police force was regarded as nothing but a nest of paid governmental spies.

Before 1829, changes to the parish and watch systems had been blocked by a coalition of right-wing 'county' elements joined by their opposite numbers, the political Radicals. Both groups feared, for different reasons, that a professional force would destroy civil liberties, bring in a system of secret-service spying to consolidate political power and introduce what was, in effect, a standing army. In short, they believed the new police would be 'expensive, tyrannical, and foreign', and most people felt they would 'rather be robb'd ... by wretches of desperate fortune than by ministers'. Nonetheless, the Home Secretary Sir Robert Peel, a political operator of brilliance, persuaded many that the rise in crime made some sort of solution imperative. There probably was no such rise – there was a rise in prosecutions, the consequence of a change in social expectations, and a growing intolerance of disorder; there were also more governmental surveys and early attempts at statistical analysis of crime figures. Together these created an appearance of increasing crime. Peel may or may not have understood that this was a difference in perception, not reality; in either case he used this perception to promote his end.*

For the most part, over the previous two decades high-profile stranger-murders requiring this new type of policing had been rare: the Ratcliffe Highway murders, the death of Spencer Perceval, and

---

* I will deal with policing and enforcement practices as they related to the crimes I discuss, but the major change – how the centralization of policing led to it becoming part of the apparatus of state – needs another book.

Burke and Hare. The other cases that had attracted attention were domestic, and were easily dealt with by older methods – Corder, Fenning (pp.183–200), Scanlan (pp.130–39), even Thurtell had killed an acquaintance. But the times were uneasy, people apprehensive. The end of the French wars had seen the return of large numbers of suddenly unemployed men inured to violent death; high food prices and chronic unemployment were producing ever more incidents of civic unrest, from machine-breaking to the Corn Bill Riots, the Spa Field Riots, bread and wage riots and Peterloo. Now the police were presented as agents who would prevent civic disorder.

Thus on 29 September 1829, parishes within twelve miles of Charing Cross saw the first 'new police' on the streets: five divisions, with 144 Metropolitan Police constables apiece. Within eight months there were 3,200 men, all dressed in blue. The Bow Street Runners had worn red waistcoats, but otherwise dressed in civilian clothes. The new police's uniforms had been carefully chosen to indicate their professionalism, while at the same time the colour had been selected to reassure the population that, unlike the red-coated army, this was a civil, not a military force. (Not that the new colour choice made much difference: the police were quickly dubbed 'raw lobsters' or 'the unboiled'. An unboiled lobster is blue; when it is put in hot water it turns red. Thus a policeman was only 'hot water' away from being a soldier.) The uniform was also protective: the stock at the neck was leather, not linen, and the rabbit-skin top hat had a reinforced leather top and bracing; according to one policeman's memoir, it weighed eighteen ounces. (In 1864 it was replaced by the 'Roman' helmet that is still worn.) The only weapon carried was a baton, with a rattle (replaced by a whistle in 1884) to summon aid.

Peel's instructions for the new police stressed that constables 'will be civil and obliging to all people', while being 'particularly cautious not to interfere idly or unnecessarily in order to make a display of his authority'. 'The object to be attained is the prevention of crime,' yet the police also had what today would be called 'caring' roles in their communities: looking after 'insane persons and children', ensuring that street nuisances (rubbish, waste, building materials) were

In 1829 Sir Robert Peel's New Police were instructed to be 'civil and obliging to all people'; their uniform, a blue coat of ordinary dress cut, was designed to reassure the population that they were not soldiers in disguise. Most declined to be reassured, however, as this mocking illustration to a song demonstrates.

removed, enforcing Sunday trading laws and preserving public order. The middle classes quickly came to accept this ideal as the reality, while the working classes were less persuaded, frequently with good reason. The early recruits were not exactly the *crème de la crème*, and of the initial intake of 2,800 men, 2,238 were swiftly dismissed, 1,790 for drunkenness.

This distrust came to a head in three separate incidents in 1833. The first was what became known as the Cold Bath Field riot. In May a group of workers calling themselves the National Political Union organized a rally in London. Lord Melbourne, the Home Secretary, ruled it an unlawful assembly, and flyers were posted warning the population not to participate. On the morning of 13 May about seventy-five constables were stationed near Cold Bath Field, the planned rallying point, with reinforcements backing them up – altogether, about 450 men were on call. When the workers arrived, the police superintendent moved his men in. Bricks were thrown, baton charges were led, many were injured, three constables were stabbed and one died. The policeman in command, Superintendent Mays, claimed he and his men had marched slowly down the street towards the speakers' platform, planning to arrest the leaders and give the crowds time to leave under their own steam. They only charged, he said, when bricks and stones were thrown; he also claimed that the rioters had guns (although everyone agreed that no shot had been fired). On the other side, eye-witnesses reported that the police had charged immediately, indiscriminately attacking men, women and children, many of whom had nothing to do with the rally, but were simply passers-by. The officers made no attempts to rein in their men, and the crowd response was purely self-defence. The jury at the inquest on PC Robert Culley reached a verdict of justifiable homicide, noting that the Riot Act had not been read, which made the police charge illegal.* This verdict was quashed on appeal, and a subsequent parliamentary inquiry found that the police had not used excessive force. This was decidedly not the public's view. The caricaturist Robert Cruikshank wrote a savage attack on the authorities, inflating the number of police to eight hundred, and suggesting that Culley had

---

* The Riot Act (1 Geo. I St.2. c.5) of 1715 permitted 'tumults and riotous assemblies' to be broken up after strict procedure was followed: the Act had to be read aloud, using a set form of words, to those whom the officials wished to disperse. The crowd then had one hour to leave the area. Force was not permitted until that hour had elapsed.

probably been stabbed by another policeman. He ended by parodying Peel's instructions with a set of his own 'Necessary Qualifications' for policemen: 'He must be utterly destitute of all feelings of humanity ... He must qualify himself for action, by knocking down, every half hour, all the poor fruit-women he can find and other peaceable hard-working people, who endeavor [sic] to get an honest livelihood to support their large families ... If able to perjure himself with a *clear conscience* he may depend upon speedy promotion ...'

While the inquest and inquiry were continuing, public outrage was exacerbated by the ongoing case of Popay, known generally as 'the police spy'. William Popay was a police sergeant sent to infiltrate the National Political Union. He pretended to be an artist and attended meetings in 'coloured clothes' (plainclothes), acting as an *agent provocateur*, inciting his supposed fellow workers to illegal actions. When he was unmasked, earlier fears about the true nature of the police force seemed to be justified. It was, said the Radicals, nothing but a government-sanctioned spy network, paid for, to add insult to injury, out of working men's taxes. Another select committee was set up, but before it could deliver its report the death of John Peacock Wood suddenly assumed significance.

Wood should have had no fame at all. He was a waterside character in Wapping, by the London docks, an amiable drunk, a man of no trade or settled way of life. But he was harmless. On the night before his death he was drinking at the White Hart tavern with a friend, his wife and the landlady. According to witnesses at the inquest, a squabble arose over who was to pay for a pint, and this attracted the attention of a policeman, who 'laid hold of the deceased, and shoved him "right slap" into the street', where he fell on the pavement. A succession of witnesses agreed that Wood had been knocked down by a policeman, while another constable was seen with 'a stick in his hand', and another 'lift[ed] the man up, whose head fell again to the pavement; the blow was violent'. It was not the first blow, either: the policeman's hands were 'stained with blood'. Somehow it took four policemen an hour to carry Wood the 250 yards from the tavern to the police station. A man in the cells saw him dragged by his feet into

a cell ('A deep murmur and expression of horror here burst forth'),
where he was left until ten o'clock the next morning, at which point
a doctor was sent for. Wood was treated and taken home, but he died
that afternoon of a fractured skull caused, said a doctor, not 'by a
lateral fall, but … by a large round stick'.

It was not just the death, but the behaviour of the police and the
coroner at the inquest that incensed the population. The police swore
that the cells' other occupant could not have witnessed Wood's treatment, because he had been discharged at six (said the charge book), or
maybe it was 2.30 (the inspector). The police were permitted to sit in
the court before they testified, unlike the other witnesses, which meant
that they would be able to tailor their evidence. (The coroner stoutly
protested that no policeman would think of doing any such thing.) At
an identification parade the constables arrived dressed in street clothes,
rather than their uniforms – to evade recognition, thought many.

The fractious bickering between jury and coroner continued for
thirteen hours on the first day. On the second, four doctors testified
that Wood's fracture had been caused by a truncheon-shaped object.
Another witness testified to seeing him being chased by the police, but
the coroner refused to accept this evidence, dismissing it as 'disgraceful'. A juror snapped back, 'If an honest perseverance to elicit the truth
was disgraceful, he would admit that their conduct throughout the
whole proceedings was disgraceful indeed.' The coroner backed down,
mumbling that it was 'the firing and cross-firing' of questions that he
had been referring to, before adjourning the sitting.

On the third day, another twelve hours was spent on the case. A
number of policemen testified to the very great care they had lavished
on the unconscious Wood. One 'burst into tears, and said he had an
aged mother, whose feelings had been much hurt by his name being
mixed up with the affair'. A juryman, unmoved, asked him if it were
not true that he had previously 'broken a man's head with his truncheon'. The coroner refused to let him answer the question, and the
court was adjourned in uproar once again.

On day four, a witness agreed with the police account, testifying
that she had seen Wood carried carefully. On cross-examination,

however, it was found that her evidence matched nothing that anyone else had seen that night, that it followed a private interview with the police inspector before the hearing, and furthermore that she had been seen drinking with another policeman only that morning. The coroner said he had received a note suggesting that Wood's head 'might have been accidentally struck against a beam at the entrance of the station-house', but even the police agreed that that was not possible, and 'the Foreman of the Jury observed – "The writer of the note must have had a beam in his eye." '

On the fifth day, a witness who testified against the police was so confused and contradictory that the jury showed their independence of mind by saying they refused to believe a word. The solicitor watching proceedings for the police leapt up and asked that the witness be committed for perjury, at which the jury noted sourly that none of the police witnesses who had obviously lied had been so threatened. The coroner, not knowing when to let well alone, smugly commented, 'I hope that the eyes of the Jury are now opened. I cannot but say from my heart, that there is not a tittle of evidence that can be relied on against the police: not a tittle that can be placed in comparison with the manly, straightforward evidence given by the police themselves ... I cannot help saying, that since the Court was opened, the Jury have pursued a course such as I have never before witnessed in the course of my life, and such as I hope never to see again.' The jury cried, '"Shame, shame!" and with clenched fists approached the Coroner ... An indescribable scene of confusion followed ... The people in the room united in the vociferations of the Jury, and the crowd in the street ... expressed their approbation by loud shouting and clapping of hands.' The coroner realized the position he'd put himself in, and added hastily, 'I feel deep sorrow for having expressed myself in a manner disagreeable to the Jury, whose conduct, it is my duty to state, as far as the ends of truth and justice are concerned, does them great credit: I did not mean in what I said to censure them morally.' The jury were having none of it, and the foreman responded: 'We stand here as honest men, having characters to support, and I can say before God, that I came into this room unbiassed against the police. Nothing that can be said to us, in the way of censure, can affect our verdict … If we are to be taxed with having a bias against the police, I, for one, would lay down my fine of 10*l*. [for refusing jury service], and walk home.' Then the coroner tried to speak, but one of the jury interrupted him: 'You have called us biassed men; we have been ill treated by you individually and collectively: your conduct has been most partial [great confusion].' The inquest was once more adjourned.

When it resumed, the coroner finally summed up: 'When I found that some members of the Jury endeavoured to degrade my office [the Jury here exclaimed that they did not], and to impugn my impartiality – when I perceived the spirit of persecution in which the examinations were conducted [cries of 'No, no!'], and the intemperate manner in which all interference on behalf of the police was resisted – I felt bound by every obligation … to extend the broad shield of the Judge over the devoted heads of the policemen, and protect them from the cruel inquisition to which they were exposed.' He then admitted that he might have been led into 'some warmth of expression', which he regretted. The jury took three hours to consider their verdict (this in an age when death sentences were routinely agreed in twenty minutes), returning with a verdict of 'Wilful Murder against some policeman unknown', adding a rider that the death certificate should be altered to read 'We are of opinion [sic] the murder was committed with a truncheon by a policeman of the K Division.' The coroner responded coldly: 'The verdict is yours, and not mine, and on you rests the responsibility.'

And there the case rested: no one was ever identified, so no one was ever charged. But a few weeks later, the House of Commons reported on Popay, condemning his behaviour as 'highly reprehensible' and blaming his superiors for their lack of proper supervision. The public too made its feelings known: on Guy Fawkes Night, the two police commissioners, Richard Mayne and Charles Rowan, were burnt in effigy on local bonfires, together with a third guy, labelled 'Justifiable Homicide'.

The following year, the police distinguished themselves even less, demonstrating the limitations of preventative policing. This time it was not the murder of a friendly drunk, but of a respectable member of the merchant class. Thomas Ashton, the twenty-two-year-old son of a mill owner, had left the family house at Gee Cross, near Ashton-under-Lyne (now part of Greater Manchester), at 7.30 one evening in 1834 to deputize for his brother at their father's Apethorne factory (Ashton usually managed another family mill, at Woodley). Minutes later, a messenger from the mill rushed in: 'He believed Mr. Thomas was down in the lane, and hurt.' Mr Thomas was not hurt, but either dying or dead, having been shot at point-blank range. At the inquest, a nine-year-old girl said that she had seen three men on the road, and thought one of them had been carrying a gun, which he tried to conceal as she passed. A book-keeper from the mill testified that three men had been sacked the week before, 'for irregularity in their general conduct', but none of them was known to have made any threats against any of the Ashton family, and one had already been rehired. This was a time of great labour unrest, and there was some discussion about whether the men had belonged to the Spinners' Union, but no evidence was offered, and in any case the Ashton mills were in full employment. Mention was made of a 'piece of thin and soft blue or purple paper' which had probably been used as wadding in the gun that was fired, but this clue seemed to lead nowhere. The jury brought in a verdict of 'wilful murder against three persons at present unknown', and the government offered a £600 reward.

The *Manchester Guardian* said that the perpetrators must have been outsiders: not only had no one recognized them, but they had made no attempt to hide their faces, as though they had no fear of recognition. The case remained in limbo for three years, until William (or James, depending on which newspaper you read) Garside, in gaol for stealing tools, told the authorities that he knew something about the murder. He refused to speak to the magistrate, however, until a three-year-old copy of the *Hue and Cry** was found, to prove to him

---

* The *Hue and Cry* was the official police publication, founded in 1786 by a Bow Street magistrate, a bi-weekly four-page paper which itemized crimes, described wanted criminals, listed stolen property and publicized government rewards.

that the government was offering a reward (now raised to £1,500) and a pardon to anyone except the person who had actually fired the gun who could give information leading to the discovery of the murderers. Garside could not read, but the offer was read aloud to him. As a result he admitted to being present at the crime, and named two brothers, Joseph and William Moseley, as the perpetrators.

All three were committed for trial. Although the newspaper reports are not explicit, it looks as though William Moseley turned king's evidence and testified against the other two. Joseph Moseley and Garside were committed for murder, William Moseley for aiding and assisting. Each of them blamed the others. William Moseley said he had been looking for employment near Macclesfield when he met a man named Stanfield or Schofield, who was with Garside and Joseph Moseley. The three men talked, and William said he caught the words 'the union'. Garside and Joseph then told him that they had agreed to shoot one of the Ashtons, 'because of the turn-outs' (strikes), and they would be paid £10 for the murder. He said they signed a book, and he made his mark. 'We then all went down on our knees, and holding a knife one over the other, said … "We wished God might strike us dead if we ever told." ' Garside said Joseph Moseley was the one who fired the gun, while Joseph Moseley, who had no legal representation, simply said that his brother William had committed 'many crimes', while Garside would swear to anything for the price of a drink. As to himself, 'It is not likely that he should shoot a man that he never saw or knew any ill of.' This was his only defence. The jury took a few minutes to decide that Garside was the actual murderer, but that Joseph Moseley was equally guilty. They were sentenced to hang. William was found guilty as an accessory, but later reprieved.

The resolution of this three-year-old crime caused a sensation among all classes and types. The *Stockport Advertiser* couldn't keep up with demand, and was driven to produce single sheets of the trial transcript. It was anti-climactic, therefore, when the executions were delayed into the following year, after legal wranglings over jurisdiction. Thus, while the *Manchester Guardian* dedicated nearly 27,000 words to the trial, by the time the two men were finally executed it was no longer topical, and the paper did not cover it at all.

This sad little case would merit no more than a mention in a history of labour unrest, were it not for two works of literature that it spawned. As a preliminary, however, in 1842 came a novel that in no way qualifies as literature. *William Langshawe, the Cotton Lord* was written by the daughter of the owner of the *Manchester Chronicle*, whose previous work, the title page advertised, was *The Art of Needlework*. The book reads pretty much as one would expect from the authoress of *The Art of Needlework*. Although set among the cotton mills, *William Langshawe* has a heroine who dresses in 'a gossamer robe of spotless white', a hermit with a secret sorrow (of the sort so often seen in the industrial heartlands) and the occasional outbreak of Italian banditti. The important thing about the book for our purposes is that there is a millhand named Jem, who loves another millworker, Nancy, who has ideas above her station and is conducting a flirtation with the son of a factory owner. Jem, in his anguish, turns to 'The Union', a fearful organization that plans turn-outs in order to reduce 'beneficent and liberal masters ... to the very edge of ruin'. Twenty pages before the end a factory owner's son sets off for his mill, shortly after which 'a sudden knock was heard at the hall door', and, just as with Thomas Ashton, a messenger comes in to say, 'I'm afeard he is down in the loan [sic], much hurt.' The young man is 'borne in by the men – a corpse', while 'not a clue, not the remotest trace of the villains remained'. There is a footnote: 'Let not my readers image [sic] that this awful incident has been invented ... A few years ago a young cotton manufacturer of the highest respectability, and most excellent character, was murdered even so, and as suddenly, as we have described, by order of the Spinners' Union.'

That readers could have forgotten the Ashton case was confirmed in 1848, with the publication of one of the great works of nineteenth-century fiction. Mrs Gaskell's *Mary Barton* used the incidents of the case, but while many reviewers commented on her fictional interweaving of the realities of industrial unrest and the battles between the owners and the workers, none seems to have recognized the origin of her story. In *Mary Barton*, Mary, a milliner's assistant, is loved by Jem Wilson, a factory mechanic. She initially rejects him in favour of Harry Carson, the son of the local mill owner, although she soon realizes she loves Jem and breaks off with Carson. He and Jem fight, and are stopped by a policeman, in whose hearing Jem threatens Carson. Meanwhile, the millworkers are striking. Mary's father, John Barton, takes part in a plan to murder one of the owners, for which lots are drawn. John Barton goes to Glasgow to talk to the workers there; Jem simultaneously agrees to accompany his cousin Will Wilson on the walk back to his ship in Liverpool. That night, Harry Carson is found shot dead in the lane. The gun is identified as Jem's, and he is arrested. The wadding from the gun is found by Mary's aunt. It is part of a valentine Jem sent Mary, but Mary alone knows this is evidence of his innocence, and her father's guilt – she had given the paper to her father.* She sets out for Liverpool to get Will to return and testify to Jem's alibi, the only way to save Jem without endangering her father. Will's ship has left, and Mary goes out in a small boat, shouting up to him that he is needed. His captain refuses to give him leave, but Will arrives to give his evidence in the nick of time, Jem is saved and Mary declares her love for him. John Barton, now dying, confesses to Carson's father, who forgives him.

The novel was quickly acclaimed as being by an 'author in the very front rank of modern novelists', but it was not recognized that the author had used reality as the basis for her (or, as this reviewer thought, his) art. Even the *Manchester Guardian* failed to recognize

---

* The wadding clue in the Ashton case spawned a number of fictional descendants. In *Bleak House* (1852–53) Dickens has his police detective, Inspector Bucket, recognize the wadding found near the murdered lawyer Tulkinghorn as 'a bit of the printed description of your house at Chesney Wold'. In Andrew Forrester's early 1860s story 'The Judgment of Conscience', Miss G., his female detective, builds her entire case around wadding made from a page of *Johnston's Chemistry of Common Life*, an East End cobbler's constant companion (for more on Miss G., see pp. 300–301). Reality only caught up with fiction in 1884, when John Toms was convicted of murder on the evidence of a piece of wadding recovered from the body of his victim, which was identified as matching a broadside in his possession.

THE INVENTION OF MURDER

the case it had reported so thoroughly a decade earlier. Instead, it says that while *Mary Barton* is well written and well constructed, 'the authoress has [?erred – semi-illegible] against truth, in matters of fact'. Her tale of murder was a libel on the workers, it went on, because 'they never committed a murder under any such circumstances', and a libel on the owners, 'who have never been exceeded ... in acts of benevolence and charity'.

While Thomas Ashton may have been forgotten, Mary Barton's story became hugely popular among the working classes. Three plays, all at minor theatres, were based on Mrs Gaskell's novel, and two scripts survive. In the script of the 1850 version, the Examiner of Plays has scored through all the political references – gone is the workers' delegation to Parliament, and no longer is Barton a Chartist delegate. Gone too is the scene where the workers conspire to kill Carson (which must have made the plot difficult to follow), and in the final courtroom scene, respect for sacred personages meant that the swearing-in of witnesses takes place in dumbshow. After the acquittal of James (not Jem in this version), the dying Barton begs Carson: 'Oh sir, say you forgive me the anguish I have caused you. I care not for death, but oh man forgive me the trespass I have done thee ... I die, oh ... The world fades from me, a new one opens to you, James and Mary,' and the play ends with a final tableau.

For many theatres, spectacle was the essential ingredient, with various types of lighting and stage effects used to create the required 'sensation-scene', the high point of the evening, full of special effects and new technology. The stage manager at the Britannia reminded himself of what was needed for one scene:

> Ring Down [curtain] when shower of fire out.
> Screams & yells & all sorts of noises. Coloured fires burning.
> Braces falling on sheet iron. [clanging noises of battle]
> ... sparks from Dragon Mouth.
> ... Red Lights full up.

Quite how realistic these effects were is difficult to judge. In 1871, a melodrama at the same theatre had a scene in which the heroine, trapped on an ice floe with the villain, is rescued by a passing steamer. This sounds technically astonishing, until one reads the stage manager's diary entries:

> 21 AUGUST: 'This night our large steam-ship in the last scene ... stuck ... on the stage midway & would not come down.'
>
> 22 AUGUST: 'This night our large steam-ship broke through the stage, & stuck fast mid-way.'
>
> 23 AUGUST: 'This night *our large steam-ship* broke through a plank at the back of the stage and would not come any further ... on Tuesday night, the wheels caught in the shaking waters & clogged & wouldn't come down ...'
>
> 25 AUGUST: 'Tonight it stuck *at the back of the stage* & would not come forward at all ...'
>
> 26 AUGUST: 'Tonight it broke through the Vampire Trap!'

In *Mary Barton, or, The Weavers' Distress* at the Grecian Saloon in Shoreditch in 1861, the high point was the sensation-scene in which the workers set Carson's mill alight, and Jem roars in to rescue the trapped Henry. Then Mary has a dramatic speech – 'I see naught but Jem, a dying man on the gallows. I hear naught but his groans ringing in my ears' – Will arrives in the courtroom on cue and the drama ends with a rousing speech from the judge – 'I tell you, that you are bound to give the Prisoner the full Benefit of the slightest doubts you may have on your minds, such is the Law of England, such is the Law of humanity ...' – and Barton's revelation that it was not he who killed Carson after all, but another character who never appears in the play, and is anyway dead: a murder where no one is to blame.

It was Dion Boucicault (1820–1890) who returned Mrs Gaskell's story to the middle classes. *The Long Strike* (1866) followed Boucicault's great success, *The Colleen Bawn*, another play based on a murder (see pp.130–33), and he went back to the elements that had worked for him in the past. The fire that had thrilled the Grecian audiences is gone, but Boucicault knew better than to deprive his audience of a sensation-scene. He himself played Johnny Reilly, the renamed Will. When his captain refuses him permission to go ashore, Reilly cries, 'Jane [the Mary character in this play] has called me back, and back I'll go,' and 'goes to the window, throws out coat and hat, takes stage to foot lights, runs up, springs through window, disappears'. In Act IV comes the great innovation. Jane no longer walks to Liverpool – that is far too old-fashioned. Instead, she and the lawyer Mr Moneypenny plan to send a telegram from the 'Telegraph Office – Messages sent to all parts of the United Kingdom'. They arrive, only to find that the line is closed for the night. Much still needed to be explained to the audience about this miracle of the modern world, so the clerk laboriously spells it out: 'The telegraph is a private enterprise, and maintained for profit. The business coming in after nine o'clock would not pay, except on the main lines.' Moneypenny ratchets up the drama: '… that wire was the thread on which the lad's life was suspended, and it fails her'. The operator is sympathetic and says maybe, just maybe, they can get through. The tension is heightened by the slow relaying of and replying to the messages coming and going, but then – miraculously – a signal!

Boucicault, a great admirer of French theatre (or, as his many enemies had it, a frequent plagiarizer of French plays), may have known of a play Dickens had seen in Paris ten years before. *La Rentrée à Paris* was, said Dickens, barely a play at all, but while 'There is nothing in the piece … it was impossible not to be moved and excited by the telegraph part,' where, in a Paris railway station, the crowds wait for the soldiers returning from the Crimea. There is an electric telegraph office to one side, and a 'marquis' offers:

'Give me your little messages, and I'll send them off.' General rush …
'Is my son wounded?' 'Is my brother promoted?' etc. etc … Last of all, the widowed mother … 'Is my only son safe?' Little bell rings. Slip of paper handed out. 'He was first upon the heights of Alma.' General cheer. Bell rings again, another slip of paper handed out. 'He was made a sergeant at Inkermann.' Another cheer. Bell rings again, another slip

of paper handed out. 'He was made colour-sergeant at Sebastopol.'
Another cheer. Bell rings again, another slip of paper handed out. 'He
was the first man who leaped with the French banner on the Malakhoff
tower.' Tremendous cheer. Bell rings again, another slip of paper
handed out. 'But he was struck down there by a musket-ball ...'
Mother abandons all hope; general commiseration; troops rush in ...
son only wounded, [enters] and embraces her ...

Boucicault's version was similarly effective, so much so that at the end
of the century some variety bills were still running the scene on its
own, amputated from the rest of the play.

'Amputate' is the key word for the next horror that titillated the reading public. On 28 December 1836, a labourer walking past a building
site on London's Edgware Road saw a sack tucked under a flagstone
propped at the side of the road. Upon investigation it proved to
contain the body of a woman 'in a horridly mutilated state'. When the
report said 'body', it meant 'body': it was a torso (complete with
arms), packed in with some towelling, a child's dress and a piece of
shawl. No identification could be made, and nothing further happened
until 6 January 1837, when a lock-keeper at Regent's Canal lock in
Stepney, in the East End of the city, found his gates blocked. He felt
around with his boat-hook and, to his horror, pulled up a human
head. One of the eyes 'was quite cut out, by means of a blunt instrument', and the earlobes were slit, as though earrings had been torn
out. The head was taken to Paddington workhouse, where it was
judged to be a match for the torso. Both were preserved in spirits, and
kept for viewing by those who were searching for missing friends or
relatives. On 2 February, a pair of legs was dredged out of a bed of
reeds near Coldharbour Lane, in Brixton, south of the river, wrapped
in a sack on which the letters 'eley' and 'erwell' could be read.

Although the police force's role was officially only preventative,
detective work, and forensic science, were beginning to develop. The
constable on the beat at Edgware Road, PC Pegler, traced the sacking
to a Mr Moseley, a corn chandler in Camberwell. The parish surgeon

added his information: the torso was that of a woman, about five feet six inches; her skull had been fractured, and he thought that most probably her eye had been knocked out before death, but the decapitation had been performed after. He judged that the head had been in the water for four or five days. (The parish surgeon in Paddington was less helpful: he reported that the torso had been dead only twenty-four hours, and then added, confusingly, that that meant three or four days.)

Even with this information, nothing further transpired until 20 March, when a man named William Gay provisionally identified the head as that of his sister, Hannah Brown, a washerwoman. Mrs Brown had been engaged to a cabinetmaker named James Greenacre, and they were to marry on Christmas Day, with another cabinetmaker, named Davis, to give her away. Mrs Brown sold off her mangle and laundry equipment, and on Christmas Eve she moved out of her lodgings. Late that night, Greenacre appeared at Davis's house to tell the family the wedding was off: 'He had discovered that she was without property, which she had led him to believe she possessed,' they had 'had some slight words', and she had left him. He was 'much agitated', but given the circumstances there was nothing odd in that, nor in 'his having a bundle under his arm … as he might have been providing for his Christmas dinner'. When Mrs Brown failed to appear at the Davises' that night as expected, they assumed she was embarrassed.

The police asked Davis to view the head, and he agreed it was Mrs Brown. When the police arrived at Greenacre's lodgings he denied all knowledge of her. A woman named Sarah Gale was living with him, and she seemed to the policeman to be hiding something. He asked to see it, and it turned out to be two rings, a pair of earrings and a pawnbroker's ticket for two silk dresses, which were identified as Mrs Brown's, as was the jewellery. In the next room, Sarah Gale's boxes were found to contain part of a child's dress which matched the piece of fabric that had been found with the torso. Greenacre and Mrs Gale were both arrested.

Interest was at fever pitch, as was hostility to the two supposed murderers. *The Times* took the lead in producing a positive waterfall of vicious rumour: that Greenacre had advertised for a wife after Hannah Brown's death (shades of Corder); that he had murdered his illegitimate child (he didn't appear to have had one); that he had previously been charged with 'administering a drug to a female ... for the purpose of procuring abortion' (why, if he was so ready to kill children?); that he had had a boy apprenticed to him for a high fee, then accused him of stealing, so he could discharge him but keep the premium; that there were two more illegitimate children, one of whom he had left at a workhouse door, the other he had 'made away' with; that he was one of the Cato Street conspirators (who had planned the mass assassination of the entire cabinet sixteen years before); that he had encouraged someone to kill the Duke of Wellington; and that he had put 'inflammatory bills' and 'the King's speech, turned upside down' in his shop windows, signs of incendiary radicalism. A broadside further claimed that Greenacre had made 'overtures ... of a base kind' to the daughter of a friend, and when she resisted he 'made a forcible attempt' on her. His friend protested, and Greenacre in revenge got the man's son to summons his father, claiming he wasn't being taught his trade, as set out in his indentures. This was disproved immediately, and the son's remorse was so great that he 'did not survive, and died a maniac'. (This beautifully moral story is embellished with a gory picture of Greenacre cutting off Mrs Brown's head.)

At the magistrates' hearing, Greenacre said that Mrs Brown 'had often dropped insinuations in my hearing about her having property enough to enable her to go into business, and that she had said she could command at any time 300*l.* or 400*l.* I told her I had made some inquiry about her character and had ascertained that she had been to Smith's tally-shop [which gave goods on credit] in Long-acre, and tried to procure silk gowns in my name, she put on a feigned laugh, and retaliated by saying she thought I had been deceiving her with respect to my property by misrepresenting it.' They had been drinking, and he struck her, whereupon she fell off her chair, hit her head and died. At which point, 'I unfortunately determined on putting her away.' Then he backtracked: she had arrived at his lodgings already 'rather fresh from drinking' and 'was very aggravating ... I own that

I tilted the chair with my foot, and she fell with her head against a clump of wood, and appeared insensible; I shook her, and tried to restore her, but she was quite gone.' His main concern in every statement was to stress that Mrs Gale knew nothing of the matter. She had not been there, and Mrs Brown's body was gone by the time she returned; he told her they were keeping her belongings in payment of a debt. But both were committed for trial, Greenacre for wilful murder, Mrs Gale as an accessory after the fact. As they left the court, the mob had to be held back by the police: 'thousands of persons' followed the coach 'the whole of the way to Newgate, with the officers of police, their staves out, running by the sides and after the coaches'.

At the trial a surgeon testified that the blow to Mrs Brown's head had definitely taken place before death, and worse, her eye had also been knocked out before she was dead. Even worse still, 'the head had been severed from the body *while the person was yet alive*'. This may or may not have been the case – forensic science was still very basic – but it was generally believed. It took the jury only fifteen minutes to find Greenacre guilty of murder, and Sarah Gale as an accessory.

Soon after his conviction, Greenacre confessed, although he still insisted the death was accidental. He said that he had waved a wooden towel-jack at Mrs Brown, to frighten her, and had inadvertently put out her eye; she fell, and he found she was dead, so he dismembered her to get rid of the body. He took two omnibuses to reach the canal, sitting quietly with the head wrapped up on his lap. He later walked towards the Edgware Road with the torso in a sack until a passing cart gave him a lift some of the way. For the last stage of the journey he said he had taken a hackney cab.

The newspapers fell on these details. The *Champion and Weekly Herald*, a Chartist paper run by William Cobbett's two sons (including the one who had supposedly learned to read by keeping up with news of Thurtell), gave all four of its pages to the trial. The *Figaro in London* satirized the financial bonanza: 'Greenacre positively established two weekly papers ... and it is a well known fact that had this murderous wretch been acquitted, a piece of plate would have been presented to him by the proprietors ... for his invaluable services in advancing [their] interests ...' This is a joke, but the idea was valid: four months later the *Age* was only half-satirical: 'every line that came from [Greenacre's] mouth was worth at least threepence'.

Yet Greenacre broadsides were not selling well. One patterer* was wise after the event: 'Greenacre didn't sell so well as might have been expected, for such a diabolical out-and-out crime as he committed; but you see he came close after Pegsworth [who murdered a draper over a £1 debt], and that took the beauty off him. Two murderers together is no good to nobody.' But this didn't mean no one was interested. While the trial was pending, two men charged sightseers 3*d.* to see Greenacre's rooms, especially 'the arm-chair and block of wood which it was said the unfortunate woman fell on. This sum was readily paid by an immense number of persons.' Catchpenny works proliferated, including one claiming to be an autobiography (almost certainly a journalist's confection), and another, the partial title of which was: 'GREENACRE, OR, THE EDGEWARE-ROAD MURDER. *Presenting an Authentic and Circumstantial Account of This* MOST SANGUINARY OUTRAGE of the Laws of Humanity; and Showing, upon the CONFESSION OF THE CULPRIT, the Means he Resorted to, in Order to Effect HIS BLOODY PURPOSE; *Also his Artful and Fiendlike Method of Mutilating his* MURDERED VICTIM ...'

Greenacre was also popular in penny-gaffs. James Grant, a journalist, reported that 'the recent atrocity known by the name of the Edgeware murder, was quite a windfall' to them, theatres choosing 'the most frightful of the circumstances' to display 'amidst great applause'. Current murders were popular because, as the audiences already knew the stories, they could be pared down to the most sensational episodes. This suited the gaffs, which crammed in as many daily shows as the market would bear – one performer remembered that he did twenty-one shows in twelve hours on Boxing Day in 1835 – and

---

* A patterer sold broadsides – 'pattering', or reading from them, and teaching the tunes to the songs. A standing patterer had a fixed pitch; a running patterer roamed a district with his goods.

therefore concision was essential. Likewise, for current events, a script could be dispensed with and the company simply ad-libbed: 'Number one is told, "You, sir, play the hero and have to frustrate the villain in all and every scene. You, number two, are the villain, and must pursue the lady, make love, stamp in fury when you are refused. You, number three, are the juvenile … make love, embrace, weep and swear to die for her you love … Now you, madam … you are the heroine, and must rave and roar when you refuse the villain's proffered love, and mind you scream right well." '

The middle classes loved to condemn this sort of working-class entertainment, believing it led to vice. In 1844 the chaplain of the Brixton House of Correction said that 'almost all' of the boys there had first been led astray by visits to penny-gaffs or fairs, where they had watched depictions of crimes 'calculated to inflame the passions'. Yet no one regarded Greenacre as fearful in the way Burke and Hare had been fearful; for some reason, he was funny. Greenacre's whole

The murder of Hannah Brown became a sensation after her chopped-up body parts were found across London. Here the murderer, James Greenacre, is shown with Sarah Gale at the grisly task.

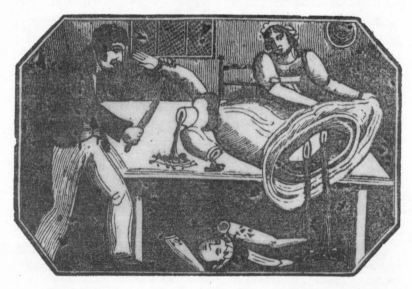

life had been marked by 'treachery and deception – in small matters as well as great', claimed *John Bull*: when he took Mrs Brown's head on the omnibus, it solemnly revealed, he had asked what the fare was. 'Sixpence a head, sir.' He paid his sixpence, 'thus paying only for one head instead of two'. *Bell's Life* filled its correspondence columns with answers to readers' questions about the betting on whether or not Greenacre would hang. (These columns printed only the editor's answers; the questions must be inferred.) A report on a prize fight in the same paper uses the word 'Greenacre' quite casually to mean a blow – 'the Black thought he could not do better than again try to pop in another "Greenacre" under Preston's left ear ...' Even the intelligentsia joined in: Jane Carlyle thought a portrait of her husband Thomas had 'a gallows-expression ... I have all along been calling it Greenacre-Carlyle'. And the Revd R.H. Barham's *Ingoldsby Legends* commemorated Greenacre in jingly nursery-rhyme rhythms:

> ... So the Clerk and the wife, they each took a knife,
> And the nippers that nipp'd the loaf sugar for tea;
> With the edges and points they severed the joints
> At the clavicle, elbow, hip, ankle, and knee.

> Thus, limb from limb they dismember'd him
> So entirely, that e'en when they came to his wrists,
> With those great sugar-nippers they nipp'd off his 'flippers'
> As the Clerk, very flippantly, termed his fists.

> ... They determined to throw it where no one could know it,
> Down the well, – and the limbs in some different place.

> ... They contrived to pack up the trunk in a sack,
> Which they hid in an osier-bed outside the town,
> The Clerk bearing arms, legs, and all on his back,
> As that vile Mr. Greenacre served Mrs. Brown ...

The crowd at Greenacre's execution was large, vocal and perfectly good-humoured, purchasing 'Greenacre tarts' from a pie-seller while they waited. Seven weeks later, Princess Victoria became Queen Victoria, and public opinion began to change.

THREE

Entertaining Murder

One of the most influential stories of murder throughout the Victorian age was not Victorian at all, but had taken place while Queen Victoria's great-great-grandfather was on the throne. Yet this 1745 crime resonated as late as the 1880s, when the actors Henry Irving and Ellen Terry toured in a heavily romanticized version of the life and death of Eugene Aram.

Eugene Aram was born in the West Riding of Yorkshire in 1704, the son of a gardener. He received a fairly good education, and by the 1730s he was living in the town of Knaresborough, Yorkshire (today on the edge of Harrogate), married, with four or five children, and employed as steward to a local landowner. Daniel Clark was a shoe-maker, about twenty-three years old, doing well in business, and with a fiancée who was known to have some money. He was thus able to order plate and silver on credit for his forthcoming wedding break-fast, to be held on the night of 7 February 1745. He also ordered other goods, probably more than he should have, but nothing sinister. Not sinister, that is, until the night before his wedding, when he told his brother-in-law he was going to visit his fiancée, and vanished. It was quickly discovered that £200 in cash and plate had gone with him, although his horse had not. Two men had been seen with him earlier that evening: Richard Houseman, a flax-dresser (someone who wove linen), and Eugene Aram. Their reputations were poor, and when their houses were searched, goods identified by the creditors were found. Aram said Clark had asked him to keep the things for him, and he was released, although it was noted that he had recently paid off a mortgage, and was unusually flush with cash. Soon afterwards, he abandoned both Knaresborough and his family. And that was the way things remained. He got a succession of jobs, first in London, ultimately in King's Lynn, Norfolk, as an usher in a school (an usher was a junior teacher, with little respect attached to the position, and even less money).

Fourteen years later, a labourer digging in a field outside Knaresborough found a skeleton. Daniel Clark's abandoned fiancée's brother claimed that it must be that of Clark, as no one else had gone missing from the area in the previous two decades. Eugene Aram's wife Anna gave evidence at the inquest on the bones, and said quite straightforwardly that she believed her husband and Houseman had murdered Clark. The jury's verdict was that 'from all apparent circumstances, the said skeleton is the skeleton of Daniel Clark'. Houseman protested: an eye-witness had seen Clark a few days after his disappearance. When questioned, however, this witness turned out only to have heard from a third person that yet a fourth person had said that he had once seen someone who resembled Clark. Houseman was arrested, and evidently began to think of how to save himself. He said that the skeleton was not Clark's, because he knew where Clark's body really was, and he sent officials to a local beauty spot called St Robert's Cave, where another skeleton was duly found. Houseman claimed that he had last seen Clark heading off to Eugene Aram's house on the night of his disappearance, while he, Houseman, had been left with the goods Clark had ordered, which they planned to fence. The next day his story had altered: he now said that he, Aram and Clark had all gone to St Robert's Cave together to divide up the goods, and Aram had killed Clark there. At the reconvened inquest Mrs Aram testified to seeing the three men set out in the early hours of the morning, after which Aram and Houseman had returned alone and burnt some clothing in the fire. The jury found that Daniel Clark had been murdered by Eugene Aram and Richard Houseman.

There are many versions of how Aram was found, usually involving the miraculous workings of providence. In reality, the speed of his arrest suggests that everyone had known where he was, but for the previous fourteen years hadn't much cared. Later rumour said he was living with a woman whom he passed off as his niece; others suggested it was his daughter; still others that he was living incestuously with his daughter. It could simply be that his daughter or niece was keeping house for him, and that that was how he was located. The warrant was delivered to the King's Lynn Justice of the Peace and MP, and he accompanied the constables to the school where Aram was employed. Aram denied knowing Clark at all, and claimed never to have been to Knaresborough. He was arrested nonetheless. By the time he was taken to York Castle (the nearest gaol to Knaresborough), he recalled that he had known Clark, but otherwise amnesia ruled his life: he couldn't remember when he had last seen Clark, nor that he had been friends with Houseman, nor what they were doing on the night Clark vanished, nor that he had paid off his debts afterwards. The only thing he could remember was that both his brothers had seen Clark after his disappearance, but, like Houseman's eye-witness, this came to nothing. Later his memory improved: Houseman and Clark had planned the fraud with another man, he said, and the four of them had gone to St Robert's Cave, but he had remained outside the cave, and when the others came out without Clark, they had told him that he had gone away.

Either Houseman or Aram was going to have to turn king's evidence if the prosecution was to succeed. Houseman was the logical choice, as Mrs Aram's testimony was crucial. Later accounts claimed that Houseman was found not guilty, but in fact the prosecution against him was withdrawn in order for him to testify against Aram. Houseman claimed pretty much what Aram had at the magistrates' hearing, just shifting the characters around: they had all gone to the cave, but now it was Aram who killed Clark, while Houseman remained outside. At the trial there were fourteen witnesses against Aram, while his defence, in later legend held up as a model of its kind, was in actuality poor.* In an age when character – reputation – meant

---

* In George Borrow's novel *Lavengro* (1851), Thurtell boasts that he is 'Equal to either fortune', which was said to be a quote from Aram's defence speech. Most commentators

a great deal to perceptions of guilt and innocence, Eugene Aram could not find a single witness to vouch for him. And a legal historian has noted that he could think of no other defence that 'condescends so little to any notice of so vulgar a thing as evidence'. Most defendants, he suggested, 'do make some endeavour to meet the case against them', but Aram did – or could – not. Instead, in his defence he set out his life history, trying to act as his own character witness; then he claimed he had been too ill at the time, too 'enfeebled', to commit murder (perhaps he hoped no one would remember the witnesses who had seen him walk several miles to St Robert's Cave two nights in a row); then he simply stressed the unreliability of circumstantial evidence. To no one's surprise, he was found guilty and sentenced to death. Initially his body was to be anatomized after his execution, as was standard, but such was local feeling that the jury asked to have the punishment increased: Aram would be gibbeted – hanged in chains after death, for his body to decay slowly in front of the local population.

That was the end of Eugene Aram, but only the beginning of the romance. In 1794, thirty-five years after the trial, the philosopher William Godwin published *Caleb Williams*, planned as a fictional counterpart to his *An Enquiry Concerning the Principles of Political Justice*. This endeavoured to show how those who lived in an unequal society were victimized by it, but it is Godwin's links to Aram that matter here. Godwin grew up only twenty-five miles from King's Lynn, and later studied at the Hoxton Academy under Andrew Kippis, who was working on a *Biographia Britannica* which included an entry for Eugene Aram, taking the standard eighteenth-century view that he was a thief and murderer. But when the story reappeared later in the *Newgate Calendar* it focused more on Aram's self-education, sliding over the fact that he was a receiver of stolen goods, and concentrating instead on the picture of a man with a thirst for learning,

---

have taken this to indicate that Thurtell was acquainted with the details of the murder of Daniel Clark. All it really means is that Borrow, the author who put these words into Thurtell's mouth, was familiar with Aram's defence, and since as a young man he had compiled a six-volume edition of *Celebrated Trials*, this is hardly a surprise.

oppressed by a rigidly hierarchical society. In *Caleb Williams*, Godwin expands this theme: when hiding from his unjust persecutors, Caleb finds 'a general dictionary of four of the northern languages' and determines 'to attempt, at least for my own use, an etymological analysis of the English language'. This is the earliest linkage of Aram to linguistics or philology, and thereafter virtually no recounting of the story was complete without a breathless recapitulation of his brilliance as a scholar.

In 1828 the poet and comic writer Thomas Hood added to the growing myth with 'The Dream of Eugene Aram', a ballad that was to shape ideas of Aram for the rest of the century. One pleasant summer, 'four and twenty happy boys/Came bounding out of school'. As they

The eighteenth-century murderer Eugene Aram gained a second audience in the nineteenth century after the wild success of Thomas Hood's 1828 poem 'The Dream of Eugene Aram' described his crime, committed by 'Two sudden blows with a ragged stick,/And one with a heavy stone'.

frolic, however, 'the usher sat remote from all,/A melancholy man', watching a boy who is reading 'The Death of Abel'. He winces, tormented, telling the boy 'Of horrid stabs in groves forlorn,/And murders done in caves'. He himself dreamed of murdering 'A feeble man and old ... here, said I, this man shall die,/And I will have his gold!' Then, retribution: 'That very night, while gentle sleep/The urchins' eyelids kiss'd,/Two stern-faced men set out from Lynn,/Through the dark and heavy mist/And Eugene Aram walk'd between/With gyves upon his wrist.'

Now, instead of a ruffian who killed a fellow criminal when dividing up their spoils, Aram is depicted for the first time as a tormented, repentant sinner. By casting the act of murder as a dream, Hood was able to ignore entirely the mercenary element, making the criminal more important than the crime. The enormous success of the poem swept away more down-to-earth retellings. In the *Manchester Times*, the ballad was reprinted with a preface telling readers that 'The late Admiral Burney [brother of the novelist Fanny Burney] went to school ... where the unhappy Eugene Aram was usher ... The admiral stated, that Aram was generally liked by the boys; and that he used to discourse to them about murder in somewhat of the spirit which is attributed to him in this poem.' (Burney had been dead for seven years when this report appeared, so was not in a position to confirm or deny it.) Three years later, from 'generally liked', the *Examiner* now said firmly that Aram was 'beloved'. This is no longer a comment on the poem, but is presented as a biographical fact.

The next person to handle Aram's story was the most influential. Bulwer, fresh from his triumphs with crime and criminals in *Pelham* and *Paul Clifford*, in 1832 took on Eugene Aram. Bulwer begins his story in Grassdale, where Aram, a reclusive scholar-genius, falls in love with Madeline Lester, the squire's daughter. All are pleased except her cousin Walter, who is in love with Madeline himself, and who now travels to forget. In a saddler's shop in the north, he recognizes his long-vanished father's whip. But he is told it was owned by a man named Daniel Clark, a villain who was later murdered. Walter meets Houseman, who incautiously connects Clark's murder to Aram.

Walter thunders home to prevent the wedding of his cousin to a murderer, Aram is arrested, tried and convicted, and Madeline dies of grief. Aram confesses: he was 'haunted with the ambition of enlightening my race', but was prevented from making 'a gigantic discovery in science' by 'the total inadequacy of my means'. He decided, therefore, that it was 'better for mankind – that I should commit one bold wrong, and by that wrong purchase the power of good'. His crime was further diminished: Clark was a vicious aristocrat who had raped a 'quiet, patient-looking, gentle creature', who subsequently killed herself. Aram's repentance, such as it is, entirely revolves around the shame he has brought to the noble family of Lester, out of remorse for which he then commits suicide.

Bulwer aimed to make Aram a tragic figure: a noble man destroyed by a single flaw. To do so he had to rewrite almost all the known facts, apart from the long-undiscovered crime itself.* Clark, instead of a young labouring man, is now, melodrama-fashion, an upper-class despoiler of women; Aram's abandoned wife and half-dozen children vanish without a trace; while Aram himself is no longer a humble usher, but a scholar of international renown.

This fiction quickly displaced fact. In 1832, the *Trial and Life of Eugene Aram; several of his Poems, and his plan and specimens of an Anglo-Celtic Lexicon, with copious notes ...* worked backwards from the novel, using Bulwer's fictional account of the trial as though it were a verbatim court report. The *Leeds Mercury* commented admiringly on Aram as 'a man of most extraordinary talents and character', and the *Gentleman's Magazine* agreed that he was entirely innocent. It was widely reported that Archdeacon Paley had pronounced Aram's defence to be one 'of consummate ability'. (A modern scholar has noted that Paley was an adolescent at the time, so if he had made the remark at all, it wasn't a hugely mature judgement; later in life he said that Aram had 'got himself hanged by his own cleverness'.) The

---

* While Bulwer may have thought his novel a moral portrait, Pierce Egan was more clear-sighted. After its publication he called on Bulwer to present him with his treasure, the caul of Thurtell, as a tribute to a man he obviously thought of first and foremost as a murder specialist. Bulwer was appalled.

journalist Leigh Hunt went even further in his praise: 'Had Johnson been about him, the world would have attributed the defence to Johnson.' Bulwer's biographer later claimed that Bulwer's creation, Madeline Lester, was also based on reality, 'taken word for word, fact for fact, from Burney's notes'. As Burney had been eight years old at the time, we might assume that his memories of an impoverished usher yearning after the local squire's daughter might not be terribly reliable, if they ever existed.

Of the success of Bulwer's novel, however, there could be no doubt. Within its first year, the *Morning Chronicle* noted, as well as French and German translations, the book sold over 30,000 copies in the USA. The *Hampshire Telegraph and Sussex Chronicle* published a plea from the Library and Reading Room in Queen Street, Portsea, in which it 'earnestly requested that their subscribers who have [borrowed] the first volumes ... of Eugene Aram ... will return them forthwith ... as detaining them so long prevents that accomodation [sic] which they wish should be received by all'.

Others rushed to elaborate the subject. Although he would have been disgusted to have his work categorized as fiction, there is nowhere else to put Norrisson Scatcherd's highly coloured *Memoirs of the Celebrated Eugene Aram* ... Scatcherd, a barrister who devoted his life to antiquarian and local-history research, claimed to have become interested in Aram in 1792, when he was about twelve, on a visit to Harrogate, and he says it was then that he began to interview locals who had known Aram thirty-three years before. In his version, Aram was 'modest', 'amiable', 'beloved and admired'. His wife, however, was 'a low, mean, vulgar woman, of extremely doubtful character', who was unfaithful, and thus Aram's doubts of their children's paternity made it perfectly natural that he should be 'disposed ... to neglect them'. According to Scatcherd, Clark was Mrs Aram's lover, and in addition he and Houseman were planning to rob and kill a pedlar boy. Aram helped Clark dishonestly order plate and goods, but only because he was 'wretchedly poor, having a family to support'. The three men went to St Robert's Cave, but it was obvious to Scatcherd that it was Houseman who murdered Clark, because Aram was 'a man of moral habits, delicate health, prepossessing countenance, slender form,* and unassuming deportment'.

Scatcherd's account was well-received. A review in the *Leeds Mercury* said he had 'corrected some important errors', and Aram could now be seen as an 'amiable and accomplished murderer'. There appears to be no irony intended in that phrase: the newspaper repeated Scatcherd's views on the justice of the killing owing to Mrs Aram's infidelity, and implied that as both Clark and Houseman were robbers and murderers themselves, the killing of Clark was really not so very terrible. As late as 1870, Scatcherd was still commended for having 'done much to ... rescue' Aram's name; the murderer was now merely 'imprudent' for having 'associat[ed] himself with persons beneath his own standing'. In the *Daily News* in 1856, the Metropolitan Board of Works considered the possibility of renaming some London streets to avoid multiple streets with the same names, and some alternatives are suggested: Ainsworth, Keats, Southey and Bulwer are among them, as are Richard Mayne (the commissioner of the Metropolitan Police) and Eugene Aram.†

The great success of these accounts of Aram's case brought theatrical adaptations in their wake. W.T. Moncrieff's version opened at the Surrey in February 1832; within a month it was advertising additional performances, 'Owing to the complete overflows'. Soon the Royal Pavilion and Sadler's Wells had their own versions, with another at the Royal Grecian by the end of the year. There were also productions in Edinburgh, Wakefield and Sheffield. The Surrey version continued the Bulwer/Scatcherd trend of turning Aram into an anguished, noble and excessively learned murderer: he 'perfected himself in ... Hesiod, Homer, Theocritus, Herodotus, Thucydides' before he 'began to study Hebrew', not to mention 'the Chaldee and Arabic' and 'Celtic ... through all its dialects'. He is introduced to the audience as 'Master

---

* Even in today's size-zero world, I don't think anyone has defended themselves against a charge of murder by claiming they were too thin to have done it.

† At first I thought this must be satire, but it doesn't appear to be; the basic information was reprinted the following day in another context.

Aram, the great scholar', while Houseman is 'guilty-like', and so repellent that all who see him 'turn aside – as from a thing infect [sic]'. Aram confesses that 'poverty and pride' had led him to commit the crime: 'I yearned for knowledge but had no means to feed that glorious yearning.' Madeline dies of grief at his feet, promising to wait for him in heaven, and Aram then kills himself, as 'I have been no common criminal; – Eugene Aram renders to the scaffold! his – *lifeless* body – pardon – pity – all.' This was an authorized adaptation of Bulwer's novel, and he himself attended the first night.* The *New Monthly Magazine* highly recommended the production, although by an astonishing coincidence the editor of this magazine was one E.L. Bulwer, author of *Eugene Aram*.

Two years after these theatre adaptations, the young novelist Harrison Ainsworth published *Rookwood*, which was very much the love child of *Eugene Aram* and *Paul Clifford* crossed with gothic tales, and this led the way to a new kind of fictional criminal-hero. Ainsworth was not concerned, as Bulwer claimed to be, with examining the motivation of criminals, and society's responsibilities. He was not even terribly concerned with facts: it was in *Rookwood* that Dick Turpin first made his epic ride from London to York on Black Bess, although the historical Turpin had only ridden as far as Lincolnshire – a sixty-mile trip instead of two hundred. Ainsworth wanted to entertain, and his highwaymen are debonair and dashing, usually men of rank cheated out of their birthrights. As Ainsworth's Turpin says, 'It is as necessary for a man to be a gentleman before he can turn highwayman, as it is for a doctor to have his diploma, or an attorney his certificate ...'

Turpin, hanged in 1739 for horse-stealing, had from about 1800 been turned into popular entertainment in coarse and inexpensive chapbooks, and in 1818 in an onstage incarnation, as *Richard Turpin, The Highwayman*. By 1823 his name was already a byword for a

* Before 1832, copyright in a novel did not extend to other art forms: anyone could write and produce a play based on any fiction. After 1832, legislation protected plays that had been published from being re-produced by other theatres, but if the play was staged without the script being published, then it too was fair game.

The eighteenth-century highwayman Dick Turpin regularly appeared onstage. This playbill focuses on the moment when Black Bess, Turpin's trusty steed, leaps the turnpike gate on his wild ride from London to York.

dashing, brave criminal. Thurtell had boasted to his brother, 'We are Turpin-like lads, and have done the trick.' From the 1830s penny-bloods returned again and again to his story. One of the most popular was *Black Bess; or, The Knight of the Road*, which appeared in 254 numbers over five years: Turpin was not executed until page 2,207. Dick Turpin, Jack Sheppard, Eugene Aram and others made up the subjects for series like Purkess's Library of Romance and Purkess's Penny Plays. These publications were so popular, the police complained, that vagrant boys spent their leisure time playing cards and dominoes and reading *Jack Sheppard* and *Oliver Twist* 'and publications of that kind', the implication being that this reading material would in and of itself lead to crime.

Rookwood was filled with songs – twenty-three in the first edition, and more later. Ainsworth may have been thinking of theatrical adaptations from the first: they certainly followed quickly, and nearly every one of them included the song he had written in 'flash', or thieves' slang, which 'travelled everywhere ... It deafened us in the streets, where it was ... popular with the organ-grinders and German bands ... it was whistled by every dirty guttersnipe, and chanted in drawing-rooms by fair lips ...'

> In the box of the Stone Jug [prison] I was born
> Of a hempen widow [my father was hanged] the kid forlorn.
> > Fake away [Go on, steal].
> My noble father as I've heard say
> Was a famous merchant of capers gay.
> Nix my dolly, palls [Nothing, friends], fake away.
>
> The knucks in quod [thieves in prison] did my school-men play
> And put me up to the time of day.
> > Fake away.
> No dummy hunter had forks so fly [pickpocket had fingers so
> > nimble]
> No knuckler so deftly could fake a cly [pick a pocket]
> Nix my dolly, palls, fake away.

But my nuttiest lady one fine day
To the beaks did her gentleman betray.
    Fake away.
And thus was I bowled out at last,
And into the Jug for a lag was cast [and was sent to prison].
Nix my dolly, palls, fake away.

But I slipp'd my darbies [fetters] one morn in May
And gave to the dubsman [turnkey] a holiday.
    Fake away.
And here I am, palls, merry and free,
A regular rollocking Romany.
Nix my dolly, palls, fake away.

In 1835 *Rookwood* was adapted for Astley's Amphitheatre, which specialized in staging hippodramas – spectaculars with vast numbers of horses, riders and extras. It was retitled *Turpin's Ride to York and the Death of Black Bess*, taking the element that people had enjoyed the most. (It is notable, two years after Cold Bath Field, that Black Bess no longer dies of exhaustion after her epic journey, but is shot by the wicked Bow Street Runners.)

The success of *Rookwood*, both onstage and as fiction, led to even more novels in which criminals were glamorized, with Ainsworth's next book revolving entirely around a historical criminal: the eighteenth-century thief and gaol-breaker Jack Sheppard. Serialization began in *Bentley's Miscellany* just as another story in that magazine, also about a boy-criminal, also illustrated by Cruikshank, was ending, and for four episodes they overlapped, so it was natural to think of them together. The second tale was *Oliver Twist*, by Charles Dickens. Today it is surprising to think of *Oliver Twist* as a crime novel, but stripped down to its bare bones, the plot is very similar to Bulwer's *Paul Clifford*: the orphan who is, unknown to himself, from a 'good' family but is left to be raised by criminals. Similarly, Ainsworth's *Jack Sheppard* is the story of an apprentice who becomes a thief, with a parallel story of a good apprentice cheated out of his inheritance by an evil relative; Oliver Twist is an apprentice who has ostensibly gone bad by joining Fagin's gang, while he is unlawfully kept from his inheritance by his evil half-brother. (The name 'Twist' in the title would also have tipped off contemporary readers that this was a book about crime and criminals: 'to twist' was underworld slang for 'to hang'.)* These books were classed together as 'Newgate novels', connecting the stories both to the *Newgate Calendar* and also to the gaol from which Sheppard himself so famously escaped.

Some critics left Dickens out of their discussions of Newgate novels, which were condemned for portraying criminals sympathetically. As the *Edinburgh Review* summed up, Dickens 'never endeavours to mislead our sympathies – to pervert plain notions of right and wrong – to make vice interesting in our eyes … We find no … creatures blending with their crimes the most incongruous and romantic virtues.' This praise of Dickens was, very obviously, also a poke at Bulwer. *Punch* magazine, too, condemned Newgate fiction in its drawing of 'The Literary Gentleman' surrounded by thoughts of 'Murder', 'Gallows heroism', 'Burglary' and 'Robbery'. On his desk is a dagger, a gallows, a broadside printed with a 'Dying Speech', a copy of the *Newgate Calendar* and another of the *Annals of Crime*. The verse that follows mocks:

---

* Dickens is 'literature' now, and it takes an effort to see him through different eyes. Yet the number of murders and otherwise unnatural deaths that occur in his novels is astonishing: *Oliver Twist* has a murder, an accidental death by hanging, an execution, and a dog's brains are smashed out for good measure; a murder, a violent riot leading to many deaths and a double execution appear in *Barnaby Rudge*; a murder, attempted murder and suicide by a murderer in *Martin Chuzzlewit*; while in *A Tale of Two Cities* there is a guillotining, and Madame Defarge shoots herself; *David Copperfield* has two accidental drownings and one suicide; a character falls down an abandoned mineshaft in *Hard Times*; *Bleak House* has two deaths from exhaustion, one suicide, one murder and one spontaneous combustion; in *The Old Curiosity Shop* there is one death by drowning, one from exhaustion; the first person killed by a train in literature appears in *Dombey and Son*; *Our Mutual Friend* has a double, murderous drowning, another accidental death on the river, and two attempted murders; in *Great Expectations* there are two attempted murders and one death by drowning; in *Little Dorrit* a house crushes a self-confessed murderer. In the unfinished *Edwin Drood* it is perfectly clear that the eponymous Drood has been murdered, but Dickens himself died before that murder was unravelled.

... you, great scribe, more greedy of renown,
From Hounslow's gibbet drag a hero down.
Embue his mind with virtue; make him quote
Some moral truth, before he cuts a throat.*

Bulwer was a punchbag for everyone. For now Eugene Aram's name – even without reference to Bulwer – was being used for anything, even a toothache cure. This advertisement appeared regularly in both the London and the provincial papers, making a segue from a murderer to a patent medicine seem bizarrely normal:

> EUGENE ARAM. – It will be in the recollection of most of our readers that after the murder of Daniel Clarke, Eugene Aram resided many years at Lynn, in Norfolk, in fancied security and seclusion. – Sweeting's Tooth Ache Elixir has also found its way to the same place. In the advertisement in another part of this paper respecting this deservingly popular medicine, will be found a letter from the agent at Lynn, from which we may conclude that while it is giving peace and ease from pain to many, yet (like Eugene Aram), it will not be allowed any rest for itself.

To dissociate himself from this type of thing, in 1840 Bulwer produced a second edition of *Eugene Aram*, with numerous changes, blandly assuring his readers that 'the legal evidence against [Aram] is very deficient'. The most important alteration was that Aram was no longer a murderer, but had simply fretted himself to a shadow for fourteen years over a murder committed by another man, Bulwer's response to the fear that, as with Thurtell and Turpin, Newgate novels would lead the young to emulate their heroes. This was of even more concern with stage versions, which had larger audiences than the printed word. *Oliver Twist*'s huge popularity – there were six stage adaptations

---

* *Punch* really had its knife out for Bulwer, and ran a series triggered by *Eugene Aram*, in which parallel columns compared Bulwer's romanticized version of Aram's life with the rather sordid facts. It later mocked Bulwer's many names by referring to him as 'Sir E. L. B. L. BB. LL. BBB. LLL.'

in London even before the end of the book was serialized, and the Surrey alone claimed that 300,000 people had seen its production in its first year – meant that most people's ideas of the story were based not on the novel, but on stage versions speedily mounted in small theatres. From 1839 to 1859 there were at least sixteen productions of *Jack Sheppard*,* and a dozen of *Oliver Twist*. *Eugene Aram* was not particularly popular in London, but was a perennial favourite outside the capital: at least thirty productions appeared in those two decades. Plays that were performed by fairground companies, fit-up companies and booth theatres (travelling companies that carried their own stages with them) have little recorded history, but they were what most people saw. Today we can only record their existence from rare survivals (like the Maria Marten marionettes), or from moments when the theatre companies met the authorities, as when in 1857 the *Leeds Mercury* reported that in Great Horton, outside Bradford, the owner of a booth theatre had been charged with performing *Eugene Aram* without a licence.

There were probably many dozens of productions like this, and in 1859 the Lord Chamberlain decided that enough was enough. *Jack Sheppard* was considered to be the worst offender: *Oliver Twist*, after all, featured a middle-class child who didn't want to be a thief, while Eugene Aram was a gentrified, remorseful murderer. Sheppard was working-class and repeatedly escaped from gaol, thumbing his nose at authority. All stage productions of *Jack Sheppard* were therefore banned, apart from the one that had first been licensed. Not coincidentally, this version had originated in the West End, where the respectable middle-class audience could be counted on not to take away an inappropriately immoral lesson. Yet the *Oliver Twist* productions, at least the non-West End versions, perhaps did not have the

---

* After the success of the play, the grave of a completely unrelated Jack Sheppard, who had been buried in Willesden cemetery two centuries before the gaol-breaker, was overrun with visitors, and the cemetery's wily sexton chipped off bits of the headstone to sell. (The criminal Jack Sheppard was buried in the workhouse of St Martin-in-the-Fields, now under the site of the National Gallery. In 1866 the remains of the cemetery's inhabitants were transferred to Brookwood, in Surrey.)

moral content the Lord Chamberlain assumed. The manager of the Gaiety Theatre remembered seeing *Oliver Twist* at the Victoria in the 1840s: 'Nancy was always dragged round the stage by her hair, and after this effort Sikes always looked up defiantly at the gallery ... He was always answered by one loud and fearful curse, yelled by the whole mass ... Finally when Sikes, working up to a well-rehearsed climax, smeared Nancy with red-ochre, and taking her by the hair (a most powerful wig) seemed to dash her brains out on the stage ... A thousand enraged voices, which sounded like ten thousand ... filled the theatre.'

It was commonly assumed that different audiences would take different messages from the entertainment, depending on their class background. The middle classes were almost unanimous in condemning working-class penny-bloods. *Punch* reflected the middle-class viewpoint in the cartoon overleaf (the 'likeness' in the caption is a portrait of the murderer). The *Derby Mercury* claimed that there were 'one hundred distinct publications' with titles like *Dick Turpin, The Bold Smuggler, Jack Sheppard, Claud Duval, or, The Dashing Highwayman*, which contained 'every variety of tale of vice, murder, and obscenity'. In 1846 the *Leeds Mercury* reported that a druggist and his wife had been found 'insensible and frothing at the mouth', and shortly died of opium poisoning. At the inquest, the woman's mother reported that the previous night the druggist had been reading *Eugene Aram* aloud. It was clear from the report that the couple drank heavily and were in debt, but it was *Eugene Aram* that was highlighted – reading about crime was a sign of bad character in the working classes. In 1870, one middle-class journalist who specialized in reports from the wilder shores of the underclasses called the bloods a 'plague of poisonous literature ... packets of ... poison'.

What was left unspoken was that the audience for these 'packets of poison' could read. In *Oliver Twist*, as early as 1837, Dickens had simply taken for granted that Oliver, brought up in a workhouse, would be literate, as were all the underworld characters (Fagin even reads the *Hue and Cry*), unlike Garside, the murderer of Thomas Ashton, a skilled factory operative but illiterate. In a survey in

Newsvendor – 'Now, my man, what is it?'
Boy – 'I vonts a nillustrated newspaper with a norrid murder and a likeness in it.'

Edinburgh Gaol in 1846, out of 4,513 prisoners, only 317 could not read at all, while 379 could read well or very well, and presumably the rest were somewhere in between. Even the upper echelons of the police were struggling. Originally Richard Mayne had planned that all divisional superintendents would be responsible for their own correspondence, but to his shock he found that illiteracy frequently made this impossible. Lower down the ranks, the rules had originally permitted entry to the force only for men under thirty years old, over 5 feet 7 inches, 'intelligent' and able to read and write 'plainly'. But from 1869, when promotions were won by competitive examination, it was found that many of the entrants could not read or write well enough to sit the exams, and classes had to be instituted across the force.

Those who could read well, the middle classes, were considered immune to the 'packets of poison'. *Oliver Twist* continued on its successful way, as did the licensed *Jack Sheppard*. (Although Lord Melbourne had complained that *Oliver Twist* was all about 'workhouses, and Coffin Makers, and Pickpockets ... I don't like them in reality, and therefore I don't wish them represented.' Queen Victoria, by contrast, thought the novel 'excessively interesting'.) Furthermore, from the 1830s, prosperous children were happy consumers of paper toy theatres, sheets of coloured card printed with sets and various characters, with abridged play texts that were remarkably similar to the penny texts published for the working classes. The main difference was that these sheets initially cost up to 6*d*. for a set (although by the 1850s the toy theatre price had dropped to as little as a ½*d*.). *Jack Sheppard* was as popular in toy theatres as it was in real ones: one version had sixty-four sheets of characters and sets. There were also many versions of *Oliver Twist*, with a good range of characters. In one set, 'Sykes' [sic] looks rather gentlemanly, in a blue jacket and dashing yellow tie. 'Fagan' [also sic] has a very big nose, a red cap, a black beard and a dressy knee-length purple coat. Nancy looks sweetly pretty in red and green with a prim apron, and a 'Pauper' woman wears a nice red dress, blue apron, cap and shawl: without the label under her figure it would be impossible to know she was a pauper. By contrast, the thieves are all smoking pipes, a clear indication of bad character.

Now that *Jack Sheppard* was banned, the Bulwer-influenced Aram story, with its comforting gentrified elements, began to dominate. Knaresborough became a sort of Eugene Aram theme park, and was even considered suitable for Sunday-school outings: a group of Wesleyan 'Sunday scholars' from Hunslet, near Leeds, went on an excursion to St Robert's Cave, 'where Daniel Clarke [sic] was said to have been murdered', before going to Harrogate to take the waters and go donkey-riding. Even the *Penny Magazine*, published by the improving Society for the Diffusion of Useful Knowledge, described St Robert's Cave primarily as 'the scene of the murder' in an article on the beauties of the region. Similarly, at least one racehorse was named Eugene Aram after Hood's poem was published, while greyhounds with the same name appeared after both Bulwer's novel and, later, the stage adaptations appeared.

There was also a second wave of novels based on Aram-like themes. The first was *Amy Paul* in 1852, an anonymous novel of orphans, inheritances, blackmail and a long-suppressed crime, all wrapped up in a love story and a depiction of genteel middle-class life. It had almost nothing to recommend it, but *John Bull* noted 'a family likeness to *Eugene Aram*', and thought 'The moral is well worked out.' It is certainly very moral, but not very interesting: 'The good ended happily, and the bad unhappily. That is what Fiction means,' said Oscar Wilde's Miss Prism, and she would have had no trouble with *Amy Paul*.

The next novel, in 1855, is a much better book: Caroline Clive's *Paul Ferroll* is the story of a squire whose bad-tempered wife is found murdered. A gardener is accused, but Ferroll nobly hires a lawyer to defend him, and he is acquitted. Ferroll meanwhile remarries, this time to his childhood sweetheart, whom he had dearly loved before he had foolishly married his first wife. Years pass; in a cholera epidemic Ferroll shows his true worth by working heroically to save lives. During a bread riot he is threatened by a mob and kills a man; given the circumstances, his magistrate neighbours can do nothing but praise his action, but he asks his much-loved wife, 'Suppose they were to make it out that I had committed a murder; suppose I were called a murderer ... could you be faithful still, love me, no matter what I was ...?' It turns out that the noble man murdered his first wife for love of his second.* Unlike in Bulwer's novel, neither the murderer nor the narrator attempts to explain or justify the crime. This may be why the reviews praised the work, and failed to mention its Aram-like murderer.

The next to reflect Aram influence, however, was not simply a fairly good book, but was a masterpiece – Dickens' *Our Mutual Friend*. Here

---

* In case someone else was accused of the crime after his death, Ferroll had deposited a confession in his first wife's coffin. How, the reader asks, was anyone supposed to know to exhume his first wife in the hope that a confession might have been buried with her? Answer comes there none.

Bradley Headstone has Aram-like features, although Dickens is more influenced by Thomas Hood than by Bulwer. Headstone is a poor schoolmaster, as Aram had been, and as Hood's poem had represented him. Dickens can therefore stay close to reality as he describes the frustrations of a man whose intelligence and abilities have lifted him out of his original class, but have left him stranded and socially ambiguous, in the middle class but not of it. There are other parallels. The name Eugene is transferred from the murderer to his intended victim, Eugene Wrayburn: from the schoolmaster to the gentleman he wanted to be. Headstone attacks Wrayburn with a stick, as Hood has Aram deal Clark 'Two sudden blows with a ragged stick'. The chapter in which Headstone attempts to shift the blame for his crime is entitled 'Better to be Abel than Cain', just as Hood's pupil reads 'The Death of Abel', and his Aram says 'murderers walk the earth/Beneath the curse of Cain'. Headstone cools his fevered head in a stream, as Hood's Aram 'washed my forehead cool', and he returns to his schoolroom, as Hood's Aram 'sat among the urchins young,/That evening in the school'. There are differences too. Hood's Aram deeply regrets the crime; Headstone simply regrets that his murderous attack failed. In Hood, the schoolboys sense something wrong, and gaze wonderingly at their master; in Dickens, the schoolboys are as self-absorbed as children usually are, and notice nothing. Instead of the single schoolboy looking sorrowingly on at Aram's remorse, here Headstone's favoured pupil thinks only of what Headstone's disgrace will mean to his own ambitions.

Hood's version also held sway in the visual arts, with a number of paintings based on his work, from Alfred Rankley's 1852 Royal Academy piece *Eugene Aram in the Schoolroom* and *Eugene Aram's Dream*, a bas-relief by Matthew Noble that was chosen to represent British Art at the Paris Universal Exhibition of 1855. (As late as 1889, reproductions of this work were still being advertised.) Rankley's piece was praised in the *Athenaeum* for its depiction of an Aram 'gnawed by the conscience-worm that never dies', and the same publication was even more enthusiastic about 'two weird drawings' on the subject by Mr Rossiter, which show 'the scared murderer coming to the well-known place in the wood, and finding that a mighty wind has laid bare the body. The bare wounded head and clutched hand protrude through the shrinking leaves.' The story had evidently evolved: a fourteen-years-dead body still showing a wound? What wood? Yet a wood, and a recently murdered victim, had become the dominant pictorial image: at the 1872 International Exhibition praise was given to Alfred Elmore's picture of Aram in a wood, 'startled by the half-revealed body of the murdered man lying among the treacherous leaves'. There were further versions on the same subject over the next decades, by A. Dixon, John Pettie (whose murderer was condemned by the *Era* as looking like a 'country clergyman ... telling the little boy to be sure and come to church next Sunday') – there was even an image by Thackeray.

The story was now part of middle-class moral education, and Hood's poem became a favoured party piece for children: Aubrey Beardsley recited it at school in the 1880s, and Lord Alfred Douglas even claimed that Oscar Wilde's *Ballad of Reading Gaol* 'owed something to that fine poem' too. A vicar in Sunderland lectured on 'Eugene Aram: his life, trial, condemnation, and execution' 'under the auspices of the Baker-street Young Men's Mutual Improvement Society'.* A Social Reform Society's weekly entertainment included a reading of Hood's ballad. The poem was regarded by some as a bit suspect, though, smacking too much of theatre, and too little of moral uplift. The Revd J.C.M. Bellew was condemned by the *Birmingham Post* for performing it too dramatically: 'A less demonstrative reading would have been ... more suitable.' Others disagreed:

* Vicars had a penchant for the story. A sale of autographs collected by the late Revd F.W. Joy included a letter from Aram after his arrest, as well as a letter from Bulwer authenticating it (although why Bulwer, born more than half a century after Aram died, should be an expert on his handwriting, is unclear). There were also 'relics': a box made from the wood of Aram's gibbet, a bone from his skeleton, another box made from a beam from Daniel Clark's house, as well as a portion of his skull (this time authenticated by the governor of York Castle), and there was a letter from Aram 'relating to a recent tour on the Continent'. The idea of a poor school usher making a grand tour is so risible that it is hard to take the rest of the collection seriously, but people did. It was estimated to sell for £19, while a letter from Robert Burns was valued at £13, and an entire manuscript in Carlyle's hand a sad little £3.

'Penny Readings for the People' at Mechanics' Institutes frequently included the poem.

There were also professional performances of the work. In 1858 'Mr Walter Montgomery' appeared at the Music Hall, Broad Street, Birmingham. On the first night he recited 'from Memory, the whole of SHAKESPEARE'S TRAGEDY OF "MACBETH", ASSISTED BY AN EFFICIENT CHOIR'. The next night too was devoted to 'the BEAUTIES of SHAKESPEARE AND OTHER CELEBRATED AUTHORS', including 'Little Jim: a Tale of the Collieries (by desire)', Poe's 'The Raven', and Hood's 'The Dream of Eugene Aram'. Hood seemed not to work in music hall: I have found only one reference to a performance, and the review says the choice was 'very injudicious', being 'long' and 'heavy … altogether out of place'. For those who wanted theatre, but could not attend because of religious or moral scruples, Aram was available elsewhere. The Gallery of Illustration in Regent Street staged one-man entertainments from 1850, and in 1873, when a new theatrical adaptation of *Eugene Aram* opened at the Lyceum with Henry Irving and Ellen Terry, the *Era* reviewed the Gallery's last night of the season, which included 'a new drama, performed for the first time on any stage, entitled *Impeached*, written apparently ['apparently' is wonderful] in blank verse, and in artistic style, by Miss H.L. Walford, who takes for her plot the leading incidents of Eugene Aram'.

Ultimately Henry Irving took over as the supreme reciter of Hood's poem. At a time when it was still the norm to have two plays on the bill every evening, he performed it in the break between the two; he also frequently performed it separately in mixed programmes. He also had years of success in *The Bells*, an adaptation of a French play called *Le Juif polonais*, in which he played a burgomaster who, fifteen years before, had robbed and murdered a man. This long-undiscovered secret is threatened by his guilty conscience, which transforms some passing sleigh-bells into those on the murdered man's sleigh. Shrieking, 'The bells! The bells!' he falls into a fit, is later hypnotized and betrays himself. To follow this success, in 1873 the playwright W.G. Wills took the story of Aram, as glamorized by Bulwer, and turned it into classy West End fare by removing the melodrama: there is no trial, no criminal awaiting execution; Aram is not only not executed, he doesn't even kill himself. Instead, he just somehow dies, romantically, in a moonlit churchyard in his fiancée's arms. Perhaps, mocked the *Saturday Review* critic, 'he caught cold by sleeping in a damp churchyard'.* By the 1890s, Irving was reciting Hood's verses with 'Dr. Mackenzie's incidental music'. (Alexander Campbell Mackenzie was the principal of the Royal Academy of Music, as well as a conductor and composer.) In 1896, Granville Bantock wrote a four-act opera based on Bulwer's novel.

Opera was the logical culmination of music and melodrama. Initially, music had been essential to melodrama, as licensing laws barred spoken dialogue in the minor theatres. After speech was reintroduced, music continued to play a major part, not only in the form of songs, but to underscore the emotions of the characters. Every theatre orchestra had its own 'agits' (that is, *agitatos*, music indicating fear or distress), 'slows' (slow music for grave moments), 'hurries', 'pathetics', 'struggles' and more. As late as 1912, the catalogue of Samuel French, the theatrical publisher, listed: 'Incidental Music Suitable for Lively Rise of Curtain, Entrance of Characters, &c., Hurry, Combat, Apparitions, Pathetic Situations, Martial, &c.' The critic Percy Fitzgerald, who had been one of Irving's assistants, noted that at transpontine theatres, 'what so natural as that when smugglers, or robbers, or captives trying to make their escape should, when moving lightly on tiptoe past the unnatural tyrant's chamber, be kept in time by certain disjointed and jerking music?'†

As late as 1890, Aram was still attracting novelists. Mary Elizabeth Braddon (author of one of the first sensation-novels, *Lady Audley's Secret*, pp.296–7), now with nearly sixty novels to her name, and an

---

* Wills had a knack for turning theatrical fiction into untheatrical theatre: his adaptation of *Jane Eyre* drops the novel's dramatically interrupted wedding scene; instead, Jane is informed of Rochester's previous marriage *in a letter*.

† Gilbert and Sullivan parodied this in *Ruddigore* (1887), which had dialogue accompanied in melodrama fashion. (The West End audiences were bemused, failing to recognize the convention.)

invalid husband to support, produced *One Life, One Love*. In it she repeats the long-hidden-murder motif, enmeshed in a story of the Paris Commune, double-identity, heroines regularly going mad and a plot so confusing that there is no real resolution, because, I strongly suspect, the author could not quite work out what had happened, and understandably did not want to read it over again. The Aram theme was briefly touched on in 1894, in Catherine Louise Pirkis's 'The Murder at Troyte's Hill', in which a lodgekeeper is murdered after decades of blackmail, and the case is solved by the lady detective Loveday Brooke. The murderer is writing a treatise on Aram's legendary subject, philology, 'a stupendous work ... a work that will leave its impress upon thought in all the ages to come' (for more on this story, see p.402).

And then there was a final, extraordinarily derivative theatrical version. *After All* (1895) was written by Freeman C. Wills, W.G. Wills' brother. Aram was played by Martin Harvey (later Sir John Martin-Harvey), who had worked for Irving for fourteen years, and Ruth (the Madeline character) by Mabel Terry-Lewis, Ellen Terry's niece. It had, remarkably, a happy ending: Houseman denounces Aram, Aram defends himself, and Walter in a gentlemanly way accepts his apology. It is not surprising that no one chose to follow this.

The constant renewal of Aram's story contrasts sharply with another eighteenth-century murder case that also achieved a blaze of interest in the nineteenth century, but as quickly sputtered out. In 1739, a Mr Hayes stopped at Jonathan Bradford's Oxfordshire inn. In conversation Hayes disclosed that he was carrying a great deal of money, and, two guests overhearing this, a robbery was planned. That night the two men entered his room, only to find Hayes dead and Bradford standing over the body, bloody knife in hand. Bradford's defence was that he had gone in to rob his guest, but had found him already dead, and had just picked up the knife that was lying beside the corpse when the two men discovered him. This unlikely story was given short shrift at his trial, and Bradford was found guilty and hanged. Eighteen months later, so the story goes, Mr Hayes' servant confessed on his deathbed: he had murdered and robbed his master, and Bradford had appeared just as he fled. There is little contemporary material to allow a balanced assessment of the case, but four inhabitants of an inn all set on robbery on the same night sounds more like art than life.

Kirby's Wonderful Magazine, a hodgepodge miscellany which reprinted the story in 1804, felt it needed an injection of realism, so it made the two guests enter the room because they heard a noise, not because they too were planning robbery. Several newspapers picked up the story, although with no great sense of urgency – the *Ipswich Journal* ran it two years later, mixed in with paragraphs on the slave trade and on the reported death of the explorer Mungo Park, and a report that a pointer had had a litter of seventeen pups.

The novelist Amelia Opie used the basic scenario for a short story in 1818. In 'Henry Woodville', Woodville is a clerk to a prosperous merchant. At an inn he and David Bradford, an ex-colleague who had been sacked for dissipation, quarrel. That night the inn's waiter robs and murders Bradford, knowing that Woodville will be suspected because of the quarrel. Woodville is found guilty, but as he is about to be executed the waiter, now repentant and dying, appears at the foot of the scaffold to assure the crowd, 'I – I murdered Bradford! – I am the real murderer!' before collapsing. There were no detective, suspense or procedural motifs in this version – none of the elements that, half a century later, would be the main purpose of any similar tale.

It was perhaps the still undeveloped nature of detective fiction that made Bradford of more interest to theatre. There was a token nod in 1811 in *Killing No Murder*, by Thomas Hook. One of the characters is named Bradford, the play is set in an inn, and another character is told to report his own pretended death. Otherwise it is a standard farce, with everyone in love with someone else, all at the same time pretending to be their own cousins or uncles or valets. In 1826 Drury Lane's *The Murder'd Guest* had a very Jonathan Bradford-like set-up, with an Oxfordshire inn, a guest who arrives with his servant and is put in a room next to two strangers, and a murderer who is pre-empted. This was followed in 1830 by *The Murderers of the Round*

Tower Inn, a 'Nautical Drama' at the Royal West London Theatre. It too had a Bradford-like innkeeper, whose stepdaughter innocently wonders, 'What can be the reason of his always sending me to bed so early, whenever Travellers sleep in the house?' 'Dreadful groans and noises in the night', combined with the travellers' complete absence in the morning, fail to enlighten her.

It was in 1833 that the story of Jonathan Bradford finally found fame, when David Osbaldiston, the manager of the Surrey Theatre, turned to Edward Fitzball for a new work. Many years later, Fitzball claimed that a theatre manager had once advised him: 'Look into the papers' for a subject; the daily crime-sheets had 'incident enough *invented* there'. This was standard procedure for many dramatists. For most of the century, playwrights barely scratched out a living, while churning out vast quantities of work. For authors, drama did not pay. A century earlier, Dr Johnson had received nearly £300 for the performing and publishing rights for a play that ran nine nights. By 1829 Douglas Jerrold was paid £5 a week as house author at the Surrey, and was expected to write at least one play a month; George Dibdin Pitt, the man who brought Sweeney Todd and his murderous barber-chair to the stage in 1841, produced twenty-six plays in 1847 alone. Dickens claimed that W.T. Moncrieff had written seven melodramas for £5 each.*

In terms of content, the result, *Jonathan Bradford, or, The Murder at the Roadside Inn*, was not much different from earlier evil-innkeeper melodramas. Fitzball definitely knew Mrs Opie's story,

---

* Dickens had a history with Moncrieff and stage adaptations, however. In 1837 Moncrieff had written an adaptation of *The Pickwick Papers* before the serialization had reached its conclusion. Dickens took his revenge in *Nicholas Nickleby*, with a depiction of a 'literary gentleman' who had 'dramatized ... two hundred and forty-seven novels as fast as they had come out – some of them faster than they had come out'. Given this type of speedy hackwork, it is not surprising that many authors stuck to newspapers. C.H. Hazlewood, the house author at the Britannia, regularly filleted the newspapers, magazines and penny-dreadfuls, précising the stories and filing 'sundry axioms, aphorisms, and moral sentiments' alphabetically under headings such as 'Ambition' or 'Kindness of Heart'. When he began a new melodrama, he merely took one of his précis and filled it in with relevant quotations. Fitzball, receiving his commission from the Surrey, similarly went back to an old story.

because two years earlier he had adapted another story from the same collection. He also used some standard elements from stage and penny-bloods: there was an underground crypt borrowed from gothic romance, a devil-may-care Irish highwayman and a comic Cockney apprentice. The key to the play's extraordinary success was the completely novel staging devised by Fitzball. He set the four rooms of the inn all onstage at once, in cross-section, and wrote the murder scene so that the action took place simultaneously across them. Or, as one advertisement had it, 'In this peculiar scene an effort will be made (never yet attempted on any stage) so to harmonize four actions as to produce *one striking effect.*' Fitzball later remembered how the mutinous actors petitioned Osbaldiston 'to insist on my leaving out this perplexing, unexampled, undramatic, unactable four-roomed scene'. Osbaldiston too was unenthusiastic, but finally agreed to let Fitzball make the attempt. On the opening night, 'the audience looked at each other exactly in the same fashion as the actors had done'. But then, 'as if convinced, on reflection, that there was something original to applaud ... they took the lenient side, and applauded unanimously'.*

The play was a smash. Its hundredth performance, or 'centenary', got a notice in *The Times*.† Ultimately the play closed in December, after a run of 161 consecutive performances (excluding Sundays). It was the first play ever to achieve this, and the record that was held for over two decades. Smaller populations had produced a repertory-based system reliant on the repeated attendance of the same people, rather than the infrequent attendance of different ones. In the 1840s, only four plays ran in London for more than a hundred nights and

---

* So popular was this novelty that it was quickly turned to satire. Only two weeks later, *Figaro in London* announced that Sadler's Wells was planning a play 'in which there is to be a scene showing twenty rooms at once, with a different tragedy acting in ten of them, operas in five, and the remaining five representing as many perfect comedies'.

† Another way of measuring the play's success was the appearance of racehorses named after the murderer. The Earl of Burlington ran a gelding named Jonathan Bradford at the 1834 Derby, and on the second day of the meeting a Mr Breary was listed as the owner of another horse with the same name.

they were not consecutive. Short runs in 1833 did not necessarily signify failure, only the small theatregoing population. *Jonathan Bradford* was staged in Dublin in November and, at least according to the advertisements, was received with 'rapturous and unbounded applause', but it only appears to have had three performances. The play was revived over and over again – advertisements for different versions continued to appear as late as the 1880s.

Within months of the London opening, there were productions across the country – Edinburgh, Oxford, Liverpool, Ipswich, Dublin and Belfast newspapers all carried advertisements, although only the *Hampshire Telegraph* mentioned the novel staging, the original selling point. Instead, many theatres interpolated local speciality acts. In Portsmouth, audiences were promised 'a Parody on the popular Song of "The Sea, the Sea, the open Sea"', as well as the appearance of Miss Parker to sing 'A Kind Old Man Came Wooing'.

By 1839, the novelty staging was used in other plays. A production of *Jack Sheppard* at Sadler's Wells had a similar compartment set to show Sheppard's escape from Newgate: 'Four Cells, two above and two below … doors, leading from one cell to the other – a fire-place at the back'. As the audience watches, Sheppard frees himself from his fetters, scrapes away at the brickwork until he can wrench out the bar blocking the chimney flue, which he then climbs into and vanishes from sight. In a moment, a hole opens in the cell above, and Sheppard appears once more. He then breaks down the cell door and vanishes through it, to reappear above, on the flat roof of the prison. This was very obviously of enormous drama, for at that moment, instead of escaping, Sheppard says, 'Ah! my blanket! I had forgotten it,' and makes the entire trip in reverse: through the two cells, down the hole in the chimney and back into the condemned cell. He collects his blanket, and the audience watches as he makes the trip a third time. On the roof he then tears up the blanket and is finally seen through the cell window abseiling down the side of the gaol.

Given Fitzball's triumphant success, it is a surprise to see almost no subsequent fiction based on Bradford's story. The only adaptations of any repute are three versions all by Sheridan Le Fanu, the Irish novelist and ghost-story writer.* He approached it first in 1848, in 'Some Account of the Latter Days of the Hon. Richard Marston', then again three years later in *The Evil Guest*. A third version, *A Lost Name*, appeared in 1868. All were variants on the same story: a man of bad character is found dead at a friend's house. A faithful servant is suspected (and in one of these versions confesses), but it was the friend who killed him, after which the servant came into the room to find him dead, as in *Bradford*. When a memory of the penny-blood version cropped up in Dickens' 'The Holly Tree Inn' (1855), it was as 'a sixpenny book with a folding plate, representing in a central compartment of oval form the portrait of Jonathan Bradford, and in four corner compartments four incidents of the tragedy'. What had lingered in Dickens' memory was the staging.

Instead, it was the penny publications that picked up the story, following the stage version closely, rather than inventing facts or characters to beef up the eighteenth-century story on their own. The real crime had by now been almost entirely forgotten. In the 1850s, in publishers' lists of penny-bloods, *Jonathan Bradford* appeared together with fictional titles like *The Poisoner, or, The Perils of Matrimony. Jonathan Bradford, or, The Murder at the Road-side Inn. A Romance of Thrilling Interest* was published in eighteen parts, attributed to 'the author of "The Hebrew Maiden", "The Wife's Secret", &c. &c.', who is thought to be Thomas Peckett Prest, a prolific penny-writer who had had a hand in the original version of *Sweeney Todd*. This was very much a story aimed at the working classes, in that throughout it is the petty bourgeoisie who thwart the good honest working people. An unpleasant, officious lawyer casts suspicion on all the good characters, while Dan Macraisy, the highwayman, although condemned in somewhat perfunctory fashion for being a murderer, offers the justification that 'perhaps if this Mr. Hayes had not gone about with so much gold in his pocket, he might

---

* There is also a story by Mrs Gaskell, 'A Dark Night's Work', begun in late 1858, which begins as though Mrs Gaskell might have read of Jonathan Bradford. It is said, however, that she based her story on a Knutsford case of a lawyer who vanished.

have been alive at this moment'. It was the victim's fault for being rich while others were poor.

And finally, *Jonathan Bradford* cropped up regularly in police reports when penny-gaffs were raided, or booth-theatre proprietors were prosecuted for performing without a licence. *Household Words* also published a reminiscence of childhood ½d. peepshows, describing a showman who carried a box on his back. 'The interior was lighted up with a candle in the middle of the day, and the different highly-coloured tableaux were let down with a heavy flop by strings at the side ... wonderful atmospheric effects were introduced at the back, by lifting a lid, and the whole was made more interesting by a running description ... by the proprietor.' The shows that were mentioned by title were *Mazeppa* (Astley's most popular hippo-drama) and *Jonathan Bradford*.

The most lasting, and most important, contribution of the Jonathan Bradford story was to extend our ways of seeing. In 1852, the playwright Dion Boucicault adapted a French play as *The Corsican Brothers*. Originally it had been a very ordinary melodrama of a murdered man and his brother's revenge. Two elements, both descendants of Fitzball's *Jonathan Bradford*, lifted the piece out of basic genre and made audiences see anew. Acts I and II of the play were to be understood to occur simultaneously, seen from the perspective of each brother; furthermore, at the end of Act I, the actions that would take place at the climax of Act II were, with the aid of new stage technology, played out at the back of the stage as a ghostly pre-vision.

In 1858 the idea of simultaneity of view was taken further by the painter Augustus Egg. His *Past and Present* triptych is a morality tale, set, like a theatrical melodrama, in a middle-class home. And, like *Jonathan Bradford*, it shows in its tripartite structure actions that take place in different – and simultaneous – times. The centre panel shows the moment a wife's adulterous liaison has been discovered by her husband. Egg's depiction could be a tableau from any melodrama, with the husband holding the telltale letter, the woman in a swoon at his feet. (Over his shoulder is a painting of a shipwreck by Clarkson

Stanfield, a noted set designer, tying the story even more tightly to the theatre.) It is the outer wings of the triptych, however, that make the work so innovative. Both are set some time after the central scene. On the left, the adulterous woman, reduced to destitution, sits under the arches by the river, contemplating suicide as she gazes at the moon. On the right, her two soon-to-be-motherless children are alone in their attic room, also staring at the moon, which is covered with the identical cloud formation that the mother is staring at, indicating that the two panels are depicting the identical moment in time. As both the children and their mother face inwards, to the central panel, Egg also conveys that they are, simultaneously, all thinking of that day when their world collapsed.

By 1871, *The Book of Remarkable Trials* gave only one page to Bradford (Jack Sheppard had twenty, Eugene Aram seventeen), and the author excused the scanty coverage: 'The details of this case reach us in a very abridged form; and we have been unable to collect any information on which any reliance can be placed.' The next murderer, John Scanlan, was even more completely subsumed into his dramatic *doppelgänger*.

Dion Boucicault had had a huge success with *The Corsican Brothers* in 1852, that play of double identities and duels, revenge and apparitions, with a famous double role for the actor-manager Charles Kean. But the two men quarrelled, and Boucicault and his actress wife went to New York, where in 1860 he wrote and they both starred in *The Colleen Bawn*. In triumph, they returned to London, to produce an amazing ten-month run of the play at the Adelphi Theatre.

The Colleen Bawn tells the story of Hardress Cregan, a young Irish squire who is smitten by the beautiful but poor Eily O'Connor, the 'Colleen Bawn', or fair maid (played by Agnes Robertson, Mrs Boucicault). In the face of her purity and goodness, Cregan is unable to seduce her, and agrees to marry her. His mother, meanwhile, is being wooed by the evil Squire Corrigan. When she repudiates him ('Contemptible hound, I loathe and despise you!'), he threatens to foreclose on her mortgage. She sees a way out of her money troubles by marrying Hardress to Anne Chute, the daughter of the local land-owner; Anne, however, loves Cregan's college friend Kyrle Daly. Hardress is now regretting his marriage: Eily speaks in dialect, is poor, and has 'low' friends, including Myles-na-Coppaleen (played by Boucicault), once a horse dealer, but now, brought down by unrequited love for the Colleen Bawn, a smuggler and poacher. The crippled Danny Mann, Hardress' loyal servant, tells him: 'do by Eily as wid the glove there on yer hand … if it fits too tight, take the knife to it … Only gi' me the word, an' I'll engage that the Colleen Bawn will never throuble ye any more.' Hardress is shocked, but Mrs Cregan overhears and tells Danny that Hardress has agreed to Eily's death. Danny takes Eily out in his boat at night, and tries to get the marriage licence from her, but she refuses. 'Then you've lived too long. Take your marriage lines wid ye to the bottom of the lake.' He tosses her overboard and rows off. Myles, who is out checking on his illegal still, shoots wildly at Danny, before dramatically leaping from the cliff to rescue Eily. In the last act, Danny thinks Eily is dead, and confesses all to Father Tom. Meanwhile, Hardress has agreed to marry Anne, but on their wedding day Corrigan, who overheard Danny's confession, arrives to arrest him for murder. In the nick of time, Myles appears with Eily. Mrs Cregan asks forgiveness, and Hardress, transformed by this trauma, swears eternal love for the Colleen Bawn. Anne and Kyrle Daly find each other, Corrigan is thrown in the horsepond, Myles is acclaimed a hero and everyone is happy in time for the final curtain.

It is hard to know quite what made *The Colleen Bawn* such a smash. Partly, it was its Irishry, which made the characters foreign but not too foreign; *The Times* noted with approval that the rogue Myles-na-Coppaleen was a 'plebeian Irishman of scampish propensities, who alternates native shrewdness and pathos after a fashion familiar'. Partly it was the balance of melodrama and comedy. And mostly, as with *Jonathan Bradford*, it was the sensational staging. The attempted drowning of Eily, with Myles' dramatic leap, routinely stopped the show. It is not entirely clear how this was done: the lake was blue gauze, manipulated by twenty boys standing in the wings, through which the drowning Eily dropped into an open trapdoor. Boucicault's leap from the cliff, routinely described as a 'header', was probably carefully aimed between the gauzes at an open trap lined with a mattress or padding, onto which he would somersault. However it was done, it was thrilling enough that the Boucicaults had to stop and take a bow each night before proceeding.*

Only infrequently had theatres been sites of subsidiary commercial activities: at performances of *Jack Sheppard* handcuffs for children, and bags holding 'a few pick-locks … a screw driver, and iron lever' were offered for sale; *The Woman in White*, the staging of Wilkie Collins' 1859–60 novel, had produced Woman in White bonnets and Woman in White perfume. But it was *The Colleen Bawn* that developed the commercial merchandising opportunity. Sheet music had been sold in conjunction with popular shows before, but this was something else again. In 1861 alone Mr William Forde's popular Irish airs were dedicated to Mrs Boucicault and illustrated with 'a well-designed sketch of the most striking episode in the drama'; there were at least another dozen similar pieces, including a 'Morceau de salon sur des mélodies Irlandaises'. Later there was the Colleen Bawn Polka, the Eily O'Connor Polka, Your Colleen Bawn, the Colleen Bawn Overture and the Colleen Bawn Quick-Step.

That was only the beginning. 'Colleen cabs' stood outside the theatre on the Strand, waiting to collect playgoers. Fashion adored the Colleen Bawn: by the spring of 1861 the women's papers were filled with advertisements for 'THE COLLEEN BAWN, the Mantle of the Season, price 3s. 6d.'; the 'Colleen Bawn cloak', which is 'simple, but very pretty'; even the 'Colleen Bawn manteau', 'trimmed at the bottom by five rows of narrow black velvet; the hood is ornamented by two agrafes [clasps] in silk passementerie, also black' – not precisely what a poor Irish girl might be expected to wear. Closer to reality was the adoption by the fashionable of the Irish countrywoman's red cloak, made from better-quality fabric and renamed the Colleen Bawn. The

* In 1896, Bernard Shaw saw a production at the Princess's Theatre in which real water was used, which he felt destroyed the illusion, although 'the spectacle of the two performers taking a call before the curtain, sopping wet, and bowing with miserable enjoyment of the applause', was something 'I shall remember … while life remains'.

Colleen Bawn also permeated the leisure world. Mr Sydney Hodges exhibited his pair of paintings, the *Colleen Bawn* and the *Colleen Ruadh* (the red-headed girl). A greyhound at the Worcester Club Croome Meeting in 1861 was named the Colleen Bawn, as was a four-oared boat that raced at the Victoria Rowing Club. There was also a racehorse, but this was a three-year-old in 1861, which meant either that its name had been changed, or that it had been named for an earlier Colleen Bawn – which was not as odd as it may sound today.

For Dion Boucicault did not dream up the Colleen Bawn. The origins of Eily O'Connor are to be found in 1819, when the real Eily was drowned, with no Myles-na-Coppaleen to perform a header to save her. Eily was in reality Ellen Hanley, aged fifteen, the orphaned niece of a shoemaker (in some accounts, a rope-maker). She had somehow met John Scanlan, a retired lieutenant of the marines, and substantially above her in social status: the Scanlans probably belonged to Munster's Catholic semi-gentry. On 29 June 1819, the couple eloped – in some accounts, they were married, in others, married by an excommunicated priest, which Scanlan (wrongly) believed would not be binding. Or Scanlan may simply have seduced Ellen, and she may have called herself 'Mrs Scanlan' in hope rather than fact. In any case, she stole her uncle's savings and ran off. A few days later, Ellen Walsh, a local woman, took passage in a boat crossing the Shannon near Kilrush, with Scanlan, his boatman/servant Steven Sullivan and a woman who called herself Mrs Scanlan. They all stayed overnight at Mrs Walsh's, where Mrs Scanlan showed off her fine new clothes. The next day Ellen Walsh saw Sullivan pull a ring off Mrs Scanlan's finger, and the day after she noticed the trunk in which Mrs Scanlan's new clothes had been packed sitting in Sullivan's lodgings. Scanlan told her that Mrs Scanlan had run away with a ship's captain, and she later overheard the two men arguing, with Sullivan saying, 'Mr. John, I have as good a right to the money as you have.'

On 6 September, a body washed up on shore; it had been in the water for weeks, and was badly decomposed, with no hair or flesh on the skull, and with a broken arm and leg. Ellen Walsh, before she saw the body, described the missing Ellen Hanley, her clothes, and the fact that she had a curious pair of double eye teeth. She was shown the stays that had been found on the body (the remainder of the clothes had probably been lost during its prolonged immersion), and thought they resembled Ellen Hanley's, but could not say more. All the teeth in the head had been knocked out, whether before or after death was not known, but on examination it was found that there were double sockets where the eye teeth would have been. Another woman came forward with clothes that matched Ellen Walsh's description, which she had purchased from Sullivan. Sullivan ran away before an arrest could be made, and Scanlan was charged with murder.

Scanlan's family had some influence and money, and he was represented by Daniel O'Connell, who would one day be 'the Liberator' of the Irish, but who was in 1819 one of the county's most successful barristers. There are barely any newspaper reports of the trial itself, and later the *Pall Mall Gazette* claimed that family influence had hushed up the scandal. The *Belfast News-Letter* in its report omitted Scanlan's name altogether, and most of the papers covered the case only when Sullivan was caught and tried, in July 1820. It is therefore difficult to put together an account of the trial, but even with a barrister of O'Connell's abilities, there was not much defence to be made. The circumstantial evidence was unanswerable: the two men were the last people to be seen with Ellen Hanley, Scanlan was identified as the purchaser of the rope that was found tied to the body, Sullivan's sister still had some of her clothes, and his landlady had others, received from Sullivan in lieu of rent. A local minister said that within a few days of the elopement, Scanlan was already obviously bored with his young 'wife'. Scanlan blamed the missing Sullivan, saying he himself had had nothing to do with Ellen Hanley's disappearance and death, that Sullivan had taken her out in a boat and returned without her. But he wasn't believed. He was quickly found guilty, and even his own lawyer was untroubled by the verdict: 'It is very unusual with me to be so satisfied,' O'Connell wrote his wife, 'but he is a horrid villain.'

Some months later, Sullivan was picked up for passing forged banknotes. In prison he was recognized as Scanlan's servant, and he was brought to Limerick for trial. Unlike Scanlan, he had no legal representation. When he was asked if he had counsel, he replied: 'I have no money to fee counsel or attorney, my Lord, and have nobody to look to but you and the great God to give fair play for my life.' The prosecution simply proceeded, calling its first witness, not an unusual situation for a working-class defendant. Sullivan's 'defence' consisted of him asking one witness two questions of no seeming relevance at all, and after fifteen minutes he was found guilty. Before his execution he confessed, saying that Scanlan had wanted to get rid of Miss Hanley because 'she always called him her husband', and he had asked Sullivan to take care of it. Sullivan claimed that it was 'some days' before he agreed – as though that made it better – and then he 'bought a boat for the express purpose of destroying her, and got an iron chain and ring made by a smith in Kilrush, to tie around her neck ... Scanlan settled the rope, and spliced a loop to it, which he put round a large stone, in order that I should lose no time, and left everything ready for me.' On the water, Sullivan hit Ellen with his musket, missing her head and breaking her arm, 'then beat her with the gun till she was quite dead ... tied her right leg to her neck, to which a large stone was attached', and threw her overboard.

So, no pretty, scenically-painted death in a red cape. Just two brutal men who used and threw away a child because they thought she didn't matter. Romanticization quickly set in, however. First was M.J. Whitty in 1824. His *Tales of Irish Life* included a story based fairly accurately on Ellen Hanley's life. Sally is the daughter of a humble but hard-working peasant. She is, of course, wonderfully beautiful, intelligent and 'docile'. She works hard, gives her father her earnings, and his 'approving kiss was the best reward of duty'. One day a stranger stops to ask for a drink of water, and tips her; she takes her first step on the downward slope by not handing the cash over to her father, but spending it on fashionable fripperies. She runs off with the stranger, and he marries her, choosing a 'rejected' priest whom he thinks will accidentally-on-purpose forget to register the marriage; but unfortunately he has not chosen well, and the marriage is valid. Within weeks he tires of her, takes her boating with his servant, and that is the end of her. Sally's father and abandoned fiancé are on his trail, however, and see the murder take place, although they are too far away to prevent it. The husband is arrested and found to be 'allied to some families of the highest respectability in Ireland, whose interest with the executive was so powerful, that the judge who tried him, acting in a manner which would have immortalized a Roman, ordered his immediate execution lest a reprieve might be obtained'. (Summary execution as a civic good?)

Gerald Griffin, a struggling journalist, may have read this story, but it was Griffin's novel *The Collegians* that marked the real beginning of the legend. Now Ellen Hanley becomes Eily O'Connor, while Myles Murphy, a farmer who sells Kerry ponies, is nicknamed Myles-na-Coppaleen, Miles of the Ponies. Here is Hardress Cregan, who has run through his inheritance and is sponging off his friends; Danny Mann appears too, although here he has a sister, 'Fighting Poll of the Reeks', 'a fearless, whisky-drinking virago, over six feet in her stocking vamps', whom Boucicault wisely decided would be too much for delicate West End sensibilities. Anne Chute and Kyrle Daly appear for the first time, and Daly is equipped with a comic servant named Lowry Looby. Mrs Cregan pushes her son to marry Anne: 'If you wed as I desire, you shall have all the happiness that rank, and wealth, and honour, and domestic affection, can secure you. If against my wish … whether I live or die … you shall never possess a guinea of your inheritance.' Hardress omits to tell his mother that he is already married. But as weeks go past (not the mere days that it took the real Scanlan), he tires of Eily, and Danny has a number of suggestions: sending her back to her father, shipping her off to Quebec, or killing her. Hardress spurns them all, then gives a series of contradictory orders, until it appears he barely knows what he wants. Danny however understands, and takes Eily out on the water, returning alone. Hardress confesses to his mother, and when the body is found, and Danny flees, she plans to buy her son's way out of trouble. Danny refuses to betray his master until, thinking Hardress has double-crossed him, he confesses all. Hardress is arrested, but is not considered entirely culpable – did he or did he not tell Danny to kill her? He is transported, Danny is hanged, and Mrs Cregan lives on to do 'austere and humiliating works of piety, which her church prescribes for the observance of the penitent'.

The novel was hugely successful – Griffin was said to have made £800 from it – perhaps because he set the story in the eighteenth century, a distancing effect that made the details appear less brutal. He also prettied things up: Eily doesn't steal from her guardian, and she definitely marries. She and her family are classed-up, too: her uncle is no longer a rope-maker, but the parish priest, 'educated at the university of Salamanca'; she speaks in standard English, not dialect, and is as 'superior in knowledge as she was in beauty' – no double teeth for Eily – as well as being a regular churchgoer.

With these adjustments, the theatre took Eily to its heart. By 1832 two Eily O'Connor plays had appeared in London: one by J.T. Haines at the City of London Theatre in Bishopsgate, *Eily O'Connor, or, The Foster Brother*; another by Thomas Egerton Wilks, *Eily O'Connor, or, The Banks of Killarney!* at the Coburg, complete with the characters as they appeared in Griffin. (Wilks in places barely troubled to alter Griffin's punctuation, much less his words.) Despite – or because of – its similarity to *The Collegians* (and despite lines like, 'Yonder comes Mr. Hector Creagh, the polished duellist'), this play was the one to survive until Boucicault came and blew everyone else off stage (Queen Victoria loved it so much she went three times in a fortnight).

There was recognition that Boucicault's play was based on *The Collegians*, but much less that it was based on fact (the *Manchester Times* commented in 1860 that it was 'a melodrama ... founded on facts', but that was a rarity). Boucicault started legal proceedings against the Britannia, claiming that C.H. Hazlewood's *Eily O'Connor* was a lightly rewritten version of his play. The Britannia did not try to defend itself with reference either to *The Collegians*, or even to reality; instead it offered Boucicault a fee to allow them to continue the run, which he accepted. But he couldn't sue everyone, and there was a positive lakeful of imitations: an anonymous *The Colleen Bawn: or, The Collegian's Wife*; *Cushla Ma Chree* (also anonymous); and even a French adaptation, *Le Lac du Glenaston* (in which some of the characters head for the California goldfields).

Parody versions of theatrical successes were a commonplace, but Eily O'Connor attracted more than her fair share. Within two years of *The Colleen Bawn* opening, there were at least three successful mainstream satirical takes: *The very latest Edition of The Cooleen Drawn, from a novel source, or, The Great Sensation Diving Belle*, an anonymous parody at the Surrey; Henry J. Byron's *Miss Eily O'Connor. A New and Original Burlesque*, at Drury Lane; and Andrew Halliday Duff's *The Colleen Bawn Settled at Last. A Farcical Extravaganza*, at the Lyceum. They all have renamed characters: Hardress is 'Hard-up', or 'Heartless', Kyrle Daly is naturally enough Curl Daily. The Surrey version was in verse, and filled with contemporary local jokes: 'Callagain', the Squire Corrigan figure, is a policeman, complete with puns:

> My name's not Robert tho' I Bobby am
> So about Bob I pray no Bobbery, Ma'am
> Tho' in the Mayne force not the Royal Blues,
> I'll use no force, but what I'm forced to use ...

Eily and Danny appear in a washing tub, and she turns up alive for the finale, to join in the dancing and the singing. The West End versions were not much more sophisticated. In Byron's version, when Danny tries to drown Eily, she pops back up repeatedly – 'Here we are again!' – before catching cold from her ducking. *The Colleen Bawn Settled at Last* was more of a West End play, its humour based on the exquisitely comic notion of an Irish peasant girl married into the gentry, and the hilarious mistakes she makes across the class divide. Lord Dundreary, a character from Tom Taylor's 1858 play *Our American Cousin*,* wanders in, and Eily turns out to be his long-lost daughter and therefore a well-born heiress, something that happens frequently in melodrama, if not in life.

There were also 'narrative entertainments' of *The Colleen Bawn*, for those who wouldn't go to the theatre. Mr and Mrs German Reed,

---

* *Our American Cousin*'s main claim to fame today is that it was the play Abraham Lincoln was watching when he was assassinated.

specialists in the genre, advertised a musical version. Upmarket, Julius Benedict wrote an opera version, *The Lily of Killarney*, in 1862. Downmarket, a penny version of the play appeared, for those who couldn't afford the gallery seats, or who wanted a more permanent souvenir; this included Lowry Lobby [sic] and Michil [sic] O'Connor, misspelled characters from *The Collegians* who had failed to make the transfer to the stage, which is an indication of the source. The frontispiece is suitably dramatic, with Danny poised to wallop Eily, who sits with ferociously glowering eyebrows in a small boat. The play was popular at fairgrounds too: there is evidence of a marionette version being performed in Sunderland in the early 1860s; in the 1870s the D'Arc marionettes had a 'Cave [i.e. lake] Scene [that] is a work of art', according to the *Era*. In the 1880s, Bryant's marionettes were performing the rescue scene at the Britannia.

Ellen Hanley may have had a grim life and a worse death, but as Eily she lived on and saw the century out. By that time she had long left the world of murder and crime behind her. Others could not, and would be remembered only for how they changed crime – and crime policing – for ever.

FOUR

Policing Murder

One man, perhaps, can be credited with the creation of Scotland Yard, although he did not live to see it, and would not have enjoyed it if he had. That man was Daniel Good, and he was not a policeman or a politician, but a murderer; not the hunter, but the hunted.

Until 1842, the police saw themselves primarily as performing the function Parliament had established them for: prevention of crime. It was hoped by Peel and his supporters that this emphasis would encourage an initially reluctant populace to view the new police as protectors of the weak and the oppressed, instead of a tool of the powerful. Up to a point, this had happened. Even with the Cold Bath Field riot a vivid memory, police crowd-control was quickly discovered to be much more satisfactory than calling out the army – truncheons got the same results, with far less damage, than mounted dragoons with sabres. One of the earliest attempts at crowd-control by the new police was in 1830, three years before Cold Bath Field, when a week of rioting followed the Duke of Wellington's rejection of parliamentary reform. Seven thousand troops were held at the ready, but were never deployed; instead, 2,000 London policemen marched. The mobs targeted them, shouting 'Down with the New Police ... Down with the Raw Lobsters!' Handbills were distributed: 'These damned Police are now to be armed. Englishmen, will you put up with this?' Yet there were no deaths, nor even any broken bones. 'A week's rioting in a city with a population nearing 2 million had for the first time in English history been suppressed ... by a ... civil force armed only with pieces of wood,' wrote one modern historian.

There were, however, limitations to this preventative role, and the eruption of Daniel Good into the national consciousness highlighted the one-sided nature of Peel's force. The police were paid to prevent violent crime. What happened afterwards, if prevention failed?

Daniel Good was a coachman employed by a Mr Quelaz Shiell in the hamlet of Roehampton, south-west of London. He had been keeping company with Jane Jones, a laundress who lived in Manchester Square, who was known as 'Mrs' Jones, even though there was no Mr Jones and her eleven-year-old son called Daniel Good 'Father'. But in 1842 Good met Susan Butcher, and Mrs Jones had come to hear of it. To soothe her, Good invited her out to Roehampton, while the boy was sent overnight to a friend. The next day, Monday, 6 April 1842, Good visited a pawnbroker in Wandsworth, where he bought a pair of black knee breeches. As he was leaving, however, the pawnbroker's assistant saw him take a second pair of trousers. The pawnbroker went to the police in the Wandsworth, or V, Division to report the matter.

A constable was assigned this case of trouser-theft and two days later, accompanied by two stable boys (Good had a reputation for violence), he went out to talk to Good. He found him in the stables, and in an emollient frame of mind, immediately offering to return to the pawnshop with the constable to pay for the goods. The constable said that was not in his orders; he was there to search for the stolen trousers. He began in the harness room, where, moving a truss of hay, he saw what he thought was a dead goose. At that moment he heard the stable door slam, turned around and found that Good had fled, locking him and his companions inside. The constable now realized that the goose was actually a woman's torso, without legs, arms or head, 'the belly … cut open, and the bowels taken out'. He and the stable boys broke down the door, but once free, instead of pursuing Good, who at that point had been gone less than a quarter of an hour, the constable resumed his search of the barn, finding a bloodstained mattress. Only then did he send off for reinforcements, waiting for them at the stable. When they arrived, they too showed little desire for the chase, and instead everyone returned to Wandsworth police station for further orders.

When, nearly two hours later, more senior police arrived, they too thought their first task was to search the stable. Evidence of a horrible crime was readily found: an axe, saw and knife covered with blood, together with a fire that showed signs of having recently burnt fiercely – 'there were pieces of wood, coal, and straw, a great quantity more than was necessary for any common fire' – while in the ashes underneath were pieces of bone. Only now was Mrs Jones's young son questioned, and the police heard that he had been sent away for a night. The gardener's son added that he had seen Mrs Jones that same day at Roehampton, wearing a blue bonnet.

In the late 1830s Commissioner Richard Mayne had instituted a city-wide system of 'route-papers' for the dissemination of police information. Every morning, the superintendent of each division had to write a complete summary of all unsolved crimes that had occurred in his district over the previous twenty-four hours, with full details, including whatever information was available concerning the suspects. A copy of every route-paper was sent daily to all divisions, so that each superintendent had a list of every unsolved crime throughout London, plus information about wanted men, suspects and so on, information which was in turn passed to the constables on the beat.

No route-paper was written on the missing Daniel Good for twenty-four hours. And when it was, there being no overall detective organization, each division that held a piece of the jigsaw started work on its own. Nine divisions followed different leads, with no coordination. Putney police discovered that Good had been seen quarrelling with a woman at the Spotted Horse tavern in Roehampton. Meanwhile in Marylebone, D Division learned that Good had spent the night at Mrs Jones's lodgings, but by the time they arrived at the house he was long gone, taking with him Mrs Jones's bed, trunk, a box and a hatbox. The cab driver who had driven him away was identified, and he said he had driven his passenger to Whitcombe Street, near Pall Mall. As this was not in D Division's area, Marylebone police took no further action. C Division covered Whitcombe Street, and they printed handbills describing Good, and posted placards throughout London and the suburbs detailing the crime and Good's appearance. Witnesses reported that Good had gone from Whitcombe Street to the Spotted Dog pub in the Strand, before moving on to Spitalfields, in H Division. C Division therefore lost sight of him. It was only on yet another search of the stables that a letter from Mrs Butcher, from an address in Woolwich, was found. V Division forwarded this information to R Division at Greenwich, who questioned Mrs Butcher at her lodgings. On the day the murder was discovered Good had visited her, leaving behind some clothes he said had belonged to his dead wife. The items included a blue silk bonnet and a reticule, both of which had been described by the Manchester Square residents as belonging to Mrs Jones. The bonnet, furthermore, looked very much like the one the gardener's son had seen Mrs Jones wearing. Good had also told Mrs Butcher about a mangle she might have, although she could not remember precisely where he had said it was. The police may not have been able to find Good, but here was confirmation that they were hunting the right man: the day before the discovery of the body, Good had been giving away Mrs Jones's possessions. He, at least, appeared to think she would no longer want them. The police offered a £100 reward for information, to which on 12 April, four days after the discovery, the Putney magistrates added another £50.

After the discovery of what was presumed to be Mrs Jones's body, the coroner for the district had initially requested that it be kept *in situ* at the stable, for identification purposes – the assumption was that Good would be rapidly captured, and that the inquest jury would visit the scene of the crime. Very shortly, however, her body was instead playing a part in the entertainment world, as it was displayed to the curious. *The Times* was eloquent on the subject. On 8 April it commended the viewings: 'very properly', the police were permitting entry only to 'the principal inhabitants of the neighbourhood'. Four days later, however, 'vehicles of every description, from the aristocratic carriage to the costermonger's cart' were permitted to enter, and with the arrival of these working-class spectators the display had now become a 'disgusting exhibition'.

By 15 April the newspapers, while still revelling in every detail of the crime, began to concentrate on the failure of the police to put their hands on the wanted man. *The Times* continued its now traditional path of convicting the accused long before the trial. Good's career, it asserted, had been one 'continued course of crime'. He had stolen 'coats, cloaks, muffs, boas, &c.', he had once killed a horse, and had been 'discharged from the service of a gentleman connected with the Deaf and Dumb Asylum for a felonious act'.* Then the paper moved its sights from the still-on-the-run villain, to take aim at the police. There was, it said, 'a feeling ... of unmitigated indignation, against the police authorities for not using such diligence as must have had ... the effect of placing a monster in custody'. Reports were pouring in from all over. A man at the Swan Tavern, London Bridge, had acted in a very suspicious manner by sighing when he asked about a steamer to Hull. Another report said Good was selling apples in Cornhill, disguised as a woman. He was also in Spitalfields. And in Gray Eagle Street. And Nottingham. And at Sheerness. He had been found drowned in the Thames. He had been in prison at Leeds, except that he had escaped. Luckily he was also in the County Gaol in Derby – and 'his appearance in every particular answers the description given of him in the posting-bills' – that is, he was precisely five feet six. By the sixteenth, *The Times* was foaming: 'the public had a right to expect better' of a police force 'maintained at so heavy a cost to the country'.

While the newspapers were united in their views of the obligations of the police, the course of action they should take was, to the police themselves, much less clear. The commissioners were at loggerheads. Charles Rowan, a former army officer, thought that their job was to wait until Good was picked up: the force's duty was prevention, not detection. The more expansionist Richard Mayne, sensing an

---

* *The Times* was not alone in its rush to judgement. The Green Row Rooms, in Portsmouth, advertised on 9 May that they had a waxwork model of 'the notorious Murderer Daniel Good'. At this stage Good had been arrested, but the magistrates' hearing at which it would be decided if there was a true bill against him was not for another two days; the trial itself not until 13 May.

opportunity, disagreed. Since the Bow Street Runners had been disbanded three years before, there had officially been no detective force in the capital. Unofficially, however, Mayne had been developing a proto-detective department. In 1840 he had signed an order allocating 'an active, intelligent man in each division' to trace stolen goods, nominally collecting information on past crimes in order to prevent the commission of future ones. Mayne also had another two men under his own supervision. All these men were, quietly, detectives. Now he recognized that the outcry over Good's escape was the perfect opportunity to come into the open. He took his two secret detectives, plus an Inspector Pearce, whom he seconded to headquarters for special duties, and charged them with the task of tracing Good.

Pearce picked up Good's trail at the Spotted Dog. Yet even now there was duplication: a local inspector from C Division traced the same route and located the cab driver who had taken Good to his next stop. Instead of reporting it, he went to Good's destination in Spitalfields on his own initiative. There he found a woman named Molly Good, who claimed that she was Good's wife, but that she had not seen him for years. Police initiative went only so far: he believed her, and dropped the lead. When Pearce also found Mrs Good, he was less credulous. Questioning the neighbours, he found that Good had been using Spitalfields as a safe haven, and that Mrs Good had even vouched for him to a local pawnbroker, where the inspector found more of Mrs Jones's possessions.

Mrs Good was arrested, and Pearce was now on the right track: from Tooley Street, in the Borough, he traced a suspect to Deptford, and then to Bromley, in Kent. In the end, though, he was pipped at the post. A railway worker in Tonbridge, who had formerly been a constable in V Division, thought that a bricklayer's labourer looked familiar, and his suspicions were strengthened by hearing the man speak in Irish. He notified the railway police, who took the man in for questioning. At his lodgings, bundled up with his clothes, was a copy of the issue of *Hue and Cry* that contained the original notice of the murder. Ten days after Jane Jones's body was found under the straw, Daniel Good had, finally, been captured.

The trial was something of a foregone conclusion. Witnesses placed Mrs Jones with Good at the stables the day before she vanished, wearing the bonnet later given to Mrs Butcher. The gardener's son, who slept over the harness room, had heard the crackling of a fire there as he came downstairs the morning after her disappearance; Mr Shiell's cook added that that morning Good had been covered in soot, like 'a sweep'. Medical evidence estimated a recent time of death – it was only possible to say it had taken place within days rather than weeks – and added that it looked as though Mrs Jones might have been pregnant. Much of the medical testimony was devoted to a discussion of whether the dismemberment had taken place before or after death, a matter of little consequence; almost no time was spent in discussing whether the bone fragments found in the fireplace were human, and if they were, whether they belonged to the torso that had been found.

Good had a lawyer, who pointed out that this was all circumstantial evidence. There was not even any evidence that Mrs Jones had been killed by violence, much less that the killing had been carried out by Good. He reminded the jury that Good had no reason to murder Mrs Jones: they weren't married, she had no claim on him, and if he had wanted to leave her, he could have just gone. The jury found him guilty nonetheless, and then Good made a statement. He said Jane Jones had killed herself in the harness room, and that when, horrified, he had found her dead body, an itinerant match-seller had happened by, who offered to dispose of the body. (It was probably sensible of the defence not to present this argument.)

The crime was discussed by all strata of society. A broadside, 'The Life, Trial and Execution of D. Good for the murder of Jane Jones', printed a series of unconfirmable rumours: that Good had spent his childhood torturing dogs; that he had been sentenced to the hulks for robbery;* that 'he has been known to twist a whipcord round a horse's tongue, and tear it out by the root'. The 'Apprehension of D. Good at Tonbridge for the Murder of Jane Jones' concentrated on snappy

* Hulks were ships that were no longer fit for active service, docked and used as floating prisons.

images: one, captioned, 'Stop, is not your name Good? why, you are the murderer of Jane Jones!' depicts two men in fashionable man-about-town outfits, even though Good had been dressed as a labourer when he was recognized, and his nemesis had been a railway worker. The *Illustrated London News*, founded shortly before Good's arrest, and aiming itself resolutely at the domestic middle-class market, nonetheless thought it essential to include a portrait engraving of Good, although it felt it necessary simultaneously to issue a rather shame-faced apology: 'It is not our intention to disfigure the pages of the "Illustrated News" with engravings, especially connected with crime and its consequences; we do not profess to be of the "raw head and bloody bones" school ... but he [Good] has only a few hours to live ...'

While Daniel Good was now safely arrested, tried and convicted, further crimes – a constable shot and killed in Highbury, north London, a second and third assassination attempt on Queen Victoria – kept the need for detection to the fore. Only two months after Good's arrest, Mayne approached the Home Office with a plan for the establishment of a new division to concentrate on detection. The example of Good had altered governmental perception, and on 14 June 1842, the 'Detective Department', consisting of two superintendents and six sergeants, opened for business. (Scotland Yard, just off Whitehall Place, was the address of the headquarters of the Metropolitan Police; after 1842 it also became a shorthand reference to the Detective Department, renamed the Criminal Investigation Department, or CID, in 1878.) Officially, police work was now about both the prevention of future crimes and the detection of past ones.

Despite the public outcry over police failures during the search for Good, many people remained conflicted over the role of the police. An earlier letter in *The Times* had suggested that there was a case to be made for some policemen not wearing a uniform, in order to go about their business more successfully; two years later this idea still seemed radical, even underhanded, to many: the newspaper fulminated against those policemen who, in tracking down a gang of counterfeiters, had 'assume[d] various disguises, – such as the dresses of cobblers, itinerant greengrocers, and costermongers', in a 'practice ... sanctioned and encouraged by the authorities'. This not only displayed 'consummate subtlety' (a negative, not a positive attribute), but also made the police 'themselves parties to [the] commission [of crime]'. By using plainclothes decoys, 'the two kings of Scotland-yard [Mayne and Rowan] have transgressed the law and violated the constitution'.

The law itself, however, was changing. Outside London the Municipal Corporations Act of 1835 had permitted all boroughs that had an elected council to appoint their own watch committee, staffed with 'sufficient' men to preserve the peace. But with no central funding, by 1837 only ninety-three of the eligible 178 boroughs had troubled to do so. Two further acts, the Police Act and the Rural Constabulary Act, both in 1839, had permitted magistrates to set up police forces in their counties. Again, by 1841, only twenty-four out of fifty-six had bothered. It was, in particular, Birmingham, Manchester and Bolton – industrial areas with vastly increased populations – that set up new forces. Now the first police commissioner of Birmingham, a solicitor named Francis Burgess, was appointed, and with 293 men, more than double the number of the old watch, he focused on prevention, particularly of crimes against property (always more widespread than crimes of violence), even more specifically counterfeiting, a Birmingham speciality because of the predominance of metal workers in the city. Mayne and Rowan established their Detective Department on 14 June; by August, Burgess too had a divisional superintendent and four plainclothes men.

Not that they were always appreciated. Burgess's men in 'coloured' clothes watching 'the well known thieves' at the local horse fair in 1841 might have been welcome, but to many of the city's population, the police were not simply preventing crimes, but enforcing new middle-class norms of behaviour on every class, a pattern emerging across the country. In 1843 the Manchester council charged the police with enforcing laws against dog-fighting and bear-baiting; they were also expected to prevent Sunday drinking. In Leeds, the council wanted the police to give evidence against all who 'prophane [sic] the Lord's day'. Changing expectations were turning what had been

merely unpleasant actions – or even merely working-class pastimes
– into criminal ones. Hawking without a licence, musical performances in unlicensed premises, being drunk and disorderly, perpetrating
low-level violence – all this was now not simply undesirable, but illegal.
In the slang of the time, the police were now 'blue drones', 'blue idlers',
'blue locusts' – they were parasites, living off the working classes.

This was well represented in flash songs – street songs linked to the
underworld of thieves and rogues:

> At Shoreditch, t'other night,
>> In a concert room we [the police] back'd in,
> And put 'em all to flight,
>> For singing songs, and acting.
> We collar'd all we chose,
>> And guv'd them such a drilling –
> Five bob we find [sic] the 'proes',
>> And the audience round a shilling …

* * *

Two murders in 1848–49, however, changed many people's perceptions: the first because the victims were prosperous, civic-minded
middle-class citizens, the second because the police, unlike in Good's
case, functioned as an efficient detective force.

In 1848, James Blomfield Rush, a tenant farmer in Norfolk, was in
financial difficulties. Rush had always been of wavering respectability.
He was born around 1800, the illegitimate son of a prosperous gentleman farmer and a mother who sued for breach of promise.* By 1836
he held the leases on two farms, Felmingham Farm and Stanfield Hall
Farm. His landlord, and the owner of the Stanfield Hall estate, was
Isaac Jermy, the Recorder of Norwich (a Recorder was a barrister who
served as a judge in some cities). Jermy had previously been known as
Isaac Preston, but on inheriting Stanfield Hall in 1838 he had changed

---

* Engagements were oral contracts; a broken engagement was a broken contract, and a
woman's loss of reputation could be financially quantified.

his name. There were, however, two other claimants to the estate: Thomas Jermy, a gardener, and his cousin, John Larner.

In his battles against these claimants, Isaac had used Rush as his right-hand man. Now, however, Jermy discovered something 'irregularly drawn up' in Rush's leases, and they were replaced with new ones, at higher rents. Rush's wife died in 1842 or 1843, leaving him with nine children. Then in 1844 his stepfather died. (Killed, so later report had it, by a gunshot wound when only he and Rush were present. It is hard to know how true this was, given the type of newspaper rumour that was then so common. The inquest found accidental death.) Most of Mr Rush senior's money was left to his widow, but Rush borrowed £1,500 from her soon after the death, and then another £200. Mrs Rush did not survive long, and in her will the money was left to Rush's children, with a codicil granting him the power to administer the property. He hired Emily Sandford as governess for the younger children, although before long he set her up in lodgings in Pentonville, in London, where he visited regularly in the guise of her 'uncle'.

Rush became further indebted to Jermy when he bought the lease of Potash Farm, borrowing money from Jermy against the mortgage, with an agreement that the loan would be repaid on 30 November 1848. By 1847, the rent on Stanfield Hall Farm was in arrears, despite the cash infusion from Rush's mother, and Jermy 'put in a distress' (a legal action to recover the rent). Rush was evicted and moved to Potash Farm. Jermy brought a further action, for bad cultivation of the farm, which he also won. In May 1848 Rush was declared bankrupt. Now he had become Isaac Jermy's implacable enemy, and was plotting with the aggrieved Stanfield Hall heirs, Larner and Thomas Jermy. He introduced them to Emily Sandford, whom he described as a 'lady of some means', saying she would offer financial backing to help them recover their property. They agreed that, in return for the help of Rush and Mrs Sandford, when they inherited they would reassign Rush's lease at a much-reduced rent. Five months after this meeting, Rush gave Mrs Sandford a memorandum of an agreement signed by Isaac Jermy, extending the lease of Potash Farm for twelve years; she signed it as a witness, despite not having been present when

Jermy had signed. A month later, Rush produced more memoranda signed by Isaac Jermy, one postponing by three years the repayment of the loan of the money for Potash Farm, another promising, on receipt of all the documentation Rush possessed concerning Stanfield Hall, to cancel the loan altogether, and renew the Felmingham Farm lease. Again, Mrs Sandford witnessed these documents despite never having met Jermy, nor seen the papers signed.

The situation for Rush in November 1848 was not promising: he was bankrupt; he had twice been successfully prosecuted by Jermy; the debt for the loan he had taken on Potash Farm was due imminently; he had documents from both sides of the inheritance dispute, both agreeing that if he helped them they would ensure his financial future; and he had documents of dubious legality signed by Isaac Jermy.

On 27 November, Rush's son, daughter-in-law and servants, all of whom normally lived at Potash Farm, were sent away, and only Rush and Mrs Sandford remained. That day, Rush instructed his servant to cover the entire path between Potash Farm and Stanfield Hall with straw. Mrs Sandford later claimed that Rush was agitated; before seven o'clock in the evening he went out for two hours. At Stanfield Hall, Jermy left his son and daughter-in-law drinking tea and playing cards, and went out onto the porch for his regular after-dinner cigar. A man 'with something black round his head' appeared, took out a gun and shot him dead. Jermy's son, the unfortunately named Isaac Jermy Jermy, rushed out on hearing the shots and was also killed. Mrs Jermy then appeared, followed by her maid, Eliza Chestney; the two women were shot at in turn, and then the gunman fled. A paper was found by the bodies: 'There are seven of us here, three of us outside, and four inside the hall, all armed … If any of your servants offer to leave the premises or to follow, you will be shot dead … we are … come to take of the Stanfield Hall property. – Thomas Jermy, the owner.' Despite this threat, the butler, unmolested, ran for help to the neighbours.

The two women, who were wounded but not dead, were carried upstairs, and by 2 a.m. the police had arrived from Norwich. No one was in much doubt as to the identity of the perpetrator: the next morning Rush and Mrs Sandford were taken for questioning. Initially Mrs Sandford said that Rush had been at home all evening. Then she said that that was what he had told her to say. Her position in this case is difficult to assess in retrospect. There is no question that at the trial she was a hostile witness against her former lover. But her father had been a solicitor's clerk, and it is worth considering whether she herself was the fabricator of the many documents that she had witnessed. The magistrate described her as untrustworthy, although this may merely have been because of her position as a woman living in sin.

The trial was, for its time, a drawn-out affair, lasting nearly a week. Most of the delay was caused by Rush representing himself; the judge permitted him a great deal of leeway in his questioning. With legal counsel, Rush might have been acquitted, for the evidence was not strong: two servants identified him as the murderer, but both had only had glimpses of the gunman; Mrs Sandford's enmity towards Rush might have been turned in his favour; the remaining witnesses – the stationer who identified the paper the threatening note was written on, locals who had seen Rush that day, witnesses to Jermy's handwriting – might all have had a harder time of it under a lawyer's questioning. As it was, Rush was by turns aggressive and foolish. His bullying questioning of Mrs Sandford made her an object of sympathy. He claimed that all the witnesses were dishonest, that 'nothing could exceed' one for 'lying', that another had 'grossly perjured himself', but he produced nothing to back any of this up. Instead he quibbled over witnesses' statements, highlighting tiny inconsistencies, as if this nullified their main purport: for example, he bickered with a policeman over whether it had been his left arm or his right that the man had held when he was arrested. He refused to hear one witness, claiming that he was prejudiced, but then called on another to contradict the statement the first one had not been permitted to make. The jury took five minutes to agree that he was guilty as charged: the only surprise was that they bothered to leave the room to make their decision.

People of all classes followed the story. One published transcript carried advertisements for other titles available from the publisher,

At the trial of James Blomfield Rush, the wounded servant Eliza Chestney was brought into court to testify in a litter enclosed in a tent (*centre rear*). Rush (*standing, centre right*) defended himself, and the hectoring, aggressive style of his questioning is caught in his posture (which contrasts with the debonair pose of the prosecution barrister, to the right of the litter).

including Eugène Sue's *The Mysteries of Paris*, a version of Dick Turpin, some pirate and shipwreck stories, a *Cricketer's Hand-Book*, *Wrestling and Pedestrianism, Modern Boxing*, ranging in price from 1*s.* to 2*s.*6*d.*: thus for a moderately prosperous audience. For those who wanted something a little more worthy, the local vicar, who had made prison visits to Rush, announced that 'If spared', he would 'give a little sketch of my interviews in the cell' in his next sermon. On Sunday, a large congregation waited for him. 'You are mistaken,' he said. 'I intend to speak of Rush in the afternoon.' 'We are come to secure seats for the afternoon,' was the response. Another vicar published a sermon on covetousness, and its effects on Rush, as a 2*d.* pamphlet. Dickens visited Potash Farm even before the trial, and reported back to his friend John Forster on the police search for the pistol (he thought they were not up to London standards). For those who couldn't make a tourist visit themselves, Staffordshire potteries produced the highlights, and people could collect the protagonists: not only Rush and Mrs Sandford (there may also have been a figurine of Eliza Chestney, the maid, although none seems to have survived), but also the venues – Potash Farm, Stanfield Hall and Norwich Castle. The city of Norwich took a certain pride in its home-grown villain: the local museum purchased a portrait 'medalet' of Rush, struck to commemorate the execution.

Nothing was too insignificant to report. The *Ipswich Journal* reprinted a note from the imprisoned Rush to the landlord of the local inn about his meals: 'any thing you like except beef … the tea

Punch magazine ran a vociferous campaign against Madame Tussaud's Chamber of Horrors: here it equated the perfectly respectable middle-class pastime of looking at murderers' likenesses with giving children murderer dolls to play with.

" SEE, DEAR, WHAT A SWEET DOLL MA-A HAS MADE FOR ME."

in a pint mug ... if you could get a small sucking pig ... send plenty of plum sauce with it'. After the trial began, the *Examiner* reminded its readers that the previous week it had reported 'nearly the whole' of the proceedings right up until press time, and now, 'In order that our country subscribers may have the narrative of the case perfect we repeat the same in this week's first edition' – over five entire pages.

Up to 13,000 people attended Rush's execution, with special excursion trains bringing eager viewers from Yarmouth and further afield. The newspapers frequently referred to the gallows as a theatre, and an execution as a theatrical spectacle. Rush seemed to provoke this metaphor more than most. 'The drop,' noted the *Examiner*, 'is literally the stage of crime for its last theatrical performance,' while the *Ipswich Journal* reported that the spectators were 'passing the interval [before Rush was brought out] very much in the same manner as the galleries of the great theatres do between the acts'. And in their view at least, Rush himself joined in. When he appeared, 'On catching sight of the scaffold he lifted his eyes to Heaven, raised ... his pinioned hands, and shook his head mournfully from side to side ... The pantomime was perfect, conveying ... a protest of innocence, combined with resignation.'

Executions as theatre were immediately turned back into genuine theatrical representations. Unusually, neither the main melodrama houses nor the legitimate theatres had much time for Rush's story: there was a mention in December 1849 of a theatre manager in Stockton-upon-Tees who was prosecuted for an unlicensed production of a play about the case, but that was one of the very few theatrical references to appear. But if Rush was not reproduced in the mainstream theatres, the fit-ups, the peepshows and the travelling showmen all loved him. These shows toured the country in caravans all summer, doing circuits around the local fairs and wakes, then came to London in October. 'People is werry fond of the battles in the country, but a murder wot is well known is worth more than all the fights. There was more took with Rush's murder than there has been even by the Battle of Waterloo itself,' said one showman.

Whether the source was fiction or true crime, the main element in melodrama was the black-and-white nature of the characters: good was good, evil was evil. Anything, almost, could be melodrama. Old Wild's booth theatre performed a 'melo-dramatisation' of *Macbeth* in the 1840s. But it was Dickens, with his exaggerated characters, who was most frequently the source of melodrama. By 1850 there had been nearly 250 productions based on his works; by 1860 the number had risen to more than four hundred. Dickens understood the link: 'Every writer of fiction,' he said, 'though he may not adopt the dramatic form, writes in effect for the stage.' His use of coincidence was similar in function to the providential workings of a melodrama: in *Oliver Twist*, the first pocket Oliver picks belongs to his lost father's best friend. His vocabulary, too, has theatrical elements – Sikes snarling 'Wolves tear your throats!' could be taken from any minor theatre stage. And stage devices are woven, unspoken, into the novels. In *Martin Chuzzlewit* Nadgett, the private detective, appears suddenly at the side of the suspected murderer, 'as if he had that moment come up a trap', that is, a trapdoor on a stage. Yet at this point, crime onstage and in fiction was still not about detection, but about the control of villainous characters who were marked by their villainy as being outside society. It was more comfortable to think of Rush in this way: as a stage villain in topboots.

One report said that at least six, perhaps eight, ballad-sellers were at Rush's execution. These ballads gave pleasure for more than the moment – families clubbed together to afford the penny price, and one patterer remembered seeing, long after the execution, 'eleven persons, young and old, gathered around a scanty fire' where an old man was reading aloud an account of Rush's final moments. One writer proudly claimed, 'I did the helegy … on Rush's execution. It was supposed … to be written by the culprit himself, and was particular penitent.' The ballad-sellers did well with a supposed confession of Rush's, in which he admitted to murdering his grandmother fourteen years previously, burying her in the garden, and then killing his wife for good measure. Another assessed Rush in financial terms: 'I lived on him for a month or more. When I commenced with Rush, I was

14s. in debt for rent, and in less than fourteen days I astonished [everyone] by paying my landlord all I owed him.' Another agreed: 'Rush turned up a regular trump for us … Irish Jem … never goes to bed but he blesses Rush the farmer; and many's the time he's told me we should never have such another windfall as that. But I told him not to despair; there's a good time coming, boys, says I.' And sure enough, he went on, 'up comes the Bermondsey tragedy'. The Bermondsey tragedy, or the story of Maria and Frederick George Manning, was to bring 'good times' to murder-mongers everywhere.

What makes one murder catch the interest of the public, while another leaves it cold, is a mystery. Henry Mayhew's patterer had various explanations: it might be that one murder occurs too close to another – 'Two murderers together is no good to nobody'; or too many patterers piling in on the same story could mean that attention was diluted; sometimes, he said, the weather was too wet, or too hot, or too something. Yet if this were the case, logic would say that the murder of Patrick O'Connor by Maria and Frederick Manning would have been a matter of general indifference, for it took place in the middle of one of the worst cholera epidemics ever known in Britain. At the time of James Rush's crime, between October and November 1848, a thousand people had died of cholera in England; by the time the Mannings came to the attention of the newspaper public, that was the merest trifle: between June and October 1849 14,000 people had died of cholera in London alone. In Bermondsey, a working-class district where poverty and overcrowding meant the disease was rampant, one out of every fifty-nine residents died that summer.

Yet this exerted less hold on the public imagination than two murders. Soon after Rush's execution, the *Bury Herald* noted some uncanny parallels between Rush and John Thurtell: the two, it reported breathlessly, had been at school together (unlikely – Rush was at least six years younger); they had both conducted their own defence; and both were executed for murder. This seemed so very remarkable that the *Preston Guardian* not only picked up the story, but printed it again on 18 August. In the same column it listed that in the previous three days, 3,015 people had succumbed to cholera; 1,253 had died. On the day the murder of Patrick O'Connor was discovered, the *Morning Chronicle* reported another 336 dead, and on the next page it mentioned, with no sense of incongruity, that 'last night hundreds of persons were congregated in front of the house' where O'Connor's body had been found. Of course, there was then no known way of preventing cholera, while in theory murder could be prevented, or if not prevented, detected and 'cured' by execution. The *Morning Chronicle* listed some of the treatments for cholera – 'chloroform, carbonic acid, ether, calomel and opium, camphor, ammonia, wine, brandy ... applications of cayenne pepper, mustard, turpentine, and other species of artificial heat'. Science could solve a single crime, but not thousands of deaths. It was more comforting to think of the former than of the latter. As with Good, the hunt for the murderers of O'Connor was to be prolonged, but unlike Good, everything worked perfectly for the police – the detective force functioned exactly as its founders had planned, while new technology (trains, telegraphs) was as much use to the pursuers as to the pursued. In a world where people were healthy one morning, dead the next, this must have been reassuring.

Maria Manning was born Marie Roux (sometimes 'de Roux') in Vaud, Switzerland. By 1843 she was working in Britain as a lady's maid for the wife of an MP in Devonshire. After her mistress's death, Marie – now anglicized to Maria – was employed by Lady Evelyn Blantyre, the daughter of the Duke and Duchess of Sutherland. (The Duchess was Mistress of the Robes, a position of some importance in Queen Victoria's household, and this touch of high life was always included in later tellings of the story.) Maria probably met Frederick George Manning when she lived in Devonshire. He was originally from Taunton in Somerset, and had been a guard on the Great Western Railway. Soon after their wedding in 1847, Manning left the railway, possibly because of suspicion of involvement in a series of train robberies, and with his wife's savings set up as landlord at the White Hart Inn in Taunton.

The marriage was not happy, nor was the pub successful. Mrs Manning now either became friendly, or continued a friendship from before her marriage, with Patrick O'Connor. O'Connor had arrived in London in the 1830s from his native Ireland, and had had a somewhat dubious, although financially lucrative, career. In his early days he told a barrister that his money came from smuggling (the barrister later claimed that O'Connor had attempted to defraud him, so how much of this is true, and how much aggrievement, is unknown). At some point he found legitimate work, first as a tide-waiter, a customs official who examined ships for contraband as they waited for the tide to turn; later as a gauger, an exciseman concerned with official measures. He was also said to have had a profitable sideline as a small-time usurer, and been involved in dockyard protection rackets.

By the early to mid-1840s, he and Mrs Manning were meeting frequently, and she may even have left Manning and lived with O'Connor at some point. In 1849 the attempt to earn a living from the inn in Taunton was abandoned, and the Mannings moved to London, eventually taking lodgings at 3 Minver Place, Bermondsey, south of the river. Mrs Manning worked as a dressmaker, a big step down from her grandeur as a lady's maid in a titled family; Manning was unemployed. On 9 August, O'Connor, who was proud of his friendship with a woman who had worked for a duchess's daughter, was seen crossing London Bridge, heading, he said, to his lady friend's for dinner. That evening, Mrs Manning visited his lodgings alone. His landlady, having frequently seen them together, permitted her to wait for some time in his room. The next day, he failed to appear at work. Nothing happened for three days, and then the police appeared at Minver Place, looking for O'Connor. Later that day Mrs Manning left the house with luggage, and the following day the furniture, and Manning, went too. When the police returned that evening, abandoned possessions were found scattered across the rooms, but there was nothing that belonged identifiably to O'Connor. Another two days passed, and the police returned once more, this time with a plan to dig up the small yard. They found nothing there, but on entering the kitchen, one sharp-eyed constable noticed that there was a thin line of discoloration running between two flagstones in front of the hearth. The flagstones were lifted, and underneath was earth that had recently been disturbed. Under this was the naked body of a man, trussed up and embedded in quicklime. Patrick O'Connor had been found, but the Mannings were gone.

Now the machinery that Mayne had worked so hard to establish showed what it could do. Already the two police divisions whose districts included O'Connor's and the Mannings' lodgings had been working together. A notice was published asking for information on 'Maria Manning, a native of Geneva, 30 years old, 5 feet 7 inches high, stout, fresh complexion, with long dark hair, good looking, scar on the right side of her chin, extending towards the neck, dresses very smartly and speaks broken English. Has been a lady's maid and dress-maker.' Everyone felt they were part of the hunt. A journalist found two cards at Minver Place, one listing sailing times to New York, the other with 'Mr. Wright, passenger to New York' written on it. These were handed to the constable on duty, who tore them up, announcing grandly that 'it was not very likely that if they had intended to go to New York they would have left those cards behind'. The journalist went down to the docks to check the passengers on the *Victoria*, one of the listed ships. No Manning appeared on the passenger manifest, but a baggage clerk said that six boxes had been delivered in that name. This information was sent to Scotland Yard, which showed more interest than the local bobby. A steamer was sent after the ship, which had by this time passed Plymouth, with an inspector on board who knew Manning by sight. The suspected murderers were not, however, on the *Victoria*.

O'Connor's lodgings were searched, and his family supplied a list of missing valuables, including railway scrip. The police also found the cab driver who had taken Mrs Manning and her boxes away; he had driven her to London Bridge station, where the boxes had been left, marked 'Mrs. Smith, passenger to Paris. To be left till called for.' They were still there, and when opened they were found to contain clothes and other possessions identified as O'Connor's, and some clothes or fabric with reddish-brown stains. Another cab driver came forward to say that he had driven a woman provisionally identified as Mrs Manning from London Bridge to Euston station. There, a Mrs

Smith had taken a ticket for Edinburgh. The police now telegraphed their counterparts in that city.

The telegraph was a wonder of modernity. The first criminal had been caught by it only four years previously (see pp.329–32). *Punch* called it 'God's lightning' – a swift and sure retribution: 'Murder has hardly turned from its abomination … when the avenging lightning stays the homicide.' The *Illustrated London News* highlighted two modernities, telegraph and railway: the 'guilty wretch, flying on the wings of steam at thirty miles an hour, is tracked by a swifter messenger'. And that is what happened to Mrs Manning. She had fled north, to Edinburgh, where she had commissioned a stockbroker to sell some shares, and asked him to find out if payment could be made on some railway scrip she held. The following day she returned to collect the scrip, saying she had been unexpectedly called away. The day after that, a notice was circulated itemizing the stolen scrip. The broker immediately contacted the police with 'Mrs Smith's' address. As the *Glasgow Herald* marvelled, the arrest was 'almost miraculous': a description had been sent from London 'at ten minutes before one o'clock', and 'a few minutes after one' the police were at her door. Then, 'before the clock had struck two' a telegraph was on its way back to London to report her arrest; 'so magically had all this been effected' that the police in London had barely returned to Scotland Yard from Euston station before the news of Maria Manning's arrest was with them.

Locating her husband was less straightforward. Manning had agreed the sale of the furniture with a broker for £13, but after that his trail went cold. There were almost as many sightings of him as there had been of Good, but finally a credible report put him in the Channel Islands, and he was traced to Jersey. The police arrested him there at the end of the month, and escorted him back from St Helier to Southampton, and then by special train to Vauxhall, where hundreds of people stood waiting to see him. It was reported that on his arrest Manning had been urbane: 'Ah, Sergeant, is that you? I am glad you are come … If you had not come I was coming to town to explain it all. I am innocent. Is that wretch taken?' (There are typographical

indications that the word 'wretch' was a polite newspaper substitution, one assumes for 'bitch'.) Manning's line from the moment of his
arrest did not vary: 'She is the guilty party. I am as innocent as a lamb.'
He claimed that his wife had shot O'Connor, and he had fainted in
horror: by the time he came to, the body had vanished.

The press kept everyone up to date. The *Morning Chronicle* was
both smug about its reporting – 'the earliest information ... was given
in this paper exclusively' – and peeved that its exclusive 'was transferred to the columns of nearly all our contemporaries, and in no one
instance was the source ... acknowledged'. *Lloyd's* meanwhile reported
receiving information that a 'clairvoyante' had seen three cellars under
the Mannings' house, in one of which was to be found the pistol that
had been used to kill O'Connor: 'What makes this letter extraordinary,' added *Lloyd's*, 'is that there are three large cellars.' Penny-
dreadful gothic cellars were not in fact found under the small terraced
house, and the newspaper moved on to a report that two pistols and
a 'bullet mould' had been traced to a Bermondsey pawnshop, producing bullets that matched those which killed O'Connor. The newspapers, at least, felt there was 'no doubt' that these were the murder
weapons, although they did not say how the pawnshop had been
located.

Meanwhile Manning's attempts to pin everything on his wife – the
'Lady Macbeth on the Bermondsey Stage', as *The Times* called her –
were doomed to failure. At the inquest, evidence was heard from a
constable who had collected the household goods Manning had sold.
The coal shovel, he testified, still had 'blood and ashes with human
hair attached'. The Mannings were committed for trial.

The trial opened on 29 October 1849, and a procession of witnesses
appeared. William Massey, a medical student who had lodged with
the couple, said that Manning 'asked me ... what drug would produce
stupefaction, or partial intoxication, so as to cause a person to put pen
to paper ... just before, or just after, he mentioned the name of
O'Connor he said he should like to get O'Connor to sign a promis-
sory-note for a considerable sum of money, 500*l*'. Two clerks from the
stockbrokers' offices that had dealt with O'Connor could not testify

– both had been stricken with cholera, and one had died – but a woman identified Manning as the man who had bought a bushel of lime from her, saying it was to kill slugs. When she had asked him what kind of lime he wanted, he replied, 'that which would burn the quickest' – hardly a necessity for slugs. A porter gave evidence that when he delivered a crowbar Manning had ordered, Manning, meeting him in the street, complained that it had not been wrapped up, and he made the porter wait while he went into a shop and bought paper to cover it. The furniture-broker's wife added that after they had bought the furniture, Manning had told her, 'I would not sleep there [in the house] to-night for £20.'

The medical evidence to prove that the body was that of O'Connor, and that he had been murdered, was less strong. At the inquest the police surgeon had testified to the victim's wounds, but although he had sent the viscera to Alfred Swaine Taylor, the lecturer on medical jurisprudence at Guy's Hospital, Taylor had refused to carry out an analysis, as the Surrey and Middlesex coroners had previously failed to pay him for work he'd performed for them; the remains had been thrown away. Further testimony involved stains on Mrs Manning's dress. William Olding identified himself as a 'practical chemist', and went on to explain that he was the son of the police surgeon, had studied chemistry for five years, and was now twenty years old. Although he had 'arrived at the conclusion that the stains [on the dress] are blood', he then went on, with no apparent sense of contradiction, 'there is no direct chemical process which will identify blood stains … I cannot swear it was blood.' The most he could say was that, when the fabric was soaked in water, it had given off 'a smoky red colour, from which I afterwards obtained a precipitate indicating albumen, one of the constituents of the blood'. As the red discharge 'was not any colouring matter with which I am acquainted', and as it contained albumen, he therefore felt happy to swear it was blood.

Manning's defence was that it was all Mrs Manning's fault – she was the guilty party, he had known nothing beforehand, he had bought the lime and the crowbar on her instructions, and had only become aware of her plans when he saw O'Connor lying dead in the kitchen. Mrs Manning's defence was just as weak. Her barrister first condemned Manning's barrister for describing her relationship with O'Connor in terms he thought 'coarse', and then outlined what he said were the two possibilities in this case: either Maria was a woman of 'abandoned character', in which case she would have been kept by O'Connor, and didn't need to kill him; or she was 'a woman of kindly feelings and disposition', and thus would not 'lend herself to such a transaction' (it is not clear if the 'transaction' was murder or adultery). The rest of the defence speech was pretty much the same as Manning's: each blamed the other.

The jury considered for forty-five minutes before coming back with a guilty verdict. When asked if they had anything to say, Manning was silent, but Mrs Manning burst out: 'There is no justice and no right for a foreign subject in this country. There is no law for me. I have had no protection – neither from the judges, nor from the prosecutors, nor from my husband ...' She then claimed that O'Connor had been her dearest friend in the world. When the judge began to sentence the pair, she burst out once more, shouting, 'No, no; I won't stand it. You ought to be ashamed of yourselves. There is neither law nor justice here,' before attempting to leave the dock. She was prevented, but probably they should have let her go, as she then cried, 'Shameful', and 'Base England', before snatching up the bunches of rue that were, by tradition, placed on the bench in front of the dock, and throwing them down in what was clearly meant to be a gesture of contempt towards the court.

This was as good as any melodrama, and the comparison did not escape contemporaries. *Punch* illustrator Richard Doyle together with Percival Leigh produced a mock Olde-English series on places of amusement – the zoo, the flower show, and so on. Then, 'did take my Wife ... to the Old Bailey, my Wife having a great Longing to fee a Prifoner tried, efpecially for Murder ... the Place look[ed] as fine almoft as the Opera. But in Truth it was as good as a Play, if not better, to hear the Barrifters fpeak to the Jury, efpecially the Counfel for the Prifoners, making believe to be mightily concerned for their Clients ... pleading their Caufe, as though they were injured Innocents, with

Richard Doyle's illustration of Madame Tussaud's. Edward Oxford was one of the seven who tried to assassinate Queen Victoria during her reign; John Thom, alias 'Sir William Courtney', tried to rouse the working classes into rebelling against their masters, but his forty followers fled when he murdered a constable in 1838 (he is the large bearded figure in the background: Thom also had messianic delusions). Baron Trenk, centre rear, was probably Franz von der Trenck, an Austrian mercenary who fought in the war of the Austrian Succession, in a paramilitary regiment known for perpetrating civilian atrocities.

fmiting of the Breaft, and turning up of the Eyes, more natural than I remember I did ever fee any Actor ...'

The verdict surprised no one, although it must have gladdened the hearts of newspaper proprietors everywhere. *The Times* had carried more than seventy stories on the case between the discovery of the crime in August and the execution of the Mannings in November. It tacitly acknowledged this glut, saying demurely that 'certain examples' of crime took 'a stronger hold than others', creating a 'more continuous interest'. So they did, and not only in the home market. *Household Words* noted advertisements from as far afield as Vienna, where 'READERS OF ALL CLASSES' were offered the opportunity to learn 'THE DARK DEEDS OF CIVILISED MAN ... "The Murder of Mr. O'Connor by the Mannings, Husband and Wife", and "The Fourfold Murder by James Bloomfield [sic] Rush".' The *Illustrated London News*, so apologetic about printing a single portrait of Daniel Good in 1842, published twelve illustrated articles on the Mannings. The *Lady's Newspaper*, specializing in 'lively and serious poetry, the fashions, directions for making and working those nameless elegancies, in collars, cuffs, mantelets, purses', featured the story regularly, while *Lloyd's Weekly* sometimes devoted as much as half its editorial space to the murder.

By 1837, only murder, attempted murder, high treason, wrecking, rape, piracy, arson on inhabited premises and 'unnatural offences' continued to be punishable by death. And after that year, only three people in the entire century were hanged for anything other than murder or high treason in wartime. Even for murder, executions were uncommon. In the West Midlands between 1835 and 1860, for example, there were 14,686 guilty verdicts for all indictable offences. Of these, thirteen people were sentenced to death, and of those so sentenced, only four were executed – four hangings in twenty-five years.

If executions were a rarity, executions of women were even rarer, and double executions of husband and wife were unimaginably rare. Throughout the sixty-three years of Victoria's reign, 26 per cent of convicted murderers were men who killed their wives, while only 1 per cent were women who killed their husbands. And eight out of every ten female homicide victims were killed by a husband, lover, or would-be husband or lover. Even for lesser crimes, women as a proportion of those tried, much less convicted, were in a tiny minority, and a minority growing smaller every year.

This rarity created a bonanza for broadside-sellers. It was claimed that 1.6 million broadsides had been sold for each of the cases of Corder, Greenacre and Good, but Rush and the Mannings were more popular still – the figure for them is 2.5 million broadsides each. In 1838 the legal requirement that executions take place within forty-eight hours of sentencing had been abolished, in order that appeals could be heard, and this gave broadside-sellers an extra window, and the 'Sorrowful Lamentations' of the criminal contemplating his doom flourished. 'Before that … there wasn't no time for a Lamentation; sentence o' Friday, and scragging o' Monday' was no use to the patterer.

There was a definite class divide in how murder news was digested. One standing patterer, who had done 'uncommonly well' with the Mannings, noted that 'Gentlefolks won't have anything to do with murders sold in the street; they've got other ways of seeing all about it,' while for those who bought broadsides, 'we picture them in the highest colours we can'. One elderly man in 1923 recollected that as a schoolboy during the Manning trial he had watched 'men carrying … rudely painted canvases on staffs on both sides of which were portraits and scenes and incidents of the murder, the bearers gathering a harvest of coppers by describing the crime in stentorian tones to crowds at street corners'. For really popular crimes, some patterers produced brightly coloured boards, with a series of boxed illustrations from the story: the murder itself, the discovery of the body, the trial and the execution, and any particular details that had captured the public imagination. One patterer described his board, with its image of Mrs Manning 'dressed for dinner' and firing a pistol at O'Connor, who was washing his hands before the meal: 'The people said … "O, look at him a-washing hisself; he's a doing it so nattral, and ain't a-thinking he's a-going to be murdered."'

The detail on these boards was not replicated in the broadside illustrations themselves, which used generic images, many lifted from completely unconnected sources. Henry Mayhew reported one 'likeness' of O'Connor that was, judging by the fur collar on the sitter's coat and the order and insignia on his breast, a portrait of William IV. Another broadside (overleaf) reproduced a standard, anonymous execution scene, with a single body hanging from a gallows; next to it, very obviously scratched onto the block at a later date, is a series of black blobs, indicating the second body. The text in many of the

broadsides published before the trial was also generic. One that was headed 'Apprehension of Mrs Manning' had no information about her arrest at all – it dealt entirely with earlier events – but word of the arrest must have arrived as it was going to press, so that simple piece of up-to-the-minute news was added, in the same way newspapers later carried 'Stop Press' columns.

After the verdict the broadsides could be more expansive, pleasurably chewing over the details. Several stressed Mrs Manning's foreignness (although quite a few claimed she was Swedish) and her brute villainy: 'We beat him dreadfully upon the floor,/We washed our hands in his crimson gore.' Others carried the usual manufactured confessions, including one almost anti-confession written as if by Mrs Manning (who never actually confessed, to many broadside-writers' disgust)* in an imaginary letter to her husband, claiming that

---

* A patterer told Mayhew: 'Every day I was anxiously looking for a confession from Mrs. Manning. All I wanted was for her to clear her conscience afore she left this here whale of tears (that's what I always calls it in the patter), and when I read in the papers ... that her last words on the brink of heternity was, "I've nothing to say to you, Mr. Rowe [the prison governor], but to thank you for your kindness," I guv her up entirely – had completely done with her. In course the public looks to us for the last words of all monsters in human form, and as for Mrs. Manning's, they were not worth the printing.'

O'Connor was actually 'shot by that young man from Guernsey, who was in the back parlour smoking'. For not bringing this mystery man forward at the trial she chides Manning in the tone of a put-upon wife whose husband has yet again forgotten to let out the cat. Other broadsides stuck more closely to Manning's repeated assertions that his wife had shot O'Connor, and then threatened to shoot him too if he refused to help her bury the body. Many liked the 'fact' that the grave had been dug the previous May, and covered with a board in the interim: they shiveringly reported how O'Connor must frequently have walked over it going to and from the sink.

For those who could manage it, the place to be on 13 November 1849 was at the execution, outside Horsemonger Lane Gaol. Even in an age when popular hangings drew thousands, the interest in the Mannings was exceptional. Three days earlier the police had already cleared the streets, barricading the space in front of the gaol and blocking off the smaller streets. (The Surrey parish authorities later recorded that £180 had been spent on barricades – the amount a small tradesman could expect to earn in a year.) Local householders saw an opportunity for even greater commerce than at an 'ordinary' hanging, and many sold seats at their windows, and on their roofs, for up to two guineas each. The American novelist Herman Melville recorded in his diary that he and a companion had 'Paid half a crown each for a stand on the roof of a house adjoining ... Police by hundreds. Men & women fainting. – The man & wife were hung side by side – still unreconciled to each other – What a change from the time they stood up to be married, together! The mob was brutish. All in all, a most wonderful, horrible, & unspeakable scene.' Extraordinary demand also saw 'tickets' issued ('Admit the bearer to one front seat at Mr —— —'s, Number — Winter Terrace'). Many landlords whose buildings faced the gaol erected scaffolding to create even more view-ing areas. *The Times* claimed that window seats commanded 'a Californian price' – a reference to the gold rush under way in the same year. (Similarly, the waiting crowd amused itself by breaking into choruses of 'Oh, Mrs Manning, don't you cry for me' to the tune of 'Oh Susannah', the marching song of the Forty-Niners.)

On 11 November, those without seats began to crowd the front of the gaol, where the scaffold was to be erected; *The Times* estimated that by noon on the 12th there were possibly 10,000 people waiting. On the day itself, estimates of the numbers present ranged widely, from 30,000 to 50,000, with five hundred police in attendance,* the crowds sustained by perambulating food- and drink-sellers and 'hundreds' (claimed the *Examiner*) of basketmen selling 'Manning's biscuits' and 'Maria Manning's peppermints'.

Among a group who had taken 'the whole of [a] roof … for the extremely moderate sum of Ten Guineas' was Charles Dickens, who after havering for some time, finally decided to attend together with four friends, one of whom was the *Punch* illustrator John Leech, who quickly produced 'The Great Moral Lesson at Horsemonger Lane Gaol' for the magazine. Dickens and his friends were well up in all the details of the case, real and imaginary. Dickens reported that Manning had said of O'Connor, 'I never liked him and I beat in his skull with the ripping chisel' (a curious flashback to the Ratcliffe Highway murders), while John Forster, the literary critic and later Dickens' biographer, wrote to Bulwer that 'Lord Carlisle (she lived in his sister's family, you may remember) says she was *always singing* in the house – and that all the ladies adored her, while her fellow servants detested her'.

Many were similarly fascinated. The wife of the art and social critic John Ruskin wrote to her mother from Venice to thank her for her letter 'telling me about the Mannings. We were all much interested …' Forster was greatly caught up in the events, seemingly entranced by the attractive appearance and formidable character of Maria, as many were.† He had earlier attended at least one of the police

---

* Counting crowds was always difficult, and was always an expression of political bias. The wide – and wild – disparities can be seen in reports of the last public execution at Lincoln, in 1859, when the *Stamford Mercury*, a Liberal paper, saw 'several hundred' people in attendance; the Tory *Lincolnshire Chronicle* numbered the same crowd at between 12,000 and 15,000, while *The Times*, establishment to the teeth, said there were 'about 25,000'.

† The artist William Mulready had attended Southwark Police Court in order to sketch both the Mannings. Daguerreotypes were also taken of the two at the same time, and advertised at a shilling a photo.

examinations, for Thomas Carlyle wrote enviously in early October that 'Fuz [Forster] … had *seen* Manning, happy Fuz.' After the execution Forster was in ecstasies, even noting that Maria had worn 'gloves on her manicured hands' on the scaffold. It would obviously have been impossible for a spectator on a rooftop to have seen her hands, bare or gloved, yet the excitement was such that this passed as a worthwhile comment. Maria was, Forster went on, '*beautifully dressed*, every part of her noble figure finely and fully expressed by close fitting black satin'.* He was only one of many to note her impressive figure: her sexuality was a constant under-refrain. More than half a century later, Thomas Hardy, recollecting the 1856 execution which was an early trigger for *Tess of the d'Urbervilles* (see pp.361–2), wrote, 'I remember what a fine figure she showed against the sky as she hung in the misty rain, & how the tight black silk gown set off her shape as she wheeled half-round and back.' This was supposedly a memory of Elizabeth Martha Brown, a labourer's wife, who was unlikely to own a silk gown. Hardy was only nine when the Mannings died, but his description is much closer to Maria than to a poverty-stricken farmhand's wife.

As with Hardy, much of the extended coverage stressed Maria's fashionable dress, so much so that *Punch* found it worth parodying: 'At the elegant *réunion* on the occasion of the late *Matinée Criminelle* at the Old Bailey, the lovely and accomplished LADY B— carried off "*les honneurs*", by her lovely *Manteau à la* MANNING … *Corsage, à la condamnée* … has a very tight body [that is, a bodice], which pinions the arms to the sides, giving that interesting air to the wearer which is so much admired on the scaffold …'

---

* For over a century and a half commentators have repeated the assertion that, by wearing black satin to her execution, Maria Manning had ensured the eclipse of that fabric and colour combination for decades. Her biographer, Albert Borowitz, has gone through the fashion journals of the day and found that, on the contrary, black satin remained an item of fashionable wear throughout the following decades. In 1850, one draper alone had twenty-five advertisements that mentioned black satin; at the Great Exhibition two years after the execution, seven black satins won prizes in the textile categories.

Dickens was more concerned with the mental state of the spectators. He had been to executions before,* and he now wrote, for publication, a letter on what he saw outside Horsemonger Lane Gaol. He
was not, he said, going to discuss capital punishment – he believed
that murderers should receive the death penalty, but their deaths
should be 'a private solemnity'. What disturbed him was that the
crowds found entertainment, not moral lessons, at the scaffold:

> When the sun rose brightly … it gilded thousands upon thousands of
> upturned faces, so inexpressibly odious in their brutal mirth or
> callousness, that a man had cause to feel ashamed of the shape he wore,
> and to shrink from himself, as fashioned in the image of the Devil.
> When the two miserable creatures who attracted all this ghastly sight
> about them were turned quivering into the air, there was no more
> emotion, no more pity, no more thought that two immortal souls had
> gone to judgment, no more restraint in any of the previous obscenities,
> than if the name of Christ had never been heard in this world, and
> there was no belief among men but that they perished like the beasts.

For the hundreds of thousands who would not have dreamt of going
to an execution, there was still plenty of Manning entertainment. In
Manchester, J. Springthorpe, 'Artist', displayed waxwork figures of the
couple in an exhibition to 'highly amuse, delight and highly instruct'.
And Madame Tussaud's, which had set up a permanent exhibition
space in London in 1836, was creating a whole new arena for murder
– a 'Chamber of Horrors'. From Madame Tussaud's earliest days there
had been a 'Separate Room' which initially displayed replica heads of
those executed in the French Revolution, together with a model of the
guillotine and the Bastille, but it was not until 1820, in Leeds, that a
criminal addition to her show was advertised: 'the celebrated notorious ARTHUR THISTLEWOOD' (one of the Cato Street conspirators,

---

* Dickens watched Courvoisier's execution in 1840 (see pp.200–209), attended a behead-
ing in Rome in 1845 (and refused to attend a double execution in Genoa in the same year),
and may have seen another execution in Switzerland before the Mannings'.

The murder of Maria Marten in the Red Barn was of all-consuming interest: sermons were preached, plays were written, puppet shows performed, and even Staffordshire figureware produced. These examples date from soon after the trial in 1828, and were purchased by the more prosperous – the bucolically pretty Red Barn piece (*top*) in particular was elaborately produced, as Maria approaches her doom, with Corder, her murderer, beckoning enticingly from the door. The figures show Corder and Maria (*below left*) in happier times, and Corder (*below right*) supposedly at his trial.

Act 1st Scene 4th in King Richard III. time, 1828.

Hare............ *Come, shall we kill him as he sleeps?*
Burke. *No; he'll say 'twas done cowardly, when he wakes.*
Hare. *When he wakes!— why, fool, he shall never*
Wake, until the great judgement-day:—
Remember our reward, when the deed's done.
Burke. *Come, he dies; I had forgot the reward.*
Hare. *Where's thy Conscience now?*
Burke. *In the Anatomist's purse.*

No. V.

R. H. Nimmo's Lithog. Edinburgh.

Burke and Hare's 'body-business' – selling to anatomy schools the bodies of the paupers they had murdered – produced a raft of pamphlets and books after its discovery, including this anonymous 'Wretch's Illustrations of Shakespeare', which drew parallels between the murderers and Shakespeare's villains.

After the murderer Thurtell was executed, his body was sent to St Bartholomew's Hospital for dissection by the faculty of medicine and its students. The caricaturist Rowlandson satirized the gruesome interest in 'The Lancett Club at a Thurtell Feast' (*above*). Note how the doctor doing the dissection is caricatured, but Thurtell himself is almost classically handsome. The artist William Mulready, who sketched Thurtell (*below left*) and his partner Joseph Hunt (*below right*) at their trial, gave a more realistic depiction.

The eighteenth-century murder of Mr Hayes by the innkeeper Jonathan Bradford got a new lease of life in 1833, when the playwright Edward Fitzball created the scenic novelty of a set that showed the four rooms of the inn all onstage at once, in cross-section (*above*), writing the murder scene so that the action took place simultaneously across all the rooms. This was the great selling point, and even a decade later the playbill for the Royal Pavilion Theatre in Whitechapel (*left*) focused on 'The Four Room'd Scene'.

Fitzball's innovation influenced high as well as popular art. The central panel of Augustus Egg's triptych, *Past and Present* (1858), depicted a middle-class home at the moment the husband discovers his wife's adultery; in the left-hand wing of the triptych the woman, cast out and cradling her illegitimate child, gazes at the moon and contemplates suicide; in the right-hand image her two children simultaneously gaze at the same moon as, orphaned and alone, they huddle in their garret.

London, Published by B. Pollock, 73, Hoxton Street Hoxton

Sykes   Dodger   Toby   Policeman   Mob

Fagan   Nancy   Sykes   Artful Dodger   Oliver

The popularity of crime as a subject for theatre meant that many toy theatres also revolved around murderous plots. *Oliver Twist* was a perennial favourite (the top two rows show two different versions, both created by Pollock's Toy Theatres); *The Maid and the Magpye*, reflecting the tragic tale of Eliza Fenning (*below*), was also a perennial favourite.

Annette going to the place of Execution.

London, Published by B. Pollock, 73, Hoxton Street, Hoxton.

The story of the eighteenth-century murderer Eugene Aram became wildly popular in the nineteenth century, first with Bulwer's novel, and then with various stage versions. The most enduringly famous adaptation starred Henry Irving, although it was made genteel by removing the melodrama – no trial, no execution, just Irving expiring of remorse in a country churchyard (*above*). This success followed an earlier melodrama, *The Bells*, in which Irving played a burgomaster who, fifteen years before, had murdered a man, and now betrays himself, overcome by a guilty conscience (*right*).

THE COLLEEN BAWN;

OR,

THE COLLEGIAN'S WIFE.

A Popular Melo=Drama,

IN THREE ACTS (AS PERFORMED AT THE LONDON THEATRES).

Father Edward
Anne Chute
Nelly
Kyrle Daly
Myles
Lowry Lobby

THE COLLEEN BAWN GALOP.

DEDICATED TO
DION BOUCICAULT ESQ.
BY
T. BROWNE.
LONDON, METZLER & Co 37, 38 & 35, Gt MARLBOROUGH ST. W.

Dion Boucicault's play *The Colleen Bawn*, based on the murder of a working-class Irish girl by her upper-class seducer and his servant, was wildly popular. Soon dozens, if not hundreds, of songs celebrated the beautiful Eily O'Connor, on stage not dead at all, but rescued in the nick of time by her unrequited lover, the horse-dealer-turned-poacher Myles-na-Coppaleen (played by Boucicault himself).

who had just been hanged). Then Corder was added, his face supposedly taken from a death mask made by Madame Tussaud. In 1829 'BURKE THE MURDERER' went on display, heralded in a very apologetic advertisement: 'some', it feared, might consider the exhibition 'improper'. By the 1840s Madame Tussaud's was well on the way to becoming an institution – more than 30,000 catalogues a year were being sold, which might indicate an attendance of ten times that level. Now the Separate Room was renamed the Chamber of Horrors, and Madame Tussaud's apologized no longer. Less than three weeks after the Mannings' execution it advertised: 'Maria MANNING, George Manning, Bloomfield [sic] Rush, taken from life at their trials, a cast in plaster of Mr. O'Connor, with a plan of the kitchen where he was murdered ...' It was this type of opportunism, and the buying up of 'relics' to go with the displays, that produced the public perception of Madame Tussaud's, whether it was condemned as a social evil, or admired for its good commercial sense, as with the patterer who complained that 'that there Madam Toosow' had damaged his sales of Daniel Good broadsides: 'You see, she ... guv 2*l.* for the werry clogs as he used to wash his master's carriage in; so, in course, when the harristocracy could go and see ... the werry identical clogs ... why the people wouldn't look at our authentic portraits of the fiend in human form.'

Two years later the notorious French detective Vidocq, now in his seventies, took this to a logical conclusion, opening a 'curious museum' which included the 'costumes' of 'swindlers, rogues, thieves, and plunderers', Vidocq's own disguises and a host of fearsome weapons. The poet Robert Browning went along, and reported to his soon-to-be wife Elizabeth Barrett: 'Vidocq ... did the honours of his museum of knives & nails & hooks that have helped great murderers to their purposes – he scarcely admits, I observed, an implement with only one attestation to its efficacy; but the one or two exceptions rather justify his latitude ... – thus one little sort of dessert-knife *did* only take *one* life ... "but then" says Vidocq, "it was the man's own mother's life, with fifty-two blows and all for" (I think) "15 francs ..." So prattles good-naturedly Vidocq ...'

173

This was too much for *Punch*. Six weeks before the Mannings' trial it worried that 'The rag-pickers of crime are at work ... London reeks with the foulness of the Bermondsey Murder. There, in words of ink-black blood, it stains the walls; there it is gibbetted in placards, and is carried shouting, in the highway ... Good MADAME TUSSAUD, devoting art to homicide, turns to the pleasantness of profit the abomination of blood. With her so much murder is so much counted money ...'

Madame Tussaud's knew its market, however: Maria Manning's model remained on display for a record 122 years. She became a figure of legend, of fear – and sometimes of comedy. In 1851, only two years after the events in Minver Place, the Kingston Assizes heard a case of two feuding neighbours: one 'had caused a number of scaffolds to be erected upon his piece of land, from which were suspended tea-kettles, tea-boards, watering-pots, horse-collars, horses' and bullocks' heads, and also a figure representing Maria Manning ... some of the witnesses said they were ... afraid to pass by the spot unless they were accompanied by a policeman'. During the hearing, a model of the alleged nuisance was revealed to the court, 'and the sight of it convulsed the court with laughter'. From the Lady Macbeth of the Bermondsey stage to convulsions of laughter in only eighteen months.

Mrs Manning the building-site bogey was unusual. More common were Staffordshire figures of the couple – at least two sets were produced. There was also a greyhound named Maria Manning, whose offspring – surely a joke – were named Hero and Peace. This was middle-class whimsy, but there was also hard commercial gain to be found in the Mannings. G.A. Sala, the ex-penny-blood-author-turned-respectable-journalist, wrote of one of his old colleagues: 'He had been a man all tattered and torn, but so soon as the remains of poor Patrick O'Connor had been identified ... the lucky reporter blossomed into a brand-new coat ... New plaid pantaloons followed, a glossy silk hat shone upon his head, Wellington boots adorned his lower extremities, and the bows of a satin necktie floated on his chest. The only thing he lacked was a waistcoat; but alas! The Mannings

The search for Maria Manning was concluded with what appeared to be magical swiftness, thanks to the telegraph. In Robert Huish's novelization of the story, the illustrations of the rather stylish detectives show how the public's attitudes to the police had altered in the past decade.

were hanged ere [he] had secured that much-coveted vest, and afterwards, murders being rare, he drifted gradually into his old and normal condition of dismal seediness.'

Sala implied that the indigent author was James Malcolm Rymer, but Rymer left an estate worth more than £7,500 on his death. It seems more likely that the penny-a-liner was Robert Huish. His Manning volume, *The Progress of Crime, or, The Authentic Memoirs of Maria Manning*, all 832 pages of it, appeared in twenty-four 6d. parts, and then in a single volume, in 1849. The early sections gave the heroine an imaginary Swiss background, in which a traditional melo-drama Marie succumbs to temptation, but from weakness rather than evil nature. *The Progress of Crime* linked up with reality only after she was employed as a lady's maid in Devonshire, and even then the story continued with the standard fictional portrait of a seduced and betrayed innocent, rather than a woman who murdered for money. The main point of interest in retrospect is Huish's admiration for the police. The detectives here are no longer villainous thief-takers or rustic boobies, but efficient and professional, presented for the read-er's admiration in both text and stylish illustrations.

Dickens wrote several articles for *Household Words* in the early 1850s eulogizing the new detective force. In 'A Detective Police Party' he reminded his readers of that exciting moment the previous year when the police had pursued the *Victoria* looking for the absconding Mrs Manning: a detective 'went below, with the captain, lamp in hand – it being dark, and the whole steerage abed and sea-sick – and engaged the Mrs. Manning who *was* on board ... Satisfied that she was not the object of his search, he quietly re-embarked in the Government steamer alongside, and steamed home again with the intelligence.' Dickens' admiration for the police was such that even this blind alley was presented as a coup.*

Shortly afterwards, in *Bleak House* (1852–53), Dickens created Mr Bucket, who has been described as the first fictional detective. It was in this novel that Dickens also immortalized Maria Manning, as Hortense, Lady Dedlock's maid. Dickens gave her all of Maria's char-acteristics (although she is French, not Swiss): she is dark, 'handsome',

---

* Sheridan Le Fanu used the same episode in *A Lost Name*, published nearly twenty years later, and otherwise based loosely on Jonathan Bradford (see pp.123–30).

with 'good taste' in her dress, and she abuses Bucket at the end in a similar manner to the abuse Maria hurled in court, 'With a stamp of her foot, and a menace', and a 'tigerish expression … her black eyes darting fire'.

Dickens had been progressively feeling his way towards detective-story elements from his early Newgate novel days. In *Oliver Twist* Mr Brownlow uncovers a mysterious plot against Oliver as detectives would do later on: he examines clues, produces witnesses, confronts the villain and explains the mystery to the listening characters and the reader. Yet Mr Brownlow was pre-modern: he had no intention of entering the legal forum of the police or the courtroom, or of exposing the child under his protection to the public gaze. The law was permitted to deal with Fagin, a lower-class, outsider villain;* Monks, Oliver's half-brother and therefore an upper-middle-class villain, is dealt with privately. The police, in the guise of the Bow Street Runners, have only a comedy role, and detect nothing. In *Martin Chuzzlewit* (1843–44), begun four years later, there are once more amateur detectives, John Westlock and Martin Chuzzlewit himself, who follow up clues in order to expose the perpetrator of a murder. Again, they solve their own problems, and never contemplate turning their information over to the police. Instead it is Nadgett who comes close to the prototype of the professional detective. At first he seems like an old-fashioned, Vidocq-ian informer, but slowly the reader learns that the ostensible spy is really on the side of the heroes.

In 1849, 'Recollections of a Police-Officer' by the pseudonymous 'Thomas Waters' (William Russell) had begun to appear in *Chambers's Edinburgh Journal*. These stories were perhaps the first to have a policeman protagonist, although in spirit they remain close to melodrama. In 'The Gamblers', for example, the narrator is a gentleman who turns policeman after being bankrupted by swindlers. He is assigned to break up a gambling ring, whose leader providentially turns out to be the 'glittering reptile in whose poisonous folds I had

---

* For artistic reasons Fagin was sentenced to hang, although as a fence his crime no longer carried the death penalty.

been involved and crushed'. No detection is involved.* The main difference between these stories and melodrama is that now the police are professional, doing a job 'which can scarcely be dispensed with'.

In *Bleak House* Dickens laid out how that job was done, now elaborating some of Nadgett's traits into the more rounded figure of Inspector Bucket 'of the Detective'. Nadgett had been all-seeing – 'every button on his coat might have been an eye; he saw so much'; he had been professional – the 'man, at a pound a week' who makes the 'inquiries'; and, as the best fictional detectives were soon to do, he was perpetually whipping in and out of disguises – he was, in dizzying succession, a coal merchant, wine merchant, commission agent and accountant. Mr Bucket develops these traits further: he is 'a sharp-eyed man – a quick, keen man – [who] takes in everybody's look at him, all at once, individually and collectively, in a manner that stamps him a remarkable man'. He can materialize in an almost ghost-like fashion: 'Time and place cannot bind Mr Bucket ... he is here today and gone tomorrow ... looking here and there, now from this side of the carriage, now from the other, now up at the house windows, now along the people's heads, nothing escapes him.'

It is generally accepted that Inspector Bucket was drawn from the mannerisms and appearance of Inspector Charles Field of the Detective Department, or 'Inspector Wield' as Dickens had dubbed him in 'A Detective Police Party'. 'Wield' was 'a middle-aged man of portly presence, with a large, moist, knowing eye, a husky voice, and a habit of emphasizing his conversation by the aid of a corpulent fore-finger, which is constantly in juxtaposition with his eyes or nose'. Mr Bucket, in turn, was a 'stoutly-built, steady looking, sharp-eyed man', whose 'fat forefinger seems to rise to the dignity of a familiar demon. He puts it to his ears, and it whispers information; he puts it to his lips, and it enjoins him to secresy [sic]; he rubs it over his nose, and it sharpens his scent ...' Dickens denied any connection – in 1853, when

---

* How far these stories still are from modern conventions can be seen in another story in the series, when the narrator policeman and his colleague capture a thief: 'with a dexterous twist [I] hurled him violently on the floor; another instant and my grasp was on the throat of Levasseur, and my pistol at his ear. "Hurrah!" we both shouted.' Hurrah indeed.

The Times wrote that he had used Field as a model, he responded, 'Allow me to assure you ... I found nothing more entirely and completely new to me than [this fact].' However, the letter is carefully worded: Dickens wrote that he did not 'avail' himself of 'that officer's experiences'; he did not say he had not availed himself of his person. The link was soon to be too well established in people's minds to be broken by a simple denial. A decade later Mark Lemon, the editor of *Punch* and a friend of Dickens, was telling people that 'Charley Field the detective, with his flabby hand and cool tongue ... traced Mrs Manning to a lodging, and tapped at door [sic] "Only me – Charley Field – so just open the door quietly, Maria." ' A fun story, even though Mrs Manning had actually been arrested by two Edinburgh officers, a Mr Moxey and his colleague.* Such was the fame of Dickens' creation that 'Inspector Field' by now almost meant 'detective'.

The most innovative use of Bucket was in the authorial voice Dickens used to tell of his investigation. For the most part, melodrama was driven by a plot that was deliberately laid out, and solved by coincidence, or the workings of providence. In *Bleak House*, at first the story has an omniscient narrator, so the reader has an overview of everyone's actions, but by the end we discover that Mr Bucket had suspected Lady Dedlock's maid Hortense all along. The trick ending, where all is revealed, soon a standard of detective literature, here appears for the first time: now the reader becomes fascinated not by the crime but by its solution, by the detection of crime.

As well as the novel's middle-class readership, *Bleak House* found a wide audience as a popular fairground marionette play. Unusually, a script for one version has survived. In *Poor Joe* most of the plot has been thrown overboard, and the story focuses on Inspector Bucket and his tracking down of the murderer, with the subplot given over to the death of Jo the crossing-sweeper. The marionettes, like the penny-gaffs where they often performed, gave performances lasting only

---

* Moxey was awarded £30 by the Treasury, and his assistant £5, 'for their active part in accomplishing the capture of Maria Manning'. Moxey divided his reward money between three charities.

twenty minutes each. Old Wild, one of the larger touring proprietors, had a ten-minute version of *The Dogs of the Plantation, or, A British Sailor in His Glory* that included six duels and a set of performing dogs. Inspector Bucket would have had little time to detect in his outings.

Dickens was not the only writer – not even the first writer – to use Mrs Manning as fodder for fiction. In 1851, the year before *Bleak House*, *The Gold-Worshippers: or, The Days We Live in. A Future Historical Novel* appeared. Here the anonymous author (Emma Robinson),* in the midst of what is primarily a social satire, has her main character, Mrs Sparkleton, visited by her ex-lady's maid. Mrs Redgold is 'a French femme de chambre, who had married an English railway guard', has 'a figure ... so tastefully and artistically dressed that it must have excited admiration in all' and lives in 'a little hovel of a residence in the Borough' (which is in Bermondsey). Nothing more is heard of her for a few hundred pages, when Mrs Sparkleton recollects that 'poor Mrs. Redgold is going to be hung to-day, and her husband with her ... They murdered some sort of an exciseman, or custom-house-officer for – for his railway Scrip,' having invited him to 'a dinner – for which she made no other preparation than a grave and a loaded pistol'. Then she vanishes again – she is simply a piece of murder tourism, or at best a symbolic warning against greed.

Murderous lady's maids with a physical resemblance to Mrs Manning had a small vogue around the mid-century, in both litera-ture and penny fiction. George Eliot, in her novella *The Lifted Veil*, depicts a tall, dark lady's maid, 'with a face handsome enough to give her coarse hard nature the odious finish of bold, self-confident coquetry', who buys poison in order to kill her mistress's husband. In Mrs Braddon's penny-blood *The Black Band, or, The Mysteries of*

---

* Emma Robinson (1814–90) published a series of historical novels before *The Gold-Worshippers*. In 1864 she returned to female murderers once more in *Madeleine Graham*, which was a highly coloured version of the life of Madeleine Smith (see pp.281–6). Little is known of Robinson's life. She was the daughter of a bookseller, wrote at least sixteen novels and died in the London County Lunatic Asylum, where she had been resident for some time.

Midnight, Rosine Rousel, a mysterious French lady's maid, previously in the employ of a titled family, 'attired in a black silk dress, which fitted tightly', attempts to murder her mistress. She is, like Mrs Manning, the brains of the operation, although as this is a penny-blood, it involves a pan-European criminal network. In other references the Mannings became shorthand for evil, or simply for a murderer. In Surtees' *Plain or Ringlets?*, a men's club is described as 'a place where they would very likely cut you up into quarters and drop you quietly over Blackfriars Bridge in the dead of the night,* or shoot you through the head and bury you in the back kitchen, as somebody did Mr. Manning, or Mr. Manning did somebody, I forget which way it was'.

In *The Woman in White* (1859–60), Wilkie Collins' phenomenally successful sensation-novel, one of the narrators, Marian Halcombe, records in a diary entry dated 15 June 1850 (that is, seven months after the Mannings were executed), 'I have asked whether Henry the Eighth was an amiable character? Whether Pope Alexander the Sixth was a good man? Whether Mr. Murderer and Mrs. Murderess Manning were not both unusually stout people …' This may be a feint, to lead the reader to assume that the Mannings were only of passing interest to the novelist. But Collins used the now-familiar details of Maria Manning's life for the back-history that is revealed when the fictional amateur detective approaches the 'Woman in White's' mother: Mrs Catherick had been a lady's maid in a grand family, involved with another man before she married and continuing in the relationship afterwards, and she used her husband as her dupe in her crime, while she was the controlling intelligence. Mrs Henry Wood, another sensation-novelist, used a similar character to Dickens' Hortense in *Mrs Halliburton's Troubles* (1862): Mlle Varsini, the governess in the family of a country solicitor, murders one of the sons in error after his brother has trifled with her affections. Like Mrs

---

* This was a reference to an 1857 case known as the Waterloo Carpet-Bag Mystery, in which a bag was found on Waterloo Bridge containing the cut-up body of a man. He was never identified.

Manning and her fictional sisters, she is dark, passionate and vindictive, and murders for reasons that can safely be isolated as 'foreign'.

Despite these frequent uses of Mrs Manning in fiction, she and her husband did not make good theatre. There were two versions of the story at the Britannia, *Marie de Roux, or, The Progress of Crime* in 1860, and *Hidden Guilt* in 1864. No copy of the latter seems to have survived, but *Marie de Roux* is a splendid farrago of melodramatic episodes, which keeps fairly closely to the story of the murder, apart from making Marie a young girl destined for a convent by her pious father, who manages (by accident, of course) to shoot him dead before she runs off with a vile seducer ('She is mine! Ha! Ha!'), her avenging brother hot on her trail.

As newspapers elaborated the Mannings' deeds, as broadsides gloated over the details, as theatres turned tragedy into melodrama, the perception became more pervasive that murder was ever-present, and in particular that female murderers were ready to kill on the slightest provocation. A series of panics swept the country – fear of poisoning being the most rampant, and the most fatal to the accused.

FIVE

Panic

It was odd that public anxiety fixated on poison, because murder by that means was barely a reality. In 1849 there were over 20,000 deaths in England and Wales that were unexplained or suspicious. Of these, 415 were linked to poison. After suicide and accidental poisonings were removed, charges were brought in only eleven cases involving possible murder by poison, and not all of these resulted in guilty verdicts. Intentional poisoning was thus suspected in fewer than 0.003 per cent of cases of suspicious deaths.

But poisoning was frightening because it involved intimacy. A stranger might bludgeon a passer-by to death – that was bad luck, being in the wrong place at the wrong time. To poison someone, the poisoner had to be intimate enough to give the victim food or drink. Who more natural to give food and drink than those who nurtured you – your family, or your servants? The idea of servants with malevolent intent was particularly frightening: servants lived with a family, they prepared the family's meals, washed the family's clothes, knew everything about the family's lives, but the family rarely knew much about their servants. A great deal could be projected onto this blank.

Eliza Fenning found this out. Her terrible story was inextricably bound up with class anxiety, with fear of the mob, with hierarchy and social structure. Eliza Fenning was born in 1793, the only surviving child of an Irish-born soldier-turned-potato-dealer living in London. She went out to service aged fourteen, and at twenty-one became cook in the household of Robert Turner, a law-stationer in

Chancery Lane. Only six weeks later, on 21 March 1815, after eating some dumplings, five people – Mr and Mrs Turner; Mr Turner's father, the wonderfully named Orlibar (sometimes Haldebart) Turner; Roger Gadsdell, the Turners' apprentice; and Eliza Fenning herself – all became violently ill. John Marshall, the family's apothecary-surgeon, arrived to find Mrs Fenning lying on the stairs 'in great agony'. 'I directed her to drink some milk and water,' he later testified, and for the family he prescribed Epsom salts and a mild purgative, and put them on a diet of milk, soda water and mutton broth. Soon everyone had recovered. Everyone recovered. No one died.

Orlibar Turner 'had a suspicion of arsenic' – why, is not recorded – and the following day he located the leftover dumpling mixture. 'I put some water into the pan, and stirred it up with a spoon ... upon the pan being set down for half a minute, upon my taking it up slowly, and in a slanting direction; I discovered a white powder at the bottom.' He showed this to John Marshall, who already distrusted Mrs Fenning: she had, he noted, 'most obstinately resisted all remedy' (that is, treatment from him), which he thought was sure 'proof of her guilt'. Marshall now cut up a leftover dumpling, put a slice 'on a polished halfpenny, and held [it] over the flame of a candle on the blade of a knife'. It exuded a garlicky smell, the knife turned black, and after it cooled the coin had 'a silvery whiteness'. When these powdery grains were put between polished copper plates and heated in the fire, they again gave off 'the alliaceous smell' and left a 'silvery whiteness' on the copper.

Marshall had no doubt that this indicated arsenic, although at the time it was possible to isolate arsenic in foodstuffs only if it was present in very large quantities.* About five times the lethal dose could be detected; smaller doses, which would still kill, were completely untraceable until 1836, when the Marsh test made it possible to isolate as little as a three-thousandth of a grain of arsenic (a

---

* Bernard Knight, a Home Office pathologist and professor of forensic pathology, doubts very much that any of Marshall's tests would indicate the presence of arsenic.

further refinement, the Reinsch test, was developed in 1841). Nevertheless, on 15 April 1815 Eliza Fenning was tried at the Old Bailey, charged with four counts of attempted murder.

The trial was heartbreaking. Modern ideas of what constitutes evidence have been so firmly internalized that it is difficult to see through to an earlier mindset. But it was only in the eighteenth century that legal and philosophical systems began to grapple with what constitutes proof, apart from directly witnessing an action. It was not until later in the nineteenth century that mathematics came to outweigh less tangible kinds of knowledge, such as perceptions of character. Before this there was no systematic attempt to address probability, or even plausibility, or the difference between presumption and proof. Eliza Fenning was born too early.

Charlotte Turner, the law-stationer's wife, testified first. Three weeks before the poisoning she had 'observed [Mrs Fenning] one night go into the young men's room partly undressed' (these men were Turner's two apprentices, who slept on the premises). After being reproved, Mrs Fenning 'failed in the respect that she before paid me', Mrs Turner found. She said that Mrs Fenning had been very pressing about making dumplings; although she did not particularly want them, she gave way. She thought that the dough had looked 'singular', and noticed it had failed to rise. Sarah Peer, the other servant, had not been in the kitchen while the dumpling dough was being made, she said, and she herself had been in and out. At dinner, 'I found myself affected in a few minutes in the stomach after I had eaten; I did not eat a quarter of a dumpling; I felt myself very faint, and an extreme burning pain, which increased every minute. It became so bad I was obliged to leave the table.'

After this, both the Turner men, father and son, testified that after eating they too had been sick. Orlibar Turner was asked by the prosecution if Mrs Fenning had given any assistance; 'None in the least,' he replied. He then went on to tell how he had found grainy material in the dumpling pan, which he had set aside for Marshall. He had asked Mrs Fenning if she had put anything in the dumplings, and she said the milk Sarah Peer had fetched had gone off. He also said there was a paper twist of arsenic in the office, which had been bought to kill rats, and was carefully marked 'poison'. Eliza Fenning, it was noted with some disapproval, could both read and write, and she might have opened that drawer in search of wastepaper to use when she lit the fire. He then produced from his pocket the two knives that had gone black to show the court.

The apprentice, Roger Gadsdell, said he had eaten some dumpling in the kitchen, together with some leftover bread and gravy. After Robert Turner told him he had been ill, Gadsdell said he had too: 'I was taken ill about ten minutes after but not so ill as to vomit.' He said he knew that the arsenic had been in the desk, and had gone missing about a fortnight previously. Sarah Peer testified that she had taken the yeast in when the brewer delivered it. John Marshall was the final witness: he said that he had arrived at the Turners' house at 8.45 that evening, sent for 'in a great hurry', that he found Mr and Mrs Turner 'very ill' ('Mr' here appears to refer to Robert Turner; Orlibar had perhaps already recovered), and showing symptoms 'such as would be produced by arsenic; I have no doubt of it by the symptoms; the prisoner also was ill, that was caused by the same'. Then the next day, when Orlibar Turner showed him the pan, 'I washed it with a tea-kettle of warm water ... decanted it off' and 'found half a tea spoon of white powder; I washed it a second time; I decidedly found it to be arsenic'.

That was the prosecution's case. At this period no summing-up by the defence was legally permitted; until the Prisoners' Counsel Act of 1836, those standing trial for felonies were forbidden access to any legal counsel at all, although this was, to a degree, permitted unofficially. The Fenning family did have legal advice, for which they paid two guineas, although their barrister left before the end of the trial. Four witnesses swore to Mrs Fenning's good character, and she made her own defence speech. It was, in its entirety: 'My lord, I am truly innocent of all the charge, as God is my witness; I am innocent, indeed I am; I liked my place, I was very comfortable; as to my master saying I did not assist him, I was too ill. I had no concern with the drawer at all; when I wanted a piece of paper I always asked for it.'* After conferring for ten minutes, the jury found her guilty, and Eliza Fenning was sentenced to death.

The case became a *cause célèbre*. Newspapers, now just coming into their own as independent sources of both news and opinion (not always particularly well separated), divided into two ferociously opposed camps. The *Observer*, a Loyalist paper, was against Mrs Fenning, and for the government and the legal establishment, as represented by the courts; the government-subsidized *Morning Post* was, unsurprisingly, of the same view. The *Examiner*, a Radical paper, was on Mrs Fenning's side, as was the *Traveller*, edited by the reformer and Radical publisher William Hone. *The Times* and the *Morning Chronicle* were less obviously biased in either direction, although they were happy to print any rumours that surfaced, and tended to the view that a middle-class person was to be believed before a working-class one. But it was early for newspapers really to get their teeth into the subject – that had to wait for Thurtell and Corder – and for the most part the crossfire was carried out in books and pamphlets. John Marshall wrote a pamphlet setting out a detailed case for the guilty verdict; almost all the other pamphlets (at any rate, almost all the ones that have survived) protested Mrs Fenning's innocence.

Marshall's pamphlet was extracted in *The Times*, which followed up with a précis of the various indications 'corroborating ... the guilt of Eliza Fenning'. These included: blushing when Mrs Turner told her that 'the dumplings were by no means what she expected', asking 'repeatedly' beforehand if Mr Turner were to dine at home, even eating the dumplings herself carried 'the strongest proof of her conviction; as, knowing she was the cause of the mischief, she was determined to destroy herself to evade justice'. There was more, said Marshall: Mrs Fenning's guilt was evident from the fact that she had not gone to Mrs Turner's assistance, 'as she naturally would have done

---

* This kind of defence was not unusual. Five years before Eliza Fenning's trial, the defence speech for Elizabeth Hinchcliff, a fourteen-year-old servant accused of attempting to poison her mistress and two others (again, there were no deaths), was, *in toto*: 'My mistress ill used me.' She was found guilty and sentenced to death, but unlike Eliza the jury added a recommendation of mercy 'on account of her age, and her parents being honest people'.

had she been innocent'; that when her box was searched after the accusation, she was found to possess 'an infamous book ... that explained the various methods of procuring abortion'; and, finally, that 'she having been frequently heard in the kitchen to say "She would have her spite out with her mistress", further illustrates the idea of premeditated revenge, and shews the depravity of her morals'. Altogether, *The Times* concluded, 'These facts serve to illustrate how greatly Mr. Turner and family have been exposed to unmerited rancour, by the artful and revengeful conduct of the wretch who has inflicted on them so much suffering and anxiety.'

The *Observer*, which was almost hysterically anti-Fenning, ran a series of articles including the 'facts' that '*her father and mother are both from Ireland,* and that they are BOTH ROMAN CATHOLICS', that she was from her youth onwards 'wayward and vicious', that she had been expelled from school for 'lying and lewd talk', that she had tried to poison a previous employer, and that she was of 'a very *amorous inclination*'. After the trial, it reported triumphantly, 'even in prison she showed evidence' of her bad character by writing 'lewd' letters 'in the most voluptuous language' to a fellow prisoner.

The *Observer* followed this up by refusing to carry advertisements for *The Important Results of an Elaborate Investigation into the Mysterious Case of Elizabeth Fenning ...*, written by John Watkins. Here, fourteen years before the founding of the Met, an ordinary jobbing author acted more like a detective than the police would as late as the 1840s. The pamphlet reproduced the trial transcript above Watkins' running commentary, in which he highlighted inconsistencies, improper questions or answers that made no sense. There were plenty of these. Orlibar Turner had testified that Mrs Fenning had not eaten any of the dumpling; Watkins noted that all he could properly testify was that he had not seen her eat any – Mrs Fenning, as a servant, ate separately from the family, in the kitchen. Watkins also noted that John Marshall, who was so vehemently convinced of Mrs Fenning's guilt, had not arrived for five or six hours after the first episode of sickness; another doctor had first treated the family, but had not been called as a witness, whether because his evidence did not suit the prosecution, or simply because they had failed to interview him, was not known.

Watkins went on to discuss things that occurred during the trial which were not taken down by the shorthand writer (this, therefore, is evidence we have from him alone). He recorded that Mrs Fenning's father had wanted to give evidence of the Turner family's earlier hostility to his daughter, but the Recorder, Sir John Silvester, had refused to permit this. Silvester had summed up heavily against Mrs Fenning, giving much weight to the fact that she had not gone to the aid of Mrs Turner: 'If poison had been given even to a dog, one would suppose that common humanity would have prompted us to assist it in its agonies.'* Watkins reminded his readers that the second servant, Sarah Peer, was there, a doctor was there, and Mrs Fenning herself was ill – a fact never denied by the prosecution. He further pointed out that hearsay evidence had been permitted; that no evidence of poisoning had been submitted; that the charge of attempted murder legally required that 'felonious intent' be shown, but no attempt had been made to do so. He added that both the clerk who took down the early depositions and the solicitor to the prosecuting barristers were both friends of Mr Turner, while John Marshall was a friend of their barrister.

But the real excellence of the pamphlet was in Watkins' examination of the scientific merits of the case. This was almost the first time in history that such forensic work was displayed in detail. John Marshall said that he had drawn off about half a teaspoon of arsenic from the leavings of the dough in the pan. This, estimated Watkins, would indicate that the four dumplings made from the dough had contained some 1,800 grains of arsenic. Five grains was generally considered to be a fatal dose (although occasionally death has occurred from as little as four grains). Therefore Mrs Turner would

* Silvester has been described by a modern historian as a notoriously prejudiced judge even in an age of prejudiced trials; he was also generally thought to exchange favourable verdicts for sexual favours. Even the *Morning Chronicle*, as fervent a believer as Silvester in law and order over the rights of citizens, acknowledged that he was not 'peculiarly calculated to inspire respect for the judicial office'.

have ingested enough to kill ten people, and Orlibar Turner enough to kill 120; yet, miraculously, neither had died. Watkins stated flatly that Marshall's proof for the presence of arsenic, that it turns a knife black, was wrong. (He also failed to note that Marshall wrote that yeast itself 'may tinge iron black', which, if true, would mean that any dumpling would turn a knife black.) Mrs Turner had presented the fact that the dumplings had not risen properly as evidence that they were poisoned; that, too, wrote Watkins, was not true: there was no evidence that arsenic stopped the action of yeast.

The courts had accepted statements from respectable (that is, middle-class) witnesses at face value, without questioning motives or sources of information, and the newspapers continued to do so. The *Morning Chronicle* thought that an employer should be believed by virtue of the fact that he was an employer. The *Observer* chose a more circular argument. There was no point in listening to Mrs Fenning or her supporters, it wrote: 'The ultimate fate of the criminal is the best proof that [her protestations of innocence have] no foundation in truth' – that is, Mrs Fenning was guilty because she had been found guilty.* Watkins disregarded social background and went looking for evidence. After Mrs Fenning's execution, Mr Turner made public a letter which stated that she had tried to poison one of her previous employers, a solicitor, and had attempted to cut the throat of another. Watkins questioned the solicitor, who said he had written this letter not because Mrs Fenning had tried to poison him, but because 'he thought Mr *Turner* had done what was proper, in *hanging the girl!* – as nobody would be safe if these *Irish* wretches were suffered to get into respectable families'. The woman whose throat she had attempted to cut told Watkins that she had never met Eliza Fenning, she had therefore never employed Eliza Fenning, and nobody, Eliza Fenning included, had ever attempted to cut her throat. Watkins followed up yet a third rumour – another case where it was claimed Mrs Fenning

* In 1867 Dickens commented on this type of view: 'The argument that the Government of the day hanged her [and therefore she must have been guilty] is stark imbecility. The Government of the day would have hanged anyone.'

had tried to poison an ex-employer – to find that this story originated with a man who remembered an incident one day when the water in his kettle frothed strangely, so it had been thrown away. He said, 'I don't say it was *Eliza Fenning* as did it; – it *mought* [sic] have been her, or it *mought* not; – I DON'T KNOW AS SHE LIVED WITH US AT THE TIME.'

There were other details Watkins missed that a twenty-first-century detective-fiction reader picks up automatically. Orlibar Turner went to the police office himself to fetch the police the day after the 'poisoning'. So despite his being ill for the five days he claimed, he was well enough the next day to go out. Much was made of the fact that Mrs Fenning was alone in the kitchen during the time the dumplings were made, but in court Mrs Turner testified that she had been in and out herself; Sarah Peer, she said, had not been there at all, but Mrs Peer said she had taken the yeast into the kitchen. Roger Gadsdell, the apprentice who had claimed to have been among those poisoned after eating a dumpling, had also grabbed – 'licked up' was Mrs Turner's phrase – 'three parts of a boat of sauce' and some bread. Having eaten his own dinner of beefsteak pie, he then went into the kitchen and illicitly gobbled down cold leftovers, including almost an entire sauce-boat of gravy. He was, he said, not as sick as Turner; he did not vomit. This appears to be a greedy boy who ate too much too quickly, and had a stomach ache.

In the aftermath of the trial several petitions were circulated, including at least two from the ministers and congregants at the chapel where Mrs Fenning worshipped (despite the *Observer*'s anti-Papist rhetoric, the Fennings were Dissenters). An unnamed man, whom Watkins identified as someone who had helped with the arsenic experiments, asked Orlibar Turner to sign a petition for mercy. Turner and his son both agreed to do so, until (here Watkins is the only source) Silvester warned them that if they did so, '*it will throw suspicion on the rest of your family!*'

Watkins was excoriated by many who saw danger in any questioning of authority. The *British Critic* began its review of the pamphlet: 'Of all the wretched attempts which have ever been made to shake the confidence of the people in the administration of public justice, this is the most audacious.' The review ended by rejecting reliance on physical evidence: whether arsenic turned knives black or prevented dough from rising was immaterial; what mattered was that it was 'well known' that Mrs Fenning was immoral, dissolute and untruthful, and, most tellingly, she had steadfastly refused to confess 'any of those sins of which she had been notoriously guilty'.

Fear of the mob was a major component in why no pardon was forthcoming. Fear of servants might have been mixed in too. Eliza Fenning was twenty-one at the time of the incident, relatively old by the standards of servants for lower-middle-class families (most worked through their adolescence, saved up and married in their early to mid-twenties). She had been in service for a third of her life. Charlotte Turner was only a year older, and had been married for eight months – both women were uneasily aware that Mrs Fenning knew more than Mrs Turner about running a house. According to *Eliza Fenning's own Narrative* (which was almost certainly not written by her), 'Mrs. Turner told me not to leave the kitchen, but I did not pay any attention to her in that respect, knowing I must leave it to do the remaining part of my work.' And as to Mrs Turner's testimony to the 'singular' appearance of the dumplings, 'it surprises me to think she pretends to know more about them than myself'.

Then there was the problem of her literacy. One of the newspapers cited by Watkins quoted a previous employer (the one whose water boiled so strangely) who said that he and his family had never trusted Mrs Fenning: there was nothing concrete against her except that she was 'deep' and she spent time '*reading*' – she even owned some 'handsome' volumes, which she claimed a previous mistress had given her, but 'was it *likely* that a *mistress* would give a SERVANT ... *such books* as them?' She was, in short, above herself. This was in tune with the general air of social menace. The day before the Turner family was taken ill, Napoleon had entered Paris after his escape from Elba. That same month, the House of Lords passed the hated Corn Laws: 42,000 residents in Westminster alone signed a petition in protest; the parish of St George's, Bloomsbury (the Fennings' vestry ward) sent another.

In June, while Mrs Fenning was awaiting execution, the battle of Waterloo could be said to have marked the end of Revolution and the embracing of reaction. The Radical press's linkage of Eliza Fenning with political disenfranchisement did not go unnoticed.

No one was going to step in to save this servant girl, who had no resources, financial or political. There was no mileage in it, and there was rather a lot of mileage in ensuring that 'the mob' saw what would happen to those who stepped out of line. The crowd outside Newgate on the day of Mrs Fenning's execution was vast – some reports put the figure as high as 45,000. Unlike many other executions, here was no ribaldry, no fairground atmosphere. This was widely felt to be judicial murder, and the spectators saw their presence as a gesture of solidarity with the Fenning family. Mrs Fenning had her own sense of drama, and dressed entirely in white. (When she was told that she might pray before leaving the prison, she carefully removed her overskirt, so that it would not be dirtied when she knelt.)

Because she had been convicted of attempted murder, not murder, after the execution her body was given back to her parents. (Or rather sold back. In a piece of bureaucratic savagery, the Fennings were presented with a bill for 14s.6d for 'Executioner's Fees, &c. Stripping [the body], use of Shell [a rough, temporary coffin]'.) Back at her parents' house, people queued for four days to file past her body. The *Observer*, still harping on the Catholic theme, reported that the family was holding a wake, and furthermore was charging viewers. Some visitors did give money: after the expense of the trial the bill for the executioner's fees was beyond her parents' resources, and they had had to borrow the cash to buy back their child's corpse.

Outside their house, the government forces – called the police by the newspapers, but probably a mixture of the watch and soldiers – blocked access, telling sympathizers that 'The *magistrates* have ordered that *nobody* shall go into the house.' When a few brave souls replied that 'The magistrates have no *right* to give such an order: it is … *illegal*,' they were threatened with 'much insulting language'. On 31 July Eliza Fenning's body was taken on its last journey. Up to 10,000 people used this opportunity to express their views. 'The streets were nearly impassable, every window was thronged, and in many places the tops of the houses were covered with spectators, most of whom appeared to sympathize in the feelings of her deeply afflicted parents.' *The Affecting Case of Eliza Fenning* gave the order of the funeral procession:

> The undertaker, with a white hat-band,
> THE BODY, IN A GREY COFFIN,
> carried by six men in black,
> covered with a rich pall, which was borne by
> Six young women dressed in white ...

The procession travelled from the Fennings' home in Red Lion Street, through Bloomsbury 'in a steady and solemn pace, with great propriety and decorum'. Even at the cemetery Eliza Fenning's parents were not allowed to mourn. Once more the papers reported police harassment, and 'soon after the corpse was lowered into the grave, a man dressed in livery [a servant], without a hat,* in violation of all decency, made use of an expression which excited the indignation of the crowd'. What he said is nowhere recorded, but the response to it is. The crowd, very decently considering how high emotions were running, waited until the family had left the graveyard. Then '"Shame! shame!" proceeded from every mouth, and many women followed him and spit several times in his face; the men shook him and pulled him by the ears; and all he could urge in extenuation of his offence was, that it was a *common saying*.'

Eliza Fenning was dead, but that did not mean she was forgotten. Many used her name for their own purposes. Anti-capital-punishment campaigners frequently referred to her case. So did a new campaign gathering force in the 1830s. Until this time, most coroners were either men of some social position, or legal professionals. Thomas

---

* It is hard to bear in mind quite how unrespectable appearing without a hat was. Had the man not been in livery, his hatlessness might have suggested that he was a beggar; dressed as he was, it might perhaps be used to indicate that he was drunk – there would be few other reasons for a respectably employed person to go hatless.

Wakley, the crusading founder of the medical journal the *Lancet*, was the spearhead of a movement to install medically trained coroners on the bench (himself included). T.W. Wansbrough, who in 1815 had published *An Authentic Narrative of the Conduct of Eliza Fenning …* *By the Gentleman who Attended Her*, in 1830 was the signatory of an open letter endorsing Wakley in his attempt to become Coroner for West Middlesex (a key position, as it covered much of London). The letter was printed as a bill, for posting in public places, and it prominently cited Eliza Fenning's well-known history, as 'it bears importantly on the question … *Ought not a Coroner to possess* CONSIDERABLE MEDICAL INFORMATION?'

Only the previous year the details of Mrs Fenning's story had been raked up again when Robert Turner died, supposedly making a death-bed confession to having poisoned the dumplings himself. Lurid details were now added, including a story that he had tried to buy arsenic, but was refused because he was showing obvious signs of insanity. (No one seems to have remembered the packet in his desk at home. It took a long time for John Watkins' lessons to be learned.) Another supposed deathbed confession was bruited about in 1857, when newspapers printed reports that a minister at Finsbury Chapel, in London, who had 'conversed and prayed' with Mrs Fenning in 1815 in Newgate, told the credulous that a baker, dying in a workhouse, had confessed to the crime. This story has all the hallmarks of newspaper fiction: the workhouse was unnamed, no reason was given for the poisoning, and the baker and minister evidently thought someone in the Turners' house had died as a result of the supposed crime. Finally, the report was at fourth hand – the baker told the matron who told a chapel elder who in turn told the minister who, by one of those providential coincidences that melodrama so loved, had prayed with Mrs Fenning forty years before. The appearance of this story in the summer of 1857 probably had more to do with the ongoing trial of Madeleine Smith for the murder of her lover in Glasgow (see pp.281–6) than with Eliza Fenning, dead for nearly half a century. Yet for all that, Eliza Fenning was a name to conjure with. Unlike Eugene Aram or Jonathan Bradford, no greyhounds or racehorses that I can discover were named for her, but the shipping lists do note that in October 1855 the *Eliza Fenning* was sitting 'off port Queenstown', having arrived from 'Caliao', Peru (now Cobh and Callao, respectively).*

Eliza Fenning the servant was vanishing, and a tidied-up, classed-up, version was appearing in her place to suit the entertainment market. In *The Affecting Case of Eliza Fenning*, the frontispiece of the dead woman was captioned 'Engraved from an Original Miniature Painting in the Possession of her Friend'. The woman wearing a stylish bonnet, an elegantly trimmed dress and a pearl necklace, and with an elaborate hair-do, is no more a picture of Eliza Fenning, even one drawn after the event, than the images adorning the penny broadsides.

A similar transformation was taking place in the theatre. In 1815, the month after Mrs Fenning's execution, Samuel James Arnold's *The Maid and the Magpye, or, Which is the Thief? A Musical Entertainment*, was produced at the Lyceum, in London, an adaptation of *La Pie Voleuse, ou, La Servante de Palaiseau*, by Louis-Charles Caigniez. In Arnold's version, Annette, a servant maid, is falsely accused by her mistress of stealing a silver spoon. Unable to explain that the spoon she has sold to a pedlar belonged to her father, an army deserter in hiding, she nobly says nothing, and only at the foot of the gallows is the thieving magpie's nest found, with her mistress's spoon still in it.†
The play was a success, with many productions in various adaptations over the next four decades, but in the months following Mrs Fenning's death this and two further adaptations were understood to have topical reference to the case. To ensure no opportunity was missed, William Hone published a script of *La Pie Voleuse. The Narrative of the Magpie; or, The Maid of Palaiseau … Founded upon the circumstance of an unfortunate female having been unjustly sentenced to death,*

---

* This is the only ship I have found named for a murderer (or attempted murderer). That it refers to this Eliza Fenning is almost beyond doubt: a name-search through the British Library's nineteenth-century British Newspapers database, which at the time of the search contained near-complete runs of forty-six newspaper titles, produced no other Eliza Fennings.

† Opera-goers will recognize that the French original was also the basis for Rossini's *La Gazza Ladra*, or *The Thieving Magpie*, which premiered at La Scala in 1817, and at the Haymarket Theatre in London in 1821.

on strong Presumptive Evidence. In this version Hone added, 'The sentiments principally applauded by the [theatre] audiences are printed in *italics* and CAPITALS.'

Soon, however, the play's connection with Eliza Fenning vanished from the consciousness of audiences, and it was frequently staged as a Christmas pantomime, while Pollock's added it to its toy-theatre productions. In this children's version, the printed stage sets and characters were in standard melodrama styles: the set for the farm is a routine pastoral view, the gaol cell would do credit to the dungeons of the Bastille in size and gloom, complete with jug of water on the floor and enormous fetters scattered about; while the paper performers include men with flags and women with garlands, presumably for a dance interlude, and Annette swoons as she is led to the gallows, followed by weeping women and a row of soldiers tippytoe-ing behind.

By 1823, jokes about Mrs Fenning could be made, at least theatrically. The Olympic's *Dolly and the Rat* was an anonymous burlesque set in a butcher's household. Dolly is the servant, loved by 'an amorous Tallow-Chandler', but she has eyes only for Dick, an apprentice boy. Mrs Brisket's white cap is stolen, appropriately for London, by a large rat rather than a magpie, and when she accuses Dolly of theft she is as unimpressed by notions of evidence and proof as the prosecutors of Mrs Fenning had been, saying: 'If it's no where [sic] to be found, it is as good as stolen to *me*.' Dick: 'That's a rum way of making people *thieves*.' As with *The Maid and the Magpye*, the animal thief is detected and everyone ends up happily ever after.

In 1837 there was an attempt to stage a version of the Fenning story at the Pavilion Theatre, but it was prevented by threats of legal action by the now-adult ex-apprentice Roger Gadsdell. 'Nothing would satisfy Mr. Gadsden [sic] but the withdrawal of the piece, on pain of criminal information. How we marvel that so shrewd a manager as Farrell, seeing that the drama contained nothing in the slightest degree prejudicial to the character of Mr. Gadsden, and his name having been taken out altogether, did not laugh at his threat, and proceed quietly with the representation of the piece,' wondered the *Satirist*.

In 1844, the Britannia produced *Charlotte Hayden, the Victim of Circumstance, or, The Maid, the Master and the Murderer*, a melodrama by George Dibdin Pitt. This is the story of a poor workhouse girl who is threatened by Enoch Grifford, the son of the workhouse master (there is also a dig at Marshall in the character of the workhouse doctor, whose patients '*obstinately recovered*' despite his treatments). Grifford senior, we learn, was bailiff to Charlotte's grandfather, and ruined him financially before driving him to suicide, after which he produced a forged will leaving everything to him. Now Charlotte's grandmother, also a workhouse inmate, has found the real will, and Enoch plans to murder her, leaving clues pointing to Charlotte. Charlotte flees to London, where she finds work as a servant. Enoch tracks her down and threatens her with exposure if she doesn't assist him in robbing her new employers. Charlotte, fleeing once more, is taken in by a kind publican. When Enoch rolls up looking for a drink, conveniently not only are the police hot on his trail, having captured his burglarious confederates, but he has foolishly neglected to destroy the will he murdered Charlotte's grandmother to obtain, and is now carrying it with him. Through a long concatenation of circumstances, a confession is forced from Enoch, the London employers show up to testify to Charlotte's goodness, all the other characters tumble back onstage to mutual cries of joy, horror or teeth-gnashing rage, as appropriate, and Charlotte makes a curtain speech to the audience, warning them not to judge by appearances.*

---

* It was this sort of melodrama that Jerome K. Jerome so sweetly mocked in the 1880s. He warned the melodrama villain about that risky last scene: 'In nine cases out of ten you would get off scot free but for this idiotic custom of yours [returning to the scene of the crime]. Do keep away from the place. Go abroad, or to the seaside when the last act begins, and stop there till it is over.' He also gave a list of rules of melodrama-land, which apply to *Charlotte Hayden* as well as many other melodramas:

'That if a man dies, without leaving a will, then all his property goes to the nearest villain ...

'That the accidental loss of the three and sixpenny copy of a marriage certificate annuls the marriage.

'That the evidence of one prejudiced witness, of shady antecedents, is quite sufficient to convict the most stainless and irreproachable gentleman of crimes for the committal of which he could have had no possible motive.

'But that this evidence may be rebutted, years afterwards, and the conviction quashed without further trial by the unsupported statement of the comic man.'

In the mid-1850s, another wave of interest in Eliza Fenning drew theatregoers. A playbill for *The Life and Death of Eliza Fenning! The Persecuted Servant Girl* at the Pavilion Theatre in 1854 stressed the innocence and goodness of 'the persecuted Servant'. 'The weeping Audience nightly testified by their tears and approval, their appreciation of this beautiful Drama of Real Life!' In the centre of the playbill was a picture of Mrs Fenning, with her arms pinioned, and a caption that read, 'I am innocent innocent.'

Eliza Fenning, The Victim of Circumstances picked up the phrase 'the victim of circumstances' from *Charlotte Hayden*, which was now closely linked to the Eliza Fenning story, particularly in the minor theatres, where much of the audience must have frequently felt themselves the victims of circumstances. This version is far more formulaic, opening in a rustic idyll, where the beautiful Eliza is the daughter of a retired sailor, while Squire Gordon, a villain and libertine, tells his steward to 'hire some ruffians, set fire to [their] cottage and hurl them all to destruction'. There follows a standard melodrama plot, until Eliza is found working as a servant, and the Eliza Fenning story is replayed. The trial and conviction are perfunctory, taking far less time than the scenes of rustic happiness or the comic interludes. In 1857 the Victoria produced another version, there was yet another at the Standard, in Shoreditch, and at least one more, at the Royal Colosseum in Leeds. The Victoria version is today perhaps most notable for Eliza muttering ominously, 'I never lived in a family where they had so many dumplings.'

These plays were all much of a muchness. After the initial *Maid and the Magpye* productions in the West End, Eliza Fenning's story became an entirely working-class subject. All the plays were melodramas, moving from expulsion from rural idyll to the evil city, where the virtuous girl is adrift and alone. Then, just as this rash of melodramas began to fade, Wilkie Collins produced a story for Dickens' decidedly middle-class *Household Words*. 'The Poisoned Meal', headed 'from the records of the French Courts', appeared in September–October 1858, and was later republished in *My Miscellanies* in a slightly abridged version. Collins told friends that he found the idea in Maurice-Méjan's

Receuil des Causes célèbres, 'a sort of French *Newgate Calendar* ... In [which] I found some of my best plots. *The Woman in White* was one.'

Collins was, however, being disingenuous. Firstly, he claimed he found 'the' volume on a French bookstall, although the edition with the *Woman in White* source is in twenty-one volumes. While major plot lines of *The Woman in White* did indeed derive from this source (see pp.289–93), Collins was using it as a distraction: the main source throughout 'The Poisoned Meal' is Eliza Fenning's story. Marie-Françoise-Victoire Salmon works as a servant for the Duparc family and Madame Duparc's parents, Monsieur and Madame de Beaulieu. She makes a hasty-pudding, Madame de Beaulieu dies after eating it, and the Duparc family claim to have been poisoned. Then the plot follows the original Fenning story much more closely than many of the British plays. There is bogus or tainted scientific evidence – the accuser claims to smell burning arsenic in the kitchen, although, 'When ... subsequently questioned on the subject ... he was quite unable to say what burnt arsenic smelt like' – and the 'white and shining' substance found in Marie's pockets is cavalierly handed around among all comers, as the blackened knives were. A maliciously prejudiced solicitor echoes Silvester, and the fear that reprieves bring justice into disrepute is repeated. This may have been the story of Marie-Françoise-Victoire Salmon, as Collins claimed – but it is impossible not also to see the story of Eliza Fenning.

There were, of course, servants who, unlike Eliza Fenning, did murder their employers. In 1840 the whole of upper-class London was convulsed when, in a small street off Park Lane, the body of the seventy-three-year-old Lord William Russell was found with his throat slit. Russell was the younger brother of the Duke of Bedford, and had had a fairly typical aristocratic life, representing the borough of Tavistock (a Bedford stronghold) in Parliament, and also living abroad for many years.

Russell, a widower, kept, by his family's standards, a small household: himself, a cook, a housemaid and his Swiss valet, Benjamin-François Courvoisier. Courvoisier had only worked for him for a little over a month when the murder occurred. On the day of the crime, Courvoisier told the housemaid that 'His Lordship is too fussy,' and that he was going to look for another position; later, he offered to go and buy the two women's evening beer, something he had never done previously. On the morning of 6 May 1840, the housemaid, always the first downstairs, found a warming pan lying in the hall outside Russell's bedroom door; the drawing room had been ransacked, and a trinket box lay by the front door, which was unlocked and unbolted. She roused the household, and Russell was found dead in his bed. Courvoisier, to his auditors' horror, exclaimed, 'My God, what shall I do? ... I will never get a place again!'*

Lord William's status demanded a response from the top, and Richard Mayne himself arrived when the local constable sent for a more senior policeman. Mayne appointed a detective from his Reserve division – those unofficial detectives who operated under his supervision. It was to be another two years before the Detective Department was established, but detective brains were already operating. The back door of the house had been forced, and initially it was thought that the front door had been used as the exit route. But the back was sheltered, while the front was overlooked – why had the thieves not left the way they had arrived? The intruders had been into the drawing room – the desk there had been ransacked – so why had none of the valuables in that room been taken? There were bloodstains on a carving knife, but it was found in its proper place on the sideboard: would an outsider have remembered the precise location, or was it more likely to have been replaced by someone who habitually put it there?

The police quickly decided that the marks on the back door had been made from the inside. The three servants were therefore separated and put under surveillance, while the house was searched for the stolen goods. Nothing was found, so Mayne went through lists he kept

* Dickens remembered this two decades later. In *Little Dorrit*, when Merdle, the crooked financier, commits suicide, his butler says, '... that is very unpleasant to the feelings of one in my position, as calculated to awaken prejudice; and I should wish to leave immediately'.

of policemen with special skills, and identified two who were particularly good at searches. It was, however, three days before a cavity
behind a pantry skirting board was discovered, stuffed with medals,
rings, gold and £10; then another cache, with more jewellery, was
located above a pipe. Courvoisier's room was searched twice, and
nothing – no stolen items, no bloodstained clothing – was found.
After the discovery in the pantry, a third search was made of his room,
and this time the police found a pair of bloodstained gloves in a box
under his bed. The box was examined a fourth time the next day, and
a bloodstained handkerchief and dicky (detachable shirt front) were
now discovered.

Courvoisier's guilt was by no means a given. The goods and the
bloody clothes were found in his room, but his very able defence
counsel* pointed out that it would be just as easy to believe that the
housemaid had committed the murder and then in the intervening
days had moved the items; or possibly the repeated searches only
slowly revealed incriminating items because the police, frustrated
at the lack of evidence, had planted them. Courvoisier's character
was vouched for in court by irreproachable sources, all of whom
had employed him over a period of time: a titled lady, an MP and
the impeccably prosperous owner of a hotel. The view was that he
may have been a thief, but it was not at all clear that he was a
murderer. Then, on the last day of the trial, a Madame Piolaine,
who managed a French hotel in Soho, identified Courvoisier as the
man who had left a sealed parcel with her the day after the murder.
Inside this parcel was Lord William's missing plate. This still proved
only that Courvoisier was a thief. But the new evidence shifted the
emotional weight of the trial. Courvoisier's cunning was extrapolated from his trip to buy beer for his fellow servants – people
speculated that he had drugged it, to give him a free hand. A guilty
verdict followed swiftly.

* Courvoisier's legal representation was provided by Sir George Beaumont, the art patron
whose paintings were a foundational gift to the National Gallery: his butler was
Courvoisier's uncle.

Legal discussions continued for some time after the trial, because after Madame Piolaine testified, Courvoisier may have admitted to his barrister, Charles Phillips, that he was guilty – or he may simply have admitted to the theft. Then as now, if he had admitted to murder, his barrister had a legal obligation to report this to the court. If, however, he had admitted only to theft, his counsel had no such obligation, as the charge was murder, not theft. We will never know, because Phillips at different times said that Courvoisier had confessed only to theft, or that he had confessed to murder, but not until the judges were ready to enter the court, when it was too late to notify them. Phillips was also criticized for asking one of the judges for advice on Courvoisier's confession. He agreed that he had asked for advice, but only from one of the judges who was sitting as an adviser. (This cannot be true: at the time of the case, but not of Phillips' later claim, all the judges sat together.) Phillips also complained that he had not been warned beforehand, as defence counsel was legally obliged to be, of Madame Piolaine's evidence; he was justifiably aggrieved that it was nonetheless allowed. After this trial Phillips moved into legal administration, abandoning his role as 'the prisoners' counsel', but his reputation was immortalized by Dickens as Mr Jaggers in *Great Expectations*: as a character Jaggers is hardly attractive, but in his unswerving commitment to his clients he could be said, ambiguously, to be heroic.

Despite Courvoisier's speedy arrest and conviction, the public response was critical of the police: 'The prevailing opinion seems to be that they [the police] have been very remiss in doing the things that they ought to have done, and there is much suspicion that they have been rather zealous in doing things that they ought not to have done.' This, in the *Satirist*, was a roundabout way of saying that in its view the police had planted the evidence. But then, as it noted, 'It doesn't follow, because Courvoisier is guilty, that the police might not have taken undue means to prove him so' – that is, just because the police acted illegally, it did not mean that Courvoisier was innocent. This was a popular take on the case, although Dickens was horrified by this slur, which 'stigmatis[ed] the men who, in the discharge of their duty, had been actively and vigilantly employed'. But the police were not blameless: after the trial one inspector was reprimanded for negligence, and two constables were sacked.

This might have been for poor searching, rather than corruption or evidence-planting. But the system of paying rewards for information leading to arrests and conviction to police as well as to disinterested citizens was seen as a problem. The rewards paid by the police to their own men on the satisfactory winding-up of a case tended to be small sums, as in the case of the Edinburgh officers who arrested Maria Manning. The public perception, however, came from fiction and the theatre, where the police not only received, but expected to receive, large sums by way of reward. As late as 1890, in the second outing for Sherlock Holmes, when the fleeing villains dump their stolen treasure overboard into the Thames, the police inspector says, 'There goes the reward!'

Throughout Courvoisier's case, interest was widespread, the more so because of the aristocratic background of the victim. The trial had been graced by a royal duke, an ambassador and countless upper-class ladies and gentlemen. Many more went sightseeing: 'Numbers of nobility,' reported the *Morning Chronicle*, 'have called at the house, in the hope of being allowed to see the room in which the murder was committed.'* A story circulated that Landseer had been commissioned by the Duchess of Bedford to paint a posthumous portrait of Russell, and that after 'he and the Duchess only were shut up with the murdered man', he was so overwhelmed that he 'went mad at his task and has never recovered his mind from that dreary date'.† For less aristocratic patrons, images of both Russell and Courvoisier were also readily available. One could purchase portraits of Courvoisier, Edward Oxford, one of the attempted assassins of Queen Victoria, 'Bailey' and

---

* No one saw this type of voyeurism as anything to be ashamed of: in *Bleak House* the three female heroines all pop their heads round a door to see where the mysterious Nemo died; in Mrs Braddon's *One Life, One Love*, a daughter even makes a detour to see the room where her own father was killed.

† Landseer did have a breakdown at this time, but less sensational triggers might have included a decade of overwork and the death of his mother a few months previously. Later in life he had no evil memories of these sessions: 'I like murders,' he said simply.

'R. Gould'.* 'Order the "SKETCHES IN NEWGATE!"' encouraged the advertisement.

Courvoisier's execution was socially dazzling. Noblemen, foreign aristocrats, including the Russian diplomat Count Nesselrode, a number of MPs, and the famous actor Edmund Kean all applied to watch it from the prison. Seats in nearby windows were going for five guineas each. Both Dickens and Thackeray were among the spectators. This was Dickens' first execution, and as with the Mannings nine years later he was revolted by it, describing it as 'a ghastly night in Hades with the demons', and writing four letters to the *Daily News* giving his reaction. Thackeray too transformed the experience into journalism, publishing 'Going to See a Man Hanged' in *Fraser's Magazine* a fortnight after the event. He had spent much of the night watching the crowd, particularly a rooftop full of 'tipsy, dissolute-looking young men'. He was thoughtful about how repeated horrors could numb the viewers' emotions: when the Cato Street conspirators had been executed in 1820, they were decapitated after death, and each head was held up to the crowd in turn, to display in time-honoured fashion the fate that awaited all traitors. Thackeray reported that the first head had produced a shudder of horror among the spectators; the second, interest; by the time the executioner fumbled the third, a wag in the crowd yelled 'Butter-fingers!' (Other accounts report the fumble, but not the joke, which is probably better interpreted as Thackeray's one-word distillation of the crowd's emotional temperature.)

The public executioner then had been John Foxen, who had died in 1829 and had been replaced by his junior, William Calcraft. Calcraft stayed in his post until he was forcibly retired in 1874, at the age of seventy-four. He was paid £50 a year, with an additional annual five-guinea retainer from Horsemonger Lane Gaol. Each execution there earned him one guinea, and he received £10 per execution elsewhere

---

* 'Bailey' may have been Richard Bailey, sentenced to death the previous year for the attempted murder of his wife. There were four 'R. Gould's who were found guilty at the Old Bailey alone in the previous twelve months, but none for murder.

in England. He probably earned far more than this in perks – the clothes of the executed were his to sell, as was the rope, and there were those who believed that touching the hand of an executed man would cure ailments, and were happy to pay the executioner for access. (The politician Gathorne-Hardy remembered as a boy in the late 1820s or early 1830s seeing people waiting to touch the hand of an executed man in Shrewsbury.)

Attitudes towards the hangman are vivid in traditional Punch and Judy shows:

JACK KETCH: Now, Mr. Punch, you are going to be executed by the British and Foreign laws of this and other countries, and you are to be hung up by the neck until you are dead – dead – dead …

[*Exeunt Hangman behind Scene, and re-enter, leading Punch slowly forth to the foot of the gallows. Punch comes most willingly, having no sense.*]

KETCH: Now, my boy, here is the corfin, here is the gibbet, and here is the pall.

PUNCH: There's the corfee-shop, there's giblets, and there's St. Paul's.

KETCH: Get out, young foolish! Now then, place your head in here.

PUNCH: What, up here?

KETCH: No; a little lower down …

PUNCH (*dodging the noose*): What, here?

KETCH: No, no; in there (*showing the noose again*) …

PUNCH: Please sir … do show me the way, for I never was hung before, and I don't know the way …

KETCH: Very well … Here, my boy! now, place your head in here, like this … this is the right and proper way … I'll take my head out, and I will place yours in … and when your head is in the rope, you must turn round to the ladies and gentlemen, and say – Good-bye; fare you well …

PUNCH (*quickly pulling the rope*): Good-bye; fare you well. (*Hangs the hangman*) …

That would have been a merciful death to many, for Calcraft was notoriously inept. He used the old-fashioned short drop, which strangled his victims slowly, rather than quickly breaking their necks. William Bousfield was an extreme example of the horrors of such an execution. In 1856 Bousfield was found guilty of murdering his wife and children. After his conviction he had had attempted suicide by throwing himself on the fire in his cell, and he was so badly burnt he had to be carried to the scaffold and placed in a chair over the drop. Calcraft had apparently received a threatening letter, so he fitted on the cap and rope, ran down under the scaffold, quickly drew the bolt and scurried off into the prison. Bousfield, from his seated position, could reach one of the wooden supports through the open drop, and propped himself up. Three times a warder pushed him off the support; three times the terrified man managed to find another foothold. Finally Calcraft returned, and while a warder pushed the doomed man from above, Calcraft grabbed his legs and held on to him until he had strangled to death.

In his essay on Courvoisier's death, Thackeray unconsciously relied in part on the vocabulary of the newspaper reports of executions. In newspapers, no one just walked to the scaffold, they walked with a 'firm step'; they either 'moaned piteously' or spoke their last words in a 'firm tone'. Thackeray did not free himself of this mindset entirely, but his description of Courvoisier as he emerged from the prison was horrifyingly, novelistically, believable: 'He opened his hands in a helpless kind of way … He turned his head here and there, and looked about him for an instant with a wild, imploring look. His mouth was contracted into a sort of pitiful smile.' That pathetically smiling figure haunted Thackeray. 'I must confess then … that the sight has left on my mind an extraordinary feeling of terror and shame … I came away … that morning with a disgust for murder, but it was for *the murder I saw done.*' Two weeks later, he continued to feel 'degraded at the brutal curiosity which took me to that brutal sight; and … I pray to Almighty God to cause this disgraceful sin to pass from among us, and to cleanse our land of blood'.

Some remained untouched by these stories, or at least kept their sympathy and their interest in different pockets. The ballad and broadside market did well with Courvoisier, particularly after a rumour began to circulate that in one of his confessions (he made three) he said that he had been influenced by reading about Jack Sheppard.* Broadsides poured out. 'The Awful Murder of Lord William Russell, MP' appeared on the day of the inquest, although the place of the inquest was given as 'Norwich', a fairly obvious error for Russell's London address, Norfolk Street, and a sign of the speed with which the sheet was produced. It reported Courvoisier giving evidence and then, further down the page, the breaking news that 'a man who had been in the service of the late Lord, has been taken into custody, but nothing has yet transpired as to the grounds of his apprehension'. The sheet (above) included an illustration of a man dead in his bed, but it was a stock image of a working-class room, with a rough

---

* This was reported everywhere, and did much to contribute to the banning of Jack Sheppard plays. *The Times* said that Courvoisier himself 'declared that he was indebted for the idea of committing this atrocious crime to *Jack Sheppard*'. A fortnight later, however, the paper printed a letter from Harrison Ainsworth, *Jack Sheppard*'s author, who indignantly rejected the entire story: 'I have taken means to ascertain the correctness of this report, and I find it utterly without foundation.' The following day, a Sheriff of London and Middlesex wrote to the *Morning Chronicle* contradicting Ainsworth, and a bad-tempered yes-he-did, no-he-didn't correspondence followed. The result, however, was that both the newspapers and the authorities began to attribute a swathe of crimes to the influence of fictional boy-bandits.

wooden bed, the only other furniture a crude chest of drawers, and a chair holding the owner's clothes. Similarly, a weekly journal illustrated Courvoisier's arrest with a portrait of him that replaced the reality of the liveried servant with an image of a prosperous, fashionably dressed man, with a high collar, elegant waistcoat and carefully curled hair. The visceral reality of the execution that Dickens and Thackeray reported was, by the time it reached print, infinitely malleable: a duke's brother's bedroom was reduced to a working-class lodging; a servant was transformed into a fashion plate. Death turned it all into journalism.

Sarah Thomas was another servant who killed her elderly employer, but her story inspired nothing but sympathy. Like both Eliza Fenning and Courvoisier, she had barely settled into her new place in Bristol when Elizabeth Jefferies, a notoriously sour and bad-tempered spinster, was found beaten to death, her house ransacked, in March 1849. Her dog had also been killed, and pushed down the privy, and her servant of seventy-two hours' standing had vanished. Sarah Thomas was seventeen or eighteen, with a 'round chubby face', and from a respectable labouring family. The police immediately searched her family home, where she was found hiding in the coal hole, together with a gold watch and chain, twenty-seven sovereigns and some change, a silver gravy spoon and five tablespoons, engraved with the initials 'EJ'.

At the magistrates' hearing, the neighbours reported that they had heard screaming from the house on the night when the murder was presumed to have taken place, but Miss Jefferies' 'infirmity of temper was well known', and they just banged on the wall with a stick. The next day Miss Thomas came bearing an apology from Miss Jefferies, claiming that the noise had been a cat yowling. The neighbour said she thought it had been the maid herself. 'I have heard you crying out in the yard,' she said, but Miss Thomas denied it, although she added, 'She is such a good-for-nothing woman ... that I can't live with her.'

The inquest reaffirmed the general view of Miss Jefferies. Her brother testified that he had not seen his sister for a year because of her bad temper. Lucy Chard, a previous servant, said that Miss Jefferies had refused to let her sit in any room that had a fire, and fed her only on rice, or a potato or two. The manager of an employment agency said she had sent servants daily for over a week, but either they refused to stay, or Miss Jefferies rejected them. Miss Thomas, without legal counsel, gave her story at the inquest: she had been sitting in the house when a former servant, whose name she gave variously as Maria Lewis or Maria Williams, appeared, saying that Miss Jefferies had refused to give her a character and that she was going to kill her. Snatching up a stone from the kitchen she disappeared upstairs; on her return, she made pancakes before killing the dog and vanishing into the night. An even more outlandish story was told by a child who said she had been at the pub next door with her uncle, a blind street musician, when a rifleman had entered Miss Jefferies' house, killing her with his sword, and hanging her head 'up to dry' before returning to the pub, where he sat placidly drinking. At this point the child had hysterics, and her uncle told the court that she was an epileptic, and insane.* The child added, as if in confirmation, 'I've seen many people killed ... The Rifles generally kill them.' She was dismissed and Sarah Thomas was charged with wilful murder.

At her trial the following month, the evidence of Miss Jefferies' appalling treatment of her servants piled up. The next-door neighbour had heard shouting and crying, and Miss Jefferies screaming that her new maid was a 'dirty hussy'. The former servant also appeared, with an alibi that made it impossible for her to have committed the murder, or even to have cooked pancakes, on the night in question. She did, however, confirm Miss Jefferies' behaviour: she herself had worked there less than two weeks. Lucy Chard testified that Miss Jefferies had threatened to beat her twice. Miss Thomas's defence now was that she had murdered her mistress, but as a reflex response, hitting out when Miss Jefferies beat

* Before the discovery of anti-convulsant drugs, frequent seizures led to progressive brain damage.

her.* The judge summed up unsympathetically, calling her story 'improbable'. The jury, while finding her guilty, added a recommendation to mercy because of her youth. The judge retorted tartly that he saw no reason to pass on the recommendation, and it took two men to remove the weeping girl from the court. After she had gone, the judge allowed that he would, after all, agree to the recommendation.

In gaol, Miss Thomas confessed to the crime once more, saying that the day after she arrived, Miss Jefferies had tried to hit her, then locked her in the kitchen all night. The next morning at five Miss Jefferies came downstairs to order a fire for her own room. That night Miss Thomas was told to sleep on the floor in her mistress's room, and the following morning she had crept down to the kitchen for the stone. Unlike the judge, most felt for the girl. Her parish priest wrote to the Queen; the Quakers petitioned the Secretary of State, as did the Young Men's Society. Three and a half thousand Bristol women – approximately 8 per cent of the women in the city – signed a petition for mercy.

The newspapers were one-sided for the murderer and against the victim. The *Era* editorialized that people too easily spoke of servants as 'the greatest plague of life'; while many of them were just that, many more were 'ill-used ... treated as mere animals ... tested sorely and severely ... poor, friendless, and almost helpless, women by nature, slaves by accident ... taken foul advantage of, and seldom appreciated'. On the employer's side, it added, 'Her fate was a terrible one ... [but] For MISS JEFFERIES, there is no sympathy. She lived miserably, and died deplorably, poor woman!' Like the *Era*, the *Manchester Guardian* described Miss Jefferies entirely negatively: she was 'tyrannical, peevish, and violent, and degraded herself by beating her servants'. She had been killed by 'three blows of a pebble' – an extraordinarily dismissive way to speak of being beaten to death. The

* It is not clear if she had legal representation. At the assize court, her counsel asked the judge if the money that had been found on her when she was arrested could be used for her defence. The judge asked if there was any evidence that she had been paid her wages; on hearing that there was not, he ruled that 'She has been in the service of Miss Jefferies but a very short time. I do not see that the money can be applicable to her defence.' There is no indication whether the counsel withdrew for lack of funds. Possibly her parents managed to find the requisite sum.

Observer also reported rumours which implicated drinkers at the pub next door and an unnamed ex-servant in a botched robbery – perhaps the only nineteenth-century murder case where the wild post-crime rumours were deployed in defence of the murderer.

This support made no difference. The legal establishment and its officials persisted in seeing Sarah Thomas as a stereotypical working-class murderer, evil and cunning rather than impulsive. During the inquest, the *Bristol Mercury* (otherwise very sympathetic) noted, in a standard phrase newspapers used for young, working-class accused, that she 'appeared to regard the investigation with indifference', interpreting dazed terror as hard-boiled criminality. Similarly the prison governor was offended by her behaviour on her last day of life. She was given paper and pen to write a farewell letter to her parents, but instead of the formal catalogue of contrition and remorse he expected, she drew a picture and printed the letters of the alphabet. She was, to a modern eye, a functional illiterate. The governor's middle-class sense of propriety was also disturbed when Mrs Thomas asked him to ensure that her child's clothes were returned to the family after her death; he lectured her on her 'want of feeling', but she failed to show 'correct appreciation of the advice'. Just as, evidently, he had no appreciation of the value represented by the clothes to a family who had probably sold all they had to pay for legal representation.

The execution was unimaginably horrible, even by the standards of the day. The *Bristol Mercury* described it as judicial murder, a 'public strangling'. In the run-up, as usual, there were plenty of commercial activities. The lessee of the Prince's Street bridge was outraged that the gaol had permitted barricades to be erected, blocking the view from the bridge, and thus preventing him from selling viewing spaces (he sued for compensation). More *ad hoc* activities were found in such fairground diversions as weighing machines, a 'standard' (yardstick) for measuring height, gingerbread- and nut-sellers, and broadside-sellers. To counter this atmosphere, the Bristol Religious Tract Society handed out 6,000 handbills.

The *Liverpool Mercury* estimated the crowd at 25,000 (Bristol's population was then approximately 135,000). When the governor went to fetch Sarah for the walk to the scaffold, 'She appeared greatly excited, stamped her feet, exclaimed several times, "I will not go! I will not go!" and added, if they meant to hang her, it should only be by force. The chaplain then tried his office with her, entreating her to be calm, and not to resist the execution of the law, but she persisted in her refusal ... [the governor] begged her to act on the chaplain's advice. She became quite frantic.' It took more than six officers to half-carry her, and 'She still resisted with all her might ... uttering piercing cries ... With great difficulty, and amidst a scene of the most painful nature, she was got into the press-room, where her arms were pinioned and she was ... implored to go to the gallows quietly, but she still said she would not.' She was finally carried up the stairs to the scaffold by two officers, screaming and struggling to the end. 'Though our reporter,' said the *Liverpool Mercury*, 'has witnessed many public executions, he states that this was the most harrowing and disgusting that he ever saw.' The *Daily News* followed its report of this dreadful death with a letter commenting on it: 'What a specimen would it be for some future historian of English civilisation, of English humanity ... [a] girl of 20 [she was in fact seventeen or eighteen], driven nearly to insanity by the appalling prospect of a violent death to one so young and so weak ... shrieking and desperate ... while the representative of civilised justice and the minister of a Christian creed looked on at the [legal] murder ...'

In the following year, two more cases emphasized the precariousness of a servant's life rather than her employer's. Mary Anne Parsons was, said *The Times* straightforwardly in March 1850, 'tortured to death' by her master and mistress, Robert and Sarah Bird, a farmer and his wife in north Devon. They had hired Mary Anne, a robust and healthy fourteen-year-old, from the Bideford Union workhouse at the end of September 1849.* On 4 January 1850 her corpse was discovered at the farmhouse, and a surgeon itemized bruises on her legs,

---

* Workhouse servants got lower wages than any other: they had no 'character', no references from other respectable middle-class people, and they had also lived in institutions, often for their whole lives, so they had no knowledge of how to run a middle-class house.

arms and chest, abscesses on one arm, the nails on one hand 'gone', the bone of one finger protruding through the skin, wounds on 'the posterior part of the hips', a bruise on the back of her head, and a head wound which was the direct cause of death.

At the trial, Mrs Parsons explained that she had placed her daughter in the workhouse after her husband had sailed for the West Indies four years previously, and had never been heard from again. After her child's death, she said, Mrs Bird had knelt, begging, 'Think … on me and my poor children, what will become of them [if there is an inquest]?' The local constable said he had heard Mr Bird tell Mrs Parsons that 'he would be a friend to the deceased's mother as long as she lived' if she said that her child should be buried without further investigation. The master of the workhouse, who had examined Mary Anne's body after death, said that he had been in the army, and recognized a flogging when he saw one. The rod with which she was beaten was described: it consisted of eighteen leather thongs tied to a stick, and was three feet long. Three witnesses testified to seeing the Birds inflict cruelties on the child; one saw her wiping away blood after she was 'corrected'. The defence case was that Mary Anne had been subject to 'giddy spells' and had fallen and hit her head on the fender. The Birds' solicitor argued that there was no evidence that any beating they had administered had caused her death, and if Bird 'had exceeded in a slight degree the limits … for the correction of his servant, there was no proof of … ill-will'.

The problem was the judge. *Bell's Life* said bluntly that the trial under his direction was a farce, and 'no man in his senses' thought the Birds innocent. The judge however told the jury that legally, 'as there was no means of knowing which of the two actually consummated the crime, they must both be exonerated'. This was recognizably wrong in law only four months after the Mannings were executed, each having claimed the other had killed O'Connor. But the jury, apparently reluctantly, felt obliged to acquit the Birds. The magistrates attempted to appease local outrage by committing them on another charge, 'felonious assault', but their solicitor successfully argued that this was double jeopardy. In August they were indicted again, charged with 'intent to wound … with the intent by such wounding to do her some grievous bodily harm'. They were, on an eight–six decision, found guilty, and while they were not given a custodial sentence, their solicitor asked if they might stay in gaol nonetheless: he was afraid they would be lynched as they left the court.

The case of Mary Anne Parsons caused national outrage, if only briefly. She was, however, immortalized by Dickens in *Bleak House* as Guster (Augusta), the workhouse child employed by Mr and Mrs Snagsby. They are not violent towards her, but Guster has fits, as Mary Anne had 'giddy spells'. Similarly Charley, the child laundress in the same novel, might perhaps have been drawn from the story of another oppressed child. In *Bleak House* the Smallweeds, a family of money-lenders and usurers, spend much care and time ensuring that Charley is fed as little as possible, putting together the dregs of teacups and scraps of mouldy bread for her meals. There is some resemblance here, in the lack of food, to Jane Wilbred, who like Charley happily did not die, but was rescued by the kindness of strangers.* Jane Wilbred, also a workhouse child, had lived for two years in the household of George Sloane, a special pleader (a type of solicitor), a man of unim-peachably good family, and his wife, an ex-dancer at the Italian Opera. One day in December 1850 a barrister with chambers in the same house as the Sloanes was told by his clerk of a girl there who looked as if she were starving; this good man questioned the porter, then followed up by consulting another lawyer. The two called on Sloane, and were admirably firm given that they were dealing with a profes-sional colleague: he 'must deliver up the girl in[to their] care, or take the consequences'. Sloane tried to bluster, but eventually handed Jane over. They called in a doctor, who reported that she was 'a mere skel-eton covered only with skin', that she was too weak to speak, and that she would inevitably have died within a few days had she not been

---

* There is, of course, a danger of overreading particular situations and cases onto fictional characters, and the link between Charley and the following case is perhaps too slight on its own; but the connection with Guster in the same novel makes the resemblance at least worth remarking on, if not stressing.

rescued. The magistrates were notified, and evidence of a sadism even more extreme than the Birds' unfolded: Jane had been surviving on a basin of broth daily; neither her single dress nor her bedding had been washed in two years, nor had she been paid; she had sometimes been forced to eat mustard, or pepper; she was not permitted to drink anything, including water, and as a consequence had once been beaten for drinking the water used to boil the cat's meat; Mr Sloane had 'often' watched when she was beaten; she had been forced to work naked from the waist up, while Mr Sloane watched; she had been refused permission to use the chamberpot more than once a day; when she had been unable to control her bowels to schedule, Mrs Sloane had made her 'eat [her] own dirt', Mr Sloane holding her while Mrs Sloane forced it down her throat.

The workhouse officials made a poor showing: at the first magistrates' hearing, the clerk to the West London Union (the workhouse) refused to appoint legal counsel on behalf of Jane Wilbred, 'as the expense would in all probability fall upon myself'. One of the aldermen indignantly pointed out that the Union had placed Jane in the Sloanes' house, and thus bore a moral responsibility for her well-being. 'The [parish] guardians are unwilling to move in the matter,' was the sole response. As Jane Wilbred was not dead, the Sloanes could be charged only with a misdemeanour. They pleaded guilty, and therefore no details emerged in court. They were sentenced to two years' imprisonment (without hard labour), and *Punch* gave·vent to most people's feelings: 'What a pity that [Jane Wilbred's] box ... had not been as roughly handled as JANE WILBRED'S suffering body! Had ... a riband valued twopence ... been taken therefrom by either of the SLOANES; then would the law have arrayed itself in tremendous terrors; then would it have pronounced imprisonment – transportation it might be ... But it was only human flesh that was striped; only human feelings that were outraged ... How lucky for the SLOANES that they ill-used only JANE WILBRED, and spared JANE WILBRED'S box!'

Jane Wilbred briefly became a national heroine. Three hundred pounds was collected for her, together with the offer of a 'respectable' situation. A racehorse was named for her – the only racehorse that I am aware of named for a victim, rather than for a murderer.* One broadside-seller at least reported that the Sloanes were a paying proposition, and worth producing an elaborate illustration board for, although 'Sloane was too disgusting for the gentry'. Some broadsides found even the extraordinary facts not extraordinary enough, and suddenly 'We discovered, because we must be in advance of the papers ... Jane Wilbred was Mrs. Sloane's daughter by a former husband, and was entitled to 1,000*l.* by rights.' Shortly after the Sloanes were sentenced, *Reynolds's Miscellany* published the story of 'Bertha Grey, The Parish Apprentice-Girl; or, Six Illustrations of Cruelty'. In July the Bower Saloon in the East End staged *Bertha Grey, the Pauper Child, or, The Death Fetch* (a fetch was a ghostly apparition of someone still living). This framed the story of an evil woman maltreating her parish servants – 'We have whips, chains, and cellars for the refractory' – in a standard melodrama, so that now Bertha becomes the missing daughter of a baronet.

The parish's cool response to Jane Wilbred's torture was not unexpected. While that case was being heard, another was vividly demonstrating the lack of legal obligation to ensure that those under parish oversight were protected. As we saw with the Mannings, 1849 was a cholera year. Yet Tooting, in the south-west corner of London, was a relatively healthful spot. No one in the neighbourhood showed any symptoms of cholera. No one, that is, except the children who were lodged at Drouet's asylum. 'Asylum' was the formal name for what were colloquially known as baby-farms – places where unwanted babies were farmed out. Sometimes a baby-farm was a woman looking after a handful of children in her own lodgings; at others, as with Drouet, the farm operated on an industrial scale. In general, the smaller farms looked after the children of parents who worked long hours, and thus could not care for them, or the illegitimate children of unmarried women, or the children of women with second

---

* A greyhound was named for Maria Marten, but to my knowledge no horse.

husbands who did not want to spend money on the offspring of a previous husband. The larger farms were stocked by parish workhouses. Under the Poor Laws, pauper children were trained to go out to work as swiftly as possible, and for large workhouses in big cities, farming the children out for a subsidy was often cheaper than raising them until they were old enough for full-time employment, the asylums acting as middlemen, finding work that the small children would do in the name of 'training', and keeping the cash.

Bartholomew Peter Drouet had first come to the attention of Holborn Union in 1847, when he offered to take as many children as the workhouse wanted to farm out. He had, he said, 'five schools conducted by competent teachers, and the Chaplain; various trades are taught by well-conducted masters ... the girls being carefully instructed in needlework, laundry, washing, and the general household work'. The parish clerk responded positively, offering 4s. per child per week: 'they are earning us, and will be earning you, very considerably', he reminded Drouet. The Holborn Union decanted eighty-one children aged between six and fourteen onto Drouet that month; another thirty the following week. At the end of the month the clerk, six Poor Law guardians and the chairman visited Tooting to inspect 'every part' of Drouet's 'school', and reported their 'entire satisfaction at the whole of the arrangements'. More and more children flowed from Holborn to Tooting.

In May 1848 the board visited once more, and this time noticed that some of the children looked sickly, which 'induced us to question them as to whether they had any cause of complaint as to supply of food or otherwise'. Forty clearly very brave boys held up their hands – the parish overseers had asked this question in Drouet's presence, and so confident was he of his position that despite the presence of the board members, he 'became violent' and threatened to flog the children then and there. When the guardians protested he told them he would be only too happy to return the children to their workhouse. The guardians crumpled, or, in the clerk's more face-saving words, 'To avoid further altercation, we left' – leaving, he neglected to mention, the children to their fate. Different officials appeared a few days later, and without apparent qualm signed a report saying that they had inspected everything, and all was in order. It was only the cholera outbreak that summoned the Holborn guardians back. They removed 155 of the children, leaving behind thirty who were too ill to be moved. One of the 155 died almost immediately, and more followed. A post-mortem on the first child showed signs of emaciation 'produced doubtless by being improperly ... fed, clothed and lodged; the appearances were consistent with that'.

Luckily the child had died in Middlesex, where Thomas Wakley was the coroner. Another eighty children had died in Tooting, but the Surrey coroner had seen no need for inquests. When Wakley began to investigate, the scale of the horror, and its confinement to Drouet's children, became clear. There was no cholera in Tooting itself, and the disease infected only one of the fifty adults at the asylum: something had made the children terrifyingly prone to infection, and unable to fight off the disease once it struck. Furthermore, the children who had been removed from Tooting for the most part recovered, while a quarter of those left behind died. Inspectors arrived to examine not only the dead and dying, but also their food and water, and their living quarters. There was, they noted grimly, a stagnant ditch at the back of the asylum, measuring three feet by twenty and full of 'filth and refuse' (human waste and rubbish) despatched routinely from the County of Surrey Lunatic Asylum, a quarter of a mile away, and collected by Drouet to be resold as manure.

On 8 January 1849, a surgeon reported that 160 children were lying ill four or five to a bed at the asylum; he did not blame Drouet directly, but did indicate that 'inadequate' medical treatment 'at the outset', and children being weakened by being 'too much exposed to the cold', were responsible. By 9 January the finger of blame began to find its target. Drouet attributed the outbreak to a fog that had been hanging over the district (at this stage medical wisdom attributed cholera to atmospheric causes). The Chairman of the Board of Directors of the parish of St Luke's (which had also farmed children out to Drouet) replied tartly that if fog were responsible, why was no one else in Tooting stricken? It was, he said, 'principally, if not entirely from overcrowding on the one hand, and poor living on the other'. He added that they were paying Drouet 4s.6d. a week per child, and that with the income of the children's labour, Drouet ought to be making 1s. a week per child, after feeding and clothing them. (If this was true, Drouet's income would have been in the region of £3,000 a year, a fabulous sum.)

On 10 January, the surgeon employed by Drouet announced that the cholera was decreasing. The *Daily News* revealed the breathtaking cynicism behind this statement: the absolute number of cholera cases in the asylum *had* dropped sharply – because a thousand children had been removed by their parishes. By the thirteenth, the newspapers were referring to the 'Massacre of the Innocents': that day the inquest opened on the first Holborn Union child, and Thomas Wakley went on the attack. The Medical Inspector of the General Board of Health read a report on conditions at the asylum: Drouet employed one doctor, aged twenty-five, for 1,370 children. There were thirty-five ill boys in twenty-five beds, in a room ventilated by one window and lit by a single candle. The girls were even worse off, lying four or five to a bed, in a room awash with vomit and faecal matter (cholera causes both diarrhoea and vomiting). After the parish doctor made strong representations (the report implies he had repeatedly to ask for this), two nurses were brought in to look after 178 patients; the four female wards had one nurse between them. The Medical Inspector had told Drouet that each ward of more than twelve needed four nurses; Drouet took this to mean four nurses for the 1,370 children. The inspector finished up by accusing Drouet of 'great neglect', indifference to the orders of the Poor Law commissions, and obstructing the inquiry. The inquest now heard of systematized neglect, cruelty, and of intimidation of the children. The jury quickly found a verdict of manslaughter, and added a rider that the guardians of the Union were negligent. Wakley approved of both the verdict and the additional comment. The spectators applauded.

The cholera broke out at Drouet's asylum, concluded the *Examiner*, 'because it was brutally conducted, vilely kept, preposterously inspected, dishonestly defended, a disgrace to a Christian community, and a stain upon a civilized land'. The rhythm and swing of this should identify its author: yet again, Charles Dickens in the thick of a murder. Dickens' friend Forster had written reviews for the paper (and would later be its editor). It was a logical place for him to publish his passionate views on Drouet, and he reported from the early deaths to the trial verdict.

The trial, sadly, was a farce, and Dickens' third piece, 'A Recorder's Charge', was written specifically to counter the opening speech of Baron Platt, the Recorder. Wakley, as pioneers will, had made many enemies; he was also a Chartist, which no doubt offended the Tory Recorder. The charge against Drouet was not for neglect, but for 'felonious killing', and the Recorder was very obviously on Drouet's side: he refused to hear evidence on the treatment of the other children who had died, and rejected questions about what had happened to the children's warm clothes when they arrived (the implication was that Drouet sold them). When a poor-law inspector said he had seen no ventilation holes in the children's rooms, the Recorder said he would allow the comment to go on the record only if the inspector was ready to swear absolutely that there were none, not just that he had seen none. He rejected ancillary evidence about the condition of the wards, because no one could say which ward the dead child had been in. The defence was simple: the prosecution could not prove that the child would not have died by disease alone, and in truth the absence of any care at the asylum ensured that there were no witnesses to testify to contributing factors. Drouet was therefore acquitted.

General opinion was that he had, literally, got away with murder. (Not for long: he died three months after the verdict.) The working classes cynically understood what respectability could buy. *The Times* reported that a woman charged with being part of a gang of robbers had 'with much impudence' said that 'Had I committed as many murders as Mr. Drouet I should have been acquitted.' Schools and other establishments that looked after children long remained bywords for suspicion. As late as 1902, in *The Hound of the Baskervilles*, Conan Doyle strongly indicated that a character was going to turn out to be the villain by making him the proprietor of a school where 'a serious epidemic broke out ... and three of the boys died', a school which had come 'to grief under atrocious circumstances'.

Dickens did his best to ensure that these small hostages to fortune were not forgotten. He had long written about the lack of care for orphaned or unwanted children – *Nicholas Nickleby* (1838–39), with its depiction of the infamous Dotheboys Hall, was the most memorable. Now he was perhaps impelled by his own memories, writing the articles for the *Examiner* just three months before the serialization of *David Copperfield* began, in which he wrote for the first time, albeit in fictional form, about his miserable, lonely childhood months working in the blacking factory after his father's imprisonment for debt. In non-fiction, in the *Examiner*, he berated 'Mr Baron Platt ... [who] took the very first opportunity of siding with the stronger. Witnesses that required encouragement ... he brow-beated [sic]; and witnesses that could do without it, he insulted or ridiculed.' (On the contrary, stoutly riposted the ultra-High Tory *John Bull* – its motto: 'For God, the Sovereign, and the People' – Platt was a 'fearless and determined lover of justice, and one specially anxious to prove himself such on behalf of the poor and oppressed'.) He returned to the subject three times in *Household Words* in 1850, and once more in 1853. Finally, and most enduringly, he created Jo the crossing-sweeper in *Bleak House*. After a case in Lewes in 1852, where a child was not permitted to testify because he was said not to understand the meaning of swearing an oath, Jo, similarly, at the 'inkwich' [inquest] in *Bleak House* can only say, too, that he does not know what an oath is, although he knows 'a broom's a broom, and ... it's wicked to tell a lie. Don't recollect who told him about the broom or about the lie, but knows both.' In the same novel, Guster, the little maid-of-all-work, was partly drawn from Mary Anne Parsons, but was also given Drouet as her fictional guardian, having been 'farmed or contracted for, during her growing time, by an amiable benefactor ... resident at Tooting'. In one of Dickens' most delicate moments of grace, when she meets Jo, the starving crossing-sweeper, 'this orphan charge of the Christian saint whose shrine was at Tooting' gives him a piece of bread and pats him on the shoulder, 'the first time in his life that any decent hand has been so laid upon him'. Thus the offscouring of the parish, flushed out to Tooting as waste, was raised above her parish masters in her understanding of the meaning of faith, hope and charity.

The death of children was one thing: children held down jobs and earned money. The death of infants was something else. Perhaps unexpectedly Punch and Judy best reflect the attitude to the murder of babies for much of the nineteenth century. An 1854 Punch and Judy script has Punch holding the baby, who begins to cry.

> PUNCH (*hitting him*): Be quiet! Bless him, he's got his father's nose! (*The Child seizes Punch by the nose.*) Murder! Let go! There, go to your mother, if you can't be good. (*Throws Child out of window ...*)
> [*Judy enters*]
> JUDY: Where's the boy?
> PUNCH: The boy?
> JUDY: Yes.
> PUNCH: What! didn't you catch him?
> JUDY: Catch him?
> PUNCH. Yes; I threw him out of window. I thought you might be passing.
> JUDY: Oh! my poor child! Oh! my poor child!
> PUNCH: Why, he was as much mine as yours.
> JUDY: But you shall pay for it; I'll tear your eyes out.
> PUNCH: Root-to-to-to-to-oo-it! (*Kills her at a blow.*)
> PROPRIETOR: Mr. Punch, you 'ave committed a barbarous and cruel murder and you must hanswer for it to the laws of your country.

Mr Punch is arrested and charged with murder when he kills Judy. No one mentions, then or later, the murder of the baby. This was not simply comedy. Sir James Fitzjames Stephen said to the Royal Commission on Capital Punishment in 1866, 'The crime [of infanticide] is less serious than other kinds of murder.'* In 1870, the *Pall Mall Gazette* indicated that public opinion was in accord: 'Juries … have never regarded infanticide quite as murder.' For the act to be 'not quite' murder, a particular set of social circumstances had to obtain: the baby had to be newborn; it had to be killed by its own mother; and usually the mother had to be unmarried. If these conditions were not met – if an older child were killed, or a woman killed someone else's child, or her own legitimate child – then popular opinion regarded the act as murder.

Public opinion aside, legally there was no crime called infanticide: murder was murder, said the 1803 Offences Against the Person Act. If it could be proved that a child had been born alive, then killing it was murder; if a live birth could not be proved, then from 1828 a charge of 'concealment of birth' could be brought against the mother. The law, however, failed to define what constituted a live birth: if the baby cried? breathed? While it was generally accepted that the laws governing infanticide were not clear, no effort was made to clarify them: their fuzziness permitted leeway in handing down verdicts on women who had few options.

And for many women, all their options were as desperate as murder. Children taken into the workhouse were separated from their parents and raised as institutionalized waifs, constantly told what a burden they were, or farmed out to Drouet clones to survive as best they could. Servants could not have children living with them. If there were no relatives to care for a child, then a quick death for the child might seem a better solution than slow starvation for both the mother and child.

Thus the sudden death of an infant frequently suited everyone: it cost the parish nothing; the mother could go back to work; and employers did not lose their servants. The Church, too, sometimes appeared to agree that it was better all round if these children died. A

---

* At the time of this Royal Commission, Stephen was a successful barrister, had published *The General View of the Criminal Laws of England* (1863), and was also a contributor to the *Saturday Review* and the *Pall Mall Gazette*. He would later become a High Court judge, and he worked closely on the legislation for the creation of a court of appeal.

clergyman preaching after the death of Maria Marten in the Red Barn told his congregation that, although she was a fallen woman, 'a forbearing Providence still dealt kindly with her. The child she bore was taken from her by death – leaving her in a situation, in which ... she might very easily have returned to the path of honest industry.' It is easy to see from this why women might think the death of a baby would be ignored if possible. If a death was brought to official attention, then the woman was frequently charged with concealment, which carried a light sentence, if any: at the Old Bailey between 1840 and 1860, sixty concealment charges saw not one guilty verdict. This was the pattern everywhere. In Kent, no woman was convicted of murder of a newborn between 1859 and 1880; and while 62 per cent of those charged with concealment were found guilty, of these, 86 per cent received a sentence of less than six months.

Wherever possible, judges and juries tried to acquit. In one example of many, Mary Weston, a nineteen-year-old servant in Staffordshire, was charged with murdering her baby in 1842. She had gone into labour in her employers' house, and asked a fellow maidservant for help, but the girl was frightened and left her to give birth alone. She put the baby in an 'earthenware vessel' (presumably a euphemism for a chamberpot) and tried to bury it, but the ground was frozen, she was discovered and charged with murder or concealment. Her fellow servant said she had heard the baby cry, so it had been born alive, but the judge disagreed: even if the child had been born alive, the mother might not have known, and therefore malice, a necessary part of a murder conviction, could not be proved; at the same time, she could not be convicted of concealing the birth because she had asked for help – the very opposite of concealment. Thus she was acquitted. Even when convictions were unavoidable, sentences could be light. Julia Moss, a servant in south London, gave birth secretly at work (this is a recurring motif in infanticide cases: 83 per cent of women charged with concealment were servants). She put the baby in a box and threw it out of the window onto a neighbour's roof, where it was found. The baby's skull was fractured, which possibly contributed to the guilty verdict. The sentence: three months' hard labour.

Yet while the crime was, in general, both sympathetically under-stood – these women were not killing out of viciousness, but in order to survive – and hardly ever prosecuted with full rigour, at the same time two opposing forces were attempting to have infanticide treated with more seriousness. Thomas Wakley was one of the leaders of this campaign. Police records were more comprehensive after 1829, and together with the growing number of newspapers, this produced an increasing number of stories of babies 'found dead'. Wakley estimated that there was probably one additional undiscovered death for every death brought to official notice, giving an estimated three hundred suspicious infant deaths a year in London. Others were less measured: twenty years later, Wakley's successor as coroner, Edwin Lankester, suggested that in London the number hovered around 12,000 suspicious infant deaths a year.*

Part of the problem of ascertaining the true quantity was that the magistrates of each district controlled the expenses of inquests. Thus doctors were frequently told that there was no money to pay for post-mortems. In 1845, after Sarah Freeman's illegitimate child had died (see p.237), the local surgeon was told by the coroner that 'the magistrates were particular as regarded the expenses', and would refuse to pay for a post-mortem.

The press, naturally, followed their own sensationalist agenda, anxious to interpret any unexplained death as suspicious. In this they were aided by men like Lankester, and the Revd Henry Humble, who reported in 1866: 'Bundles are left lying about the streets, which people will not touch, lest the too familiar object – a dead body – should be revealed, perchance with a ... woman's garter around its throat.' He then repeated Lankester's figure of 12,000 suspicious

---

* This makes Lankester sound a bit mad. The Middlesex magistrates had refused to fund his plans to promote improved health and social care; his inflated figure may have been an attempt to make it impossible for them to withhold the money. If for nothing else, Lankester should be remembered as the parish official who supported John Snow in 1849, when he isolated the Broad Street pump as the source of the cholera ravaging the district. Lankester persuaded his fellow vestrymen to pay for a 'cholera committee' to investigate the results of an epidemiological report he commissioned, and also his own microscopic examination of the contaminated water.

infant deaths in London every year, which, he clarified, meant that 'one in every thirty women … is a murderess'.

Instead of considering how unlikely this was, the newspapers produced ever more elaborate tales of wanton infant murder. Whichever way you looked at infanticide, there was a possible – or probable – overreaction. Infant mortality rates in some parts of the country were as high as one in every two children born; illegitimate children had even less chance, with 60 to 90 per cent dying before the age of five. But did this indicate murder, or simply poverty and its inseparable friends, crowded housing, poor food, contaminated water, failing hygiene and rampant disease? Were the low conviction rates for concealment, and the almost non-existent conviction rates for murder, an indication that juries were anxious not to convict guilty women, or an indication that over-zealous inquest juries were committing innocent women for trial? In 1857 Thomas Laycock, a professor of clinical medicine, published a series of introductory lectures for medical students: 'You have to collect evidence,' he told them, '… penetrate disguises … sift conflicting statements … reconcile impossibilities.' Just as the police needed to be more rigorously scientific, so the scientists had to detect better. The question remains: was there anything to detect? Evil people perpetrating evil deeds were more comfortable to contemplate than the reality of poverty, chronically low wages, and lack of a structure to support the children of working women. These things would be hard to solve; accusing a wicked parent was easy. This may have been the precipitating factor in the creation of the idea of infant-murder for gain – the burial-society murder, which soon became almost completely unquestioned.

In the eighteenth century, Friendly Societies had been devised to help the prudent cope with misfortune: for a small weekly sum, a worker could protect himself and his family against the consequences of unemployment or illness. Sometimes professional companies, but more frequently informal groups run out of taverns or by undertakers, were established so that, in case of death in the family, the funeral expenses were paid for from a general fund in exchange for as little as ½d. a week per person. The Anatomy Act of 1832, aiming to end the resurrection trade, had established that, as well as the bodies of executed criminals, any body buried at the parish's expense could be handed to anatomy schools for dissection. This was a further goad to be prudent and guard against the expenses of sudden death.

By 1858 there were 20,000 registered Friendly Societies in Britain, with two million members. But there were many more informal organizations, and these were the ones around which rumours swirled. Most clubs would not insure a child at birth – infant mortality was too high for that – and the more respectable the insuring body, the later the age at which it would accept enrolment. The Prudential took children at three months, and paid out only if the child died after a 1*d*. contribution had been made weekly for at least three months – even then, the payment was only 10*s*. After a year, that rose to £1, and £2 at two years. Many children were enrolled in more than one scheme. This could be for devious reasons – to collect more money at their death than any single institution would pay out. Or it could be for pragmatic ones – many small clubs were bankrupted by epidemics, or were prone to mismanagement or embezzlement by their unlicensed officials. Spreading the risk was a sensible way to proceed.

It was the case of Robert and Ann Sandys that first taught the public to fear the burial clubs. In Stockport in 1840, the beginning of the decade of economic hardship known as the 'hungry forties', the couple, impoverished Irish immigrants, lived with their family in a cellar. Initially a woman named Bridget Riley was arrested, suspected of murdering Robert and Ann's four-year-old daughter Mary Ann. At the inquest, evidence was presented that Mrs Riley had 'some time ago' bought arsenic to kill rats, keeping what was left in a mug. Mary Ann and her brother had visited Mrs Riley, who gave them bread and tea; on the way home Mary Ann began to vomit, and shortly afterwards died. Suspicion lighted on Mrs Riley, as she and Mrs Sandys, once close friends, had fallen out. No post-mortem had been carried out, however, and there was no evidence that the child had been poisoned. The jury refused to return a verdict, and the inquest was adjourned. When it reconvened, the coroner opened the session by stating that, 'since they last met, circumstances had come to light which would probably ... show that the mother of the child was the guilty person, in causing the death' not only of Mary Ann, but also of Elizabeth, her six-month-old sister, who had died some time before. The inquest heard that the children had been enrolled in a burial club, which had made a payment of £3.10s.6d. on the death of each child. A week later, Robert Sandys' brother and sister-in-law, George and Honor Sandys, were also included in the charges, accused of poisoning their daughter Catherine, who they said had died of measles. A doctor testified that he had treated Mary Ann and 'Jane' (probably Elizabeth). 'He thought there was very little inclination on the parents' part to give the children any medicine' – or perhaps very little money to pay for it? – and that they showed 'great indifference towards the children'. A collector for the burial society testified that Robert had asked repeatedly how soon Mary Ann would be eligible for the payout. This could suggest wicked intent, or fear that he would be unable to pay for his child's burial, and she would end up dissected by surgeons. Whatever the case, on 11 October 1840 the collector told him Mary Ann was now eligible; she died on the thirteenth. Another doctor gave evidence that he had examined a child who might have been Elizabeth (the report is unclear), and did not think she had been poisoned; meanwhile an analyst said he had 'little doubt' that she had been, even though the tests on the viscera had not been completed.

The coroner reminded the jury that 'The whole of the parties were Irish. Though he did not wish to draw any invidious distinction, yet he wished the jury to understand, they were catholics, *and, on that account, might probably not attach that seriousness to the commission of a crime which parties of a different religion might do.*' Even so, the jury took two and a half hours to reach a verdict. Ann was charged with the wilful murder of Elizabeth and Mary Ann; Robert, George and Honor with aiding and abetting in the deaths of Elizabeth and Mary Ann; while Honor was charged with the wilful murder of Catherine.

At the trial for the death of Mary Ann, no evidence was actually presented that the child had been murdered. The prosecution relied instead on Mrs Sandys' statement that only she and her husband had fed the child during her illness, as an obvious indication of guilt. They also presented evidence that Mrs Riley had bought half a pound of arsenic, and that on the day of Mary Ann's death some had gone missing, although it was unclear what this was supposed to add – Mrs Riley was not on trial, and there was no evidence that she and Ann Sandys were colluding, or even on speaking terms. It took fifteen minutes for the jury to find Robert and Ann Sandys not guilty. The next day they were tried again, for the murder of Elizabeth. The prosecution this time used Sandys' questions to the collector of the burial society as evidence of his guilt, together with the fact that he had given the registrar of deaths and the church sexton two different causes of death. His defence was that no one had produced any evidence that Elizabeth had been murdered. This time the jury found him guilty, but Mrs Sandys innocent. Honor and George Sandys had by now vanished from the record, and it appears likely that the charges against them had been dropped. Fortunately for Sandys, the requirement that executions be carried out within forty-eight hours of sentencing had been abolished. His lawyers submitted arguments for an 'arrest of judgement' on a point of law, his sentence was 'respited' and he was eventually transported.

Despite an entire lack of evidence that any child had been poisoned, much less been intentionally killed, this was the case that convinced much of the population that scores – hundreds – thousands – of the poor routinely murdered their children for cash. Even in cases where the money element was entirely missing, the burial-club bogey was superimposed. In 1847 Mary Ann Milner was found guilty of the murder of her sister- and father-in-law. *The Times* printed a report that before her death she said that she had done it because her sister-in-law 'was continually vexing her, and making herself unpleasant to her; and that, in revenge, she determined to rid both herself and brother of the wife and child', while her mother- and father-in-law 'came to her house on all occasions, as though it was their own, and took and did what they liked, without regard to her; and also that her husband gave them money and things ...'* Yet before her execution,

* I have only found this one report of her 'confession'; that it appears in *The Times*, which had a long history of fabricated reports of criminals, suggests it may not be true. I include it simply because no other motive was ever ascribed to her.

the *Morning Chronicle* editorialized: 'The only imaginable motive for the conduct of the wretched woman ... was the obtaining moneys from burial-clubs on the deaths of the deceased.' At neither trial had there been any mention of money, nor any suggestion that Mrs Milner had tried to claim anything on their deaths, nor even evidence that the deceased had been insured.

It was not just newspaper gossip: serious thinkers considered the reality of mass burial-society murder to be indisputable. In 1843, soon after Robert Sandys' sentence was commuted, Thomas Carlyle reminded his readers of 'The Stockport Mother and Father': they think, 'What shall we do to escape starvation?' and then look at 'starveling Tom', who would be better off 'out of misery', and the money used to keep 'the rest of us ... alive[.] It is thought, hinted; at last it is done.' (As the coroner had done, he also laid stress on their nationality.) A couple of years later, burial-society deaths were now simply assumed to be part of the natural order. In Disraeli's *Sybil*, a poor woman, needing to repay a loan, promises that 'we shall have a death in our family soon: this poor babe can't struggle on much longer. It belongs to two burial-clubs ... after the drink and the funeral, there will be enough to pay all our debts.' The idea of vicious working-class parents making money out of their children's misery appeared in all sorts of guises. A broadside, 'A Copy of Verses on Mary Arnold, the Female Monster', tells of a woman who blinded her daughter to make her a more lucrative beggar by placing beetles in nutshells and tying them over her eyes until they ate through. This was presented as a true story, although it was actually lifted from Reynolds's *Mysteries of London*.*

* 'Cocks', or false stories, in broadsides were not uncommon. They are usually recognizable from the lack of specific detail – the names of towns, or gaols – or the extreme nature of the claim, such as 'The Life of the Man that was Hanged, but is now Alive'. Sometimes real people were the starting point. Mayhew reported that a patterer had told him that he 'had twice put the Duke of Wellington to death, once by a fall from his horse, and the other time by a "sudden and myst-erious" death ... He had twice performed the same mortal office for Louis Phillipe ... each death ... by the hands of an assassin; "one was stabbing, and the other a shot from a distance". He once thought of poisoning the Pope, but was afraid of the street Irish ...'

In 1854, a parliamentary select committee on the Friendly Societies questioned this unswerving belief in mass murder. The committee noted how few cases there were where there was any evidence, and how many there were of unsupported assertion – cases that included the phrases 'everyone knows', 'I was told of a case', 'you hear it everywhere'. The writer Harriet Martineau, in *Once a Week*, a family magazine, wrote in exactly these vague terms: she 'knew of' a woman who had murdered her eight babies by putting arsenic on her breasts. She added darkly that there were many (unnamed) parents who told doctors they could not pay their bills right away, but would when the burial-society money arrived – as if paying doctors' bills was not exactly what insurance was designed for. Even those who should have known better felt no need of hard evidence. Alfred Swaine Taylor, Professor of Medical Jurisprudence at Guy's Hospital in London, reported in 1851 that there had been 185 arsenic poisoning cases in England in 1837–38; 'We have not seen any statistics of the last year or two,' he added blithely, 'but we certainly think the number must have increased.'

This was the beginning of a new panic that began a few years after the Sandys case, when a conviction took hold that dozens, if not hundreds, of cases of domestic poisoning were taking place every year. The idea of the 'secret poisoner', a cunning fiend who utilized a 'poison ... so rare that the greatest chemist shall find no trace of it', suddenly became widespread. The last quote is from an 1860 stage version of *The Woman in White*, in which the master criminal Count Fosco puts a mysterious substance into a glass of water, waves his handkerchief over it and gives it to his victim to drink. In the real world, however, it was not some mythical unknown poison that was feared, but arsenic. Arsenic was colourless, odourless, tasteless, and, most of all, cheap. It was also found in dozens of household items: in paint, dyes, soaps and patent medicines. It was used for pest control, as a fertilizer and weedkiller, in stables as a wash for horses' coats, and on farms as sheepdip. Once newspapers picked up the idea, the ubiquity of arsenic made it terrifying; as they printed more (and more sensational) cases, it appeared that poisoning cases were on the rise.

Arsenic was feared partly because it was omnipresent in the Victorian house. Among many other uses, it was supposed to be a complexion-enhancer, and arsenical soaps were advertised into the twentieth century.

Medical journals, and professionals like Taylor, should have been calming influences, but instead they drove these fears on. Today, the statements from the professionals appear little different from those of the newspaper sensations. The *Annual Register* wrote in 1847 that poison 'appears to have become fearfully prevalent'; *The Times* countered that in some places arsenic was 'a weapon in the hands of the weaker vessel'; while the *Illustrated London News* warned that 'the women of England of the lowest and most ignorant class are proved to be addicted to this crime, for the sake of pecuniary profit'. Compare this to the Coroners' Society, which in 1855 'urged its members to be vigilant against the rising tide of secret poisoning', while the *London Medical Journal*, edited by Taylor, ran a series in 1847 entitled 'On the Increase of Secret Poisoning', and in 1855, Taylor reported that 'he himself [had] received annually ... from 100 to 150 confidential cases [of secret poisoning]'.*

What these widely disseminated stories made it impossible to realize at the time was that at most, in the 1840s two cases a year in England and Wales revolved around murder or attempted murder by poison, and that number remained stable for twenty years. These figures were available, but no one, not even the medico-legal fraternity, was reading them with an unclouded mind. How could they, given newspapers reporting murder rings operating across the country? Everyone saw the increased numbers of poison trials: from 1829 to 1838 the Old Bailey held seven, while from 1839 to 1848 there were twenty-three, and from 1849 to 1858 there were seventeen, before dropping back to seven in the following decade. But more trials – even more guilty verdicts – did not necessarily mean more poisonings. An increased level of newspaper rumour encouraged more fear; more fear brought more accusations; more accusations saw more trials.

The newspapers laid great stress on women poisoners, particularly working-class women poisoners. An early prototype can be found in 1816, the year after Eliza Fenning was hanged. Matthew Holroyd, a weaver, lived near Ashton-under-Lyne with his wife Susannah and

---

* Taylor's convictions of secret poisoning frequently overrode scientific evidence. In 1849 he testified at the trial of Mary Ann Geering, who was accused of administering arsenic to her son. The local doctor gave evidence that he had prescribed mercury pills. Taylor, having performed an analysis of the remains, agreed that the corpse was full of mercury, but not arsenic, but he was convinced all the same that the man had died of secretly administered arsenic, rather than doctor-prescribed mercury.

their three children. In April, their eight-year-old, their newborn and Holroyd all died. Mrs Holroyd earned her living by nursing illegitimate children while their mothers worked, and one of these mothers now gave evidence that a fortune teller had promised Mrs Holroyd that, within six weeks, three funerals 'would go from her door'. According to her evidence, when Holroyd had complained that his gruel tasted peculiar, his wife urged him on, saying 'it was the last gruel she would ever prepare him'. Many of the elements that were to recur in the mid-century poison cases are present in these few bare details: the women mostly lived in small rural communities; there was little or no evidence that a murder had taken place; there were reports of an angry snatch of conversation which could in hindsight be interpreted as a threat to kill; superstition of some sort frequently played a role; and the accused was often an outsider, in some way deviant – Mrs Holroyd nursed illegitimate children, other women accused were sexually promiscuous, had too many children they could not support, or were simply sharp-tongued or bad-tempered.

The only thing missing from Mrs Holroyd's story was possible monetary gain, and this was not always a constant. Women were accused by their families, by their neighbours, or by people who bore them a grudge, and these accusations were listened to. The similarities between such cases make an overview possible.

In 1843 a report of what was presented as mass murder within a family came from Wrestlingworth, in Bedfordshire. Sarah Dazley (sometimes Dazeley) had been married before, to Simeon Mead, with whom she had had a son, Jonas. Four months after the birth, Mead was taken ill and within a week was dead, and Jonas died later that year. No suspicions were voiced. Two years later the widow married William Dazley, and she got on with him no better than she was reported to have done with Mead. When Dazley became ill, his wife mixed him a rhubarb powder (a purgative), and was reported to have said, 'It'll make him better or worse.' Worse was the answer, for he died the following day. Even now, nothing much was thought about it. It was only when the banns for a third marriage were posted that rumours began to circulate. The local vicar, who clearly fancied himself as a detective, was 'chiefly instrumental in carrying through the investigation', before turning his findings over to the coroner, at which point the police became involved.

The witnesses at the inquest gave a picture of an ordinary unhappy life: members of Mead's family testified that the couple had quarrelled frequently. She had once had a shilling and had refused to give it up, whereupon Mead knocked her down and she responded, 'D— him, I'll poison him, but what I'll get rid of him!' His sister said that she had 'frequently' wished her husband was dead. But the analysis found no poison in his remains, and the inquest jury was instructed to find that there was no evidence to show how he had died. The inquest on Jonas's remains brought more neighbourhood gossip: she had frequently wished the child dead, said one; she was 'a brute of a mother ... and never washed or kept [the child] clean like other mothers'; she gave the child a powder she said she got from a doctor; she was not friendly with the neighbours. The accumulation of petty remarks had its effect, and Mrs Dazley was indicted for the wilful murder of Jonas Mead.

The Times reported these inquests extensively, but despite the transcripts having been reprinted in full on the same page, the accompanying articles ranged freely among the rumours, even when their own reports directly contradicted them. It was reported that Mrs Dazley was 'suspected of being accessory to the death of her former husband and of her daughter, by administering a quantity of arsenic', despite it having been stated earlier in the same piece that no arsenic had been found in her husband's remains, and that the 'daughter' was a boy named Jonas. *The Times* gloried in sensational invention – Mrs Dazley was known 'throughout the county of Bedford by the name of the "Female Blue Beard" ' – but the paper felt no obligation to deal in hard fact: there were articles on the inquest and the rumours, but nothing on the trial itself. Mrs Dazley was found guilty, although she went to her death swearing her innocence.

Many of these poison cases operated primarily at local level, although there the interest was intense. When Mary Ann Geering was executed in Lewes, Sussex, in 1849 for the murder of her two sons, the

Daily News, a London paper, dismissed the crowd of three or four thousand as a paltry gathering. Yet Lewes's population two years later was 9,533. Even allowing for a large number of spectators travelling from surrounding areas, possibly one out of every four inhabitants of the town attended the execution.

To a modern reader Sarah Dazley's crime appears to have been promiscuity. Promiscuity may also have been the root of the accusations against Sarah Freeman, in Shapwick, near Bridgwater in Somerset. She was the daughter of 'a decent man', but was herself of 'loose character'. She had left home some years before, and had had an unknown number of illegitimate children, all of whom had died young. Towards the end of 1844, she asked her family if she could come back, but they refused. Shortly afterwards her mother and brother died while she was visiting to plead her case. After an inquest on these two, rumour forced another, on one of her illegitimate children. This was the second such inquest: one witness explained that there had been an earlier one 'because the neighbours thought there ought to be' – that is, local gossip had made it necessary. At her trial, her lawyer complained that portions of the evidence had been produced after the depositions were taken, and he had therefore been unable to rebut them. But the trial went ahead, and Mrs Freeman was found guilty of murder.

It was reported in shocked tones that when she was pressed to confess in gaol, Mrs Freeman told the authorities 'very snappishly' that she was innocent and, in effect, to stop nagging. A modern sensibility cheers her on: to be convicted of murder was one thing; to have relays of the well-meaning pressing endlessly for a confession must have been like being pecked to death by beady-eyed fowl. Confessions were an integral part of the emotional narrative of trial, conviction and execution. For much of the first half of the century, confession was seen in its religious aspect: the sinner repented, and was therefore, after an earthly punishment, forgiven by a beneficent God. By the late 1840s, however, one senses a change. The desire for confessions now appeared to be more a wish for confirmation that the condemned really was guilty. It may even have been this series of poison trials that crystallized for many a previously unspoken discomfort. By 1856, the newspapers were highlighting the 'weakness' implicit in the public's desire for a confession. In one case, the *Examiner* 'regretted that endeavours were made to extort a confession, for the assumption should always be that the crime has been proved beyond a doubt by the process of law ... To solicit it is to imply that the verdict of guilty wants verification.' But this was what was wanted: reassurance of guilt, not certainty of eternal redemption.

Deaths like that of Mary Gallop made reassurance of guilt doubly necessary. Twenty-one years old, Miss Gallop was the daughter of a carpenter (or in some reports a railway worker) who also acted as the local medicine man. Her mother had killed herself six months previously, after many years of aberrant behaviour. Miss Gallop too was troubled: her father feared 'she was going like her mother'. She had an understanding with an apprentice in Liverpool, of whom her father did not approve; then her father conveniently died. Evidence was presented that she had bought arsenic for rats, but there was nothing to show that she had administered it. Her father could easily have taken it himself, as he was in the habit of dosing himself as well as others; furthermore, he had been ill for six weeks, while the prosecution claimed that the poison was fed to him only on the day before his death. Unlike most poisoners, Miss Gallop's reputation was good – she was a Sunday-school teacher – and her young man had barely figured in the prosecution's case. Nonetheless, the judge in his summing-up identified unlawful, unregulated sexual desire as the motivating force: it was well known, he said, that 'there were instances where women would go to great lengths to gratify their passions'. The jury found her guilty without even retiring. Mary Gallop had one of those hideous executions that gave even proponents of public hangings pause. She was so frightened that she couldn't walk, and had to be carried to the scaffold. Once there, she was unable to stay on her feet for sheer terror, and was placed in a chair. Because of this, the drop was miscalculated, and 'the mortal struggle ... was of frightful duration'.

At least, it probably was. The case of Mary Ann Milner three years later is a salutary reminder of how much reliance should be placed even on multiple eye-witness reports. Mrs Milner had also been found guilty of poisoning members of her family, and according to the *Morning Chronicle*, the government's mouthpiece, at her execution 'she conducted herself with much composure. The usual preliminaries were quickly adjusted, and the drop having fallen, the wretched murderess, after struggling a few seconds, ceased to exist.' *Jackson's Oxford Journal* used the same words; so did *John Bull*. The only problem was that Mrs Milner was not executed: she had committed suicide in her cell the previous night. The *Bristol Mercury*, which had reported her execution, later issued a correction, with an implicit shrugging off of responsibility: the first story had been 'copied from a London contemporary [paper]'. Most of those who reported the execution-that-wasn't saw no need even to print a correction.

These women seemed part of a trend to their contemporaries. In Essex, however, three cases became so entwined in the public mind as to produce the terrifying idea of a 'poison ring', a group of women who were trading tips for murder, helping each other, and their friends, to rid themselves of troublesome family members. In the village of Clavering, Sarah Chesham, a washerwoman who also took in babies to nurse, was arrested in 1846 for the murder of her two sons. The boys had died two months before, around the same time as the illegitimate infant of a local farmer. As with so many of these cases, the deaths at first roused no particular interest. After rumours began, an inquest was set in motion. The local doctor testified that he had not seen the sick children, although their father had called in for medicine, and he had given him first a purgative, then when that had no effect, mercury, also a purgative, and opium. (The practice of dosing patients without seeing them was common – doctors' visits were expensive.) Two witnesses testified that Mrs Chesham had asked them to buy some arsenic for her; neither had agreed to do so, and one could not even recall if the request had been made before or after the boys' deaths. Lydia Taylor, the mother of the farmer's illegitimate child, admitted that while she had said 'perhaps the mother might have poisoned the children', she had really 'had no reason to say so'. The farmer, Thomas Newport, confirmed that he had sacked one of

Sarah Chesham's two boys for stealing eggs, and had had no contact with either of the children since; he did, however, possess arsenic.

Before the jury could reach a verdict, there was a sudden adjournment. Five weeks later they returned to find that Mrs Chesham was now charged with poisoning Newport's child too. The resumed inquest heard evidence of the various times she had shouted at her children, all laced with innuendo to suggest homicidal intent. A neighbour said that Mrs Chesham had prophesied, 'I shall soon hang on the Chelmsford gallows and be buried underneath it.' The coroner felt this 'clearly established' that the children had been intentionally poisoned, and it was only up to the jury to decide if it had been Mrs Chesham who was 'the person whose hands prepared the fatal meal'. No evidence of when or how the poison had been administered had been offered, and the coroner accepted that no connection had been made between Sarah Chesham and Newport, but while no purchase of arsenic had been traced to Mrs Chesham, 'at the same time he … begged to observe that it had been clearly traced to be in the possession of Thomas Newport' – the man he had just said Mrs Chesham had no connection to. The jury followed his lead and found her guilty of wilful murder, and she was committed for trial.

At the trial for the murder of one of the two boys, the neighbour who had reported Mrs Chesham's expectation of dying on the gallows now admitted that she was very deaf, and that Mrs Chesham might actually have said that 'those who died of hard work' might as well be buried under the gallows for all the reward they got. The defence was simply that there was no evidence that Mrs Chesham had possessed arsenic. The jury agreed, and she was acquitted. She was then retried the next day for the murder of the second boy; the evidence was the same, as was the verdict. And then the third trial began, for the murder of Thomas Newport's child by Lydia Taylor. The prosecution case was that Mrs Chesham had visited Lydia and the baby twice, in January and June 1845; she had given it something to eat, and 'from that time [on] it appeared that the child was continually ill', although it only died three months after her last visit. No poison having been found in the exhumed remains, the prosecution withdrew its case and the jury was directed to bring in a verdict of not guilty.

Three years later the poor woman was indicted once more, for the murder of her husband Richard. The newspapers by this stage had no doubt at all that Mrs Chesham was a ringleader in 'the extraordinary and fearful system of poisoning', and they salaciously reported rumours that had continued to be passed around Clavering since her triple acquittal. At the inquest, Alfred Swaine Taylor presented his analysis of Richard Chesham's remains as clear evidence of 'secret poisoning': he had found arsenic in the remains, he said, but not enough to cause death; since, however, the man had died, Taylor attributed his death to arsenic acting on a system weakened by 'consumptive symptoms'. All the local witnesses, however, had testified that suspicion was first aroused because of Chesham's great good health before his sudden illness: there was no history of consumption. The jury acquitted Sarah Chesham once more. *The Times* was furious: 'There was a vast amount of prevarication, with a view apparently to screen the guilty party.' The magistrates were equally unwilling to accept that Mrs Chesham might perhaps not be a murderer after all. They re-questioned a witness who had originally testified to her love for her children, and under their prodding she now said that she had seen her hide poison under a tree stump. The magistrates held a closed hearing, and the evidence is therefore not on the record, but it was widely reported that this same witness testified there that Mrs Chesham had told her that if she had a bad husband she should make him a pie, bring it to her, and 'she would season it for her'. Mrs Chesham had apparently also told her 'it was no sin to bury such husbands'. A cousin of Mrs Chesham's testified that two years before the deaths he had given arsenic either to Mrs Chesham or to her husband – he could not remember which of them it had been, and anyway, when he'd asked Chesham about it, he'd replied that it was used up. After this evidence, the magistrates decided they had enough to commit Mrs Chesham for trial.

The Times' report of the trial presented all the evidence that had previously acquitted her as an indication of her guilt, and added that since the 'murders' she had also been implicated in 'another charge of poisoning'. This was a reference to Newport's baby, in whose remains Taylor had been unable to find any poison. The prosecution made no attempt to produce evidence that Mrs Chesham had ever had arsenic, or that any of the supposed victims had even died of arsenic, or any poison. The charge was no longer murder, but attempted murder, a tacit admission of the poverty of the prosecution's case. The Treasury Solicitor phrased the official view discreetly: 'The material testimony certainly is not so decisive of the cause of Death as could be wished.' Taylor, however, was firm: 'Morally speaking there can be little doubt of arsenic having been the cause of these ... attacks.' But even he admitted that 'There is a want of ... strong *medical proof.*' That lack, however, did not prevent him testifying for the prosecution.

Sarah Chesham now had no legal representation. Her defence consisted of her stating that she had never had any poison, and that she had never killed anyone. The judge, in his summing-up, found the prosecution's case 'overpowering', especially as Mrs Chesham had, he said, 'confessed to having murdered two of her children'. Except that she hadn't: she had said she was entirely innocent. But after three inquests, one magistrates' hearing and four trials, this poor, exhausted woman was finally sentenced to death.*

The piece of evidence that decided the jury was not a fact, but a rumour. It was reported, by *The Times* among other papers, that Sarah Chesham had been in league with Mary May. She hadn't. They lived in different parts of Essex, and were not of the socio-economic level that travelled. But the name Mary May was enough. Three years before Mrs Chesham's final trial, Mrs May had been accused of poisoning her half-brother, 'Spratty' Watts. The evidence was typical: Watts, who lived with his sister and her family in Wix, near Harwich, had died after Mrs May had taken a mysterious paper from a locked drawer. Also typically, he had died and been buried with no questions

---

* She was given no rest even in death. After her execution her body was returned to her family, who sent it back to Clavering for burial. The vicar refused to conduct the service, so her body was placed in a temporary grave, from which it was promptly stolen. I have found no report of what happened after that.

asked. Following local rumours, there was an exhumation. Taylor once more did the analysis, and found arsenic in his remains. Watts, who had been nearly fifty when he died, was found to have been insured by Mrs May with two burial clubs for a total of £9 or £10. She had insured him under the name of 'William Constable', and given his age as thirty-eight. A neighbour reported that Mrs May had said she was going to use the burial money to buy a horse and cart and turn higgler (an itinerant trader). One newspaper now rather over-excitedly reported that she had murdered fourteen of her sixteen children (she had two, both alive and well). The *Morning Chronicle* did not even trouble to itemize: Mrs May 'is said to have been implicated in *all* the suspected cases [of murder] *more or less*' (my italics). The trial heard more of the same, and Mrs May was found guilty and executed in August 1848. In June 1851 the banns were read for the marriage of her widower to the neighbour who had testified that Mrs May had been looking forward to the burial-society money. However, May committed suicide the following month, shortly before his fiancée's illegitimate child was baptized. Village life and village feuds had deep roots.

The real excitement, however, was that at the trial testimony was heard not only about Mrs May, but also about her sister, Hannah Southgate, who, it was suggested, was an assassin for discontented village wives. An inquest was opened on her first husband, Thomas Ham, and her ex-servant testified that Mrs Southgate had told her, 'It's a good job [he was dead], for I always hated him; he was a nasty little blackguard.' Two months after that she married John Southgate. Her servant also added ominously that Mrs Southgate had had six children, of whom five were dead. Another witness testified to hearing Mrs Southgate and Mrs May talking before Ham's death. Mrs May said, 'If it was my husband I would give him a pill,' and Mrs Southgate responded, 'Yes, I'll be d—d if I don't give him a dose one of these days.' Luckily for Mrs Southgate, she had money for a good barrister – possibly her second husband, described as a farmer, had both the cash and the intelligence to hire Mr Ballantine, an Old Bailey regular. He devastated the prosecution's case. Under his cross-examination

Mrs Southgate's servant was forced to admit that, like Mrs Southgate, she too had had five children, of whom four were dead, and that Mrs Southgate had sacked her for theft and drunkenness. Thomas Ham's mother, who had painted a picture of a virago who had beaten her son with a whip, less luridly acknowledged that Mrs Southgate had only attacked him after he got drunk and stole her money. And a third witness, who had heard Mrs May say, 'If he were mine, I'm d—d if I wouldn't give him a pill,' was revealed to have been evicted from a cottage owned by Mrs Southgate's father. Ballantine won a very rare acquittal for his client. In the one case where the defence could afford a good barrister, this cannot be coincidental.

Unlike the excitement that surrounded the Essex poisoners, Eliza Joyce, the wife of a gardener in Boston, Lincolnshire, aroused little interest, local or national. In 1844, just before the May–Southgate story took off, Mrs Joyce had pleaded guilty to murdering her step-daughter and her daughter; she had previously been charged and

The illustration to a 'Sorrowful Lamentation' on the supposed murders of the working-class Sarah Chesham was a stock image, showing an upper-class woman (note the fur-trimmed jacket) sitting by a bed that has a large sweep of curtain beside it.

SARAH CHESHAM'S LAMENTATION
For the MURDER of RICHARD CHESHAM, her Husband, by Poison.

acquitted of murdering her stepson, but she now admitted to killing him and the two girls. It may be that the lack of interest reflected the lack of the elements that most of these murder cases included: promiscuity, money, wise women – there was not even any backbiting among her neighbours. Instead, when asked why she had committed the murders, Mrs Joyce replied simply: 'I don't know, except I thought it was such a thing to bring a family of children into this troublesome world.' Perhaps this was too raw to be fun to read.

The stories of these sad, impoverished women were not much fun in general. There were no plays about them, and few waxwork exhibits – Madame Tussaud didn't bother with any of them. A broadside after Mrs Chesham's death said that 'agents for Madame Tussaud's Chamber of Horrors' had tried to gain admission to the 'dead-house' to view her body, but no model of Mrs Chesham appears in the guidebooks to Madame Tussaud's. Almost immediately after the first report came from Clavering, and long before her final trial, Sarah Chesham lent the name of her village to the villainess in Bulwer's novel *Lucretia*, but for characterization and plot he relied on a vastly more upmarket murderer (see pp.253–4).

Punch satirized the poison panic in the 1840s, not because it recognized that it was a media confection, but as part of a campaign to control access to poisons in order to stymie these poison rings. In 1849, during the height of the panic, it ran a mocking little playlet in dialogue form, in which a small girl asks Bottles, the chemist's assistant, for 'twopence-halfpenny' of arsenic 'to kill rats'. He replies, 'Rats! – eh! Father belong to a burial club?' If further reinforcement were needed, a cartoon (see following page) hammered away at the same theme.

As a result of newspaper agitation, and the trials of these women, in 1851 the Sale of Arsenic Act was passed, restricting the sale of the drug to those over twenty-one, and either known to the dispensing chemist, or vouched for by someone who was. Their names and addresses had to be recorded and the purchase signed for. If the purchase was for less than ten pounds of uncoloured arsenic (that is, for domestic rather than industrial use), a witness had to endorse the

FATAL FACILITY; OR, POISONS FOR THE ASKING.

Child. "PLEASE, MISTER, WILL YOU BE SO GOOD AS TO FILL THIS BOTTLE AGAIN WITH LODNUM, AND LET MOTHER HAVE ANOTHER POUND AND A HALF OF ARSENIC FOR THE RATS (!)"
Duly Qualified Chemist. "CERTAINLY, MA'AM. IS THERE ANY OTHER ARTICLE?"

signature. Originally, it had been planned to restrict the sale of arsenic to adult males, but John Stuart Mill protested at this 'gross insult to every woman … If the last two or three murderers had been men with red hair, as well might Parliament have rushed to pass an Act restricting all red haired men from buying or possessing deadly weapons.' The clause was dropped. Yet even as it stood, the Act dealt only with

246

arsenic, and only arsenic in its raw state; the drug was still utilized in many household goods that could be purchased with no restrictions.

By the 1860s, however, *Punch* had moved on. Now it mocked the huge readership that these grim deaths attracted, with a parody advertisement for a new magazine, to be entitled the *Sensation Times*: it would be, *Punch* promised, 'devoted chiefly to ... Harrowing the Mind, Making the Flesh Creep, Causing the Hair to Stand on End ... and generally Unfitting the Public for the Prosaic Avocations of Life ... Murder, of course, will have in these columns the foremost place ... Arsenical Literature will find in these columns its best exponent, and all Poison Cases will be watched by a staff of special reporters who have been medically educated ...'

For by now the panic had long faded. By the time Eliza Foxall and Mary Anne Scrafton were charged with attempting to murder Henry Foxall in Durham in 1887, no one was much interested. The Foxalls had been unhappily married for two years, and after Foxall was taken ill, a friend of his wife took a letter to the police. Mrs Scrafton, a fortune teller, had written to Mrs Foxall: 'I know that if the dose was strong enough it will do for him. You did not say in your letter if he was ill; but I do not think it will be long, and then you will be free.' Mrs Foxall admitted that she had paid Mrs Scrafton 5s. for a charm 'to put him away': if she placed her shoes in the shape of a T before bed, refrained from eating between ten o'clock and midnight, and didn't speak after 11.45, 'all would be right'. She was sentenced to five years, Mrs Scrafton to seven, harsh enough punishments for putting your shoes in a T, but compared to the poison-panic sentences four decades earlier, this response to supposed working-class poisoners was almost lenient.

Middle-class poisoners, however, could expect different treatment.

SIX

Middle-Class Poisoners

Before the poison panic, a certain sort of poisoning case could be considered exciting: if it was not likely to happen to you, it was fun to read about. One such case was that of Thomas Griffiths Wainewright, whose trial took place in 1837, but whose aura, promoted and enhanced in theatre and literature, remained a potent force throughout the next wave of poison fears.

Wainewright had inherited a small annual income from his grandfather, the founder of the *Monthly Review*, a prestigious literary journal. He studied first under a portrait painter, then, 'ever to be whiled away by new and flashy gauds', as he later wrote, he 'postponed the pencil to the sword', buying a commission in the army. He saw no active service and, like many young men, regarded his military career largely as an opportunity to swagger about in quasi-fancy-dress. By 1815 he had sold his commission, and was once more a would-be artist and writer (he never quite made up his mind). He contributed essays to the *London Magazine* under the pseudonym 'Janus Weathercock', but was more interested in 'the diamond rings on our fingers, the antique cameos in our breast-pins ... our pale lemon-coloured kid gloves': dandyism as art. Although his affected, facetious style is almost unreadable today, it was admired by a circle that included the critics Thomas de Quincey and William Hazlitt, essayist Charles Lamb and Thomas Hood.

In 1822 he married, and the couple moved into rather grand lodgings in Great Marlborough Street, which had once belonged to the tragedian Sarah Siddons. This alone, without any other expensive

248

habits, was far beyond his modest income. Even before his marriage Wainewright had been in financial difficulties, which he had temporarily resolved by forging the signatures of his trustees to gain access to the capital sum on which his income depended. He obtained half of the capital immediately, and a second forgery the following year procured the rest. This carried him through until an uncle died in 1828, but despite great expectations he inherited only a few thousand pounds and a large house that he could not afford to run.

The household now consisted of Wainewright and his wife; Mrs Abercromby, his mother-in-law; and his wife's two young sisters, one of whom, Helen, at Wainewright's urging, insured her life. She told the insurers that there was a chancery suit in her name, which was likely to end in her favour; the insurance was to give temporary cover in case she died before it was settled, so her heirs would benefit. With Wainewright accompanying her, she insured herself with two different companies. In 1830, Mrs Abercromby died suddenly and unexpectedly. Later that year Helen applied to another seven insurance companies for cover. She was, by the end of the year, the possessor of policies that would pay out £12,000 on her death, and on 12 December she signed a will in favour of her sister. On 14 December she was taken ill; 'a chill on the stomach', thought the doctor. On 20 December she was dead.

The insurance companies refused to pay out, claiming that the policies had been obtained by fraud. In some cases Helen and Wainewright had said no other cover had been obtained; there was also, contrary to her statement when buying the policies, no chancery suit; and Wainewright was the beneficiary, despite Helen having told the companies that the policies were to benefit her sister. Wainewright brought a suit against the Imperial Insurance Company for non-payment, but his own tangled finances meant that he could not await the outcome. He fled to France to avoid arrest and bankruptcy proceedings, and for the next few years, everything we know of him is based on rumour. At some point, however, one of the trustees of his inheritance applied to the Bank of England for Wainewright's French address, assuming the bank would be forwarding payments to him.

This image has been described as a self-portrait by Thomas Griffiths Wainewright.
However, many contemporaries described Wainewright as fat and bald, so either
the image is not a self-portrait, or Wainewright merely hoped that this was how
he would be remembered.

Only now was it discovered that the entire sum had been embezzled
in 1824; in 1835 a warrant for forgery was sworn out.

Meanwhile, the civil case against the insurance company was
proceeding, despite Wainewright's continued absence. The prosecution's case was that Helen Abercromby had been murdered. As
Wainewright could not have afforded to continue paying the

premiums, he must have planned all along to kill her. The judge ruled that this was irrelevant: Helen Abercromby did not insure herself with the intention of being murdered, and therefore she had perpetrated no fraud. The jury failed to agree a verdict, and a retrial was necessary. This time the insurance company stressed fraud rather than murder, and won; in his absence, Wainewright's house was sold and his goods auctioned off.

For reasons that were never clear, Wainewright returned to England in 1837. Legend has it that he was arrested by one of the most famous detectives of the day, Daniel Forrester, and it may be so. Forrester was said to have recognized him despite his new 'large tuft of mustachios and beard'. He 'ran up, and tapping him smartly on the arm, said, "Ah, Mr. Wainright [sic], how do you do? Who would have thought of seeing you here?"' Rather dramatically, *The Times* claimed that Wainewright was carrying 'a small dirk in a sheath', but the next phrase was probably more realistic: he was entirely 'without money or friends', and was taken to a debtors' prison. The next day he was charged with fraud on the Bank of England, and transferred to Newgate, bank fraud and forgery being capital crimes. Very sensibly therefore Wainewright agreed to plead guilty to passing a forged cheque, which was not a capital crime, in exchange for the Bank of England dropping its prosecution. He was sentenced to transportation to Van Diemen's Land (Tasmania), and in 1847 he died there. At no time was he tried for, much less convicted of, murder.

That was no reason to rein in the imagination. Wainewright, according to popular views, had definitely murdered Helen Abercromby; and her mother; and his uncle. As one end-of-century author shrugged, 'The evidence … is not conclusive, nor, indeed, very strong, but in the face of his subsequent actions there can be little doubt of his guilt.' This author then repeated two murder stories he said straightforwardly that he didn't believe. One was that, after fleeing to France, Wainewright supposedly murdered a man in Calais, and another in Boulogne, the latter merely because the man had secured a loan on an insurance policy from the company that had refused to pay Wainewright. Other versions suggested there was no motive for this murder at all – Wainewright just liked killing. One source said he had used a 'poison ring', which had a hinged compartment in which he 'always' carried strychnine, 'a poison almost tasteless' (strychnine is not tasteless: it is harshly bitter). After Wainewright's death in Tasmania, more murders in Hobart were added to the list. There were also reports that he kept a diary in which he gloated over his crimes 'with a voluptuous cruelty and a loathsome exultation'. This diary was frequently cited, although no one ever saw it, nor is there any reason to believe in its existence. The only part of the legend that would probably have pleased Wainewright was that in most of these stories he was no longer, as in reality, short, fat, bald and with a speech defect, but had elegant raven locks, and a sinister, glamorous presence resembling that of a stage vampire: John Camden Hotten reported 'snakish eyes' which glowed with 'unearthly fire'.

Hotten was the publisher in 1870 of Dickens' 'Hunted Down', based on Wainewright's supposed murders. Dickens had long been interested in Wainewright. In 1837 he had even briefly seen him in gaol before his transportation. He, John Forster, the illustrator 'Phiz', the barrister and writer Thomas Noon Talfourd and the actor William Macready were visiting Newgate – Dickens was researching a piece – when suddenly Macready stopped and said, 'My God! there's Wainewright.' Talfourd later elaborated this glimpse: 'On some of the convicts coming down into the yard with brooms to perform the compulsory labour of sweeping it, he raised himself up, puffed down his soiled wristbands, and exclaimed … "You see those people; they are convicts like me; – but no one dares offer me the broom!" '

Six years later, in *Martin Chuzzlewit*, Dickens produced his first portrait of Wainewright. Jonas Chuzzlewit attempts to murder his father; when he marries he tries to insure his wife's life, even though he 'didn't consider myself very well used by one or two of the old companies in some negotiations I have had with 'em'. He wants, he tells Tigg Montague, his crooked companion, to insure her without her knowledge, 'for it's just in a woman's way to take it into her head, if you talk to her about such things, that she's going to die directly'.

Jonas, like his close namesake Janus, was an ambiguous murderer: he fails to kill his father (although he thinks he has succeeded), while he ultimately kills Tigg Montague, under the impression Tigg knows of this murder-that-wasn't. Wainewright may have killed; he may not have. Dickens was at this stage content to see uncertainty in his roguery. The play adaptations of the novel were more straightforward in their accusations of murder. In 1844, two versions, for the Queen's Theatre and the New Standard Theatre, both concentrated on the insurance-murder theme. When Jonas Chuzzlewit insures his wife's life, Tigg taunts him: 'Surely she can't be *poison* to you yet. You don't want to get rid of her do you? bless my soul – what's the matter. How white your lips are.'

Bulwer had no time for moral ambiguities in *Lucretia, or, The Children of the Night*, which appeared in 1846. Six years earlier he had rewritten *Eugene Aram* to remove any indication of criminality on the part of the murderer. Now, in the preface to *Lucretia*, he stated that his two murderous protagonists were based on real people, in whom 'there appear to have been as few redeemable points as can be found in Human Nature ... Yet ... their sanguinary wickedness was not the dull ferocity of brutes; – it was accompanied with instruction and culture' – thus giving himself licence to glamorize. But Bulwer insisted, 'There has been no exaggeration ... even that which seems most far-fetched', like the poison ring, was founded on 'literal facts' (sic). Nor, he added, had he 'much altered the social position of the criminals'. Thus he countered criticism in advance by claiming that he had merely drawn from life.

Bulwer had access to the facts of Wainewright's case, having been given all the documents held by the Eagle Insurance Company, which had sent its agent, Henry Smith, to recover them from France after Wainewright's arrest. The second murderer in the novel, the Lucretia of the title, was seen by many people to be a portrait of a Frenchwoman, Marie-Fortunée Lafarge, who had been convicted in 1840 of poisoning her husband with arsenic. It was one of the first cases to use the Marsh test, and there were as many conflicting views on the result as in the case of Eliza Fenning. Madame Lafarge's memoirs had been translated into English in 1841, and she was a popular figure of dread.

Merging these stories, together with a quick gallop around the French Revolution (Varney, the Wainewright character, is forced as a child by his father to watch the guillotining of his mother), Bulwer produced a glamorous story of upper-class poisoning, money, royalist plots and betrayal. The two villains are Varney and his stepmother, Lucretia Clavering. Varney perpetrates a forgery on the Bank of England, arranges for a character named Helen to insure her life and then, with Lucretia's help, slowly poisons her. As in the best melo-dramas, Lucretia murders a beggar, discovering only as he is in his death throes that he is her long-lost son. She goes mad, Varney tries to claim the insurance money, is arrested for an earlier forgery and is transported, leaving Lucretia abandoned in an asylum.

Soon melodrama would be overtaken by sensation-fiction, and in *Lucretia* we can already see the first shoots. No longer set in dens of low-class vice, sensation-novels kept all the excitement of gothic horror, but situated the stories squarely in the middle-class home, which was now seen to be a den of infamy, filled with madness, forgery, bigamy and murder. Bulwer still clung to the older genre's focus on the aristocracy, but his depiction of outward respectability masking inward evil in realistic settings sometimes led his readers astray, and his highly coloured picture of wholesale death was taken seriously by many who should have known a great deal better. Alfred Swaine Taylor's *London Medical Journal* cited the novel as a 'hand-book on poisoning' which instructed 'wretches who employed this mode of assassination' how to avoid detection, while encouraging the 'weak and the criminal'.

Lucretia was a precursor: as well as the vicious female poisoner that sensation-fiction was to revel in from the 1860s, the novel also drew an early portrait of the sophisticated, suave, upper-class murderer, and created the type of elaborate insurance-scam murder thought to be perpetrated by the prosperous. Four years later, *Chambers's Edinburgh Journal* published a series of stories narrated by an attorney who took the role that would later be given in fiction to the amateur detective.

One case revolved around insurance fraud: a child dies shortly after being heavily insured; the insurance company queries the death but, after a satisfactory post-mortem, pays out. Some time later, the boy's godfather in India dies, leaving him a fortune. The child's father now confesses to the attorney that his son is not actually dead: when his lodger's son died of cholera he allowed the substitution in order to claim the insurance money. It is not the rather banal story itself that is of interest, but the use of insurance fraud as a quotidian middle-class crime – as well, of course, as the use of the attorney as detective.

In Caroline Clive's *Paul Ferroll* (1855), the long-undiscovered murder has links to Eugene Aram, but the character of the murderer – the upper-class man whose 'name and fame as an author were some of the best parts of his existence' – was much closer to Varney/Wainewright. Soon after the appearance of that novel, Dickens returned to Wainewright, this time as the blackmailer and all-round villain Blandois (or Rigaud – he uses both names) in *Little Dorrit*. Dickens drew on a French murderer, Pierre-François Lacenaire,* for most of the details of Blandois, but the similarity to Talfourd's description of Wainewright in Newgate is unmistakable. In prison, Blandois asks rhetorically, 'Have I ever … touched the broom, or spread the mats, or rolled them up … or put my hand to any kind of work?' Dickens was not the only one to be fascinated by the 'gent' element in Wainewright's story. In Surtees' *Ask Mamma* of the same year, he too reiterated Talfourd's phrase: 'They don't set me to make my bed, or sweep the yard … they treat me like a gentleman,' although he added, practically if fictionally, 'They think I'm in for ten thousand pounds.'

Even now, Dickens had not worked Wainewright out of his system, and in 1870 he produced 'Hunted Down'. Dickens was a friend of the same Henry Smith of the Eagle Life Assurance Company who had provided Bulwer with Wainewright's papers. By 1848 a story was

---

* Lacenaire (1800–1836) was, like Wainewright, a writer, and his crimes too inspired many artists, from Dostoyevsky in *Crime and Punishment* to Marcel Carné, who in 1945 depicted him in the film *Les Enfants du Paradis*.

current that Smith had been in love with Helen Abercromby, and had gone to France not for the Eagle, but for vengeance. Dickens scribbled out a rough idea for a story: 'Devoted to the destruction of a man … The secretary in the Wainewright case, who had fallen in love … with the murdered girl.' From this he created Julius Slinkton, who insures the life of his surviving niece after her sister mysteriously dies; she too is now ailing – 'The world is a grave!' he sighs mournfully. Slinkton is unmasked by an actuary, who was in love with the dead niece, and afterwards made it his life's work to expose Slinkton. He ensures that her sister is spirited away to safety, and Slinkton commits suicide. The introduction to the 1870s edition was signed 'J.C.H.', John Camden Hotten, and he appended his own highly coloured version of Wainewright's story – 'It was death to stand in his path – it was death to be his friend – it was death to occupy the very house with him' – crediting him with at least five more forgeries, and a full complement of murders.

Throughout the 1860s these elements – the glamour of the man, his gentlemanly status, and the murders, always by poison, sometimes via a poisoned ring – were repeated over and over, as in Mrs Braddon's *The Trail of the Serpent*, in which the villain commits suicide 'by means of a lancet … concealed in a chased gold ring of massive form and exquisite workmanship'. In Wilkie Collins' *The Moonstone* the villain is revealed to have embezzled a trust by forging both the power of attorney and the trustees' signatures on the order instructing the bank to pay out. In *The Haunted Hotel*, Collins returned to the insurance scam with a glamorous, scoundrelly Continental wastrel, Baron Rivar, who murders a peer and swaps his body with that of a dying servant in order to profit from a £10,000 policy. In 1877, Dickens' magazine *All the Year Round* rehearsed the story once more, and the following year in Mrs Braddon's *Charlotte's Inheritance* a stockbroker facing financial ruin persuades his stepdaughter Charlotte to insure her life. As with Helen Abercromby, he escorts her to the insurance offices. She begins to fade, and, as in 'Hunted Down', she is spirited out of the house by her concerned friends, after which she recovers to marry happily.

The theatre took to Wainewright too, although many plays involving poison were retrospectively said to have been influenced by his crimes, when they were in fact more consistent simply with straightforward melodrama. The drama critic Chance Newton wrote that in his youth *Who Did It?* at the Britannia was based on Wainewright's crimes, but the surviving playscript shows no such resemblance – it is about a poisoner, but there is no insurance element at all; instead the poisoner kills before he is cut out of a will. Similarly, in 1898 there was said to be a portrait of Wainewright in *The Medicine Man*, written for Henry Irving. It is difficult, again, to discern any Wainewright elements apart from an aura of stylish evil. Tregenna (Irving) is a society doctor who practises hypnotism (although it is never referred to as such), gaining the confidence of Sylvia, the daughter of his lost love, in order to be revenged, after a quarter of a century, on the man who stole her away from him. After alienating Sylvia from her father and her fiancé, Tregenna discovers that her father never knew his wife had a previous love, and twenty-five years of hatred vanish like the morning mist. (At the moment the scales fall from his eyes he is rather unfortunately murdered by a patient, but it's the thought that counts.)

Thus, by the end of the century Wainewright no longer meant forgery, or insurance poisoning, but simply an urbane, cultured man committing gratuitous murder. As early as de Quincey, Wainewright was considered to be a 'murderer of a freezing class; cool, calculating, wholesale in his operations'. This became the predominant motif. Oscar Wilde, in 1889, celebrated him not merely as 'a poet and a painter, an art-critic, an antiquarian … and a dilettante of all things delightful, but also a forger … a subtle and secret poisoner … powerful with "pen, pencil, and poison"'. Wilde stressed his dandyish airs, his foppish dress and his fine discrimination. By this time, the actuality was far enough in the past for Wilde easily to conflate two myths, repeating the tale of Wainewright claiming proudly in gaol that his cellmates had never 'offer[ed] me the broom', and adding that he was imprisoned alongside 'the agent of an insurance company' – a misremembering of Henry Smith of the Eagle Insurance Company.

The following year the writer Havelock Ellis used Wainewright in his sociological study *The Criminal* as an example of 'the perfect picture of the instinctive criminal in his most highly developed shape ... a moral monster'. To back this up, he repeated the now-familiar myths: the Abercromby murders (plural), the French murders, the supposed diary. Ellis also added his own flourish, that Wainewright had 'admitted ... with extraordinary vanity and audacity, his achievements in poisoning'. As, not unnaturally, Wainewright preferred not to be executed, he had done no such thing.

By mid-century, however, Wainewright's crime appeared minor compared to the many atrocities laid at the door of Dr William Palmer. Palmer's crimes seemed extraordinary, and extraordinarily evil, to the respectable professional classes because he was one of their own. As one noted: 'No one cared to cast the first stone ... A family that includes in its members a clergyman, a surgeon, and a lawyer, would ... require as cautious handling as a hedge-hog.' But, once in the public consciousness, these middle-class murderers began to appear ubiquitous: 'A London man of business is disposed of, in a crowded train, returning to his home in the suburbs; a medical practitioner poisons his relations under the eyes of the Glasgow doctors; a child is found mysteriously dead in the bosom of a respectable family; a young lady buys arsenic, and her lover dies.'*

William Palmer was born at Rugeley, in Staffordshire, in 1824, the son of a prosperous timber merchant who left his children possibly as much as £10,000 apiece. Palmer trained at Bart's (St Bartholomew's Hospital Medical College) in London; by 1846 he was a member of the Royal College of Surgeons and practising in Rugeley. He married and had five children, although only one survived infancy. Palmer kept racehorses, and devoted far more time to the turf than to medicine; by 1852 he had essentially given up his practice. In 1854,

---

* The murderers here referred to are, in order, Franz Müller, Edward Pritchard, Constance Kent and Madeleine Smith; see below.

overwhelmed by debt, he insured his wife's life for £13,000 (some said £30,000). Soon after the first premium was paid, she was dead. That same year, Palmer attempted to insure his brother Walter's life. Walter, an alcoholic, had been rejected by two companies. One finally agreed to insure him, and in August 1855 Palmer bought prussic acid from a chemist; his brother died two days later. Soon afterwards Palmer recommended as a candidate for insurance George Bates, a 'gentleman ... with a famous cellar of wine', suggesting a £25,000 policy. The insurance company sent an investigator, only to discover that Bates was actually Palmer's groom. Foiled, Palmer forged a bill to get ready cash. The bill would have fallen due on 20 November, but by then circumstances had changed.

On 13 November John Cook, a racecourse friend of Palmer, had a big win with his horse, Polestar, at Shrewsbury races. That evening Palmer and Cook sat drinking brandy and water, although Cook complained of the taste, and later that night he was taken ill. After two days he had recovered enough for the two men to travel to Rugeley, Cook staying at the Talbot Arms, across the road from Palmer's house. On 17 November, Palmer ordered coffee for Cook, who was immediately stricken with the same symptoms he had suffered at Shrewsbury. That day and the next, Palmer dosed the vomiting Cook, and ordered special broth for him. On the second day, Palmer consulted Dr Bamford, aged eighty-two; he diagnosed, with Palmer's help, 'bilious diarrhoea', prescribing purgatives and morphia. Palmer went to London, and Cook improved; when Palmer returned, Cook declined. Palmer had bought strychnine while he was away, and the following day he purchased more strychnine and some opium. Finally, on the night of 20 November, Palmer dosed Cook once more, and within half an hour he vomited, suffered a series of terrible convulsions, and was dead. Dr Bamford signed a death certificate giving the cause of death as apoplexy.

Cook's stepfather, a man named Stevens, arrived shortly after the death, to find Palmer making preparations to bury Cook in Rugeley without any of his family present. Stevens asked for Cook's betting book and papers, but Palmer brushed him off: 'It's of no manner of use ... when a man dies, his bets are done with; and besides, Cook received the greater part of the money on the course.' Cook's papers had vanished, as had any cash, despite his recent large win and his immediate illness, which made it impossible that he had ever spent the money. Unsurprisingly, Stevens pushed for an investigation.

A post-mortem was scheduled, and Palmer, in a gesture of bizarre professional courtesy, was permitted to attend. When the viscera were removed, to be sent for analysis to London, Palmer jostled the doctor, and the stomach contents spilled out; later the jar with the organs disappeared; when it was located, the seal covering it had been cut through; even after that, the inn's pot-boy reported that Palmer had offered him money to upset the chaise carrying the jars to the station. By the time the jars arrived in London, the stomach contents had vanished. The following week the analyst Alfred Swaine Taylor wrote to the coroner with his preliminary findings, only for the postmaster to hand the letter over to Palmer before it was delivered (the postmaster was later prosecuted). Palmer also sent the coroner a gift of some game, and £10.

Despite this, the resumed inquest might have gone either way on the medical evidence. Taylor was unable to isolate any strychnine (the only poison Palmer was known to possess that would have caused the tetanic convulsions Cook suffered), and instead found a small trace of antimony, although not enough to result in death. Antimony poisoning causes dizziness, headache and vomiting, not convulsions. As always, however, Taylor was prepared to commit himself on contradictory (or no) evidence. He therefore ignored the poison he had actually found, and instead gave a judgement based on the poison he could not find: Cook had 'died from tetanus, and that tetanus was caused by medicine given to him shortly before his death', in pills containing strychnine. The jury took less than ten minutes to find a verdict of wilful murder of Cook by Palmer.

Two weeks later, the bodies of Palmer's wife and brother were exhumed. A solicitor arrived for their inquest with a watching brief for twenty insurance companies. Taylor again testified, this time that Anne had been poisoned by antimony; the jury again found for wilful

The Times illustrated its report of the trial of William Palmer with this portrait of Alfred Swaine Taylor (*right*) and his colleague George Rees.

murder by Palmer. At Walter's inquest, the boot-boy of the hotel where he had lived told how Palmer had given him alcohol for Walter (who was supposedly drying out), and was later seen putting something in the bottles. Taylor this time announced that Walter had definitely been poisoned, although he had been unable to find any poison at all in his remains, and added that prussic-acid poisoning and alcoholism produced the same symptoms. (They don't.) The coroner, the man Palmer had tried to bribe, brushed aside the insurance question and summed up for apoplexy, but after a long two hours the jury found a third time for poisoning by Palmer.

It was not only Palmer who played fast and loose with judicial etiquette. Taylor wrote two articles for the *Lancet* in January and February 1856, months before the trial, stating that Mrs Palmer had 'died from the effects of tartar emetic [antimony], and from no other cause'. His sole concession to professionalism was that he coyly refused to give his reasons until the trial itself. He had already been reproved at Cook's inquest after reports of his analysis had appeared in the *Morning Post* and *The Times*. Taylor denied releasing the details, and it is possible that the report was leaked by the police. But even if he had said nothing then, he was entirely responsible for an interview he gave to Augustus Mayhew, which appeared in the *Illustrated Times*. Taylor claimed that he had no idea Mayhew was a journalist, and that he had presented himself as the representative of an insurance company.* One leaked report may have been unfortunate; four press spreads in a matter of months cannot be coincidental. At Palmer's trial, before Taylor gave his evidence, the defence used these indiscretions as a way of undermining him on the witness stand, reminding the jury that he 'had used expressions towards the prisoner which, to say the least, were not discreet'.

Long before the trial in May 1856, the newspapers went into overdrive. This was the first major sensation since the newspaper tax had been abolished. Before 1855, only *The Times* sold more than 10,000 copies a day, although many working men and women would have read the papers had they been affordable. Some clubbed together to buy a single copy, others read the papers in pubs or coffee houses. In the mid-1850s 3–4*d*. bought a bed in a poor lodging house in London's East End, including access to shoe-blacking, brushes and soap; a newspaper was 'almost always' included in the price. Once the heavy newspaper tax was removed, circulation skyrocketed: the *Telegraph* halved its price to 1*d*., and circulation immediately rose to 27,000 copies a day, rising again to 141,700 copies daily within the next six years, while *The Times*, still selling at 4*d*., had only half the readership. By 1860, 3 per cent of the population regularly read a daily paper, and

---

* Mayhew responded on the day Palmer was convicted, writing in the *Illustrated Times* that his letter of introduction had named the journal he was writing for, he had asked permission to publish, and he had shown Taylor a proof of the interview, which Taylor had corrected himself. Mayhew's response appended a letter from another journalist, who confirmed that he had been present when Taylor had agreed to the publication of the interview.

another 12 per cent did so on Sundays. Then along came what may have been the biggest murder news since Thurtell. A special 'Rugeley Number' doubled the circulation of the *Illustrated Times* to 400,000; *Lloyd's* bought two new rotary presses simply to keep up with demand.

Truth became an irrelevancy. The *Manchester Times* claimed that Palmer had owned a horse named Strychnine, which figured 'mysteriously on the Turf'. (Palmer had no horse named Strychnine, and I have yet to work out what a horse must do to be mysterious.) The *Era* claimed that he had tried to kill the boot-boy at an inn near Rugeley, to prevent him giving evidence (of what, or to whom, did not appear); it added that he had tried in a fit of delirium tremens to cut his own throat (this possibly referred to his brother Walter). An article in *Lloyd's* showed how anything at all about Palmer was considered fit to print: the paper claimed that Palmer had been seen with the Lord George Bentinck, a well-known habitué of the turf, on the day Bentinck died suddenly, and that Palmer had then claimed that Bentinck, whose betting book was missing, just like Cook's, owed him a large sum. In the next paragraph, the article contradicted everything it had just said: Bentinck's betting book was not missing, no one resembling Palmer had visited him on the day he died, and he had died at home, of a heart attack. Then it segued smoothly into a story of a missing commercial traveller, friendly with Palmer's mother, who had vanished suspiciously after having been seen with her son. In the late 1830s, the Revd R.H. Barham had already mocked such reports:

> The newspapers, too, made no little ado,
> Though a different version each managed to dish up;
> Some said 'The Prince Bishop had run a man through,'
> Others said 'an assassin had kill'd the Prince Bishop.'

The pamphlet and book market also fattened itself on Palmer. One pamphlet, *The Doings of William Palmer*, appeared four months before the trial, advertising Palmer's 'public frauds and private trickeries'. It reported that his children died 'very, very young', that his father-in-law's 'brains were blown out, but by whom was never discovered' (his father-in-law had committed suicide), and added a story of a man who had died mysteriously after making a large loan to Palmer. Meanwhile, *The Illustrated Life and Career of William Palmer of Rugeley* reported yet another racing man who had died mysteriously after a win, and whose betting book and money too were missing, while Palmer's mother-in-law went on her last visit to her son-in-law with the words, 'I know I shall not live a fortnight!'

Palmer's defence protested that he would not receive a fair trial in Staffordshire.* The *Manchester Examiner* reported that while the defence may have wanted a change of venue, the people of Stafford – particularly those connected to the 'victualling interest' – 'loudly protest against this, as a violation of what they conceive to be their just rights'. Despite the grievances of the catering trade, it was agreed that it was perhaps not always 'expedient to the ends of justice' to hold a trial where local feelings ran high, and what was colloquially called Palmer's Act was passed, which permitted a venue change for any defendant where it was feared that this might prejudice a trial's outcome. Given the national newspaper coverage of Palmer's case, it is not certain that a jury anywhere else would be any less influenced. Certainly the social status of the spectators at the Old Bailey was remarkable: the Duke of Cambridge, Lord Lucan, Lord Derby, Gladstone, the Marquis of Anglesey, Earl Grey, Lord Denbigh, Prince Edward of Saxe-Weimar and three sons of the Duke of Richmond were all reported to have attended at least once during the twelve-day trial. Prince Albert was known, or said to be known, to be following the case, and 4*d.* copies of *The Times* with the trial transcripts reportedly changed hands for 4*s.*

The trial revolved almost entirely around scientific evidence. This was the first time that strychnine was suggested as a cause of death in

---

* Palmer was routinely referred to as 'the Rugeley Poisoner', much to the town's disgust. One story claimed that the locals petitioned the Prime Minister for permission to change their town's name to escape the notoriety. 'By all means, gentlemen,' he genially responded, 'so long as you name your town after me.' (The Prime Minister in question was Palmerston.)

a criminal trial in England, and it was also the first time that the mass-newspaper-reading public had watched the role of medical and scientific experts unfold in a judicial setting. Taylor's belief in strychnine poisoning was, to modern eyes, based on faith rather than reason. On opening Cook's viscera, he said, 'There was no smell of opium, of prussic acid, nor of spirits, nor of henbane, nor, indeed, of any poison ... In the intestines and stomach there was nothing to indicate the cause of death ... there was only a slight trace of antimony on the parts examined, and there was no trace of any other substance ...' He continued, 'We have no evidence before us to enable us to form a judgment' on whether antimony 'was or was not the cause of death'; but still, he was certain that 'the pills administered on Monday night and Tuesday night contained strychnine'. This he based on the fact that strychnine acts quickly, and Cook had been 'drawn up like a bow' (that is, his body had been convulsed in a rigid, tetanus-like arc). He agreed that the anatomists who had examined Cook's spine and brain had said their appearance was not consistent with strychnine poisoning, and finished off by admitting that 'I have never witnessed [strychnine's] action on a human subject.'

This was the problem. None of the prosecution's nine experts had ever examined a body poisoned by strychnine. Instead, experiments on rabbits had shown them that strychnine metabolized very quickly, and was not always detectable after death (three-quarters of a dose of strychnine metabolizes within a hundred minutes of administration). The prosecution therefore claimed that the failure to find evidence of strychnine simply meant that it metabolized too quickly to be detected, and presented Cook's symptoms as evidence that the poison had been administered. The defence's fifteen experts countered that the failure to detect strychnine indicated simply that no strychnine had been ingested. The great names of forensic science of the day went head to head: Taylor was the lead for the prosecution; William Herapath, one of the founders of the Bristol Medical School, Thomas Nunneley, surgeon and lecturer at the Leeds School of Medicine, and Henry Letheby, City of London Medical Officer of Health, all appeared for the defence.

The defence produced a letter Taylor had written after his original analysis, saying that, as the contents of the stomach were missing when the viscera were delivered to him, he could not find for or against strychnine. Another witness suggested that Cook's symptoms might be attributable to 'a delicate constitution', syphilis, 'disease of the lungs', 'mental depression and excitement', or even a rare form of epilepsy where the patient retains consciousness, although he had to admit that he had never heard of such a thing. Unlike Taylor, both Nunneley and Herapath had actually anatomized bodies known to have been poisoned by strychnine (in Nunneley's case, he said he had had experience of sixty cases over thirty years), and Herapath testified he had never failed to find post-mortem evidence of strychnine. The defence, however, had to proceed cautiously. They needed to maintain that Taylor was skilful enough to have discovered strychnine if it had been administered – if they suggested he was completely incompetent, it might imply that poison had indeed been present, but he was not clever enough to find it.

The judge leant heavily towards the prosecution, claiming that Herapath and Letheby were not expert witnesses, but 'advocates' for Palmer. This was indignantly denied: 'Why are one half of these gentlemen to be held up to indignation for doing just what they all came to do?' The remaining, non-scientific, witnesses were damning for Palmer: the two druggists' assistants who had sold him strychnine; the apothecary who claimed he had asked him how much poison was needed to kill a dog; Cook's stepfather and his tale of the missing betting book and cash; various servants at the Talbot Inn who synchronized Cook's recurring bouts of illness with Palmer's visits; Palmer's behaviour at the post-mortem; his bribery of the coroner and postmaster; his parlous financial situation. Every piece of evidence on its own was weak, but the combined effect was overwhelming, and Palmer was convicted.

Yet no one considered the case had been proved. The *Morning Chronicle*, among others, agitated that the verdict was a miscarriage of justice, not because Palmer had not committed murder, but because the trial had failed to prove that murder had been committed. The case became an obsession, particularly among the medical profession. The *Lancet* produced a stream of articles on poisoning, medico-legal proof in general, and strychnine in particular, including 'Notes on Three Lectures on the Physiological Action of Strychnia' and 'The Physiological Test for Strychnia', and a promise that an analysis of the medical evidence would be forthcoming. This was followed by 'On the Detection of Strychnia in Solution with Potassio-Tartrate of Antimony', an editorial on medical and scientific witnesses at trials, a letter on the 'Detection of Strychnine', and a paper by Henry Letheby on 'The Medico-Legal Chemistry of Strychnia'. At this time the Crimean War was raging, with its high death toll from typhoid, and Florence Nightingale's well-publicized nursing crusade was under way. This generated a single article, 'The Sanitary Condition of the British Army in the Crimea', and a few essays on battle surgery, but nothing captured the attention of the doctors like Palmer. The *Medical Times* had even had its own dedicated reporter at the trial, and gave fifty-six columns to its coverage.

Palmer had erupted into public consciousness just as doctors were beginning to present themselves as professionals, separating their higher calling from the lower-status apothecaries and surgeons, culminating in the Medical Registration Act (1858), which permitted only those licensed by specific schools to call themselves doctor. Palmer was a medical man, trained at a prestigious medical school; yet he had used his professional status not only to poison, but also to certify for insurance policies for the purposes of fraud. At the end of the century Sherlock Holmes encapsulated the feelings this aroused: 'When a doctor does go wrong, he is the first of criminals. He has nerve and he has knowledge.' He then added, 'Palmer and Pritchard were among the heads of their profession' (Pritchard was executed in 1865 for the murder of his wife and mother-in-law in Glasgow). This was not remotely true, but the idea of the rogue physician was potent. (By the time Conan Doyle was writing, strychnine, in 1856 so mysterious, was familiar even to an army doctor-cum-general practitioner like Watson. In *The Sign of Four* Holmes describes the convulsions and 'distortion of the face' of a murdered man, and Watson immediately recognizes the symptoms of 'some powerful vegetable alkaloid ... some strychnine-like substance which would produce tetanus'.)

After such a confused trial, more than ever it was hoped that the criminal would confess before his execution – not for the sake of his soul, but to confirm that justice had been done. The *Journal of Medical Science* reported that 'Palmer was persuaded, entreated, implored day by day, almost hour by hour, to confess his crimes, not to God, but to man.' But he remained mute. He was returned to Stafford Gaol to await execution, which despite heavy rain* was attended by perhaps as many as 100,000 people (the *Morning Chronicle*'s estimate), although it may have been half that – still a huge number for a town with a population of 45,000. The *Staffordshire Advertiser* said that between midnight and six o'clock on the morning of the execution, the main road into town was 'a complete procession' of all types of vehicles, as were the roads leading from the Potteries. One man claimed to have walked home to Accrington, seventy-five miles away, after the execution. And one journalist complained that 'Perhaps no criminal of celebrity was ever executed in so inconvenient a place, so far as the facility for obtaining a view is concerned.'

Three years earlier, a German traveller had been told by an Englishwoman that if he wanted to see 'Our popular festivals ... Go to Newgate on a hanging day.' This was the middle class's view; and many of the working-class publications echoed it (in large part because they too were written by middle-class authors). In *The Boy Detective*, a penny-dreadful for boys, one character laments, 'I allers

---

* According to the governor of the gaol, on the way to the scaffold Palmer 'minced along like a delicate schoolgirl, picking his way and avoiding the puddles ... anxious not to get his feet wet'. This appears in the reminiscences of Henry Hawkins, a notoriously poor judge known to almost universal contempt as 'Hanging Hawkins'. The *Oxford Dictionary of National Biography* thinks his book is unreliable, and was almost certainly not written by him (the four chapters narrated by his dog were also, I suspect, not by the dog). The book was published in 1904. I wonder if George Orwell, born the previous year, ever read it. In his 'A Hanging', published in 1931, he described seeing an execution in Burma in 1926 where the condemned man, on his way to the scaffold, 'stepped slightly aside to avoid a puddle on the path'. Whether or not Orwell attended an execution is disputed – he claimed that he had, but he also said that it was 'only a story'. Whatever the case, he had certainly read Thackeray's 'Going to See a Man Hanged' – perhaps he had read Hawkins too.

was unlucky ... now, arter I made the loveliest weal pie, and put a new feather in my pork pie 'at ... that little snake is respited! ... Ain't it provoking? Sich a day's pleasure, too ...' The crowds at Stafford seemed to agree that an execution was 'a day's pleasure', yet Palmer's guilt continued to be in doubt. As late as 1874, the novelist Anthony Trollope had a lawyer say, 'We were delighted to hang Palmer, – but we don't know that he killed Cook.' It was said that Palmer's final words were, 'I am innocent of poisoning Cook by strychnine.' This sentence was analysed forwards and backwards. Was he saying that he was guilty of poisoning Cook by some other means? Or that he was guilty of poisoning someone else by strychnine? Or that he was innocent?

From the moment of Palmer's conviction, trial reports were snapped up by eager amateur detectives. A copy of the *Illustrated and Unabridged Edition of* The Times *Report of the Trial of William Palmer* in the British Library has newspaper reports pasted in at relevant points, as though its owner wanted to provide an 'I was there' running commentary. While the cases of Eliza Fenning and others had produced books and pamphlets by journalists claiming to be written by the convicted themselves, for Palmer, publications supposedly written by others appeared. His brother, the Revd Thomas Palmer, indignantly denied that he was the author of *AN INQUIRY INTO the CHARGE of LORD CHIEF JUSTICE CAMPBELL, on the LATE TRIAL of WILLIAM PALMER, illustrative of its dangerous tendencies as destructive to the long enjoyed rights and privileges of all British subjects*.* The coroner Thomas Wakley similarly repudiated authorship of *The Cries of the Condemned: Proofs of the Unfair Trial of William Palmer*. Less than two weeks after Palmer's execution, one C.J. Collins, author of *Dick Diminy* (1853), a fashionable tale of the turf, wrote to the *Racing Times* to warn readers that the illustrations had been lifted from his novel to adorn a life of Palmer as though they were portraits.

---

* Another brother, George, complained to the press that his perfectly ordinary insurance transactions were reported in a libellous manner, insinuating that, as a Palmer, he must have ulterior motives. The *Daily News* agreed that it was disgraceful, and took the opportunity to repeat the allegations.

Other publications were more authentic. Alfred Swaine Taylor published *Poisoning by Strychnia, with Comments on the Medical Evidence Given at the Trial of William Palmer* ..., which should more accurately be entitled 'The medical evidence at the trial, with comments on poisoning by strychnia', such is the author's concern to justify his trial evidence via a succession of straw men set up by himself, so that he can with some authority knock them down. By page 2, he is already warning the unsuspecting reader that Palmer's defence used 'an unusual amount of sophistry ... misrepresentation ... [and] personal attacks on witnesses whose evidence was of vital importance'. He also alludes darkly to the 'attempted intimidation of the jury', but produces no evidence.

Others just enjoyed the story: the anonymous *The Most Extraordinary Trial of William Palmer*, which went through four editions in less than a year, was published by a specialist in pennybloods. Other publications advertised in the endmatter all have titles like *Sylvester Sound, the Somnambulist*, or are highwayman tales, or melodramas, or tales of pirates, shipwreck, and the occasional smuggler. At Southwark Police Court the month after the execution, a woman was convicted of shoplifting two titles from a bookstall in a railway station – she had stashed *The Christmas Tree* and *The Illustrated Life of William Palmer* under her shawl, despite being a woman of 'considerable property', with 'highly respectable' friends. Perhaps she was ashamed of her interest. It wasn't only the English who were interested. A Greek-language publisher in the City, Stephanos Xenos, published a hefty two-volume work in Greek, the first volume of which was a vindication of his father, who had been accused of forgery; the second was entirely taken up with the trial of Palmer, with many plates of the people and events, including a splendid spread of Polestar winning at Shrewsbury Races.*

---

* The work is published under the pseudonym Ch. V. Cavour, but it appears to be by Xenos himself. Xenos was an active member of the London Greek community, writing a couple of historical novels and a book on the Great Exhibition, and in 1860 founding the *British Star*, a weekly paper in Greek.

The sporting connection was, indeed, among the elements of the case that continued to fascinate. In January 1856, long before the trial, the *Racing Times* reported briefly on betting for the Derby, and at much greater length on the presence at Epsom of Captain Hatton, the Chief of the Staffordshire Constabulary. The paper appended a notice requesting 'Any gentleman who paid the late Mr. Cook money at Shrewsbury Races, or who had, or witnessed any money trans-actions with him at that time' to get in touch with Hatton. According to *Household Words*, the gamblers of the Stock Exchange were 'offer-ing long odds' on Palmer being acquitted. Even after the verdict, according to the *Racing Times*, 'the turfites' merely thought of Palmer as 'a black sheep', and added that his horses, now sold to pay his creditors, were doing very nicely; in October, one of them, previ-ously known as Chicken, but now the more aggressively named Vengeance, won the Cesarewitch, with Cook's erstwhile horse Polestar coming an ironic second. Another of Palmer's horses was renamed Gemma di Vergy, which, the *Racing Times* noted, was the name of a 'very notorious murderer' in an opera. (In fact, Donizetti's Gemma di Vergy is a blameless heroine whose husband is murdered by a slave.)

Other forms of murder sightseeing were possible for those not attracted to the turf: in June, the *Daily News* reported special trains from the Potteries to Rugeley 'for the express purpose of enabling persons to visit the scenes of the murder!' A photographer rented Palmer's house, and advertised his studio 'at the rear of the PREMISES LATELY OCCUPIED BY W. PALMER'. Madame Tussaud's had a waxwork in place the day after the execution; Allsop's in Liverpool was advertising a display five days after that; by 1859 the Royal Parthenon in Trongate had also added its own model of Palmer. If anything, his crimes grew greater rather than less. In the 1869 cata-logue to Madame Tussaud's, Palmer's 'victims' are plural but unquan-tified; by 1873 'he was believed to have poisoned more than a dozen persons'. There were also, as had now become routine, Staffordshire figurines of Palmer, and another of a generic Georgian building care-fully labelled 'Palmer's house'.

For sheer nastiness, however, it was difficult to compete with a fair-ground show at the Wilmslow Races, in Cheshire. Here, four months after Palmer's execution, John Fletcher advertised that he had

... secured the services of
John Smith,
of Dudley, the executioner of the late
William Palmer,
at Stafford; and also been fortunate, through a friend,
of procuring from Liverpool a
cast of his face and features,
forming an exact model of the culprit, dressed in
corresponding clothes, as he appeared on the morning of
execution. There will be the
scaffold and beam,
with a company of trained officials, who will perform and
go through the ceremony of
Hanging!
Twice each morning of the races.
Performances commencing at ten and twelve o'clock.
Admission 1s. each, 6d. to be returned in refreshments.

The press and public remained obsessed by Palmer for the remainder of the century. The *Sporting Times* was particularly smitten. From December 1879 to February 1881, over forty issues, it published weekly verbatim transcripts of the trial. In 1886 it highlighted Palmer as a 'Turf Celebrity' in two issues, returning a month later with 'Palmer's Love Letters' (two rather dull letters he had written several decades before). It mocked – itself? its readers? – with little asides such as 'we shall get [Palmer] comfortably hanged by about Easter'. This was different only in quantity, not kind, from the *Pall Mall Gazette*, which claimed to have seen 'the poison bottles of Palmer' at Madame Tussaud's – even though anyone who had followed the case had to know they could not be authentic. Perhaps, given this, it should not be surprising that a report appeared in the *Liverpool Courier* in 1875 claiming that Palmer, 'the Rugby [sic] poisoner', was 'brother of an ex-Lord Chancellor'. The 1st Earl of Selborne felt obliged to point out that, as 'the only person named Palmer who has had the honour to fill the office of Lord Chancellor', he was not 'even remotely related to that notorious criminal'. 'Palmer is not a very uncommon name,' he added plaintively.

Yet in theatre, Palmer was barely represented. The verdict was delivered on 27 May 1856; on 29 May the Britannia submitted a melo-drama, *Monti the Poisoner*, to the Lord Chamberlain for approval. This was a typical recipe of evil squires, betrayed lovers and comic servants, except that the gypsy fortune teller warns the abandoned wife to insure her life. Finally, when good wins out over evil, 'Oliver kneels C[entre] with children, Stephen points to Policy Insurance which he's holding up. The others group round him as the curtain descends.' This play did not last long, and the success or otherwise of *The Rugeley Tragedy, or, the Life and Death of William Palmer!!* at Oldbury is unknown, but its playbill promised that it would conclude with 'MUSIC AND DANCING, AND A LAUGHABLE FARCE!' These appear to be the only traces of Palmer onstage.

Novelists briefly used Palmer's name as shorthand for a generic murderer, as they had for the Mannings, as in Mrs Braddon's *Aurora Floyd* in 1863: 'If Mr. William Palmer had known that detection was to dog the footsteps of crime, and the gallows to follow at the heels of detection, he would most likely have hesitated long before he mixed the strychnine-pills for the friend whom, with cordial voice, he was entreating to be of good cheer.' The same author's *Birds of Prey* and *Charlotte's Inheritance* (1867–68) were involved tales of insurance and murder based on a mishmash of Wainewright and Palmer details.

But before there was any real opportunity for the novelists to get to grips with Palmer, they were brought up short. For only three years later, the whole thing happened again: a medical man was accused of murder, this time within the family.

Thomas Smethurst was reported to have been a hydropathic prac-titioner at a spa who gave up his practice on his marriage to a

273

prosperous, and much older, woman.* By 1858 the Smethursts had rooms in Bayswater, where Isabella Bankes was a fellow lodger. She was a woman of some small property – £1,700 outright, and the income on a lifetime interest in £5,000. After a brief period of time, and a lot of gossiping among the lodgers, she moved to new lodgings in Richmond, and shortly afterwards she was followed by the doctor. The couple went through a bigamous form of marriage, and three months later the new and not-quite-legitimate Mrs Smethurst became ill, was treated by several local doctors called in by Smethurst, but continued to decline. Her sister was informed – it was the first the bride's family had heard of her marriage – and after a single meeting, Smethurst wrote to say that Mrs Smethurst's doctor had forbidden future visits. A month after the illness first manifested itself, Smethurst gave a solicitor a draft will leaving everything to him after his 'wife's' death (he said the draft had been drawn up by a barrister, but later it was proved to be in his own handwriting). At Smethurst's urging, the will was, unusually, executed and signed on a Sunday – an indication of the need for speed. The doctors now suspected 'unfair treatment', and had Mrs Smethurst's 'evacuations' tested, at which point the police were called in, and Smethurst was arrested. A letter to his first wife was found, which indicated that they remained on harmonious terms, and that he expected at some point to return to her. The magistrates decided that the case against Smethurst was not strong enough, and he was discharged, only to be rearrested the next day after the second Mrs Smethurst died.

The trial followed the pattern set by Palmer's, with much emphasis placed by both sides on the medical evidence. Alfred Swaine Taylor

---

* 'Reported to have been' is the closest I can manage. Smethurst at his trials in 1859 was said to have been forty-eight years old, and to have married in 1828, which would have made him seventeen at the time. His wife, reported not terribly reliably to have been between seventy and seventy-three in 1859, was definitely substantially his senior, for her son by a previous marriage was four years older than Smethurst. But how Smethurst could have been a medical practitioner, even of the quackish type prevalent at watering places, and even with a medical degree that he probably purchased, *before* his marriage at seventeen, is a question to which I have found no solution. Perhaps the newspapers, which reported the age gap between himself and Mrs Smethurst as anything between eighteen and thirty years, were themselves confused, and he practised after, rather than before, his marriage.

was, once more, expert witness for the prosecution, and he testified to finding arsenic and antimony in the medicines Isabella Bankes had been taking, as well as antimony in the viscera. However, he was obliged to confess to the court that the arsenic in the medicine had been introduced by himself in error: he had contaminated the samples by using a copper gauze for the Reinsch test, the gauze itself containing arsenic.* He somewhat nullified this admission, however, by adding that the potassium chlorate Mrs Smethurst had been taking had contained enough poison to kill her, and was of a type that dispersed rapidly in the system. Thus, he suggested, the very fact that he could find no poison was in itself evidence that she had been poisoned. The defence responded by highlighting the absence of any symptoms of arsenic or antimony poisoning; furthermore, the quantities of arsenic found in the dying woman's faeces could easily be accounted for by her various medicines. Other possibilities they suggested were that the symptoms were those of dysentery; Mrs Smethurst's ex-landlady testified that she had had a history of bilious illnesses. Or, possibly, as she was forty-three years old and pregnant, vomiting should be expected.†

The judge did not rely entirely on the medical evidence in his summing-up. Instead, it was Smethurst's bigamy that weighed most heavily: the judge repeated the word 'felony' six times in referring to the bigamous marriage. It made sense to focus on this, for otherwise there was no motive. Smethurst inherited Isabella Bankes' £1,700, but her income – about £200 a year, or the wages of a senior clerk – terminated on her death. His first wife was prosperous, and they had lived very comfortably on her money for over thirty years. They were on good terms, she appeared to have no trouble with the idea of a second

---

* A contemporary writer on nineteenth-century medico-legal proof notes dryly that the expert Dr Taylor had been using copper gauze in his arsenic tests for *fourteen years*. In his testimony, Taylor acknowledged that he had been using this method 'for many years'. Fortunately for him, if not for those other accused, both the judge and the defence failed to highlight this alarming fact.

† A modern commentator has suggested Crohn's disease, the symptoms of which were not described until 1902, or categorized as a single illness until 1932.

Mrs Smethurst. What was he killing for? The jury didn't pause long, however, finding him guilty in twenty minutes.

Immediately, the public and the newspapers began to worry away at the verdict. *Tait's Edinburgh Magazine* pointed out that while there were grounds for suspicion, the prosecution had not proved that Isabella Bankes had been poisoned at all, much less that she had been poisoned deliberately, and even less that Smethurst had done so. The *Leader* summarized the pros and cons. Against the verdict: the scientific evidence was, at best, inconclusive, given Taylor's blunder with the copper gauze, and poison could therefore only be considered as 'affording a probability that required corroboration'. For the verdict: the bigamous marriage, which would be revealed sooner or later, while Isabella Bankes' death would cover it over; and the money she left. The article then went on to Smethurst's bad character: he had committed bigamy, he had lied about not being able to afford a nurse, he had kept his second wife's family away, he had made her sign her will in her maiden name,* and on a Sunday, too.

The *Daily News* carried a stream of letters questioning the verdict, and noted other questionable elements. The defence had objected at the very start of the trial to the Lord Chief Baron acting as judge, as he was 'an intimate personal friend of Dr. Taylor'. The judge had brushed this aside: he had 'not seen [Taylor] for a considerable time', and anyway all of the legal confraternity knew the analyst. Then a juryman at the start of the trial said he was 'strongly prejudiced against the prisoner'. The judge told him he should have mentioned it before, and he was now legally powerless to dismiss him. After the Palmer verdict the newspapers had begun to look at the role of the expert witness. With Smethurst, the *Telegraph* began to question the use of assertion: statements were not proof, it said, highlighting the fact that Taylor had not only not proved that poison was present, he hadn't even attempted to do so.

---

* Smethurst had told the solicitor who drew up the will that they were not married, and his wife had signed it in her legal name. I am not sure that telling the truth is necessarily a definitive sign of bad character.

With the developments in forensic science, the newspapers had printed blow-by-blow descriptions of post-mortems and analyses, educating their readers as the cases progressed. In the case of William Richardson, acquitted in 1848 of murdering his son (who was also his grandson: he had fathered the child on his daughter), the *Daily News* gave columns of description of the processes the child's remains were subjected to:

> decomposition had taken place, and [the viscera] had become a pasty mass. [The analyst] took the whole of this mass, which he boiled in distilled water ... he acidulated it with pure muriatic acid, and again boiled it, conducting the operation in a porcelain vessel, and then filtered it through new calico ... A portion of the liquid [the] witness then mixed with an equal portion of muriatic acid, mixed it with an equal quantity of distilled water ... He then took two pieces of bright copper, which had been carefully cleaned in nitro-sulphuric acid. These two pieces he then boiled, the one in the distilled water and muriatic acid, and the other in the liquid in which the body had been boiled, the effect of which would be, that if arsenic were present, it would give to the copper a dark colour, similar to iron; but if no arsenic were present, the copper would remain comparatively clean and bright ...

This is a small extract only – the full report went on for columns. Yet as the century progressed, and particularly during these high-profile poisoning cases, the public became increasingly disillusioned with experts. The *Lancet*, after the Palmer case, thought rather optimistically that 'juries will learn how ... authoritative the decision of Medicine may be ... and the public will perceive ample reason for placing firm reliance upon science for the detection and prevention of crime'. What the public actually saw was a group of men, all claiming absolute knowledge, and all contradicting each other bad-temperedly. Even when they didn't disagree, they were frequently and obviously both arrogant and ignorant. At Mrs Brown's trial in Beaminster for the murder of her husband (see pp.359–62), in the same year as Palmer, the prosecution's expert rejected her claim that her husband had been kicked in the head by a horse: the wound had to have been produced by a blunt instrument, such as a hatchet, he stated categorically. On cross-examination, he admitted that he had never seen a fractured skull, nor had he seen a wound caused by the kick of a horse, nor, for that matter, by a blunt instrument, nor even a hatchet. His fellow surgeon agreed nevertheless: 'I know there have been remarkable instances' when people with serious head injuries recovered, 'but in this case it is morally impossible'. Dickens may have resuscitated the phrase, if not from this rather obscure trial, then from others (see Alfred Swaine Taylor's moral certainty on p.242). In *Edwin Drood* (1870), when Drood goes missing, Mr Datchery asks if there are 'strong suspicions of any one?' 'More than suspicions, sir … all but certainties,' replies the pompous mayor. '… But proof, sir, proof must be built up stone by stone … It is not enough that Justice should be morally certain; she must be *im*morally certain …' 'Immoral. How true!' says Mr Datchery. The reading public learned to be distrustful of evidence, and even more distrustful of experts.

The *Daily News* encapsulated the public's ambivalence over Smethurst. It reported that in 'high quarters' it was considered 'a case for conviction, but not one in which the capital punishment should be carried out'. If half a grain of arsenic had been found in Isabella Bankes' stool after constant diarrhoea for weeks, then she should have been riddled with the stuff, yet nothing was found in any of her organs. And despite Smethurst's entire life being raked over, no one had found any debts, any need of money, or anything against him at all. Having printed this, the *Daily News* changed sides a couple of days later, suggesting now that Smethurst had an obviously guilty demeanour. He had been cool and calm at his trial; it would need cool and calm to poison a bigamous wife; *ergo*, the cool and calm man was a killer. The following day the paper swapped sides again, arguing that it was only circumstance that made Smethurst appear guilty: his calm made him look guilty in the dock, but had he been in the witness box, no one would have thought his behaviour at all suspicious.

In the normal course of events, if an appeal were made, the Home Secretary reviewed the case and made a decision. But with Smethurst he devolved responsibility, handing everything over to Sir Benjamin Brodie, a distinguished surgeon, first President of the General Medical Council, and Serjeant-Surgeon to the Queen (Brodie had also appeared as a prosecution witness against Palmer, so perhaps was not entirely objective). On 4 September, Brodie's verdict was delivered, with fourteen reasons for and against Smethurst, of which only six were medical or scientific. So, although Brodie had been brought in as a sort of superior expert witness, his judgement was based not on his expertise at all, but simply on the fact that 'the impression on my mind is that there is not absolute and complete evidence of Smethurst's guilt' – to determine which was legally the job of the jury.

Smethurst's appeal was allowed, but he was immediately arrested, this time on a charge of bigamy. The *Morning Chronicle* pointed out the hypocrisy of the public, who wanted Smethurst to be punished, but only a little bit. The bigamy charge was 'an expedient for repairing the failure' of the first trial, 'or as a means of satisfying a public moral feeling'. Smethurst, at this new trial, claimed that the first Mrs Smethurst had earlier been married to a man named Johnson, and therefore they had not been legally married, but he offered no proof. The jury refused to believe him, probably rightly: if his first marriage was invalid and he believed himself to be legally married to Isabella Bankes, why had her will been drawn up in her maiden name? Smethurst was found guilty of bigamy, and sentenced to a year in prison.

Dickens, a great popularizer but not a great populist, was appalled that public opinion could so sway a verdict, and satirically suggested some amendments to the law, to deal with likeable poisoners. The jury, he suggested, should be given second- or third-hand accounts of the evidence, and could then 'constantly write letters about it to all the Papers', while doctors who had neither treated the victim nor performed any analyses chipped in with their opinions. In private as well as public he fulminated against the reprieve: 'I saw the beast of a prisoner (with my mind's eye) delivering his cut-and-dried speech ...

no one but the murderer could have delivered or conceived it.' The case 'needed no medical evidence either way', he was convinced; Smethurst, with his calm, collected demeanour, was a 'black scoundrel' and well deserved the gallows.

The very ordinariness of these medical poisoners disturbed him most. The year after Palmer's execution he had written: 'everywhere I see the late Mr. Palmer with his betting-book in his hands. Mr. Palmer sits next to me at the theatre; Mr. Palmer goes before me down the street … I look at the back of his bad head repeated in long long lines on the race course, and in the betting stand … and I vow to God I can see nothing but cruelty, covetousness, calculation … and low wickedness.' The essential here, as with Smethurst, was that Palmer was a villain, and yet he looked no different from anyone else. Dickens wanted a villain in life who looked and sounded like a villain in melodrama or fiction, even as he recognized that 'Cunning … secrecy, cold calculation, hard callousness and dire insensibility' were the tools of a murderer – a killer who looked and sounded like Bill Sikes would have a short career. Many similarly wanted their murderers to resemble O. Smith, a melodrama actor best known for playing villains. Smith had, according to one historian of melodrama, the perfect collection of villainous mannerisms: 'a half-crazed look and manner, a stealthy step, a hollow voice, and a piercing eye … His trump card … was his laugh, a taunting, deliberate basso-profundo effect in three syllables … That laugh … became a convention in the interpretation of villain roles.'

While most people continued to think of murderers as marked by such idiosyncrasies, in the last of these high-profile poison cases of the 1850s, the accused was not a man, not a thug, and also not a doctor, but something even more startling: a young woman from a good family. In contrast to the fears aroused by working-class poisoners, this middle-class female poisoner was, somehow, not frightening at all. Thousands of young ladies just like the one on trial could not get enough of the details. In the year of Smethurst, Emily Eden in her novel *The Semi-Detached House*, represented the attitude to middle-class domestic murder. Genteel, elderly Mrs Hopkinson tells her daughters: 'there is such a grand murder in the paper ... a whole family poisoned ... It was really very interesting, and I like a good murder that can't be found out; that is, of course, it is very shocking, but I like to hear about it.'

Many middle-class ladies like Mrs Hopkinson were reading about murders, both fictional and real. From the 1840s a number of magazines for working-class women and their families had begun publication, with titles like the *Family Herald* and the *Family Library*, or *Home Circle*. They cost between ½*d*. and 1*d*., and as well as recipes, housekeeping advice and other similar matter they also carried serial fiction which, said the *British Mother's Magazine*, a more upmarket publication, 'if weighed in the balance of strict Christian principle, would be found miserably wanting'. Perhaps, but by 1859 Dickens, always attuned to the *zeitgeist*, had started his new magazine, *All the Year Round*, with a serialization of *A Tale of Two Cities*, a violently bloody melodrama. This was followed over the next few years by many more middle-class family magazines: *Once a Week*, *Macmillan's*, *Cornhill* (edited by Thackeray), *Temple Bar*, *Argosy* (edited by Mrs Henry Wood, author of one of the most sensational of all sensation-fictions, *East Lynne*), *Belgravia* (edited by Mrs Braddon). All of them carried serial fiction, and, given the culture of the times, and their editors, much of that fiction was sensation-fiction.

Back in the real world, the many Mrs Hopkinsons followed every detail of the murder of Emile L'Angelier. Madeleine Smith, who was charged with his murder, was the daughter of a successful Glasgow architect. At seventeen, she had finished her education at Mrs Gorton's Academy for Young Ladies, near London, and had returned to Glasgow to live the life of an upper-middle-class girl, paying social calls with her mother and sister, doing decorative needlework, and having a disturbingly exotic private life, unknown to any of her family. Miss Smith had met Emile L'Angelier, who had seen her on the street and forced a reluctant acquaintance to introduce them without her parents' knowledge. L'Angelier was a twenty-six-year-old shipping clerk from Jersey, hard-working, if a little vain, steady, reliable, and a churchgoer. He was also earning £50 a year, which put him, to his great discontent, in the ranks of the very lowest middle class; he spent most of his income on fancy clothes, in order to look like a gentleman. He was no match socially for the Smith family, but a secret life appealed to the bored girl's sense of the dramatic – she could play at having a great passion thwarted by bourgeois parents. In her more than two hundred surviving letters to him, found on his death, Miss Smith quoted poetry, claimed to carry his letters next to her heart, and coyly refused to give him a lock of her hair because she had once promised a person 'now in the cold grave' never to do so, and 'a promise to the dead is sacred'. Not promises to the living, however. In early 1855 she told him that she had spoken to her father, and been forbidden to see him again; in 1856 this was repeated, with her mother now given the role of the heartless parent. Miss Smith blackmailed one of the family servants, who had an illicit follower of her own, to smuggle letters between the pair, and by 1856 they had become lovers. L'Angelier's letters suggest that Miss Smith took the lead here, while he was more cautious: 'I am sad it happened … We should indeed have waited till we were married.' In January 1857 the imagined future evaporated when Miss Smith's parents produced William Minnoch as a potential husband. Minnoch was a partner in a trading firm, prosperous, the equal of the Smiths in status and income. By February Miss Smith's letters began to prepare L'Angelier for the break. But he refused to follow her script, and threatened to go to her father. Her letters hastily resumed their affectionate 'one day' fantasies.

On 19 February Miss Smith attended the opera with Minnoch. (In a nice touch, they went to see Donizetti's *Lucrezia Borgia*: many would appreciate this later, including the eagle-eyed Mrs Braddon, who three years after the murder reproduced the episode in her novel *The Trail of the Serpent*. One of her characters condemns the opera as setting 'a dangerous example … we don't want our wives and daughters to learn how they may poison us without fear of detection'.) Later that night, L'Angelier talked to her through the kitchen window, their frequent assignation spot. She gave him a cup of hot chocolate and he later suffered a gastric attack, which passed; so did a second one after another meeting, three days later. On 12 March Miss Smith and her

parents set a wedding date; on 21 March, she made another assignation with L'Angelier; on 23 March, he was dead.

On his death, Miss Smith's letters were found; little detective work
was needed to discover that she had made two purchases of arsenic,
one 'to send to the gardener' at the Smiths' house in the country, the
other to 'to kill rats'. Nearly ninety grains of arsenic were recovered
from L'Angelier's body. The story was initially reported far more
discreetly than murder cases normally were. The *Glasgow Herald*
headlined its article 'Painful Event', and almost apologized for having
to report it at all. It had refrained from any mention of the case until
the 'names of the respective parties' were 'in the mouths of everyone',
and added that 'We fervently trust that the cloud which at present
obscures a most respectable and estimable household may be speedily
and most effectively removed.' A pamphlet struggled to find the
appropriate idiom, reporting Miss Smith in prison awaiting trial, 'her
hours ... spent in light reading, with occasional regrets at the want of
a piano'. Her 'equanimity' under such a charge was praised, 'and her
demeanour is certainly not that of a guilty person', wrote the *Daily
News* – the paper that had thought Smethurst guilty precisely because
of his coolness. *The Times*, too, was convinced that 'a highly and vir-
tuously bred young lady' could not be a killer: that was 'too appalling
for belief', and the report assured its equivalently middle-class readership that 'the possession of arsenic' was 'compatible with entire innocence' – probably the first time that newspaper had ever written those
words in the same sentence. Others, privately, were less convinced that
a middle-class demeanour meant virtue. Jane Carlyle reported that
'Miss Madeleine Smith said to old Dr Simpson, who attended her
during a short illness in Prison, and begged to use "the privilege of an
old man, and speak to her seriously at parting" – "My dear Doctor! it
is *so* good of you! But I wont [sic] let you trouble yourself ... for I
assure you I have quite made up my mind *to turn over a new leaf*!!!["]
That is a fact!' And whatever their opinions, everyone was reading
about it: Henry James, then only fourteen, knew about it; Nathaniel
Hawthorne said the reports were read out loud by guests in hotel
lounges in the Highlands, where he was on holiday.

The trial rapidly altered perceptions of the young lady's respectability. There were two big legal battles in court, one won by the defence, one by the prosecution. The defence's win probably saved Miss Smith's neck; the prosecution's destroyed her reputation. L'Angelier had kept a diary, which the prosecution failed to have admitted in evidence. Miss Smith's letters, however, were admitted, and her frank admissions of sexual pleasure were met with titillated fascination. The prosecution used the letters with discretion: they were read out when necessary, ensuring that no one could view the woman in the dock as a sweet young girl, but what were described as 'gross and indelicate allusions' and 'particular words' were censored to ensure that no one in court was offended – and even more, perhaps, to ensure that the jury's imaginations were allowed to run luridly free.

Public opinion was as divided as it had been with Smethurst. John Blackwood, an Edinburgh publisher, wrote to George Eliot: 'She is a nice young woman ... I really doubt whether she did poison the beast and at all events he deserved anything. I wish the dog had died and made no sign ...' Many were encouraged to think like this by the defence, whose unspoken theme throughout the trial was that a vulgar, lower-class foreign clerk had tried to raise himself by despoiling a pure middle-class girl, a girl just like the jury's and newspaper readers' sisters and daughters. While all this was only suggested, Miss Smith's barristers entered in evidence that L'Angelier had been rejected by women before, and had talked of suicide then; that he had a history of gastric attacks; that he took arsenic as medicine; that Miss Smith had spoken to friends about arsenic as a complexion-enhancer, on which subject articles had appeared in both *Blackwood's* and *Chambers's* magazines.*

Every bit as good as Miss Smith's defence was the inadequacy of the prosecution (and the incompetence of the judge). The prosecution

---

* Advertisements for arsenic-enhanced products continued to appear for the rest of the century. Dr. Mackenzie's Arsenical Toilet Soap 'with special ingredients' was promoted as 'a Beautifier of the Skin ... guaranteed to contain Arsenic' (see p.233). One of the celebrities recommending it in the accompanying copy was the actress Ellaline Terriss, whose own father was murdered, although not by arsenic (see pp.351–6).

failed to prove that poison had been administered; failed even to enquire what type of arsenic was used – Miss Smith's purchases had been coloured with indigo dye or soot (this was commonly done, precisely to prevent accidents or murder), and the analysts had not been asked to report on dye in L'Angelier's viscera, which might have determined the source of the poison. Miss Smith's letters were undated, and no particular care was taken by the prosecution to ensure that they were kept in the original envelopes, rendering the dates of the couple's meetings even more uncertain. The judge added to this woeful display by permitting one witness to provide entirely hearsay testimony, relaying conversations she had not herself heard. The prosecutor had also had a preliminary meeting with her, with 'no sheriff present to restrain improper interference'. The judge was aware of this, but made no attempt to prevent her evidence being heard. Most egregiously, the prosecution entirely failed to prove that Miss Smith had seen L'Angelier on the evenings before his gastric attacks. The best they could do was show that she had *hoped* to see him at those times: there were letters asking for meetings, but without the diary, there was no proof that these had taken place. The first meeting before the first gastric attack could be proved, but there was no evidence for the other two. The judge, notably prejudiced and even more notably muddled, summarized: 'In the ordinary matters of life, when you find the man came to town for the purpose of getting a meeting, you may come to the conclusion that they did meet; but, observe, that it becomes a very serious inference ... to draw. It may be a very natural inference, *looking at things morally*. None of you can doubt that she waited for him again, and if she waited the second night after her first letter, it was not surprising that she should look out for an interview on the second night after her second letter.' As far as this can be untangled, he appeared to be suggesting that if a person has performed an action once, it can be taken as a given that they will repeat the action under similar circumstances another time; and that while therefore it could be taken as a given that Miss Smith had met L'Angelier on the second and third nights, it would be wrong to take it as a given that she therefore poisoned him; and yet the jury might assume that she had done so, not because it was proved, or even because it was logical, but because she was an immoral hussy.

Many agreed with the judge. George Eliot responded to John Blackwood: 'it is a pity Palmer is not alive to marry her and be the victim of her second experiment in cosmetics – which is too likely to come one day or other'. Eliot's partner, G.H. Lewes, agreed: 'I see absolutely *no* trace of goodness in her. From first to last she is utterly bad.' Bad or not, the verdict after the eight-day trial was the Scottish in-between one, 'not proven'. As Lewes wrote to Blackwood, 'it is very lucky for that miserable girl that her victim was a Frenchman and she a Scotchwoman. Under any other circumstances she must have been hanged … the evidence against her was overwhelming.' The *Glasgow Herald* was only one of many voices reflecting this nationalistic, even xenophobic, view: L'Angelier, it reminded its readers, 'was of French extraction, if not French by birth', and 'The French … are notoriously addicted to the use of cosmetics,' therefore L'Angelier may have introduced 'the Scottish girl' to arsenic. In fact, the murder was altogether the victim's fault, for 'there were many circumstances … which gave the whole proceedings … an un-British character'. Class and gender also played their parts. L'Angelier was a foreigner, a seducer and a social climber, and it was frequently implicitly suggested that he was also a blackmailer. Scottish law accepted marriage by witnessed oath, and by sexual congress, and L'Angelier could thus have blackmailed Miss Smith, although there is no evidence that either was aware of this fact.

While the verdict was initially welcomed, opinion soon swung against Miss Smith. The *Glasgow Herald* blackened L'Angelier's reputation during the trial, but by the end of the month reported that he had been 'exemplary, amiable, and studious', and had the 'good opinion' of his employers, his relationship with Madeleine Smith being 'the only stain on his reputation'. In this ambivalent aftermath, various subscriptions were raised for the people involved in the case. From the days of Burke and Hare, monetary collections had been made for those who could not afford the necessary help when involved involuntarily in a legal situation, the amounts raised unwittingly reflecting public attitudes. After the discovery of Burke and Hare's crimes, the *Caledonian Mercury* collected less than £10 for Mr and Mrs Gray, the couple who had discovered the body of Mrs Docherty (the same amount, ironically enough, that Knox had paid the burkers for a single body); when Gray died the following year, his widow had to beg money to bury him. In 1849, £3,361.8s. was subscribed to a fund for Eliza Chestney, the maid who had rushed to the aid of Mrs Jermy when Rush attacked, while Emily Sandford, who might have been complicit in Rush's financial chicanery, if not in murder, had £2,101.10s. pledged to help her. In a later case, in 1874, the widow of the murderer Henry Wainwright (see pp.336–43) was the object of 'A great deal of sympathy', and £1,200 was raised for her, while the man who had unmasked the murderer, literally running halfway across London to alert the police, received £30. In Madeleine Smith's case, a group of local tradesmen made a presentation to her father to demonstrate their 'sympathy for his family under their present affliction', circumstances which 'reflect no discredit on him'.* A subscription was also raised for 'this unfortunate girl', said to amount to £10,000, although this is probably newspaper hyperbole. Not everyone approved. The *Era* reminded its readers that Miss Smith's 'moral reputation' was now 'out of the pale of deserved commiseration'. But whatever pieties the newspapers preached, the subscription for L'Angelier's widowed mother, who had relied financially on her son, amounted to a derisory £89.9s.3d. And ten days after the verdict Mr F. Bell of Thirsk named his bay filly Madeleine Smith, by Hermit out of La Femme Sage – 'Wise Woman' – a thumbed nose at morality if ever there was one.

Even more outrageous was 'Madeline [sic] Smith's Dream in Prison', a long, wildly pro-Miss Smith poem that describes the

* Others felt differently. Miss Smith's two sisters remained unmarried, perhaps coincidentally. Miss Smith herself had a more adventurous life. At some point in the next few years she found work as an embroiderer with Morris & Co., William Morris's design firm, and in 1861 she married George Wardle, Morris's bookkeeper, draughtsman and 'utility man generally'. In her late fifties – although claiming to be thirty-six – she moved to the USA; by her late seventies she was bigamously married to a builder thirty years her junior (and two years older than her son by Wardle).

accused woman imprisoned, and dreaming of her dead 'dearest friend', comparing herself to 'Christ our Lord', who was 'crucified,/Yet innocent of blood', while her 'loved one' is referred to as 'He', printed with a capital H, as Christ or God would be. The reunited couple share 'ardent kisses' and travel 'The Sovereign Highway ... That led to Paradise and God', where they are met by welcoming angels, before the prisoner is rudely awoken: 'For lo, it was a Dream'. Even to Miss Smith's supporters, the poem must have appeared blasphemous – it still does.

More mainstream were the Madeleine-Smith-influenced novels. In the early 1860s, Emma Robinson, who had dropped a cameo of Mrs Manning into *The Gold-Worshippers*, now built an entire three-volume novel around the story of a respectably brought-up young poisoner. Her Madeleine Graham reads about arsenic-eaters in the Austro-Hungarian empire, at the Misses Sparx's Finishing Educational Establishment for Young Ladies, and is befriended by the French mistress, who we know, because she is French, is a woman of loose morals. So it proves, and through her Madeleine meets a poor Frenchman named Camille LeTellier, while also keeping the rich Mr Behringbright dangling. The plot then closely follows the outlines of the Smith story, although much of it is set among landed estates in Ireland, with stag hunts and other upper-class joys unknown to a Glasgow architect's daughter. When Madeleine attempts to end her relationship with LeTellier, he blackmails her, having 'scores on scores of *letters* from you, which he could show to prove *everything*'. Madeleine immediately offers him a cup of coffee – 'You seem fond of coffee,' she purrs ominously. Ultimately her evil plot is foiled, and she is married off to the recovered LeTellier against her will and forced to live in Lyons, possibly considered by the novelist to be a fate worse than death.

This middle-class romance had been preceded by the anonymous 1857 *Story of Minie L'Angelier, or Madeleine Hamilton Smith*, a book returning to the earlier style of fictionalized accounts of true crime, similar to those that had appeared with the Burke and Hare murders, and with Greenacre and Maria Manning. This was not quite fiction, but not quite trial reporting either; instead it is a dossier, with a narrator's voice guiding the reader through each person's story, and suggesting an appropriate response to each episode. The book is only important for the influence it may have had on another, far greater, writer.

Wilkie Collins' *The Woman in White* (serialized 1859–60) is frequently called the first sensation-novel, and it is possibly the one with the greatest pretensions to 'literature'.* Collins followed this in 1868 with *The Moonstone*, one of the starting points of detective fiction. To a degree, it can be said that these genres grew out of the heightened emotions surrounding the poison trials of the 1850s. Collins told a friend that the narrative structure of *The Woman in White* occurred to him after attending a trial in London in 1856, noticing how each witness held a single strand of the story, which when woven together formed a dense narrative. He did not name the trial, but it is unlikely that if he had been trial-going in London in 1856 he would have missed Palmer's, the biggest of the decade.

Whichever it was, *The Woman in White* is shaped as a series of overlapping voices, with additional 'voices' from diaries, documents and depositions. 'As the Judge might once have heard it, so the Reader shall hear it now,' says the omniscient narrator in one of his few appearances. There is no evidence that Collins knew *The Story of Minie L'Angelier*, but this method of switching between reality and fiction in crime reporting was not the novelty he made out. In 1855 the author of *Paul Ferroll* had pasted trial transcripts in albums for reference, and the year after the publication of *The Story of Minie L'Angelier* she wrote of her readers as a jury who have 'to answer Yes or No'. Even the popular press routinely moved between reportage and fiction. One journalist at Madeleine Smith's trial saw a man leaning against the ledge of the courtroom gallery, who 'recalled to mind irresistibly the picture of Rigaud sitting at an upper window in the

---

* Or that is our judgement now. In 1862, *Blackwood's* magazine classed Dickens' *Great Expectations* as a sensation-novel, and as a less successful one than *The Woman in White*, at that.

concluding number of *Little Dorrit* (which had just ended its serial publication).

Similarly, the magazine serials had their preoccupations echoed in non-fiction articles in the same issues. As episodes of *The Woman in White* appeared in *All the Year Round*, articles in the rest of the magazine mirrored the preoccupations of the characters: when Marian Halcombe was stricken with a mystery illness in the novel, the magazine printed an article on nervous diseases; a chapter on the fictionally neurasthenic Mr Fairlie was mirrored by a non-fiction piece by a former resident of Bedlam. These shifting lines between form and function, fiction and non-fiction, were not unique to Collins. Mrs Braddon's *The Trail of the Serpent* used the casebook formula pioneered in memoirs like Vidocq's. Many other novels incorporated fictional trial transcripts, their style familiar to every newspaper reader.

Truth, the newspapers and journals constantly told their readers, is every bit as strange as, if not stranger than, fiction. Collins admitted to his friends – and flatly denied in print – that he used real crimes in his fiction. *The Law and the Lady* reversed the Madeleine Smith story, with a man, Eustace Macallan, receiving a verdict of 'not proven'. Collins possibly also made use of J.H. Burton's *Narratives from Criminal Trials in Scotland*, which dated from before the Smith trial (he is known to have owned a copy), but Madeleine Smith's case was more obviously the moving force. Macallan's revealing diary is read out in court, as Miss Smith's letters had been; he buys arsenic, claiming he wants to kill rats, as Miss Smith had done; his wife's schoolfriends testify that she had spoken of arsenic as a complexion-improver, as Miss Smith's had. Another case, less well known in Britain, triggered *The Woman in White*. The book by Maurice-Méjan that Collins had used in his retelling of the Eliza Fenning story also included the story of the Marquise de Douhault, whose brother had defrauded her of her inheritance. When she attempted to take him to court, she was drugged and awoke to find herself incarcerated under a false name in the Salpetrière, the Parisian Bedlam, while her brother announced the sad news of his sister's death. It was two years before she was able to smuggle out a letter which led to her being freed. This is in essence the plot that Collins' villain, Count Fosco, conceives in *The Woman in White*. Even the detail of the white dress that marks out the Woman in White of the title had its source in the French case: when the Marquise was finally released from the Salpetrière, she was handed back the white dress she had been wearing on admission two years previously.

To his reading public, Collins continued to be disingenuous about these links to reality. In his 1866 novel *Armadale* there is perhaps the most teasing of his hall-of-mirrors 'it was true' formulations. Collins claimed that it was only after he had planned the novel's denouement – when his villainess attempts to murder Allan Armadale by wafting poison gas into his bedroom – that he read of three nightwatchmen on a ship called the *Armadale*, berthed at Liverpool, who had died of 'carbonic acid gas'. A modern scholar has noted, however, that *The Times* mistakenly printed 'carbonic acid gas', rather than carbon monoxide, and Collins replicated the mistake: he had copied the news report, whatever his protestations. Again, in 1871, in the dedication to *Poor Miss Finch* (which used, in the backstory, details from the Rush murders), he wrote that 'one of these days, I may be able to make use of some of the many interesting stories of events that have really happened ... Thus far I have not ventured to [do so] ... The true incidents are so "far-fetched"; and the conduct of the real people is so "grossly improbable". Yet to his friends he acknowledged that while the plot of *The Woman in White* had 'been called outrageous', 'It was true.'

The plot of *The Woman in White* is complex, and appears even more so because of the overlapping narratives. Late one night near Hampstead Heath, Walter Hartright, a poor artist, meets a mysterious woman dressed in white, and helps her to escape from her unidentified pursuers. He takes up a position teaching drawing to two half-sisters in Cumberland, Laura Fairlie, an heiress with whom he falls in love, and Marian Halcombe, masculine (she has a moustache) and intelligent. Laura loves Walter, but is engaged to Sir Percival Glyde (obviously a villain, from his penny-blood name, and also from the fact that *All the Year Round*, in which this was serialized, placed another article by Collins, on Vidocq, close by). Soon after their marriage Laura discovers that Glyde is heavily in debt. We now discover that the mysterious woman in white was Anne Catherick, Laura's unknown half-sister, who has been incarcerated in an asylum by Sir Percival to prevent her revealing his closely guarded secret. To get access to Laura's fortune, Count Fosco, Sir Percival's friend and co-villain, plans to have Laura incarcerated under Anne's name, while Anne, who has a weak heart, will conveniently be allowed to die and be buried as Laura. Marian discovers their plot, and with Walter panting in her wake (he, as the man, is the nominal prime mover, but he is a pale shadow compared to the heroic Marian) sets out to rescue Laura.* Laura is freed, but is still legally dead, so Walter seeks out Sir Percival's secret, which is that he is illegitimate, and therefore not 'Sir' Percival at all. Sir Percival is burnt to death while attempting to destroy the parish register that would expose him, Fosco is forced into a confession that permits Laura to recover her fortune, and is then assassinated in a timely fashion by a member of the Carbonari, the Italian secret society he had betrayed decades before, who just happens to have discovered him at this opportune moment.

The plot of *The Woman in White* is no more plausible than those of many penny-bloods or gothic romances. Laura, an educated upper-class woman, is presented in the asylum as a village girl with no education; she could speak French, play the piano, paint – it was not possible that they could be confused. Likewise, although she is a typi-cally mid-Victorian weedy heroine, frequently ailing, she is carefully tended by those who wish her ill before being imprisoned in an asylum. Why isn't she simply allowed to die? The question of why this book found lasting success while books with equally implausible plots were forgotten has two answers. One is that the gaps in the plot are more than covered over by Collins' superb narrative drive. More

* Marian's primacy was recognized by many. Men were reported to have written in to the magazine offering themselves in marriage to the original, and Edward FitzGerald, adapter/translator of *The Rubáiyát of Omar Khayyám*, named his boat the *Marian Halcombe* in her honour.

important than that is the character of Count Fosco. The villain of the piece should have been the evil Sir Percival, but he is of the melodrama school – he is a villain because he is bad, and bad because he is a villain. Fosco, a fat, amiable, chuckling monster, represents a new, more psychologically reflective type of villainy, one in which a superficially respectable – a likeable – man, a man you would invite into your home, turns out to have a completely separate, secret personality. He bursts on the world as a new type of fictional malefactor: the man who smiles, and smiles, and is a villain.

Fosco is the source of the new archetype of the master-criminal, an archetype which would lead to Sherlock Holmes's rival Moriarty, and even James Bond's Blofeld. The master-criminal was now a gentleman; he was not only educated, he was cleverer than anyone around him. Fosco was medically trained, had knowledge of secret poisons, and esoteric skills in sudden death. But in his public persona, every bit as important as his secret criminal life, he was a connoisseur of art and music (like Madeleine Smith, he attends a performance of *Lucrezia Borgia*), a man of charisma and charm. Collins may have plotted himself into a corner towards the end of the book – Fosco's plan is so elaborately successful that Collins has to make him confess. In terms of plotting, the situation is awkward, but Fosco, no less than Falstaff, is one of those characters whose life force enables him to break free of the book that holds him. His malevolent glee at his own cleverness, his posturing, preening, glorious – and gloriously comic – egotism are what matter.

Other sensation-novels using similar source material were more conventional, relying on older fashions. The Irish writer Sheridan Le Fanu's *Uncle Silas* (1864) had an isolated house, home to Uncle Silas himself, a traditionally sinister villain who regularly falls into drug-induced trances, and who is guardian to the innocent heiress Maud. The backstory, however, was a reprise of Palmer's murder of Cook. Silas, when young, was a reckless gambler who entertained Mr Charke, 'a gentleman of the turf' who had won large sums from Silas, only to be found with his throat slit in a room locked from the inside, while his 'memorandum book in which his bets were noted' and much of his money were missing. Disconcertingly to the historian looking for archaeological traces of murder in fiction, some of the elements that seem to have been so obviously drawn from the Palmer case had in reality been created independently by Le Fanu. In 1838 Le Fanu had published 'The Murdered Cousin', the story of a gambler murdered in a locked room, whose 'double-clasped pocket-book' listing his host's debts vanished after his death. (This locked-room puzzle story appeared three years before Edgar Allan Poe's 'The Murders in the Rue Morgue', supposedly the 'first' locked-room story.)* In *Uncle Silas*, twenty-five years later, these fictional details were adjusted to fit more closely to the subsequent facts of Palmer's crime, while the locked-room element was subordinated: in a stage adaptation of *Uncle Silas* at the end of the century, Le Fanu's cunning solution to the locked room – a revolving window frame – is present, but Charke is murdered in the room next door, entirely missing the point.

Gradually, however, it was the detective element that prevailed, while the true-crime element faded into the background. Soon people were less interested in what crimes were committed than in how they were solved, copying, in fictional form, the earlier movement of policing from prevention to detection. To satisfy this desire for 'how', stories with detective heroes began to appear. Originally, many presented themselves as memoirs; a few were, but more were fictional constructs. In keeping with the general interest in police work, and with the expansion of magazines and newspapers that carried fictional tales of murder right next to crime reports, Edgar Allan Poe's 'The Murders in the Rue Morgue' appeared in 1841. It is often put forward as the first detective story, and has many of the elements we now expect of the genre. Dupin is the prototypical amateur sleuth† with razor-like deductive abilities who outpaces the slow-thinking police,

* It is useful to be reminded that pretty well all 'firsts' are nothing of the kind – Inspector Bucket as the 'first' detective was preceded by the stories of Thomas Waters; *The Moonstone* as the 'first' detective novel was preceded by Braddon's *The Trail of the Serpent*.

† The word sleuth, to mean detective, would not appear for another half-century. Originally short for sleuth-hound, or bloodhound, it only gained its secondary meaning in Britain early in the twentieth century.

and whose obscure technical knowledge leads him infallibly to the truth. (For example, he recognizes that a piece of ribbon left at the crime scene is tied with a knot 'which few besides sailors can tie, and is peculiar to the Maltese'.) Other elements of the story site it more firmly in the early nineteenth century, such as the penny-blood gothic window-dressing peeping out of Poe's description of the narrator's house, 'a time-eaten and grotesque mansion, long decayed'. The 'Recollections of a Police Officer' by the pseudonymous 'Thomas Waters' had appeared in *Chambers's Edinburgh Journal* from 1849, the same year in which Dickens depicted Inspector Bucket in *Bleak House* and Collins published 'A Terribly Strange Bed', another early locked-room puzzle, in which a gambler wins big and is persuaded to sleep the night in the gambling den, whereupon the canopy over his bed mechanically descends, threatening to squash him so that his winnings can be reappropriated by the house.* The story, however, is narrated by the gambler, so the reader sees what is happening as he does, rather than having the solution presented at the end: there is no detective, and no puzzle.

Sensation-fiction implied a world in which every respectable person had a potentially unrespectable secret life, while crime fiction reassured the reader that only one person did, and that she or he would be separated from the respectable at the end. Sensation-fiction was about mystery; crime-writing was about certainty. Increasing urbanization had created a world where large numbers of strangers lived side by side in ignorance of others' real natures: sensation-fiction, with its aura of menacing domesticity, might be seen as a response to this. *Bleak House* contained a policeman and a 'solution', but it was also full of people silently watching, attempting to read the

---

* Conan Doyle might have known this story, or as a small boy he might have read *The Poor Boys of London* (see p.378), a penny-dreadful in which at one point the policeman is trapped by the villain in a room where the floor becomes red-hot and the ceiling comes down to crush him (our hero escapes). The premise is mirrored in Doyle's 'The Adventure of the Engineer's Thumb', in which an engineer is asked by counterfeiters to repair a faulty mechanism in their press. After he has done his work, they attempt to murder him in a room with a descending ceiling.

truth behind their neighbours' façades: characters have 'a silent way of noticing', they 'never tired of watching', are full of 'private researches … watchings … listenings'.* Tulkinghorn the lawyer sets the plot in motion with his determination to uncover Lady Dedlock's secret. He is the old-fashioned type of detective, the thief-taker – he is in it for personal gain – while Bucket is the new, professional kind. But while the new type is depicted, the novel adheres to the older forms.

Sensation-fiction also implied that anyone could be a detective. The lawyer in *The Woman in White* sends a servant to track down a missing woman, while in Le Fanu's *A Lost Name*, a vicar is requested to 'examine' a crime scene. More commonly, it was assumed that the appropriate person to take on the detective role was a concerned family member. This was standard in melodrama: Pharos Lee, the Bow Street Runner in the Maria Marten plays, is driven by family loyalty, not by professional duty: 'On my father's grave I took the oath of vengeance to hunt you down,' he tells Corder. 'I joined the law to complete my task.' Later, Robert Audley unmasks Lady Audley in order to protect his uncle, as well as to locate his missing friend. In life rather than fiction, James Fitzjames Stephen, in an essay on 'Detectives in Fiction and Real Life', rejected the reality of the working-class detective, and said that Palmer's crime had been uncovered owing entirely to Cook's father's suspicions.

One of the most commercially successful amateurs appeared in 1861, with Mrs Braddon's *Lady Audley's Secret*. This was sensation-fiction in full, rip-roaring glory, with a melodrama plot, sensation-scenes, penny-dreadful scenarios, all neatly tucked under a tidy domestic surface. As Mrs Braddon herself said, 'the amount of crime, treachery, murder and slow poisoning, & general infamy required [by her readers] … is something terrible'. Terrible, but, apart from slow poisoning, all appear in *Lady Audley's Secret*. George Talboys, having made his fortune in Australia, returns to England to discover that

---

* In a series of so-called detective stories that appeared in *Household Words*, 'detection' is almost entirely equated with watchfulness. As late as 1897, in *Dorcas Dene, Detective*, when a private detective asks Dorcas to help him, she is initially repelled: 'You want me to … watch people?'

Helen, the wife he left behind, has died. To distract him, his oldest friend, Robert Audley, takes him down to visit his uncle, Sir Michael Audley, newly married to Lucy Graham, a much younger, poor but beautiful governess. At Audley Court, the new Lady Audley unaccountably avoids her guests, and George mysteriously vanishes. Robert, against his will, is forced to investigate his friend's disappearance, amid his growing suspicion of his uncle's wife. He discovers that she is in fact Helen Talboys, George's supposedly dead wife; to keep her secret she burns down the inn where he is sleeping. This fails to kill him, and she admits that she was George Talboys' wife, but pleads in mitigation that he went off to Australia, leaving her with a small child and no means of support. This cuts no ice: Sir Michael, understandably upset to discover that he has married bigamously, abandons her, and Robert has Lady Audley declared insane after she admits that she pushed George down a well when he confronted her. Only now is it revealed, in a deathbed confession by the innkeeper, that George was rescued, and is alive. He returns, and after some neat tidying up of the romantic subplots everyone (except Lady Audley) ends happily ever after.

In this sensation-novel Robert is forced to turn detective, in the way Walter Hartright and Marian Halcombe were in *The Woman in White*, not for the love of the chase, or for abstract notions of justice, but as a consequence of friendship. Dickens, in the same year as *The Woman in White*, drew a similar portrait, with the detective in 'Hunted Down' remorselessly tracking Slinkton for love of the murdered woman. It is fortunate, but not essential, that he is 'an observer of men' who finds himself noticing each 'little key [that] will open a very heavy door'. He is drawn into detection by emotion, but solves the crime by observation. Observing was an equal-opportunities occupation in fiction. It may be because so many plots revolved around righting a family wrong that there was a plethora of fictional women detectives. In sensation-fiction there were countless of these avenging fiancées, wives and daughters: Valeria Woodville in *The Law and the Lady* finds the real murderer of her husband's first wife; Marian Halcombe in *The Woman in White* searches for her sister; Anne

Rodway in 'The Diary of Anne Rodway' discovers her fellow lodger's killer; Magdalen Vanstone in *No Name* fights for herself and her sister after her parents' death – and those are only Wilkie Collins' women.

A bridge from these family-burdened women to professional women doing a job is Mrs Bucket, who helps her husband in *Bleak House* by keeping watch on Hortense, the Maria Manning surrogate, 'night and day'. She is 'a lady of natural detective genius', declares her proud husband. A decade later, the professional female detective was born. She was a sharp contrast to the reality of policing, which was entirely male until two women were hired to look after female prisoners at police stations in 1883. The legal system was even more testosterone-only: not only were judges and lawyers all men, so were juries until 1919. Yet in the early 1860s the female detective arrived on the page full-blown. In Edward Ellis's* penny-dreadful *Ruth the Betrayer* (published in fifty-two numbers, 1862–63), Ruth Trail is 'a female detective – a sort of spy we use in the hanky-panky way when a man would be too clumsy'. She is not of the regular police, but 'attached to a notorious Secret Intelligence Office, established by an ex-member of the police force'. (Rather wonderfully, it is so secret that the office has a brass plaque on the door: 'Secret Agent', it reads.) Similarly, in *Armadale*, the private inquiry office in Shadyside Place has 'women attached', who easily disguise themselves as servants, or milliners, to go into places male detectives might not be able to.

Ruth precedes what are frequently called the first fictional female detectives. It is believed that the pseudonymous Andrew Forrester published his *Revelations of a Female Detective* sometime in 1864. Forrester's lady detective, referred to as 'G' by her colleagues in what appears to be a private inquiry office, hires herself out, usually disguised as a dressmaker or milliner. She is coy about who or what led her into this profession: 'It may be that I took to the trade ... because I had no other means of making a living; or it may be that the

---

* Edward Ellis was the pseudonym of Charles Henry Ross, possibly writing with Ernest Warren.

work [sic] of detection I had a longing which I could not overcome. It may be that I am a widow working for my children – or I may be an unmarried woman, whose only care is herself.' These stories appeared almost simultaneously with the anonymous *The Experiences of a Lady Detective* (the author is thought to have been the journalist William Stephen Hayward). Here the lady detective is Mrs Paschal, who is widowed, and forced to work at this unwomanly task from economic necessity. The reader is clearly supposed to understand that she works for Scotland Yard – her superior is a colonel, as was Scotland Yard's real Commissioner, Charles Rowan. Mrs Paschal is a curious mix. Her superior approves of her because she shows 'prompt and passive obedience', but the front cover has a woman raising her skirt to show her ankle, while holding a cigarette (unimaginably modern twenty years before one book still thought it necessary to explain that cigarettes were 'paper cigars').

This ambivalence was not for women detectives alone. The police, as we have seen, were both admired and distrusted. Early-nineteenth-century fiction, together with its eighteenth-century forefathers, had understood the law to encompass punishment, not detection, and its professionalism had a negative connotation: money corrupted justice. In Godwin's *Caleb Williams* the detective's motive is, according to de Quincey in 1845, 'vile eavesdropping inquisitiveness'. G.W.M. Reynolds, in *The Mysteries of London*, put it more simply for his working-class readers: a policeman 'doubtless had several golden reasons for not noticing anything' in a rich man's house, while he 'instantly ran ... after a small boy who he suspected to be a thief, because the poor wretch wore an uncommonly shabby hat'. In *Martin Chuzzlewit*, likewise, Chevy Slyme joins the police on purpose to be 'bought off'.

While Inspector Bucket in 1852 had done much to dispel this attitude, it was an earlier series of stories, begun in 1849, that was the first native-born foray into detective fiction for the sake of detection. These pseudonymous *Recollections of a Police Officer* appeared in *Chambers's Edinburgh Journal* over four years, and were presented as the memoirs of a real policeman. However, 'Charles Martel's' *The*

Detective's Notebook, similarly presented as a memoir in 1860, is a mix: some of the episodes are old-fashioned chase stories, but others start to develop the idea of detection as a skill.

The main way of telling fictional memoirs from real ones is to look at the crimes. A real detective, James McLevy, who joined the force in Scotland in 1833, claimed to have worked on more than 2,220 cases by the time he produced two volumes of reminiscences, *Curiosities of Crime* and *The Sliding Scale of Life*, both in 1861. The cases he described included the theft of hens and tobacco, a mugging, a pickpocketing. All except two, one a concealment of birth, the other a murder, were property crimes, and the sentences ranged between sixty days (for the theft of some ducks), nine months (the concealment of birth) and fourteen years' transportation (the murder, reduced to culpable homicide). The volumes were reprinted a few times, but had no great success. How different were the stories of James McGovan, whose *Brought to Bay* was published in 1878 and sold 25,000 copies.* McGovan claims that McLevy was his 'old friend', and presents his work as reminiscences too, but here the stolen ducks are superseded by vast jewel thefts, a murder disguised as suicide, a counterfeiting ring run from 'Fegan's'. These are romances, tales of plucky young lads, broken-hearted mothers, noble sisters. Here there is no place for a crime such as McLevy reported, a man who stole 4½d. from an old woman – every penny she had in the world. McLevy's world is the real world, a world where Helen Blackwood, a Glasgow prostitute, shared a room measuring eight feet by six feet inches with her lover, two other prostitutes who stayed there intermittently and two homeless boys, aged nine and eleven, whom she let sleep under her bed. This was reality.

For some time the working-class reading population remained ambivalent about detective fiction. *Ruth the Betrayer* was the heroine, but was 'degraded by the hateful calling of spy and informer'. Forrester's middle-class Miss G. fought back: 'I am quite aware there

---

* While these stories were finding such success in Scotland, Arthur Conan Doyle was a medical student in Edinburgh.

is something peculiarly objectionable in the spy, but ... we detectives are necessary,' she states. And slowly the working class came to agree, at least some of the time. In *The Boy Detective* Ernest Keen is absolved of this horrible taint: 'Our hero ... could use dissimulation as a shield or sword when dealing with powerful enemies. In common life such conduct would be detestable, but Ernest Keen was the BOY DETECTIVE ... in his own character there was not a franker, more impulsive lad in the world.' *The Boy Detective*, too, was one of the earliest penny-dreadfuls to teach readers how to detect vicariously: when Keen's boss, Inspector Hawks, looks for clues he explains how one must not walk over ground where there might be footprints, how to match the suspect's shoes against these prints, how to check for bloodstains and more.

The Boy Detective was driven by the success of *Lady Audley's Secret*, of which there were at least four London productions and one provincial one within twelve months of its first serialization. A West End production spoon-fed the audience explanations for all the novel's mysteries by playing out each scene: Lady Audley's backstory, and her connection to Helen Talboys, only slowly revealed in the book, were straightforwardly recited in the opening scene. The version at the Victoria entirely distrusted the audience's ability to follow the plot, and spelled out the mystery elements – Lady Audley relates her entire history in soliloquy before pushing George down the well in view of the audience.

It was only in 1866, at Astley's Amphitheatre, that the audience finally watched a detective detecting. This new focus was signalled by the title, which no longer concentrated on the villainess but, as *The Mysteries of Audley Court*, highlighted the puzzle element. Now Robert Audley instructs the audience about his job, which is to gather 'a scrap, a shred, the fragment of a letter, an incautious word, a shadow ... links of steel in the wonderful chain forged by the science of the detective officer'. This was only shortly after the *Englishwoman's Domestic Magazine* noted stories 'called "detective" novels', which place the reader 'in the position of a Bow-street runner, panting and breathless to join in the "hue and cry", and to run down imaginary crime'.* This was, significantly, not in an article entitled 'Detective Literature', but in one entitled 'Sensation Literature'. For the moment, the two forms were not distinct.

The following year, Wilkie Collins turned once again to Madeleine Smith's story, merging elements with that of Smethurst, in *Armadale*, his incredibly complicated and thus frequently overlooked novel. Two men, one rich, one poor, are both named Allan Armadale, the poor one travelling under the name Ozias Midwinter after running away from his unhappy, abused mother and cruel stepfather. He becomes friends with the rich Allan Armadale without knowing that the father of rich Allan Armadale was the murderer of his own father. Both Allans fall in love with the glamorous and obviously bad Lydia Gwilt (she, like Lady Audley, has red hair, now a villainess-indicator;† her surname, only one letter away from 'guilt', is a clue too). Lydia marries Midwinter: she knows he is really named Allan Armadale, and she plans to murder the rich Allan so that she, legally 'Mrs Allan Armadale', can claim his estate. She is foiled by Midwinter, and dies. (The book is actually much better than this summary makes it sound, once past the initial trauma of all the Allan Armadales.)

In Lydia Gwilt's backstory, we are told that she poisoned her first husband, a gambler who beat her. Emile L'Angelier was similarly believed by many to have deserved his end, for his temerity in approaching a girl outside his class. In *Armadale* too the victim is perceived as the evil-doer: 'I say he deserved it!' Unlike Miss Smith, Miss Gwilt was found guilty, yet, as with both Miss Smith and

---

* The *Oxford English Dictionary*, surprisingly, dates the first print usage for 'detective novel' to 1924.

† Although these red-headed women were regarded by the reading and theatre-going public as epitomes of evil, they were remarkably inefficiently evil. Lady Audley tries to kill George Talboys, Robert Audley and Luke Marks (the innkeeper), and fails each time. Lydia Gwilt tries three times to kill Allan Armadale, and doesn't succeed either.

   Miss Gwilt demonstrates one difference between sensation-fiction and melodrama. In melodrama, any character with a mysterious past turns out to be a baby switched at birth, or stolen by gypsies, or the daughter/sister/wife of one of the other central characters. Miss Gwilt, however, springs out of nowhere. In this novel of a family curse passed down through the generations she alone has no family, and her existence and place in the world is never explained – something that would have been unthinkable in the older style.

Smethurst, she was 'alive and hearty … free to … poison at her own entire convenience, any man, woman, or child that happens to stand in her way'. Collins makes this parallel plain in a long passage describing what happened after her trial:

> On the evening of the Trial, two or three young Buccaniers [sic] of Literature went down to two or three newspapers offices, and wrote two or three heartrending leading articles … The next morning the public caught light like tinder … All the people who had no personal experience whatever on the subject, seized their pens and rushed … into print. Doctors who had *not* attended the sick man, and who had *not* been present at the examination of the body, declared by dozens that he had died a natural death. Barristers without business, who had *not* heard the evidence, attacked the jury who *had* heard it … The general public followed the lead of the barristers and the doctors, and the young Buccaniers who had set the thing going … the Home-Secretary, in a state of distraction … [had] the conflict of medical evidence submitted to one great doctor; and when the one great doctor took the merciful view, after expressly stating, in the first instance, that he knew nothing practically of the merits of the case, the Home-Secretary was perfectly satisfied … the verdict of the Law was reversed by general acclamation; and the verdict of the newspapers carried the day.

Then, once Miss Gwilt was reprieved, 'A general impression prevailed directly that she was not quite innocent enough, after all, to be let out of prison then and there! Punish her a little – that was the state of the popular feeling.' And so she was re-tried, this time 'for the robbery, after having been pardoned for the murder'.

Although the initiating moment of *Armadale*, a dream in which the action of the novel is foretold, closely resembles old-fashioned melodrama from Mrs Marten's dream of the Red Barn onwards, *Armadale* more generally looked forward to the new detective genre. Like *Bleak House*, it is a novel where everyone spies and is spied on. There is James Bashwood, a professional private detective; Armadale hires someone to spy on Lydia; Lydia in turn spies on Armadale and his

putative fiancée; a solicitor investigates Lydia's friend Mrs Oldershaw.*
With all of that, Collins shared the common view of professional
detectives. *Armadale*'s detective operates out of an office on 'Shadyside
Place', and in case that isn't clear enough, he is described as a 'vile
creature ... a man professionally ready on the merest suspicion (if the
merest suspicion paid him) to get under our beds, and to look through
gimlet-holes in our doors'. Allan Armadale, headstrong and naïve,
initially rejects all detective methods of investigating Lydia's background, calling them 'meddling in her private affairs'. His solicitor,
less sympathetic but more pragmatic, calibrates levels of detection: 'a
man from Scotland Yard' is less objectionable than a private
detective.

This *de haut en bas* attitude was exacerbated by the fact that the police
could be hired by any private individual. 'At any moment you might,
on the application of any individual in the country who chose to pay
the costs, be sent to any part of the United Kingdom, or even out of
it,' wrote a Scotland Yard inspector in 1890. This private hiring (and
therefore firing) of detectives survived even longer in fiction, consoli-
dating the idea that detectives were like petty tradesmen, there when
needed by the middle classes, dismissed when they were no longer
wanted. In Mrs Gaskell's *North and South* (1854–55) the police investigating a death are fired by the northern manufacturer to protect the
heroine; they are fired again in Mrs Oliphant's *Salem Chapel* (1862),
by Dickens once more, in *Our Mutual Friend* (1865), and by Collins
in *The Moonstone* (1868).

    The Moonstone was a halfway house for attitudes to police, and
fictional detectives. The jewel of the title (really a huge diamond),
stolen from a Hindu shrine during the Indian Mutiny, is bequeathed
to Rachel Verinder, from whose bedroom it is stolen. The suspects are

---

* Mrs Oldershaw is yet another real criminal fictionalized by Collins: she is a portrait of
Madame Rachel, otherwise Rachel Leverson, the owner of a cosmetics shop in Bond Street.
She was convicted of blackmail after *Armadale* was published, but even before it was
generally suspected (and Collins was happy to reinforce the suspicion) that she was also
an abortionist and procuress.

Rachel herself, Rosanna Spearman, a maid with a dubious past, a group of Indian 'jugglers' who have been performing in the neighbourhood, and Franklin Blake, Rachel's cousin. Sergeant Cuff suspects Rosanna, who commits suicide; after she is posthumously cleared his suspicion lights on Rachel, at which point Lady Verinder pays him off and sends him away. It takes the local scientific amateur to deduce that Franklin Blake stole the diamond in an opium-induced trance; he was seen by Rachel who, for love of him, has kept silent, leading to her suspicious behaviour. The diamond is re-stolen by Geoffrey Ablewhite, another suitor for Rachel's hand, who turns out to be an embezzler and a pious fraud. Ultimately, the Indian jugglers, high-caste Brahmins in disguise, murder Ablewhite and steal the stone a third time, to return it to its rightful place in the shrine.

On his first appearance in the Verinder household, Sergeant Cuff adapts himself admirably to the people he interviews: with Mrs Yolland, a friend of the maid Rosanna, he discusses the royal family, Primitive Methodism, and the price of fish: 'In about a quarter of an hour ... good Mrs. Yolland was persuaded that she was talking to Rosanna's best friend.' But she is working-class. With the upper classes, things are not so easy. Cuff is outside his area of expertise, which is criminals, who by definition are of the 'dangerous', or working, classes (even though all the thieves in the novel turn out to be gentry). Thus he mistakes the evasions of Rachel Verinder, the daughter of the house, who is shielding the man she loves, for criminal knowledge. In spite of his professionalism, he still sees his function as that of a smoother-over of middle-class problems: 'I had a family scandal to deal with,' he says, 'which it was my business to keep within the family limits.' There is no difference between this professional man and the strictly amateur Mr Brownlow of *Oliver Twist* thirty years earlier. Sergeant Cuff would have arrested a guilty housemaid; a guilty daughter of a titled family would have had her crime kept 'within the family limits', at least as presented by a middle-class novelist for his middle-class audience.

Anthony Trollope's *The Eustace Diamonds*, begun the year after the serialization of *The Moonstone*, although only published in 1871–73, has been described as a parody, or inversion, of that earlier novel. Instead of Rachel Verinder stealing her own jewel, in *The Eustace Diamonds* Lizzie Eustace pockets the diamonds which are the property of her dead husband's estate. The family lawyer is stymied: 'Had it been an affair simply of thieves, such as thieves ordinarily are, everything would have been discovered long since; – but when lords and ladies with titles come to be mixed up with such an affair, – folk in whose house a policeman can't have his will at searching and brow-beating, – how is a detective to detect anything?'

This was the question that had confounded real detectives from the beginning. In 1851, following the lean years of the 1840s, and the 1848 revolutions in Europe, there were fears that the mob, the working classes, would rise up in some way at the opening of the Great Exhibition in London. *Household Words*, therefore, followed 'The Metropolitan Protectives' for three days, and commended the force's 'patience, promptitude, order, vigilance, zeal, and judgment'.* The unspoken assumption of the piece, however, was that the force was watching the working classes in order to protect the middle classes; the idea of their watching the middle classes was so alien it appears never to have entered the authors' heads. In the case of Constance Kent (see pp.362–79), where a middle-class home was subjected to scrutiny, Samuel Kent, the head of the household, automatically limited the access of the police, resenting, said his solicitor, 'an uncourteous intrusion'. Two years later, in Mrs Henry Wood's *Mrs Halliburton's Troubles*, a fictional detective found himself in a similar situation. He hears of a sudden and violent death in a middle-class house, and, says the notably nettled authorial voice, he entered, 'possibly to gratify his curiosity; possibly because he thought his services might be in some way required'. First comes the idea that the policeman is gratifying his vulgarly lower-class curiosity, only second the thought that he might be needed. The idea that it was his *duty* to interfere, a more modern notion, is entirely absent. Similarly, when in

* The piece began with an unintentionally counterproductive typographical error, referring to 'the Defective Police'.

the novel the police sergeant comes to arrest the suspected murderer, a middle-class solicitor's son, he is told, 'You are overstepping –'

A decade later, another murder case would bring the public back to the doors of the middle-class home. But for some reason, despite an extraordinary series of bizarre details, the case of Christiana Edmunds never really caught the popular imagination.

In August 1871 the Brighton papers reported that a number of locally prominent families had received parcels of fruit, cakes and sweets, each with an accompanying note: 'A few home-made cakes for the children, those done up are flavoured on purpose for yourself to enjoy. You will guess who this is from; I can't mistify [sic] you, I fear. I hope this will arrive in time for you to-night while the eatables are fresh.' Everyone who ate from the parcels became ill. The recipients included Mrs Beard, a doctor's wife, a magistrate and a journalist. Then the story became even more sensational. Earlier that year, readers were reminded, four-year-old Sydney Barker had been visiting Brighton when he was given some chocolates purchased from Maynard's confectionery. Within twenty minutes he had died of strychnine poisoning. The child was working-class, with no money to leave anyone; no one disliked him, and he came from a happy home. At his inquest, Mrs Cole, who ran a nearby grocery, added to the mystery by testifying that she had twice in the previous three months found chocolates in her shop, apparently forgotten by customers: one eaten from the first parcel had made its taster ill. Then Christiana Edmunds testified. She said she had twice bought chocolates from Maynard's, and twice been made ill. She said she had told Maynard this, but he had brushed her off. She had had the chocolates analysed, and found they were laced with zinc. Oddly enough, however, she never confronted Maynard with this evidence. The inquest jury returned a verdict of accidental death, adding that, as 'chocolate manufactories are much infested by rats', some rat poison might have mistakenly been mixed in with the chocolates that were then sold to Maynard.

At the magistrates' court hearing on the mysterious poisoned boxes, Mrs Beard told how she and her husband had been friendly with Miss Edmunds, a spinster, and her widowed mother. Miss Edmunds, however, had fallen in love with the doctor, writing him passionate letters, and in September 1870 she had given Mrs Beard a sweetmeat which 'acted injuriously'. Dr Beard warned Miss Edmunds that he knew she had tried to poison his wife. He said he would not take legal action, to protect his reputation, but he wanted to have nothing further to do with her. (It seems possible, perhaps even likely, that they had been having an affair, hence the doctor's reluctance to go to the police.) According to the Beards, Miss Edmunds protested her innocence, but they broke off all contact. After the inquest on Sydney Barker, Miss Edmunds wrote to Dr Beard, asking if they could not be friends again – she had bought the sweetmeat for Mrs Beard at Maynard's, and surely it was now clear to him, she said, that the shop was to blame if there had been anything wrong with it.

Maynard, however, had been vigilant since the inquest – his repu- tation had been seriously damaged – and he noticed that Miss Edmunds had frequently bought chocolates from him which she then returned, saying she didn't like them. When he mentioned this to her, she stopped, but he found that she was paying boys to bring packets back to his shop. After the poisoned parcels appeared in households across Brighton, Maynard went to the magistrates with his suspicions. A chemist identified Miss Edmunds as the woman to whom he had sold strychnine 'to kill cats', who had given a false name and address. He had also received orders from other chemists ordering strychnine, while a messenger had recently brought a letter from the coroner asking for the loan of his poisons book (the book that customers who purchased poison needed to sign with their names and addresses). The book had been given to the boy, and when it was returned some of the pages had been torn out. The coroner's and the chemists' letters proved to be in Christiana Edmunds' handwriting. A box that held one of the gifts of fruit and cake was shown to have belonged to her. A dog she had played with had died of what looked like poisoning. On the second day of the hearing, she was charged with the murder of Sydney Barker. The prosecution's case was that she had wanted to get rid of Mrs Beard; when she failed, and Dr Beard cut her off, she had set in motion random poisonings to prove her innocence and regain his friendship. She was committed for trial on four counts: the murder of Sydney Barker, and the attempted murders of three recipients of the parcels.

On 5 November, an effigy of Miss Edmunds was burnt on the Lewes Guy Fawkes bonfire; pictures of her were widely available in the shops of Brighton, Arundel and other Sussex towns. The trial was therefore transferred to the Old Bailey, and Miss Edmunds was moved to Newgate, which was a shock: she complained vociferously that she was not allowed to wear her bonnet to chapel: 'she had always been brought up as a lady, and ... it was quite impossible she could ... submit to attend the chapel service without wearing a bonnet'. By the end of the month, many of the newspapers were suggesting that Christiana Edmunds was insane. At this distance, it is hard to know if her complaints about her bonnet (she appealed to the ordinary, the governor, and threatened to take the matter to the sheriffs) were simply middle-class propriety taken to extremes or a true disconnection from reality. Or if she simply had good legal advice.

Her trial lasted a single day. Her defence was, to a modern eye, curious. Her barrister stated that 'He did not pretend that on certain occasions she did not give poisoned chocolate creams to several children; but in regard to this charge the Jury must be satisfied that the chocolate cream which caused the death of the boy was given indirectly by the prisoner.' (Did he mean that she had poisoned children, just not this one? Or that she was not responsible because there was an intermediary who unknowingly handled the poisoned chocolates?) He stressed the ten-day gap between the return of the chocolates to Maynard's and Sydney Barker's death: if Maynard's was as successful as he claimed, he said, how did the poisoned chocolate come to be sold so long afterwards? (She would have poisoned better, and more efficiently, if Maynard hadn't sold stale chocolate?) And he told the jury that they would find the accused was 'of impaired intellect': her father had died in an asylum, while her brother, also dead, had been 'an epileptic idiot or lunatic'; both grandfathers were 'perfectly imbecile', and 'other relations were afflicted with insanity.

Her sister suffered constantly from hysteria, and had attempted to commit suicide.' 'Her age was given as 34 ... but he should show that her real age was 43.' (A sure sign of insanity: a woman who lied about her age.) The chaplain of Lewes Gaol agreed that, although her conversation was 'perfectly coherent', that in itself was 'extraordinary', given her situation. Her coherence was thus a sign of insanity. And that was the end of the defence.

After an hour, she was found guilty. She protested: 'It is owing to my having been a patient of [Dr Beard], and the treatment I received in going to him, that I have been brought into this dreadful business. I wish the jury had known the intimacy, his affection for me, and the way I have been treated.' The sentence of death was passed, but was quickly commuted, by reason of insanity, to life in Broadmoor, to the subsequent disgust of a Brighton town councillor, who was outraged to discover that the commutation of the sentence left the town 'saddled, as long as Miss Edmunds lives, with the expense of her maintenance! I say this is one of the grossest pieces of injustice ever perpetrated!'

Most newspapers reported the case with sympathy, and thought the commutation appropriate. The *Telegraph* said Miss Edmunds was a 'wretched, half-crazed creature', and her execution would have brought 'disgrace upon British justice'. *Reynolds's Newspaper*, however, always a Radical voice, dissented: '*She* is a genteel murderess, and the gallows is not for such as her,' it said, while four men who had been executed that week were of the 'lower classes'. That information, it added tartly 'was needless, for if they had belonged to the "upper orders", some of them would never have been hanged'.

It is hard to understand why this case of indiscriminate poisoning, philandering doctors, unrequited love and madness didn't catch the imagination of the public, but it didn't. The only trace that may perhaps – and only perhaps – be found is, surprisingly, in George Eliot's *Middlemarch*, which began serialization four months after the magistrates' hearings. The novel is set in the early 1830s, and Tertius Lydgate, the reforming young doctor, is a proponent of the medicalization of the coroners' courts that Thomas Wakley had endorsed.

From her notebooks we know that Eliot read intensively to learn what a doctor would know in 1830; she also read up on the various diseases and illnesses, and their contemporary treatments, that figure in the novel. But there is one anachronism, when Lydgate says: 'The coroner ought not to be a man who will believe that strychnine will destroy the coats of the stomach if an ignorant practitioner happens to tell him so.' The first strychnine poisoning case was not heard until 1856, with Palmer. Had Christiana Edmunds' recent trial been on Eliot's mind in her final months of creation?*

For the rest, perhaps madness was too frightening. Or the idea that any packet of chocolate might contain strychnine? Whatever the case, Christiana Edmunds lived out the next thirty-five years imprisoned, whether by her own mind or by bars. By the time of her death, in 1907, her name was long forgotten, as another doctor, and another female poisoner – or possibly not – had captured the public imagination.

Adelaide Bartlett had a background that sounds suspiciously like that of a penny-dreadful heroine. Some contemporary crime historians have suggested that she was the illegitimate daughter of a son of the Duc de la Tremoille and an Englishwoman; others gave her an English father and a French mother. Whatever the case, she was born in about 1855, in Orléans, and by 1874 she was living in Kingston, in Surrey. In 1875 she married Thomas Edwin Bartlett, a devout Methodist grocer more than ten years her senior. The marriage may well have been arranged, and Adelaide's dowry appeared to have been used to purchase another grocery shop, in East Dulwich. At this point, as was not unusual at the time, the young girl, still not nineteen, returned to school for another two years. After her education had been completed, she moved in with Bartlett, living above his shops, which now numbered six, in different districts of south London. In 1883 or 1884

---

* A further link to Palmer in *Middlemarch* can be found in the death of Raffles, the black-mailer, who is hurried to his death when his victim gives him alcohol, which has been strictly forbidden, just as the heavily insured Walter Palmer was said to have been plied with alcohol by his murderous brother. The same detail appears in Dickens' 'Hunted Down' of the same year.

the couple moved to Merton, near Wimbledon, where they became close friends with the Revd George Dyson, a Wesleyan minister. Soon Dyson was spending long days tutoring Mrs Bartlett in Latin and mathematics, with her husband's approval, while he was at work. Bartlett also paid for Dyson to go on holiday with them, and when the couple moved to Pimlico, Dyson continued his tutorials, although, noted the parlour maid, he brought no books with him. He also kept a house jacket and a pair of slippers in their house, indicating a shocking level of intimacy. In December 1885 Bartlett began to be unwell, and became convinced that the cause was an infected tooth, although one doctor thought it was mercury poisoning, perhaps from the numerous patent remedies Bartlett was dosing himself with. By the end of the month, whether owing to medical supervision or because he had had a number of his teeth extracted, Bartlett was much improved. On the evening of 31 December he felt well enough to eat some jugged hare, oysters, fruit cake, mango chutney and bread and butter, and to request haddock for his breakfast. He did not live to enjoy it; during the night he swallowed a lethal amount of liquid chloroform, and died.

Mrs Bartlett, like any good wife, had been sitting up by her ailing husband's bedside; she had dozed off, she said, and when she awoke, he was dead. However, it was quickly revealed that Dyson had recently purchased chloroform at the request of Mrs Bartlett, who had wanted it for her husband's 'bad spells'. Bartlett's father, who very obviously detested his daughter-in-law, revived an allegation he had made some years before: that Adelaide had had an affair with his second son, her brother-in-law. When he had first made this accusation, Thomas Bartlett had been enraged, and had forced his father to apologize to his wife in writing, and to sign a legal document stating that there was no truth in the story. Now Mr Bartlett reaffirmed his original statement, and both Mrs Bartlett and Dyson were arrested.

Mrs Bartlett's defence was perhaps the most remarkable – and imaginative – that had been seen that century. She claimed that she and her husband had lived in a celibate marriage; that he believed that every man should have two wives, one for friendship and one for 'use', and she had been the former. However, she had wanted a child, so there was one 'episode' of sexual congress, from which she became pregnant. Instead of a doctor, Bartlett had taken her to the wife of Dr Nichols, the author of *Esoteric Anthropology, or, The Mysteries of Man*, which explained birth control. (The dissemination of birth-control literature was considered legally equivalent to the dissemination of obscene literature, and was a prosecutable offence.) Dr Nichols had recommended a nurse, Annie Walker, but the child had been stillborn. From that time, said Mrs Bartlett, she had used chloroform to ward off her husband when he became amorous. Furthermore, her husband, fearing that he would not live long, had 'given' her to Dyson to become his wife after Bartlett's own anticipated death.

At the trial, Mrs Bartlett was defended by Edward Clarke, QC, MP, very prestigious legal representation, paid for, rumour had it, by her supposedly noble family. The charges against Dyson were formally dismissed as the trial began, so Mrs Bartlett appeared alone in the witness box. She was, for the time, oddly dressed: instead of being in deep mourning for her recently deceased husband, as custom demanded, she wore a silk dress, with no hat, and with her hair cropped short. I can find no explanation for this remarkable appearance, which, given her defence team, must have been at the very least sanctioned. For the evidence against her was formidable, and her team handled it immaculately.

The prosecution set out to paint Adelaide Bartlett as a liar and a hussy. Her father-in-law repeated his assertions about her, saying that she had run off with Fred, and had only returned to her husband when Fred emigrated to America. He added that until the last month of his life, Bartlett had been in good health, contrary to his wife's statements, and that they had lived together as man and wife. He also asserted that the signature on his son's will was forged (despite the two witnesses testifying to watching Bartlett sign it), and displayed a letter written to him by his daughter-in-law, refusing him permission to visit his son without express invitation, adding, 'understand that I have neither forgotten nor forgiven the past'. When he asked her to call in another doctor for a second opinion on her husband's illness, she refused on the grounds of cost. Dyson, appearing as a prosecution witness, said that Mrs Bartlett had told him that her husband had an 'internal complaint' which she soothed with chloroform supplied by Annie Walker, Dr Nichols' nurse, and that she had asked him to buy chloroform because Mrs Walker was in America. She also told him, he said, that Nichols had said Bartlett had at most a year to live. Nichols rebutted this: he had never seen either of the Bartletts, nor had he, therefore, made any diagnosis. Furthermore, Annie Walker said she had only looked after Mrs Bartlett after her pregnancy, had never bought chloroform for her, and had never gone to America. Dyson did, however, admit that Bartlett had spoken to him of his two-wife theory, and had told him he did not expect to live. The minister added bitterly that he had been 'duped by a wicked woman'. The prosecution laid stress on the dubiousness of Mrs Bartlett's statements on the celibacy of her marriage, presenting evidence that Bartlett had condoms in his possession (no one appears to have considered that they might have been for use elsewhere). The prosecutor also hammered away at the change to Bartlett's will only months before he died. An earlier version had left everything to his wife on the condition that she did not remarry; the new one left her everything outright, and made Dyson Bartlett's executor.

Clarke's defence dealt with both the practical administration of chloroform, on the one hand, and the moral questions on the other. First he concentrated the jury's minds on the fact that no one had ever before been intentionally poisoned by swallowing chloroform. Chloroform has a strong taste, a pungent smell, and it burns. It was implausible, therefore, that Bartlett could have drunk it unknowingly; as he was a strong man, it appeared impossible that his wife should have forced it upon him. The prosecution had suggested that Mrs Bartlett had administered it while Bartlett was unconscious, but there were no burn marks on his windpipe to indicate that she had done so, nor had he vomited, which was the normal reaction. An analyst from the Home Office deposed that he had three times tried to administer chloroform to an unconscious patient, and had managed to do so only once. In contrast to the failure of this skilled doctor, an unskilled woman had supposedly managed the feat with no trouble, perpetrating a crime 'absolutely unknown in the history of medical jurisprudence'. Why, Clarke demanded, if she wanted to kill him, had she not simply let the unconscious man breathe in the drug until he overdosed? He also held up Dyson's testimony about Annie Walker and Dr Nichols to ridicule: there was no evidence for any of it except the minister's word, which was now as discredited as his reputation. Clarke's second line of defence was to put the dead man on trial: his peculiar views on marriage, his complaisance relating to Dyson's visits to his wife, his recourse to Nichols and his disgusting book. (Later in life Clarke outlined the case in his memoirs, and it is clear that he thought Mrs Bartlett was having an affair with Dyson. He noted that Dyson called her by her first name, kissed her when her husband was present, she visited his lodgings, and they went for walks together – all, apparently, infallible signs of immorality.)

If Adelaide Bartlett had killed her husband so she could be with her lover, she would have been a statistical anomaly. Of the forty-seven women accused of murder between 1828 and 1900, only three fall into this category (Sarah Dazley, Mary Ann Cotton (pp.387–94) and Hannah Southgate, the latter of whom was acquitted). Statistics show that men kill women for adultery, and not vice versa; men kill their wives' lovers, and not vice versa. In Mrs Bartlett's case, however, the jury took an hour to consider, returned to question a legal point, then conferred again. Finally, they pronounced cautiously: 'Although we think there is the gravest suspicion attaching to the prisoner, we do not think there is sufficient evidence to know how or by whom the chloroform was administered.' The judge was forced to ask, 'Then you say, gentlemen, that the prisoner is not guilty?' and only then did the foreman formally declare, 'Not guilty.' The court erupted. *Lloyd's* felt obliged to report that it was 'one of the most disgraceful scenes ever witnessed in an English court of justice', but nonetheless its reporter very obviously approved the spectators' 'Cheering, shouting, and clapping of hands … *on the bench a number of men excitedly waved their hats*, while shouts of "Bravo!" rang through the building …'

Bell's spelled out the reasons for its approval: 'There is no hanging,' it wrote, 'on suspicion.' Did Bartlett die of chloroform poisoning? 'The medical evidence tends' in that direction, but 'by no means makes it certain'. Was Bartlett murdered? 'There is not one item of evidence that he was; and we must remember that the prisoner is not called upon to prove that he was not; it is for the prosecution to establish the charge.' Even if Bartlett had been poisoned, it continued, there was no evidence that Mrs Bartlett had done the deed.

A year later, a novella was published in *Beeton's Christmas Magazine*, spelling out the public's feelings towards medical experts and their unpleasant practices. In this story, a disabled army doctor is looking for someone to share the cost of lodgings. A friend takes him to meet an acquaintance who is in a similar position, but warns the doctor: the man 'is a little too scientific for my tastes – it approaches to cold-bloodedness. I could imagine his giving a friend a little pinch of the latest vegetable alkaloid, not out of malevolence, you understand, but simply out of a spirit of inquiry in order to have an accurate idea of the effects. To do him justice, I think that he would take it himself with the same readiness.' Medical experts may be clever, was the popular feeling, but they do not share a common humanity, and are to be distrusted. (Although the public learned not only to trust but to love this particular medical expert: the disabled doctor was one John Watson, the inhuman scientific machine a certain Sherlock Holmes.) *John Bull* was in agreement with this distancing of medical experts from 'us', stressing that the experts at the trial had failed to understand the home life of a decent middle-class woman. If anything, it urged, the fact that Mrs Bartlett had been alone with her husband by his bed when he died proved she was innocent: it was 'where she ought to be – watching at the bedside with a wifely devotion'. The evidence that confirmed to middle-class journalists that a middle-class woman was innocent was the very same evidence that had hanged so many working-class wives: she was alone with her husband when he died of poison.

It was less the did-she/didn't-she aspect that attracted public interest; it was the details of the Bartlett–Dyson ménage. Even the *Lancet*, while claiming to be interested in the 'physiological and medico-legal bearings' of the case, in fact cosily circled around the Bartletts' marriage, dwelling on the expected outcome of a relationship 'When the principles of *Esoteric Anthropology* are made the guide', a book 'fit only to be burned by the public hangman'. A few pages on, an article on 'Feminine Pruriency' brought the medical mind to bear on the 'vice' of women attending trials.

All the newspapers (and the judge, who made 'strong remarks' on the subject) were shocked that nearly two-thirds of the trial spectators were women. This was a long-running complaint (although it is noticeable that these same newspapers did not object to female readers buying their papers). 'Feminine Pruriency' stated that it was the presence of women that had 'reduced' the court 'to the level of a place of public entertainment of the lowest description ... Why were extra seats provided, or, being provided, why were they allowed to be occupied by women?' *Bell's* did not see the presence of women as the factor that turned a courtroom into theatre, but it had no doubt, however, that it was a theatre all the same: 'The most successful dramatic entertainment during the past week has been the Bartlett trial. At every representation of this sensational drama the theatre – I beg pardon, the court – has been crowded to the doors ... The play was very fascinating ... but ... the tone was morbid, and the dialogue often of a very indecent kind ... I think I may venture to assert that had the piece been submitted to the Lord Chamberlain ... it would have been suppressed.' If crime had become theatre, theatre now acknowledged crime. Clarke attended the Lyceum on the night of Mrs Bartlett's acquittal, and was given a standing ovation by the audience. And it would only be another decade before that type of accolade was given to a fictional detective. After Holmes unravels one mystery, Dr Watson and Inspector Lestrade 'with a spontaneous impulse ... both broke out clapping as at the well-wrought crisis of a play ... [Holmes] bowed to us like the master dramatist who receives the homage of his audience.'

A sixteen-page penny publication, *The Life of the Reverend George Dyson and his Strange Adventures with Mrs. Bartlett*, even had section titles that mimicked the playbill descriptions: 'The Actors', 'The Wife's Tutor', 'Gave His Wife Away!' The tone is one of genial amusement, and there are two morals: 'Dangerous Drugs Should be Used Only by Doctors', as they were too tempting in an unhappy home; and 'Marriage is All a Lottery ... for every one prize there are a thousand blanks.'* Don't, the author urged, neglect your wife, 'And above all, don't leave her to take Latin lessons from a younger, better educated, and more handsome man than yourself.' Good advice, surely.

Other publications were crueller, yet always with the tone of comedy that prevailed across the Bartlett saga. During the trial, Dyson, poor man, was revealed to have written verse to Mrs Bartlett:

> Who is it that hath burst the door,
> Unclosed the heart that shut before,
> And set her queen-like on its throne,
> And made its homage all her own?
> My Birdie.

Wits quickly supplied additional verses: 'Who is it my poor heart disturbs/With chloroform and Latin verbs?'

As Madeleine Smith's case had generated a rash of fiction, so too did Adelaide Bartlett's. *Tempest-Driven*, a three-volume novel by the Irishman Richard Dowling, appeared first. Dowling usually wrote tales of Irish peasants, and was used to working fast – between 1879 and 1884 he had produced nine novels. *Tempest-Driven* opens with a wife in an otherwise deserted house who calls to a passing stranger when her husband dies after inhaling chloroform, which she says he used to help his asthma. The stranger, who is most conveniently a doctor, immediately thinks, 'I hope this is not a case of foul play.' Mrs Bartlett's distrustful father-in-law is here a brother-in-law, there is the lover in the wings, and a deceased husband with peculiar ideas. The wife is not prosecuted because at the post-mortem the dead man is

---

* I assume that the sexual innuendo was intentional, given Mrs Bartlett's pregnancy following her one 'episode' with her husband.

found to have swallowed a suicide note,* and his wife conveniently goes mad.

Three years later, *The Fatal Phryne*, by F.C. Philips and C.J. Wills, tells a similarly Bartlett-ish story. An older man marries a young wife in an arranged marriage in Paris. He seems to condone his wife's liaison with a younger, more attractive man, although as it turns out he is secretly ferociously jealous, and administers one of those fictionally common poisons that does not kill, but destroys the younger man's appearance. The husband then discovers that his wife has been true to him all along, and dies, apparently of mortification, mouthing the word 'Forgive.'

Neither of these books was interested in the question of how the chloroform had been administered, the mystery that has preoccupied most commentators ever since. It was the peculiar private life that they rehearsed; science would have to wait.

---

* This may trump Paul Ferroll's confession left in his wife's grave for 'least likely place to leave a confession'.

SEVEN

Science, Technology and the Law

The Bartlett trial had finished on a note of forensic mystery. Yet much
of the nineteenth century can be read as one of continuing education,
for the legal establishment and for the rapt public. At the beginning
of the century, the situation had looked very different.

In Warwickshire in November 1817, Abraham Thornton was
accused of raping and murdering Mary Ashford; the subsequent trial
demonstrated to a shocked public just how out of touch – how medi-
eval – the law could still be. Thornton had met Miss Ashford, a
gardener's daughter, at a dance; the couple was seen later that night,
at about 3 a.m., sitting on a stile. At four o'clock Miss Ashford called
in at the house of a friend to change into her working clothes for the
walk home. At some point between then and five o'clock she had sex,
whether consensual or forced, and died. In the morning her body was
found in a pond, or a water-filled pit, near a footpath. Thornton had
been seen with her that night, his shoes matched prints left near the
path, and when questioned by the magistrates he admitted that they
had had 'connexion', but claimed it was consensual. At his trial, he
produced nine witnesses who had seen him between four and five.
(One of the fascinating sidelights of this trial is the high level of activ-
ity on a dark November night, all apparently considered entirely
routine.) No evidence was presented to prove that Miss Ashford had
been murdered: she might have accidentally fallen into the pit and
drowned, or she might have thrown herself in after a sexual assault,
or out of remorse for consensual sex. The defence relied entirely on
witnesses who independently confirmed that Thornton had been

320

elsewhere at the time of her death, and he was acquitted. He was immediately rearrested and re-entered into the dock to be tried for rape, but since the complainant was dead, no evidence was offered and he was formally cleared.

Thornton might have thought that was the end of the matter, but William Ashford, Mary's brother, was pointed in the direction of an almost obsolete law, 'appeal of murder', which permitted a family member to appeal against a not-guilty verdict without double jeopardy being invoked. Thornton was arrested once more, but luckily for him he had a very clever lawyer. When the appeal came to be heard, 'when called upon to answer, whether guilty or not guilty', Thornton read: 'Not guilty: and I am ready to defend the same with my body.' He took a pair of gauntlets, put one on, throwing the other on the floor in front of the bench for Ashford to take up, 'in pursuance of an old form'. The prosecution was unprepared: 'I must confess I am surprised ... the trial by battle is an obsolete practice ... it would appear to me extraordinary indeed, if the person who has murdered the sister would ... be allowed to prove his innocence by murdering the brother also ...' stuttered his lawyer. The judge, who was probably equally uncertain, replied feebly: 'It is the law of England ... we must not call it murder.' William Ashford did not care what it was called: he was only a boy, while Thornton was a vigorous, powerful man. (Some reports referred to him as a bricklayer, others said he was the son of a small builder. Given the ingenuity of his legal representation, the latter seems more likely.)

Several more hearings were needed to deal with this legal remnant of feudalism in a modernizing world. Eventually it was agreed that the boy, 'from his youth and want of bodily strength', was legally incompetent to accept the challenge, so as a formality Thornton was re-arraigned, his lawyer entered a plea that he had already been tried and acquitted, and he was released a final time. Shortly afterwards Thornton emigrated to the USA, and he seems to have led a perfectly ordinary life thereafter, while the law was hastily amended. In 1819 the right of 'appeal of murder' was abolished, and with it the right to trial by combat.

All of this was followed closely by the public. The *Observer*, which specialized in crime reporting of the nastier sort, had printed the first ever illustration in a newspaper in 1815, a wood engraving of St Helena when Napoleon was exiled there. In 1818 it produced its second: a portrait of Thornton. The *Ladies' Monthly Magazine* also covered the case, even though it was 'impossible consistently with delicacy to state even the substance of the evidence'. Instead it printed a 'portrait' of the gardener's daughter, implausibly dressed in a fashionable gown, her hair carefully arranged. The vicar of Miss Ashford's parish found a way around the indelicacy, producing *A Moral Review of the Conduct and Case of Mary Ashford ...*, which ended with a 'proposed epitaph':

AS A WARNING TO FEMALE VIRTUE,
This Monument
is erected over the remains of
MARY ASHFORD,
a young Woman, chaste as she was beautiful,
Who, in the 20th year of her age,
having, incautiously repaired to a Scene of Amusement,
without proper Protection,
was brutally violated and murdered
on the 27th of May, 1817,
in the Parish of Aston.

Only a month after the court's ruling the Coburg Theatre opened, staging as its very first production *A Trial by Battle; or, Heaven Defend the Right*, by William Barrymore. The play tells of the beautiful but poor Geralda, who is abducted by a band of brigands on the orders of the wicked Baron Falconbridge. Her noble brother and her stalwart lover, Henrie (sic), attempt to rescue her, and in so doing are accused by the Baron of committing the crimes he was himself guilty of: 'a guilty man found innocent – acquitted – turned loose upon the world, and no other chance left of meeting with his deserts, but getting his head cracked in a trial by battle ...' The trial by battle is played out onstage, and good triumphs over evil. (The play was revived in 1871, when the now renamed Victoria Theatre reproduced its first ever production as a historical curiosity. One reviewer called it 'the most ridiculous farrago ever served up'.)

Another, anonymous, version of the story, *The Murdered Maid*, was published in Warwick in the year of the trial, sanitized for family viewing: 'every disgusting circumstance is carefully omitted', the preface assured the anxious, and 'additions' had been made to reinforce 'that great moral lesson ... That although vice may for a time triumph, a merciful but just God fails not to punish ... the perpetration of a crime.' The play is set in France, and Thornton becomes Thornville, a 'noted rake'. 'I despise your insidious language, as much as I do the motive of it,' Marie hisses at her would-be seducer. She flees, he chases, 'A shriek is heard, and followed by a noise, as of one falling into Water, – the Stage becomes dark ...' Thornville, we learn, had earlier preyed on Marie's sister, as Thornton was similarly reported to have 'known' Miss Ashford's sister, while Marie's aged grandfather stages a dramatic confrontation, drawing back a curtain to show the body of Marie on her bier, calling for *'Justice, justice, justice, on the murderer, justice, justice!'* Finally Thornville offers Marie's brother, Guillaume, the 'Wager of Battel' (sic), and, carrying a shield inscribed 'Avenge Marie', Guillaume attacks the stronger man, who conveniently suddenly goes mad, experiences a heavenly vision and then shoots himself. Happy family entertainment, as the preface promised.

A less professional version still, *The Mysterious Murder; or, What's the Clock*, was probably performed at fairs and exhibitions, and may have been written by the prompter at the Theatre Royal, Birmingham, who published it himself ('at the earnest request of his Friends'). Maria is here 'a giddy, thoughtless girl', Thorntree a rich cad, Quibble the cunning lawyer. The script follows the real story fairly closely (if we accept that there was a murder, and that Thornton committed it), ending in a churchyard where Maria is buried under 'a white marble MONUMENT' that was 'erected by her Friends, to perpetuate the fatal effect of Inordinate Passions'.

Thornton's story continued to resonate. In 1826 Walter Scott reported a conversation at a dinner with Lord Liverpool and the Duke of Wellington at 'Mr Peele's' (Robert Peel, not yet Sir Robert): 'We canvassed the memorable ... case of Ashford. Peele almost convinced me of the man's innocence.' More than a decade later, *Figaro in London* published 'The Somnambulist', a short story presented as a first-person narrative of a visit to the 'Allegany [sic] mountains'. A traveller lodges at a remote house, waking to find the owner walking in his sleep, repeating the phrase 'Not guilty!' and 'making an action as if drawing a glove upon his right hand, and flinging its fellow upon the floor'. Then, with a smile 'of demoniacal triumph' he vanishes. The narrator recognizes Thornton, and hurries away from the 'contaminating atmosphere'.

There was definitely a 'contaminating atmosphere' in Bristol when Mary Ann Burdock, a landlady, came up for trial in 1835 for the murder of her lodger, Clara Smith. Mrs Smith had died in 1833, and Mrs Burdock had organized her funeral, telling the undertaker her lodger had had neither money nor family, and to bury her 'at as little expense as possible'. Onlookers were surprised: it was believed that Mrs Smith had both family and cash, while Mrs Burdock, in contrast, had been very poor, and was now claiming to have inherited 'a large property' from an uncle of whom no one had previously heard. In December 1834 Mrs Smith's relatives came calling and, aghast at finding no property, began an investigation. The body was exhumed, arsenic was identified and Mrs Burdock was arrested.

At the trial, witnesses testified to buying arsenic for Mrs Burdock; her servant said she had seen her pour powder into Mrs Smith's gruel, before washing her hands twice in two changes of water and scrubbing her nails. She had also used 'abusive epithets' about her lodger, referring to her as a 'drunken old bitch'. Mr Burdock had later been seen with gold rings and a gold bottle for smelling-salts, even though he had been unemployed when Mrs Smith died, at which point he set himself up in business. (He himself had since died.) Mrs Smith's solicitor contradicted Mrs Burdock's report of her lodger's indigence, saying she had received £700 in 1829, and had an annuity as well. Mrs Burdock had made a will after the death of Mrs Smith, being in possession of £500, although only a short time before she had told a witness that 'she had not a shilling in the world'.

Mrs Burdock's counsel was particularly active for the period. Before the trial her solicitor attempted to get the venue altered because of local bias – a remarkably innovative idea two decades before Palmer's Act. He also attempted to keep out of evidence the witnesses who had seen Mrs Smith's possessions in Mrs Burdock's keeping after her death, arguing that this was a trial for murder, not theft. He failed, but for the time and for a working-class client it was notable that he even tried. He also produced witnesses who backed up Mrs Burdock's version of events, that Mrs Smith was indigent, drunk and behind on her rent. The chemist from whom Mrs Burdock was supposed to have bought arsenic testified that she could not have done so: he had had no shop at the relevant period.

It was the scientific evidence, however, that was new, and newly presented. The Recorder, Sir Charles Wetherell, addressed the jury before the trial.* Mrs Smith, he noted, had died in October 1833, and was only exhumed in December 1834. 'I am not aware of any parallel case having ever transpired' where so long a period had elapsed between death and investigation, he said. But, 'You will have the testimony of several eminent medical men, and that also of some able chemists, who will state to you the results of certain experiments and tests.' The idea of detecting poison quickly was well known; long-delayed exhumations after violent death had even been dramatized. In the melodrama *The Murderers of the Round Tower Inn* (1830) the plucky hero Tom Topmast returns from sea to find his father has died. Suspecting his mother's second husband, Hamlet-like, he takes

---

* Wetherell was making his first visit to Bristol since 1831, after the failure of the Reform Bill. He had been a noted opponent of reform, and Bristol was one of the many cities that would have achieved better representation in Parliament had the Bill passed. When in 1831 he arrived to open the Assizes he injudiciously threatened to imprison protesters. At that they rose up, and Wetherell was forced to flee in disguise as a woman. But that was the last comic moment. Riots continued for the next three days, until the dragoons were brought in. Later a Lieutenant-Colonel was court-martialled for 'leniency' in commanding his men to use swords rather than open fire on the rioters. He committed suicide before the verdict, and a hundred rioters were tried and four executed.

himself to the cemetery, where, conveniently enough, a grave is being dug next to his father's, and thus his father's skull is accidentally exhumed: 'Oh horror! horror ... the dreadful truth now comes to light. Captain, my friend, look here! look here! (*he draws a long nail out of the skull just at the crown*).' Now, the Burdock case demonstrated that poison could be identified as easily as a nail in a skull.

The trial began with an attempt to exclude the medical experts from the court while others gave evidence. After consideration, it was decided that they could remain, as they were not witnesses to the events that had transpired, but were simply providing scientific testimony. Just as legal procedures were not yet codified, so the best method of conducting post-mortems had not yet been established. Two of the doctors present at Mrs Smith's autopsy had never before examined a person who had died of poison; they relied entirely on tests by William Herapath to identify arsenic, as from their own experience they were unable to identify any marks of poisoning. Herapath represented the future. He attended the exhumation and the post-mortem, and analysed the viscera, and in his evidence he not only told the court of his results, but explained carefully how each test had been performed, and what the results meant. He also brought sections of the body into court, to demonstrate each point.

All of this was carefully relayed to the reading public. For example, Herapath described how 'The stomach and abdomen were laid open ... and it was discovered that the integuments had been converted into adipocire [sic], which is a hardening of the fat, or animal soap ...' explained one report. Another confirmed that 'The bowels are in a glass case, and the head of the unfortunate Mrs Smith are [sic] ... ready to be produced' if needed.

The first quotation is taken from a middle-class sporting paper, *Bell's Life*, the second from a working-class broadside, but there is little to distinguish the two – both were concerned to instruct their audiences on how to read the evidence, in exactly the same way the scientists were instructing the jury. The attitudes reflected in both newspapers and broadsides contrast with the views sometimes imposed retrospectively on the working classes by the more educated.

In *Middlemarch* (1871–72), set the year before Mrs Smith's death, the inn landlady speaks for many when she condemns the 'advanced' doctors who go about 'cutting up everybody before the breath was well out o' their body'. The evidence of the broadsides, however, indicates a greater sophistication than this in the response of the public. They explained court procedure, repeating the prosecutor's address to the jury on their legal responsibilities, they analysed the Recorder's decision not to grant a change of venue, and explained how 'Mr. Herapath and the Medical Gentlemen' had 'taken up' the body and 'chemically analysed' the stomach contents to find 'above 20 grains of arsenic … although it was 14 months ago since her burial'. One execution broadside even fell into verse on the scientific analysis:

> … nought was heard,
> About the Murderer,
> 'Till December seven, thirty four, [sic]
> Oh! then it came to light,
> Her Stomach it was analyzed,
> And the Arsenic found so bright …

This was the period in which broadsides flourished, and they did not expect their readers to rely on them exclusively – at least one simply noted that 'newspapers throughout the Kingdom have enlarged their columns with the narrative of this tragic affair'. Many others cannibalized themselves, taking the same text and laying it out differently, or using generic pictures of little relevance: a Regency female, a funeral image, a clergyman in front of a country house (overleaf). Yet there was sufficient market that one local printer found it profitable to produce a broadsheet every day during the trial, as well as at the more standard high points – the confession, sorrowful lamentations, dying speech and execution broadsides.

In 1890 a skeleton was discovered when the foundations of a building in Bristol were being dug, and it was immediately 'believed by many to supply a missing link' between Mrs Burdock and a baker's son who had vanished, although the only apparent connection is that

both events took place in 1833 – evidence, perhaps, of the extreme rarity of murder. Mrs Burdock was the first woman to be executed in Bristol in thirty-five years, the twentieth of either sex, including the four rioters.

* * *

When Mrs Burdock stood trial, the idea of scientific analysis was new. By the time John Tawell was accused of murdering his mistress Sarah Hart, in 1845, it was a commonplace, and a tool of the defence as well as the prosecution. But Tawell's case had another novelty: he was the first person to be arrested by means of that newfangled invention, the telegraph.

John Tawell, of Berkhamsted in Hertfordshire, presented a sober face to the world. He was over sixty, a pious Quaker, respectably married and doing well in business. Yet behind this façade, a more dubious man lurked. In his youth Tawell had been transported for forging a bill for £1,000 (the sum given in some newspapers; another, less excitingly but probably more accurately, said £10). Whatever the amount, he was sentenced to fourteen years' transportation and, having worked out his sentence, lived in Sydney as an increasingly prosperous druggist, becoming a Quaker and ultimately returning to London. At some point his wife died, and he began a relationship with his children's nursemaid. When he married a rich Quaker widow in 1841 he pensioned off the nursemaid, Sarah Hart, paying her £1 a week and continuing to visit her at her new home in Slough.

On the day in question, the next-door neighbour saw Mrs Hart's visitor arrive; she later heard a scream, and then saw the man leave. Concerned, she went next door and found Mrs Hart lying on the floor, dead. As well as the police, the local vicar appeared on the scene. He gave evidence at the inquest: 'Hearing ... that a person in the dress of a Quaker was the last man who had been seen to leave the house, I proceeded to the Slough station, thinking it likely he might proceed to town by the railway. I saw him pass through the office, when I communicated my suspicions to Mr. Howell, the superintendent at the station ... Mr. Howell then sent off a full description of his person, by means of the electric telegraph, to cause him to be watched by the police upon his arrival at Paddington.' At Paddington, the railway police spotted Tawell in his distinctive clothes, and followed him home. He was arrested the next day, at which point he denied having been in Slough or knowing anyone who lived there, and haughtily tried to quell the working-class policeman: 'My station in life must rebut any suspicion that might be attached to me.' The policeman was impervious to this argument, and Tawell was escorted to Windsor, where he said he now remembered Mrs Hart: she had been his servant, and was in the habit of writing begging letters and threatening suicide if she did not receive help. He had travelled to Slough, he continued, to tell her that she could expect no further help from him, at which point she drank the contents of a phial, throwing the rest, conveniently enough, into the fire. 'I did not think she was in earnest,' he ended.

At his trial, Tawell was shown to have twice purchased prussic acid, and an 'analytical chemist and lecturer on medical jurisprudence' testified to his belief that prussic acid was the cause of death, although, as was so frequently the case at this time, he had never before seen the action of prussic acid on a human body – 'my knowledge is theoretical only'. The defence claimed that small traces of prussic acid occurred naturally in apple pips, and Mrs Hart had been eating an apple before her death. (Small traces of cyanide do occur naturally in some fruit pips, but not enough even to cause illness.) The jury gave more weight to Tawell's newly discovered money troubles, and to Mrs Hart's threat to confront his wife, and found him guilty.

Tawell's was one of those executions that did so much to promote the campaign against capital punishment. *Bell's* simply noted that he came out, knelt, prayed, and was dead 'in a short time'. *John Bull*, however, printed a more detailed report, which unfortunately is also therefore more likely to be true: the drop was miscalculated by the executioner, and spectators watched in horror as the elderly man in sober Quaker dress 'struggled most violently. His whole frame was convulsed; he writhed horribly, and his limbs rose and fell again repeatedly, while he wrung his hands ... and continued to wring his hands for several minutes ... still clasped as though he had not left off praying. It was nearly ten minutes ... before the contortions which indicated his extreme suffering ceased.' It was, the paper said, 'torture'.

Broadside-sellers did well with Tawell, enjoying his criminal past. Three patterers told Mayhew that they had written Tawell's

John Tawell was recognizable by his distinctive Quaker dress, and many broadsides focused on that, rather than on the victim, or the circumstances of her death.

confession, in which he admitted to two earlier murders in Van Diemen's Land (despite the fact that he had been transported to mainland Australia, and was not known ever to have set foot in Tasmania), as well as to robbing the captain of the ship on which he returned to England. The waxworks liked him for his clothes. At the penny end of the market, a stall on Clerkenwell Green in London showed Tawell just two days after his execution; the Saloon of Arts in Great Windmill Street, with an admission price of 1s., catered to a very different level of society, but it too had an effigy of Tawell, together with a 'Centrifugal Railway' (an early form of rollercoaster, most likely), Miss Gulliver, who was thirty-six inches tall, and Wilkison Kirk, 'the American Spotted Wonder' (no further explanation). According to *Punch*, Madame Tussaud's had been extremely keen to get its hands on Tawell's clothes, offering £25 for the Quaker coat, although its bid appears to have failed.

But it was the 'telegraphic communication' that people remembered. Some time after the execution, an 'exceedingly respectable looking man' stared out at the telegraph wires by the side of the track as his train approached Slough and 'muttered aloud, "Them's the cords that hung John Tawell!"'

Tawell had travelled by train, and had been caught by telegraph; the first murder *on* a train was not to occur for another two decades. At that time railway carriages had doors to the platform only; once the train was in motion each carriage was entirely cut off from the rest of the train. This created either a feeling of safety if one was alone in a carriage, or of danger if one was locked in with a dubious stranger.

In the 1850s a new reason to fear strangers emerged, a scare similar to the poison panic of the 1840s, but involving not murder but garrotting. Garrotting originally meant murder by strangulation; then it was modified to mean that the victim was merely caught about the throat and choked; by the late 1850s it simply meant any sort of mugging. In 1862 an MP was garrotted while walking down Pall Mall (this incident was used by Trollope in 1867 in his novel *Phineas Finn*). Newspapers fanned the hysteria: to set foot on the street was to court death, they warned. A chaplain of Newgate wrote in to suggest that garrotters were haunting the British Museum to learn thuggee skills from the sculptures dedicated to Kali. Contemporary police statistics did show an increase in arrests for street robbery, but only after the panic began. Fear caused arrests, and the rising statistics reflected the panic, they did not cause it.

The idea of stranger-murder, by violence, in public places, was therefore on people's minds when *The Times* carried a headline in July 1864: 'MURDER in a FIRST-CLASS CARRIAGE on the NORTH LONDON RAILWAY'. Now nowhere was safe, not even a first-class carriage (trust *The Times* to focus on class). Two clerks entered an empty compartment on the 9.50 from Fenchurch Street station to Chalk Farm to find a walking stick, bag and hat (a 'gentleman's hat', said *The Times*). They called the guard, who further noticed that the seat cushions, the window and the door handle were covered in blood. Half an hour later, a driver returning to the depot saw something beside the line between Hackney Wick and Bow. He got out to have a look, and found a desperately injured man, who was carried to a nearby pub. There he was identified as Thomas Briggs, in his late sixties, the chief clerk of Roberts & Co. bank. He died the following day. His watch, chain and gold spectacles were missing, but the bag and stick in the train were identified as his; the hat, however, was not. This one was of beaver, not silk, and was presumed to belong to the murderer, who had perhaps knocked Briggs' hat off in the attack, and grabbed the wrong one as he fled.

The government, the North London Railway and Briggs' employers each offered £100 rewards for information. A jeweller named Death came forward. (The name is not as extraordinary as it appears: there are more than two hundred people named Death on the electoral register today, sometimes spelt De'Ath.) Two days after the murder, he said, a German had come into his shop in Cheapside and asked if he would exchange a gold chain for another less expensive one, together with a gold ring. A week later a cabman named Matthews approached the police, having just heard some other cabmen discussing the crime. (His wife later said that he would have seen the report in *Lloyd's* on Sunday as usual, had they not had visitors; it went without saying in her explanation that working people had time to read the papers only on Sundays.) Matthews had recognized Death's name, for a tailor named Franz Müller had recently given one of his children a box with that name on it to play with. Müller had been friendly with the cabman's daughter, and had come to say goodbye to the family

333

before he emigrated to America. Mayne's force was now operating like clockwork: Matthews gave his information at his local station; he was immediately taken to a superintendent, who took him straight to Mayne himself, who sent him on to Inspector Tanner in Stepney. Matthews identified the hat from the train: he had bought it for Müller after Müller had admired his own. He also, and this was handy for the police, had a photograph of the German, which Death immediately identified.

The police went to Müller's lodgings, only to find that he had sailed for New York the previous day. His landlady said he had been out on the night in question, and had later shown her his new gold chain. With this confirmation Inspector Tanner, a detective sergeant, with Death and Matthews in tow for identification purposes, headed for Liverpool and a government steamship to New York. (Müller was on a sailing ship; the pursuing party could expect to arrive at least two weeks, possibly more, in advance.) And so it played out. When Müller's ship docked in New York, the police and witnesses boarded, Müller was identified, his box was searched and Briggs' watch found, together with a silk hat that had been cut down to remove the maker's label. The telegraphed news triumphantly announced that the first train murderer had been captured by the first steamship pursuit.

The prosecution had plenty of witnesses. As well as Death and Matthews, the hatter who had sold the hat to Matthews identified it: he had used the lining in the hat found on the train on only two or three occasions, as an experiment. Then Dr Letheby gave what scientific evidence was possible: Briggs had died from multiple head wounds, partly from a blunt instrument, possibly a walking stick, and partly from being thrown from the train. He was unable, however, to confirm that the blood on the walking stick was human, much less Briggs' – tests to distinguish animal from human blood would have to wait until the twentieth century. He did his best, however, noting that the stains 'contained also particles of brain matter'.

Müller was well represented, his legal fees being paid for by the German Legal Protection Society. His defence was that there was no evidence that Briggs had been wearing the hat that had been found in

Müller's box on the day in question; that there was no proof that the hat found on the train had ever been Müller's; that Matthews' testimony had been very obviously motivated by the £300 reward, and, given that Matthews had purchased the hat, it could just as easily have been him in the train, and his hat;* that Müller was a small, slight man, and Briggs, despite his age, a large, heavy one, but nonetheless Müller was supposed to have robbed, murdered and thrown him from the train, all in the three minutes between two stations; that a witness had given evidence that two men, not one, had been seen in Briggs' compartment earlier; and, surely the clincher, that at the time the murder was taking place, Müller had three witnesses who put him in Camberwell, six miles away. The Solicitor-General, appearing for the prosecution, dismissed this last, seemingly unbreakable alibi, stressing that the three people were a woman 'of the unfortunate class' and her landlord and landlady – that is, a prostitute and brothel-keepers. No reliance, he was sure, could be placed on a clock found in such a location, nor an alibi provided by such people. The judge apparently agreed, summing up strongly against Müller. It took the jury only fifteen minutes to find him guilty.

There was much post-trial discussion of the correctness of the verdict, but it was agreed in the newspapers that science had triumphed. Müller refused to confess right up until the last minute, saying, 'I should be a very bad fellow if I had done it.' The German chaplain who attended him to the scaffold claimed that he had, at his insistent questioning, replied, 'I HAVE DONE IT,' just before the drop opened. Perhaps he did. The newspapers reported that his confession was 'immediately' forwarded to the Home Secretary and to Sir Richard Mayne, which suggests a level of doubt among both readers and the legal establishment.

Some were able to look at the case light-heartedly. A broadside claimed that 'Thousands of pounds was betted ... That he would be

---

* Matthews, after the event, proved to be a dodgier customer than first appeared: he did indeed get the reward money, but it was paid over to his creditors, who were numerous; he had previously been imprisoned for bankruptcy, and was declared bankrupt again after Müller's death.

acquitted,' while the *Glasgow Herald* reported a local shop offering 'Hats Muller'd here'. The teenaged Robert Louis Stevenson wrote to his mother that when an elderly man behaved erratically in his train compartment, 'At first I expected to be Mullered.'* And at a regatta in Northumberland, the *Franz Muller* came in second in the races for ballast keelboats. In the 1890s the London and South-Western Railway sponsored a charity bazaar that displayed a model of the compartment in which Briggs was murdered. New-style carriages, with corridors giving access to the rest of the train, appeared in the 1880s. Perhaps the subliminal message was that this type of murder could no longer happen.

At the time, however, the press reproduced the pervasive atmosphere of fear. *The Times* linked the murder of the day with the fear of the year by reporting that the 'mysterious, dull sound' that had been heard outside Newgate 'all night' before Müller's execution was 'the sound caused by knocking hats over the eyes' of anyone who appeared prosperous, 'and while so "bonneted" stripping them and robbing them of everything. None but those who looked down upon the awful crowd ... will ever believe in the wholesale, open, broadcast manner in which garrotting and highway robbery was carried on.'

Forensic science was seen to take another great leap forward in 1875, with the trial following the discovery of human remains in a disused warehouse in Whitechapel Road in London. In September 1875 Henry Wainwright (not to be confused with Thomas Griffiths Wainewright, with an 'e'),† thirty-eight years old, the bankrupted owner of a brushmaking business, was working for a corn merchant.

---

* The word survives today, usually in a sporting sense – 'He absolutely mullered that ball.' This may be from Müller, or it may be extrapolated from a muller-stone, used to crush or grind painters' colours or apothecaries' drugs.

† More than one reader commented on the similarity of the names. Edward FitzGerald thought this later Wainwright 'a nasty thing' compared to 'that famous Man of Taste'. The poet Swinburne, too, felt parodic 'deep grief' that the 'honoured name' of Wainewright was 'associated with a vulgar and clumsy murder, utterly inartistic and discreditable to the merest amateur'. He sounds, consciously or not, very like de Quincey.

Alfred Stokes, his former employee, worked with him, and Wainwright asked him to help move a couple of parcels from his old warehouse in Whitechapel Road. They carried them to the street, and Wainwright went to fetch a cab, leaving Stokes with the parcels. Stokes smelt something nasty in the parcels, and suspected Wainwright was stealing human hair, which was used in brushmaking. After Wainwright's business failed, his stock had been sold, but it was still stored in the warehouse. Stokes lifted one of the waterproof coverings, saw not hair, but a hand, and 'had the presence of mind to *kiver* it up again quick'. Admirably, he managed to maintain a calm façade when Wainwright returned with the cab. They loaded the parcels into it, and Wainwright drove off, with, unknown to him, Stokes following along behind on foot. Wainwright stopped briefly to collect a woman; Stokes heard him tell the driver, 'As fast as you can over London Bridge to the Borough,' and the procession of cab and runner set off again. At Leadenhall Street in the City Stokes saw two policemen, and tried to explain what was happening; they refused to take him seriously, and rather than lose the cab he set off again. On the south side of London Bridge he saw the cab stop and Wainwright go into a pub named the Hen and Chickens. He found another two policemen, who this time were interested in his story of body parts waiting in front of a pub these local men knew to be no longer in business.

The police asked Wainwright what he was doing: 'Ask no questions and there's £50 for each of you,' he rashly offered. Instead, they suggested he open the parcels. He raised his offer to £200 to pretend that the last ten minutes had never happened. The police ignored this and opened the parcels and, finding a number of body parts, immediately arrested Wainwright, along with his companion, Alice Day, a dancer at the Pavilion Theatre, situated only doors away from the warehouse in Whitechapel Road. At the warehouse the police found what looked like an open grave filled with chloride of lime, and a hammer, a chopper and a spade nearby. Wainwright was charged with murder, his brother Thomas, the failed licensee of the Hen and Chickens, and Alice Day as accessories. (Miss Day was discharged after the inquest.) While the body could not immediately be identified, local rumour soon suggested it was that of Harriet Lane, who had been missing for a year.

Harriet Lane had been a milliner working in the Whitechapel Road when she met Wainwright, then a prosperous merchant, in 1871. He was already married, but soon an advertisement appeared in the local newspaper announcing Mr and Mrs Percy King's 'marriage', and the new Mrs King moved into lodgings. Mr King was understood to be a commercial traveller, and was therefore frequently absent, but the couple had two children; meanwhile Wainwright lived under his own name with his wife and five children, who were also under the impression that he travelled for work. He gave Mrs King £5 a week (£250 a year was a good middle-class income), and she invited a Miss Wilmore, a fellow milliner, to live with her and help with the children.

This double life was only sustainable while Wainwright remained prosperous. In 1874 his brother William dissolved their partnership: Wainwright owed him substantial sums, and he owed others even more.* Wainwright became unable to maintain his second family, and Mrs King was forced to pawn her possessions, even her wedding ring. She also began to drink, turning up distraught at Whitechapel Road, threatening to go to Wainwright's wife. Finally he gave her £15 to redeem her pawned possessions, pay her debts and – her landlady having tired of her drinking – move to new lodgings. On 10 September 1874 Mrs King told Miss Wilmore that she was going to Whitechapel Road. She never returned. That same day, Wainwright purchased half a hundredweight of chloride of lime, to be delivered to the warehouse. And at some point around that time – they were later unable to date the event precisely – three workmen near the warehouse heard gunshots.

Miss Wilmore, with two children not her own, and no money, approached Wainwright for advice. He told her that Mrs King had

---

* Poor William, the respectable member of the family, a churchwarden, and the master of his Masonic lodge, did not end happily either. His wife left him, he started drinking, and in 1892 he shot himself in a train.

run off with an auctioneer named Teddy Frieake, and sure enough, Miss Wilmore soon received a letter from Mr Frieake, followed by a telegram from Mrs King, saying they were setting off for a new life abroad. Wainwright sent money for the children when he could, and there matters rested until his business finally failed and the mortgage on his warehouse fell in. Wainwright and his brother Thomas bought lengths of waterproof cloth, a chopper and a spade, and on 11 September Wainwright asked Stokes for help.

The combination of details – the length of time between the death and its discovery; the cast-off mistress; the double life; the epic run of Alfred Stokes – all went to make this crime a crowd-pleaser. 'Harriet Lane' became a slang phrase for tinned meat.* Many newspapers leapt upon the report that Wainwright had been a great supporter of the Pavilion Theatre: at a benefit he had played, according to one story, an amateur Shylock, demanding his pound of flesh with vigour; even more widespread were the stories of his amateur performances of 'The Dream of Eugene Aram'. This was possibly the most newsworthy crime since Palmer. The *Telegraph* devoted 125 columns to the case – that paper and *The Times* together, at 216 columns, gave more space to Wainwright than they would to Jack the Ripper thirteen years later. The weeklies loved it too – *Lloyd's* gave the magistrates' hearing three pages, while the first day of the trial took up nearly 50 per cent of the editorial space. They were only supplying what the crowd wanted: the *Daily News* reported that the morning arrival of the jury at the Old Bailey during the trial drew 'numbers of people' to watch these twelve ordinary men merely walk up the street.†

At the trial, Wainwright's inability to support two families was demonstrated; witnesses identified 'Teddy Frieake', Mrs King's caller,

---

* This grisly joke had a precedent: 'Sweet Fanny Adams', a child murdered and dismembered by Frederick Baker in 1867, had also given her name to tinned meat (see p.383).

† For a few days these spectators might also have spotted the playwright and poet W.S. Gilbert among the lawyers. Gilbert, trained as a barrister, had been a professional playwright for a decade, and had recently inaugurated his collaboration with Arthur Sullivan when, to his annoyance, he was summoned for jury duty. Gilbert asked a friend to give him a brief for a few days on the Wainwright case, so he could claim exemption as a practising barrister.

as Wainwright himself; and Frieake's letter to Miss Wilmore was proved to be in his handwriting. But it was the forensic work that made the trial so important. The first thing was the identification of the year-old, decomposed and dismembered body. The prosecution was helped by the lime that had been used to mask the smell: it had done that efficiently, but it also delayed decomposition. The soil was sieved, and body parts, as well as buttons, pins, a ring and a piece of rope, were found. Harriet's family described her as small, with brown hair, a decayed front tooth, pierced ears, and a scar on her right knee. She had been twenty-four when she died, and the wisdom teeth found were judged consistent with this. The face of the corpse was too decomposed to identify, but the single ear that remained was pierced; the hair had been damaged by the lime, but it was almost the same colour as that described, and more of the same colour hair was on the spade; the decayed tooth, too, was intact, and a scar was found on the body's right knee. The remains measured approximately four feet eleven inches; the forensic team (as it might now properly be called) estimated from a photograph that Harriet had been just over five feet tall. Two bullets were found in the skull, and the throat had also been cut, although it was not possible to tell if this had occurred before or after death.

The defence had a hard time against this array of evidence. One line was to say that the prosecution had not proved the remains were Harriet Lane: the height was not quite right; the prosecution had claimed that the deceased had borne a child, but the defence said it was impossible to know; the body had a scar on both knees, casting doubt on Harriet's father's claim that her right knee was scarred; there was no mark on the left hand to show that she had habitually worn a wedding ring. A second line was that Harriet had committed suicide. The prosecution asked disdainfully if she had then slit her own throat, before burying herself, and a year later digging herself up and dismembering her own body. Doggedly, the defence claimed that Wainwright had panicked when he found her dead, had buried her, then dug her up when the warehouse was going to be sold. The judge summed up strongly against Henry Wainwright, but suggested that Thomas had been his brother's dupe, and was therefore less culpable. The jury took less than an hour to find Henry Wainwright guilty; Thomas was found guilty as an accessory after the fact and sentenced to penal servitude for seven years.

Executions were no longer public events. Since 1868 they had been held in private inside the prison, but 'private' was a flexible word – a hundred journalists were admitted to watch Wainwright die, and they shared their experience with their readers. Public interest did not fade away with his death, either. Subscriptions were opened to support his wife and the children of his two families, all left in poverty. Six hundred *Times* readers alone sent contributions said to amount to £700, and in March another paper claimed that £1,232.18s.10d. had been raised. Alfred Stokes too was rewarded – the trial judge gave him £30, and after an outcry in the press at the discrepancy between his reward and the funds raised for Wainwright's family, journalists raised more. Initially Stokes did not find life easy; Wainwright's supporters physically threatened him, and a friend of his was attacked. It must have been a serious assault: the man was sentenced to seven years' penal servitude, five years' police supervision, and twenty-five lashes. Stokes, however, found a vicarious fame afterwards. In court he said he had opened the parcel because he thought Wainwright was stealing. By January 1876 he was assuring the world that he had opened it because a spectral voice had told him to; soon the spectre had even called to him the traditional three times.

The *Illustrated Police News* published a penny-pamphlet, 'From the Footlights to the Prison Cell', ostensibly by Alice Day, although probably by the authors of a similar pamphlet, 'The Whitechapel Tragedy', both of which went on sale within weeks of the execution. Theatre too dabbled in the story, although most of the productions appear to have been unlicensed, and probably did better at fairs than in more mainstream venues. The Royal Clarence Theatre, Dover, had *The Whitechapel Tragedy* running for a week. The following year a theatre in Market Harborough produced either the same play or a variant of it – its only trace is a newspaper report of the execution scene, which appears to have been played out in full onstage (another indication

The long tradition of broadsides showing the 'last moments' at the scaffold inured readers to images of execution, even after they became far more realistic than broadsides had ever been. This image of the final moments of Henry Wainwright appears to have caused no disquiet among readers, although today it is shocking to see even an illustration.

that it was unlicensed): the stool slipped and the actor-Wainwright nearly went the way of the real one.

While Wainwright was soon forgotten, the display of how science could be used to catch a murderer was not, and after the trial the 'science' in detective fiction became even more elaborate. In *Almack, the Detective*, an 1886 penny-work, Tom Rawdon's sister is murdered by a tramp as she visits the poor. Rawdon has her body 'frozen hard – my object being to examine it myself scientifically'. He finds 'bright particles' in the skull wound, which means that 'The instrument that struck the blow must have been of steel.' He also does a blood analysis which finds 'an appearance which is unique in the human race, and never before observed', deducing that this must be the murderer's blood (although why the murderer was bleeding, the reader never discovers): 'I am certain, that, could I obtain a single drop of her murderer's blood, I could unhesitatingly prove him guilty of the crime.' That was the year before Sherlock Holmes appeared in *A Study in Scarlet*, analysing the bruising of a body after death. Wainwright's main legacy was to forensic science, fictional and real, and it became relevant two years later, with the case of Harriet Staunton.

In 1874, Louis Staunton, a twenty-three-year-old auctioneer with ambitions, began to court Harriet Richardson, the daughter of a deceased Church of England clergyman. She was ten years older than her suitor, plain, and, according to her mother, 'simple' and 'of weak intellect'. She did, however, have some money of her own. Her mother, now married to another clergyman, named Butterfield, attempted to have her declared a ward in chancery to prevent the marriage, but she failed, and in June 1875 the couple married. In July Mrs Butterfield paid a brief formal call, but shortly afterwards she received a letter from her daughter severing relations. In March 1876 Mrs Staunton gave birth to a son, and some time later the couple moved, and Mrs Butterfield lost sight of her daughter's whereabouts.

In February 1877 she saw Alice Rhodes at London Bridge railway station. Mrs Butterfield and Miss Rhodes were tenuously related: Miss Rhodes was the stepdaughter of Mrs Butterfield's nephew, and her sister Elizabeth was married to Louis Staunton's brother Patrick. Miss Rhodes told Mrs Butterfield that her daughter was in Brighton. The worried mother noticed that Miss Rhodes was wearing a brooch that belonged to Mrs Staunton, and when she commented on it, Miss Rhodes offered it to her; she refused, but was puzzled – the brooch had been one of Mrs Staunton's favourites.

This preyed on her mind, and she set to work and traced her daughter to Halstead, near Cudham in Kent. She travelled down, and by chance met Patrick Staunton at the station as she set off. To her anxious queries he replied, 'Damn your daughter, I know nothing about her,' adding, for good measure, 'If you come to my house I will blow your brains out.' Nothing daunted, she went on to Halstead and found directions to Little Grays, the farm Louis Staunton was renting. Elizabeth Staunton opened the door, but was immediately joined by Louis, who called his mother-in-law an 'old bitch' and refused to allow her in. Mrs Butterfield begged: 'If you will only let me hear her voice or see her hand on the banisters, I shall then go away content,' but he threatened her, and she was forced to return to London. She continued to try to reach her daughter, applying to the magistrates both in London and in Kent, to no avail.

Two months later, in April, in a post office in the south London suburb of Penge, a man named Casabianca overheard a stranger enquiring where he should go to register the death of a woman named Staunton. This was an unfortunate coincidence for Louis Staunton, for Casabianca was married to Harriet Staunton's sister, and he knew of Mrs Butterfield's unsuccessful attempts to find her. He went to the local police, who initially followed up only as a matter of form. They found that a couple and another woman had taken lodgings the day before in preparation for the arrival of 'an invalid lady'. They had asked for a local practitioner to visit her, and were referred to Dr Longrigg; the invalid, the doctor was told, was feeble-minded and partially paralysed. When he arrived she was unconscious, emaciated and dirty. He arranged for a nurse, but said there was no hope, and the patient died later that day. Based on the information given to him by the caring couple who called him in, he certified 'cerebral disease and apoplexy'. After the police appeared, the doctor hastily revoked the certificate and notified the coroner.

At the inquest, a sinister picture emerged. Louis and Elizabeth Staunton were identified not as a married couple, but as the husband and sister-in-law of the deceased, while the role of Miss Rhodes appeared dubious. The post-mortem revealed that the dead woman, now named as Harriet Staunton, had been lice-ridden, and, despite being five feet five inches tall, had weighed only seventy-four pounds on her death. There was also some suggestion of an irritant poison. Louis Staunton claimed that he and his wife had separated because of her heavy drinking, but the post-mortem found no sign of liver disease, and no witnesses could be located who had ever seen Mrs Staunton drunk.

It was now disclosed that a week before Mrs Staunton's death, Patrick and Elizabeth Staunton had appeared at Guy's Hospital in London with a seriously ill child, saying the mother couldn't care for it. Either that day or the next, the child died, and Louis arrived at the hospital the following day. He identified the boy as 'Henry Stormton', the son of a carpenter, who was 'away'. He said he was there to arrange the funeral on Stormton's behalf, and gave his own name as Harris. The funeral, he added, should be performed as cheaply as possible. This, it now appeared, was Harriet and Louis' child. The shocked inquest jury found a verdict of death by starvation and neglect against the three Stauntons and Miss Rhodes.

The trial opened at the Old Bailey in September 1877. Edward Clarke was the barrister for Patrick Staunton, and he led the defence of all four of the accused. Mrs Butterfield was the first to testify for the prosecution. She told how her daughter was not 'fit' to marry and of her attempts to see her, which had been thwarted by the Stauntons. Then the court heard the medical evidence, of the post-mortem state of the corpse and the analysis which found no poison. The doctor in Kent said he had never been asked to treat Mrs Staunton; another doctor said that Miss Rhodes had given birth to a child while living with Louis Staunton. A solicitor testified that Louis had sold the reversionary interest of his wife's inheritance, and had the money signed over to him.

The bombshell, however, was the evidence of the housemaid Clara Brown. At the inquest she had merely said that Mrs Staunton had lived perfectly contentedly with her husband. Now she turned on her employers. 'I noticed,' she said, 'that Mr. Louis Staunton and Alice Rhodes were too affectionate to one another – I am not quite sure that

Alice Rhodes always slept in her own bed – I found her night dress in a chest of drawers ... in Mr. Louis' room.' She went on to tell the enthralled court how Miss Rhodes and Louis Staunton had moved to Little Grays together, while Mrs Staunton remained with Patrick and Elizabeth Staunton, a mile or so away. After her husband left, Patrick Staunton had kept Mrs Staunton confined, even locking away her hat and jacket to prevent her leaving the house (respectable women did not go outdoors in indoor dress). Just before Christmas 1876, Mrs Staunton was confined to her room, and Patrick was heard to threaten her: 'You must not come down-stairs you damned cat, or I will break your back,' while Elizabeth, less harshly but no less unkindly, told her, 'We don't want you down here.' Clara also reported that Patrick hit his sister-in-law when she failed to obey him. Her room, she said, contained nothing but a bed, a chair-bedstead (a rough bedside table) and two boxes. She added, 'There was no basin or jug or mode of cleaning herself – I was there when the policeman afterwards examined that room – other things had been put into it after she was taken away.'

Other witnesses reinforced the maid's testimony. The driver of the fly that had brought Mrs Butterfield to Little Grays said that Louis Staunton had shouted at his mother-in-law, 'You shall not see her if you live for a thousand years, you old bitch,' before threatening her with a knife. The police had found a draft letter, in Louis' handwriting, but apparently for his wife to copy, that read: 'Mrs. Butterfield, – I really am astonished at your audacity and impertinence after your shameful and unnatural behaviour ... I would cast myself into a lion's den to be devoured at once rather than come within arm's length of you, having come to the fullest determination to have nothing to do with you or your family. I have been again to my solicitor to-day, and we have given instructions for you to be taken into custody at once should you continue to molest me ...' Mr Butterfield had received a letter from Louis, threatening to report him to his bishop, and warning that Mrs Butterfield would be given in charge if she ever approached him again.

For the defence, Clarke produced evidence to show that the corpse's emaciation and dirt could have been produced by tubercular meningitis, diabetes or Addison's disease. He dismissed Clara Brown's evidence, reminding the jury that she had sworn the exact opposite at the inquest. He did a good job, but he was unfortunate in that Mr Justice Hawkins, trying his first big case, was not much impressed with the idea of medical experts: 'Why make these examinations in pursuit of something you have no reason to believe existed?' was his dismissive view. (This was the same Hawkins whose dog was to contribute to his memoirs.) Instead he focused his summing-up on Mrs Staunton's financial situation, and how the moment her money was paid over to Louis he immediately left to join Miss Rhodes in their 'illicit' (Hawkins used the word a lot) relationship. Even the *Sporting Gazette*, which admired Hawkins, thought that the 'grim persistence with which the judge dwelt upon the prosecution side', and 'almost ignored' the defence, was 'cruel'. The jury, at any rate, was crushed, and brought in a verdict of 'guilty of murder, but recommended Elizabeth Ann Staunton and Alice Rhodes to mercy, the latter strongly'.

The *Lancet* immediately organized a petition signed by six hundred doctors. Medical evidence was routinely based on post-mortems performed by general practitioners, men with no medico-legal training. (In 1870 one doctor had testified that he had found nothing at a post-mortem to account for the death of a man, and he rather thought, therefore, that he had died of fright. Although, he added as an afterthought, the man had fallen out a window and 'that might have been another cause of death'.) The *Lancet* warned that Mrs Staunton's post-mortem had been 'inefficient and the practitioners inexperienced and the results obtained most unsatisfactory, owing to the absence of some eminent Pathologist who … would have demonstrated with greater accuracy the presence of disease'. The entire case, it concluded, 'was bad in fact and therefore … bad in law … [T]hat the deceased died of starvation is not only unproved, but entirely unsupported by the evidence.'

The *Examiner* did not agree with the *Lancet*'s insistence on the primacy of medical evidence. The Stauntons had imprisoned and ill-treated their victim, and no amount of tubercular meningitis would change that, in the newspaper's view. But after a pause, non-medical views swung against the convictions, led by a campaign in the *Telegraph* spearheaded by the novelist Charles Reade. Reade's first letter to the newspaper, two weeks after the convictions, was head-lined 'Hang in Haste, Repent at Leisure'. Hawkins had said in his summing-up that whoever had had 'the charge' of Mrs Staunton and had failed to protect her was guilty of murder. But, Reade pointed out, only Patrick had 'the charge' of her. Elizabeth Staunton was brutalized by her husband, and anyway legally a wife who had abetted her husband in a criminal act could be sentenced only to two years' imprisonment. Miss Rhodes did not have Mrs Staunton in her 'charge' – she lived separately. Louis had paid his brother £1 a week to care for his wife, which wasn't much, but was enough for food: if Patrick had failed to look after her, that was not Louis' legal responsibility.

The other newspapers agreed, as did their readers – virtually all the papers daily carried letters protesting against the verdict. Perhaps the *Maidstone and Kentish Journal* best summarized the feelings of middle-class readers: the original charges had been brought to 'show disapproval' of the Stauntons; a conviction was the last thing that had been expected, and the jury had been led into giving the wrong verdict for the type of people in the dock. Hawkins, seemingly surprised by the outcry, 'upon consideration' thought that perhaps the capital penalty was too strong. The Home Secretary, under the weight of media and professional opposition, gently caved in. Miss Rhodes was pardoned and immediately released, and Elizabeth, Patrick and Louis Staunton had their sentences commuted to penal servitude for life. But as *Reynolds's* pointed out, if they were guilty, they should by law be executed; if they were innocent, they should by law be released. They could not be a little bit guilty. 'The fact is, the Home Secretary has done his best to get Hawkins out of the mess his reckless and intemperate charge had plunged him into.' Most, however, were satis-fied that the result reflected the gravity of the crime while taking into account the medical uncertainty. Harriet Staunton had been brutal-ized, and permitted to die, even if she had not been murdered; the consensus was that her tormentors should suffer too.

Patrick Staunton died in prison three years later. Elizabeth served six years and was quietly released in 1883. Louis served the longest, spending twenty years in Dartmoor. When he was released, still only forty-six years old, he married Miss Rhodes and they had another two children. He received financial help from Edward Clarke – who offered him the choice of receiving £2 a week for two years, or a lump sum of £100 to set himself up in business, 'about the same as the amount of the fees I had received in the case, which had brought me great rewards', said the barrister – and he returned to his previous occupation of auctioneer, living to the venerable age of eighty-three.

Medico-legal advances, in this case, were on balance accepted. But there was something about the story that pulled people back to older attitudes towards crime. Broadsides, which had been in decline from mid-century, made a comeback to sing the doom of poor Mrs Staunton. 'No one to love her, no one to care,/For the poor starving wife in secret despair', chorused one, a distinct improvement on another, which bumpily proclaimed: 'Poor Harriet Strnnton [sic] tho' born well to do,/Has died in such misery it hardly seems true/It is said she's been starved and cruelly used,/Worse than a dog has she been abused.' This was published before the inquest was over, and ended with 'a warningtobad husbands wesay [sic]/Not to treat wives in an unmanly way'. The household at Little Grays was broken up and the goods sold by auction, with hundreds of eager souvenir-hunters buying the 6d. catalogue, and 'thousands' attending the sale itself, as thousands had done half a century before at Probert's cottage.

But there was novelty too. After the verdict, but before the commutations, the deputy governor at Maidstone prison, where the four were held, had the prisoners photographed 'In accordance with the regulations'. The Prevention of Crimes Act 1871 had formalized the photographing of criminals; in the first year 30,463 photographs were taken – so many that by 1876 only 'habitual' criminals and paroled prisoners were routinely photographed. Owing to their notoriety, the Stauntons were an exception. While photography in prison was relatively new, the images were immediately used in an old-fashioned way – the Staunton brothers asked for copies to give to family members as souvenirs, just as Courvoisier and others had signed bits of paper from their condemned cells.

If technology was selling, so too was quackery. Dr Monck, 'the celebrated medium' (celebrated among the legal confraternity too, as he had recently served a sentence for fraud), announced that 'a distressed spirit came to our *séance*, and, giving astounding proofs of her identity as Harriet Staunton, solemnly declared that if the condemned prisoners are hung they will be wrongly executed, *for they were not her intentional murderers, but her death was occasioned by disease alone*'. Monck followed this, somewhat oddly, with the promise that 'even though the spirits know the truth, he will never tell', because 'the spirits are not detectives, not sleuth-hounds baying on the track of human blood'.

Given the lurid details, it is astonishing that only one fictionalized version of the story appeared: *Harriet Staunton, or, Married and Starved for Money*, a penny-dreadful in sixty parts, was advertised in 1878, entitled a 'romance'. (I have been unable to find a surviving copy.) Apart from this, only small traces of the story were used, two of them linked to Sherlock Holmes. In 1899 William Gillette produced his lasting contribution to theatre, *Sherlock Holmes*, which he wrote and also starred in, first in the USA, and then at the Duke of York's in London.* The first act opens in a mysterious, slightly decaying house, where the Larrabee siblings are discussing Alice, and her stubborn refusal to hand over some documents.

LARRABEE: We ought to be able to make her tell.
MADGE: We've tried haven't we? ... Starving isn't any use – that's certain ... She's so weak now she can scarcely stand – and as obstinate as ever ... What's the use of hurting the girl any more. You've tried all *that*.

---

* It was Gillette who inextricably linked Holmes with the calabash pipe, its great curved stem replacing the straight-stemmed pipe seen in the magazine illustrations. A legend grew up that Gillette chose it because it was easier to speak with the curved stem clenched between his teeth, but it is more likely that, as he said on another occasion, a straight-stemmed pipe would have hidden his face – a true actor's reason.

LARRABEE: Well I'll try something else …
MADGE: … Remember – nothing that'll *show*. *No marks* …

Conan Doyle was named with Gillette as joint author, but it is thought that the work is almost entirely Gillette's. The next reference, however, is Doyle's own. In his short story 'The Disappearance of Lady Frances Carfax', Lady Frances is duped by a conman, who takes her to a south London suburb where he refuses her worried family access, while he and his wife nurse a dying servant, whose death an unsuspecting local doctor willingly certifies. (In the nick of time Holmes stops the funeral and has the coffin opened; Lady Frances is found inside together with the dead servant.)

It was, appropriately enough, an actor who ushered in twentieth-century technology with his murder. In 1897 William Terriss was performing in another Gillette vehicle, *Secret Service*, at the Adelphi Theatre. Terriss had the kind of biography that movie stars would later fabricate. Born in 1847 to a barrister father, he joined the merchant navy, jumped ship, worked as a tea-planter in Assam, and a sheep farmer in the Falklands; on his return journey on board a whaler, the crew mutinied and elected the twenty-four-year-old Terriss captain, or at least so he said. By the 1880s he specialized in playing gallant British tars in popular West End melodrama, inter-spersed with a number of soldiers, also gallant, for variety. He excelled in parts where he could dive about the stage athletically, often performing daring rescues, and his debonair charm won him the nickname Breezy Bill. Terriss had played Shakespearean parts as support lead to Henry Irving (and had once played the murderer Houseman to Irving's Eugene Aram), but he had little interest in seri-ous drama: in 1895 Shaw wrote *The Devil's Disciple* for him and his co-star Jessie Millward, but Terriss fell asleep during the reading.

On the night of 16 December 1897, Terriss and a friend had just reached the actor's private entrance to the Adelphi when he was approached by a man in evening dress and an Inverness cape. The stranger appeared to thump him twice on the back in a friendly way.

William Terriss (left) – 'Breezy Bill' – in character at the Adelphi Theatre in 1894.
This was typical of the cartes-de-visite that actors posed for to promote their
images. After Terriss's murder three years later, his found a ready new market.

Terriss turned, and was struck once more. He called out, 'My God, I
am stabbed,' and his friend grabbed at the man with the knife, calling
to a policeman who happened to be passing. Terriss was carried into
the theatre, and laid on the floor by the door. A doctor was
summoned, but in a matter of minutes Terriss was dead. The

policeman escorted the murderer the few dozen yards to Bow Street police station. 'What could have induced you to do such a cruel deed as this?' he later reported asking. 'Mr. Terriss would not employ me, and I was determined to be revenged,' was the murderer's response. At the station he added, 'That's what I stabbed him with,' and handed over a knife.

Richard Archer, who called himself Richard Prince, was a failed actor from Dundee. Ten years previously he had been an extra in *Harbour Lights*, with Terriss starring. He then got odd jobs in small provincial theatres, although he was usually sacked fairly quickly; he was incompetent, and most people who came into contact with him thought he was insane. His sister, from the guarded references to her in the press, was probably a prostitute in London (although she may simply have been living with a man: the tone would be the same). For a time Mrs Archer, as she was known, was supported by an actor at the Adelphi, and he helped Prince find work. But the siblings were soon estranged – Prince claimed to have met his sister in the street a few hours before the murder and begged for help, to which he said she replied, 'I would rather see you dead in the gutter.' This was probably true, for when the police notified her of the murder, she responded by telegram: 'Mrs. Archer declines to have anything to do with him.' Prince in turn believed she was 'in league with Terriss in blackmailing me'. What he thought Terriss was blackmailing him with or for could never be clarified, and he added that Terriss had arranged for him to be poisoned 'at Chester, Greenwich and Plymouth'.

At the police court hearing Prince's landlady testified that he was virtually starving. The Actors' Benevolent Fund had made several payments to him, at Terriss's urging, but had recently informed him they could help him no further, which he took as a sign of increasing malignancy on Terriss's part. A theatre manager from Newcastle testified to Prince's erratic behaviour, saying that company members had refused to work with him: he could not learn his tiny part, and when taxed with this he suggested that they shut the production down until he was better. 'His brain was gone,' he concluded. The stage-door-keeper had seen Prince hanging about the Adelphi for a couple of months, and had purposely told him that Terriss used the stage door, when in fact he used a private door further along Maiden Lane.*

At the trial at the Old Bailey, Prince's mother told of her son's long history of erratic behaviour, persecution complexes and delusions – he insisted at one stage that he was Jesus Christ, although, Mrs Archer told the court pathetically, 'he did not say that very often'. She also said he had a half-brother who was 'silly'.† She protested feebly that he was not violent, but admitted that he had attacked his brother with a poker and a knife. Later a foreman at the works where Prince had been employed as a labourer said that when he lost his temper he 'would not be quietened down, and the white foam was at his mouth and we had to lock him down'. Prince was found guilty but insane, and was sent to Broadmoor. From there he continued to write letters, including several to the editor of *Lloyd's Weekly*, who remarked dryly that 'they did not exhibit more delusions than are common with newspaper correspondents'.

Lloyd's had had closer dealings with Prince than the editor was willing to recall in his memoirs, however: a man named Eayres was arrested for forging an order of admission to Holloway, in order to interview Prince. He had succeeded, and only his hubris in selling the piece to *Lloyd's* led to his discovery. (He got £20 for the article, of which he said £12 had gone to Prince, with the remaining £8 to follow, but if that were the case, what was in it for him? One wonders if Prince ever saw the first sum.) Other newspapers, without *Lloyd's* exclusive, spent less time on the sad, crazed murderer. Instead, the crime provoked a raft of stories of precognition. Terriss's understudy gave interviews to the press: 'I dreamt I saw Mr. Terriss lying in the landing surrounded by a crowd, and that he was raving … It was a horrible dream … I tried to forget it … but to-night … when I came to the theatre, I was going down Bedford-street when something

---

* There is, today, a blue plaque marking the spot where the murder occurred.

† Another brother, a cab driver, was said in court to have died of general paralysis brought on by insanity. 'General paralysis (or paresis) of the insane' denoted syphilis, but as he died after falling from a cab onto his head, the diagnosis appears to have been influenced by his brother's subsequent notoriety.

seemed to say, "Don't go there" ... a few minutes afterwards I heard a great noise, and found that he had stabbed Mr. Terriss.' Jessie Millward likewise claimed she dreamed before his death that Terriss cried out, 'Sis! Sis!' warningly from behind a locked door. In the new year another story was picked up by many magazines: on the night of Terriss's death, Mrs Terriss was at home at the bucolically named 'The Cottage' in Chiswick, when, at 7.20 precisely – the very moment the fatal blows were struck – her dog leaped off her lap and ran frantically around the room. The journalist who reported this in *Country Life Illustrated* seemed less than entirely convinced, ending his report, 'Whatever the cause', the dog's behaviour 'has added one more touch of pathos to the terrible tragedy with which England has but lately been ringing'. Another journalist, however, was so overwhelmed by this synchronicity that he suggested the dog should be taken to court to confront the murderer, for identification purposes.

Meanwhile, many of the newspapers broke into verse. Broadsides were long dead, but the valedictory poem was finding a place in the mainstream press. A number of the poems had no more connection to reality than the old execution broadsides sold under the gallows had had. In the *Daily News* the poet and man of letters Richard Le Gallienne lamented the loss of 'London's young Galahad ... Romance's own proud image of a lad' (young Galahad was in fact fifty when he died). *Fun* and *Punch* caught more accurately the aura Terriss had projected – 'Poor Terriss will ne'er charm again,' said the former, while the latter said farewell to 'Splendid Will!', 'our hero', 'BREEZY BILL!' Madame Tussaud's had a model, but of the victim, not the murderer – only Maria Marten, perhaps, had had such a profile.

Breezy Bill's funeral was a production in itself. Six hundred flower arrangements were received from theatre aristocracy and real aristocracy, including the Prince of Wales, two Rothschilds, as well as the staff of Charing Cross Hospital and the Otter Swimming Club. Fifty-eight carriages followed the hearse to Brompton Cemetery, and the procession was estimated to be half a mile long. The newspapers reported that at least 10,000 people gathered at Turnham Green station to watch the cortège leave Terriss's house; at Hammersmith

Broadway station another 15,000 stood silently as it arrived, and several thousand more were at the cemetery gates. Street hawkers worked the crowds, selling funeral cards for 1*d*. – the execution broadside of the 1890s.

But the new century was coming, and with it new means of entertainment. The *Era* advertised: 'We have succeeded in taking a good Cinématograph Film of the Funeral Procession of this lamented actor passing from the hearse to the grave, embracing a large number of his personal and professional friends.' Music halls now included short films as part of the evening's entertainment, and in the same issue of the *Era*, 'Joe Hasting's Unparalleled Combination' was advertised as already showing 'Mr Lear's Biograph with the Funeral Procession of the Lamented Actor Mr William Terriss'. New technology was selling the old stories.

EIGHT

Violence

What class the murderer was, what class the victim was, how the death occurred, all these things made a great deal of difference to public interest. In 1848, at the height of the poison panic, when seemingly anything concerning working-class women murdering their husbands was of interest, Harriet Parker's back-street murder of her two step-children produced resounding apathy. Absolutely no one was interested. And yet the story was pathetic enough.

In 1845 Robert Blake, a twenty-six-year-old grinder (he sharpened blades), deserted his wife in Birmingham and ran off to London with Harriet Parker, aged thirty-five, taking his two children, Amina and Robert, aged six and three, with him. They lived in the inappropriately named Cupid's Court, a tenement behind Golden Lane, in the City, and were averagely unhappy. At 4 a.m. on New Year's Day 1848 a distraught Mrs Parker banged on her neighbours' door, calling, 'Oh, Mrs. Moore, I have done it ... I went out with Blake last night, intending to go to the play, when he met with a little strumpet, and took hold of her arm, and he immediately left me!' An exhausted Mrs Moore more or less said that four in the morning was not the time for visiting. Mrs Parker's response ensured sleep was banished: 'I have murdered the two children.' And they were indeed both lying dead in their bed.

The story as it unfolded was a sad, ordinary one, with only the violence at the end making it extraordinary. Blake had been a good provider, a steady, reliable worker. But he had taken up with Jane Jones, spent less time working, and Mrs Parker was not only rampagingly jealous, she and the children were going hungry. On New Year's Eve Blake had come home, saying brusquely: 'Make haste and get the tea, and get me some water to wash me for I'm in a hurry, and have got to meet a girl at the top of Old-street. I'm going to take her to a play.' He meant to be provocative, and Mrs Parker rose to the bait. When he went out, she followed him openly, and at a milestone in the road he goaded her, saying, 'I'll kiss [the milestone] for the sake of them I'm going to see,' and 'He did kiss it,' said the desolate woman. She followed him into the local pub, where they sat briefly drinking gin before Blake managed to slip away. 'He shall repent this, I will do something before morning ...' she said. Later that evening she told her neighbour, 'There will be a pretty spectacle for him when he does come home.' She made no secret of her action, telling the police after her arrest: 'I doted on the ground he walked on,' but 'I blew the candle out, jumped on the bed and killed the girl. After I had killed her, I felt as though I could have killed a thousand children ... I turned round, saw the boy, and showed him no mercy, and I want none shown to me.' She later summed up the situation as she saw it: 'Him and that woman have been the cause of all our misfortunes, and the death of the children lies at their door. Until he became acquainted with her we had plenty, but during the fortnight he knew her, me and the children had nothing to eat but bread and dripping. That is all.'

At the trial, Blake admitted to sleeping with at least six other women during his relationship with Harriet Parker, although, he added truculently, 'there was no cause for her being jealous'. He agreed that he had goaded her by telling her about other women, and that on the night of the murders he had been with Mrs Jones. He only heard of the deaths when he returned to his house the next morning at eleven (a clear indication that he was unemployed – artisans started work by seven at the latest).

Mrs Parker was unable to afford legal representation, and the sheriffs had 'out of charity' arranged someone to represent her, but from the record little was actually done. The trial was quickly over, and the jury had no choice but to find her guilty; but they added a strong recommendation to mercy, 'in consideration of the unparalleled provocation under which she perpetrated the crime'. The judge was terse: 'The children gave her no provocation.'

The newspapers wanted no part of this story. *The Times*, that usually indiscriminately murder-loving newspaper, didn't cover the execution. Most Birmingham papers ignored the case altogether, even though the participants were from that city. The *Observer* attempted some formulaic characterizations – the murderer was 'a repulsive, downcast looking woman', while Mrs Jones was 'genteel looking' – but its heart wasn't in it. The *Morning Chronicle* published what it said was a letter from Mrs Parker to Blake while she was awaiting execution, but it sounds as if it had been lifted from a sorrowful lamentation: 'My days are numbered; this day fortnight I shall be *silent* in the *grave*,' followed by more routine aspirations: that she would be redeemed in death etc., etc., God in his wisdom etc., etc., while living in sin has 'brought us to misery, shame, and sorrow' and more.

An even more violent and bloody, and even less discussed, story was that of Elizabeth Martha Brown, who was executed for murdering her husband in 1856. Her story was so ordinary, and therefore so disregarded, that if there had not been one transformative eye in the crowd at her execution, she would not figure even here. Mrs Brown lived in Beaminster, in Dorset. She was forty-four years old and married to John Anthony Brown, a nineteen-year-old carrier (he conveyed goods and parcels from towns and villages, along fixed routes). They had been servants at a farm together, and it appears that the older woman may have had enough money to set the young man up in business when they married. They too appear to have been unhappy in a routine fashion: Brown drank, and was cheating on his wife with a woman named Mary Davies. He was also violent. On 5 July 1856 he was seen giving Mrs Davies a lift on his cart; he then joined a friend and drank and played skittles all afternoon, before drinking, without the skittles, until midnight. At five o'clock the next morning, Mrs Brown arrived at a house nearby: at about two o'clock, she said, her husband had arrived home covered in blood, gasped out, 'The horse,' and collapsed on the floor, clutching her dress so tightly in his death-grip that she had only just been able to release herself.

But no blood could be found anywhere outside the house, there was no blood on Brown's face, no dirt on his clothes or hands – Mrs Brown's story, that he had been kicked by his horse, looked dubious. At the post-mortem, the doctors agreed that his wounds were not consistent with a kick from a horse, while they were consistent with being struck by a poker or a flat-iron. In addition, they stated, their extensive nature would have knocked Brown out: he could not have walked with a head wound such as he had. Mrs Brown was arrested on a charge of murder.

Unlike Harriet Parker, she did have competent legal counsel. Her barrister demonstrated that the doctors, so certain in their post-mortem diagnosis, had never seen a fractured skull, nor a skull kicked by a horse, nor even a skull wounded by a poker or flat-iron. He also forced them to admit to knowledge of cases where the most extra-ordinary head wounds had not disabled their victims, who had walked and talked long after a supposedly fatal blow. Finally, he reminded the jury that her husband was Mrs Brown's sole source of income: with his death she was completely impoverished. In fact, he did his job so well that, in an age of rapidly achieved verdicts, the jury took a notably prolonged three hours to reach theirs. But they still found Elizabeth Martha Brown guilty. She probably would have done better had she used as a defence her confession from gaol. She said Brown had come home drunk and vicious; he had hit her, then reached for a horsewhip and started to lash her with it, threatening to 'knock your brains out through the window'. She grabbed at the hatchet she had been using to break up the coal, and struck out. 'I had never struck him before, after all his ill-treatment, but when he hit me so hard ... I was almost out of my senses and hardly knew what I was doing.'

Mrs Brown was unfortunate in her timing. Attitudes to male brutality were changing, and had she committed her murder a decade later, she would almost certainly have been acquitted. Previously, male violence towards women had been considered a private matter, but by 1846, *The Times* noted with disapproval a case where a man found his wife drinking and hit her with a brick, killing her, to be sentenced to

only three months' hard labour. The *Examiner* agreed, highlighting
the following year a sentence that suggested it was 'one of the marital
rights to kick and beat a wife to death'. The *Daily News* berated the
courts for continuing to believe that wife-murder was 'at the best,
justifiable homicide, at the worst, manslaughter'. While the courts did
not yet reflect public opinion, the newspapers do show less acceptance
of private violence.

These were all wife-murders. The commentary on husband-
murders reflected much more harshly on the women, but did not
necessarily reflect reality. From the 1840s to the 1890s, the number of
women charged with murdering their husbands dropped from twenty
per decade to seven, while the number of men charged with murdering their wives rose from seventy-seven to 158. Only seventeen women
were executed for husband-murder in the sixty years from 1840, and
five of those were poison-panic cases. Mrs Brown was unlucky in
being found guilty: the conviction rate for husband-murder was only
46 per cent. She was even unluckier in being executed: of the women
sentenced to death for murder after 1843, only 13 per cent were
hanged.* Mrs Brown was one of only twenty-four women throughout
the Victorian period to be hanged for killing her husband.

Despite its rarity, contemporaries viewed the story as ordinarily
brutal, and it aroused little interest. The *Morning Chronicle* reported
a 'concourse ... not very large' to watch the execution in Dorchester,
although the *Bristol Mercury* thought the crowd was 'large ... in spite
of the thick, hazy rain which was falling'. Among those watching was
a sixteen-year-old apprentice architect who in 1926 still remembered
Mrs Brown's 'fine figure'. Later he added, 'I saw – they had put a cloth
over the face – how, as the cloth got wet, *her features came through it.
That was extraordinary.*' That apprentice grew up to become the
novelist Thomas Hardy, and it has long been suggested that the death
of Mrs Brown was transformed, three decades later, into the image

---

* This compares to a figure of nearly 59 per cent for men, useful to bear in mind when
reading of female vs male killers. Women attracted far more vitriol in print, but were less
often treated to the full majesty of the law.

presiding over *Tess of the d'Urbervilles*, subtitled 'A Pure Woman, Faithfully Presented'.*

By the time Hardy came to write *Tess*, both he and his readers had long been accustomed to executions taking place behind prison walls. The heroine of the novel is therefore executed offstage, unlike Mrs Brown, and Hardy used the watchers' response to produce the effect that was generated by Mrs Brown on Hardy himself that dank day in 1856:

> Upon the cornice of the tower a tall staff was fixed ... A few minutes after the hour had struck something moved slowly up the staff, and extended itself upon the breeze. It was a black flag.
>
> 'Justice' was done, and the President of the Immortals, in Aeschylean phrase, had ended his sport with Tess ... The two speechless gazers bent themselves down to the earth, as if in prayer, and remained thus a long time, absolutely motionless: the flag continued to wave silently. As soon as they had strength, they arose, joined hands again, and went on.

*   *   *

The murdered Francis Savile Kent was only a bit younger than little Robert Blake, who had been smothered by his father's common-law wife in a back street. No one wrote about Robert Blake, but when 'a child is found mysteriously dead in the bosom of a respectable family', as *Blackwood's* noted, people paid attention, and hordes descended on the quiet village of Road on the Somerset/Wiltshire border.† As Mrs Braddon wrote, a murder 'uncommonly cruel, cowardly, and unmanly, and moreover occurring in a respectable rank of life' was always bound to create interest. Francis was killed by – well, by whom was a question that convulsed Britain for half a decade.

On the morning of 29 June 1860, Elizabeth Gough, a nursemaid, tapped on the door of her mistress's bedroom, looking for

* Although see p.171 for a connection to Maria Manning.

† The village's name is now spelt Rode, and the county boundary has since been redrawn.

three-year-old Francis. He was not there, and a wider search was quickly under way: the four children of Samuel Kent's first wife, the cook and the nursemaid all hunted through the house; Samuel Kent rode off to fetch the Trowbridge policeman; the inhabitants of the nearby cottages searched the grounds. On Kent's return he was met with the news that the toddler had been found thrust down the outside privy, his throat cut, and with a stab wound in his chest. Kent, a sub-inspector of factories for the west of England, took charge. He told the police which areas they might and might not search – not in the house, for example, for 'the murderer would not be found there'. He pushed them towards the locals, who resented, he said, his limiting their fishing rights, and to 'former nursemaids' who might have wanted to take revenge. He even suggested that old melodrama staple, the gypsies.*

It is not clear what revenge he thought the nursemaids might feel owing to them, but Samuel Savile Kent had left some vengeful feelings behind as he passed through life. The son of a carpet manufacturer, he had married the daughter of a City merchant, who gave him two daughters and a son before developing signs of insanity. This slowed him down not a jot, and he fathered another six children on her. By 1852, when she died, of those children that survived, the youngest daughter, Constance, was eight. The family moved house, and the nursemaid, Mary Pratt, the daughter of a greengrocer, moved too – into Kent's bed, shortly to emerge as the second Mrs Kent. Possibly because of this, the family had a bad reputation: the Board of Factory Commissioners had earlier questioned Kent about his first wife's seclusion; it was also whispered that the family could not keep servants – a hundred were said to have passed through the house in only four years. There was no question that the Kents were living well beyond their means. Kent earned less than £400 as a factory inspector; he may have had another £300 or £400 in private income; and while

---

* The force's submission to the factory inspector reflected social reality. West Country police were paid badly even compared to police in the rest of the country: the superintendent of the Wiltshire County Constabulary earned less than £80 per annum.

£700–800 a year would place him among the middle of the prosperous middle classes, his large house and several servants required much more. Then there was the treatment of his first wife's children: neighbours spoke openly of their stepmother's harshness towards them. Three years previously Constance and her brother William had run away from home; Constance – a true scandal this – had cut her hair short and *dressed as a boy*.

The police decided right away that the murder had been committed by one of the household. Mrs Kent was very advanced in pregnancy, and would not have been able to carry the toddler from his nursery, through the house, and outside to the privy; her two other children were too young. That left as suspects Mr Kent, the four children of the first marriage, the nursemaid, the cook and the housemaid. The nursemaid was the focus of police attention: she slept in the same room as the child, but claimed to have heard nothing during the night; she also said that when she woke and saw he was gone, she assumed he had been taken by Mrs Kent, even though she had never done such a thing before. The sixteen-year-old Constance Kent was also an object of suspicion: she resented the second family, her nightgown had gone missing on the night of the murder, and a bloody shift had been found jammed in the scullery boiler. This second, or first, shift was passed around like a parcel in a children's game. It was found in the first place only because, in the excitement of the morning, the housemaid had forgotten to light the boiler. When the local police saw the bloody garment, they appear to have assumed that it was stained with menstrual blood, and, embarrassed, ignored it. When Miss Kent's nightgown was discovered to be missing, attention returned to the shift. Kent arranged for the police to stake out the kitchen overnight (although not, for unexplained reasons, the scullery where the shift had actually been found), to ambush anyone who came to retrieve it. However, when Kent went to bed he quietly locked them in, with no access to the scullery or the rest of the house. By the time they were released in the morning, the shift had vanished, and between the embarrassment of menstrual blood and the embarrassment of being locked in by a suspect, the shift was never

James Blomfield Rush, a failing tenant farmer who murdered his landlord and son, created a sensation when he defended himself (unsuccessfully) in court. Even Dickens travelled to Norfolk to see the site of the murders. This medallion was produced to commemorate Rush's execution.

Eliza Fenning, a servant, was accused of attempting to poison the family who employed her. Despite no evidence that anyone was even poisoned (nobody died), she was hanged nonetheless. East End theatres such as the Pavilion in Whitechapel Road had great success with the tales of her persecution by her social 'betters'.

Maria and Frederick Manning were the sensation
of 1849 when the body of Maria's lover was
found buried beneath their kitchen floor. Madame
Tussaud's did a roaring trade when it exhibited
their likenesses, claiming that Joseph Tussaud
himself had taken them from the living criminals
while they awaited execution. The drawings by
William Mulready, however, suggest that a certain
amount of artistic licence was taken in wax.

Madame Tussaud's outdid itself in ingenuity when it came to William Palmer. Palmer, a doctor, was convicted of murdering John Cook, a racetrack character. Dozens of further murders were soon laid at his door, although he was never charged with any of them. Madame Tussaud's, however, produced his 'poisons box' – although nothing like it had been produced in evidence. That Palmer was a doctor made it unsurprising that he had many drugs in his surgery: a fact that troubled none of Tussaud's visitors, who were also thrilled to see an ordinary mourning card printed by Cook's family, as was the custom.

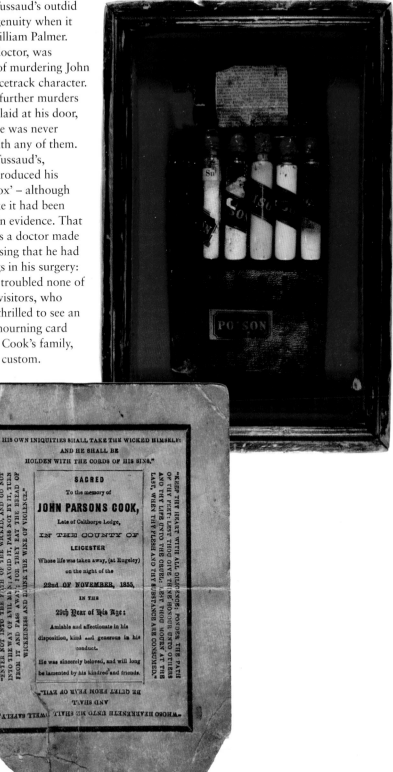

Middle-class female murderers could expect very different treatment from that meted out to working-class women like Eliza Fenning and Maria Manning. Madeleine Smith (*opposite*), a Glasgow architect's daughter, was accused of murdering her secret lover, and despite her explicit letters to him being read out in court, shaming her family irreparably, her legal defence was adroit, and the verdict was the Scottish 'not proven'. Adelaide Bartlett (*above right*) also had a brilliant lawyer, who saw her acquitted of her husband's murder, although he cheerfully announced to many that he thought her entirely guilty. The mystery of who murdered toddler Francis Saville Kent was not to be solved for five years, until his sister Constance (*below right*), long under suspicion by the police, and then living in an Anglican convent, finally confessed.

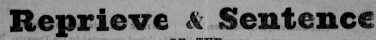

Reprieve & Sentence
OF THE
PENGE CONVICTS.
(Paadon of Alice Rhodes, the 3 Stauntons imprisonment fo r life)

Who were sen-
tenced to be
hung at Maids-
tone, on Tuesday
Oct. 16th, 1877,
f.r the cruel
shocking murder
of Harriet Staun-
ton.

JUSTICE

IN

ENGLAND

The death of Harriet Staunton aroused public revulsion when her husband, his mistress, his brother and sister-in-law were all accused of imprisoning her and starving her to death. Medical experts were less certain, and the verdict was ultimately a legal fudge, although magazines such as the *Illustrated Police News* had few doubts.

After Eleanor Pearcey was found guilty of murdering her lover's wife and child, pushing their bodies in the baby's pram before abandoning them in the street, Madame Tussaud's swooped in, buying up the furniture from her lodgings, and the victims' clothes and the pram from the bereaved husband. A toffee found in the pram, thought to have been in the child's mouth at her death, takes pride of place under a glass dome on the mantelpiece in this photograph of the display. Madame Tussaud's knew its audience: 75,000 people visited in the first three days.

The crimes of the unknown person dubbed 'Jack the Ripper' have probably had more written about them than any since Cain killed Abel. Among the many suggestions for the role of the murderer was a mad occultist; anarchists of various nationalities and beliefs; a clergyman; a rogue policeman; and a 'scientific humanitarian' who was killing prostitutes in order to improve the world. The *Pall Mall Gazette* plumped for an army doctor with sunstroke who had been too heavily influenced by *Dr Jekyll and Mr Hyde*, currently onstage. Its star, Richard Mansfield (*left*), transformed himself from the respectable Jekyll to the evil Hyde in front of the audience, relying solely on changes in posture, feature and gait, and thus exacerbating fears that an urbane professional man could, with no warning, suddenly become a ravening beast. Dozens of publications fed off this theme, as in this broadside (*below*).

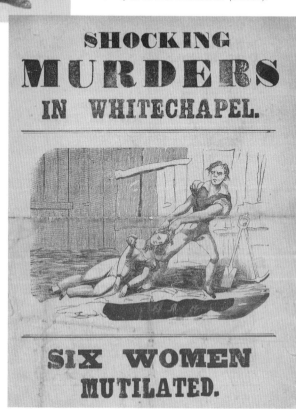

mentioned when twelve days after the crime a Scotland Yard detective arrived.

The Wiltshire magistrates had requested help a week after the crime, but 'Now that the County Police is established, the assistance of London officers is seldom resorted to,' the Home Office replied. The inquest was, at best, incompetent. The coroner refused to permit a routine adjournment for police investigation; he prevented the doctor who performed the post-mortem from describing the wounds, so no cause of death could be recorded. The Kent family was only questioned at the jury's insistence – the coroner thought it unseemly to imply suspicion of such a respectable family. He also failed to present the alternatives of manslaughter or murder to the jury, nor did he give them the opportunity to state their own verdict, but simply told them to countersign a form he had himself filled out. The Home Secretary changed his mind and arranged for Scotland Yard to step in.

Inspector Jonathan Whicher of Scotland Yard appeared before the magistrates primed by Samuel Kent and his friends with stories of Miss Kent's eccentricities, including an episode three years earlier, when she was thirteen, and had secretly read the *Times* reports on the shocking Miss Madeleine Smith. Then there was the missing nightgown; Whicher thought it had been worn by Miss Kent when she killed her half-brother, and later destroyed because it was covered in blood. He asked the magistrates to have her arrested, and somewhat dubiously they agreed, to the horror of the middle-class world – arrest the daughter of a middle-class house purely on suspicion? Whicher appears to have assumed that Miss Kent, once arrested, would confess, but she simply sat mute. The magistrates' hearing the following week was as blatantly slanted to favour the Kents as the inquest had been: the family was not required to give evidence, or even to attend the hearing; jurymen known to be hostile to the Kents were removed; the foreman was a friend of Samuel Kent, who said it was his 'duty to spare the feelings of the family as far as possible'. The evidence presented to suggest Miss Kent's guilt was only her jealousy of her father's second family and the missing nightdress, coupled with her earlier attempt to run away from home. Her very able solicitor then highlighted her mother's insanity, before presenting Whicher to the magistrates as a presumptuous working-class meddler who was mixing with decent middle-class families in a case beyond his understanding. Even so, the magistrates were half-persuaded by the prosecution's case, and released Miss Kent only on recognizance of £200.

Most of the newspapers crowed that Miss Kent had been found innocent, overlooking the fact that this was a preliminary hearing, not a trial. Whicher returned to London with his reputation destroyed: *Punch* later mocked him as Inspector Watcher of the Defective Force. That this was a class response cannot be in doubt. After Miss Kent was released, the nursemaid Elizabeth Gough was in turn arrested, and soon also released for lack of evidence. While *The Times* had berated Whicher for his 'indecent' mentions of Miss Kent's nightgown, the same paper speculated at length on a possible solution to the crime revolving around the nursemaid and an unknown lover being discovered in bed by the child, whom they accidentally smothered in an attempt to prevent him waking the house. While this is as plausible a scenario as any, what is striking is the newspaper comfortably imagining this scene of illicit sex involving a working-class woman, while ferociously rejecting the word 'nightdress' in connection with a middle-class girl.*

The working classes were no happier with the police's work than their middle-class counterparts. As the Kent case continued unsolved, another murder, in London, hit the headlines. Mrs Emsley, the prosperous widow of a local builder (and, it was suggested, a ruthless small-scale slum landlady in her own right) was found dead at home, her head beaten in. On the testimony of one George (sometimes James) Mullins, a shoemaker named Emms, who collected rents for

---

* Dickens was one of many who believed in the theory of the nursemaid and her lover, and he put a name to the man, writing in October 1860 to Wilkie Collins: 'Mr. Kent, intriguing with the nursemaid, poor little child wakes in Crib, and sits up, contemplating blissful proceedings. Nursemaid strangles him then and there. Mr. Kent gashes body, to mystify discoverers, and disposes of same.' Many agreed, noting that the present Mrs Kent had once been the older Kent children's nursemaid, and assuming that what had happened once could happen again.

Mrs Emsley, had his shed searched, and items identified as coming from her house were found. But very swiftly the evidence was turned on its head. Emms was shown to be a man of unimpeachable character, while Mullins had worked undercover for the police spying on suspected members of an Irish secret society, using forged documents and attending clandestine political gatherings. He had also, it was discovered, served a sentence for robbery. He was ultimately convicted of the murder himself, and of planting the evidence in order to claim the reward. The general opinion was that such behaviour was all that could be expected of a police spy. Andrew Forrester's *Female Detective* used this episode as a curious little prologue to another story, about a kidnapped child. Here 'a lady of somewhat solitary and reserved life' is found brutally murdered, and the police receive information that the goods stolen from her home are to be found in a shed; they are commended for making 'a wonderful series of fortunate guesses and industrious inquiries' – even at this stage, 'fortunate guesses' are a praiseworthy part of detective work.

The guesses concerning the Road murder, however, were making a much greater sensation. One broadside warned that 'On some there lies a great suspicion,/Examinations has [sic] took place,/And to persecute [sic] they are determined,/Into this mysterious case.' No mention was made of Miss Kent, or her siblings, or of Mr and Mrs Kent, only: 'The nursemaid in the room was sleeping,' it noted tantalizingly. This was one of the very few broadsides on the case to appear, for by 1860 their day was past: despite its fame, the Road murder was said to have sold a scant 150,000 broadsides, compared to 2.5 million for the Mannings. (Although the *idea* of the broadside remained in people's imaginations, and in their vocabularies. Only a few years later, Wilkie Collins had Allan Armadale's prophetic dream taken down 'from my own lips ... as if it was my "last dying speech and confession" '.)

As a comedy coda to the botched inquest and stalled police investigation, a local magistrate set in motion what he called an independent hearing, which had no legal status. Anyone and everyone was invited to give 'evidence' at the local Temperance Hall. This, as

Blackwood's reported with scorn, produced only 'absurd and irrelevant gossip', with the magistrate 'covering himself with contempt'. The single piece of new information was the story of the bloody shift, which up until now the police had managed to suppress. But nothing came of this, and the fevered press speculation continued. Four months after the murder, one magazine estimated that the upmarket newspapers were still printing twenty columns a day on 'The Road Mystery'; *The Times* ran eight leaders alone on the subject by the end of the year. Even the *Lady's Newspaper*, its pages filled with ladylike topics – the 'Court Circular', 'Wedding Stationery' and 'The Opera' – kept its readers updated on the murder.

The newspapers and the police files were filled with variants on Maria Marten's stepmother's dream, perhaps caused by the dearth of concrete information. One letter to the police helpfully supplied the details of 'a dream which has given me a deal of uneasiness. I dreamed I saw 3 men making up the plot at a house near Finished Building, about half a mile from the sean [sic] of the murder ... I can give a minute description of the men I saw in my dream.' The press colluded in and encouraged this type of superstition, with the *Western Daily Press* reporting that, before Francis's funeral, the bands supporting his coffin all simultaneously snapped at the precise moment the bearers passed the fatal privy.

Miss Kent, still under suspicion, was sent to a convent in Belgium to continue her education. The newspapers printed rumours that she had confessed, then more rumours that the previous rumours were incorrect. The rest of the family, meanwhile, moved away, as sightseers, many of them of the 'respectable' classes, continued to wander through the house's grounds, and Mr and Mrs Kent were publicly jeered when they walked down the street in the nearest county town. Kent had a public sale of his possessions, like Louis Staunton before him, selling seven hundred catalogues and netting £1,000-odd. (The baby's cot, however, was held back, to keep it out of Madame Tussaud's hands.)

Pamphlets such as *The Road Murder*, by 'A Barrister-at-Law', showed great changes since Eliza Fenning's death in 1815. The anonymous barrister opened his summary of the situation after the inquest with a range of questions, itemized as though for a detective to follow up. 'Why did [Samuel Kent] ... seek a policeman at a distance, when one lived nearer?' Why was Miss Gough not suspected by the Kents? What was the story of locking the policemen in the kitchen? and more. But with no resolution in sight, the fiction market took the lead. This was the perfect meshing of subject (middle-class and prosperous) with readership and the new genre of sensation-fiction. The anonymous 'Disciple of Edgar Poe' turned to Dupin-like methods of deduction in *Who Committed the Road Murder? or, The Track of Blood Followed*. 'There are six theories,' he wrote; 'if five of them can be proved untenable, the remaining one may fairly become the subject of attention.' (Compare this to Sherlock Holmes thirty years later: 'When you have eliminated the impossible, whatever remains, *however improbable*, must be the truth.') The pseudonymous Charles Martel cherry-picked from reality in *The Diary of an Ex-Detective*, where 'The Murdered Judge' took elements from the Road mystery: two men, one a ne'er-do-well, one the son-in-law of the judge's sister, are under suspicion; the working-class suspect is taken into custody, but 'the committee was exceedingly loath to move in the matter' of the other, 'on account of [his] respectable position'.

Many novelists turned to the shattered Kent family. Mrs Oliphant's Chronicles of Carlingford novels explored the domestic vicissitudes of a country town, and in the first instalment, *Salem Chapel* (1862–63), internalized many of the elements of sensation-novels, although Mrs Oliphant herself despised the genre, writing of the fictional detective, 'He is not a collaborateur [sic] whom we welcome with any pleasure into the republic of letters. His appearance is neither favourable to taste nor morals.' Yet in *Salem Chapel* the still unsolved Kent case is mirrored when Susan, the genteel daughter and sister of Dissenting ministers, is falsely accused of murdering her supposed seducer, and is tracked by a remorseless, Whicher-like policeman. Having followed her from the scene of the crime, the lower-middle-class man is bundled out of the house by one of the town's tradesmen, who is shocked to find him physically present in a middle-class household. Susan's brother Arthur finds that the newspapers turn 'the whole terrible tale ... into a romance of real life, in which his sister's name, indeed, was withheld, but no other particular spared ... all over the country by this time, newspaper readers were waking up into excitement about this new tale of love, revenge, and crime'.

A similarly non-sensation-novel, *The Trial*, by the High Church writer Charlotte M. Yonge, in 1864 described the fallout after an unsolved crime, with a country town overrun by newsboys crying the updates, and the 'artists' of the illustrated papers who arrive with their 'three-legged cameras' as the sightseers gawp at the mill where the murder has occurred, the housekeeper 'making a fortune' out of the decent middle-class family's tragedy. Mrs Braddon's narrator in *Aurora Floyd* (1863) similarly thinks of the Kents in that 'quiet Somersetshire household in which a dreadful deed was done', and wonders 'what must have been suffered by each member of *that* family? What slow agonies, what ever-increasing tortures, while that cruel mystery was the "sensation" topic of conversation in a thousand happy home-circles, in a thousand tavern-parlours and pleasant club-rooms ...'*

No detail was too small to be turned into fiction. In Mrs Braddon's *The Doctor's Wife* (1864), a character slashes at himself with a paper-knife: 'I'm only trying whether a man would cut his throat from right to left, or left to right,' he offhandedly tells a horrified onlooker. He is, it turns out, a novelist trying to verify the details of a fictional suicide. The newspapers four years before had been filled with discussions about whether Francis Kent's throat had been cut left to right, or right to left: fictional deaths now assumed their readers' familiarity with true-crime minutiae. Later, in the Sherlock Holmes stories, the two would be considered as inextricably woven together: part of Holmes's study of crime was his 'immense' knowledge of 'Sensational Literature ... He appears to know every detail of every horror perpetrated in the

---

* These sentences were cut in later editions (and do not appear in many modern ones), perhaps because the narrator says that the secret 'never will be revealed until the Day of Judgment', instead of, as it turned out, merely 1865.

century.' (Sherlock Holmes may even have owed his name to sensation-fiction. Conan Doyle credited a cricketer as the source of his
unusual first name, but the traduced suspect of Le Fanu's *A Lost Name*
was Carmel Sherlock, a so-far overlooked source.)

Many disapproved of the predilection of sensation-writers for true
crime. In the *Quarterly Review* the Oxford theologian Henry Mansell
was shocked that 'Sometimes the incident of real life is made the main
plot of the story,' highlighting a just-published novel entitled *Such
Things Are* (published anonymously, but the first novel of Matilda
Charlotte Houstoun). 'By way of feeding this depraved taste', he wrote,
the novel 'brought again to the light of recollection a shadowy vision
of two past, but as yet undiscovered crimes' – the Road murder and
the Madeleine Smith case. There was 'something unspeakably disgusting in this ravenous appetite for carrion, this vulture-like instinct
which smells out the newest mass of social corruption'. Disapproving
as he was, Mansell did not trouble to name either case: even the most
respectable readers of this most respectable journal were expected to
recognize the two crimes by their descriptions alone.

In *Such Things Are*, one of the characters reports hopefully that
'there seems a chance at last of discovering the perpetrator' of the
long-unsolved murder. It was to be another two years, however, before
that became reality. In 1860, Inspector Whicher had been assisted at
Road by Sergeant Frederick Adolphus ('Dolly') Williamson. Five years
later, the Bow Street magistrates summoned Williamson, now head of
the Detective Department. On his arrival he found a veiled woman
accompanied by a clergyman and an Anglican nun. The Revd Arthur
Wagner, spiritual director of St Mary's Anglo-Catholic retreat in
Brighton, formally notified the magistrates that he had heard the
confession of the young girl known in the convent as Emilie Kent; that
she had given the confession of her own free will; and that she agreed
to repeat it there, under oath, on the understanding that the police
would take action based on what she was about to say. The veiled
woman, now introduced as Constance Kent, produced a written
confession affirming that she, and she alone, had murdered Francis
Savile Kent.

The police arrested her, but publicly doubts were immediately raised. She claimed that she had cut her half-brother's throat with a razor, and when he didn't bleed, had slashed his chest with it. In reality, a cut artery would have pumped blood everywhere, while the chest wounds were punctures, not gashes, and were not made with a razor. Miss Kent was at pains to stress that 'the guilt was hers alone, and that her father and others who have so long suffered most unjust and cruel suspicion are wholly and absolutely innocent'; she had definitely not been 'driven to this act ... by unkind treatment at home, as she met with nothing there but tender and forbearing love'. If anything, this strengthened the suspicion that had attached itself to Mr Kent. The *London Review* conceded only that 'as far as we know' there was no evidence for the Mr Kent/nursemaid scenario, but warned that 'the mania for self-accusation which seizes upon some minds' can lead them to make 'the most unfounded charges', suggesting that Miss Kent's mind was unhinged by hereditary insanity, worked on by religious fervour, and the 'manipulation to which her conscience was subjected' by 'those gentlemen who are playing at being Roman Catholic priests'. In conclusion, 'It is quite conceivable that it may, after all, turn out to be true. But until we have much stronger reasons for believing it than exist at present, we shall continue to regard it with extreme scepticism.'

Newspapers relied on crime – the *Examiner* had a regular column headed 'Murders and Murderous Crimes', the *Manchester Times* too ran a 'Murders' column. But now a foreign murder took precedence. Constance Kent confessed on 25 April 1865. On 26 April, *The Times* received the news of the assassination of Abraham Lincoln eleven days earlier, and the next day copies of the threepenny newspapers were changing hands for 2s.6d. The solution to this crime, so long awaited, now seemed insignificant. On 28 April an advertisement for *Lloyd's Weekly* devoted a third of its space to Lincoln, while the Road murder took up less than a tenth. But politics never held sway for long, and by summer things had returned to normal. The *London Review* reported cartes-de-visite of Miss Kent on sale 'in every petty print-shop', and a few years later, at Townhead, near Penrith in

Cumbria, in a happy event, 'Mr W. Cowper's red bitch Constance Kent' had a litter of eight pups.

This second wave of attention to the Kents, however muted by current events, was followed by a parallel wave of fiction. Some was ephemeral. An anonymous three-volume novel, *Not Proven* (actually by Christina Broun Cameron), utilizes most of the elements of the Kent case in a wildly rambling plot: Rosetta Pierce, aged seventeen, is accused of abstracting her toddler half-brother from his nursery, stabbing him, cutting his throat and shoving him down a privy. Her dressing gown is missing; she has a stepmother she dislikes; her father is jeered later in town; she has an 'unmanageable', un-feminine past history. (The novel also contains the splendid line: 'I am obliged to say now that I ... cannot marry a person whom I believe guilty of a murder.' A rule to live by.)

Not Proven also mixed in some Madeleine Smith elements – blackmailing as a consequence of letters to a lover, a 'not proven' verdict – and several novelists were to follow suit. In John Harwood's* *Miss Jane, or, The Bishop's Daughter* (1867), Jane, once a member of an Anglican sisterhood, is under the thumb of the fanatical Revd Austin Traxford. Her true love, the curate Edwy Mortimer, hears a confession from a dying parishioner that implicates Jane in murder. He asks her to deny it, and she arranges to meet him early one morning on the clifftop, where they can speak without being disturbed. There, by way of explanation, she pushes him over the cliff before gaily tripping back to the convent. A backstory tells of her illegitimate child, whom she had murdered; Traxford knew of it, and has blackmailed her ever since. The bishop's daughter ultimately dies very beautifully of shame, claiming that she was insane when she killed her child. (The author appears to have forgotten that she also murdered a curate.)

Miss Jane is a halfway house: the sensation-novel elements remain to the fore, but detection is assuming more importance. Many other novelists stuck to the classic sensation formula. In 1866 Mrs Henry

---

* Little is known of John Harwood. He published some novels in the sensation style in the 1860s; one scholar suggests that in fact he may have been a woman.

Wood focused entirely on the domestic when she rewrote her 1853 short story 'St Martin's Eve' as a novel, tightening earlier plot elements to make it resemble more closely Constance Kent's story: there is the death of a small child, murdered as a result of passionate jealousy between a first and second family, and a dose of hereditary insanity for the female murderer. Dickens transferred Miss Kent's attempt at running away dressed as a boy to Helena Landless in *Edwin Drood*. She too crops her hair (or rather, she fails to do so, and dramatically tries to gnaw it off), and she and her brother are also stepchildren, made 'secret and vengeful' by their unhappiness.

In other novels, the sensation elements were assuming less importance, while the detective elements were increasing. Andrew Forrester's *The Female Detective*, published before Constance Kent's confession, included 'A Child Found Dead', in which a barely fictionalized framing device was inserted around a straightforward recounting of what is presented under the not very disguised name of the 'Bridge' murder by a 'medical man' who is involved with the family.* In 1861 J.W. Stapleton, a medical man and friend of Samuel Kent, had published *The Great Crime of 1860*, which did everything in its power to move the spotlight of suspicion from the Kent household. In 'A Child Found Dead' 'nobody is more anxious than the father of the dead child to learn the cause', and instead of the murderer being a family member twisted with jealous rage, the crime is 'committed while the murderer was asleep, and while under the influence of murderous monomania'.

This solution leads directly to what T.S. Eliot called 'the first ... and the best of English detective-novels': Wilkie Collins' *The Moonstone*. 'The best' is a matter of taste; *The Moonstone* is not the first, although

* This story was republished as a pamphlet after Constance Kent's confession, now retitled *The Road Murder. Analysis of this Persistent Mystery*, with the name J. Redding Ware on the title page. Ware (c.1832–1909), sometimes suggested as a contributor to the *Boy's Own Paper*, was a modestly prolific playwright, and in 1880 he published *Before the Bench. Sketches of Police Court Life*. This combination of interests, together with the appearance of his name on what had originally been an Andrew Forrester story, leads me to suggest that the pseudonymous 'Andrew Forrester', until now unidentified, was in fact J. Redding Ware.

'first' is almost as hard to define as 'best': do the detectives have to be professional, do they have to belong to a police force, do they have to be the major precipitating element in the discovery of the criminal, do 'novels' include penny-dreadfuls that were then published as single volumes? Mrs Braddon and Dickens had earlier depicted professional policemen; many three-volume novels such as *Miss Jane* had private detectives as characters; Edward Ellis had a female police detective in the penny-blood *Ruth the Betrayer*; and Wilkie Collins had used both professional and amateur detectives in his earlier short stories and in *Armadale*. Where *The Moonstone* was the first was in pulling together many of the elements we now regard as crucial to the genre: the crime is committed at the beginning of the story; the detective(s) follow a series of artfully dropped clues which point to each of the suspects in turn, who are gathered together in one place; the mystery is unravelled at the end by a single person – there is even a 'sidekick' character. Not everything was yet in place: no detective solves this case, the policeman vanishing long before the halfway point; the scientist has the right idea, yet even he does not produce the solution, which is patched together by a number of participants – more like the real world, but not much like the super-sleuths of the genre.

A reviewer in the *Spectator* in 1861 described the sensation-novel as 'a host of cleverly complicated stories, the whole interest of which consists in the gradual unravelling of some carefully prepared enigma'. The sensation-novel was about buried secrets, and their revelation; the detective novel about the person doing the revealing. Wilkie Collins looked both forward and back. *Armadale* was serialized from November 1864 to June 1866, thus beginning five months before Miss Kent's confession, and ending long after. In it Collins inserted several parallels to the Kent case. Ozias Midwinter is treated harshly by his stepfather; his mother, like the second Mrs Kent, is not socially the equal of her husband; he runs away from home. When Miss Gwilt is convicted of killing her brutal husband, 'The judge sobbed', which, given the many examples of hanging judges, seems the most fictional element of all. But according to *The Times*, on sentencing the guilty Miss Kent, the judge 'was deeply affected, and spoke in accents broken by emotion'.

When Miss Gwilt leaves prison, like Miss Kent she goes to a 'first-rate establishment' in France, then to a 'Belgian school' run by nuns.

These details decorate the texture of the narrative, but are not integral to it; they were nothing compared to the use Collins made of Constance Kent's story in *The Moonstone*. There is the stained, missing nightdress; the detective, summoned from London, who fails at his task because he does not understand the upper-middle-class family, and returns to London in disgrace; Rosanna Spearman, the servant who is suspected of the crime, just as Miss Gough was; the daughter of the house who is the detective's choice for murderer. As well as these major plot elements, Collins stuck to the Kent story in the minute elements, too. Miss Kent's missing nightgown could be distinguished from those of her half-sisters because she alone in the house had a plain, unfrilled nightgown, a sign of her stepchild status; Rachel Verinder's nightgown cannot be mistaken for that of the servant Rosanna Spearman, because of the frills and lace. Sergeant Cuff, like Dolly Williamson, is a rose-grower in his spare time.* One of the local policemen in *The Moonstone* is dismissed by Cuff because he fails to follow Rosanna, as the Road police had failed to follow the mysterious person who flitted down to the scullery in the night to remove the bloody shift. Rachel Verinder, who is partly complicit in the disappearance of the moonstone, shifts suspicion to Rosanna, the way Miss Kent shifted suspicion to the laundress to whom, she said, she had given her nightdress.

At the same time, Collins turned the horrors of reality into the excitements of fiction. Readers no longer had to feel horror for the death of a toddler, viciously murdered and stuck down a privy, but could with more legitimate excitement contemplate the theft of an exotic jewel. The nightdress was stained not with blood, but with varnish from a freshly painted door. Cuff withdraws back to London after his failure, but is permitted to locate the jewel in the East End,

---

* And as Sherlock Holmes briefly, and most unconvincingly, becomes in 'The Naval Treaty' (1893), where he interrupts a recital of the details of a crime to exclaim, Cuff-like, 'What a lovely thing a rose is ...'

rather than, like Whicher, being virtually forced into retirement. And while Cuff is right to believe that Rachel knows more about the crime than she is letting on, unlike Miss Kent she is proved to be a virtuous woman defending her family and her soon-to-be husband, a good woman's role. And finally, the scientific solution to the mystery of the jewel theft, that Franklin Blake had walked in an opium-induced sleep, had not only appeared in the fiction of Forrester's 'A Child Found Dead', but also in a letter to *The Times* at the time of the discovery of the Road murder, when 'M.D.' suggested that 'the Frome murder may have been committed during the condition of sleep-walking, or somnambulism'. Not in Road, unfortunately, but in *The Moonstone* this was ultimately the comforting solution – it was nobody's fault. This was the great discovery of detective fiction as a new genre: violence could be tucked away out of sight, with the murder committed offstage (or even before the story commences), and the punishment left to occur after the story ended: all the fun was in the hunt.

The story of Constance Kent appealed more to middle-class than working-class audiences. There were a few more broadsides after her confession, but because no one felt they knew why the murder had been committed, the authors appear uncertain quite what they are lamenting. Instead, it was in a seventy-part penny-dreadful, *The Boy Detective, or, The Crimes of London*, which began publication in the year Constance Kent confessed, that Ernest Keen, the eponymous boy detective, reached a working-class readership, complete with a background like Constance Kent's. Ernest has a sister, significantly named Constance, and is driven to run away from home by his stepmother's cruelty. He goes to sea, but after he breaks his arm 'saving the life of a nice little girl' he nips back for a chat with Constance, on the same night that his wicked stepmother's secret lover, Gaspard, who is both 'the captain of a band of brigands' and a French aristocrat, is surprised by Mr Keen and murders him using Ernest's knife. We now discover that between running away from home and going to sea, Ernest 'lodged in the same house with Inspector Sharp, and did work for him so cleverly that the fly coves called him the BOY DETECTIVE!' He is therefore well suited to gather a gang of poor but honest boys to prove his innocence while bringing the evil Gaspard and his brigands to justice. (In a particularly exciting episode, Ernest goes undercover disguised as a governess.) All this happens in the first fifty pages, before the story veers off, not only from any Constance Kent elements, but from anything that has gone before, with most of the characters vanishing without explanation.

While this narrative is deeply unsatisfying as a single volume, the central character of the boy detective was part of a new trend. Penny-bloods had earlier appealed to a broad readership; now the focus narrowed, with boys the key market. In 1861 there were nine million people under the age of nineteen, out of a population of twenty million – potentially 45 per cent of the reading public were children or young adults. This led to a raft of titles like *The Wild Boys of London* (1864–66), *The Work Girls of London* (1865) and *The Poor Boys of London* (c.1866). As with so many of these penny-dreadfuls, *The Poor Boys* is about a gang of poor but deserving boys who work with the police as their unofficial helpers. In 1860, in *The Trail of the Serpent*, Mrs Braddon had advanced her plot through Sloshy, the adopted child of a mute policeman, and in *Revelations of a Lady Detective* Mrs Paschal also uses a boy as an information-gathering device. In 1868 in *The Moonstone* Collins confirmed the transfer of the type from sensation-fiction to detective fiction with Gooseberry, 'one of the sharpest boys in London'. Sergeant Cuff uses him to follow suspects, because boys can hang about in the streets without attracting attention: 'The boy – *being* a boy – passed unnoticed.' This culminated at the end of the century in Sherlock Holmes's Baker Street Irregulars: 'half a dozen of the dirtiest and most ragged street Arabs that I ever clapped eyes on', says the bourgeois Watson. But, replies the more pragmatic detective, 'These youngsters ... go everywhere, and hear everything.'

They did, and one of the things they liked, and had money enough to indulge in, was seeing themselves depicted onstage. Ernest Keen was transformed in productions at the Effingham and the Britannia a couple of years after the penny-dreadful was first published. *The Boy Detective* includes the same characters, and the story opens with the same unhappy Kent stepfamily set-up. Ernest and Constance run away, Ernest dresses up as a girl once more (this was clearly a favourite bit), and calls himself the Boy Detective, but while the word is used, and Ernest is at the centre of the drama, there is no detection in the script. Instead everything happens, melodrama-style, as a result of coincidence and providence. Detection and theatre had not yet meshed. It took some time for dramatists to believe that their audiences would enjoy being puzzled every bit as much as readers did. Even in 1877, Wilkie Collins' own adaptation of *The Moonstone* had Franklin Blake walk in his sleep and steal the jewel in a trance in the opening act, although Cuff was given a greater role in solving the theft than he had in the novel. The police themselves also understood the theatrical responsibilities of their roles – the caption of one photograph, probably from 1860, states that it shows an arrest, although it is clear that the men had posed in a studio, creating for their audience an image of what their job should look like.

For suddenly, 'detective' plays had become fashionable. The turning point was Tom Taylor's *The Ticket-of-Leave Man* in 1863.* Like the poison panic of the 1840s, and the garrotting panic in the early 1850s and 1860s, in the 1860s there was a ticket-of-leave panic, when fears became widespread that paroled convicts – men who had won their 'ticket of leave' – were reoffending on a colossal scale. As late as 1869, the Home Secretary was still receiving requests for more divisional detectives because of the 'thousands upon thousands' of criminals roaming the streets. Taylor's play opened against this background, and achieved a remarkable success, running for 407 performances. Bob Brierly, the ticket-of-leave man, was nominally the hero, in the old melodrama stereotype of the country naïf unwittingly drawn into crime. But tastes were changing, and the main interest quite quickly became Hawkshaw, 'the 'cutest detective in the force'. ('Cute' meant acute, not sweet; 'hawk' had long meant a policeman, someone who pounced on his prey – Ainsworth had used it in *Rookwood* three

* Tom Taylor (1817–80) was one of those multi-faceted Victorians who must never have slept: as well as writing seventy-four plays, he was a Professor of English at the University of London, a barrister, the editor of *Punch*, Secretary to the Board of Health and an art critic for *The Times*.

decades earlier: 'The hawks are upon us.') The opening scene is set in a tea garden, where Hawkshaw appears disguised, on the track of a counterfeiter who is setting up Bob Brierly as his 'flat', or dupe, to pass bad notes. May, a good girl down on her luck, has become a street singer, and Bob gives her money before he is arrested by Hawkshaw.* The next act takes place three years later. May has been faithfully waiting for Bob to be released from prison, and they plan to marry after he gets a job as a messenger at Mr Gibson's City firm. On their wedding day, Hawkshaw appears at the office on the trail of a gang of forgers, the counterfeiters of the first act. They recognize Bob, inform Gibson that he is a ticket-of-leave man, and he is sacked. In the last act, Bob agrees to rob his ex-employer, but it is a ruse, and he has warned Hawkshaw, who arrives to arrest the forgers, while Mr Gibson is lectured by the wounded but valiant hero: 'You see, there may be some good left in a "TICKET-OF-LEAVE-MAN" after all. [*Tableau*. Curtain.]'

Detectives were everywhere onstage. C.H. Hazlewood used the same French source as Taylor to produce *The Detective* at the Victoria; then the following year he wrote *The Mother's Dying Child*, a melodrama enhanced by the presence of a female detective, 'Florence Langton, Daughter of Sir Gervase, with a weakness for finding out secrets'. Here 'female curiosity' is comically equated with detection, and Florence bustles about saying things like, 'There's some mystery here ... and I'm determined to fish it up,' while indulging in that pastime of all stage detectives, disguise, appearing as nurse, a man and an Irish lad, as well as changing her frock (which fools everyone).†

---

* This scene became the template of stage detection, so much so that a decade later a touring version of *The Red Barn* stopped the action two pages before the denouement so that the detective could appear disguised as a street singer in a tea garden, merging two of the three roles in this emblematic scene.

† Twenty years later, these disguises were still common enough for Jerome K. Jerome to satirize them: 'A married man, on the stage, knows his wife, because he knows she wears a blue ulster and a red bonnet ... She puts on a yellow cloak and a green hat, and, coming in at another door, says she is a lady from the country ... She puzzles him ... There is something about her that strangely reminds him of his darling Nell ...' He added, in a nod to *The Ticket-of-Leave Man*'s endless productions, that by pulling his hat over his eyes and 'speaking in a squeaky voice' the detective fools the villains, who 'go into a public tea-garden, and recount their crimes to one another in a loud tone of voice'.

This deluge of detection both altered public perception of the police and reflected a change that was coming from the streets. Now even policemen on the beat – the men with whom working-class audiences were most likely to come into conflict – were shown to have hearts of gold. In George Ellis's *The Female Detective* at the Britannia, the hero, a squire's noble son cheated out of his inheritance, becomes a policeman himself, and refuses a reward: 'I did but my duty, [and] for that I am paid ... if a man can't do a kindness without expecting payment, Heaven help those who have nothing to give.' The *reductio ad absurdum* of detective fever may have come in 1876, with a performance at the Surrey of *The Dog Detective: A Dramatic Sketch*, 'written expressly for Herr Wayho and His Celebrated Dog Bob'.

Even if dogs are left out of the equation, most crimes in the real world were still being detected not by the Hawkshaws of the force, but simply through local knowledge, happenstance or plain good luck. The death of a small girl named Fanny Adams was a case in point. On 24 August 1867, Fanny and three friends were playing in a field near Alton, in Hampshire. A man gave two of the children a penny and told them to run off home, then carried Fanny away. Several hours later her mother passed a man whom one of the children identified as the one who had given her a penny. He shook off Mrs Adams' questions, telling her that if she wanted him, he would be at his office, where he was clerk to the local attorney, Mr Clements. Shortly afterwards she and her neighbours came upon a horrible sight. Fanny's head was perched on two hop poles, while on the ground was one of her legs, still with its stocking and boot on. Her right arm, then a hand, then her torso, were found nearby. Her other foot, and left arm, were in the next field. Her intestines had been removed, and were not found until the next day, together with her heart. It was reported that her eyes, which had been removed from her head, were found in the River Wey (this appears an impossibility, but was widely believed). Meanwhile Mr Clements' clerk, Frederick Baker, told his fellow clerk that 'as he came along the meadows he met with some women who asked him what he had done with the child. He further said that if anything

MURDER AND MUTILATION OF THE BODY?

The murder of Fanny Adams generated many gory illustrations of a type that had begun to disappear with the broadsides.

happened to the child it would be awkward for him.' Soon the police appeared, acting on information given by Mrs Adams. They found blood on Baker's cuffs, which he failed to account for. They also found his diary; the day's entry read: 'Saturday, 24, killed a young girl; it was fine and hot.' The general view was that Baker had sexually assaulted the child, and then dismembered her body to hide the fact. If that was his intention he had been successful, as the medical examiner at the inquest said he could not confirm 'criminal violence' one way or another.

The trial was swift, although Baker's defence was good. Alfred Swaine Taylor gave evidence for the prosecution on the bloodstains, stating that they could not be more than three weeks old, although the amount of blood on Baker's penknife was much less than he expected after a crime of that nature, and was more in line with what would be found after cutting meat, or perhaps from a nosebleed. The evidence for Baker's absence from work at the crucial time was poor – the other clerk gave conflicting statements, and Baker would have had to have dismembered the child's body with astonishing swiftness. His lawyer suggested that the diary entry was misleading: with an extra comma – 'killed, a young girl' – Baker was merely noting that a child had been killed; as to 'it was fine and hot', the *Pall Mall Gazette* later reported that the phrase occurred 164 times in Baker's diary, and except for this one occasion, always in reference to the weather. Without stretching credulity, therefore, the entry could be understood to read: 'I have heard a child was killed; the day has been fine and hot.' The judge summed up remarkably impartially, giving fair emphasis to the defence's case. Nonetheless, the jury found Baker guilty in only twenty minutes.

Despite the grisliness of the crime – and the even more grisly subsequent use of Fanny Adams' name as slang for cheap tinned meat – little public interest was aroused by this case. Baker figured in Christmas waxworks exhibitions – Madame Tussaud's included his model in their 'Public Amusements'. *Tomahawk*, a satirical magazine, observed that no doubt all 'mirth-seeking, merry Londoners' would make a special trip: 'This is obviously a Christmas treat,' and it suggested that perhaps books along the same lines could be produced for Christmas presents – *Please, Papa, Take Me to Newgate* was one idea.

The newspapers did their best, producing a series of rumours – that Baker was mad, a drunk, had been sacked for embezzling – but their hearts were not in it. Even the *Illustrated Police News* special was reduced to anodyne phrases like, 'He bears but an indifferent character in the town', and the most it could produce by way of deviant behaviour was that Baker had made 'improper overtures' to a woman, who evaded him by the simple expedient of running away, leaving him throwing stones after her. The paper made up for the paucity of really good rumour, however, with nearly a dozen illustrations over the course of the inquest and trial. 'Finding the Remains of Fanny Adams' shows a stock rustic holding a head, with an arm lying on the ground; 'Prisoner Mobbed Upon Entering Winchester' has the police almost overcome by an enraged populace; a particularly vivid portrait of Alfred Swaine Taylor gives him wild hair in a huge bouffant comb-over. Finally came the culminating images: a 'correct portrait of Calcraft', the executioner, the 'last hours of the condemned' and 'the wretched man ascending the steps of the scaffold'.

This remarkably placid reception of an extraordinarily brutal murder was echoed by an entire lack of theatrical adaptations. It was not the gore that kept authors away: audiences – the most respectable audiences – had long proved their love of gore. Even for those who found theatre morally dubious, violence was not the problem. The problem was the artifice theatre required. For many, therefore, public readings were the answer, and the most famous readings of the century, possibly of all time, were those of Charles Dickens. In the 1840s he had read sections of his new novels to friends and family, in groups, both formally and informally. He then began to think he might make 'a great deal of money' from it, although his friends were against the idea – to turn himself into a performer would, they thought, lower his standing. He did a few charity readings, and in 1857 he returned to the idea. Within seven months he had given a hundred readings, both in London and on a provincial tour, and he continued these until his death, giving between four and eight two-hour performances a week for several weeks a year, to audiences of up to 4,000 people at a time. As he had suspected, he did make a 'great deal of money': initially he earned approximately 1,000 guineas a month (the annual salary of the most successful surgeon or barrister in the land); by 1870 he had doubled that.

These early readings were either comic or 'pathetic', that is, full of pathos. Then, in 1869, Dickens introduced his most famous reading, 'Sikes and Nancy', from *Oliver Twist*, the only reading he performed that revolved around violence, horror – and murder. It is notable that this single crime-reading followed a flurry of crime stories in the press: in 1867, *All the Year Round*, Dickens' magazine, had reprinted the stories of Eliza Fenning, Corder and Wainewright; in 1868 *The Moonstone* swept the country. Henry Irving was having great success with 'The Dream of Eugene Aram'. Perhaps even more importantly, 'Sikes and Nancy' was introduced the year executions moved behind prison walls, no longer being conducted in public. Dickens' own murder novel, *Edwin Drood*, would begin serialization the year after 'Sikes and Nancy' debuted. As long ago as *Nicholas Nickleby* (1838–39) Dickens had seen the dramatic potential of bloody recitals, when Miss Petowker ('of the Theatre Royal, Drury Lane') recites 'The Blood-Drinker's Burial', with her 'bachelor friend … posted in a corner, to rush out at the cue … and catch her in his arms when she died raving mad'.

The 'Sikes and Nancy' reading began with Nancy's betrayal of the gang, and went on to include Fagin's discovery of her treachery, his incitement to violence of Bill Sikes, and Sikes' brutal battering to death of his mistress. Dickens held a trial reading of this episode in December 1868, and it left 'the company … unmistakably pale, and … horror-stricken'. When he performed it publicly, 'I don't think a hand moved … or an eye looked away.' It became the high point of his readings, and its popularity led to the Britannia taking Hazlewood's 1855 adaptation of *Oliver Twist*, snipping out the Sikes and Nancy scenes and producing them as a separate piece, *The Death of Sikes*, only two months after Dickens' first public reading of the episode.

Perhaps it was stories like these that made some real-life cases seem tame. The Alton murder was not lacking in disgusting detail, but it was short on mystery or suspense. The suspect calmly identified himself to the victim's mother, walked back to his office and awaited the police. Fiction required more. In the early 1850s Dickens had Inspector Bucket assume various disguises to track his prey: he dresses as a doctor, 'a very respectable old gentleman, with grey hair, wearing spectacles ... a black spencer [an overcoat] and gaiters and a broad-brimmed hat'. As soon as the supposed medic gains access to the premises where his quarry is hiding, 'the physician stopped, and taking off his hat, appeared to vanish by magic'. After Inspector Field's retirement from the police he set up as a private detective, and used the newspaper reports of his similarly 'cute' exploits as advertising. The *Bath Chronicle* printed a long article describing in detail how Field had traced a wanted man named Provis by disguising himself as an elderly invalid.* By the 1860s, novelists had discovered how very useful disguise was, and what glamour and drama it lent. In an otherwise forgotten novel of 1861, a detective 'turned ... a corner ... and drawing from his coat pocket a wig, he in an instant slipped it on ... He took off his coat, and, turning the sleeves inside out, put it on again, a totally different coat in shape and make. Putting on a pair of spectacles ... the detective, who had turned into that corner a slight and erect man, rather under the middle age ... emerged from it a bent and broken down person, rather advanced in years.'

Disguise was fictionally so useful that even the frequent disavowals of professional detectives failed to check disguise-mania. A departmental commission of inquiry into the detective force in the late 1870s heard that although there was a make-up room at Scotland Yard, it was used fewer than six times a year. In 1889 one policeman huffed: 'It is absurd to suppose that [detective] officers are unknown. Their features, peculiarities of dress, tone of voice ... every characteristic' were routinely recognized by criminals. Yet disguises in fiction continued to become ever more elaborate. By the 1890s, disguises in some boys' stories were assumed almost for the sake of it. Dan Hays, 'the well known detective', goes to see his client wearing a 'faultless dress suit and tall silk hat', together with 'a prodigious set of red

---

* And real life fed back into fiction: Provis was the name assumed by the convict Magwitch in Dickens' *Great Expectations*, published in 1862.

whiskers', and has himself announced as 'Col. Toddoff, Russian Service', although he has no reason to hide his identity from his own client, and she recognizes him with no difficulty. And Sherlock Holmes appears at various points as 'a respectable master mariner who had fallen into years and poverty', a groom, a clergyman, a priest, 'an unshaven French *ouvrier*' and an opium addict. In *The Return of Sherlock Holmes* the master of disguise even manages 'to take a foot off his stature for several hours' (Watson is amazed each time).

This contradictory phenomenon – disguise and its impossibility – began just as photography was becoming commonplace. The philosopher Walter Benjamin noted the coincidence of the birth of detective fiction with the birth of photography, 'this most decisive of all conquests of a person's incognito'. But at the beginning photographs did not reinforce familiarity: it was the differences in each image of the same person that were remarked on. In 1887 *The Times* reported that 'The police authorities at Scotland-yard have in their possession a series of 60 photographs of one and the same German girl ... so different are the dress, the look, the expression and the whole appearance of the subject of these photographs ... that the most clever detective might readily be imposed upon and fail to recognize the identity of the "artiste".' This new technological marvel did not at first allay fears, but exacerbated them, by displaying the extreme cunning of the criminal.

Photographs of the notorious Mary Ann Cotton existed in 1872, but they were no longer sold as souvenirs, as engravings of criminals had been ever since Thurtell. Mrs Cotton's case, for all its horror, was reported in a subdued, almost discreet fashion. Mrs Cotton was originally from County Durham, and was said to have worked as a nurse-maid and as a Wesleyan Sunday-school teacher before she married William Mowbray, a colliery worker, in 1852. They moved about the country as Mowbray found work, and together they had nine children. By the mid-1860s, five children had died, and the couple and their surviving children were living in Sunderland. Mowbray was ill, finding it harder to get work, and soon died; two more children followed him. His widow and the two surviving children moved to

Seaham Harbour, south of Sunderland, and there she was employed as a nurse at the Sunderland Infirmary. In 1865 she married George Ward, an engineer whom she had nursed, but he died within the year. She became housekeeper to James Robinson, a shipyard foreman with five children, and within six months they were married. One of Robinson's children died the week she took up her post, as did one of her two children by Mowbray. The other was living with the new Mrs Robinson's mother; in the spring of 1867 she went to nurse her mother, who died unexpectedly nine days later. Mrs Robinson returned with her child; two of Robinson's children died in April, and her own child in May, all of gastric fever. By now the couple had had two children, one of whom had died.

In October 1869 Robinson discovered that his wife had been trying to borrow money using his name, and his son told him she had been secretly sending him to pawn goods Robinson had given her. He accused her, and she left, taking with her her surviving child and the contents of her Post Office savings account. She soon abandoned the child, who was later returned to Robinson. By 1870 she was pregnant again, by Frederick Cotton, a colliery labourer and her fourth (and this time bigamous) husband. The Cottons moved to West Auckland in County Durham in 1871, with their baby and two boys from Cotton's previous marriage. Joseph Nattrass, who had been the new Mrs Cotton's lover before she met Robinson, reappeared as their lodger, and in September 1871 Cotton died suddenly. Mrs Cotton began to work for Mr Quick-Manning, an excise officer at a brewery, and in swift succession Cotton's eldest son, her baby, Nattrass and Cotton's sister Margaret all died.

In May 1872 Mrs Cotton was living with Cotton's remaining son, Charles Edward, and receiving 1s.6d. a week from the parish for his upkeep. The parish overseer asked her if she was planning to marry Quick-Manning, and later said she had replied, 'It might be so. But the boy is in the way. Perhaps it won't matter, as I won't be troubled long. He'll go like all the rest of the Cotton family.' A week later Charles Edward was dead. The overseer reported the conversation to the police and the doctor. The doctor refused to give a death certificate, and the insurance company withheld the child's burial money. At the inquest the next day, however, the finding was death by natural causes.

But the newspapers did not drop the story, and pushed the authorities into ordering an analysis of the viscera (the doctor had reported without a scientific analysis at the inquest, old-style). Traces of arsenic were found in Charles Edward, and on 18 July, six days after his death, Mary Ann Cotton was arrested. A neighbour reported that Mrs Cotton had asked her to buy arsenic, to kill bedbugs, and that she had helped clean the bedstead, in which, she gossiped, she had seen no bugs (she had seen bugs in the mattress, but that made a less good story). Now Nattrass was exhumed – he had signed a will in Mrs Cotton's favour, leaving her £10 in savings, plus 15s. in sick pay, a watch and his clothes. Poison was found in his body. Two Cotton children were exhumed, and more arsenic was found. Frederick Cotton's body could not be located: he and the children had probably been buried on the parish, and paupers' graves were not marked. A dozen coffins had been uncovered before the ones with the children's names painted on the lids were finally found, and it was decided to look no further for Cotton. Likewise, the authorities decided that they would not investigate the earlier Mowbray, Ward and Robinson deaths.

Mrs Cotton was seven months pregnant with Quick-Manning's child, and the trial was accordingly postponed. In February 1873, the murders of Nattrass and two Cotton children were added to the charges. In March, at the Durham Assizes, Mary Ann Cotton came to trial. To say that the defendant had legal representation would be a gross overstatement. G.F. Smith, a solicitor's clerk from Bishop Auckland, had offered to act for her, but what he seems to have been particularly adept at was collecting money for the goods Mrs Cotton arranged to sell in order to pay his fees. She wrote to a neighbour, 'Smith had lead me rong. He told me not to speake A single Worde [at the committal hearings before the magistrates] if i Was Asked Ever so hard or Ever so mutch ... [But] He has never brote forth Won Witness fore me ... I do not Want nothing but the trouth of Every Won then

ie Would have A Chance fore my Life … if it had not been for smith
ie should make 5 or 6 of them stand With thar toungs tyde.'*

When the court received a letter from a local man offering to pay
for a barrister, Smith said he had already briefed counsel, although
none ever appeared. At the end of February the *Northern Echo*
announced that a fund to pay for Mrs Cotton's defence had been
established. Two days before the trial opened, when no one had come
forward, the judge appointed a barrister, who had only minimal time
to discuss the matter with his client, and no time or money at his
disposal to gather witnesses. (How little Mrs Cotton understood of
what was going on can be seen by a letter she wrote after the trial:
Smith had assured her that 'Mr Blackwell And greenhow Would be
thare to defende mee When ie Went in to the docke' – Greenhow was
in fact the lawyer for the prosecution.)

This was two decades after the Palmer case had established the
right to move jurisdiction in the case of local prejudice, but there was
neither the time nor the money for such niceties. Prejudice, however,
there was no lack of. The *North Wales Chronicle* gave Mrs Cotton
fifteen children, all murdered, and added an extra lodger to her tally.
Long before the police court hearings, much less the trial, the *Yorkshire
Post* listed nineteen deaths attributable to her. In November 1872, the
Illustrated Police News began an article with two sentences that almost
guaranteed that its report would be filled with wild rumours: 'At
present it would be unjust to speculate upon the probable issue of this
long-pending inquiry. The law … justly holds every person to be
innocent until proved guilty by the clearest evidence.' Then comes the
key word: 'Nevertheless'. Mrs Cotton, the article continued, 'a woman
whose life is one long chapter of crime', had carried out acts that
would have made Burke and Hare 'pale in horror'. It credited her with
five recent murders, and then added an additional nineteen – not
saying she was responsible for them, but that they had taken place

---

* The newspapers, it must be remembered, claimed that Mrs Cotton had taught at Sunday
school. The Wesleyans were generally very well educated: the newspapers appear to have
stuck to their own brand of truth.

'under her roof, all of which she had some [financial] interest in'. The Home Office, although aware of the newspaper reporting, shrugged off responsibility: 'The Secretary of State cannot prevent the publication of such paragraphs.'

Yet by the time of her committal hearing, in February 1873, there were only sixteen reporters present, six of them local. The local papers continued to cover the story comprehensively, but even those national papers that lived on crime had dropped it. *Lloyd's*, *Reynolds's* and the *Daily News* had only eight or nine stories each over the eight months between the arrest and trial, some only a few lines long (the *Leeds Mercury*, by contrast, ran twenty-three). Even *The Times* carried only nine stories, although they were longer than most. The *Illustrated Police News* gave the case no coverage between November 1872 and March 1873, not even reporting the trial. It was only after the verdict that it returned to the subject, with illustrations of 'Last Hours of the Condemned', 'The Execution' and 'Hoisting the Black Flag'. The accompanying article was just over a column long, and the following week there was not even any text, only pictures: 'Strange Spectre Appearances of the Poisoned Victims of Mary Ann Cotton' showed a cemetery where a feeble spectre waggled its arms at two even more feeble innocents. For Constance Kent, more pressing international news had driven her story off the pages. This was not the case here. Mary Ann Cotton, supposed poisoner of twenty-odd, was replaced in the press by a 'Fatal Fall from a Ladder'.

The trial itself was a foregone conclusion: a working-class woman with no effective legal representation, accused of mass murder among family members. In a replay of the earlier poison panic, Mary Ann Cotton was an outsider, sexually promiscuous, with too many children, at least some of whom were maintained by local taxes. The prosecution's case was that she had killed her stepson because he was ill, which prevented her from working; that the insured child was 'worth' £8 in burial money; that she was the only person who fed him, and the analysis suggested that he had been given repeated doses of arsenic, rather than one large one, which ruled out accidental death. (How this was deduced is not clear: today's tests, which measure the appearance of arsenic along the nail or hair shaft, were not then possible.) There was also a constant refrain regarding the 'prevalence' of child-murder and burial clubs, and repeated mentions of the succession of deaths among Mrs Cotton's family. The judge overruled her counsel's objections: the prosecution was 'entitled to show the history of others in the house when under the same circumstances they had died of poisoning', despite there being no evidence at all that anyone *had* died of poisoning.

The defence case was strong. Mrs Cotton's barrister pointed out that there was nothing to show that she had been the one to administer poison, and there was no evidence, despite the many newspaper reports, that any other family members had been murdered. The proof that anyone had been deliberately poisoned was weak, given the prevalence of arsenic in household goods at that time. Mrs Cotton, the jury was reminded, relied on her lodgers for much of her income. Nattrass had not only been her lodger, he was planning to marry her – two very good reasons to want him alive. Local gossip claimed she had brutalized her children; her counsel pointed out that this 'rested mainly on the evidence of three or four gossiping women, every one of whom, it appeared ... had a belt, a whip, or a "taws", which they used to [sic] their own children'. The prosecution had produced a chemist who swore that Mrs Cotton had bought arsenic from him in 1869, but under cross-examination it became evident that the police had shown him her photograph before they took him to the gaol to identify her. However, the defence overlooked the prosecution's charge that when Nattrass was ill Mrs Cotton had refused to bury her dead child, saying that if she waited the two could be buried together, which suggested she expected Nattrass to die shortly. In fact the baby had died on a Thursday, and was buried on Sunday, while Nattrass had died the day after the baby's funeral. With proper defence, much of the prosecution's evidence could probably have been shown to be similarly a mass of hearsay, hysteria and spite. No matter. The judge dismissed the defence's case in his summing-up. Considerations of motive, or its lack, he told the jury, had no place in their deliberations; the law was concerned only with the 'moral certainty' that a 'reasonable man' could have. The jury came back with a guilty verdict.

Despite a petition for clemency signed by her employers at the Sunderland Infirmary, despite the stress on the prejudicial nature of the newspaper reports and her lack of proper legal representation, Mary Ann Cotton's execution went ahead. The last execution of a woman in Durham had been in 1799. Then the rope had snapped, and the execution was rescheduled, the woman being hanged twice in an hour. Mrs Cotton was no luckier. Calcraft still used the old-fashioned short drop, and her death was reported to have been slow and painful.

The middle-class response was muted, but an older working-class form of commemoration returned: broadsides had almost completely vanished from the market, but for Mrs Cotton the genre briefly revived. One repeated the story of her waiting for the death of Nattrass before burying her baby, another told how 'She applied for coffins for her victims,/Before their limbs were cold'. Some broadside writers appear to have lost the facility for catchy verse that their predecessors had had – one rejoiced, 'How happy is it that seldom we hear/Of women poisoning their children so dear.' This one was surmounted, in the old style, with an unrelated image, of a woman wearing a Scotch bonnet and plaid, who may originally have been Flora Macdonald. Some, though, were more up-to-date: one broadside replaced the old image of the scaffold with one of the gaol with a black flag raised, the new sign of a private execution accomplished.

There appear to have been no melodramas about Mrs Cotton, although the year of her arrest saw a new touring version of *The Red Barn*. This new version may offer some explanation. In it there were no heartless seducers, no prides of the village. The revised story was much more like a detective novel, with motivations and reasons for the villain's descent to crime. Perhaps Mrs Cotton was too much a melodrama villainess for the new detective dramas. Madame Tussaud's had only a mild interest in the woman it catalogued as 'Mary Anna Cotton'. It advertised her model for a couple of months after her execution, but although it continued to be displayed into the 1890s, it was never the main attraction. A makeshift show at a colliery near Thornley in County Durham had a model of her in the year following her death, but we know of it today only because a newspaper reported the destruction of the exhibition in a freak storm. There may have been other penny-shows like this one that were below the radar even of the local press. A few traces can be found: 'a great moral drama – The Life and Death of Mary Ann Cotton' was staged at the New Gaiety Theatre of Varieties in West Hartlepool almost immediately after the execution. A greyhound named Mary Ann Cotton ran in competition in Northumberland the following year. And, finally, a children's skipping rhyme survived into our own century:

> Mary Ann Cotton
> She's dead and she's rotten
> She lies in her bed
> With her eyes wide oppen [that is, pronounced
>   with the same short 'o' as 'rotten']
> Sing, sing, what can I sing?
> Mary Ann Cotton is tied up with string.
> Where, where?
> Up in the air,
> Selling black puddens a penny a pair.

* * *

No one turned Alfred Monson into a nursery rhyme, but no one took him very seriously either. Monson came from an upper-middle-class family, although he had done his best to neutralize any benefits that might have brought him. His uncle had been the British ambassador in Paris, he himself had been a civil servant in South Africa, but by the late 1880s he had descended to the not very glorious position of tutor to young men who were cramming for army entrance exams, living well beyond his very scanty means, with a large house, horses and servants. In 1889 he had been introduced by a man named Tottenham to a Major Dudley Hambrough, who had a life interest in estates that produced £4,000 a year. Hambrough had borrowed so heavily against his income that he had been forced to mortgage this interest to an insurance company, and the company had foreclosed. Tottenham was supporting him, and attempting to work out a way to return the life interest to Major Hambrough. Meanwhile Tottenham arranged for Monson to tutor the Major's son Cecil. Just as some sort of dubious scheme was behind Tottenham's support of the Major, so too some sort of dubious arrangement had been made between Tottenham and Monson – Monson didn't even pretend to tutor the young man.

Over the next year or so, convoluted financial arrangements were repeatedly put in place and then collapsed, as Monson finagled to become the 'owner' of the Major's life interest, even as he himself received handouts from Tottenham, who was in turn attempting the same financial arrangements. No one was honest. In 1892 Monson rented Ardlamont House in Scotland. He was not able to sign a lease himself, as he had recently been made bankrupt; as a minor, Cecil Hambrough could not sign either; so 'Mr Jerningham', his 'guardian and trustee', was sent to sign. When the household moved to Ardlamont (rent £450 per annum), Monson was so hard up he had to borrow the train fare from Tottenham, and his wife left their linen behind because there was no money to pay the laundress. In July, Monson attempted to insure Hambrough's life in Mrs Monson's favour, but insurance companies were by now chary of legatees who had no obvious connection to the insured person's life. A week later he tried another company, and failed again. In early August he told the Mutual Assurance Co. of New York that Hambrough was the heir to a £200,000 fortune that he would inherit the following year, when he turned twenty-one, that the young man wanted to purchase Ardlamont, and that Mrs Monson was going to advance the money until he was of age and inherited; the insurance was to cover the period in between, in case he died before he could repay the loan. Somehow, only a month after not being able to pay his laundress, Monson had enough cash for the first premium, £194. The policy was confirmed on 7 August. On 10 August, Cecil Hambrough was dead.

Two days earlier, a man named Scott had arrived at Ardlamont, introduced as an engineer who was advising Monson on the purchase of a yacht. The next evening, Monson and Hambrough went fishing. Monson could swim well, Hambrough not at all. The boat capsized, and Hambrough was rescued and brought to shore. Monson claimed the boat had hit a rock and foundered, although locals were puzzled: there were no rocks in the bay. The next morning, none the worse for their unexpected dip, Monson, Scott and Hambrough went out shooting. Estate workers heard a shot, and saw Scott and Monson return to the house. It was ten minutes before they re-emerged, without their guns, to announce that Hambrough had accidentally shot himself. The outdoor workers rushed to the spot where the body lay, on a turf dike beside a ditch. Monson now said that he and Scott had heard the shot, rushed over and found Hambrough lying in the ditch, from which they had lifted him before returning for assistance. Monson telegraphed Tottenham, although not Hambrough's parents, and when they finally arrived, according to the Major, Monson had told him that their son had been the only one to have a gun, had been entirely alone, and that he had attempted, but failed, to insure Hambrough's life.

The Procurator Fiscal had been prepared to declare the death an accident until he discovered that Hambrough's life, contrary to Monson's statement, had been insured in Mrs Monson's favour. Only on 24 August, therefore, did a proper investigation begin, two weeks after the young man's death. It was found that the doctor who examined the body had never seen a gunshot wound to the head before; that Scott had vanished soon after the discovery of the body, and no one knew where he was or, even more suspiciously, who he was; no scorch marks were found around the wound, casting doubts on the theory that Hambrough had shot himself. Monson was arrested and charged with murder on 30 August; on 30 October another charge, of attempted murder by drowning, was added.

This crime had everything: a hunting lodge, high (and low) finance, an upper-class family, a mysteriously vanishing witness, and more. Throughout October and November the newspaper rumour-mill

went into the kind of overdrive it had displayed in only a few exceptional cases. Scott had not been found, said *Woman* magazine, because
he was in reality 'a woman in man's guise'; the *Aberdeen Weekly*, by
contrast, thought he was 'a scion of a noble English family', while
Lloyd's couldn't decide – he was a bookmaker known as 'Long Ted', or
Monson's valet, or in prison. According to the *Aberdeen Weekly*, when
the Procurator Fiscal asked Mrs Monson to identify a photograph
which he thought might show Scott, she replied that it was her
deceased brother, and then threatened her questioner with a pistol.
The *Daily News* denied a report that a portion of a skull had been
found, saying it was a hoax: some 'friend or foe of Monson' had
obtained another human skull (according to the paper this was 'easy'),
and had planted it to confuse the investigation. Several newspapers
discussed Monson's influence over Hambrough, and reported that his
father had attributed it to hypnotism. The *Daily News* wanted to have
its cake and eat it, reporting and denying wild rumours in the same
article: 'It is not true', it said sternly, that Major Hambrough had ever
had a shooting estate where a mysterious fatality had occurred. The
Glasgow Herald took a similar tack, denying its own rumour that
Monson had been appointed guardian to Cecil by Major Hambrough's
father (who had actually died eleven years before Cecil was born).
Reynolds's was not even sure if the crime was popular or not. It
reported that 'the Ardlamont mystery has not turned out the boom
that was expected', before going on to say that 'young fellows' in
Edinburgh were so anxious to attend the hearings that they dressed
up as lawyers. These were the highlights: most papers contented
themselves with rumours of financial profligacy, attempted frauds,
possible arson and more.

At the trial all the witnesses agreed that they had seen no blood in
the ditch, while blood had pooled under Hambrough's body, suggesting that he had died on the dike, and not falling into the ditch as
Monson claimed. Then there were Monson's financial confusions. Mr
Jerningham, who had signed the Ardlamont lease as Hambrough's
trustee, was shown to have no connection to him, but was instead
supported by Tottenham, now identified as a moneylender. Scott still

remained unidentified, and unlocated. Finally, much emphasis was placed by both sides on the forensic possibilities. Had the nearby trees been marked by shot, as if by a man shooting from a distance, or were the marks just weather damage? At what distance would a skull shatter as Hambrough's had? The actual trees were dug up and transported to Edinburgh and entered in evidence. To demonstrate their theories, both sides produced models and actual skulls (some reports claimed they were horses' skulls, others that they came from 'some known person' so as to avoid Hambrough's skull being displayed in court in front of his parents).* Dr Joseph Bell, an Edinburgh surgeon and Conan Doyle's acknowledged source for Sherlock Holmes, testified for the prosecution on gunshot wounds, together with his assistant Dr Watson (first name not John but, exotically, Heron).

The trial lasted an astonishing ten days, and frequently appeared to be more a theatre, a place to be seen, than a courtroom. The *Weekly Herald* even set out its advertisements like a playbill, with the participants described as if in a cast of characters: the 'IMPECUNIOUS LANDOWNER', the 'MYSTERIOUS SALLOW MAN'. Nearly seventy journalists attended the trial, with another twenty 'colour writers' and fifteen artists, and between them they telegraphed over 1.6 million words to their various newspapers.† (Compare this to Jessie King, an impoverished working-class woman charged with murdering three babies in her care in Edinburgh four years previously: *The Times* had devoted a whole twenty-three lines to her case. The same paper carried nineteen articles, over thirty-five columns, on Monson.) The *Aberdeen Evening Express* had an extra edition out on the street ten minutes after the verdict was given in court. The *Aberdeen Weekly* had reported

---

* In a Victorian display of propriety, while this skull – whether a horse's or a person's – was openly passed around in court to show where the shots entered, the guns that Monson and Hambrough had carried were brought into the courtroom decently covered in black crêpe – the fabric used for mourning dress.

† The importance of the telegraph to the press was indicated by its special rates. A private telegram cost sixpence per dozen words; but for the press, it was a shilling for seventy-five words, or a hundred words at night.

that Edinburgh bookmakers were giving odds of 9–4 on a guilty verdict, but Monson slipped through the net: in less than an hour the jury came back with a verdict of 'not proven', and he was released.

Monson was now in the unusual position of being able to turn himself into entertainment. Not for him shy retirement from the public gaze. Only days after the end of the trial, the *Daily News* reported that he had been offered £40 a week to give talks on his experiences, and a month later he was scheduled to deliver 'the first of a course of lectures' at the Prince's Hall in Piccadilly, with 'scenery, and … realism without stint. The trial, the tragedy, and life in gaol will all come in.' Monson, however, failed to appear as promised, although he did show up at the Westminster Aquarium in 1895, to give a twenty-minute description of his travails, which ended by him pathetically assuring the audience that his life had been 'ruined' by 'a malicious system of law'. It may be that that lecture went off well enough for him to be encouraged to do more, for three months later advertisements appeared in the newspapers challenging him to undergo hypnosis onstage, to 'solve' the mystery. These, it became clear, were placed by a theatrical producer named Morritt who was secretly working with Monson.

In the interim, the mysterious Scott was finally discovered to be a bookmaker named Edward Sweeney. He too capitalized on the public's interest, and with the ubiquitous Mr Morritt staged a performance at the Prince's Hall, which sounds extraordinarily pointless: 'Scott is pinioned to the seat … which is then suspended by pulleys to the back of a sloping easel, the chair and subject remaining … in full view of the spectators. A pistol shot is fired, the stage momentarily darkens, and the subject has disappeared, while a chair drops from the clouds on to the floor.' Evidently people were going simply to see one of the actors in the Ardlamont drama – what he actually did was of less matter. The *Graphic* even thought this was worth illustrating (overleaf).

Long before this, waxworks exhibitions across the country had greeted the case with delight. McLeod's Wax-Works in Aberdeen advertised 'Up-to-date Sensation! Realistic Representation of the

Plantation with young Hambrough lying shot dead! The Rowan and Lime Trees, Turf, and Earth', complete with a tableau of Monson, Mrs Monson and Scott 'in consultation in the Drawing-room'. In Liverpool, 'REYNOLDS'S Grand Xmas Carnival' included 'A correct Likeness of ALFRED. J. MONSON' alongside marionettes, a humorist, a wizard, a hypnotist, and 'England's EDUCATED FLEAS', which made a simple 'representation' of 'the discovery of Hambrough's body' in Cardiff sound tame.

The entertainment industry was walking a narrow line, however, as Madame Tussaud's (and its cousinly arm, Louis Tussaud of Birmingham) found to its cost. By the end of the first day of the trial, Madame Tussaud's had a model of Scott on display, together with a scene of the shooting. A few days after the verdict, Louis Tussaud advertised in the *Birmingham Daily Post*:

The CHAMBER OF HORRORS ...
Just Added – VAILLANT* and MONSON.

Monson filed for an injunction against both exhibitions, claiming that by displaying him in the Chamber of Horrors, they were implicitly stating that he was guilty of murder, despite the not proven verdict. At the hearing, Louis Tussaud's lawyers said that 'a gentleman' had arrived one day, claiming to be a friend of Monson's and warning the exhibition's secretary that it was illegal to show a person without his consent. When the secretary robustly replied that it was no such thing, the friend changed tack and said Madame Tussaud's in London had offered Monson 'a large sum of money' to reproduce him in effigy. 'The secretary, not believing this, laughed, and asked why Monson did not accept.' When no fee was forthcoming, the incensed friend threatened legal action. Tussaud's lawyers mildly added that as Monson had agreed to give lectures and write a book, it could hardly be said that he wanted no publicity: he just wanted to make sure he saw the financial rewards himself. Madame Tussaud's in London added that Monson's figure was not in the Chamber of Horrors, but in 'Napoleon Room No. 2', together with Napoleon, Mrs Maybrick, Wellington relics and Piggott, an Irish adventurer and forger. Monson's lawyers countered that Mrs Maybrick had been found guilty of murdering her husband, and that her model and Monson's were placed entirely apart from Napoleon and the Duke of Wellington. And while Louis Tussaud, too, had placed his model 'adjacent' to the Chamber of Horrors, his advertisements made no such distinction.

Monson's injunction was granted, but on appeal Madame Tussaud's added evidence that Tottenham had offered, on Monson's behalf, to sell them Monson's gun and clothes for £50; for another £50 he

* Auguste Vaillant, a French anarchist, had thrown a bomb from the gallery of the Chamber of Deputies in 1893.

offered that Monson would sit for his model. After the first £50 was paid, and the gun and suit handed over, Tottenham wrote to say that Monson 'declined to recognize or consent' to this agreement, and returned the cheque, asking for the gun and clothes back. Madame Tussaud's refused, having bought the items in good faith. In court the waxworks' lawyers noted that while Monson was claiming that Tottenham had stolen the items from him and sold them against his express intention, Monson had at the very same time signed a contract with Tottenham to write his story: 'Tottenham had practically stolen your clothes, and you were entering into a contract with a thief?' Monson: 'Yes.' The judges reversed the previous decision, and declined to allow the injunctions.

Monson, never one to give up the smell of cash, now sued for libel, having been defamed, he claimed, by having had a model of himself placed in the company of murderers. One of his complaints was the use of the word 'mystery' in the phrase 'the Ardlamont Mystery', which implied doubts that Hambrough had shot himself. He was forced to admit, however, that his own pamphlet was entitled *The Ardlamont Mystery* (this apparently had not occurred to him previously). After endless testimony of Tottenham and Monson lying, cheating, forging, doctoring letters, reneging on agreements, defrauding each other and anyone else within sight, the judge reminded the jury that libel had to lower a man's reputation in the eyes of the world. The jury found that Monson had been libelled, and valued the damage to his reputation at one farthing: one-quarter of a penny, the lowest possible denomination.

It may have been fear of litigation that kept others away from the story. There appear to have been no plays, and only one story, Catherine Louise Pirkis's 'The Murder at Troyte's Hill' (1894), with the female detective Loveday Brooke saving the day. Set in Scotland, it tells of Sandy, Mr Craven's lodgekeeper, who is found shot dead. Craven's son Harry is 'as much a gentleman-blackleg as it is possible for such a young fellow to be', and suspicion falls on him. Sandy had been with the Craven family in South Africa, where Monson had worked in the civil service before becoming a tutor.

Monson remained in the public gaze, which may have kept writers away from his story. In 1896 an Alfred Wyvill, living on the Isle of Man, claimed on his insurance after a fire at his house; he was revealed to be Monson, and was prosecuted for perjury. In 1898 he was again charged with attempting to defraud an insurance company, and finally went to gaol, sentenced to five years' penal servitude.

Cecil Hambrough died an ugly death, but Monson, with his cheap shyster life, had distracted attention from that, and focused it instead on the money scramble. The case of Eleanor Pearcey, however, was not about money. Her brutal, violent crime was somehow not even seen as threatening. Eleanor Pearcey became one of Madame Tussaud's most popular exhibits, and a subject for many jokes.

At seven o'clock on the evening of 24 October 1890 a man was returning home in north London when he noticed a woman lying at the side of the road. It would have long been dark, the area was only partly built-up, and the road had no street lamps as yet. Still, there was enough light for him to see her by. 'At first,' reported the newspapers, 'he paid no particular attention to what he had seen, but continued his way homewards.' The world was then a harsher place, and a 'very respectably dressed' woman, in a black cashmere dress and an imitation fur jacket, could lie in the dark on the road without causing alarm. It was only 'on reflection' that the home-bound clerk decided that perhaps the woman was not drunk, but had been taken ill, and turned back to have a closer look. When he approached, he found her head wrapped in a 'cardigan jacket'. Removing that, he saw by the light of a match that she was neither drunk nor ill; she was dead, with her throat cut.

The next morning, Mary Eleanor Pearcey and Clara Hogg appeared at the police station. Miss Hogg feared that the dead woman might be her sister-in-law Phoebe Hogg, who was supposed to have gone to see her sick father, but had never arrived. Having read that morning's newspaper report of the finding of an unidentified woman whose clothes were marked 'P.H.', her husband Frank had sent his sister to Mrs Pearcey, whom Mrs Hogg had been going to visit, and the two women had set out for the police station together. At the mortuary Mrs Pearcey immediately said that the body was not that of Mrs Hogg, and tried to drag her friend away. Miss Hogg was uncertain; she recognized the clothes. The police washed the blood off the woman's face* and asked her to look again, and now Miss Hogg had no doubts. It was her sister-in-law. When the police heard that Mrs Hogg had set out the day before with her child, Miss Hogg and Mrs Pearcey were asked to go to another police station, where an abandoned blood-stained pram was being held; it had been found in St John's Wood, over two and a half miles from Mrs Pearcey's lodgings. Miss Hogg immediately identified the pram as that of her brother and sister-in-law's eighteen-month-old child, also named Phoebe. They were asked to return to Hampstead police station, stopping en route to collect Frank Hogg. He was searched, and a key (later found to belong to Mrs Pearcey's rooms) was found on him.

Mrs Pearcey's behaviour at the mortuary had aroused suspicion, and she was escorted back to her lodgings. There the police found knives covered in blood, and blood splashes on the ceiling, the floor, the window and a rug. There was blood and hair on a poker, and blood splashes on the firewood, which suggested that all this blood had been recently produced. Two windows were cracked. A policeman 'took the knives and poker into the parlour where [Mrs Pearcey] was sitting. She whistled and assumed an air of perfect indifference.'† Further searching found a card case belonging to Frank Hogg

---

* Truly it was a harsher world. The police had not cleaned the corpse before it was viewed by members of the public hoping to identify friends or family.

† Later newspaper reports turned this whistling into playing the piano and singing throughout the search, but it was not only the papers that were unreliable. When Melville MacNaghten, the head of the CID at the time, came to write his memoirs in 1914, this scene was elaborated into Mrs Pearcey 'strumm[ing] away at popular tunes'; 'When the musical hostess was asked for an explanation [of the blood] ... she chanted a reply, "Killing mice, killing mice, killing mice," and went on with her piano-playing.' The police inspector who actually performed the search, however, testified at her trial that 'she was not whistling tunes, she was whistling to herself'. Twenty years after the event MacNaghten also remembered that her home had been searched 'from garret to basement', quite a feat as she lived in three small rooms. And he thought the baby had been found in its pram on Hampstead Heath; the pram had been found in St John's Wood, the baby two miles away from the Heath.

in her bonnet box. The police asked her when she had last seen Mrs Hogg. She said, 'Mrs. Hogg did come here at six o'clock, and asked me to lend her two shillings and to mind the child. I told her I could not lend her the money as I had none, and I could not mind the child as I was going out. I told Clara Hogg about it, and she advised me to say nothing ... it would be such a disgrace if people thought her husband kept her short of money.' The blood, she explained, was owing to a recent nosebleed, while the scratches on her hands were from killing mice. The other lodgers in the house all said they had heard an altercation the previous night, and seen a pram in the hall. Eleanor Pearcey was arrested. Meanwhile, a baby's body had been found by a hawker on some waste land just off the Finchley Road.*

At the police court hearing and then at her trial, the evidence piled up. Mrs Pearcey's mother testified that her daughter, née Mary Eleanor Wheeler, had left home in her teens, and had vanished for a year, coming back to say that she was working 'in the fur line' in Stepney, although later she said she was working abroad as a servant. She had married – that is, she had lived with and taken the name of – John Charles Pearcey, a carpenter, although he had left her when she had started seeing Frank Hogg. She was now supported by a Mr Creighton or Crighton, although Hogg continued to visit. Hogg, who worked for his brother in his furniture-removing business, had known Mrs Pearcey for about five years. Three years after the relationship started, he had married Phoebe, who was three months pregnant. Letters from Mrs Pearcey to Hogg were found: 'Do not think of going away,' she had written, 'for my heart will break if you do ... I would see you married fifty times over ... I could bear that far better than parting with you ...' He introduced Mrs Pearcey to his new wife as a friend of the family, and the two women had become friends – earlier that year,

---

* It is never stated precisely how the child died: some reports imply it was of exposure, others suffocation. I don't know if the reports are unclear because the cause of death was uncertain, or if it was simply an oversight in the reporting. Mrs Pearcey was charged only with the murder of Mrs Hogg, and therefore no discussion of the cause of the infant's death appears in the trial transcript.

when Mrs Hogg had been ill, Mrs Pearcey had shared the nursing, staying with the couple for some weeks.

Contrary to Mrs Pearcey's statement that Mrs Hogg had arrived to borrow money, testimony was heard that Mrs Pearcey had twice written to Mrs Hogg, asking her to visit with 'our little darling'. The post-mortem said that Mrs Hogg had been hit on the head, then her throat was slashed several times, one of the cuts being savage enough to sever the windpipe and the spinal cord. Her hands and wrists were marked, as though she had tried to ward off an assault. A neighbour had heard glass break, and a child scream; another 'thought it best not to interfere. Mrs Pearcey was always very ladylike and kind-speaking.' Two witnesses saw her that evening, pushing a pram piled high with what they thought was laundry. A police searcher from Kentish Town police station had given evidence at the magistrates' court that when she was waiting to take Mrs Pearcey's clothes to the Inspector, Mrs Pearcey had said, 'As we were having tea Mrs. Hogg made a remark that I did not like. One word brought up another –' Then she stopped herself: 'Perhaps I had better say no more.' At the trial, the defence belittled this statement, pointing out that the woman had failed to mention these suspicious words until just before the hearing. She had not known it was important, she responded. The defence reacted with incredulity: how could it not be important? Desperately, she continued, 'I don't know exactly the meaning of the word "important" – Yes, I do know ... I was instructed not to repeat anything the prisoner said,' she stumbled on. 'Do you mean to say that after being a searcher for five years you believed that when you were told not to repeat anything ... it meant you must not tell your inspector?' 'Yes.'

The prosecution had, however, put together a formidable forensic case: at Mrs Pearcey's lodgings they found human hair matching Mrs Hogg's on a broom and a bottle of paraffin (this, of course, was a visual match only). A button found in the ashes in the dustbin matched those on Mrs Hogg's jacket, which was missing one; a pair of bloodstained curtains was soaking in the wash-house; the remains of a hat were found in the grate, while Mrs Hogg's hat was missing; the cardigan that had been wrapped around Mrs Hogg's head had been left behind by John Pearcey when he moved out; a brass nut, which fitted a screw in the pram, had been found near Mrs Hogg's body. The police had even tested a duplicate pram to ensure that it would bear the weight of a woman and child, wheeling it along the passageway and into the kitchen to prove it could be done.

The defence called no witnesses at all. Before the trial, Mrs Pearcey's mother was reported to have said that she would have to sell her daughter's belongings to pay for a defence. There was, she said, 'a great deal' that could be done for her daughter, if only she had the money. It appears, from the trial transcript, that that money cannot have been forthcoming. The speech for the defence began: 'there was nothing but circumstantial evidence against the prisoner', at which point the judge interjected: 'It was clearly shown Mrs. Pearcey was a party to a plan to destroy Mrs. Hogg, and the matter must not be cavilled with.' A more prosperous accused would have been able to launch an appeal

Mrs Pearcey was sketched a she appeared in the dock, possibly by the *Vanity Fair* caricaturist 'Spy' – Leslie Ward.

on that statement alone, but Mrs Pearcey's counsel had to plough on. He examined the evidence that had been presented by the prosecution, noting that it was all entirely circumstantial: the two witnesses who had seen a woman pushing a pram had given two different descriptions of her; Mrs Hogg's body bore signs that she had struggled violently with her attacker, but Mrs Pearcey showed no similar marks (she did, actually – the scratches she attributed to 'killing mice'); Mrs Hogg's wedding ring had vanished, but Mrs Pearcey was never shown to have had any ring but her own. There was no motive: her relationship with Hogg was continuing, so she had no particular reason to want his wife dead. Finally he pointed out that Mrs Pearcey was a slightly built woman, who was supposed to have severed her victim's spinal cord, then to have had the strength to push a pram loaded with the victim and the victim's child up a steep slope – nearly two miles to the point where Mrs Hogg was found, nearly three miles to where the pram was found, and then finally to have carried the baby, at night, in the dark, another quarter of a mile before walking the three miles back home.

The judge summed up firmly against Mrs Pearcey; he warned the jury not to heed the defence's comments on the weakness of circumstantial evidence – if some elements of the chain of evidence had broken down, he stated blithely, the others could still indicate guilt. He added that if Mrs Pearcey had merely known of the murder, but had not committed it herself, she was as guilty as if she had been the murderer. The jury agreed: guilty.

Many newspapers assumed that Mrs Pearcey had not acted alone. Her size was one element (although the unreliable MacNaghten, from a distance of two decades, remembered that he had 'rarely seen a woman of stronger physique than Mrs. Pearcey'). *Lloyd's* reported that the police had 'information' that would soon implicate a second person; the *Liverpool Mercury* agreed that 'There is now absolutely no doubt' a second person was involved, although it nominated another woman as the second murderer. Most looked to Hogg. *The Times* said that 'there will always be a doubt ... as to how the woman can have done the deed alone', and 'indeed, it would seem from one or two

expressions used by the Judge that he himself is not quite convinced
... But the man HOGG had a complete alibi.' The *Western Mail* went
even further, suggesting that Mrs Hogg had been starved when Mrs
Pearcey had nursed her, and that, ominously, 'on one occasion she
refused to touch a custard ... fearing that some one had tampered
with it'. The report ended, 'The Central News learns on inquiry that
Mr. Hogg is in even better health and spirits than usual. The statement that he has gone mad is entirely unfounded.' This permitted the
paper to suggest that he was a raving madman (who might therefore
easily have committed a murder), and at the same time that he was a
heartless beast, being in good 'health and spirits' after his wife and
child had been brutally murdered. The public agreed that Hogg was
culpable. As he followed the two coffins to the cemetery, 'there was a
furious outburst of yells and execrations that might have made the
stoutest heart quail ... So threatening and excited' was the crowd that
the police – 150 of them – had to form a cordon to stop it overturning
the mourning coach. During the funeral itself, Hogg was jeered and
hissed.

By the 1890s, women on trial at the Old Bailey represented less
than 10 per cent of defendants. And as time progressed, those
convicted could rely with more confidence on a reprieve. In 1849
there were six convictions for murder by a woman; five were executed.
By 1880, when seven female murderers were convicted, none was
executed. Between those two dates there was no year in which there
was more than a 30 per cent chance of a woman murderer actually
being executed if found guilty. Mrs Pearcey, however, was not one of
the fortunate majority.

Even after her execution, the rumour-mill continued to grind every
piece of chaff that came its way. One of the most persistent rumours
was that she had been married secretly (and implicitly to someone in
a higher station of life), and that she had requested her solicitor to
place the following 'in the Madrid papers: "M.E.C.P. Last wish of
M.E.W. Have not betrayed".' *Lloyd's*, three months later, was still
running with this story, claiming that it now had firm information
that on the night of the murders Mrs Pearcey had met with Mrs Hogg

and an unnamed gentleman, had knocked Mrs Hogg out with the poker, and then 'ordered her male visitor to cut the wretched woman's throat'. They dumped the bodies before the strangely obliging murderer vanished to Spain. Then, in a fine example of newspaper double-think, the report continued: 'Inquiries of the police show that they attach no importance whatever to the above statement.'

Lloyd's had a proprietorial interest in the story. A 'young artist' had been passing when Mrs Hogg's body was found, and that very night he approached *Lloyd's* with a sketch and details of the discovery. Fortunately for him, the crime had occurred just before the weekly edition went to press, and the staff inserted his description, although his illustration had to wait until the following week. 'This gave us a start that, followed up, helped to increase largely the demand for the paper.' After the illustration of the discovery of the body, other pictures followed: the kitchen, the pram, the broken windows. By November, pictures of both the Hogg and the Pearcey lodgings appeared, showing groups of spectators staring up at the notorious premises. Soon it was advertising 'CORRECT PORTRAITS' of Mrs Pearcey and Mrs Hogg, 'cabinet size, mounted together'. In the same issue Mrs Pearcey's mother lamented that she would have to sell her daughter's possessions, but 'I would ... be satisfied if I could only get that photograph of her in evening dress which appeared in *Lloyd's Newspaper*.' The reporter promised at once and in print to get her a copy. The 'photograph' was a middle-class flight of fantasy, for Mrs Pearcey of a certainty did not possess evening dress. When she made her first appearance at the police court hearing she was wearing a workhouse dress, because her own was still being examined for bloodstains. The inescapable conclusion is that Mrs Pearcey had only one dress, which was not unusual for a woman in her economic bracket.

Lloyd's inserted itself wherever possible into the story: it quoted the woman who did Mrs Pearcey's mangling, who claimed to have seen her pushing the pram on the relevant night: 'I was reading *Lloyd's* newspaper ... and saw that there had been a murder ... I said to my mother, "Why, mother, I saw her just under the railway arch, going along with a bassinette very heavily loaded."' In November a reader excitedly wrote: 'Sir, – As a reader of *Lloyd's* ... I wish to state for your information that it is reported here that Hogg brought the prisoner with a furniture van through the town some few days before the murder. – I am, sir, yours, A BEDFORDSHIRE READER', and 'a portrait they had since seen in *Lloyd's Newspaper*' enabled 'shocked' residents to identify 'the alleged murderess'. Naturally, there was a reported incident of supernatural prescience: 'When bedtime came the ... young lady ... who was to have occupied the other bed [in the room where Mrs Pearcey was sleeping] ... felt convinced that there was something so seriously wrong with her that she was afraid to sleep in the same room ...'

While *Lloyd's* readers were enjoying their quasi-proximity to noto-riety, the more middle-class newspapers were worrying again about women's interest in crime. Four years before, at the trial of Adelaide Bartlett, the *Evening Standard* had complained that the courtroom had been 'filled with well-dressed women and girls armed with ... sherry, sandwiches and eye-glasses'. This trio of accoutrements was symbolic of a certain type of woman, and at the trial of Eleanor Pearcey they reappeared: 'Hour after hour did these ghoulish women, armed with opera glasses, sherry-flasks, and sandwich boxes, hang with eager curiosity upon every movement and look of their miser-able sister ...' Now however this kind of aspersion was no longer permitted to pass without comment, and the *Women's Penny Paper* responded tartly: 'an eye-witness has seen fit to write to the daily press objecting to the presence of women in the court ... Is it not time that men learned ... that where women cannot go unharmed is no right place for themselves, and since a *woman* is in the dock it is not women but men who ought to be excluded?'

Male or female, middle- or working-class, all were gripped, and Madame Tussaud's was ready. Only 'hours' after the verdict was deliv-ered, 'Hey Presto!' wrote *Lloyd's*, Mrs Pearcey's model was on display in the Chamber of Horrors. This was a slight exaggeration, but it was no exaggeration to say that Madame Tussaud's knew a commercial opportunity when it saw one. It had earlier discovered that, as well as waxwork models of the participants, more theatrically staged settings were popular. In 1878, Madame Tussaud's had purchased the gallows from Hertford Gaol when it was demolished. Now it bought up all Mrs Pearcey's belongings – clothes, furniture, ornaments. It was stated that it paid £200 (some reports said £500), which went towards her defence. Hogg sold Madame Tussaud's the baby's pram (for a reported £25) and the clothes his wife and child had been wearing when they were killed. He also, at least according to the newspapers, sold them his beard and moustache for 25s. In its catalogue, the waxworks proudly boasted:

THE HAMPSTEAD TRAGEDY.
Mrs PEARCEY.
A MODEL OF THE KITCHEN, containing the identical
Furniture and Fixtures from No. 2, Priory Street, where Mrs.
HOGG and her BABY were murdered.

LIST OF FURNITURE, &c.,
TABLE, CHAIRS, OILCLOTH, COOKING
UTENSILS, CROCKERY, FIREPLACE,
GRATE, WINDOW AND FLOORING.
THE TABLE against which Mrs. Hogg was supposed to have
been leaning when the blows were struck.
THE WINDOW supposed to have been smashed by Mrs.
HOGG in her death struggles.

All the articles contained in the Kitchen have been
removed from No. 2, Priory Street, and are placed in
exact relative position as found by the Police when they
entered the premises.

Mrs. PEARCEY'S SITTING ROOM, with her identical
Furniture, Couch, Chairs, Table, Mirror, Carpet, Piano,
Ornaments, Curtains, Blinds, &c.
*The Piano is the one on which Mrs. Pearcey played whilst the Police
were searching her house.*

Mrs. PEARCEY'S BEDSTEAD AND FURNITURE.
THE PERAMBULATOR in which the Bodies were carried.
CASTS OF THE HEADS OF Mrs. HOGG AND HER
BABY, taken from Nature after death.
THE CLOTHES worn by Mrs. Hogg and Baby when
murdered.
Mrs. PEARCEY'S RECEIPT in her own handwriting.
THE TOFFEE found in the Perambulator.

The exhibition opened just before Christmas, and on Boxing Day 31,000 people queued to see this one exhibit; 75,000 were admitted in the first three days. *Punch* mocked Pearcey fever, satirically claiming to have overheard 'A Strict Old Lady' at Louis Tussaud's rival establishment in Regent Street who refused to look at models of Henry Irving and Ellen Terry: 'No – I don't care to ... that's play-actin', that is – and I don't 'old with it nohow!' In front of Cardinals Manning and Newman, she was even firmer: 'Come along, and don't encourage Popery by looking at such figures.' But: 'I *did* 'ear as they'd got Mrs. PEARCEY and the prambilator somewheres. I *should* like to see that, now.'

It was probably easier to find entertainment in a female murderer, simply because they were so rare. In 1841 the ratio of husbands to wives as spouse-killers was 5:1; by 1900 it was 14:1. The entertainment world reflected a different view: in 1889, Madame Tussaud's had four male killers for every female, and fictionally women were even more lethal. Half of the Sherlock Holmes stories have domestic suspects (the rest involve either professional criminals, such as burglars, or spies), and of these sixteen involve women as criminal or in some way deviant. Against this monstrous regiment of criminal women there are only two stories of men in similar domesticity who go rogue.

Most people knew that this was not reality, and women murderers were rare enough to be a source of comedy: 'A cynical friend ... on hearing a sympathetic acquaintance express commiseration for that wretched man, Hogg, hotly retorted, "Pity *him*, indeed! He's to be congratulated; loses his wife, his lady love, and his kid all at one fell swoop." '

This startlingly modern voice breaks through a century of more covert pleasure in blood. Perhaps the events of two years previously had changed attitudes to murder more than first appeared.

NINE

Modernity

Mary Ann Cotton was found guilty of murder, and popular opinion laid twenty-odd deaths at her door. Yet while she fits into the pattern of the poison panics of mid-century, no panic ensued. And while she was accepted as being the most prolific murderer since Burke and Hare, hers was not the name that people remembered when the most notorious murderer of the century appeared on the scene in 1888. Jack the Ripper brought with him a new kind of crime, and a new kind of fear. Mary Ann Cotton looked backward.

The murderer who was popularly described as being the precursor to Jack the Ripper had only one victim. Israel Lipski was convicted of murdering Miriam Angel in their lodgings off Commercial Street, in London's East End, just twelve months before Martha Tabram, the woman some named as Jack the Ripper's first victim, was found dead a few hundred yards away. A Polish–Jewish immigrant, Lipski had fled conscription into the Russian army and found his way to London in about 1885. Ambitious and industrious, he worked for an umbrella manufacturer until, in 1887, he took his savings, borrowed £2.5s. from his fiancée's mother and pawned his watch in order to set up a workshop of his own in his attic room in Batty Street. The day of the murder was to be his first day in business.

The lodging house was crowded, with fourteen people living in five rooms. The landlord (also named Lipski, but no relation), his wife and seven children lived in one room on the ground floor; his mother shared a room on the first floor with a Mrs Levy, and next to them was a couple who had moved in six weeks earlier: Isaac Angel, a

Polish–Jewish boot-riveter, and his pregnant wife Miriam. On the morning of 28 June 1887, Isaac Angel went to work at 6 a.m. as usual. Miriam was in the habit of going to her mother-in-law's for breakfast, and when she failed to arrive, Mrs Angel came looking for her. The door to her room was locked, but through a window on the staircase she could be seen lying on the bed. Afraid the pregnant woman had been taken ill, the landlady, Mrs Angel and Mrs Levy broke the door down. Miriam Angel was found unmoving, with yellow foam on her lips. One of the women ran for a doctor, while the house's occupants all spilled out of their rooms to see what the noise was. The doctor pronounced Miriam dead, noting the marks of a corrosive poison on both her lips and her hands. It was only when he asked the others to look for a bottle that might have held the poison that anyone realized she had not been alone in the room. Under the bed was the body of Israel Lipski, semi-conscious, and with the same marks of corrosive

Israel Lipski was found poisoned under the bed of the murdered Mrs Angel, his fellow lodger. The young immigrant would be convicted of her murder in what soon became seen as a precursor to even more terrible East End murders.

poison around his mouth. The police, reported *The Times*, 'have been unable to obtain any satisfactory solution of the affair', although they hoped that if Lipski recovered, he would be able to give them information. To this end they had an interpreter at the hospital, as Lipski spoke no English.

Lipski did recover, although perhaps he later wished he had not. His story was that for his new business he had hired a boy, Richard Pitman, who had worked with him at the umbrella-maker's, and two men whom he had met casually. One of these, Simon Rosenbloom, had come early, and Lipski had left him with Pitman in the attic while he went to buy extra tools for Isaac Schmuss, the second employee. The shop was still closed (it was not yet 8 a.m.), and he returned and went out a second time, telling Rosenbloom to fetch some brandy. On his return he saw Rosenbloom and Schmuss on the first-floor landing. They grabbed him and demanded money, forcing a piece of wood into his mouth. He told them he had just spent everything he had; even his watch was in pawn. They replied, 'If you don't give it to us you will be as dead as the woman.' They forced a liquid down his throat, and before he lost consciousness he heard one say, 'Don't you think he is quite dead.' The other replied, 'He don't want any more.' And that was the last he knew.

Lipski's statement met with incredulity, and the inquest found a verdict of wilful murder against him. At the trial, Rosenbloom said Schmuss had arrived, waited briefly and then left. Richard Pitman agreed that Schmuss had arrived and gone away in Lipski's absence, but said that first Schmuss and Rosenbloom had spoken together 'in their own language' (Yiddish), after which Rosenbloom had told him he knew Schmuss. In cross-examination Rosenbloom denied this, saying he spoke no English and Pitman no Yiddish. Pitman said that Rosenbloom had communicated in a mixture of languages, and had definitely said he knew Schmuss. Schmuss told the court that he had arrived, waited fifteen minutes (Pitman said five), and then left. 'I saw that I should not have a great chance of work there, so I did not go back,' was all the reason he gave. This, then, was the prosecution's case: that Lipski had gone to the Angels' room, although whether to steal

417

or to rape Mrs Angel was never made clear; he had either met with more resistance than he expected, or had been surprised by Mrs Angel, and therefore poisoned her with the nitric acid he had just purchased for his work, which he had in his pocket. To evade suspicion, he then took a small dose himself.

Unfortunately for Lipski, he had a perfectly terrible defence team, led by A.J. McIntyre, a Liberal MP and a barrister who had no experience in criminal trials. A great deal of evidence presented by the prosecution's own witnesses should have been used by the defence. It became clear that the man who claimed to have sold nitric acid to Lipski, and who identified him in hospital, had in reality been guided to him by the police – a policeman was sitting by his bed when the chemist was brought to the ward. He was also only willing to say that 'to the best of my belief' Lipski was the man, adding cautiously that he had been serving half a dozen people at the relevant time. The prosecution's case was that only Lipski could have murdered Mrs Angel, because her door had been locked from the inside. But a policeman testified that after the murder he had been to the Angels' room over a dozen times, entering when they were absent without difficulty: the lock barely worked, he said, 'only just to keep the wind off; if you just touched the door it came open'. Likewise the landlady said that she and two other women had broken the door down in 'seconds'. The doctor's assistant testified that the bottle of poison was 'not exactly found', but had been pointed out to the police by Rosenbloom, and that for at least ten minutes after he arrived, a number of people had been 'milling around' the room: he could not say how many, or what they had been doing. The judge, the same Sir James Fitzjames Stephen who had twenty years before said that infanticide was 'less serious than other kinds of murder', summed up dead against Lipski.* The jury had

---

* Mr Justice Stephen would continue on his merry way. Two years later he told the jurors at the trial of Florence Maybrick that they were not there to decide whether or not James Maybrick had been poisoned, but rather to judge the case of an adulterous woman who 'had already inflicted a dreadful injury [on her husband] – an injury fatal to married life'. Florence Maybrick was found guilty, but after an outcry her sentence was commuted to life imprisonment, and she served fourteen years.

no trouble either. It took them eight minutes to produce a guilty verdict.

Initially the papers had shown little interest in the case. *The Times* had carried a few small paragraphs, the *Morning Chronicle* had no reports at all, the *Daily News* only two sentences. It was the *Pall Mall Gazette* that made Israel Lipski a matter of national discussion. This was superficially surprising. While the editor, W.T. Stead, had said he wanted his paper to be 'the great tribune of the poor', the immigrant poor of the East End were decidedly not the people he meant; he and his paper were more than usually anti-Semitic, even for the time. There were, however, a number of reasons for their campaign on behalf of Lipski. The Home Secretary, Henry Matthews, was Catholic, Unionist and Conservative – everything Stead detested. Stead had also had a run-in with Stephen, while the prosecuting counsel had been the prosecutor in a case brought against Stead in 1885.* Despite these ulterior motives, the case the paper made was a good one, and it was joined by Lipski's solicitor, Jonathan Hayward, who was vehemently – almost unprofessionally, and touchingly – distraught at his client's fate. He published a pamphlet outlining the defence more cogently than Lipski's barrister had done in court, and added new details: he reminded his readers that Schmuss, who claimed to have been in great need, had not waited ten minutes for paying work; the amount of nitric acid swallowed and splashed about was far more than the chemist said he had sold; and boxes had been piled in front of Lipski under the bed, which he could not have dragged in after himself.

Stephen was sent a copy of the pamphlet, and was disturbed by its contents, admitting (said Hayward via Stead) that 'I myself did not exactly hit the right point in summing up.' The Home Secretary was firmly convinced of Lipski's guilt. The police had supplied him with

---

* This was the notorious 'Maiden Tribute of Babylon' case, Stead's journalistic crusade against child prostitution. To prove that children were easily bought and sold for sex, Stead himself 'bought' a thirteen-year-old girl. Although the uproar ultimately led to changes in the criminal law, Stead was prosecuted and, the child's father not having given his permission for the 'sale' of his daughter, found guilty on a technicality and sentenced to three months in gaol.

material not presented at the trial, and he refused to recommend that the sentence of death be commuted, or mercy shown. Two days before the date scheduled for the execution, therefore, Hayward placed advertisements in several newspapers, asking for the jurors to get in touch with him; he also organized and presented a petition, and mailed out his pamphlet without charge to anyone who requested one. Questions were raised in Parliament, and the *Pall Mall Gazette* ran a long article, headed 'Hanging an Innocent Man: Conversion of Mr. Justice Stephen', which reported the meeting between the judge and Hayward, although Stephen immediately denied that he had said most of what was attributed to him, and claimed that 'the more I think over the matter, the more fully I am convinced that he did it'. The Home Secretary, in Parliament, brushed aside Stephen's supposed anxiety – 'altogether irrelevant', he said.* Stephen then suggested that the execution be postponed for a week, giving him time to re-examine the case, although perhaps more as a public-relations ruse – 'This would remove any impression of haste from public mind,' he telegraphed the Home Secretary. He added, to his wife, 'The worst of it is that everyone will say, I was bullied into it by that blackguard Stead.'

'That blackguard Stead' kept up the pressure, with headlines every day that week. All the other newspapers now piled in with their own views. The *Telegraph*, the *Methodist Times* and the *Lancet* pressed for commutation, on the grounds that the case was not proved beyond reasonable doubt. The papers that held out for execution seemed to be doing so not from conviction, but because they were anti-Stead and anti-*Pall Mall Gazette*. 'We have been exposing the miserable tactics of [the *Gazette*],' wrote the *Evening News*, while *Lloyd's* referred to the 'screechings of one particular journal'.

Stephen re-examined the case, and came to the same conclusion as he had at the trial. Meanwhile Godfrey Lushington, the Permanent Under-Secretary of State, who had dealt with the case for Matthews, added a note to the file warning that the chemist's new report on the

---

* In fact Matthews might have been able to discover the truth more easily than either the judge or the anti-Semitic editor: an extraordinary linguist, he most unusually spoke Yiddish.

nitric acid was disturbing and should be withheld from Lipski's lawyer. The Home Office also withheld information from the defence. On the other side, seventy-eight MPs signed a petition for commutation (it was August, and only two hundred MPs were in town). All this went for nothing. On 21 August 1887, Lipski was told by Lushington that the execution would go ahead. And then he confessed.

How the confession was received pretty much depended on each person's previous stance. The Home Office, the police and the papers that had been against Stead saw it as validation of their views. Stead was furious, and gave vent to his anti-Semitic views: 'Lipski!!!! ... could any human being not a Pole and also a Jew have played the *Pall Mall Gazette* so scandalous a trick. It was a bad fall.' (Although, presumably, not as bad a fall as Lipski was about to take.) Others listened more closely to what the rabbi who had received Lipski's confession said: Lipski had asked him what would happen if the sentence were commuted, and was told he would then be imprisoned for life. Aged twenty-two, he was apparently not prepared for this, and his confession followed. He had gone into the Angels' room, he said to steal. Mrs Angel had woken up, and since 'I had long been tired of my life, and had brought a pennyworth of aqua fortis [nitric acid] that morning for the purpose of putting an end to myself', he poisoned her with it, taking the remainder himself. This was so at odds with the evidence that at this distance in time it is beyond belief. If Miriam Angel had been wakened by Lipski, he must have entered the room before eight o'clock – she normally reached her mother-in-law by 8.30. But he was seen after 8.30 by the landlady. If he had not gone to the room until closer to eleven, why was Mrs Angel still asleep? And on the same morning that he set up his own business, having decided to commit suicide, he went out, purchased the means to do so, and then stopped off for a spot of burglary?

None of this was dealt with by the *Pall Mall Gazette*, which retreated, infuriated, while the other newspapers, grateful they had not been left similarly exposed, concentrated on the journalistic débâcle rather than the potential miscarriage of justice. Stead, said the *Evening News*, had in the past 'done more to degrade the Press than any man living', but even for him, this was a 'low-water mark'. The *Spectator* thought it was 'a deep disgrace to English journalism'. The *Evening News* simply noted that on the day of Lipski's execution, up to 6,000 people stood outside Newgate, 'the largest gathering ever known since capital punishment has been performed in private', as though the size of the crowd validated the correctness of the verdict.

'The Whitechapel Tragedy', a surviving ballad sheet, was conventional in form, lamenting 'that cruel deed that I have been relating,/ Heavy on his conscience it does lie', and ending with a warning to others to learn from 'Lipsky's [sic] awful fate'. Meanwhile the *Pall Mall Gazette* reprinted a leaflet that was on sale outside Newgate on the morning of the execution. One verse ran,

> What would my poor old mother say and father could they see
> Their son to die for murder upon that fatal tree?
> Through circumstantial evidence I met a dreadful fate.
> They may find out I am innocent, alas, when it's too late.

In style this is similar to the older broadsides, in that the verses don't scan, and their quality is poor, but the stress on the innocence of the murderer is unusual, if not unique. It may be that this was the *Pall Mall Gazette*'s own parting – and anonymous – contribution.

While broadsides and ballads were now virtually antiques, the detective story was thriving, and the shadow of the Lipski case was discernible in the details of East End journalist Israel Zangwill's 'The Big Bow Mystery', published in the *Star* in 1891. The story is important in the development of crime fiction: while earlier tales had used locked rooms as part of the plot, this was one of the first to enjoy the puzzle for its own sake. More topically, it pits George Grodman, a retired detective, against his Scotland Yard successor, Inspector Wimp, who 'was at his greatest in collecting circumstantial evidence; in putting two and two together to make five'.* Grodman's neighbour

---

* I can find no meaning in the Inspector's unusual name, the slang word 'wimp' appearing to be a twentieth-century Americanism.

finds a dead lodger in her house, and asks him for help. As with Lipski, after the discovery of the body, 'The tongues of the press were loosened, and the leader-writers revelled in recapitulating the circumstances ... though they could contribute nothing but adjectives to the solution. The papers teemed with letters ...' including one in the not-very-disguised '*Pell Mell Press*'. Ultimately, Grodman himself is revealed to be the murderer. He has been so clever that the police do not discover this, and it is only when an innocent man is convicted that he confesses. The innocent man, unlike Lipski, is reprieved, and when Grodman hears this, he kills himself.

Before Grodman committed suicide in the pages of the *Star*, before Lipski decided to commit suicide on the day he set up in business, another suicide took place, before the eyes of thousands, nightly. In 1886, Robert Louis Stevenson had followed up his successful novel *Treasure Island* with the even more successful novella *The Strange Case of Dr Jekyll and Mr Hyde*. Dr Jekyll discovers a drug which allows him to become physically a second person, a person who manifests all his own suppressed evil impulses. As the repellent Mr Hyde, he roams the town, indulging the worst elements of his character, trampling a small child and murdering Sir Danvers Carew, an 'aged and beautiful gentleman', by clubbing him to death with his stick. The doctor eventually finds that he is no longer in control: Hyde appears involuntarily. As the police and his friends are on the brink of unmasking his double existence, Dr Jekyll commits suicide. This good/evil doubling had been used regularly, from Poe's 'William Wilson' to Dickens' Bradley Headstone and (probably) Jasper in *Edwin Drood*. The difference is that this was now an intentional split on the part of the good character, and it was given a modern twist by the scientific approach of the doctor.

Jekyll and Hyde was a phenomenon. By February 1886 *Punch* already had a parody version, in which 'Mr. Hidanseek' 'thought how pleasant it would be' to become 'a creature with an acquired taste for ... hacking to death (with an umbrella) midnight barons who had lost their way'. By July, nearly 40,000 copies had been sold, and vicars were using the novella as a text for their sermons. In the spring of 1887 an adaptation by T.R. Sullivan, with Stevenson's approval, was staged in Boston and New York, soon moving to London. Not everyone was enthusiastic. The *Pall Mall Gazette* thought 'Nothing more horrible has ever been seen on a stage ... Scratch John Bull and you find the ancient Briton who revels in blood, who loves to dip deep into a murder, and devours the details of a hanging.'

And in the same month that the *Pall Mall Gazette* worried about John Bull's love of blood, suddenly John Bull had the most famous murder case ever to revel in. On the morning of 7 August 1888, Martha Tabram was found dead in George Yard Buildings, just off Whitechapel High Street. The crimes of the unknown person dubbed 'Jack the Ripper' have probably had more written about them than any since Cain killed Abel. The great horror – and the great fascination – of this series of murders is that they are entirely unknowable. The date they began, or ended, is open to question; the number, and sometimes even the names, of the victims is disputed. Sometimes Martha Tabram and a number of other women are listed as victims; other times they are not. There was no arrest, no trial, no verdict to draw a line under the case, only a shadowy figure and a list of suspects that is almost comic in its inclusiveness. In October 1888 alone, the *Pall Mall Gazette* suggested that the murderer was an army doctor with sunstroke who had been too heavily influenced by *Dr Jekyll and Mr Hyde*; a mad occultist; anarchists of various nationalities and beliefs; a clergyman; a rogue policeman; and a 'scientific humanitarian' who was killing prostitutes in order to improve the world.* So wide has the net been spread that any murderer will slip easily through the holes. Of the more than fifty murders discussed in this book, only

* Time has only enlarged the number of possibilities. A twentieth-century crime historian has listed some of the 'beguilingly diverse pretenders': the Duke of Clarence; Montague John Druitt, a barrister; James Kennet Stephen, the son of the judge; a Jewish ritual circumciser; several doctors and a midwife; a magician; the Revd Samuel Barnett, the social reformer and founder of Toynbee Hall; the painter Walter Sickert; the poet Algernon Charles Swinburne and the novelist George Gissing; Gladstone; Dr Barnardo; and 'a perfectly blameless member of the late Bertrand Russell's family'. Several murderers also made the list: Mrs Pearcey, George Chapman, Thomas Neill Cream and Frederick Deeming, 'the Rainhill murderer'.

three saw no arrest shortly after the discovery of the murder – the case of the drunken John Peacock Wood, of Thomas Ashton the mill owner's son, and of Constance Kent. In each of those cases there was a closed group from which to pick – the police who arrested Wood, the Spinners' Union men, and the Kent family. Here there was no group, no single suspect to reassure the population that the ultimate crime would always be followed by retribution.

The death of Martha Tabram aroused little interest, a common fate for these women, frequently alcoholic, all of them at the outer edges of poverty. An attack of particular ferocity might attract passing attention: four months earlier, Emma Smith had been gang-raped, including with a blunt instrument 'with great force', and then robbed. The level of violence, and the supposition that her death was the work of one of the High Rip gangs, who extorted protection money from prostitutes, made her story worth a sentence or two to the news-papers. The *Daily News* merely reported Martha Tabram's death as a 'supposed murder in Whitechapel' – which since the woman had been stabbed more than three dozen times, seems to stretch the meaning of the word 'supposed' past breaking point. The *Echo* was the first, although unintentional, link between the East End murders and *Jekyll and Hyde*: its articles on the finding of the body and the inquest were separated in print by a piece noting that George Grossmith's farce *The Real Case of Hyde and Seekyll* was to open shortly. The view was that Martha Tabram had been killed by a client. She had been seen with a friend and two soldiers earlier in the evening, and her body was first spotted at 3.30 a.m. by a cab driver heading home. He did not stop to look at her – as the clerk would later not stop to look at Mrs Hogg – because 'people constantly slept on the stairs', either drunk or simply homeless.

It was on 31 August, when Mary Ann (Polly) Nichols was found dead in Buck's Row, that the press began to feel that this was a story worth following. As the press magnate Alfred Harmsworth noted, 'crime exclusives are *noticed* by the public more than any other sort of news. They attract attention, which is the secret of newspaper success.' The series of deaths which came to be grouped together as murders by a single, unknown person, were, without doubt, a circulation-booster, and for the local East End papers they were a godsend. Newspapers had always sold on crime – *The Times*, with 20 per cent of its coverage given to the subject, had a circulation of 100,000, the *Telegraph*, with 30 per cent, sold 250,000 copies, and *Lloyd's* 750,000. The *Star* was a local ½d. paper that had only started publishing in January of that year; after the murder of Annie Chapman in September, its circulation went up to over a quarter of a million copies a day, dropping back to 190,000 by the middle of the month, when no further killings took place; in early October, after Elizabeth Stride and Catherine Eddowes were murdered on the same night, the paper's circulation rose once more, to 217,000 copies, and after the final murder it reached 300,000. The *Star*, the *Evening News* and the *Echo* were said to have run their presses around the clock during the autumn and winter of 1888, rushing out new editions with updates – or to say there were none, as when the *Evening News* on 1 September had an announcement: 'The Exchange Telegraph Company, on inquiry this morning at Scotland Yard, were informed that no arrests had been made in connection with the brutal murder at Whitechapel up to eleven o'clock to-day.'

The national newspapers, as well as the local ones, began to take notice. *The Times* still assumed that Mrs Nichols would soon be revealed as simply another 'unfortunate' murdered by a High Rip gang, but most newspapers recognized that this idea was becoming untenable, and began instead to focus on the mutilations, the element that tied these murders into a single series. The *Star* headlined its piece 'A Revolting Murder. Another Woman Found Horribly Mutilated in Whitechapel. Ghastly Crimes by a Maniac', and used the word 'disembowelled' in the subhead. On 1 September it had returned to the deaths of Emma Smith and Martha Tabram, and noted the 'significant similarity' of the 'hideous mutilations'.

High Rip gangs, maniacs, these and other possibilities were discussed in the press, and already, only the day after Mrs Nichols' death, the action, or inaction, of the police had begun to attract derision. 'The theories of the police about most things connected with the detection of crime are not deserving of much attention at any time,' began the *Evening News*. 'They, therefore, showed much cuteness in not insisting too long upon the possible fact of there being a fiend in human shape, such as Mr. Stevenson describes, roaming about the metropolis.' It then went on to repeat various atrocities, historical and in fiction (some of which were nonetheless identified as 'absolute fact'), before it signed off with a final dig at the police for failing to catch either the 'maniac' or the High Rip gang members. The following day *Lloyd's* joined in, reporting that one of the first people to come across Mrs Nichols' body had found a policeman who was 'calling people up' (that is, waking them for their factory shifts, a community service that also earned the police extra money on the side). Instead of immediately going to the body, or summoning aid, 'He continued calling the people up, which I thought was a great shame.' The witness added pointedly that the body was cold enough to make it evident that 'no policeman on the beat had been down there for a long time'. *The Times* was appalled to discover that when Mrs Nichols' body had been brought to the makeshift mortuary (there was no permanent one in Whitechapel, another local complaint) it had been stripped without police supervision, or instructions on how to handle the clothes which might have provided clues.

By the end of the first week of September, the press had wrung the stories dry. Then the mutilated body of Annie Chapman was found early on the morning of 8 September. The *Star* returned to the gothic style of half a century before: 'London lies today under the spell of a great terror. A nameless reprobate – half beast, half man – is at large ... The ghoul-like creature who stalks through the streets of London ... is simply drunk with blood, and he will have more.' Two days later, the *Star* was less concerned with making its readers' flesh creep, and more with its own position. In an article headed 'The Police and the Press', it issued a denunciation, a challenge and an assertion of the importance of newspapers within the crime-detection world:

One thing is absolutely certain ... murderers will always escape with ... [the] ease that now characterises their escape in London until the police authorities adopt a different attitude towards the Press. They treat the reporters ... with a snobbery that would be beneath contempt were it not senseless to an almost criminal degree. On Saturday they shut the reporters out of the mortuary; they shut them out of the house where the murder was done; the constable at the mortuary door lied to them; some of the inspectors ... seemed wilfully to mislead them ... Reporters are not prying individuals simply endeavoring [sic] to gratify their own curiosity. They are direct agents of the people who have a right to the news and a right to know what their paid servants the police and the detectives are doing to earn the bread and butter for which the people are taxed.

The newspapers, particularly the newspapers with radical views, or a working-class audience, saw that they could use the murders as a stick with which to beat the police. There was, unfortunately, rather a lot of material to hand. Police numbers had been rising steadily: from just over 3,000 men at the foundation of the Met, to about 8,000 in 1852, and nearly 12,000 in 1886. All divisions now had a detective department of up to ten men, with the central division at Scotland Yard increased to forty-two men. Minor crimes were dealt with by local divisions; anything bigger was shunted to Scotland Yard. The Criminal Investigation Department, or CID, as it now was, had nearly three hundred men on its staff, but it was no longer the admired institution its creators had hoped. In 1878 three senior Scotland Yard detectives had been found guilty of corruption in what was known as the Turf Fraud case, and the entire department was put on probation, apart from Dolly Williamson, who was made Chief Superintendent, and his deputy. In 1880 another case revealed that a suspected abortionist had been entrapped by detectives acting as *agents provocateurs*. The judge condemned 'employing *spies* to go and lie', and the Home Office made the situation worse by issuing such a weak defence – 'As a rule, the police ought not to' – that it was clear that this was standard practice.

Col. Edmund Henderson, named Commissioner on the death of Mayne in December 1868, resigned after a rally for the unemployed at Trafalgar Square had led to the Black Monday riots of February 1886. He was replaced by Charles Warren, a soldier. He ran into the same problem in November 1887, when another rally turned into Bloody Sunday: nearly 5,000 police and soldiers blocked access to Trafalgar Square, and it was only at the last minute that a bayonet charge of the crowd was prevented. Even so, hundreds of unarmed protesters were badly injured. That was a public problem. At Scotland Yard, a more urgent internal problem was that Warren could not get on with James Monro, head of the CID. Monro complained that Warren was only interested in street disorder. The percentage of men assigned to detection in London, Monro noted bitterly, was 2.42; in Liverpool and Glasgow it was 3.5 per cent; in Birmingham, 4.5. Two weeks after Martha Tabram was murdered, Monro resigned, and was replaced by Robert Anderson, who had acted as the Home Office's 'adviser in matters relating to political crime' – he was the government's spymaster.

In the best of circumstances, the man whose job it was to break the Fenians would not have been much loved in the East End, with its large Irish Catholic population. Anderson made sure of general detestation by his complete lack of interest in the residents of Whitechapel. He started work as head of the CID on the day Mrs Nichols was murdered. At the end of his first week, Mrs Chapman was killed. The following day, he left on a month's holiday. He could just as easily receive reports from the office in Switzerland, he told his superiors; indeed (one can almost hear his aggrieved tones), he had even moved part of his vacation to Paris, for swifter communication with London. In his absence the CID was under the supervision of Dolly Williamson, who suffered from a heart condition and could no longer participate operationally, but who was kept on the force because of his vast experience. The next in the chain of command was Superintendent Shore, who was in effect running the entire CID. Thus the Whitechapel murders were handled locally, by the divisional detectives, with input from just one Scotland Yard inspector.

The newspapers ensured that their readers knew these shocking facts. Other shocking facts were slower to emerge. Until now, the press had been relatively reticent in describing sex crimes. While both the courts and the papers were far more habituated than modern audiences to body parts being displayed in court, or to detailed reports on scientific or medical testimony, sex was off-limits. The 'criminal violence' that Fanny Adams may have undergone was a reference to possible rape, not to the undoubted criminal violence of being murdered and dismembered; similarly, after Mrs Angel had been killed by a corrosive poison, the doctor said he had pulled back the bedclothes to check if 'any violence had been offered to her'. 'Outrage' was another common euphemism: in 1874 a woman had died after a gang-rape, and the *Telegraph* reported that she had been 'outraged to death'. After the inquest on Mrs Tabram, the *East London Observer* referred to mutilations in 'the lower portion of the body', and added that there were no indications of 'recent intimacy'.* Then, with the death of Mrs Nichols, *Reynolds's Newspaper* gave its front page over to a report: the mutilations, it wrote, were 'too horrible to describe or even hint at' – and then it described them, at length and in detail. By the time Mrs Chapman was murdered a week later, it would appear from the return to discretion that the police had leant on both the coroner and the newspapers. When the inquest on Mrs Chapman opened, *Lloyd's*, apparently alone, used the word 'womb'. *The Times*, the *Evening Standard*, the *Telegraph* and the *Morning Post* simply said that 'portions' were missing from Mrs Chapman's 'abdomen', while others refrained even from mentioning the area from which the organ was missing. (Other body parts were not subject to the same restraint: the *Star* blazoned, 'The Heart and Liver were Over Her Head'.) After the inquest was resumed at the end of the month, the coroner used the word 'uterus', and several papers – *The Times* and some of the weeklies that specialized in crime, such as *Lloyd's*

---

* Perhaps things change less than one thinks. In August 2009 the BBC reported that a woman suffered a potential miscarriage by saying she had experienced 'intimate bleeding'.

– followed suit. The next week the *Lancet* used the word 'vagina', while denouncing the press for feeding 'a depraved appetite for the horrible and the bestial'.

The newspapers may have printed anatomical details more freely than before, but for the most part they remained circumspect about the occupations of these women. 'Unfortunate' had been a standard euphemism for the best part of a century. At Mrs Chapman's inquest, her friend told the coroner that Mrs Chapman had earned her living by needlework or making artificial flowers, two notoriously poorly paid types of piecework; those who undertook this work were frequently compelled to prostitution. Otherwise, she added, 'she was not particular'. The newspapers repeated this innuendo-laden phrase, and added others: 'She was out late at night at times', and she would sell 'anything she had to sell'.

The 'anything' was little enough. On her last night, Mrs Chapman had had no money to pay for a bed, so had gone to the street to earn her night's sleep. Her mutilated body was found at six the following morning. Apart from the clothes she was wearing, her worldly goods at her death consisted of two combs and a used envelope. Mrs Nichols, too, was out on her last night because she had drunk her few remaining pence away: 'Never mind,' she said as she left the lodging house, 'I'll soon get my doss money. See what a jolly bonnet I've got now.' After her death her belongings were itemized: the clothes she was wearing, a handkerchief, a section of a comb and a broken piece of looking-glass.

It was not the poverty, however, that many of the West End journals concentrated on, but its by-products, as they painted the East End as a jungle, 'where well-armed Authority fears to tread,/Murder and outrage rear audacious head,/Unscanned, untracked ...' wrote *Punch*. A week later it returned to the theme in 'The Nemesis of Neglect', describing 'Dank roofs, dark entries, closely-clustered walls,/Murder-inviting nooks, death-reeking gutters ... Red-handed, ruthless, furtive, unerect,/'Tis murderous Crime – the Nemesis of Neglect.' This was accompanied by a full-page illustration by Tenniel, showing a ghostly figure, headed 'Crime', carrying a knife through a decaying alleyway.* *Punch*'s attitude was fairly typical. It made no mention of disease or poverty, only of the presence of 'thievish dens' which produced a 'vice to be nursed to violence'.

In response, the East End newspapers presented the crime as East vs West, working class vs middle class. The Home Office, said the *Star*, would long ago have offered a reward if the victims had been West End residents.† It also suggested that locals should form their own vigilance committees, as the police – who had, it reminded its readers, used truncheons against unarmed workers on Bloody Sunday – were either unwilling or unable to deal with this horror. The *Pall Mall Gazette* also used Bloody Sunday as a symbol for the uncaring nature of authority towards the poor: the police could stop workers, it suggested, but they couldn't (read wouldn't) stop a murderer. Other, less political, newspapers were happy just to indicate sympathy. The *Sporting Times* ran a 'leader' of some five lines, the thrust of which was that when 'the beast' was caught, 'we advise that he should be turned out to the Whitechapel ladies … and if there be two consecutive inches of that murderer left together, we should smile'.

Meanwhile, at the inquest on Mrs Chapman, the coroner and the doctor who had conducted the post-mortem had a set-to over what, precisely, should be revealed in testimony. The coroner's view was that 'all the evidence the doctor had obtained … should be on the records of the Court … however painful it might be' – he hoped that the newspapers would show discretion in reporting it, but did not feel that it should be withheld from the court itself. Dr Phillips, however, 'thought it would be better not to give more details'. The coroner told him pretty sharpish that this was not his decision to make. Phillips snapped back: as the mutilations were not the cause of

---

* Sir John Tenniel (1820–1894) is best known to posterity as the illustrator of Lewis Carroll's *Alice's Adventures in Wonderland* (1865) and *Through the Looking Glass* (1872). To his contemporaries, however, it was his satirical political cartoons for *Punch*, where he had been chief cartoonist since 1865, that were his calling card.

† This is probably not so. The public rewards that had been routine in the early part of the century had long been seen to encourage misreporting from those eager for the money, and had been virtually discontinued outside fiction.

death, he was therefore under no obligation to report them. Coroner: 'That is a matter of opinion.' They finally compromised, and the courtroom was cleared of women and boys before Dr Phillips gave his evidence.

The element that the press now concentrated on, however, was not so much the mutilations, as the coroner's own injudiciously stated belief that Mrs Chapman's uterus had been removed by someone who displayed some level of anatomical knowledge: 'No mere slaughterer of animals could have carried out these operations.' The newspapers immediately elaborated wildly on this phrase. *The Times* thought that the murder 'belongs to an unspeakable class of crimes which are committed in order to secure the premium offered by certain anatomists and pathologists for the possession of human bodies and human organs'. Reviving the old anatomization fear, the article mentioned Burke and Hare, merging them with the more recent burial-society panics, reminding readers that the murder of children for insurance money was 'so frequent'. Finally the newspaper quoted the coroner, who said that 'an officer of one of our great medical schools' had told him that an American had offered to pay 'the sub-curator of the Pathological Museum' £20 for each uterus he could supply, in order to 'issue an actual specimen with each copy of a publication on which he was then engaged'.

Many other newspapers reported similar stories. The *Star* carried a letter saying that it was well known that 'biologists' were so 'infatuated by their pursuits as to cause murder to be committed': this was a 'matter of history'. Therefore it was obvious, continued the letter, that 'some half-mad physiologist' was collecting tissues 'for experiments on graftation'. Another letter added that the viscera beside Mrs Chapman's body had been laid out 'as if for inspection by the demonstrator at a post-mortem examination', and suggested that 'all dissecting room or post-mortem porters of the hospitals or mortuaries and even veterinary assistants' should be checked for mental stability. (It is easy to see why the working classes felt unjustly singled out – the author did not think that mad anatomy professors, doctors or vets might be responsible, only their assistants.)

Even those papers that scoffed at the idea of a maniac killer also embraced it, seemingly without quite noticing what they were doing. The *Pall Mall Gazette* and the *Globe*, among others, returned again and again to *Dr Jekyll and Mr Hyde*, suggesting that it was the double nature of the killer that made it possible for him to escape detection. The 'maniac' looked like an ordinary person, they warned, not Spring-Heel'd Jack.* The reference to a penny-dreadful is significant. New printing technology had replaced the old-fashioned text-based play-bills with vibrant illustrated posters. New technologies, new fears. The *Illustrated Police News* began to worry that these 'highly-coloured pictorial advertisements' promoting melodramas might unbalance the unstable: 'Such pictures [have] the same effect that the taste of blood produces upon the tiger.' In a *Punch* cartoon (opposite) the devil, dressed as a bill-sticker, gloats as he pastes up the image of a man wielding a knife, while a bill in his pocket, still to be posted, is inscribed 'Murd—'.

The Whitechapel murders and the newspapers were now insepar-able. The *Bath and Cheltenham Gazette* noted that 'the excitement has been great ... but it has been largely stimulated and fed by the great and unnecessary prominence given to the subject'. The Nichols and Chapman inquests, with their adjournments, occupied much of September. The pause that followed was bad for circulation, and the newspapers acted promptly. On 29 September the Central News Agency forwarded to Scotland Yard a letter which it claimed it had just received:

---

* Spring-Heel'd Jack was perhaps the first ever urban legend. In 1837 an extraordinary figure, with bat's wings, goat's horns, a tail and springs in his heels which enabled him to leap over high walls, was sighted across south London. In 1838 a woman in Bow reported that a man had asked for a candle, before 'vomit[ing] blue and white flames', his eyes 'balls of white fire' as he tore at her dress with his metal claws. Several further attacks appeared in the newspapers over the next two months, and intermittently up to the 1920s. A penny-blood of the adventures of Spring-Heel'd Jack appeared shortly after his first appearance in 1838; the first play, at a minor theatre, was in 1840, and others soon followed. In 1867, *Spring-Heel'd Jack* (now wearing a natty scarlet suit) became a forty-part serial. In the earlier penny-bloods he had been a predator, a despoiler of women; by the 1870s, he had become a Batman-like righter of wrongs.

Dear Boss,

I keep on hearing the police have caught me but they wont fix me just yet. I have laughed when they look so clever and talk about being on the *right* track. The joke about Leather Apron gave me real fits.* I am down on whores† and I shant quit ripping them till I do get buckled. Grand work the last job was. I gave the lady no time to squall. How can they catch me now. I love my work and want to start again … I saved some of the proper *red* stuff in a ginger beer bottle over the last job to write with but it went thick like glue and I cant use it. Red ink is fit enough I hope *ha. ha.* The next job I do I shall clip the ladys ears off and send to the police officers just for jolly wouldnt you. Keep this letter back till I do a bit more work … My knife's so nice and sharp I want to get to work right away if I get a chance. Good luck.

Yours truly

Jack the Ripper

Dont mind me giving the trade name.

[in red crayon] … They say I'm a doctor now *ha ha*

This letter, and many others that followed, were almost certainly written by journalists. Some went to Scotland Yard, some to the Central News Agency. The newspapers reprinted them, even while they sometimes cast doubt on them (although they never went so far as to suggest that they were the source). *Fun* magazine's 'The Crime Cauldron', 'as brewed by certain papers', acknowledged via a *Macbeth* parody their effect on circulation. 'Enter three Editors …'

> Round about the cauldron go
> In it slips of 'copy' throw.

---

* 'Leather Apron' was one of many suspects, a local man who wore a leather apron and was reported to have mistreated prostitutes. A bootmaker named Joseph Pizer was briefly arrested; he had indeed worn a leather apron, it being the uniform of his trade. The police were convinced of his non-involvement, and he was released without charge.

† Most newspapers reprinted this letter, quite a few in facsimile. The *Morning Post* baulked at the word 'whores', however, and omitted it from its transcript.

Headlines of the largest size –
Murderer's letters – all faked lies;
And other spicy bits we've got
To simmer in our charmèd pot.
Bubble, Bubble! Crime and Trouble
Make our circulation double ...

Some papers, such as the *Observer*, did distance themselves, condemning the ridiculous reports 'which immediately tempts some silly fellow to write letters in Yankee phraseology'. But real or fabricated, these letters created the persona and tone – a catch-me-if-you-can cheerfulness and a black humour that were retrospectively superimposed upon the all-too-unhumorous murders. Many misread, or misremembered, the source of the 'Dear Boss' letter, assuming that Scotland Yard had released it for publication.

Meanwhile the chastisement of the police became louder, and more open, every day. *Punch* was typical in its not-very-subtle mockery:

A DETECTIVE'S DIARY A LA MODE

MONDAY: Papers full of the latest tragedy. One of them suggested that the assassin was a man who wore a blue coat. Arrested three blue-coat wearers on suspicion.

TUESDAY: The blue coats proved innocent. Released. Evening journal threw out a hint that deed might have been perpetrated by a soldier. Found a small drummer-boy drunk and incapable. Conveyed him to the Station-house ...

SATURDAY: ... Ascertain in a periodical that it is thought just possible that the Police may have committed the crime themselves. At the call of duty, finished the week by arresting myself!

Detectives were no longer the omniscient Inspector Bucket and Sergeant Cuff, but merely PC Plods. A disdain for the people who were supposed to catch the criminals was becoming widespread once more. Even fictionally, professional detectives were now being outpaced by their amateur rivals. In *The House on the Marsh*, an 1883 novel by 'Florence Warden' (Florence Alice Price), a policeman elaborately disguises himself, as only fictional detectives could do, but instead of being superior to the criminals he ignorantly reveals his plans to the criminal himself, and it is left to the clever amateur to catch him. Even Wilkie Collins, Sergeant Cuff's creator, by 1877 had a character 'of considerable worldly wisdom' say that the police are a 'waste [of] time and money ... who *can* believe in them, who reads the newspapers?' Instead, in *My Lady's Money* he uses a private detective, Old Sharon. Without any doubt, Old Sharon is an ancestor of Sherlock Holmes, who would make his first appearance the year before Jack the Ripper commenced work. There are differences between the two. Old Sharon is a detective because it pays – 'You give me a guinea and I'll give you half an hour.' But, like Holmes, he discovers things that the police are too stupid to work out; and he is an outsider, a bohemian: he is first seen 'through a thick cloud of tobacco-smoke ... robed in a tattered flannel dressing-gown, with a short pipe in his mouth'. Holmes, in his first outing in 1887, is also an outsider, an artist of a sort – the title of *A Study in Scarlet* would have reminded readers of the Aesthetic movement's penchant for 'mood' titles, especially Whistler's paintings, with their titles such as *Arrangement in White and Yellow*. Holmes is not prosperous, originally taking lodgings with Watson because he cannot afford rooms on his own. Furthermore, his function is not to bring criminals into the justice system: only eighteen of the sixty Holmes stories end in an arrest.

At the beginning Holmes himself was fairly dangerous and violent; very soon, however, the crimes he investigates become quirky, even whimsical, as in 'The Adventure of the Red-Headed League' (1890), where the criminal advertises for a red-headed man to copy out the *Encyclopaedia Britannica* in order to lure a red-headed pawnbroker away from his premises. It may perhaps be that this lack of blood was one of the things that made Holmes so popular. There was enough blood, enough violence, in Whitechapel, and in the newspapers. Holmes also has certainty, a vast store of knowledge that would surely enable him to put his hand on this terrifyingly elusive killer. In *A Study in Scarlet*, he recognizes that 'such an ash ... is only made by a Trichinopoly [cigar]. I have made a special study of cigar ashes'; in *The Sign of Four* he is expert in 'the tracing of footsteps' and also on 'the influence of a trade upon the form of the hand'. Eventually he is revealed as having written on the classifications of tattoos, the 'distinctiveness of human ears', ciphers, and document dating, although here he shows humility: 'I confess that once when I was very young I confused the *Leeds Mercury* with the *Western Morning News*.'*

Such certainty might be welcome after the horrors of 1888. At the end of August, after a direct instruction from the Home Office, Robert Anderson finally cut short his vacation and returned to London. As he was travelling, at 1 a.m. on 30 September Elizabeth Stride was found murdered on Berner Street; at 1.45, Catherine Eddowes' body was discovered around the corner on Mitre Square. Elizabeth Stride was a Swede, who worked when she could as a seamstress or a servant, and when she couldn't, as a prostitute. She was known to take a drink, but unlike the other victims was generally in employment, and was fairly respectable. She was found near the International Working Men's Club, a Jewish radical organization, and although she had throat wounds, there was no other mutilation. The murderer may have been interrupted, and thus gone on to kill Catherine Eddowes. Mrs Eddowes was an alcoholic, but she too worked fairly regularly, as a charwoman, and in season she went hop-picking. She was

---

* Less glamorously, he ploddingly echoes police procedure with his elaborate filing system. This sounds like a character in *A Terrible Temptation* (1871) by Charles Reade, who said every piece of paper that crossed his desk 'ought either to be burnt, or pasted into a classified guard-book, where it could be found by consulting the index ... Underneath the table was a formidable array of note-books, standing upright, and labelled on their backs. There were about twenty large folios, of classified facts, ideas, and pictures ... Then there was a collection of ... smaller folio guard-books called Indexes ... by way of climax, there was a fat folio ledger, entitled "Index ad Indices", all of which is astonishingly similar to Holmes's magisterial index books.

ferociously mutilated, and it was this double crime that truly opened the newspaper floodgates.

That night the editor of *Lloyd's* was woken by a messenger with the news, and was back in his office just after two o'clock on Sunday morning. *Lloyd's*, being a Sunday paper, was already being printed, but the editor himself went to the police stations to pick up what information there was, then moved on to Mitre Square and the mortuary, before 'spinning out' an article for an early special edition, which over the next twenty-four hours was updated by as many editions as the presses could print. The following Sunday, *Lloyd's* produced approximately 25,000 words on the subject.

All reticence was thrown aside. The *Star* reported that Mrs Eddowes had been 'ripped up like a pig in the market', her 'puberic [sic] bone ... left completely bare'. Licence for this sort of report was implicitly given at the inquest on Mrs Eddowes, where the coroner three times asked if the murderer had shown anatomical skill, with the questions phrased to imply he expected the answer 'Yes,' although the most the police surgeon was willing to say was that a butcher or a slaughterer could have known where the various organs lay. The coroner, clearly hankering after the mysterious American doctor, asked, 'Could the organs removed be used for any professional purpose?' The surgeon was adamant: 'They would be of no use for a professional purpose.' The coroner persisted: 'Can you as a professional man assign any reason for the removal of certain organs ...?' 'I cannot,' replied the surgeon. At the resumed inquest a week later, the question was asked twice more, and twice more the doctors replied in the negative, one adding firmly: 'the murderer had no particular design on any particular organ'.

This was no longer enough. Over the period of the murders, the *Telegraph*, living up to its reputation as a crime-sheet, printed nearly 400,000 words on the subject, over seventy-two columns. The *Morning Post* and *The Times* had over eighty columns each; the *Star*, a local, 115. Meanwhile the Sunday papers, despite having to compress a week's news in each issue, gave the story proportionately far more space. Four of the major Sundays (*Lloyd's*, *Reynolds's*, *People* and the

Weekly Times) expended nearly 210,000 words on the subject over four issues, while four dailies that focused on crime (*Daily Chronicle, Telegraph, Evening News* and *Globe*) had just under half a million, but over twenty-four issues. To fill this amount of space, almost anything went, and the newspapers all reported in anatomical detail what had been done to Mrs Eddowes.

There followed a range of articles suggesting that the organs had been removed for magic rituals, or religious ceremonies. The *Star* and the *Pall Mall Gazette* both printed reports claiming that candles made from human fat put people into an enchanted sleep, so they could be robbed with impunity; the *Pall Mall Gazette*, its anti-Semitism even closer to the surface after Lipski, reported that these magic candles were used to commit murder in Russia. As early as 15 September, the *East London Observer* reported popular sentiment: 'such a horrible crime ... must have been done by a Jew'. Mrs Stride was not only found outside the Jewish working men's club, but Berner Street was just one street away from Batty Street, where Mrs Angel had been murdered the year before. This was not merely newspaper pandering to popular sentiment. Otherwise intelligent people were swept away by the hysteria. On the night of Mrs Stride's death, a man claimed that someone near the spot where she was murdered had shouted 'Lipski!' at him. Godfrey Lushington, the Home Office Under-Secretary, said, '[this] increases my belief that the murderer was a Jew'.

This conviction, held by many, was encouraged by a scribbled inscription found on the wall near Mrs Eddowes' body, which may have read: 'The Juwes are the men that will not be blamed for nothing'. Sir Charles Warren quickly had the words erased, seeing them as a trigger for anti-Semitic action. In retrospect they were most likely another journalistic confection, influenced by Sherlock Holmes's first outing the previous year. In *A Study in Scarlet*, Holmes finds the mysterious word 'Rache' written in blood on the wall of the room in which the dead man lies, and recognizes it as the German for 'revenge'. The *Pall Mall Gazette* stoked up prejudice: 'The language of the Jews in the East End is a hybrid dialect, known as Yiddish, and their mode of spelling the word Jews would be "Juwes". This the police consider a strong indication that the crime was committed by one of the numerous foreigners by whom the East End is infested.' *The Times* added: 'the Talmud says that a Jew who is intimate with a Christian must slay and mutilate her', in order to be ritually cleansed. The Chief Rabbi responded by pointing out that the Yiddish for 'Jews' was 'Yidden', not 'Juwes', and that he could 'assert, without any hesitation, that in no Jewish book is such a barbarity' as *The Times* suggested 'even hinted at'. But innuendo persisted: when the deranged Richard Prince was arrested in 1897 for the murder of William Terriss, the Dundee son of a farm labourer was accused of looking 'like a foreigner', and 'loitering' in the 'shade' of a synagogue in Maiden Lane.

No one, of any age, was immune from this blanket coverage. The novelist Compton Mackenzie, five years old in 1888, later remembered that bedtime became 'almost unendurable' even far away on the other side of London, with 'the hoarse voices of men selling editions of the *Star* or *Echo* … shouting along the street … "Murder! Murder! Another horrible murder in Whitechapel! Another woman cut up to pieces in Whitechapel."' These newsboys' shouts were a common feature of memoirs and fiction. Even in France they were part of the story. In one French play the newsboy shouts, 'Demandez le crime de Whitechapel! … L'horrible assassinat de deux femmes commis par Jack l'Éventreur … Horribles détails … Un penney! [sic]'* (for more on this play, see pp.460–62).

After the double murder and their inquests, the newspapers searched again for more amusement to be had from the subject, and they found it in an unlikely place. Several of them had suggested that bloodhounds should be brought in to track the murderer, evidently not having any idea of how difficult, if not impossible, this would be in a busy city. Finally Sir Charles Warren caved in, and the police

---

* 'Ask for the Whitechapel crime … The horrible murder of two women by Jack the Ripper … Horrible details … One penny!' Jack the Ripper appears to be the only nineteenth-century murderer to receive his own sobriquet in foreign languages: Jack l'Éventreur ('*éventrer*' is 'to eviscerate', or, more prosaically, 'to gut', as with fish), Johann der Ausschlitzer, Giovanni il Squartatore, Jack o Estripador, Jack el Destripador.

borrowed a couple of hounds from a breeder near Scarborough, and, reported the *Evening News*, ran trials in Hyde Park, with Sir Charles, in a bizarre – and misguided – PR exercise, volunteering to act as the quarry. On 9 October, the *Pall Mall Gazette* combined the Trafalgar Square riots with the East End murders in 'A Ballad of Bloodhounds':

> Shall Jack the Ripper's arts avail
> To baffle Scotland-yard forsooth?
> Quick – on the flying murderer's trail
> Unleash the bloodhound, Truth!
>
> 'Where'er he skulk in hovel pent,
> Or through the streets red-handed roam,
> I, Charles, with sleuth-hound on the scent,
> Will hunt the miscreant home.'
>
> Thus boasts Sir Charles; and Truth, the hound,
> Springs from the leash, and holds not back,
> But from Whitechapel's tainted ground
> Leads westward on the track.
>
> And up and down, through thick and thin,
> While crowds collect and loafers stare,
> They speed, until their way they win
> Full through Trafalgar-square.
>
> Till last by Scotland-yard they halt,
> Where Truth, the sleuth-hound, sniffs and snarls:
> 'The trail is utterly at fault –
> What means it?' quoth Sir Charles.
>
> Just this. The reign of lawless law,
> The tyranny of stocks and staves,
> Which strikes in honest hearts the awe
> It spares to murderous knaves:

> To *this* belongs the blood that's spilt
> By fiends who know not human ruth;
> To *this* is due the heavier guilt
> Tracked by the bloodhound Truth.

In reality, the bloodhound idea had been virtually forced upon a pragmatic Warren by the clamour of the newspapers, and he refused to
purchase the two animals, which were kept quietly moping in
kennels.*

Meanwhile, Robert Anderson of the CID was outraged to hear that
prostitutes were being protected by constables on the beat, and
suggested that any woman found in the streets of Whitechapel after
midnight should automatically be arrested. It had to be explained to
him that it was not actually legal to arrest people for walking in the
streets. He countered with the proposal that it should be made clear
that the police no longer had orders to protect 'working' women,
which was agreed to.

Unsurprisingly, the police were treated even more harshly by the
papers than before. *Punch* demanded: 'Of what use was VINCENT
HOWARD in the Detective Department? ... A prize will be given for
a moderately satisfactory solution.' ('Vincent Howard' was in fact
Howard Vincent, who in 1878 had been appointed Director of
Criminal Investigation at Scotland Yard aged only twenty-nine, to
clean up the department after the Turf Fraud case.) *Reynolds's* bitterly
suggested that the procession for the Lord Mayor's Show should form
as follows:

> Waggon containing wax figures representing the condition
> of the wounded at the battle of Trafalgar-square ...
> Bevy of detectives blindfolded ...
> The victims of Whitechapel ...

---

* Sherlock Holmes evidently learned from Sir Charles Warren's difficulties. Less than two
years after the commissioner was chased across Hyde Park, Conan Doyle ensured that
Holmes's Toby, 'half spaniel and half lurcher', follows the scent of a murderer who has
conveniently first stepped in creosote in a quiet suburb.

Banner representing
Waste, Extravagance
Dirt, Disease
Misery, Jobbery ...

Even a penny-dreadful, *The Whitechapel Murders, or, The Mysteries of the East End*, which appeared at approximately this time,* was flat-out hostile towards the police. In the opening three episodes, following the style of boy's-own detective stories set up by Ernest Keen and others, the detectives are the heroes. Richard Ryder, or 'Detective Dick' as he is known 'and hailed by his superiors', is put on 'special duty to unravel the mystery'. Dick goes to the local rogues' pub, where the landlord tries to bar him: 'Nothing is private for Dick Ryder,' announces our hero, and the landlord immediately stands back: 'He knew the name too well not to respect it.' Then, in episode four, a character suddenly announces: 'We have carefully investigated the causes of the miserable and calamitous breakdown of the police system,' which can 'chiefly' be blamed on 'The inefficiency and timidity of the detective service, owing to the manner in which Sir Charles Warren has placed it, and forbidden it to move except under instructions.' (What happens after this volte-face is unknown: only the first five instalments appear to have survived.)

With no murders between 8 October and 9 November, the newspapers had to cast around for material. Many returned to the Jekyll and Hyde theme. One of the highlights of the stage adaptation at the Lyceum was the transformation of its star, Richard Mansfield, from Jekyll to Hyde, in front of the audience, relying solely on changes in posture, facial expression and gait (and probably lighting). It is likely that this feat of stagecraft exacerbated the prevailing fear, making it seem entirely possible that an urbane professional man could, with no warning, suddenly become a ravening beast. By early September, the *Pall Mall Gazette* had already referred to the unidentified killer as 'Mr.

---

* The publication can be dated solely from the cover illustration, which shows a dead woman lying below a poster that refers to four murders.

Hyde at large', and on 29 September the final performance of *Dr Jekyll and Mr Hyde* was announced. The *Telegraph* spoke for many: 'there is no taste in London just now for horrors on the stage. There is quite sufficient to make us shudder out of doors.' However Mansfield's next play was panned. In need of a vehicle, he hastily scheduled a revival of *Jekyll and Hyde* 'owing to great demand'. His poor taste was deplored by many; others saw his insistence in continuing as more sinister. 'I should be the Last to think because A man take A dretfull Part he is therefore Bad,' wrote one anonymous correspondent to the police, 'but when I went to See Mr Mansfield Take the Part of Dr Jekel and Mr Hyde I felt at once that he was *the Man Wanted ... I do not think there is A man Living* So well able to disgise Himself in A moment ... *Who So well able to Baffel the Police*, or Public he Could be A *dark man*. Fair Man. Short man. or Tall in A five Seconds if he carried a fine Faulse Wiskers &c in A Bag.'

While Mansfield does not seem to have been troubled by the police, or by a nervy populace, others were not so lucky. A drunken German accosted two women he thought were prostitutes, and a mob gathered around him, shouting 'Jack the Ripper'. (He was found guilty of 'frightening the women ... at a time when they would easily be frightened', and sentenced to a month's hard labour.) Another man was reported for suspicious behaviour because 'he carried a black bag and his actions were very strange'. The following month, still another man was suspected because he 'stared into the face of a woman in Whitechapel-road'.

Some were more complicit: a seamstress in Bradford was found to have sent a letter saying 'Jack' was planning 'a little business' in that city. And any murder of a woman was automatically attributed to 'Jack', no matter how far from the pattern it appeared. Jane Beetmoor was murdered near Gateshead, and it was thought a good use of police resources to send an officer connected with the Whitechapel murders and the surgeon who had performed the post-mortem on Mrs Chapman to Newcastle, despite the fact that Jane Beetmoor had not been mutilated, and her young man, who had been seen with her on the night of her death, had vanished. In Glasgow, reported *The*

All the newspapers were gripped by the murders committed by the unknown 'Jack the Ripper', and each new death saw their circulation soar. Here the middle-class *Illustrated London News* shows a restrained image, of the Vigilance Committee set up to patrol the streets.

Times solemnly, the police were taking 'extra precautions': if they heard 'any cry of distress, such as "Help", "Murder", or "Police", they are to hasten to the spot at once'. (What, one wonders, had their instructions been before?)

In Whitechapel, locals formed Vigilance Committees to patrol the streets. While no murders took place throughout October, 'Jack' was a busy correspondent. On 1 October, just after the double murder, a postcard was received that appears to have been written by the person who wrote the 'Dear Boss' letter: 'I was not codding dear old Boss

447

when I gave you the tip, you'll hear about Saucy Jacky's work tomorrow double event this time number one squealed a bit couldn't finish
straight off. had not the time to get ears for police ...' This harping on
removing organs to send somewhere became an actuality on 16
October, when George Lusk, of the Whitechapel Vigilance Committee,
received a parcel which contained the following note:

> From hell.
> Mr Lusk,
> Sor
> I send you half the Kidne I took from one woman prasarved it for you
> tother piece I fried and ate it was very nise. I may send you the bloody
> knif that took it out if you only wate a whil longer
> ... Catch me when you can Mishter Lusk

With this was a piece of something, although what exactly, was never
determined: the newspaper reports ranged from the view that it was
an animal kidney, to 'half of the left kidney of an alcoholic woman
aged around forty-five' (that is, a description of Mrs Eddowes), to the
Evening News' headline: '... HALF THE VICTIM'S MISSING
KIDNEY RESTORED. THE OTHER HALF EATEN BY THE
CANNIBAL ASSASSIN'.*

Fun magazine now printed a poem which blamed Scotland Yard
for all the ills of the investigation, while exonerating the beat police.
(The first verse refers to the grafitto found near Mrs Eddowes' body,
and Sir Charles Warren's action in having it removed.)

> Some horrid murders have been done
> All in the slums of Whitechapel.
> The 'Bobbies' up and down have run

---

* Sherlock Holmes reflected this aspect of the case too: in 'The Adventure of the
Cardboard Box', a spinster in Croydon receives two ears in the post, just as Mr Lusk had
received the 'kidne'. She suggests that they may have been sent by medical students for a
joke, but Holmes knows better: 'who but their murderer would have sent this sign of his
work ...?'

To find a clue, but sad to tell,
The only link, a written scrawl
Too early in the dawning day;
It was upon a dirty wall,
Some busybody wiped away.

Now Jack the Ripper, with his knife,
Goes safely down the busy street,
Alert to take another life,
Nor shirks a 'Bobbie' when they meet.
We do not mean, nor would we say,
That the police are aught to blame.
A true and trusty band are they,
As records of their deeds proclaim.

If possible to hunt him down,
They'll catch him yet upon the wing.
Tho' some may sneer, and some may frown,
And talk of red tape blundering,
'The Force' is no blind booby lot –
They're clever men, alert and 'game',
And ill deserve a sneer or blot
Upon their courage and their name.

Tho', doubtless, sometimes they may make
In all their careful best laid schemes,
A seeming blunder or mistake,
Of what the wisest never dream.
But bear in mind, they are but men
(Since first created men have erred),
One cannot do the work of ten,
And they are ruled by Scotland Yard.

Warren had had enough. He wrote an article responding to the criticism, all of which had been 'stirred up', he complained, by 'restless demagogues'. The piece is a combination of extreme tedium – a long history of the Met, the legal statutes that underpin the force, disciplinary methods and hiring practices – and a proper whinge. The newspaper mockery had clearly driven this former soldier, unused to public oversight, well past breaking point. 'Peace and order,' he warned in his opening, 'will be imperilled if the citizens ... continue ... in embarrassing those who are responsible for the security of the Metropolis.' This is a revealing elision: Warren thinks the *knowledge* of police failure would lead to lessened public safety, not the police failure itself – civil unrest by embarrassment. That this was not simply bad syntax, but something he believed, is clear, for he went on to say that the 12,000 police in the city were necessary because the public had 'an unreasoning habit of cavilling and finding fault'. Decent people, he added, should realize that bringing the police into contempt was a way of 'encouraging the mob to disorder and rapine, and it very much increases the police rate'. After this Warren was directly forbidden to publish any more. He was also in conflict with the Home Office over who would control police budgets; the Bloody Sunday riots and the failure of the CID in Whitechapel cannot have helped. Warren resigned on 8 November.

The next night, 9 November, Mary Jane (sometimes Mary Anne) Kelly was murdered, in the most savage attack yet. Mrs Kelly's death was atypical: she was twenty years younger than the other women, although she too was an alcoholic prostitute; and she was the only one to be murdered indoors. She was found in her room in Miller's Court around mid-morning. The police waited for two hours after the discovery before entering her room: they had sent for Warren's bloodhounds, not knowing that the useless animals, imposed on the CID by the baying press, had long since been sent back to their owner. Or, as one flash song said simply: 'Assistance soon arrived but as usual was too late.'

Once inside the room, the police found that the scale of the violence was truly shocking. The murderer, indoors, had been able to indulge his desire for mutilation to the extreme. At the inquest, this time it was the coroner who refused to permit a description of the mutilations to be given, but by the next day most of the newspapers carried reports which included a description of Mrs Kelly's body as it was found, and the blood-soaked condition of the room. The descriptions were detailed, and over the next week they became progressively more so – on 12 November the *Pall Mall Gazette*, which had hitherto concentrated on the lack of solution and the failures of the police, printed a positively ghoulish piece describing Mrs Kelly as she lay in the mortuary; the *Telegraph, Globe* and *Evening News* all discussed at length the state of the body, the mutilations, and whether or not organs were missing.

Other stories examined Mrs Kelly's background. As with crime victims from Maria Marten and Ellen Hanley onwards, a certain amount of tidying-away of less attractive details was done. In the half-century plus of retellings, these earlier victims had been transformed from fallen women to 'the pride of the village'; some newspapers now tried to do the same for Mrs Kelly. She was, the *Globe* advised in the week after her death, not Irish but Welsh, an important distinction, separating her from the large, predominantly impoverished Irish community in the East End. She was also – and here the reports moved into the realm of penny-dreadfuls and melodrama – 'an artist of no mean degree' and 'an excellent scholar' who had been led astray by an evil Frenchwoman. This was virtually a sensation-novel plot, but it was only an extreme version of the way the newspapers had blurred the distinction between fact and fiction. Sometimes it was overt, with the cunning murderer, according to *Lloyd's*, appearing like 'the shadowy and wilful figures in Poe's and Stevenson's novels'. Elsewhere the real and fictional characters were merged, as when the *Observer* listed its suspects: the 'highly respectable householder during the day and an assassin at night. The Socialists, an escaped lunatic, the Jews, an unknown man who murdered twelve negro women in Texas, a chimpanzee, a butcher's slaughterman, and a jealous woman ... and, finally, a dark soul who has been supping on melodrama' – *Jekyll and Hyde*, Poe (the chimpanzee) and East End melodramas.

The newspapers had been the most notable element of the entertainment industry's response to the crimes, because of the quantity of their coverage. But others had not lagged behind. Madame Tussaud's, usually so quick off the mark, found itself shut out this time, because no murderer's face was known, and the gallery had made verisimilitude its selling point.* This troubled the makeshift East End exhibitions far less, if at all. While the crimes were still continuing, a waxworks in the Whitechapel Road displayed effigies of the murdered women, as well as the unknown murderer. An illustration outside advertised the exhibition, but given the public's heightened fears, it was considered 'too strong', and removed, although no one seems to have stopped the show itself. By the spring of 1889 Jack the Ripper exhibitions were a commercial proposition. An advertisement appeared in the *Era* for 'The Wax Head of "Jack the Ripper", carefully Modelled from Sketches published in the "Daily Telegraph", Furnished by witnesses who had actually seen him, also a Wax Head of Mary Jeanette [sic] Kelly, hi[s] last victim'. From the surrounding advertisements, it appears that this was placed by a manufacturer who supplied heads to waxworks exhibitions (it follows an advertisement offering 'Seals, Guaranteed Feeders, Eighty Serpents, for Charming ...'). By 1892, D'Arc's Waxworks in Cardiff was advertising in the same professional classifieds: 'Wanted, to Buy a Set of Jack the Ripper Victims'.

Fiction writers were quick off the mark too. After the double murder on 30 September, J.F. Brewer's *The Curse upon Mitre Square* immediately took Mrs Eddowes' death and its location as its theme. The novel opens in 1530, when the monastery of Holy Trinity Church, Aldgate, is threatened at the dissolution of the monasteries. The evil Thomas Audley, Speaker of the House of Commons, is promised the proceeds from this particular monastery if he can find a plausible excuse to shut it down. Brother Martin, suffering a breakdown, meets a mysterious woman, murders her, dances on the corpse and then

---

* However, Marie Belloc Lowndes' *The Lodger*, a fine Ripper novel of 1913 (outside the time-span of this book), meshes the two when the mysterious lodger/murderer confronts the landlady who has penetrated his disguise in the Chamber of Horrors.

mutilates the body as Mrs Eddowes' would later be mutilated, before discovering that, set up by Audley, he has murdered his long-lost sister. Martin commits suicide, and the monastery falls into Audley's hands, with only a ghost to mark the spot. The second section takes place in the eighteenth century, at the Mitre Pub, where the publican and his friends mock the ghost; 'liquid fire' appears from the heavens, striking the 'fatal slab of stone', and killing ten. In the final part, we return to Whitechapel in 1888: 'Measure this spot as carefully as you will, and you will find that the piece of ground on which Catherine Eddowes lies is the exact point where the steps of the high altar of Holy Trinity existed ... Who is there so bold as to say ... that there is no *Curse upon Mitre Square?*'

Despite being published by a mainstream, middle-class fiction publisher, this story has the schlock-horror feel of a penny-dreadful. More respectable was a novel that appeared the year after the killings.* 'John Law' was the pseudonym of Margaret Harkness, who had written on the impoverished workers of the East End. This also formed the basis for *Captain Lobe: A Story of the Salvation Army*, where in one chapter the Salvation Army captain hears the deathbed confession of a Jewish butcher, who relates how his work produced unnatural longings: 'I wanted to see the blood, and feel it all warm on my fingers,' he tells Lobe. 'It grew, that thirst did ... I got to feel at last that nothing would quench my thirst but human blood, human flesh ...' He therefore murders 'a miserable-looking woman', before the shock restores him to his senses. 'I left the place, and I hid myself here among the Jews, who hate blood and never spill it. I'm not a Jew, I'm a Gentile ...' he adds, before expiring.

Many novels used elements from Jack the Ripper like this, merely trading on the sensational elements. Mrs Braddon worked out the ideas of doubling and madness more thoroughly in *Thou Art the Man* (1894), in which she revived the now slightly old-fashioned female

---

* It was, of course, only in retrospect that one could say when the series of murders ended. As late as 1890, any woman murdered by a knife, or a prostitute murdered by any method, was frequently introduced in the press as another Ripper killing.

who turns to detection to rescue her doomed lover. Brandon Mountford has 'a strain of madness in his blood' and also suffers from epilepsy; his fears that he will waken 'one day a creature of demoniac impulses, transformed from man to devil' seem to bear fruit when he revives after an attack next to the corpse of a murdered woman. When his lover helps him escape to Africa, she wonders if 'this first crime might not be the beginning of a series of murders?'

The link between the East End murders and the 'savagery' of 'darkest Africa' had already appeared in 1891, in *Back to Africa* by William Westall. Westall usually wrote historical romances, but here the narrator, the educated daughter of a doctor and a scientist herself, marries an explorer recently escaped from Africa, where he had been held captive by a cannibal tribe. Gradually it becomes clear to the reader that he had not been a captive as he claimed, but had rather been the king of the tribe, and is now continuing his cannibalistic habits in the East End. That same year, *The House of Mystery* by J.W. Nicholas also relied on a Jack the Ripper character in a melange of stolen children, mesmerism, hidden corpses, dogs that could sniff out impostors, and more.

Given the poor quality of these books, it is all the more remarkable that Jack the Ripper also influenced some of the greatest works of fiction. A novel that was originally thought of in the melodrama, or even penny-dreadful school, but whose extraordinary boundary-breaking nature was quickly recognized, appeared in 1897. On 6 October 1888, the *East London Advertiser* wrote that 'It is so impossible to account ... for these revolting acts of blood, that ... the myths of the Dark Ages rise before the imagination. Ghouls, vampires, bloodsuckers, and all the ghastly array of fables which have been accumulated throughout the course of centuries ... seize hold of the excited fancy.' In March 1890, Henry Irving's business manager made his first note for a novel about those ghouls, vampires and bloodsuckers – his name was Bram Stoker, and the novel was *Dracula*. While *Dracula* is about much more than a Ripper-type murderer, the 1888 crimes, and the sensations that surround them, are woven throughout the novel. Five women are attacked and mutilated by the vampire, as five women were murdered in Whitechapel; one character is a doctor, as the Ripper was suspected of being; the vampire-hunter van Helsing carries a black bag, as the Ripper was thought to have done; he and his friends form what Stoker in his notes calls a 'vigilante committee' to trap the mysterious being that threatens their community. And overall, the unnamed fear of the 'other', the stranger – particularly the Eastern European stranger – is as rampant in *Dracula* as it was in Whitechapel.

Perhaps, though, the strongest Ripper element was another entirely unspoken one, that of the doubling, the man who presents two faces to the world. Stevenson's *Jekyll and Hyde* created one of the archetypes of doubling, and a variation on the theme was developed by Oscar Wilde in *The Picture of Dorian Gray*, which was published in *Lippincott's Monthly Magazine* in June 1890, only two months after Stoker made his first note. Not coincidentally, it was at the same dinner party that Wilde was commissioned to write this story and Conan Doyle *The Sign of Four*. The febrile atmosphere of London during these years of uncertainty and fear, the sense that no one was what he seemed, that everyone might have a secret life, was an influence on Wilde's frank, open, beautiful Gray, with his sinister portrait hidden away. Gray has 'mysterious and prolonged absences' from home, giving rise to 'strange conjecture', while 'there are other stories – stories that you have been seen creeping at dawn out of dreadful houses and slinking in disguise into the foulest dens in London'. Ultimately Dorian becomes a murderer, killing the painter who created his portrait, and cutting up his body.

The case of Jack the Ripper also influenced fictional accounts across the world. Several novels (some truly fiction, some claiming to be 'real' accounts of the killer) were published in the USA from 1888 onwards. A particularly enjoyable example is a dime-novel (an American cousin of the penny-dreadful), *Lord Jacquelin Burkney* by 'Rodissi', the pseudonym of Jacob Ringgold, a man who had clearly never set foot in England. Burkney, the 'heir to an English Lord', is disinherited after falling in love with a poor but honest shopgirl. He moves to France, where he becomes 'the most adroit and scientific dissector in all Paris'. On his father's death he returns to Burkney Manor, 'a real Sir Christopher Wren house', where his devoted servants refer to him with remarkable impartiality as 'Your highness' or 'Your lordship'. He leaves these quaint West Country customs behind and heads for London, where he meets his old love, now a streetwalker. He murders her, using his 'old skill' as anatomizer to remove her heart, which he 'toyed with' amid 'peals of demoniacal laughter'. He then takes up slaughtering prostitutes wholesale, the locations and the descriptions matching the Ripper killings, including some of the wilder press rumours, such as the Gateshead murder, before returning to his Christopher Wren house where, after communing with his dead father, he writes a final letter: '… THE AVENGER HAS COME! I SHALL SMITE THEM ALL!'

Back in the UK, ballad-writers had been busy. By the early 1880s the street stalls on the New Cut, near what had been the Victoria Theatre (and was now a coffee room and temperance hall), each carried 'about a hundred grimy octavos', magazines and books, as well as a hundred or so ballads covering murders from Maria Marten and the Red Barn, through the more recent cases. We know little about these sheets, as few have survived. Their audiences, however, were probably wider than is generally credited. One collection of murder broadsides and pamphlets in the British Library carries a bookplate naming its original owner as Alfred Harmsworth, later the founder of the *Daily Mail*. But little remains today: just a few scattered mentions appear in the press of 'printed pamphlets relating to the Whitechapel murder', and pamphlets entitled 'The Whitechapel Blood Book' and 'A Complete History of the Whitechapel Horrors'.

One series of sheets has survived: the first is illustrated on the front with a drawing of a garishly uplit man waving a knife over a supine woman, while the reverse has a prose account of the double murder, followed by a defiantly cheerful comic song:

Now ladies all beware or you'll get caught in a snare,
They seem to say the devil's running loose,
With a big knife in his hand, he trots throughout the land,
And with all the ladies means to play the deuce,
He's a knockout I declare, here there and everywhere,
And to catch him we all know they've had a try,
He's got the laugh as yet, but his day will come you bet,
And he'll play his little game out bye and bye.

CHORUS:
As [sic] any one seen him, can you tell us where he is,
If you meet him you must take away his knife,
Then give him to the women, they'll spoil his pretty fiz,
And I would'nt give him twopence for his life.

Now they've searched the underground, and all the country round,
In every hole and corner so they say,
But he comes out of a night, and puts us all in a fright,
And he manages somehow to get away,
We can't tell if we're standing on our heads or on our heels,
While mystery these crimes still enshrouds,
We must ask Professor Baldwin to go up in his baloon,
And see if he can find him in the clouds.

Now Mrs. Pott's says she, I'd let the villian see,
If I had him here I'd sure to make him cough,
I'd chop off all his toes, then his ears and then his nose,
And I'd make him such a proper drop of broth,
His hat and coat I'd stew and flavour it with glue,
Blackbeetles, mottled soap, and boil the lot,
I've got a good sized funnel I'd stick it in his guzzle,
And make [the] humbug eat it boiling hot.

Now at night when your undressed, and about to go to rest,
Just see that he ain't underneath the bed
If he is you must'nt shout but politely drag him out.
And with your poker tap him on the head,
So look out Jack the ripper we're on your blooming track,
There's a pretty piece of rope for you in store,
We'll give you beans old bogey, then good old ripper Jack,
He'll never go out killing anymore.

There were also two songs to be sung, the reader is informed, to the tune of 'My Village Home'. A later compilation, *Jack the Ripper at Work Again*, contained five songs, including the comic song above, and appears to have been put together from earlier broadsides. In September 1888 the *Daily News* reported that 'men with verses round their hats' were singing flash songs to the tune of 'My Village Home' everywhere in Whitechapel, and the *Observer*'s 'Special Reporter' saw three 'mere girls' singing a flash song 'in praise of the dread "Jack the Ripper"'. The same reporter later heard 'itinerant vendors of street literature' shouting ''Ere you are. All about Jack the Ripper,' while another offered 'The truth about the Vitechapel murders'. MacNaghten, in those memoirs that proved so unreliable in the case of Eleanor Pearcey, remembered the following piece of doggerel in the Ripper files when he joined Scotland Yard in 1889:

I'm not a butcher, I'm not a Yid,
Nor yet a foreign Skipper,
But I'm your own light-hearted friend,
Yours truly, Jack the Ripper.

This sounds more like the refrain from a flash song than anything of use to a detective. A more middle-class approach appeared in the *Sporting Times* the week after the murders of Mrs Stride and Mrs Eddowes. It is a poem of 'slumming ... down the dark frowsy East'. The narrator recounts how

The *Tele*'s [i.e. the *Telegraph*'s] narration of each mutilation
So fascinates me since I've taken it,
That if 'Jack the Ripper' had tipped me his flipper
I really believe I'd have shaken it.
And though all this reading 'bout cutting and bleeding
Is unhealthy stuff at the best of it,
It's better than 'Marriage a Failure', and 'What
Shall we do with our girls?' and the rest of it ...

The sporting papers regularly referred to the East End rather insou-
ciantly as 'Jack the Ripper land', and in October this attitude attracted
hostility. The *Belfast News-Letter* reported that at a coursing event a
dog named Jack the Ripper was announced, to the jeers and hoots of
the crowd, which cheered when it lost. By December, however, the
dog appeared again, quietly taking its place with no comment at all
from the newspaper; in 1890 three more dogs with the same name
appear in the coursing reports, again without any editorial remarks.
From 1889 a number of horses named Jack the Ripper appeared, both
racehorses and hunters – at least ten different animals in the next
eight years. Not a single newspaper found the name worthy of
remark.*

The reality was that while the murders were terrifying to those who
lived in Whitechapel, many who lived elsewhere, and did not feel
personally threatened, were perfectly happy to accept them as part of
daily life: after the double murder, 'Zadkiel's Almanac' for 1889 was
advertised in *The Times*: 'Zadkiel foretold the rainy summer, the
Whitechapel Murders, &c.' – there wasn't much difference to the

---

* Horses seemed to receive special licence for names or phrases that would be otherwise
beyond the pale: in 1881, the racehorse Filho da Puta appeared in the lists, also without
comment. It was not until the twentieth century that the registration of racehorses' names
became established, and those that were vulgar, offensive or had unpleasant links were
banned. Today, says Weatherby's, the central administrative offices of British horseracing,
Jack the Ripper would not be permitted (much less Myra Hindley or Harold Shipman). In
1864, such censorship would have been considered an outrage: *Bell's* 'Rough Notes on Turf
Nomenclature' begins: 'It is but natural and proper that every man should call his own
horse by the name which seems best to himself.'

publisher, apparently, between the weather and violent death. Others made jokes. This wasn't something shamefaced, to be done privately. The genteel *Myra's Journal of Dress and Fashion* carried an advertisement for M.J. Haynes & Co., in Peckham, which sold 'Specialities' (below): 'The Great SURPRISE WATCH', had 'a secret spring, which liberates a noted character, namely, "Jack the Ripper", to the horror and astonishment of all beholders. Price. 1/3 each, three for 3/6.' More fun could be had from a parlour game, with, at its centre 'the familiar but sinister subject of Jack the Ripper ... The mysterious object of the policeman's vigilance and the newspaper man's imagination has to escape through a series of squares, past twelve constables and twelve reporters ... This game will hardly commend itself to heads of families,' acknowledged the *Pall Mall Gazette* in January 1889, only two months after the murder of Mrs Kelly, but it highlighted it in its 'Shows in the London Shops' column nonetheless.

Even less did theatrical versions commend themselves to the respectable. In September 1889 the British allowed themselves a frisson of luxurious disgust at the decadence of foreigners. The *Era* reported, 'Horrible but true! Jack the Ripper is to make his apparition on the stage' in Paris. The *Pall Mall Gazette* added that 'A Dutch version is filling an Amsterdam theatre nightly, and an American version is being played at the Brooklyn Opera House.' *Jack l'Éventreur*,

M. J. HAYNES & CO.'S Specialities.
EVERY HOUSEHOLDER SHOULD SEND FOR THEM.

The Famous Model STEAM DANCING NIGGER' "Rare good fun" for the long dull winter evenings. Will dance for ONE HOUR at each operation. Price, 1/9 and 2/9 each.

THE BOY'S OWN STEAM ENGINE, works splendidly. Price, 1/3 each.

The Great SURPRISE WATCH, a lovely Nickel Silver Watch and Chain; on showing same to your friends you ask them what it is worth, and so on, and just as they are about to take hold of it you press a secret spring, which liberates a noted character, namely, "Jack the Ripper," to the horror and great astonishment of all beholders. Price, 1/3 each, three for 3/6.

The Great SURPRISE CIGAR CASE, on handing same to your friend to help himself, just as he is about to take a cigar, y· u press a secret spring, when an "Old Man or Woman" instantly appears, pointing with their fingers to the nose, as much as to say, "Ah, would you!" Price, 1/3 each; three for 3/6.

"OH, LOR! WHAT WON-DERFUL NOVELTIES! SO CHEAP AND GOOD. TOO." **The Great ELECTRIC FUSEE CASE (Nickel Silver).** On handi g same to your friend he immediately drops it, as he feels a sharp electric current pass through the body, Immense fun. Price 1/9 each

The Great SINGING CANARY SCARF PIN. A Splendid Novelty, worn by Ladies and Gents, in their dress, richly enamelled; owner can cause the Bird to sing splendidly without the slightest detection whatever: Bird moves both back and tail while singing. Price, 2/6 each.

by Gaston Marot and Louis Péricaud, opened in Paris in August 1889. Sir Stevens, the head of the London police, arranges to have Ketty, the girlfriend of Jackson, the man suspected of committing 'le crime de Piccadilly', followed by one of his secret force of women detectives. Jackson has meanwhile disguised himself as 'sir Peters Wild', the New York Chief of Police. The fact that the supposed American has a title does not tip Sir Stevens off, and thus he outlines to the disguised criminal all his plans. Ketty catches Jackson in the act of killing an informer and, 'recoiling with horror', she says 'Ah!' as the curtain falls. In the next act we learn that she has attempted to commit suicide by throwing herself into the 'Tamise', after which 'La Blackornn', a procuress, reveals to her that she is in reality the long-lost daughter of Sir James Plack, stolen by La Blackornn in infancy. Ketty still wants to die, but is not brave enough to attempt suicide again, so she returns to Jackson, 'to kill myself by you'. Jackson refuses, revealing just as the police burst in that he too was stolen as a child, and that his mother is La Blackornn. This newly found mother throws herself in front of him to save him as the police fire, and is killed as Jackson and Ketty escape. In the final act, Jackson is burgling Sir James's house when Sir Stevens providentially appears: 'In the name of the Queen, I arrest you!' Jackson: 'Ah! Jack l'Éventreur dies! But Jack l'Éventreur is not dead! For others will replace him to revenge the Newgate hanged!' (According to the *Era*, this brought a round of applause from the audience.) Ketty, who has apparently undergone a conversion in the previous eyeblink, says, 'Oh, shut up! I hate you!' Jackson: 'You hate me? Then I am glad to die. (Dies.)' And the comic amateur detective gets the curtain line: 'I have saved England!' According to *Lloyd's*, Jackson wore a Glengarry cap and a tartan cape, and the orchestra played 'God Save the Queen' as he died.

It was not until 1893 that a theatrical work of any quality grew out of the subject. When it did, however – as with *Dracula* – it produced a work of seminal importance. Frank Wedekind's two 'Lulu' plays, *Erdgeist* (*Earth Spirit*, 1893) and *Die Büchse der Pandora* (*Pandora's Box*, 1904), follow Lulu, a cabaret dancer who first rises in the world then falls into the abyss, finally, as a streetwalker in London, bringing home 'Jack', and meeting death at his hands.* Jack, played by Wedekind himself in the first production, is 'A thickset figure with elastic movements, a pale face, inflamed eyes, scrofulous nose, a high, strong, forehead, and a drooping moustache, tangled side-curls, bright red hands with chewed nails.' He is, in fact, a compilation of standard stage-devil figures, with more than a touch of stage Jew (when he argues over Lulu's price, he says, 'I am not Baron Rotschild'). He takes Lulu into a back room, and she cries, 'He's ripping me open!' (Jack's part, and Lulu's when she speaks to him, are in heavily Germanified English in the original.) After her death, he reflects on his crime as he washes up: 'That is a phenomen [sic], what would not happen every two hundred years ... When I am dead and my collection is put up to auction, the London Medical Club will pay a sum of threehundred [sic] pounds for that prodigy, I have conquered this night ...'

British theatres did not follow suit. *The Doctor's Shadow*, by H.A. Saintsbury (who as an actor would later give more than 1,400 performances as the detective in Gillette's *Sherlock Holmes*), was staged in Accrington in 1896, but after a few token nods to the Ripper it relied more heavily on *Dr Jekyll and Mr Hyde*. A few music-hall performers also touched on the subject, but little information has survived. In 1889 a performance was said to be 'based on' the death of Mrs Kelly, but what that means is unknown. In 1892, at the Royal Albert, Canning Town, Miss Edith Manley, 'extempore vocalist', produced topical songs on subjects chosen by her audience, including Gladstone, Keir Hardie (who had recently become the area's MP) and Jack the Ripper, but while the reviewer judged her performance 'equal to the occasion', he gave no particulars.

The real legacy of Jack the Ripper was as an archetype, and it seems only appropriate that this faceless, internationally renowned killer should have become enmeshed with one of the most recognizable detective archetypes of all time. With Sherlock Holmes, everything

* These two plays formed the basis of two further works of art, G.W. Pabst's film *Pandora's Box* (1929), starring Louise Brooks, and Alban Berg's opera *Lulu* (1937); but they fall outside the time-span of this book.

suddenly pulled together. Holmes is, as the amateurs of sensation-fiction had been, middle-class, and he detects not for money (even though he is frequently paid) but for an abstract sense of justice, or the love of knowledge: 'I play the game for the game's own sake.' He earns his reputation not as a concerned relative, and not because of his social position, but because of his slowly and laboriously acquired knowledge, and his talents – the reader is given to understand that we could all become detectives if only we worked at it; a very democratizing idea.

Other stories missed this fine balance. *Reaping the Whirlwind*, a boys' adventure story, has its detective help the rightful heir win back his landed estate; as a reward he is made its land agent, as though a gentlemanly life in the country were every man's desire. In *Martin Hewitt, Investigator*, Hewitt is a young legal clerk who sets up on his own as a detective. But in one case, although he works out who committed a crime, he does nothing, because, 'I'm not a policeman … Of course, if anybody comes to me to do it as a matter of business, I'll take it up …'* One set of stories is aimed too high, one too low, for the middle-class audience. While Holmes frequently allows criminals to escape, he does so to fit in with his notions of justice rather than law.

In the earliest detective stories James McLevy and his cohorts wrote about the slums; Andrew Forrester and his about ducal jewel thefts. Although the later Sherlock Holmes moves up in the world, in his early days he was situated between the two, like his readers. Many of the stories are set in suburbia, where his readers lived, and tap into everyday details that resonated with them. 'It is my belief, Watson,' says Holmes, '… that the lowest and vilest alleys in London do not present a more dreadful record of sin than does the smiling and beautiful countryside.' Holmes could not have thought that in the days of

---

* Martin Hewitt also investigates a case where a runner is prevented from entering a race to benefit some gamblers. One of the characters is called Steggles, and if the schoolboy P.G. Wodehouse did not read this story aged thirteen, before going on to write 'The Great Sermon Handicap' (1922), in which a crooked bookie named Steggles rigs a bet, then I will eat my deerstalker.

The Mysteries of London, or even of *The Boy Detective* – and what is more, had he done so, the books would not have sold. But by the end of the century, in 'The Adventure of the Greek Interpreter', the interpreter, after a nasty adventure, is dumped in a dark street, and is reassured when a stranger tells him, 'If you walk on a mile or so, to Clapham Junction … you'll just be in time for the last [train] to Victoria.' It was the safety, the security of that suburban, domestic, middle-class world, with crime safely tucked away where decent people did not venture, that readers craved after the horrors of 1888.

For several years, every time a woman was knifed, the newspapers worried that another Ripper murder had occurred. Similar knife-murders in other parts of the world were also reported, with the suggestion that 'Jack' had fled to wherever that week's crime had taken place. When Mrs Hogg was found dead in 1890, *Lloyd's* meant to soothe fears: 'When the murder at first was bruited abroad the alarming rumour spread that Jack the Ripper had been at work in the locality, and had cut off a woman's head. The inquiries made by our representative, however, seem to show that this latest atrocity was not perpetrated in the manner associated with that individual's operation'.

Some could not let the matter go. Two years after the murders, a newspaper vendor was prosecuted for false pretences after he shouted, 'Another horrible murder and mutilation. Jack the Ripper at work again.' (He received thirty-one days' hard labour, ostensibly because he had a record, but surely at least in part because of the still-ready-to-be-ignited fears.) At the height of the murders, the police had received over a thousand letters a week. A year later, there were still enough arriving for Scotland Yard to use pre-printed forms to acknowledge receipt of these missives. Some of them were less repeats of the past than symbols of the future. One was said to have been marked with a bloody thumbprint. *The Times* reminded its readers that 'The surface markings on no two thumbs are alike,' and suggested that the many suspects should be summoned to have their thumbs compared with the print.

This was remarkably up-to-date. Fingerprinting had been pioneered in India, when Sir William Herschel, a magistrate in Bengal, had used a system of prints for legal documents. The scientist Francis Galton also worked on the subject, showing that fingerprints were unique to each individual, and did not alter over time. Herschel had promoted his system to a civil servant, Edward Henry, who developed a method of classification and identification that was simple to use and relatively reliable, taking in Galton's classification, storage and retrieval systems. In 1901 Henry was appointed to the CID, and within months he had set up a central fingerprint office. By 1902 the first conviction on fingerprint evidence was secured: at the Old Bailey, Harry Jackson was found guilty of stealing billiard balls from a house which, unfortunately for him, had freshly painted windowsills. In 1903, even fiction had caught up: in 'The Adventure of the Norwood Builder', Inspector Lestrade of Scotland Yard points out a mark on the wall to Sherlock Holmes: 'You are aware that no two thumb-marks are alike,' he says, showing him a 'waxen print' that he had taken from his suspect. Holmes, now sounding distinctly behind the times, murmurs only, 'I have heard something of the kind.'

But before that, in 1898, another of those not-very-good, cashing-in novels appeared. Guy Boothby's *The Lust of Hate* has a mysterious Dr Nikola who lives 'in luxury' in a disused warehouse decorated with 'at least a dozen valuable pictures', waited on by a deaf-mute Chinese servant. He kills his enemies by decoying them into a specially fitted-out hansom cab, whose cushions are filled with anaesthetic gas. Once the victim is unconscious, the seat revolves and the body drops out, to be found dead in the middle of a lonely road. The bodies are all similarly mutilated by the seat's mechanism as they fall.

The novel on its own has nothing of interest, but with this confection we have come full circle, returning once more to a penny-dreadful, a revolving chair through which murder victims are dropped, Sweeney Todd style. It is appropriate that this taste of the Demon Barber appears in a novel based on Jack the Ripper, for in many ways the two men are mirror images. While Sweeney Todd never existed, and the 1888 Whitechapel serial killer definitely did, everything we know about Jack the Ripper – his name, his persona, his reasons for killing – is the culmination of a century of murderous entertainment, of melodrama, of puppet shows, of penny-dreadfuls and more. The excitements, the fears and the sense that murder was a spectacle were all focused by the killings, and projected onto the blank screen of unknowingness created by the lack of solution to the crime. The Whitechapel murderer operated for ten weeks; 'Jack the Ripper' was the product of the entire previous century. And this mythical figure, in turn, opened the door to a new century of killing, a vastly less entertaining, and more frightening, proposition.

Murder had developed, as de Quincey had prophesied. An apparatus had developed around murder, a scaffolding: there was a police force now; there were detectives. There were stage shows featuring detectives, there were waxworks, puppet shows, songs and sketches; there were, perhaps most importantly of all, detective stories and novels. Crime fiction took this new scaffolding, and covered it with an attractive surface. Now it had a shape, and a *raison d'être*. The detective stands with his back to the fire: 'You may be wondering why I've summoned you all together,' he pronounces. No one wondered any more. Detection – in fiction, at any rate – made the world safe. The sleuth-hound would track down the murderers and bring them to justice; no longer would people have to look over their shoulders in fear. The cunning of the criminal was matched on stage, on the page, by the wisdom of the hunter.

Repeated over and over, this archetype became, in people's minds, reality. Most people in Britain had never had to worry about murder: by the nineteenth century it was vanishingly rare; by the start of the new century, therefore, a love of blood could be indulged in safely and securely, without any fear of an ugly reality bursting in. Instead, oceans of blood could cheerfully be poured across the stage, across the page, in song and sermon. Murder was, finally, a fine art.

ACKNOWLEDGEMENTS

A book of this nature is virtually a collaborative exercise, and my debts are correspondingly large. I would like to thank, for information or advice (and often both): Emily Alder, Zoë Anderson, Cathie Arrington, Peter E. Blau, Karen Amy Bourrier, Dagni Bredesen, Jen Cadwallader, Evangelos Calotychos, Honor Clerk, Natalie Cole, Julia Collins of Madame Tussaud's archive, Betty Cortus, David Crane, Matt Demakos, Barbara Dunlap, Anna Dzirkalis, Tony Fincham, Marguerite Finnigan, Sunie Fletcher, Elizabeth Foxwell, Ginger Frost, Tony Gee, the late Robin Gibson, Sheldon Goldfarb, Jonathan Green, Jill Grey, Philip Hoare, Tobias Hoheisel, Stephen Holcombe, Kellie Holzer, Jonathan Horne of Sampson & Horne Antiques, Nico Howson, Audrey Jaffe, Kathryn Johnson, Melisa Klimaszewski, Bernard Knight, Sarah LaDow, John Langbein, Bob Lapides, David Latané, Peter Lennon, John Lewis, Paul Lloyd, Michael McCaffery, Fiona MacCarthy, Carolyn McGrath, Kate Mattacks, Douglas Matthews, Chris Michaelides at the British Library, Liz Miller, Joanna S. Mink, Rosemarie Morgan, Richard Nemesvari, Gerry Newby, Katherine Newey, Robert Newsom, Lee O'Brien, Denis Paz, Caroline Radcliffe, Sharon Ragaz, Rama Rahimi, Alan Rauch, Chris Redmond, Paul Reis of Tattersall's, Malcolm Rigby, Gail L. Savage, Clemence Schultze, Patrick Scott, Malcolm Shifrin, Gary Simons, Brian Simpson, Robin Surtees, Fergal Tobin, Norman Vance, John Walker, Stephen White, Nick Wilson and Penny Parry-Williams at Weatherby's, Michael Wolff, Christian Wolmar and Frank Wynne.

Some of the above are 'virtual colleagues', members of the Victoria 19th-Century British Culture & Society mailbase, and I would once again like to record my thanks both to the listmembers and to Patrick Leary, who as listmaster creates and maintains both the content and the atmosphere of this haven of scholarly collegiality.

A great debt of gratitude is owed, as always, to Bill Hamilton: I fear this debt is not only growing, but may never be adequately repaid. Colin McDowell and Ravi Mirchandani frequently permitted me to spill gory details, and they hardly ever winced. At HarperCollins I am grateful to Graham Cook, Helen Ellis, Minna Fry, Sophie Goulden, Graham Holmes, Robert Lacey and Arabella Pike.

The Bodleian Library, the British Library (especially the staff of the Rare Books Room), Cambridge University Library, the Guildhall Library, the London Library (especially Amanda Corp, and Gosia Lawick of the inter-library loan department), the National Library of Scotland (especially Rebecca Parry and Veronica Denholm), the Victoria and Albert Theatre Museum, and their helpful staffs have provided much-needed assistance. I would like to record a particular debt of gratitude to Julie Ann Lambert, curator of the John Johnson Collection at the Bodleian Library, who ensured that I saw all the material I needed (and much that I didn't know I needed until she supplied it) while her collection was at the same time undergoing digitization.

NOTES

Magazine and newspaper references are cited by date, article title or page number.

1: Imagining Murder

1 *in the tea-urn*: Thomas de Quincey, *The Works of Thomas de Quincey*, gen. ed. Grevel Lindop (London, Pickering & Chatto, 2000–2003), vol. 6, pp.15–16.

one a year: Crime statistics for the first half of the nineteenth century are notoriously uncertain. It was only in 1856 that the Home Office began to compile national statistics; before 1843 execution figures did not even record the gender of those hanged. Interpretation, therefore, is always difficult. I have used the figures that are most generally accepted.

nearly ten million: Stanley H. Palmer, *Police and Protest in England and Ireland, 1780–1850* (Cambridge, Cambridge University Press, 1988), p.164.

62 per 100,000: The EU figures come from Cynthia Tavares and Geoffrey Thomas, 'Population and Social Conditions: Crime and Criminal Justice', in *Statistics in Focus*, 15, 2007, http://epp.eurostat.ec.europa.eu/cache/ITY_OFFPUB/KS-SF-08-019/EN/KS-SF-08-019-EN.PDF; the remaining figures are cited in *Foreign Policy Review*, September 2008.

2 *it was 113s.*: Linda Colley, *Britons: Forging the Nation, 1707–1837* (London, Pimlico, 1994), p.158.

3 *the right time*: These murders and John Williams' death have been compiled from: *Caledonian Mercury*, 14, 16, 19, 21, 28 December 1811, 4 January 1812; *Derby Mercury*, 12 December 1811; *Examiner*, 15 December 1811; *Hull Packet*, 17, 24 December 1811; *Ipswich Journal*, 14 December 1811; *Jackson's Oxford Journal*, 21 December 1811; *Leeds Mercury*, 14 December 1811; *Liverpool Mercury*, 13 December 1811; *Morning Chronicle*, 10, 11, 12, 13, 17, 18, 24, 25, 27, 28, 30 December 1811, 18 January 1812; *The Times*, 11, 12, 13, 16, 17, 21, 25, 28 December 1811; *Edinburgh Annual Register*, January 1812; *Gentleman's Magazine*, December 1811, January 1812.

4 *bloodthirsty children*: Patricia Anderson, *The Printed Image and the Transformation of Popular Culture, 1790–1860* (Oxford, Clarendon Press, 1991), p.22.

loose character and hasty temper: These broadsides are in the Bodleian Library, John Johnson Collection, in particular Crime 2.6, 2.7 and 2.8.

5 *shoes with Grecian ties*: Fairburn's *Account of the Dreadful Murder of Mr. Marr and Family, at their House In Ratcliff-Highway, on Saturday Night, December 7, 1811; including the Whole Investigation before The Coroner's Inquest, &c. &c.* (London, John Fairburn, 1811).

7 *not lame*: Cited in Thomas de Quincey, *On Murder*, ed. Robert Morrison (Oxford, Oxford University Press, 2006), pp.191–2n.

by a jury: J.J. Tobias, *Crime and Police in England, 1700–1900* (Dublin, Gill & Macmillan, 1979), p.128.

8 *to this mysterious gang*: No newspaper I have seen mentions these men after 14 December; presumably they were released for lack of corroborating evidence, or their lack of detailed knowledge of the murders.

acting on a system: Cited in Leon Radzinowicz, 'The Ratcliffe Murders', *Cambridge Law Journal*, 1956, p.40.

10 *hammer, on the stairs*: Dickens to Walter Thornbury, 15 September 1866, Charles Dickens, *The Letters of Charles Dickens*, The Pilgrim Edition, eds. Madeline House, Graham Storey, Kathleen Tillotson, et al. (Oxford, Clarendon Press, 1969–2002), vol. 11, p.247; Charles Dickens, *Dombey and Son*, ed. Peter Fairclough, intro. by Raymond Williams ([1846–8], Harmondsworth, Penguin, 1970), p.790.

undoubtedly be seen to be done: Lord Chief Justice Hewart ([1924] 1 KB 256), in the appeal to Rex v. Sussex Justices, Ex parte McCarthy.

11 *through its heart*: *Notes and Queries*, 11th ser., 5, January 1912, p.6.

Cannon Street Road: The scrapbook, with the undated reports, was cited as 'now in the rectory of St George's-in-the-East' by P.D. James and T.A. Critchley, *The Maul and the Pear Tree* (London, Sphere, 1987), p.228.

12 *Sir Thomas Lawrence*: *Pall Mall Gazette*, 'Some Relics at Mme Tussaud's', 14 August 1886. Julia Collins, the archivist at Madame Tussaud's, says that the portrait appears not to have survived.

no traces had yet been discovered: *Morning Chronicle*, 'Houses of Parliament', 18 January 1812.

such accumulated violence: Cited in James and Critchley, *The Maul and the Pear Tree*, pp.185–6.

13 *turnpike roads alone*: Palmer, *Police and Protest*, p.76.

in cases of Felony: Cited in Joseph F. King, *The Development of Modern Police History in the United Kingdom and the United States*, Criminology Studies, vol. 19 (Lewiston, NY, Edward Mellen Press, 2004), p.22.

Middlesex Justice Bill was passed: which became the Justice of the Peace, Metropolis Act, 32 Geo.III, c.53.

14 *write his own* Memoirs: Attributions of authorship of the four volumes include Maurice Descombres, L.F.J.L'Héritier and Émile Morice. See Howard G. Brown, 'Tips, Traps and Tropes: Catching Thieves in Post-Revolutionary Paris', in Clive Emsley and Hannah Shpayer-Makov, eds., *Police Detectives in History, 1750–1950* (Aldershot, Ashgate, 2006), pp.38–9; Ian Ousby, *Bloodhounds of Heaven: The Detective in English Fiction from Godwin to Doyle* (Cambridge, MA, Harvard University Press, 1976), p.46.

original English ones: Ousby, *Bloodhounds of Heaven*, p.46.

15 *Prevention and Detection of crimes*: Patrick Colquhoun, 'Treatise on the Police of the Metropolis', cited in Anthony Babington, *A House in Bow Street: Crime and the Magistracy, London, 1740–1881* (London, Macdonald, 1969), p.179.

and potential crime: J.M. Beattie, 'Early Detection: The Bow Street Runners in Late Eighteenth-century London', in Emsley and Shpayer-Makov, *Police Detectives in History*, p.20.

16 *40 per cent*: Ibid., pp.28–9.

17 *criminals and their cohorts*: Radzinowicz, 'The Ratcliffe Murders', pp.47–8.

most notorious offenders: *Morning Chronicle*, 'Houses of Parliament', 18 January 1812.

shown to be absurd: Cited in James and Critchley, *The Maul and the Pear Tree*, p.181.

Fouché's contrivances: David Taylor, *The New Police in Nineteenth-century England: Crime, Conflict and Control* (Manchester, Manchester University Press, 1997), p.19.

beleaguered fortress: Thomas de Quincey, *On Murder*, 'Postscript', p.98. This volume includes the key essays de Quincey wrote on the aesthetics of murder, which initially were published as: 'On the Knocking at the Gate in Macbeth', *London Magazine*, 8, October 1823, pp.353–6; 'On Murder Considered as One of the Fine Arts', *Blackwood's Magazine*, 21, February 1827, pp.199–213; 'Second Paper on Murder Considered as One of the Fine Arts', *Blackwood's Magazine*, 46, November 1839, pp.661–8; 'Postscript', *Selections Grave and Gay* (Edinburgh, 1854), pp.60–111. There is also a short story, 'The Avenger', which appeared in *Blackwood's Magazine*, 44, August 1838, pp.208–33.

18 *colossal sublimity*: De Quincey, *On Murder*, p.10.

an orange and a lemon colour: Ibid., p.100; clothes, p.101.

than street thug: I owe this interpretation to Laurence Senelick, 'The Prestige of Evil: The Murderer as Romantic Hero from Sade to Lacenaire', PhD thesis, Harvard University, 1972, pp.138–46.

19 *copious effusion of blood*: De Quincey, *On Murder*, p.32.

2: Trial by Newspaper

22 *more than one jurisdiction*: Kellow Chesney, *The Victorian Underworld* (Harmondsworth, Penguin, 1972), pp.267, 269.

23 *performing the part*: George Borrow, *Lavengro; The Scholar – the Gypsy – the Priest* ([1851], New York, Dover, 1991), p.157.

for their skins: Eric Partridge, *A Dictionary of Slang and Unconventional English*, 5th edn (London, Routledge & Kegan Paul, 1961).

and metropolitan thieves: George Borrow, *The Zincali; or, An Account of the Gypsies of Spain*, 4th edn (London, John Murray, 1846), p.13.

24 *damages went to Thurtell's creditors*: The newspapers covered this bankruptcy hearing thoroughly. See in particular: *Bristol Mercury*, 30 June 1823; *Aberdeen Journal*, 19 November 1823.

25 *postponed pork*: Charles Dickens, *Our Mutual Friend*, ed. Adrian Poole ([1864–5], Harmondsworth, Penguin, 1997), p.673.

26 *to do and commit*: The life, crimes, trial and execution of Thurtell are compiled from: *Aberdeen Journal*, 19, 26 November 1823; *Bell's Life*, 29 June 1823, 2, 9, 16, 30 November, 7, 14 December 1823, 11, 18 January 1824; *Bristol Mercury*, 30 June, 3, 10, 17 November 1823; *Caledonian Mercury*, 6, 8, 13, 15, 17, 19 November, 11 December 1823; *Derby Mercury*, 5, 12 November, 10, 31 December 1823; *The Englishman*, 7 December 1823; *Examiner*, 22 September 1823, 19 October, 2, 9, 30 November, 7, 21 December 1823, 11 January 1824; *Hampshire Telegraph and Sussex Chronicle*, 10 November 1823; *Ipswich Journal*, 28 June, 8, 15 November 1823; *John Bull*, 3, 10, 17, 24 November, 8 December 1823, 12 January 1824; *Leeds Mercury*, 22 November 1823; *Manchester Guardian*, 31 January, 13 March 1824; *Morning Chronicle*, 31 October, 1, 3, 4, 5, 6, 14, 17, 19, 26, 28 November, 6, 15, 29 December 1823, 7, 8 January 1824; *Norfolk Chronicle*, Supplement, 3, 17 January 1824; *Observer*, 24 November 1823; a collection of contemporary cuttings relating to the trial and execution, British Library, shelfmark 6497.d.1. There are numerous contemporary accounts. A good summary can be read in Edward Herbert, 'A Pen and Ink Sketch of a Late Trial for Murder, in a Letter from Hertford', *London Magazine*, February 1824; others include [Anon.], *Fairburn's Edition of the Whole Proceedings on the TRIAL of John Thurtell, and Joseph Hunt, for the Wilful Murder of MR WEARE, in Gill's-Hill Lane …* (London, John Fairburn, [1824]); Anon., *The Fatal Effects of Gambling Exemplified in the Murder of Wm. Weare, and the Trial and Fate of John Thurtell, the Murderer …* (London, Thomas Kelly, 1824); Anon., *A Full Account of the Atrocious Murder of the Late Mr. Weare …* (London, Sherwood, Jones, 1823); Anon., *A Narrative of the Mysterious and DREADFUL MURDER OF MR. W. WEARE, containing The Examination Before the Magistrates, The Coroner's Inquest, The Confession of Hunt, And other Particulars previous to the Trial …* (London, J. McGowan, [1824]); Anon., *The Trial of Hunt and Thurtell, for the Murder of Mr. Weare, with their Defence …* (London, B. Dickenson, [1824]); Pierce Egan, *Pierce Egan's Account of the Trial of John Thurtell and Joseph Hunt* (London, Knight & Lacey, 1824); and his *Recollections of John Thurtell, who was*

Executed at Hertford On Friday, the 9th of January, 1824; for Murdering Mr. W. Weare ... (London, Knight & Lacey, 1824). Twentieth-century sources include Eric R. Watson, *Trial of Thurtell and Hunt* (Edinburgh, William Hodge, 1920); Albert Borowitz, *The Thurtell–Hunt Murder Case* (London, Robson, 1988).

28 *nearly a century*: Thomas Boyle, *Black Swine in the Sewers of Hampstead: Beneath the Surface of Victorian Sensationalism* (London, Hodder & Stoughton, 1990), p.47; Senelick, 'The Prestige of Evil', p.81.

31 *community in the world*: Jim Davis and Victor Emeljanow, *Reflecting the Audience: London Theatregoing, 1840–1880* (Hatfield, University of Hertfordshire Press, 2001), p.44; and Michael R. Booth, *Theatre in the Victorian Age* (Cambridge, Cambridge University Press, 1991), pp.4, 79.

held 1,200 people: Mayhew, *London Labour and the London Poor* ([1861], NY, Dover, 1968), vol. 1, p.18; Douglas A. Reid, 'Popular Theatre in Victorian Birmingham', in David Bradby, Louis James and Bernard Sharratt, eds., *Performance and Politics in Popular Drama: Aspects of Popular Entertainment in Theatre, Film and Television, 1800–1976* (Cambridge, Cambridge University Press, 1980), p.69.

being the most famous: Michael R. Booth, 'Melodrama and the Working Classes', in Carol Hanbery MacKay, ed., *Dramatic Dickens* (Basingstoke, Macmillan, 1989), p.87.

32 *the ancient dramatists*: F.G. Tomlins, *A Brief View of the English Drama* (London, C. Mitchell, 1840), p.65.

at about nine o'clock: 'Mr. Ravenscaw of the Minor Theatres', *Punch*, 10 June 1843, p.239.

if I remember rightly: This letter is bound into a copy of *The Gamblers* in the British Library, shelfmark 11779h13.

33 *ha, ha, ha*: Cited in M. Willson Disher, *Blood and Thunder: Mid-Victorian Melodrama and its Origins* (London, Frederick Muller, 1949), p.123.

favourite melodies: Cited in William Knight, *A Major London 'Minor': The Surrey Theatre, 1805–1865* (London, Society for Theatre Research, 1997), p.62.

34 *Alluded to by the Daily Press*: The playbill is in the collection of the Victoria and Albert Theatre Collection.

pool of fire to be his pond: *Observer*, 'Surrey Theatre', 24 November 1823; *The Times*, 18 November 1823.

35 *truculent looking hag*: Walter Scott, *The Journal of Sir Walter Scott*, ed. W.E.K. Anderson (Edinburgh, Canongate, 1998), pp.543–4.

impossible to sustain: *Examiner*, 'The King v. The Proprietors of the Surrey Theatre', 30 November 1823.

36 *views of Probert's cottage*: The unattributed cutting is in a scrapbook devoted to the case, in the British Library, shelfmark 6497.d.1.

37 *no defence could be mounted*: William Holdsworth, *A History of English Law* (London, Methuen, 1966), p.192.

semi-literate at best: Antony E. Simpson, *Witness to the Scaffold: English Literary Figures as Observers of Public Executions: Pierce Egan, Thackeray, Dickens, Alexander Smith, G. A. Sala, Orwell* (Lambertville, NJ, True Bill Press, 2008), p.66.

Hunt and Probert had done it: His defence speech was reprinted in, among others, *Bell's Life*, 11 January 1824.

38 *the heads of the people*: 'An Account of the Last Moments and Execution of William Probert' (Gateshead, W. Stephenson, [1825]), in the Bodleian Library, Harding, B9/1.59.

Sunday newspapers' account: Marcia Pointon, 'Painters and Pugilism in Early Nineteenth-Century England', *Gazette des Beaux-Arts*, 6, Octobre 1978, p.138.

noted the Chronicle: The *Observer* advertised in the *Derby Mercury*, 31 December 1823; *Bell's Weekly Dispatch* advertised in the *Hull Packet*, 15 December 1823.

Palmer, Probert and Williams: *Bell's Life*, 28 March 1868, p.7.

39 *early in the day*: Alexander Smith, 'A Lark's Flight', in *Dreamthorp* (London, Strahan & Co., 1863), p.99.

Weare's body into the bushes: 'Scene of the Murder in Gill's-Hill-Lane' (London, J. Catnach, [1823–4]).

40 *Did drink his reeking blood*: 'The Hertfordshire Tragedy; or, the Fatal Effects of Gambling. Exemplified in the Murder of Mr. Weare and the Execution of John Thurtell' (London, J. Catnach, [1824]).

affecting beyond description: Untitled broadside, Bodleian Library, Crim 590 P186a(27).

was a murdered man: G.M. Macaulay, *British History in the Nineteenth Century, 1782–1901* (London, Longmans, 1922), p.171.

41 *worse than those who are*: George Borrow, *The Romany Rye* ([1857], Oxford, Oxford University Press, 1984), pp.275–7.

in the dissecting room: *The Times*, 'The Body of Thurtell and the Phrenologists', 13 January 1823, p.3.

in the next Number: Egan, *Account of the Trial of Thurtell and Hunt*, prelim page, unnumbered.

entirely realistic: Susan Wheeler, 'Medicine in Art: *The Lancett Club at a Thurtell Feast*, by Thomas Rowlandson', *Journal of the History of Medicine and Allied Science*, 57, 3, 2002, p.330.

42 *few windfalls like him*: William Makepeace Thackeray, 'Solitude in September', *National Standard of Literature, Science, Music, Theatricals and the Fine Arts*, 14 September 1833, 37, vol. 2 (London, Thomas Hurst, 1833), pp.158–9.

confess his being hoaxed: Broadside sales in Charles Hindley, *The Life of J. Catnach, Late of Seven Dials, Ballad Monger* (London, Reeves & Turner, [1878]), p.4. These figures should be treated with caution. In *The Catnach Press: A Collection of the Books and Woodcuts of James Catnach* ... (London, Reeves & Turner, [1869]), pp.142–3, Hindley wavers between the number of presses Catnach had for the job – four on one page, eight on the next, then back to four again; 'The Hoax Discovered' (London, W. Chubb, [1823–24]), cited in Borowitz, *Thurtell–Hunt Murder Case*, pp.89–90.

Irish Champion, Langan himself: Coburg: Allardyce Nicoll, *A History of Early Nineteenth Century Drama, 1800–1850* (Cambridge, Cambridge University Press, 1930), vol. 2, p.468; Surrey: Playbill reproduced in Borowitz, *Thurtell–Hunt Murder Case*; Langan: advertisement, *The Times*, 29 January 1824, p.2, and passim other days.

by hardened villains: Hannah Maria Jones, *The Gamblers; or, The Treacherous Friend: A Moral Tale, Founded on Recent Facts* (London, E. Livermore, 1824), pp.669–70. Biographical information, John Sutherland, *The Longman Companion to Victorian Fiction* (Harlow, Longman, 1988).

43 *botched robbery*: It has long been recognized that *Pelham* itself draws on an earlier novel, William Godwin's *Caleb Williams* (1794), for what would later be called detective-story elements – crime, pursuit, revelation – including Bulwer taking a variant of the name 'Tyrrel' from Godwin for one of his main characters. Yet Jones's entirely obscure novel *The Gamblers* is another influence on Bulwer: four years before *Pelham*, *The Gamblers* not only used the name Tyrrell, but also had a lead character named Pelham.

sold quite quickly: *The Times*, advertisement, 21 February 1824, p.1.

reading about THURTELL: William Cobbett, *Rural Rides*, ed. Ian Dyck ([1830], Harmondsworth, Penguin, 2001), pp.259–60.

44 *their own line*: Thomas and Jane Carlyle, *The Collected Letters of Thomas and Jane Welsh Carlyle*, eds. Charles Richard Sanders, Clyde de L. Ryals, Kenneth J. Fielding et al. (Durham, Duke University Press, 1970–2005), 21 January 1824, vol. 3, p.16; Watson, *Trial of Thurtell and Hunt*, p.48. The erroneous report appeared in the *Quarterly Review*, 37, 1828, p.15; its unreliability was obvious at the time, as the journalist added 'We quote from memory'; George Eliot, *The Mill on the Floss*, ed. Gordon S. Haight ([1860], Oxford, Oxford University Press, 1996), p.272; William Makepeace Thackeray, *Vanity Fair*, ed. J.I.M. Stewart ([1848], Harmondsworth, Penguin, 1968), p.796. John Harwood, *Miss Jane, the Bishop's Daughter* (London, Richard Bentley, 1867), Vol. 3, p.1.

the licence was refused: Henry Young and J.J. Cave, 'The Gipsey of Edgware, or, The Crime in Gills Hill Lane', unpublished playscript, for Marylebone Theatre, August 1862, licence refused, Lord Chamberlain's Plays, BL Add MSS 53015 (O).

wot lived in Lyons Inn: The verse, and Browning's memory of it, in Charles Kegan Paul, *Memories* (London, Kegan Paul, Trench, Tribner, 1899), p.338.

New Globe Theatre: *Observer*, 29 November 1868, p.6.

45 *co-proprietor of a girls' school*: The details of Corder's crime, trial and execution are compiled from: *Bell's Life*, 27 April, 4 May, 1, 15 June, 10 August 1828; *Manchester Guardian*, 26 April 1828; *Morning Chronicle*, 24, 25, 28 April, 1, 29 May, 8, 9, 11, 12, 30 August 1828; *Observer*, 27 April, 4 May, 10, 11, 17 August 1828; *The Times*, 23, 24, 28 April, 1, 29 May, 10, 21 June, 4, 8, 9, 11, 12, 16, 18 August 1828. Contemporary reports include: [Anon.] *An Accurate Account of the Trial of William Corder, for the Murder of Maria Marten, of Polstead, in Suffolk ... to which are added, an explanatory preface, and fifty-three of the letters Sent by various Ladies, in answer to Corder's Matrimonial Advertisement ...* (London, George Foster, [1828]); [Anon], *Advertisement for Wives* (W. Foster, London, 1828); Anon., *The Trial of William Corder for the murder of Maria Marten, in the Red Barn, at Polstead, including the matrimonial advertisement ...* (3rd edn, 1828); J. Curtis, *An Authentic and Faithful History of the Mysterious Murder of Maria Marten and A Full Development of the Extraordinary Circumstances which led to the Discovery of her Body*, ed. Jeanne and Norman Mackenzie ([1828], London, Pilot, 1948).

imprudent connexion: 'Horrible Murder. An account of a most horrid, bloody, and savage Murder ...' (John Muir, Prince's Street, 1828), Bodleian Library, John Johnson Collection, Crime 1 (47).

46 *off the track*: 'Atrocious Murder of a Young Woman in Suffolk', broadside, reprinted in Hindley, *The Catnach Press*, p.180.

its absence at the trial itself: *Observer*, 'Dreadful Murder', 27 April 1828, has mention of the dream (only twice); neither the *Observer*, 'Norfolk Circuit. – Suffolk Assizes', 10 August, nor *The Times*, 'Summer Assizes', 8 August, in their transcripts of the trial, makes any mention of it.

47 *under the Red Barn floor*: 'Murder of Maria Martin by W. Corder' (Liverpool, John White, [1828]), Bodleian Library, Firth c.17(111).

reach of scepticism: W.T. Moncrieff, *The Red Farm, or, The Well of St. Marie*, no. 611 in Dick's Standard Plays (Surrey, 1842; London, John Dicks, [1885]), p.1.

secrecy may be relied on: Reproduced in *An Accurate Account of the Trial of William Corder*, pp.5–6.

48 *razors, dogs, and hay*: Douglas Jerrold, *Wives by Advertisement; or, Courting in the Newspapers. A Dramatic Satire in One Act* ([1828], London, John Dicks, [1888]), pp.2, 3, 59.

50 *less in this town*: The congregation of 5,000 and the Stoke-by-Nayland fair: Catherine Pedley, 'Maria Marten, or, The Murder in the Red Barn: The Theatricality of Provincial Life', *Nineteenth Century Theatre and Film*, 31, 2004, pp.30, 28; the Cherry Fair and ballad-singers: Curtis, *Authentic and Faithful History*, pp.73–4; the judge's comments, *The Times*, 'Summer Assizes', 9 August 1828, and trial transcript, Curtis, *Authentic and Faithful History*, pp.118–19.

the boiling of the eggs: 'Lord' George Sanger, *Seventy Years a Showman: My Life and Adventures in Camp and Caravan the World Over* (London, C. Arthur Pearson, [1926]), pp.18–19.

51 *inquest on the child*: J.J. Tobias, *Crime and Police in England*, pp.124–5; *Bristol Mercury*, 4 October 1873, p.3.

burn all my letters: 'A Full Account of the Trial and Conviction of Wm. Corder ...' (Gateshead, Stephenson 1828), Bodleian Law Library, Crim 590 P186a (40).

53 *gesture for his readers*: Mr Hyatt, *The Sinner Detected. A Sermon Preached in the Open Air near the Red Barn at Polstead ...* (London, Westley & May, [1828]); Mr Pilkington in

Morning Chronicle, 'Polstead Sermons', 30 August 1828; Mr Hughes, *A Sermon on the Power of Conscience, with an application to the Recent Trial and Condemnation of William Corder* ... (Bury St Edmund's, T.C. Newby, [1828]); 'A Suffolk Clergyman', *An Address to My Parishioners and Neighbours on the Subject of the Murder lately committed at Polstead, in Suffolk* (London, Seeley & Son, [1828]), passim, and final service, pp.18–19; V.A.C. Gatrell, *The Hanging Tree: Execution and the English People, 1770–1868* (Oxford, Oxford University Press, 1994), p.44.

Maria and Frederick Manning: [Robert Huish and William Maginn?], *The Red Barn, A Tale, Founded on Fact* (London, Knight & Lacey, 1828); biographical details: Helen R. Smith, *New Light on Sweeney Todd, Thomas Peckett Prest, James Malcolm Rymer and Elizabeth Caroline Grey* (London, Jarndyce, 2002), pp.13–14.

54 *accelerate his death*: The Times, 'Confession and Execution of William Corder ...', reprinted in Hindley, *The Catnach Press*, p.187; Gatrell, *Hanging Tree*, p.54; 'Conduct, Confession, and Execution of Corder', 12 August 1828.

55 *without any outdoor clothes*: I am grateful to the fashion historian Colin McDowell for his reading of this word.

made plaster casts: 'A Copy of Verses, on the Execution of Wm. Corder, For the Murder of Maria Marten ...' ([no printer or place of publication], [1828]), Bodleian Library, Johnson Ballads 2416; 'A Full Account of the Trial and Conviction of Wm. Corder ...' Bodleian Law Library, Crim 590 P186a (40); *Observer*, 'Execution', 17 August 1828; Curtis, *Authentic and Faithful* ..., p.191.

56 *Camera obscura of the murder*: For information about the relics, see: *Observer*, 17 August 1828; *Morning Chronicle*, 3 June 1831; *The Times*, 20 April 1943; *Hull Packet and Humber Mercury*, 14 July 1829; *Literary Gazette*, June 1829, p.427; Curtis, *Authentic and Faithful* ..., pp.190–92; *Kaleidoscope*, September 1828, p.83; Gatrell, *The Hanging Tree*, pp.256–8.

cavalier costume: Mayhew, *London Labour*, vol. 3, p.140.

population was under twenty: Martin J. Wiener, *Reconstructing the Criminal: Culture, Law and Policy in England, 1830–1914* (Cambridge, Cambridge University Press, 1990), p.17.

57 *filled with benches*: James Greenwood, *The Wilds of London* (London, Chatto & Windus, 1874), pp.13–14.

THE MURDER IN THE COTTAGE: James Grant, *Sketches in London* (London, W.S. Orr & Co., 1838), pp.162–3, 183.

58 *even into Europe*: John and Clodagh McCormick and John Phillips, *The Victorian Marionette Theatre* (Iowa City, University of Iowa Press, 2004), p.49.

surviving Corder lived: Mayhew, *London Labour*, vol. 3, p.139; *The Times*, 29 February 1844, p.4; McCormick, *Victorian Marionette Theatre*, p.121.

lunatics, and ghosts: G.A. Sala, *The Seven Sons of Mammon* (London, Tinsley Brothers, 1862), vol. 2, pp.22–3.

59 *'respectable' fiction*: John Sutherland, *Victorian Novelists and Publishers* (Chicago, Chicago University Press, 1976), p.5.

much more blood: Cited in Elizabeth James and Helen R. Smith, *Penny Dreadfuls and Boys' Adventures: The Barry Ono Collection of Victorian Popular Literature in the British Library* (London, British Library, 1998), p.xvi.

60 *the treacherous chair*: Henry Mayhew, *London Labour*, vol. 1, p.25.

highwayman from grief: *Maria Martin [sic]; or, The Red Barn Tragedy* (London, J. Johnson, n.d.), Bodleian Library, John Johnson Collection, c.412.

shortly after the trial: H.G. Hibbert, *A Playgoer's Memories* (London, Grant Richards, 1920), p.86.

I am her murderer: Cited by Curtis, *Authentic and Faithful* ..., pp.212–19.

62 *some dancing*: For the various productions of *Maria Marten*: Cheltenham production: *Theatrical Observer*, October 1828, p.481; Weymouth and Wales productions: Malcolm Morley, in a preface to a play by Eric Jones-Evans, *Mr Crummles Presents: The Red Barn*

Murder, or, The Gipsy's Curse (Southampton, G.F. Wilson, 1966), pp.x–xi; Hull: Gilbert B.
Cross, *Next Week – East Lynne: Domestic Drama in Performance, 1820–1874* (Lewisburg,
Bucknell University Press, 1977), p.51; James Lee onstage: *Observer*, 28 July 1867, p.7;
Swansea text: reprinted in Michael Kilgarriff, ed., *The Golden Age of Melodrama: Twelve
19th Century Melodramas* (London, Wolfe, 1974), pp.204–5, 215ff; Manchester production:
Manchester Guardian, 6 August 1895; text, Lionel Ellis and George Comer, 'The Red Barn',
unpublished playscript, for performance at the Theatre Royal, Birkenhead, April 1872, Lord
Chamberlain's Plays, BL Add MSS 53497 (I).

64 *the recognizable bits first*: 'The Echo of Surgeons Square', *Letter to the Lord Advocate,
Disclosing the Accomplices, Secrets, and Other Facts Relative to the Late Murders; with a
correct account of the manner in which the anatomical schools are supplied with subjects*
(Edinburgh, 132 High Street, 1829), p.18.

66 *Hare's wife! Burke her*: 'An Account of the Liberation of Hare, the Murderer, From the Gaol
at Edinburgh …' (Gateshead, Stephenson, [1828]), Bodleian Library, Harding, B9/4.254.
reported me one of the visitors: Guy Mannering, or, The Astrologer ([1815], Edinburgh, Adam
& Charles Black, 1854), pp.297–8. Sir Walter Scott, *The Letters of Sir Walter Scott,
1828–1831*, ed. H.J.C. Grierson (London, Constable, 1936), vol. 9, pp.72, 102–3.
where they conflicted: Ibid., vol. 9, p.133.

67 *honour them for it*: The details of Burke and Hare's crimes and trial are compiled from:
Aberdeen Journal, 31 December 1828, 7, 14, 21, 28 January, 4, 11, 25 February 1829; *Bell's
Life*, 4 January, 1 February 1829; *Caledonian Mercury*, 29 December 1828, 1, 8, 12 January
1829; *John Bull*, 5 January 1829; *Morning Chronicle*, 29, 30 December 1828, 1, 3, 5, 14, 26
January, 10 February 1829; *The Times*, 22 November, 29, 30 December 1828, 1,3, 8, 17
January, 2 February 1829. The many contemporaneous publications include: [David
Paterson?], *Letter to the Lord Advocate, Disclosing the Accomplices, Secrets, and Other Facts
Relative to the Late Murders …* (Edinburgh, n.p., 1829); [Anon.], 'Confession of Burk' [sic]
(Newcastle, W. ?Boag, [1829]); [Anon.], *The Official Confessions of William Burke, Executed
at Edinburgh For Murder …* (Edinburgh, Stillie's Library, 1829); [Anon.], *Trial of William
Burke and Helen McDougal, Before the High Court of Justiciary … For the Murder of Margery
Campbell, or Docherty. Taken in Short Hand by Mr. John Macnee, Writer* (Edinburgh, Robert
Buchanan, 1829); [Anon.], *The West Port Murders. Characters Of Burk [sic], Hare, and Dr.
Knox*. From the 'Noctes Ambrosianae', *Blackwood's Magazine* for March 1829 (Edinburgh,
R. Menzies, [1829]).

68 *shaven off his body*: Cited in William Roughead, *Burke and Hare* (2nd edn, London,
William Hodge, 1948), p.66.

69 *pious thoughts for all*: Anon., *The Murderers of the Close*, p.iii and passim.
winna be Knoxed: *Aberdeen Journal*, 'Mansie Wauch's Dream', 25 February 1829.

70 *student goes mad*: René-Charles Guilbert de Pixérécourt, *Alice, ou, Les Fossoyeurs écossais*
(Paris, 'Chez les auteurs', 1829); first performed Théâtre de la Gaité, October 1829. The
translations are my own. The published edition names the authors on the title page as
Charles Desnoyer and B. Edan, but all subsequent studies refer to the author as Pixérécourt,
with no co-authors; [Anon.], 'The Victim. A True Story. By a Medical Student', *New
Monthly Magazine*, 32, 132, December 1831, pp.571–6.
sold to the doctors: Robert L. Mack, *Wonderful and Surprising History of Sweeney Todd: The
Life and Times of an Urban Legend* (London, Continuum, 2007), p.41. Mack links this to the
case of the Italian boy, Carlo Ferrari, and the 'London burkers', Williams and Bishop.
to tour further: *Examiner*, 2 October 1831, pp.634–5.

71 *hardly any parallels*: Cited in Kate Berridge, *Waxing Mythical: The Life and Legend of Mme
Tussaud* (London, John Murray, 2006), p.240. Advertisement giving date of display,
Liverpool Mercury, 13 February 1829.
BAND WILL PLAY EVERY EVENING: *Bristol Mercury*, 6 September 1831, p.1.
in Curtain Road: H. Chance Newton, *Crime and the Drama, or, Dark Deeds Dramatized*
(London, Stanley Paul, 1927), p.61; E.L. Blanchard, 'Vanished Theatres', *Era Almanack*,

476

1877, pp.88–92; theatre listings, 'The Theatres of the County of London, 1850–1950; A Directory and Bibliography of Theatres, Music Halls and Pleasure Gardens' (PhD thesis, Fellowship of the Library Association, 1966).

72 *the story of Burke and Hare*: G.A. Sala, *Gaslight and Daylight, With Some London Scenes they Shine Upon* (London, Chapman & Hall, 1859), p.346; Alexander Leighton, *The Court of Cacus, or, The Story of Burke and Hare* (London, Houlston & Wright, 1861).

student love, Duncan Grahame: [David Pae], *Mary Paterson; or, The Fatal Error. A Story of the Burke and Hare Murders* (London, Fred. Farrah, 1866).

73 *daft Jemmy*: Advertisement, *Illustrated Police News*, 10 August 1867, p.4; advertisements, *Era*, 24 February 1867, 22 March 1874, 11 October 1890, 24 September 1892.

the burkers' victims: Hugh Douglas, *Burke and Hare* (London, New English Library, 1974), pp.165–6.

killed in a brawl: Arthur Conan Doyle, 'My Friend the Murderer', first published in *London Society*, Christmas Number, 1882.

74 *long-dissected corpses*: Robert Louis Stevenson, 'The Body Snatcher', in *The Complete Short Stores: Centenary Edition*, ed. Ian Bell (Edinburgh, Mainstream, 1993), pp.419–35; first published in the *Pall Mall Gazette* Christmas extra, no. 13, London, 1884.

carrying their own coffins: Katherine Linehan, ed., *Robert Louis Stevenson: Strange Case of Dr. Jekyll and Mr. Hyde: An Authoritative Text, Backgrounds and Contexts, Performance Adaptations, Criticism* (New York, W. W. Norton, 2003), p.121; Robert Louis Stevenson, *The Letters of Robert Louis Stevenson*, eds. Bradford A. Booth and Ernest Mehew (New Haven, Yale University Press, 1995), vol. 5, p.35n.

75 *insurance money*: James McGovan, *Solved Mysteries: or, Revelations of a City Detective* (2nd edn, Edinburgh, John Menzies, 1888), p.287ff.

shake of the head: [R.S. Surtees], *Hillingdon Hall, or, The Cockney Squire; A Tale of Country Life* (London, Henry Colburn, 1845), vol. 1, pp.191–2.

buys the beef: Cited in Roughead, *Burke and Hare*, pp.7–8.

76 *property, individual safety*: 'Code des Délits et des Peines', 1795; cited in Clive Emsley, *Policing and its Context, 1750–1870* (Basingstoke, Macmillan, 1983), together with the derivation of the word 'police', p.2.

in their Language: Cited in Palmer, *Police and Protest*, p.69.

than by ministers: Cited in Ousby, *Bloodhounds of Heaven*, pp.7–8.

77 *eighteen ounces*: Cited in John Wilkes, *The London Police in the Nineteenth Century* (Cambridge, Cambridge University Press, 1977), p.15.

prevention of crime: Cited in King, *The Development of Modern Police History*, pp.50–51.

79 *1,790 for drunkenness*: G. Belton Cobb, *The First Detectives and the Early Career of Richard Mayne, Commissioner of Police* (London, Faber, 1957), p.56. For the outline of the development of the new police in these paragraphs, I have relied on: David Taylor, *Crime, Policing and Punishment in England, 1730–1914* (Basingstoke, Macmillan, 1998); Robert D. Storch, 'The Policeman as Domestic Missionary: Urban Discipline and Popular Culture in Northern England, 1850–1880', *Journal of Social History*, 9, 4, 1976, pp.481–509; Emsley, *Policing and its Context*; Palmer, *Police and Protest*; J.J. Tobias, *Nineteenth-century Crime: Prevention and Punishment* (Newton Abbot, David & Charles, 1972); and John Styles, 'The Emergence of the Police: Explaining Police Reform in Eighteenth and Nineteenth Century England', *British Journal of Criminology*, 27, 1987, pp.15–22.

not the public's view: The account of the incident is taken from King, *Development of Modern Police History*, p.56; and David A. Campion, '"Policing the Peelers": Parliament, the Public, and the Metropolitan Police, 1829–33', in Matthew Cragoe and Antony Taylor, eds., *London Politics, 1760–1914* (Basingstoke, Palgrave, 2005), pp.46ff.

80 *upon speedy promotion*: Robert Cruikshank, *Cruikshank v. the New Police, Showing the Great Utility of that Military Body, Their Employment, &c.* (London, W. Kidd, [1833]), pp.7, 30ff.

81 *a large round stick*: The transcripts for the inquest appear in *Bell's Life*, 21, 28 July 1833; *Morning Chronicle*, 17, 20, 22 July 1833; *Observer*, 14, 21, 28 July 1833.

83 *lack of proper supervision*: Parliamentary Papers, 627, xiii, 407: 'Report from the Select Committee on the Petition of Frederick Young and Others', 1833.
Justifiable Homicide: Taylor, *New Police*, p.99.

84 *publicized government rewards*: Babington, *House in Bow Street*, p.169.

85 *but later reprieved*: The inquest and trial reports appear in the *Derby Mercury*, 12, 26 January 1831, 14 May 1834, 11, 13 August 1834, *Manchester Guardian*, 8 January 1831, 9 August 1834; *Morning Chronicle*, 7, 8, 11 January 1831, 26 April 1834, 13 August 1834; *The Times*, 10 January 1831, 9, 11 August 1834.
trial transcript: *Morning Chronicle*, 'The Murder of Mr. Ashton', 13 August 1834.

86 *the Spinners' Union*: Mrs [Elizabeth] Stone, *William Langshawe, the Cotton Lord* (London, Richard Bentley, 1842), vol. 1, p.116, vol. 2, pp.159–60, 303–7.

87 *cobbler's constant companion*: Charles Dickens, *Bleak House*, ed. Norman Page ([1853], Harmondsworth, Penguin Books, 1985), p.797; Andrew Forrester, *The Female Detective* (London, Ward & Lock, [1864?]), pp.154–5.
who forgives him: Elizabeth Gaskell, *Mary Barton: A Tale of Manchester Life*, ed. Stephen Gill ([1848], Harmondsworth, Penguin, 1970).

88 *benevolence and charity*: *Observer*, 5 November 1848, p.3; *Manchester Guardian*, 28 February 1849.
Red Lights full up: Jim Davis, ed., *The Britannia Diaries, 1863–1875: Selections from the Diaries of Frederick C. Wilton* (London, Society for Theatre Research, 1992), pp.38–9.

89 *Vampire Trap!*: Ibid., p.191.
is anyway dead: Anon., 'Mary Barton: A Tale of Manchester Life', unpublished playscript, for performance at the Victoria Theatre, June 1850, Lord Chamberlain's Plays, BL Add MSS 43028 (16) ff.474–514; Thompson Townsend, 'Mary Barton, or, The Weavers' Distress', unpublished playscript, for performance at the Grecian Theatre, October 1861, Lord Chamberlain's Plays, BL Add MSS 53008 (K).

90 *a signal*: Dion Boucicault, *The Long Strike* (New York, Samuel French, [1870]), first performed at the Lyceum Theatre, London, 1866 [the name on the title page of this edition appears as 'Baucicault'], Act IV, sc. I, stage directions, pp.81–2.

91 *and embraces her*: Charles Dickens to Mark Lemon, *Letters*, 7 January 1856, vol. 8, pp.11–12.
rest of the play: Richard Altick, 'Dion Boucicault Stages *Mary Barton*', *Nineteenth-Century Fiction*, 14, 1959, p.130.

92 *found with the torso*: The account of the murder, trial and execution of James Greenacre is compiled from the Old Bailey trial transcript, ref. t18370403-917; and from: *Morning Chronicle*, 28, 29 March, 6 April 1837; *The Times*, 30 December 1836, 9 January, 4, 6 February, 8, 28, 31 March, 4, 5, 17, 19, 24, 26 April 1837; and C.J. Williams, *Greenacre, or The Edgeware-Road [sic] Murder. Presenting an Authentic and Circumstantial Account of this Most Sanguinary Outrage of the Laws of Humanity* ... (Derby, Thomas Richardson, [1837]); and Anon., *The Paddington Tragedy. A Circumstantial Narrative of the Lives and Trial of James Greenacre, and the Woman Gale, for the Murder of Mrs. Hannah Brown, his intended wife, which was brought to light by the discovery of her Mutilated Remains* ... (London, Orlando Hodgson, [1837]).

93 *cutting off Mrs Brown's head*: 'The Edgware-road Tragedy. Life, Trial, and Execution of James Greenacre' (London, Catnach, [1837]), Bodleian Library, John Johnson Collection, Broadsides, Murder and Execution 6 (8).

94 *taken a hackney cab*: 'Particulars of the Confession and Execution of James Greenacre, Who was Executed this Morning ... for the Wilful Murder of Mrs. Hannah Brown' (London, Birt, [1837]), Bodleian Library, Harding, B9/3.150.

95 *at least threepence*: *Champion and Weekly Herald*, 16 April 1837; *Figaro in London*, 'The Press and its Supporters', 9 June 1838; *The Age*, 14 October 1838.
no good to nobody: Cited in Hindley, *The Catnach Press*, pp.280–81.
immense number of persons: *Champion and Weekly Herald*, 'Examination of Greenacre', 9 April 1837.

96 *scream right well*: Grant, *Penny Theatres*, p.24; Paul Sheridan, *Penny Theatres of Victorian London* (London, Dennis Dobson, 1981), pp.56–7.
inflame the passions: *Theatrical Observer*, 'Suppression of the Penny Theatres', December 1844.

97 *Greenacre-Carlyle*: *John Bull*, 30 April 1838; *Bell's Life*, 'To Correspondents', 16, 23 April, 7 May 1837; Jane and Thomas Carlyle, *Letters*, 18–19 January 1843, vol. 16, p.23.
served Mrs. Brown: Revd Richard H. Barham, *The Ingoldsby Legends* ([1837–40], London, Richard Edward King, [1893]), pp.65ff.

3: Entertaining Murder

102 *front of the local population*: The most comprehensive eighteenth-century account of Aram's crime and trial is found in [Anon.], *The Genuine Account of the Trial of Eugene Aram, for the Murder of Daniel Clark … &c.* ('Printed by A. Ward, for C. Etherington, Bookseller in *Coney-Street*', 1759). Anon., *The Original and the Only Authentic Account of the Trial of Eugene Aram, (Late a Schoolmaster at Knaresbrough [sic],) for the Murder of Daniel Clark; With his Autobiography, and a particular account of his Studies; and literary attainments; also, several of his Letters, &c. to which is added, 'The Dream of Eugene Aram,' A Poem, by Thomas Hood, Esquire* (Knaresbrough [sic], W. Langdale, [c.1832]) is generally considered the most reliable of the later reports. Excellent modern accounts from which I have drawn include Eric R. Watson, *Eugene Aram: His Life and Trial* (Glasgow, William Hodge, [1913]), and Nancy Jane Tyson, *Eugene Aram: Literary History and Typology of the Scholar-Criminal* (Hamden, CT, Archon, 1983).
thief and murderer: Andrew Kippis, *Biographia Britannica* (London, C. Bathurst, 1778), vol. 1, pp.230–35. The links between Aram and *Caleb Williams* are explored in Nancy Tyson's *Eugene Aram*, pp.37–44.

103 *of the English language*: William Godwin, *The Adventures of Caleb Williams, or Things as They are* ([1794], New York, Rinehart & Co., 1960), p.341.

104 *gyves upon his wrist*: Thomas Hood, 'The Dream of Eugene Aram', *Gem*, 613, October 1828, p.662.
as a biographical fact: *Manchester Times*, 'The Dream of Eugene Aram', 21 November 1828; *Examiner*, 25 December 1831, p.820.

105 *then commits suicide*: Edward Bulwer-Lytton, *Eugene Aram: A Tale* ([1832], London, George Routledge & Sons, [n.d.]). This is the post-1840 edition, with the later revisions.
a murder specialist: Victor Lytton, *The Life of Edward Bulwer, First Lord Lytton* (London, Macmillan, 1913), vol. 1, p.389.
entirely innocent: *Leeds Mercury*, review of *Trial and Life of Eugene Aram*, 1 September 1832, p.7; *Gentleman's Magazine*, review of *Trial and Life of Eugene Aram*, November 1832, p.448.
of consummate ability: Cited in W.T. Moncrieff, *Eugene Aram, or, Saint Robert's Cave* (London, Samuel French, n.d.), p.7.
hanged by his own cleverness: The modern scholar is Nancy Tyson, *Eugene Aram*, p.27; Paley quoted in George Wilson Meadley, *Memoirs of William Paley, DD* (Edinburgh, Archibald Constable, 1810), pp.8–9.

106 *the defence to Johnson*: 'Eugene Aram: Mr Bulwer's New Novel', in *Tatler*, 4, 1832; reprinted in Lawrence Huston Houtchens and Carolyn Washburn Houtchens, eds., *Leigh Hunt's Literary Criticism* (New York, Columbia University Press, 1956), p.397.
from Burney's notes: The biographer is T.H. Escott, cited in Watson, *Eugene Aram*, p.32.
30,000 copies in the USA: *Morning Chronicle*, 9 May 1832, p.4.
should be received by all: *Hampshire Telegraph and Sussex Chronicle*, 25 June 1832, p.4, advertisement.

107 *unassuming deportment*: Norrisson Scatcherd, *Memoirs of the Celebrated Eugene Aram … with some account of his family and other particulars* (London, Simpkin & Marshall, 1832), pp.3–6, 9–11.

and Eugene Aram: Leeds Mercury, 2 June 1832, p.4; Ibid., 'A Stranger in Yorkshire', 4 August 1870; *Daily News*, 'New Names for London Streets', 15 December 1856.

Wakefield and Sheffield: The London productions are compiled from advertisements in *The Times, passim*, 1832. The provincial productions are listed in H. Philip Bolton, *Dickens Dramatized* (London, Mansell, 1987), p.26.

108 *pardon – pity – all*: Moncrieff, *Eugene Aram*, preface: 'Remarks', p.5; pp.12, 64, 66, 68.

author of Eugene Aram: *New Monthly Magazine*, 'The Drama', 135, March 1832, p.108.

attorney his certificate: Harrison Ainsworth, *Rookwood* (London, Richard Bentley, 1834), pp.221–3.

109 *done the trick*: *Examiner*, 9 November 1823, p.732.

110 *until page 2,207*: Michael Anglo, *Penny Dreadfuls and Other Victorian Horrors* (London, Jupiter, 1977), p.32.

publications of that kind: Cited in Philip Collins, *Dickens and Crime* (London, Macmillan, 1962), a report to a House of Lords committee, undated, p.258.

111 *palls, fake away*: Horace Bleackley and S.M. Ellis, *Jack Sheppard* (Edinburgh, William Hodge, 1933), p.99.

112 *poke at Bulwer*: The *Edinburgh Review* citation and its interpretation are both found in Keith Hollingsworth, *The Newgate Novel, 1830–1847: Bulwer, Ainsworth, Dickens, and Thackeray* (Detroit, Wayne State University Press, 1963), pp.126–7.

113 *cuts a throat*: 'The Literary Gentleman', *Punch*, 1842, p.68.

Sir E.L.B.L.BB.LL.BBB.LLL.: *Punch*, 3, 10 and 17 April, 1847, pp.136–7.

rest for itself: *Leeds Mercury*, 18 September 1841, p.6.

very deficient: Bulwer, *Eugene Aram*, p.13.

114 *in its first year*: Playbills of performances at the Surrey Theatre, London, 1810–58, British Library, shelfmark Playbills 311–13.

Brookwood, in Surrey: Bleackley, Ellis, *Jack Sheppard*, p.125.

without a licence: *Leeds Mercury*, 'The Illegitimate Drama at Great Horton', 14 April 1857.

115 *filled the theatre*: John Hollingshead, *My Lifetime* (London, Sampson Low, 1895), vol. 1, pp.189–90.

packets of poison: *Punch*, 'Parties for the Gallows', 5 April 1845, p.147; *Derby Mercury*, leader, 24 April 1850; *Leeds Mercury*, 'Mysterious Poisoning of a Man and His Wife, at Leeds', 8 August 1846; Greenwood, *The Wilds of London*, p.158.

116 *somewhere in between*: Patrick Brantlinger, *The Reading Lesson: The Threat of Mass Literacy in Nineteenth-Century British Fiction* (Bloomington, Indiana University Press, 1998), pp.77ff.

across the force: Cobb, *The First Detectives*, p.47; Smith, *Policing Victorian London*, p.39.

117 *excessively interesting*: Charles Dickens, *Oliver Twist, or, The Parish Boy's Progress*, ed. Philip Horne ([1837–8], Harmondsworth, Penguin, 2002), introduction, p.xiii.

of bad character: Pollock's Toy Theatre and Redington's Toy Theatre produced sheets with identical characters, although Redington's has an extra four backdrops; examples of both are in the Bodleian Library, John Johnson Collection, Miniature Theatres 3.5–26 and 4.22–46.

118 *adaptations appeared*: *Leeds Mercury*, 16 August 1851, p.1; *Penny Magazine*, 'The Dropping-Well at Knaresborough', 6, September 1837, p.348. Racehorse: *Derby Mercury*, 26 September 1832, p.4, and *Racing Calendar*, October 1833, p.24; greyhounds: *Preston Guardian*, 'Ridgway Coursing Club', 8 November 1856; *Newcastle Courant*, 'Yorkshire Coursing Club, Fairfield Stakes', 2 February 1877.

not very interesting: [Anon.], *Amy Paul. A Tale* (London, Colburn & Co., 1852); *John Bull* review reprinted in an advertisement in *The Times*, 27 July 1852, p.10. Oscar Wilde, *The Importance of Being Earnest: A Trivial Comedy for Serious People* ([1895], London, Samuel French, 1856), p.35.

no matter what I was: Caroline Clive, *Paul Ferroll* ([1855], Oxford, Oxford University Press, 1997), p.73.

its Aram-like murderer: See, for example, *Athenaeum*, 18 August 1855, 1451, pp.947–8; also *New Quarterly Review*, 16, October 1855, pp.420–22 and 'The Author of Paul Ferroll', *National Review*, 24, April 1861, pp.489–99.

119 *his own ambitions*: Dickens, *Our Mutual Friend*, pp.685, 729, 692–5.

120 *image by Thackeray*: Rankley: *Athenaeum*, 'Royal Academy', July 1852, p.728; Noble: *Daily News*, 'British Art Contributions', 13 April 1855, *Glasgow Herald*, 14 January 1889, advertisement, p.12; Rossiter: *Athenaeum*, 'Pictures at the French Gallery', 21 August 1858, p.240; Elmore: *Manchester Times*, 'Notes of the Day', 27 April 1872, *Leeds Mercury*, 'The International Exhibition', 29 April 1872; Dixon: *Liverpool Mercury*, 'Corporation Exhibition, Art Gallery. No. II', 9 September 1878; Pettie: *Birmingham Daily Post*, 'Exhibition of the Royal Academy. First Notice', 29 April 1882, *Era*, 'Tragedy at the Royal Academy', 6 May 1882; Thackeray: *Pall Mall Gazette*, 'Art Notes', 13 July 1892.

121 *included the poem*: Beardsley: Tyson, *Eugene Aram*, p.58; Wilde, Alfred Douglas, *Oscar Wilde: A Summing-up* (London, Duckworth, 1940), p.132. Sunderland vicar: *Hull Packet*, 2 November 1860, p.6; Social Reform Society, *Glasgow Herald*, 20 November 1861; the Revd J.C.M. Bellew: *Birmingham Post*, 15 October 1862, p.2; penny readings: *Hampshire Telegraph and Sussex Chronicle*, 27 February 1864, *Birmingham Daily Post*, 3 November 1864; the sale of the Revd F.W. Joy's collection: *Leeds Mercury*, 'A Remarkable Sale of Autographs', 30 May 1887.

incidents of Eugene Aram: *Birmingham Daily Post*, 3 March 1848, advertisement, p.3; *Era*, 'The London Music Halls. London Pavilion', 28 July 1878; *Era*, 'Gallery of Illustrations. – (Last Night.)', 25 May 1873.

122 *damp churchyard*: *Saturday Review*, 26 April 1873.

by letter: James F. Stottlar, 'A Victorian Stage Adapter at Work: W.G. Wills "Rehabilitates" the Classics', *Victorian Studies*, 16, 4, 1973, pp.401–32.

opera based on Bulwer's novel: Playbill, 18 April 1873, in the Victoria and Albert Theatre Collection; *The Times*, 2 July 1881, p.6; reviewed in *The Times*, 14 May 1894, p.14, and in the *Era*, 22 September 1900, p.17; *Glasgow Herald*, 'The Music of 1896', 31 December 1896.

and jerking music: James Glover, *Jimmy Glover, His Book* (London, Methuen, 1911), pp.240–41; David Mayer, 'The Music of Melodrama', David Bradby, Louis James and Bernard Sharratt, *Performance and Politics in Popular Drama: Aspects of Popular Entertainment in Theatre, Film and Television, 1800–1976* (Cambridge, Cambridge University Press, 1980), p.63n ; Percy Fitzgerald, *The World Behind the Scenes* (London, Chatto & Windus, 1881), pp.312–13. I am grateful to Michael McCaffery for the information on *Ruddigore*.

123 *going mad*: Mary Elizabeth Braddon, *One Life, One Love* (London, Simpkin, Marshall, Hamilton, Kent, 1890).

the ages to come: C.L. Pirkis, *The Experiences of Loveday Brooke, Lady Detective* (London, Hutchinson, 1894), p.73.

Ellen Terry's niece: Production information: Tyson, *Eugene Aram*, p.135.

124 *seventeen pups*: *Kirby's Wonderful and Scientific Museum: or, Magazine of Remarkable Characters* ... (London, R.S. Kirby, 1804), p.523; *Ipswich Journal*, 9 August 1806, p.4.

the real murderer: Amelia Opie, 'Henry Woodville', in *The Works of Mrs. Amelia Opie* (Philadelphia, Crissy & Markley, 1843), vol. 2, pp.385–411.

125 *to enlighten her*: Thomas Edward Hook, *Killing No Murder, with … the scene suppressed by order of the Lord Chamberlain* (5th edn, London, C. Chapple, 1811), p.31; Anon., 'The Murder'd Guest', unpublished playscript, December 1826, Lord Chamberlain's Plays, BL Add MSS 42881 (11) ff.526–53b. (The siting of the production at Drury Lane is from Nicoll, *A History of Early Nineteenth-Century Drama*); Anon., 'The Murderers of the Round Tower Inn', unpublished playscript, for performance Royal West London and Olympic Theatres, February 1830, Lord Chamberlain's Plays, BL Add MSS 42900 (6) ff.209–87.

for £5 each: Disher, *Blood and Thunder*, p.90; [Wilkie Collins], *Household Words*, 'Dramatic Grub Street', 17, 6 March 1858, p.267. (The authorship for the unsigned articles in *Household Words* has, throughout these notes, followed the sourcing of Anne Lohrli,

Household Words: A Weekly Journal 1850–59 ... based on the Household Words *Office Book* ... (Toronto, University of Toronto Press, 1973).) Jerrold: Michael R. Booth, *English Melodrama* (London, Herbert Jenkins, 1965), p.48; Dickens on Moncrieff: Dickens to John Forster, 7 September 1837, in Dickens, *Letters*, vol. 1, p.304.

had come out: S.J. Adair Fitz-Gerald, *Dickens and the Drama, Being an Account of Charles Dickens's Connection with the Stage and the Stage's Connection with Him* (London, Chapman & Hall, 1910), pp.83ff., 121–6; Charles Dickens, *The Life and Adventures of Nicholas Nickleby*, ed. Michael Slater ([1838–9], Harmondsworth, Penguin, 1986), p.727.

with these quotations: Kilgarriff, *The Golden Age of Melodrama*, p.239.

Cockney apprentice: Edward Fitzball, *Jonathan Bradford!, or, The Murder at the Roadside Inn!* (London, John Duncombe, [?1833]), p.33.

126 *one striking effect*: *Hampshire Telegraph and Sussex Chronicle*, 16 December 1833, p.3, advertisement. Fitzball's name appears nowhere in this advertisement, and it may be that for copyright reasons this was not his version. But the pioneering effect it described certainly was.

applauded unanimously: Edward Fitzball, *Thirty-five Years of a Dramatic Author's Life* (London, T.C. Newby, 1859), pp.239, 241.

Many perfect comedies: *Figaro in London*, 27 July 1833, p.120.

notice in The Times: *The Times*, 'Surrey Theatre', 7 October 1833.

horse with the same name: Derby runners, *Derby Mercury*, 9 July 1834, p.2.

excluding Sundays: Advertisements appear in the *Examiner* on 7 October, 1 and 15 December 1833 giving the number of performances; for the longer theatre runs in the 1850s, see Booth, *Theatre in the Victorian Age*, p.13.

127 *had three performances*: Advertisements in *Freeman's Journal and Daily Commercial Advertiser*, 14 and 18 November 1833, p.1 in both issues.

Man came wooing: Productions appear in advertisements in: *Caledonian Mercury*, 24 August 1833, p.2; *Jackson's Oxford Journal*, 7 September 1833, p.3; *Liverpool Mercury*, 25 October 1833, p.350; *Ipswich Journal*, 18 January 1834, p.3; *Freeman's Journal*, 14 and 18 November 1833, p.1; *Belfast News-Letter*, 24 December 1833, p.1; *Hampshire Telegraph and Sussex Chronicle*, 16 December 1833, p.3.

of the gaol: Thomas Greenwood, *Jack Sheppard; or, The Housebreaker of the Last Century* (London, John Cumberland & Son, [1839?]), p.15.

128 *lawyer who vanished*: Mrs Elizabeth Gaskell, 'A Dark Night's Work' (1863) in *The Works of Elizabeth Gaskell*, vol. 4, 'Novellas and Shorter Fiction III', ed. Linda Hughes (London, Pickering & Chatto, 2006); the Knutsford murder story and its Gaskell connection appears in John Geoffrey Sharps, *Mrs Gaskell's Observation and Invention: A Study of Her Non-Biographic Works* (Fontwell, Sussex, Linden Press, 1970), pp.354–5.

dead, as in Bradford: Sheridan Le Fanu, 'Some Account of the Latter Days of the Hon. Richard Marston' (1848); *The Evil Guest* ([1851], London, Downey & Co., [1892?]); *A Lost Name* (New York, Arno Press, 1977; facsimile edn of London, Richard Bentley, 1868).

incidents of the tragedy: Charles Dickens, 'The Holly Tree Inn: The Guest', *Household Words*, 12, Christmas Special, December 1855, p.5.

129 *alive at this moment*: [Thomas Peckett Prest?], *Jonathan Bradford, or, The Murder at the Road-side Inn. A Romance of Thrilling Interest* (London, E. Lloyd, [1851]), pp.110, 140. It is James and Smith who attribute the authorship to Prest, in *Penny Dreadfuls and Boys' Adventures*.

by the proprietor: [John Hollingshead], 'Street Memories', *Household Words*, 17, December 1857, p.10.

130 *world collapsed*: Martin Meisel, *Realizations: Narrative, Pictorial, and Theatrical Arts in Nineteenth-Century England* (Princeton, NJ, Princeton University Press, 1983), p.25, discusses Augustus Egg in connection with *The Corsican Brothers*, but the Jack Sheppard/Jonathan Bradford links are my own. For more on *The Corsican Brothers*, see also my *Consuming Passions: Leisure and Pleasure in Victorian England* (London, HarperCollins, 2006), pp.333–5.

482

reliance can be placed: Captain L. Benson, *The Book of Remarkable Trials and Notorious Characters. From 'Half-Hanged Smith', 1700 – To Oxford, who Shot at the Queen, 1840* (London, Chatto & Windus, [1871]), p.121.

131 *for the final curtain*: Dion Boucicault, *The Colleen Bawn, or, The Brides of Garryowen. A Domestic Drama* (London, Thomas Hailes Lacy, 1860).

open trapdoor: Richard Fawkes, *Dion Boucicault* (London, Quartet, 1979), p.118.

night before proceeding: I am grateful to Tobias Hoheisel for suggesting the possible mechanics of Boucicault's leap. *The Times*, 'The Adelphi', 27 December 1860.

while life remains: George Bernard Shaw, *Our Theatres in the Nineties*, (London, Constable, 1932), vol. 2, p.29. I am grateful to Zoë Anderson for this reference.

132 *Woman in White perfume*: Sheppardiana: Hollingsworth, *Newgate Novels*, p.140; *Woman in White* spin-offs: Deborah Wynne, *The Sensation Novel and the Victorian Family Magazine* (Basingstoke, Palgrave, 2001), p.38.

Bawn quick-step: The music for all these pieces, and many more, can be found in the British Library catalogue.

133 *earlier Colleens Bawns*: Colleen cabs: Nicholas Daly, 'The Many Lives of the Colleen Bawn: Pastoral Suspense', *Journal of Victorian Culture*, 12, 1, 2007, p.5; fashion advertisements: *Le Follet: Journal du Grand Monde …*, 1 April 1861, *Englishwoman's Domestic Magazine*, 'The Fashions', 1 August 1861, *Le Follet*, 1 August 1861, *Ladies' Monthly Magazine*, 'Le Monde Eléganté [sic]', 1 September 1861; Sydney Hodges: *John Bull and Britannia*, 22 June 1861, p.395; greyhound: *Bell's Life*, 24 March 1861, p.5; rowing club: *Bell's Life*, 28 July 1861, p.6.

134 *a horrid villain*: The details of Ellen Hanley's murder and both trials have been compiled from: *Belfast News-Letter*, 24 September 1862; *Examiner*, 25 July, 6 August 1820; *Glasgow Herald*, 14 August 1820; *Pall Mall Gazette*, 29 November 1867; *The Times*, 4, 8 August 1820; Revd Dr Richard Fitzgerald of Ballydonohoe, *The Colleen Bawn: The True History of Ellen Hanley. By One who Knew Her in Life and Saw Her in Death* ([1868], Tralee, Kerryman, 1931); Daly, 'Many Lives of the Colleen Bawn'; O'Connell to his wife: Maurice R. O'Connell, ed., *The Correspondence of Daniel O'Connell* (Dublin, Irish University Press for the Irish Manuscripts Commission, 1972), vol. 2, p.243.

136 *reprieve might be obtained*: M.J. Whitty, *Tales of Irish Life, Illustrative of the Manners, Customs, and Condition of the People* (London, J. Robins, 1824).

137 *observance of the penitent*: Gerald Griffin, *The Collegians; or, The Colleen Bawn* ([1829], London, George Routledge, [?1860]).

they appeared in Griffin: Playbill in the Fillingham Collection, British Library, shelfmark 1889.b.10/6.

times in a fortnight: M. Willson Disher, *Melodrama: Plots that Thrilled* (London, Rockliff, 1954), p.6.

a rarity: Manchester Times, 'Art and Literary Gossip', 27 October 1860.

which he accepted: Davis, *Britannia Diaries*, p.19.

138 *well-born heiress*: Anon., 'The very latest Edition of The Cooleen [sic] Drawn, from a novel source, or, The Great Sensation Diving Belle', unpublished playscript, for performance at the Royal Surrey Theatre, October 1861, Lord Chamberlain's Plays, BL Add MSS 53007 (O); Henry J. Byron, *Miss Eily O'Connor. A New and Original Burlesque* (London, Thomas Hailes Lacy, [1862]); 'Andrew Halliday Duff' [pseud. of William Brough and Andrew Halliday], *The Colleen Bawn Settled at Last. A Farcical Extravaganza* (London, Thomas Hailes Lacy, [1862]); First performed at the Royal Lyceum Theatre, July 5th, 1862; Lord Chamberlain's Plays, BL Add MSS 53014 (Z).

139 *musical version*: Bell's Life, 15 June 1862, p.3.

a small boat: The Colleen Bawn, or, The Collegian's Wife, Purkess's Penny Pictorial Play ([London, G. Purkess, n.d.]).

at the Britannia: Sunderland and D'Arc marionettes, McCormick, *Victorian Marionette Theatre*, pp.109, 121–2. Britannia Theatre, playbill dated 3 October 1881, in the Victoria and Albert Theatre Collection.

4: Policing Murder

140 *with pieces of wood*: Palmer, *Police and Protest*, pp.308–9. I am indebted to Palmer for the information and interpretation in this paragraph.

142 *constables on the beat*: Cobb, *The First Detectives*, p.102.

144 *Murderer Daniel Good*: *Hampshire Telegraph and Sussex Chronicle*, 9 May 1842, p.2.

146 *to dispose of the body*: The outline of Daniel Good's crime, pursuit and trial is taken primarily from: Old Bailey trial transcript, ref. t18420509-1705; *Bell's Life*, 10, 17, 24 April, 15, 29 May 1842; *Era*, 10, 17, 24 April, 15, 29 May 1842; *Examiner*, 9, 14, 16, 23, 30 April, 28 May 1842; *Morning Chronicle*, 11, 14, 19, 22 April, 14, 24 May 1842; *The Times*, 8, 9, 12, 13, 14, 15, 16, 18, 19, 21, 22, 23, 26, 28 April, 13, 24 May 1842; and Cobb, *The First Detectives*, pp.183ff.

147 *had been a railway worker*: 'The Life, Trial, and Execution of D. Good, for the Murder of Jane Jones' (London, Paul, [1842]), and 'Apprehension of D. Good at Tonbridge for the Murder of Jane Jones …' (London, Paul & Co., [1842]), both in the Bodleian Library, John Johnson Collection, Broadsides: Murders and Executions, Large Folder.

hours to live: *Illustrated London News*, 21 May 1842, p.30.

148 *violated the constitution*: *The Times*, 2 December 1845, p.4.

four plainclothes men: For the development of the Birmingham force, Michael Weaver, 'The New Science of Policing: Crime and the Birmingham Police Force, 1839–1842', *Albion*, 26, 2, 1994, pp.289–308.

149 *living off the working classes*: Robert D. Storch, 'The Policeman as Domestic Missionary'.

round a shilling: 'The Righteous Peeler', *The London Singer's Magazine: A Collection of All the Most Celebrated and Popular Songs as Sung at the London Theatres* … (London, John Duncombe, [1839?]), vol. 2, p.197. The British Library catalogue offers 1838 for the date of this publication, but the Police Act 1839 parodied in the lyrics indicates a date of at least 1839.

152 *guilty as charged*: Accounts of the life, crime and trial of Rush have been compiled from: *Bell's Life*, 3, 10, 17, 24 December 1848, 1, 8, 22 April 1849; *Daily News*, 4 December 1848, 23 April 1849; *Era*, 10, 17, 24 December 1848, 14 January, 1, 8 April, 13 May 1884; *Examiner*, 2, 9, 16, 23 December 1848, 31 March, 7 April, 5 May 1849, 'False Reliance'[attributed to Dickens], 2 June 1849; *Ipswich Journal*, 9, 23 December, 13 January, 31 March, 7, 28 April 1849; *John Bull*, 2, 16, 25 December 1848, 31 March, 7, 21 April, 26 May 1849; *Lloyd's Weekly*, 14 January, 1, 15 April 1849; *Morning Chronicle*, 16, 21 December 1848; *The Times*, 28, 30, 31 March, 2, 3, 4, 5 April 1849. The *Norwich Mercury's* special supplement, 'Norwich Mercury Extraordinary': Bodleian Library, John Johnson Collection, Broadsides: Murders and Executions, folder 7 (34). Anon., *A Full Report of the Trial of James Blomfield Rush for the Murder of Mr. Jermy and His Son* … (15th edn, London, W.M. Clark, [1849]); *An Introductory Narrative and a Revised Report of the Trial and Execution of J.B. Rush, for the Murder of Isaac Jermy, of Stanfield Hall Esq. … and of his Son, Isaac Jermy Jermy, Esq* … (Norwich, Bacon & Kinnebrook, 1849); *The Life, Trial, and Execution of James B. Rush, for the Stanfield Hall Murders!* (London, Birt, [1849]); *The Stanfield Hall Assassinations! Authentic Report of the Trial, Conviction and Extraordinary Defence of Jas. Bloomfield [sic] Rush* … (2nd edn, London, Cleave, [1849]); a modern outline of the trial can be found in W. Teignmouth Shore, *Trial of James Blomfield Rush* (Edinburgh, William Hodge, 1928). The idea that Emily Sandford was the source of the forged documents is my own.

153 *prosperous audience*: Anon., *A Full Report of the Trial of James Blomfield Rush*, endpapers.

a 2d. pamphlet: William Wayte Andrew, *Sermon Preached … After the Execution of J.B. Rush, for the Murder of Isaac Jermy, Esq., of Stanfield Hall* … (Norwich, Josiah Fletcher, 1849); Samuel Hobson, 'The Root of all Evil': *A Sermon preached to a village congregation on the Sunday before the Execution of James Blomfield Rush, the Stanfield Murderer* (Norwich, Charles Muskett, 1849).

154 *up to London standards*: Charles Dickens to John Forster, [2 January 1849], *Letters*, vol. 5, pp.473–4.
and Norwich Castle: The Staffordshire figures (except for Chestney) are in the P.D. Gordon Pugh Collection in the City Museum and Art Gallery, Stoke-on-Trent, with similar figures in the Brighton Museum.
155 *Stockton-upon-Tees*: *Punch*, 'The Mannings at Home', 1 December 1849.
battle of Waterloo itself: Mayhew, *London Labour*, vol. 3, pp.88–9.
156 *come up a trap*: Old Wild's production of *Macbeth*: Josephine Harrop, *Victorian Portable Theatres* (London, Society for Theatre Research, 1989), p.62; stage vocabulary in Dickens: Meisel, *Realizations*, p.302; Charles Dickens, *The Life and Adventures of Martin Chuzzlewit*, ed. P.N. Furbank ([1843–4], Harmondsworth, Penguin, 1986), p.595.
157 *up comes the Bermondsey tragedy*: Mayhew, *London Labour*, vol. 1, pp.223–4.
died that summer: The mortality figures appeared regularly in the *Morning Chronicle* and *The Times* during the epidemic. See also Albert Borowitz, *The Bermondsey Horror* (London, Robson, 1988), p.4.
158 *1,253 had died*: *Preston Guardian*, 'Miscellaneous News', 19 May 1849.
artificial heat: *Morning Chronicle*, 8 January 1849, p.5.
161 *a swifter messenger*: 'Our Little Bird', 1 September 1849; *Illustrated London News*, 1 September 1849, p.147.
164 *towards the court*: The account of the crime, pursuit, trial and execution of the Mannings is drawn from: Old Bailey trial transcript, ref. t18491029-1890; *Daily News*, 20, 21, 22, 23, 24, 28, 29, 30 August, 3, 6, 7, 8, 11, 17, 20 September, 6, 26, 27, 29, 30 October, 8, 10, 12, 13 November 1849; *Era*, 26 August, 9, 16, 23, 30 September, 4, 11, 18 November 1849 [including, ' "Boz's" Description of the Execution']; *Examiner*, 18, 25 August, 1, 8 September, 27 October, 17 November 1849; *Glasgow Herald*, 'Science and Crime', 27 August 1849; *Lloyd's Weekly Newspaper*, 19, 26 August, 2, 16, 23, 30 September, 14, 21, 28 October, 11, 18 November 1849; *Observer*, 19, 26 August, 2, 9, 30 September, 7, 14, 28 October [4-pp. supplement given over to the trial], 4, 11, 18 November 1849; *The Times*, 18, 20, 21, 22, 23, 24, 25, 27, 28, 29, 30, 31 August, 1, 3, 4, 5, 6, 7, 8, 12, 13, 17, 20, 22, 28 September, 6, 10, 25, 26, 27 October, 2, 10, 12, 13, 14 [including letter to the editor from Dickens], 13, 14, 17, 19 November 1849 [another Dickens letter]; [Anon.] *An Account of the Last Days, Confessions, and Execution of the Mannings, for the Murder of Patrick O'Connor, at Bermondsey* (Leith, C. Drummond, [1849]); *An Authentic Report of the Trial of the Mannings for the Murder of Patrick O'Connor* (London, G. Lawrence, [1849]); *The Bermondsey Murder, Containing the Discovery and Inquest on the Body. Life of Patrick O'Conner, the apprehensions and examinations of both prisoners together with the Memoirs and Confessions of the Prisoners. With the fullest particulars of the Extraordinary Conduct of Mrs. Manning, with the Trial and Sentence* (London, G. Vickers, [1849]); *The Bermondsey Murder. A Full Report of the Trial of Frederick George Manning and Maria Manning, for the Murder of Patrick O'Connor ...* (London, W. M. Clark, 1849); *Full Particulars of the Apprehension of Frederick Manning, for the Murder of Patrick O'Connor ... Also the Coroner's Inquest, and the Examination of his Wife* (London, Birt, [1849]).
165 *fee any Actor*: Rychard [sic] Doyle and Percival Leigh, *Manners and Cvstoms of Ye Englyshe* (London, Bradbury & Evans, [1849]), unpaginated.
166 *Murder by James Bloomfield Rush*: Household Words, [W.H. Wills, Grenville Murray and ?Thomas Walker], 'German [sic] Advertisements', October 1850, p.35.
high treason in wartime: Patrick Wilson, *Murderess: A Study of Women Executed in Britain since 1843* (London, Michael Joseph, 1971), p.14.
four hangings in twenty-five years: David Philips, *Crime and Authority in Victorian England: The Black Country, 1835–1860* (London, Croom Helm, 1977), pp.172, 256.
husband or lover: Carolyn Conley, *The Unwritten Law: Criminal Justice in Victorian Kent* (New York, Oxford University Press, 1991), p.73.
smaller every year: Wilson, *Murderess*, pp.315–16.

167 *2.5 million broadsides each*: These figures are given by Mayhew, *London Labour*, vol. 1, pp.284–5. No doubt they are the figures he was given by patterers and possibly by printers, but whether they were accurate is unknowable.
no use to the patterer: Mayhew, *London Labour*, vol. 1, pp.284–5.
a-going to be murdered: B.B. Valentine, 'The Original of Hortense and the Trial of Marcia [sic] Manning', *Dickensian*, 19, 1, 1923, pp.21–2; Mayhew, *London Labour*, vol. 1, pp.232, 234, 301–2.
the second body: Portrait of William IV: Mayhew, *London Labour*, vol. 1, p.277; double execution image: 'Execution of the Mannings' (no place of publication, no printer, [1849]), Bodleian Library, John Johnson Collection, Crime 2 (5).
168 *'Stop Press' columns*: 'Murder of Mr. O'Connor' (London, Hodges, [1849]), Bodleian Library, Firth c.17(265).
not worth the printing: Mayhew, *London Labour*, vol. 1, pp.223.
169 *from the sink*: 'The Execution of Mr. and Mrs. Manning. Also a Copy of an Affecting Letter to his Sister ...' (London, Ryle & Co., [1849]), Bodleian Library, John Johnson Collection, Broadsides: Murders and Executions, Large Folder; 'The Execution of the Mannings', John Johnson Collection, Crime 2 (5); 'Trial, Sentence, Confession and the Execution of Mr. & Mrs. Manning, for the Murder of P. O'Connor' (Newcastle-on-Tyne, John S. Wodson, [1849]), John Johnson Collection, Broadsides: Murders and Executions, 7 (5); one example of several, in *The Times*, 'The Bermondsey Murder. Execution of the Mannings', 14 November 1849.
spent on barricades: *Era*, 6 January 1850, p.14.
& unspeakable scene: Jay Leyda, *The Melville Log* (New York, Gordian Press, 1969), pp.330–31. I am grateful to Philip Hoare for this reference.
a Californian price: 'Admit the bearer': *The Times*, 13 November 1849, p.4; price of seats: *The Times*, 14 November 1849, p.5; erection of scaffolding: *The Times*, 12 November 1849, p.5.
170 *about 25,000*: John Tulloch, 'The Privatising of Pain: Lincoln Newspapers, "Mediated Publicness" and the End of Public Execution', in *Journalism Studies*, Special Issue: 'The Development of the Provincial Press in England, c.1780–1914', 7, 3, 2006, pp.437–51.
Manning's peppermints: *The Times*, 14 November 1849, p.5, estimated 30,000; the *Examiner*, 17 November, p.730, went for 50,000. Both agreed on the number of police, which from its consistency appears to have been issued as an official figure. Basketmen: *Examiner*, Ibid.
detested her: The ripping chisel: Dickens, *Letters*, vol. 5, p.642; Forster to Bulwer: James Atterbury Davies, 'John Forster at the Mannings' Execution', *Dickensian*, 67, 1, 1971, pp.12–15.
171 *half-round and back*: Ruskin: Mary Lutyens, ed., *Effie in Venice: Unpublished Letters of Mrs John Ruskin, written from Venice between 1849–1852* (London, John Murray, 1965), p.76; Thomas Carlyle to John Carlyle: Carlyle, *Letters*, 6 October 1849, vol. 24, p.266; Forster: James Atterbury Davies, 'John Forster at the Mannings', pp.12–15; Mulready drawings: Anne Rorimer, *Drawings by William Mulready* (London, Victoria and Albert, 1972), pp.114–15; daguerreotypes: *The Times*, 19 October 1849, p.2; black satin: Borowitz, *Bermondsey Horror*, pp.291–4. Thomas Hardy to Lady Hester Pinney, cited by Beth Kalikoff, 'The Execution of Tess d'Urberville at Wintoncester', in William B. Thesing, ed., *Executions and the British Experience from the 17th to the 20th Century: A Collection of Essays* (Jefferson, NC, McFarland, 1990), p.111; the link between Hardy, Martha Brown and Maria Manning is, however, my own.
admired on the scaffold: *Punch*, 'Fashions for Old Bailey Ladies', 10 November 1849, p.186.
172 *before the Mannings'*: Collins, *Dickens and Crime*, p.234.
perished like the beasts: *The Times*, 14 November 1849, p.5.
and highly instruct: *Manchester Guardian*, 24 November 1849, p.1; *Theatrical Journal*, 10, December 1849, p.387.

173 *where he was murdered*: Pauline Chapman, *Madame Tussaud's Chamber of Horrors: Two Hundred Years of Crime* (London, Constable, 1984), p.40. Ms Chapman was archivist at Madame Tussaud's, and much of the material in her book accepts as fact the many legends created for advertising purposes. For background information, therefore, I have relied on Kate Berridge's *Waxing Mythical*. Advertisement for Burke, 13 February 1829, Liverpool, in Chapman, *Madame Tussaud's*, pp.45–6; sale of catalogues: Berridge, *Waxing Mythical*, p.301. *fiend in human form*: Mayhew, *London Labour*, vol. 1, p.223.

good-naturedly Vidocq: *The Times*, 'M. Vidocq's Exhibition', 9 June 1845; Robert Browning to Elizabeth Barrett, 1 July 1845, Elizabeth Barrett and Robert Browning, *The Brownings' Correspondence*, eds. Phillip Kelley, Ronald Hudson, et al. (Winfield, KA, Wedgestone Press, 1984–2007), vol. 10, pp.286–7.

174 *so much counted money*: *Punch*, 1 September 1849, p.83.

convulsed the court with laughter: *Observer*, 6 April 1851, p.8.

sets were produced: P.D. Gordon Pugh Collection, City Museum and Art Gallery, Stoke-on-Trent.

Hero and Peace: *Bell's Life*, 'The Bendrigg (Open) Autumn Meeting', 16 October 1853; *Bell's*, 'Caledonian Club Meeting', 22 January 1854.

176 *James Malcolm Rymer*: Cited in Smith, *New Light on Sweeney Todd*, pp.12–13. The suggestions of the identity of the impoverished hack are Smith's. Rymer's will: probate, 24 September 1884, CGPLA Eng. & Wales, cited in *Oxford Dictionary of National Biography*.

and stylish illustrations: Robert Huish, *The Progress of Crime, or, The Authentic Memoirs of Maria Manning* (London, n.p., 1849).

with the intelligence: [Charles Dickens], 'A Detective Police Party', *Household Words*, July 1850, pp.410–11; Le Fanu, *A Lost Name*, p.247.

177 *darting fire*: Dickens, *Bleak House*, pp.209, 793–4.

178 *involved and crushed*: 'Thomas Waters', *Recollections of a Policeman* ([1849–53], New York, Cornish, Lamport, 1853) pp.10, 125.

nothing escapes him: Dickens, *Martin Chuzzlewit*, pp.662, 516; Dickens, *Bleak House*, pp.278, 361, 768.

179 *than this fact*: [Dickens], 'A Detective Police Party'; *Bleak House*, p.768; *The Times*, 20 September 1853, p.9.

open the door quietly, Maria: Cited in Collins, *Dickens and Crime*, p.344n.

between three charities: *Lloyd's Weekly*, 24 February 1850, p.7.

180 *performing dogs*: *Poor Joe*, in the Victoria and Albert Theatre Collection; McCormick, *Victorian Marionette Theatre*, pp.117–18, 67–8; Harrop, *Victorian Portable Theatres*, pp.68–9.

grave and a loaded pistol: [Emma Robinson], *The Gold-Worshippers: or, The Days We Live in. A Future Historical Novel* (London, Parry & Co., 1851), vol. 1, pp.65ff, 70; vol. 3, pp.288–90. Biographical information, Anne Humpherys, 'Emma Robinson', *Oxford Dictionary of National Biography*.

181 *pan-European criminal network*: George Eliot: 'The Lifted Veil', in *The Lifted Veil, Brother Jacob*, ed. Helen Small ([1859], Oxford, Oxford World's Classics, 1999); Braddon: [first published as written by 'Lady Caroline Lascelles'], *The Black Band, or, The Mysteries of Midnight* ([1861–2], London, George Vickers, 18[6–]7), pp.132ff, 142.

which way it was: Robert Surtees, *Plain, or Ringlets?* (London, Bradbury, Agnew & Co., [1860]), p.179.

with her affections: Collins, *The Woman in White*, ed. Matthew Sweet ([1860], Harmondsworth, Penguin, 1999), pp.218, 528ff; Mrs Henry Wood, *Mrs Halliburton's Troubles* ([1862], London, Richard Bentley, 1888).

182 Hidden Guilt: Davis, *Britannia Diaries*, pp.79–80.

She is mine!: Anon., 'Marie de Roux, or, The Progress of Crime', unpublished playscript, for performance at the Britannia Theatre, Hoxton, 1860, in Lord Chamberlain's Plays, BL Add MSS 52990 (L).

5: Panic

183 *resulted in guilty verdicts*: Ian A. Burney, 'A Poisoning of no Substance: The Trials of Medico-Legal Proof in Mid-Victorian England', *Journal of British Studies*, vol. 38, no. 1, 1999, p.69.

a grain of arsenic: A. Keith Mant, 'Science in the Detection of Crime', *Royal Society for the Encouragement of Arts, Manufactures and Commerce Journal*, 141, 1983, pp.549–55 is very useful, but while Mant discusses Eliza Fenning's case, he is unfortunately under the impression that someone died, and that it was the contents of the stomach which, when examined, blackened the knife blade and smelt of garlic.

187 *being honest people*: Old Bailey trial transcript, ref.: t18100919-37.

sentenced to death: The outline of the case and the trial can be found in the Old Bailey trial transcript, ref. t18150405-18. There are scarcely any newspaper accounts of the trial itself apart from a report in the *Morning Chronicle*, 15 April 1815. Most of the reports (see below) appeared during the publication war that followed. I am grateful to David Crane for the information on Mrs Fenning's legal councel.

before a working-class one: Patty Seleski, 'Domesticity in the Streets: Eliza Fenning, Public Opinion and the Politics of Private Life', in *The Politics of the Excluded, c.1500–1850*, ed. Tim Harris (Basingstoke, Palgrave, 2001), p.273.

protested her innocence: Citations from John Marshall are all from *Five Cases of Recovery from the Effects of Arsenic ... To Which are Annexed Many Corroborating Facts ... Relative to the Guilt of Eliza Fenning* (London, C. Chapple, 1815).

188 *suffering and anxiety*: *The Times*, 27 September 1815, p.4.

most voluptuous language: *Observer*: 'Condemned Criminals in Newgate', 23 July 1815, 'Execution of Eliza Fenning ...' and 'Republication of the Trial of Eliza Fenning for Poisoning a Family', 30 July 1815; 'Statement of the Medical Men Regarding the Guilt of Eliza Fenning', 6 August 1815, 'Eliza Fenning', 24 September 1815.

written by John Watkins: Citations from John Watkins are from his *The Important Results of an Elaborate Investigation into the Mysterious Case of Elizabeth Fenning ...* (London, William Hone, 1815).

189 *the judicial office*: Gatrell, *The Hanging Tree*, p.359.

190 *would have hanged anyone*. Dickens to Walter Thornbury, 22 December 1866, Dickens, *Letters*, vol. 11, p.288.

192 *notoriously guilty*: *British Critic*, 4, December 1815, pp.631–6.

more about them than myself: Anon., *Elizabeth Fenning's own Narrative of circumstances which occurred in the family of Mr. Turner, from the time of her going into their service until her apprehension ...* (London, no publisher, [1815]), pp.4, 7, 8.

193 *did not go unnoticed*: Seleski, 'Domesticity in the Streets', pp.275–6.

dirtied when she knelt: T.W.W[ansbrough]., *An Authentic Narrative of the Conduct of Eliza Fenning ... till her Execution ... By the Gentleman who Attended Her* (London, Ogles, Duncan, & Cochran, 1815), p.19.

use of Shell: Watkins, *The Important Results*, p.95.

insulting language: Ibid., p.97.

194 *propriety and decorum*: *Affecting Case of Eliza Fenning, Who Suffered the Sentence of the Law, July 26, 1815 ...* (8th edn, John Fairburn, [1815]), p.40.

a common saying: Ibid.

195 *CONSIDERABLE MEDICAL INFORMATION*: This is a single sheet, headed, 'CORONER. The Following Letter has just been addressed to the CHAIRMAN of MR. WAKLEY'S Committee ...' (London, no publisher, 1830), in the British Library, shelfmark 74/1880.c.1.(180.).

had confessed to the crime: *The Times*, 'New. CIRCUMSTANTIAL EVIDENCE', 21 July 1857.

196 *Caliao, Peru*: *Morning Chronicle*, shipping lists, 15 October 1855. I am grateful to Jill Grey for her information on Callao and South American shipping into Queenstown.

spoon still in it: Samuel James Arnold, trans., *The Maid and the Magpye, or, Which is the Thief? A Musical Entertainment*, 'freely translated, with alterations, from the French ... First Performed at the Theatre-Royal, Lyceum, On Monday, August 21, 1815', music by H. Smart (London, John Miller, 1815). The other two versions were: Anon., *The Magpie; or, The Maid of Palaiseau* ... 'Performed at the Theatre Royal, Drury Lane, on Tuesday, September 12, 1815' (London, John Murray, 1815); and Isaac Pocock, *The Magpie or the Maid?* 'Translated and Altered from the French ... First performed at the Theatre-Royal, Covent-Garden, On Friday, September 15, 1815. The Music Composed by Mr. Bishop' (London, John Miller, 1815).

197 *tippytoe-ing behind*: This particular version is in the Bodleian Library, John Johnson Collection, Miniature Theatres, 2, 46–52.

making people thieves: Anon., *Dolly and the Rat, or, The Brisket Family. A Burlesque, Tragic, Comic, Operatic Parody on The Maid and the Magpie* (London, Duncombe, 1823). Allardyce Nicoll, *History of Early Nineteenth Century Drama*, vol. 1, p.426, lists [Anon.], *The Brisket Family; or, The Running of the Rat*, also at the Olympic, in 1822. There appears to be no surviving copy of this title, and it is not therefore clear if this is an earlier version, the same play with a different title, or possibly not based on Eliza Fenning at all.

wondered the Satirist: *Satirist*, 'The Theatres', 8 October 1837.

198 *judge by appearances*: George Dibdin Pitt, 'Charlotte Hayden, the Victim of Circumstance, or, The Maid, the Master and the Murderer', unpublished playscript, for performance at the Britannia, Hoxton, June 1844, Lord Chamberlain's Plays, BL Add MSS 42976 (11) ff.385–464.

of the comic man: Jerome K. Jerome, *Stage Land: Curious Habits and Customs of its Inhabitants* (London, Chatto & Windus, 1889), pp.14, 3.

199 *I am innocent*: Playbill, Pavilion Theatre, 22 July 1854, Victoria and Albert Museum Theatre Collection.

so many dumplings: Anon., 'Eliza Fenning, The Victim of Circumstances', unpublished playscript, for the Britannia Saloon, September 1855, Lord Chamberlain's Plays, BL Add MSS 52956E; Anon., 'Eliza Fenning', unpublished playscript, performed at the Victoria Theatre, August 1857, Lord Chamberlain's Plays, BL Add MSS 52967 (W).

200 *White was one*: Wybert Reeve, *From Life* (London, George Robertson, 1891), p.4.

disrepute is repeated: Wilkie Collins, 'Cases Worth Looking At. II. The Poisoned Meal', in *My Miscellanies* (London, Samson, Low, Son, 1863), vol. 2, pp.114–72.

201 *to leave immediately*: Charles Dickens, *Little Dorrit*, ed. John Holloway ([1857], Harmondsworth, Penguin, 1985), p.774.

202 *butler was Courvoisier's uncle*: This detail is reported in Simpson, *Witnesses to the Scaffold*, p.98, but without a source. I have seen it in none of the newspaper reports, but it would explain how a valet could afford such a high-flying barrister.

verdict followed swiftly: The outline of Courvoisier's crime, trial and execution has been taken from the Old Bailey trial transcript, ref. t18400615-1629, and the following newspaper reports: *Bell's Life*, 10, 17, 31 May, 21, 28 June, 12 July 1840; *Era*, 17, 24 May, 12 July 1840; *Examiner*, 17, 24, 31 May, 21, 28 June, 12 July 1840; *John Bull*, 10, 17, 24, 25, 31 May, 21, 22 June, 6 July 1840; *Morning Chronicle*, 7, 8, 11, 12, 14, 15, 20, 23, 25, 28 May, 1, 8, 19, 25 June, 7 July 1840; *The Times*, 7, 9, 11, 12, 13, 14, 15, 21, 28 May, 8, 19, 22, 24, 25, 26, 27 June, 6, 7 July 1840. A twentieth-century summary is Yseult Bridges, *Two Studies in Crime* (London, Hutchinson, 1959).

203 *vigilantly employed*: *Satirist*, 5 July 1840, p.5. Dickens, *Letters*, vol. 2, pp.86–8.

204 *There goes the reward*: Arthur Conan Doyle, *The Sign of Four* ([1890], Harmondsworth, Penguin, 2007), p.121.

father was killed: Dickens, *Bleak House*, p.250; Braddon, *One Life, One Love*, vol. 2, p.168.

that dreary date: Elizabeth Barrett to Miss Mitford, April 1840, *Elizabeth Barrett to Miss Mitford*, ed. Betty Miller (London, John Murray, 1954), p.99.

I like murders: Cited in Senelick, 'The Prestige of Evil', p.95.

205 *SKETCHES IN NEWGATE*: *Odd Fellow*, 27 June 1840, p.104.

five guineas each: *Morning Chronicle*, 'Execution of Courvoisier', 7 July 1840.
206 *in Shrewsbury*: David D. Cooper, *The Lesson of the Scaffold* (London, Allen Lane, 1974), pp.21–2.
Hangs the hangman: Mayhew, *London Labour*, Vol. 3, p.57.
strangled to death: Cooper, *Lesson of the Scaffold*, pp.22–3.
207 *our land of blood*: 'WMT' [William Makepeace Thackeray], 'Going to See a Man Hanged', *Fraser's Magazine*, 22, 128, August 1840, pp.150–58.
208 *boy-bandits*: *The Times*, 25 June 1840, p.14; [letter] 7 July 1840, p.7; *Morning Chronicle*, 11 July 1840, p.5.
209 *carefully curled hair*: 'Awful Murder of Lord William Russell, M.P.' (London, Paul & Co., [1840]), Bodleian Library, John Johnson Collection, Broadsides: Murders and Executions, Large Folder; *Penny Satirist*, 23 May 1840, p.1.
211 *recommendation to mercy*: Sarah Thomas's crime, inquest, trial and execution details are compiled from: *Bristol Mercury*, 10, 17, 24 March, 7, 14, 21 April, 1849; *Daily News*, 9, 15, 16 March, 21, 23 April 1849; *Manchester Guardian*, 14, 17 March, 25 April 1849; *Morning Chronicle*, 5 April 1849; *Observer*, 12, 18 March 1849.
petition for mercy: Number of signatories: *Daily News*, 'The Execution at Bristol', 23 April 1849; I have extrapolated the number of women in Bristol from the 1851 census. The population of Bristol was c.135,000 at the time, and about 32 per cent were children under fifteen years of age; my figure has been reached by assuming that women made up 50 per cent of the population.
212 *defence of the murderer*: *Era*, 'More Murder. One Servant Too Many', 18 March 1849; *Manchester Guardian*, 25 April 1849, p.5; *Observer*, 12 March 1849, p.6.
6,000 handbills: *Bristol Mercury*, 'Abolition of the Punishment of Death', 21 April 1849; *Bristol Mercury*, 'Police Intelligence', 12 May 1849; *Bristol Mercury*, 'Bristol Religious Tract Society', 2 March 1850. It is not clear from this report if the Society was giving the tracts away or selling them.
25,000: *Liverpool Mercury*, 'Public Executions', 24 April 1849.
213 *disgusting that he ever saw*: *Daily News*, 'The Execution at Bristol', 23 April 1849; 'Death Punishment', 21 April 1849; *Liverpool Mercury*, 'Public Executions', 24 April 1849. The report from the *Liverpool Mercury* was a reprint from another, unnamed newspaper; it is not therefore clear whether 'our reporter' belongs to the *Mercury* or the original newspaper.
[legal] murder: *Daily News*, [letter], 23 April 1849. The square brackets are in the original newspaper report.
215 *lynched as they left court*: The case of Mary Anne Parsons, the inquests and trials, can be found in: *Bell's Life*, 31 March, 20 April, 11 August 1850; *Examiner*, 30 March 1851; *The Lady's Newspaper*, 15 February 1851; *Liverpool Mercury*, 21 February 1851; *Northern Star and National Trades' Journal*, 30 March 1850; *The Times*, 24, 26 March, 7 August 1850; *Trewman's Exeter Flying Post*, 17 January 1850, 30 January 1851.
216 *without hard labour*: The case of Jane Wilbred and the Sloanes can be found in: *Bell's Life*, 22 December 1850, 5 January, 9 February 1851; *Daily News*, 9 January 1851; *Era*, 15 December 1850; *John Bull*, 14 December 1850, 8 February 1851; *Lloyd's*, 8, 15 December 1850, 12 January 1851; *Morning Chronicle*, 9, 14 December 1850, 9 January, 6 February 1851.
JANE WILBRED'S box: *Punch*, 15 February 1851, p.72.
217 *daughter of a baronet*: Subscription for Jane Wilbred: *Northern Star and National Trades' Journal*, 31 May 1851, p.3; racehorse: *Bell's*, 15 February 1852, p.4, and *Racing Times*, 27 December 1853, p.522; broadside-sellers: Mayhew, *London Labour*, vol. 1, pp.225–6, 232; 'Bertha Gray': *Reynolds's Miscellany*, 'Bertha Grey, The Parish Apprentice-Girl; or, Six Illustrations of Cruelty', by Edwin F. Roberts, 6, March 1851, pp.137–9. H. Young, 'Bertha Gray, the Pauper Child, or, The Death Fetch', unpublished playscript, for performance at the Bower Saloon, July 1851, Lord Chamberlain's Plays, BL Add MSS 43036; 'Bertha Gray', a later version, with no author named on the script, appears in the same archive for

performance at the Standard Theatre, August 1859. This play is a seemingly cobbled-together revival of the 1851 version: the characters mostly have the same names, and although the general plot is more or less followed, in the 1859 version the scenes are sketchy. If the audience had no knowledge of the previous version, it would have been impossible to follow.

221 *was therefore acquitted*: The Drouet baby-farm scandal can be found in: Old Bailey trial transcript, ref. t18490409-919; *Daily News*, 9, 10, 12, 13, 16, 17, 19, 20, 24 January, 14, 16 April 1849; *Era*, 28 January, 22 April 1849; *Examiner*: 13 January, 21 April 1849; *John Bull*, 29 January, 21 April 1849; *Lloyd's Weekly*, 14, 21 January, 11 February, 22 April 1849; *Morning Chronicle*, 6, 8, 11, 13, 16, 17, 19, 20 January, 1 February, 14 April 1849; *The Times*, 13, 16, 17, 19, 20, 24, 25, 27, 31 January, 1 February, 13 April, 16 April 1849. The four articles by Dickens in the *Examiner* are: 'The Paradise at Tooting', 20 January 1849; 'The Tooting Farm', 27 January 1849; 'A Recorder's Charge', 3 March 1849; 'The Verdict for Drouet', 21 April 1849.

222 *under atrocious circumstances*: *The Times*, 'Central Criminal Court', 18 April 1849; Arthur Conan Doyle, *The Hound of the Baskervilles* ([1902], Harmondsworth, Penguin, 2007), pp.89, 160.

223 *been so laid upon him*: Dickens, *Bleak House*, pp.180, 417.

the laws of your country: 'The Wonderful Drama of Punch and Judy', by 'Papernose Woodensconce' (1854), cited in George Speaight, *Punch and Judy: A History* (London, Studio Vista, 1970), p.148.

224 *other kinds of murder*: Cited in Conley, *Unwritten Law*, p.110.

infanticide quite as murder: *Pall Mall Gazette*, 24 September 1870, p.10.

225 *less than six months*: 'A Suffolk Clergyman', *An Address to My Parishioners and Neighbours on the Subject of the Murder lately committed at Polstead*, p.5; Martin J. Wiener, *Men of Blood: Violence, Manliness and Criminal Justice in Victorian England* (Cambridge, Cambridge University Press, 2004), pp.124–5; Conley, *Unwritten Law*, p.110.

opposite of concealment: Philips, *Crime and Authority*, p.256.

three months' hard labour: Lionel Rose, *The Massacre of the Innocents: Infanticide in Britain, 1800–1939* (London, Routledge & Kegan Paul, 1986), pp.39–40.

226 *suspicious infant deaths a year*: 'Infanticide and Illegitimacy', *Journal of the Statistical Society*, 28, 1865, p.420.

for a post-mortem: *The Times*, 20 January 1845, p.3.

227 *is a murderess*: Revd Henry Humble, 'Infanticide, Its Cause and Cure', in Revd Orby Shipley, ed., *The Church and the World: Essays on Questions of the Day* (London, Longmans, Green, Reader, and Dyer 1866), p.57.

the age of five: Margaret L. Arnot, 'Understanding Women Committing Newborn Child-Murder in Victorian England', in Shani D'Cruze, ed., *Everyday Violence in Britain, 1850–1950* (Harlow, Longman, 2000), p.61.

reconcile impossibilities: Cited in Andrew Mangham, 'The Detective Fiction of Female Adolescent Violence', in *Clues*, 25, 1, 2006, p.70.

228 *anatomy-schools for dissection*: 2 & 3 Will.IV.c.75.

at two years: Rose, *Massacre of the Innocents*, pp.136–7, 138.

230 *was eventually transported*: The details of the Sandys case, the inquest and the trial can be found in: *John Bull*, 7 August 1841; *Liverpool Mercury*, 30 October 1840, 6 August 1841; *Manchester Guardian*, 21, 28, 31 October, 2 November 1840, 14 April 1841, 7 August 1840, 30 April 1842; *Manchester Times and Guardian*, 10 April 1841, 16 April 1842; *Morning Chronicle*, 5, 6 August 1840; *Newcastle Courant*, 30 October 1840; *Northern Star and Leeds General Advertiser*, 1 October 1840; *Observer*, 1 November 1840.

231 *deaths of the deceased*: *The Times*, 7 August 1847, p.5; *Morning Chronicle*, 2 August 1847, p.4.

at last it is done: 'Thomas Carlyle's Past and Present', *Tait's Edinburgh Magazine*, 10, June 1843, pp.341–8.

pay all our debts: Benjamin Disraeli, *Sybil*, ed. Sheila M. Smith ([1845], Oxford, Oxford University Press, 1981), p.158.

they ate through: Broadside reprinted in Vivian De Sola Pinto and Allan Edwin Rodway, eds., *The Common Muse: An Anthology of Popular British Ballad Poetry, XVth–XXth Century* (London, Chatto & Windus, 1957), pp.374–6.

afraid of the street Irish: 'The Life of the Man that was Hanged' and other cocks, in Hindley, *Curiosities of Street Literature*, passim; cocks based on real people, Mayhew, *London Labour*, vol. 1, pp.228–9.

232 *money arrived*: [Harriet Martineau], 'A Death-Watch Worth Dreading', *Once a Week*, 2, December 1859, pp.18–22.

must have increased: Cited in [Richard H. Horne], 'Household Crime', *Household Words*, 4, 13 December 1851, pp.277–81.

find no trace of it: Anon., 'The Woman in White', unpublished playscript, for performance at the Royal Surrey Theatre, October 1860, Lord Chamberlain's Plays, BL Add MSS 52997 (B).

234 *weaker vessel*: Both cited in Judith Knelman, *Twisting in the Wind: The Murderess and the English Press* (Toronto, University of Toronto Press, 1998), p.60.

pecuniary profit: *Illustrated London News*, 1 September 1849, pp.150–51.

Increase of Secret Poisoning: Coroners' Society reports and *London Medical Journal*, in Burney, 'Poisoning of No Substance', p.68.

of secret poisoning: Anon., 'The Doings of William Palmer, the Alleged Wholesale Poisoner: His Public Frauds and Private Trickeries …' (London, Frederick Mitchell, [1856]), p.19.

stable for twenty years: Owen Davies, *Murder, Magic, Madness: The Victorian Trials of Dove and the Wizard* (Harlow, Pearson, 2005), p.92.

the following decade: Ian A. Burney, *Poison, Detection and the Victorian Imagination* (Manchester, Manchester University Press, 2006), pp.20, 36.

235 *ever prepare him*: *The Times*, 'Lancaster Assizes', 18 September 1816. I have found no other reference to Sarah Holroyd's case in the forty-one newspapers I have based my research on. Nor is there any mention in fifty-six magazines, apart from one account in the *Weekly Entertainer, or, Agreeable and Instructive Repository*, 'Lancashire Assizes', 56, September 1816, pp.787–9.

236 *swearing her innocence*: The account of Sarah Dazley's inquests, trial and execution has been compiled from: *John Bull*, 22 April, 5 August 1843; *Lloyd's Weekly*, 23 April, 13 August 1843; *Morning Chronicle*, 22 April 1843; *The Times*, 15, 22 April, 8 August 1843.

237 *paltry gathering*: *Daily News*, 22 August 1849, p.5; population figure from Post Office Directory for Sussex, 1851.

guilty of murder: The case of Sarah Freeman, in *Age and Argus*, 18 January 1845; *Bristol Mercury*, 11, 18 January, 1 March, 12, 26 April 1845; *Era*, 19 January 1845; *Examiner*, 18 January 1845; *John Bull*, 11, 18 January, 28 April 1845; *Lloyd's Weekly*, 19 January 1845; *Morning Chronicle*, 13, 21 January 1845; *The Times*, 13 January 1845.

238 *wants verification*: *Examiner*, 'Palmer's End', 21 June 1856.

of frightful duration: Mary Gallop's trial and execution: *Era*, 22 December 1844; *Examiner*, 28 December 1844; *Hull Packet and East Riding Times*, 13 December 1844; *John Bull*, 14, 28 December 1844; *Lloyd's Weekly*, 15 December 1855; *Morning Chronicle*, 25, 31 December 1844; *Northern Star and Leeds General Advertiser*, 14 December 1844; *The Times*, 10, 30 December 1844.

239 *London contemporary paper*: *Morning Chronicle*, 2 August 1847, p.4; *Jackson's Oxford Journal*, 7 August 1847; *John Bull*, 31 July, 2 August 1847; *Bristol Mercury*, 14 August 1847.

242 *strong medical proof*: Both the Treasury Secretary and Taylor cited in Burney, *Poison, Detection and the Victorian Imagination*, p.32.

sentenced to death: The inquests, hearings and trials of Sarah Chesham: *Daily News*, 19 September 1846, 13 March 1847, 8 June 1850, 7, 26 March 1851; *Examiner*, 7 September

1850, 8, 29 March 1851; *Ipswich Journal*, 22 August 1846, 12 September, 8 March 1851; *John Bull*, 5, 19 September 1846, 13 March 1847, 7, 14 September 1850, 8, 29 March 1851; *Lloyd's Weekly*, 20 September, 25 October 1846, 9 June, 8, 15 September 1850, 13 April 1851; *Morning Chronicle*, 23 September 1850, 26 March 1851; *Northern Star and Leeds General Advertiser*, 30 January 1847, 1 June 1850, 29 March 1851; *Reynolds's Weekly News*, 8 September 1850, 9, 30 March 1851; *The Times*, 5, 19 September, 24 October 1846, 12, 13 March 1847, 5, 11, 23 September 1850, 7, 26 March 1851. There were also a number of broadsides retelling the story of Sarah Chesham – far more than for any other of these women. In particular, 'Sarah Chesham's Lamentation', in 'Ballads and Other Broadside Sheets Published by J. Pitts ... (1665–1870)', British Library, shelfmark 11621.k.4; 'Trial, Confession, and Awful Execution, of Thomas Drory, For the Murder of his Sweetheart ... Also, the Execution of Mrs. Sarah Chesham' (Gateshead, Robert Rankin, [1851]), Bodleian, Harding B.9(243); 'Sarah Chesham's Lamentation, for the Murder of Richard Chesham, her Husband, by Poison' (London, Hodges, [1851]), Bodleian Library, Firth b.25 (406); 'Copy of Verses, Written on the fate of Thomas Drory, and Sarah Chesham' (London, Ryle & Co., [1851]), Bodleian Library, Firth c.17(260); '[text missing] For the Murder of Richard Chesham, her Husband, by Poison' (London, Hodges, [1851]), Bodleian Library, Firth b.25(382).

244 *acquittal for his client*: For the inquest, trial and execution of Mary May: *Bell's Life*, 16 July 1848; *Ipswich Journal*, 29 July, 19 August 1848; *John Bull*, 29 July, 18 August 1848; *The Times*, 25 July, 15, 29 August 1848; for the inquest and trial of Hannah Southgate, *Bell's Life*, 3 September 1848; *Ipswich Journal*, 9 September 1848, 10 March 1849; *John Bull*, 2, 9 September 1848; *Lloyd's Weekly*, 11 March 1849; *Morning Chronicle*, 5 September 1848; *Northern Star and Leeds General Advertiser*, 2 September 1848; *The Times*, 31 August, 5 September 1848, 10 March 1849. Don Budds, *Arsenic and Old Wix: The True Account of Mary May and Hannah Southgate* ... (Colchester, privately published, 1995) contains excellent research into local parish archival material.

245 *this troublesome world*: Eliza Joyce's story appeared in: *Examiner*, 27 July 1844; *Hull Packet and East Riding Times*, 26 July, 9 August 1844; *John Bull*, 27 July 1844; *The Times*, 24 July 1844.

to view her body: 'Trial, Confession, and Awful Execution, of Thomas Drory, For the Murder of his Sweetheart', Bodleian, Harding B.9(243).

Bulwer's novel Lucretia: Edward Bulwer-Lytton, *Lucretia, or, The Children of the Night* (Leipzig, Berh. Tauchnitz Jun., 1846).

given the arsenic: *Punch*, July–December 1849, pp.96–7.

247 *to a burial club*: Katherine Watson, *Poisoned Lives: English Poisoners and Their Victims* (London, Hambledon & London, 2004), p.42; Knelman, *Twisting in the Wind*, pp.67–8.

medically educated: *Punch*: 'Sensation Times', 9 May 1863, p.193.

almost lenient: The case of Eliza Foxall and Mary Anne Scrafton can be found in *Northern Echo*, 14 September, 5 November 1887, and *The Times*, 14 September, 7 November 1887, 13 March 1888. None of the other newspapers or magazines I have used reported on this case at all.

6: Middle-Class Poisoners

248 *lemon-coloured kid gloves*: Cited in A.G. Allen, 'Thomas Griffiths Wainewright, Poisoner', in Thomas Seccombe, ed., *Lives of Twelve Bad Men: Original Studies of Eminent Scoundrels by Various Hands* (London, T. Fisher Unwin, 1894), p.296.

251 *he died there*: There is a lack of contemporary reportage on Wainewright, owing to the guilty plea and the charge of forgery rather than murder. Two reports can be found, in the *Examiner*, 9 July 1837, and the *Morning Chronicle*, 27 June 1838. *Reynolds's Miscellany of Romance* retold the case a few decades later, 'Wainwright [sic], the Poisoner', 11, August 1853, p.22, as did *All the Year Round*, 'Old Stories Re-told. Thomas Griffiths Wainewright

(Janus Weathercock), the Poisoner', 17, 5 January 1867, pp.34–41; at the end of the century, there was a summary, A.G. Allen, 'Thomas Griffiths Wainewright, Poisoner', in Thomas Seccombe, ed., *Lives of Twelve Bad Men*. A number of twentieth-century accounts attempt to make up for this lack. They include: Jonathan Curling, *Janus Weathercock: The Life of Thomas Griffiths Wainewright* (London, Thomas Nelson, 1938); John Lindsey, [pseud. Muriel St Claire Byrne], *Suburban Gentleman: The Life of Thomas Griffiths Wainewright, Poet, Painter and Poisoner* (London, Rich & Cowan, 1942); Andrew Motion, *Wainewright the Poisoner* (London, Faber, 2000); Charles Norman, *The Genteel Murderer* (New York, Macmillan, 1956); Marc Vaulbert de Chantilly, *Wainewright the Poisoner: An Example of Andrew Motion's 'High Scholarship'* (London, Vanity Press of Bethnal Green, 2000). All of these books, however, must be handled with caution. In the absence of objective documentation they rely on the later reputation of Wainewright, much (most?) of which is supposition and rumour. None takes into account the norms of crime reporting in the nineteenth century, and thus they unwittingly reproduce as fact many of the flights of fancy which were routine in murder cases.

252 *unearthly fire*: Senelick, 'Prestige of Evil', pp.110–11, traces the change in his appearance. The stage-vampire analogy is my own.

there's Wainewright: Cited in, amongst others, Collins, *Dickens and Crime*, p.43.

offer me the broom: Thomas Noon Talfourd, *Final Memorials of Charles Lamb* (London, E. Moxon, 1848), vol. 2, pp.23–4.

going to die directly: Dickens, *Martin Chuzzlewit*, pp.511–12.

253 *your lips are*: The main adaptations were: [T.H. Higgie and T.H. Lacy], 'Martin Chuzzlewit', unpublished playscript, for the Queen's Theatre, July 1844, Lord Chamberlain's Plays, BL Add MSS 42976 (23); E. Stirling, 'Martin Chuzzlewit', unpublished playscript, for the Lyceum, July 1844, Lord Chamberlain's Plays, BL Add MSS 42976 (15) [only Act I survives in the Lord Chamberlain's collection]; [C. Webb], 'Martin Chuzzlewit', unpublished playscript, for the New Standard Theatre, [1844], Lord Chamberlain's Plays, BL Add MSS 42976 (16); W.B. Webster, 'Martin Chuzzlewit', unpublished playscript, for the Olympic Theatre, March 1868, Lord Chamberlain's Plays, BL Add MSS 53066 (F).

position of the criminals: Bulwer, *Lucretia*, pp.vi–viii.

254 *weak and the criminal*: Cited in Burney, *Poison, Detection and the Victorian Imagination*, pp.54–5.

255 *the insurance money*: 'Confessions of an Attorney', *Chambers's Edinburgh Journal*, 355, October 1850, pp.241–4.

parts of his existence: Clive, *Paul Ferroll*, pp.18–19.

any kind of work: Dickens, *Little Dorrit*, pp.46–7, 814.

ten thousand pounds: Robert Surtees, *Ask Mamma, or, The Richest Commoner in England* ([1857–8], London, Bradbury, Evans & Co., 1872), p.335.

256 *with the murdered girl*: Cited in Dickens, *Letters*, vol. 2, p.252n.

Slinkton commits suicide: Charles Dickens, *Hunted Down. A Story, with some account of Thomas Griffiths Wainewright, the Poisoner* (London, John Camden Hotten, [1871?]).

to marry happily: Mary Elizabeth Braddon, *The Trail of the Serpent*, ed. Chris Willis ([1860], New York, Modern Library, 2003), p.396; Wilkie Collins, *The Moonstone*, ed. Sandra Kemp ([1868], Harmondsworth, Penguin, 1998), p.453; Wilkie Collins, *Miss or Mrs?, The Haunted Hotel, The Guilty River*, eds. Norman Page and Toru Sasaki ([1871, 1878, 1886], Oxford, Oxford University Press, 1999), pp.90ff; Mary Elizabeth Braddon, *Charlotte's Inheritance* ([1868], London, Simpkin, Marshall, Hamilton, Kent & Co., [n.d.]).

257 *like the morning mist*: Newton, *Crime and the Drama*, p.25; 'Who Did It? A Mystery Unmasked, or, The Track of Crime', unpublished playscript, for performance at the Britannia Theatre, August 1867, Lord Chamberlain's Plays, BL Add MSS 53061 (J); R.S. Hichens and H.D. Traill, *The Medicine Man*, published playscript (no publisher, title page), for performance at the Lyceum, May 1898, Lord Chamberlain's Plays, BL Add MSS 53658 (F).

an insurance company: De Quincey, *On Murder*, p.x; Oscar Wilde, 'Pen, Pencil and Poison: A Study', *Fortnightly Review*, 45, January 1889, pp.41, 52.

258 *achievements in poisoning*: Havelock Ellis, *The Criminal* (London, Walter Scott, 1890), pp.12–17, 127.

as a hedge-hog: Anon., *The Doings of William Palmer*, p.14.

her lover dies: *Blackwood's*, 'Switzerland in Summer and Autumn, part 2', 98, 1865, p.493.

262 *from no other cause*: [A.S. Taylor and G. Owen Rees], 'The Rugeley Suspected Secret Poisoning Cases. Evidence of Dr. Taylor ...', *Lancet*, 19 January 1856, 1, pp.78–80; 2 February 1856, 1, pp.134–5.

were not discreet: G. Lathom Browne and C.G. Stewart, *Reports of Trials for Murder by Poisoning ... With Chemical Introduction and Notes on the Poisons Used* (London, Stevens & Sons, 1883), pp.128–9; Mayhew's response: Extra Number, 'Trial of William Palmer', 27 May 1856, 'The Rugeley Poisonings. The Trial of William Palmer ... The Rugeley Number of the *Illustrated Times*' (London, 'Illustrated Times' Office, n.d. [1856]).

263 *up with demand*: Lodging-house: Mayhew, *London Labour*, vol. 1, pp.252–4; *Telegraph* and *Times* circulations: L. Perry Curtis, *Jack the Ripper and the London Press* (New Haven, Yale University Press, 2001), p.58; *Illustrated Times* and *Lloyd's*, W.F. Bynum, Stephen Lock and Roy Porter, eds., *Medical Journals and Medical Knowledge: Historical Essays* (London, Routledge, 1992), p.119.

the Prince Bishop: Barham, *Ingoldsby Legends*, p.68.

264 *was Palmerston*: The story is cited in Richard Whittington-Egan, *William Roughead's Chronicles of Murder* (Moffat, Lochar, 1991), p.318; it says something about the attitudes to Palmer, although it sounds apocryphal.

a trial's outcome: Palmer's Act was, more formally, 19 & 20 Vict.c.19.

266 *all came to do*: Judith Rowbotham and Kim Stevenson, eds., *Criminal Conversations: Victorian Crimes, Social Panic and Moral Outrage* (Columbus, Ohio State University Press, 2005), pp.15–16.

Palmer was convicted: The amount of print on the Palmer case is astounding, and a very selective overview includes: Old Bailey trial transcript, ref. t18560514-490; *Bell's Life*, 23 December 1855, 6, 13, 20 January, 3, February, 18 May, 25 May [trial supplement], 1, 15 June 1856; *Daily News*, 18 December 1855, 12, 15, 16, 17, 18, 24, 25, 30, 31 January, 1 February, 10 March, 15, 16, 17, 19, 20, 21, 22, 23, 24, 26, 27, 28, 29 May, 2, 4, 5, 9, 16 June 1856; *Derby Mercury*, 30 January 1856; *Era*, 23 December 1855, 6, 20, 27 January, 18 May, 1, 8 June 1856; *Examiner*, 14 June 1856; *John Bull*, 22 December 1855, 5, 12, 14, 19, 21, 26, 27 January, 22 March, 17, 19, 24, May, 7, 14 June 1856; *Liverpool Mercury*, 16 January 1856; *Lloyd's Weekly*, 23 December 1855, 13, 27 January, 3, 10 February, 18 May 1856; *Manchester Times*, 5, 6, 12 January, 14 May, 19, 26 June 1856; *Morning Chronicle*, 5 January, 21 March, 17 June 1856; *Racing Times*, 24 December 1855, 14, 21, 28 January, 2 June 1856. Contemporary pamphlets and trial reports include: *The Doings of William Palmer, the Alleged Wholesale Poisoner: His Public Frauds and Private Trickeries ...* (London, Frederick Mitchell, [1856]); *Illustrated Life and Career of William Palmer of Rugeley: containing details of his conduct as a school-boy, medical-student, racing-man, and poisoner ...* (London, Ward & Lock, 1856); *Illustrated and Unabridged Edition of* The Times *Report of the Trial of William Palmer ... from the short-hand notes taken in the Central Criminal Court ...* (London, Ward & Lock, 1856); *The Most Extraordinary Trial of William Palmer, for the Rugeley Poisonings ...* (4th edn, London, William Clark, 1847); [Angelo Bennett, a shorthand note-taker], *The Queen v. William Palmer: Verbatim Report of the Trial of William Palmer ...* (London, J. Allen, 1856). A good twentieth-century overview and transcript: George H. Knott, ed., rev. by Eric R. Watson, *Trial of William Palmer* (Edinburgh, William Hodge, 1923). Other useful material includes: Browne, Stewart, *Trials for Murder by Poisoning*; Ian A. Burney, 'A Poisoning of No Substance'; Michael Harris, 'Social Diseases? Crime and Medicine in the Victorian Press', in Bynum, Lock and Porter, *Medical Journals and Medical Knowledge*, pp.108–25; Thomas Rogers Forbes, *Surgeons at the Bailey: English*

Forensic Medicine to 1878 (New Haven, Yale University Press, 1985); George Robinson, *Observations on Some Recent Cases of Poisoning* (Gateshead, D. Dunglinson, 1856).
267 *Chemistry of Strychnia*: These articles and more appear in the *Lancet*, 31 May, 7, 14, 21, 28 June 1856.
to its coverage: Harris, 'Social Diseases? Crime and Medicine in the Victorian Press', p.114.
268 *would produce tetanus*: Conan Doyle, 'The Speckled Band', *The Adventures of Sherlock Holmes*, ed. Ed Glinert ([1892], Harmondsworth, Penguin, 2001), p.178; Conan Doyle, *The Sign of Four*, p.54.
but to man: Cited in Burney, *Poison, Detection and the Victorian Imagination*, p.2.
a view is concerned: *Morning Chronicle*, 14 June 1856, gives 100,000; the *Examiner* on the same day says 50,000, as did the *Era* the following day (although this article might have been taken from the *Examiner*; they are very similar); Palmer on the way to the scaffold: Henry Hawkins, *The Reminiscences of Sir Henry Hawkins, Baron Brampton*, ed. Richard Harris (London, Edward Arnold, 1904), vol. 1, p.273; George Orwell, 'A Hanging', in *The Collected Essays, Journalism and Letters of George Orwell* (New York, Harcourt, Brace & World, 1968), vol. 1, pp.44–8. Orwell's knowledge of Thackeray: Simpson, *Witnesses to the Scaffold*, p.216; population of Stafford: estimated from the 1851 and 1861 censuses; *Staffordshire Advertiser* reprinted in *Daily News*, 16 May 1856; the Accrington walker: *Liverpool Mercury*, 27 June 1856; the complaining journalist: cited by the editor of *Lloyd's*, Thos. [sic] Catling, *My Life's Pilgrimage* (London, John Murray, 1911), p.59.
269 *pleasure, too*: The Englishwoman to the German traveller: Max Schlesinger, *Saunterings in and About London*, trs. Otto Wenckstern (London, Nathaniel Cook, 1853), pp.59–60; Anon., *The Boy Detective, Or, The Crimes of London* (London, Newsagents Publishing Co., [1865–6]), p.46.
continued to be in doubt: John Sutherland, *Victorian Fiction: Writers, Publishers, Readers* (Basingstoke, Macmillan, 1995), p.39, suggests that one of the maids at the Talbot Arms was bribed to say she was taken ill after tasting Cook's broth, that the judge was 'ruthlessly biassed', and that the establishment closed ranks to secure a conviction. But the judge's remarks appear fairly standard when read in conjunction with other trials of the period; and Sutherland's main source, Robert Graves' twentieth-century rehabilitation of Palmer, is hardly unbiased itself.
he killed Cook, Anthony Trollope, *Phineas Redux*, ed. John C. Whale ([1874], Oxford, Oxford World Classics, 1983), vol. 2, p.178.
they were portraits: Anon., *Illustrated and Unabridged Edition of* The Times *Report*, British Library shelfmark 6497.b.4.(2.). The clippings have only one identifying tag, 'The Family Fri[end?]'. The books 'by' the Revd Thomas Palmer and Thomas Wakley are *AN INQUIRY INTO the CHARGE of LORD CHIEF JUSTICE CAMPBELL, on the LATE TRIAL of WILLIAM PALMER, illustrative of its dangerous tendencies as destructive to the long enjoyed rights and privileges of all British subjects* (London, T. Taylor, 1856) and *The Cries of the Condemned: Proofs of the Unfair Trial of William Palmer* (London, C. Elliot, 1856); the denials by the real Revd Thomas Palmer and Thomas Wakley: in *John Bull*, 'The Late William Palmer', 21 June 1856, and *Daily News*, letter, 9 June 1856; George Palmer: *Daily News*, 31 January 1856, p.3; the *Racing Times*, 23 June 1856, p.197, carries the letter from C.J. Collins regarding *Dick Diminy*; the correspondence squabble between the newspaper and the publisher then continues on 30 June, and in the *Era* on 22, 27 and 29 June.
270 *produces no evidence*: Alfred Swaine Taylor, *Poisoning by Strychnia, with Comments on the Medical Evidence Given at the Trial of William Palmer* ... (London, Longman, Brown, Green, Longmans, & Roberts, 1856), p.2.
at Shrewsbury Races: Anon., *The Most Extraordinary Trial of William Palmer, for the Rugeley Poisonings*; Southwark Police Court: *Daily News*, 15 July 1856, p.6. Ch. V. Cavour [pseud. Stephanos Xenos], Ὁ [ἐ]ναγης Ἰατρος ἠτοι ἡ πολυκροτος δικη του Οὐίλλιαμ Παλμερ. Ἐκ της συγχρονου Ἀγγλικης δημοσωγραφιας ὑπο. (ἐν Λονδινῳ, 1860) [*The Cursed Doctor: The Notorious Trial of William Palmer from Contemporary English Journalism*, London, n.p.,

1860]. I am greatly obliged to Chris Michaelides of the British Library for his help with this book; the background information on Xenos comes from Chris Michaelides, 'Greek Printing in England, 1500–1900 … Stephanos Xenos, a Greek Publisher in Nineteenth-century London', in Barry Taylor, ed., *Foreign-language Printing in London, 1500–1900* (Boston Spa and London, British Library, 2002), pp.212ff.

271 *murderer in an opera*: Racing Times, 'Tattersall's', and 'The Room', 14 January 1856; [Charles Dickens], *Household Words*, 'The Demeanour of Murderers', 14 June 1856, p.506; Chicken/Vengeance and Gemma di Vergy: *Racing Times*, 'Vengeance', 20 October 1856, [letter], 23 March 1857.
    labelled Palmer's house: Trains: *Daily News*, 30 June 1856, p.2; photographer: *Illustrated Life and Career of William Palmer of Rugeley*, p.103; Madame Tussaud's: *Bell's Life*, 15 June 1856, p.3 and catalogues, *Biographical and Descriptive Sketches of the Distinguished Characters which Compose the Unrivalled Exhibition and Historical Gallery of Madame Tussaud and Sons* (London, G. Cole, 1869) and ibid. (London, M'Corquodale, 1873); Allsop's, *Liverpool Mercury*, 20 June 1856, p.1; Royal Parthenon, *Era*, 4 December 1859, p.1; Staffordshire figurines: P.D. Gordon Pugh Collection, City Museum and Art Gallery, Stoke-on-Trent.

272 *returned in refreshments*: Reprinted from the *Manchester Examiner* in the *Morning Chronicle*, 'Sporting Intelligence: William Palmer of Rugeley', 12 September 1856.
    poison bottles of Palmer: Pall Mall Gazette, 'The Value of Murderers' Relics', 28 October 1892.

273 *very uncommon name*: The Times, 'Lord Selborne and the Rugeley Poisoner', 26 November 1875.
    laughable farce: Anon., 'Monti the Poisoner', unpublished playscript, for performance at the Britannia Saloon, May 1856, Lord Chamberlain's Plays, BL Add MSS 52959 (Y); *The Rugeley Tragedy*, playbill reproduced in *John Bull*, 'Stage Morals', 20 September 1856.
    to be of good cheer: Mary Elizabeth Braddon, *Aurora Floyd* (London, Tinsley Bros., 1863), p.183.

274 *before his marriage*: For the ages of Smethurst and Mrs Smethurst, see the Old Bailey trial transcripts, refs. t18590815-785 and t18591128-86, where Smethurst's age is given as a fact, and Mrs Smethurst's is estimated from her appearance by her landlady. *Tait's Edinburgh Magazine*, 'Circumstantial Evidence', September 1859, pp.548–53, suggested nearly thirty years' difference between the couple in one sentence, in the next only eighteen. The purchase of Smethurst's medical degree, Richard Altick, *Victorian Studies in Scarlet* (London, J.M. Dent & Sons, 1972), p.165.

275 *for fourteen years*: Forbes, *Surgeons at the Bailey*, pp.138–9.
    she had been poisoned: The analysis of Taylor's statements is in Rowbotham and Stevenson, *Criminal Conversations*, p.147.
    until 1932: Mant, 'Science in the Detection of Crime', p.554.

276 *in twenty minutes*: The details of the case of Dr Smethurst are compiled from: Old Bailey trial transcripts, refs. t18590704-683, 18590815-785 and 18591128-86 (the first two references are to the murder trial, the latter to the bigamy case); *Bell's Life*, 21 August, 11 September, 4 December 1859; *Daily News*, 5, 9, 14, 21, 26 May, 1, 16, 17 June, 8, 9 July, 16, 17, 18, 19, 20, 22, 23, 24, 25, 26, 27 August [and letters passim on following days, to 6 September], 1, 5, 6, 8, 12, 19 September, 10 October, 14, 21 November, 1 December 1859; *Era*, 13 November 1859; *Examiner*, 3 September 1859; *John Bull*, 20, 27 August 1859; *Leader*, 7, 14 May, 27 August, 10 September 1859; *Liverpool Mercury*, 22 August 1859; *Lloyd's Weekly*, 15, 22 May, 5 June, 10 July, 21, 28 August, 4, 11, 25, 28 September, 13, 20 November 1859; *Morning Chronicle*, 7 May, 23, 25 August, 5, 30 September, 12 November 1859.
    T.G. Geoghan's *Observations on the Medical Evidence in the Case of the Queen v. Smethurst* (Dublin, Hodges, Smith & Co., 1859) is useful, as are two summaries of the case: Browne and Stewart, *Reports of Trials for Murder by Poisoning*, and Leonard A. Parry, *Trial of Dr*

Smethurst (Edinburgh, W. Hodge, 1931). Forbes, *Surgeons at the Bailey*, is good on the forensic/medico-legal questions; and Ginger S. Frost, *Living in Sin: Cohabiting as Husband and Wife in Nineteenth-century England* (Manchester, Manchester University Press, 2008) on the questions raised by the trial.

277 *clean and bright*: *Daily News*, 4 February 1848, p.8.
prevention of crime: *Lancet*, 'The Scientific Evidence on the Trial of William Palmer', 1, 1856, p.667.

278 *morally impossible*: *The Times*, 23 July 1856, p.12.
Immoral. How true: Charles Dickens, *The Mystery of Edwin Drood*, ed. Arthur J. Cox ([1870], Harmondsworth, Penguin, 1985), p.222.
of Smethurst's guilt: Brodie cited in Browne and Stewart, *Reports of Trials for Murder by Poisoning*, p.479.
with their opinions: [Charles Dickens], 'Five New Points of Criminal Law', *All the Year Round*, 24 September 1859, pp.12–13.

280 *black scoundrel*: Dickens to John Forster, 25 August 1859, cited in Collins, *Dickens and Crime*, p.246.
low wickedness: Charles Dickens to John Forster, ?15 September 1857, Dickens, *Letters*, vol. 8, pp.446–7.
dire insensibility: Charles Dickens, 'The Lazy Tour of Two Idle Apprentices', *Reprinted Pieces and The Lazy Tour of Two Idle Apprentices*, introduction by Charles Dickens the Younger (London, Macmillan, 1925), p.396.
interpretation of villain roles: Frank Rahill, *The World of Melodrama* (University Park, Pennsylvania State University Press, 1967), pp.208–9.

281 *to hear about it*: Emily Eden, *The Semi-Detached House* ([1859], London, Virago, 1979), pp.177–8.
miserably wanting: Wynne, *The Sensation Novel*, pp.14–15.

282 *without fear of detection*: Braddon, *Trail of the Serpent*, p.161.

283 *most effectively removed*: Cited in W.N. Roughead, ed., *Classic Crimes: A Selection from the Works of William Roughead* (New York, New York Review Books, 2000), pp.149–50.
That is a fact: Jane Carlyle to Thomas Carlyle, 26 July 1857, *Letters*, vol. 32, p.201.

284 *guaranteed to contain Arsenic*: *Hearth and Home*, 13 January 1898, p.421.

286 *immoral hussy*: This demolition of the prosecution's case was performed by Alexander Forbes Irvine, 'Report of the Trial of Madeleine Smith, before the High Court of Justiciary at Edinburgh ...' *Edinburgh Review*, 108, October 1858, pp.343–76. The paraphrase of the judge's remarks at the end is, of course, my own.
not proven: For the details of the crime and trial of Madeleine Smith, see, among many other reports: *Aberdeen Journal*, 8 April, 15 July 1857; *Bell's Life*, 12 July 1857; *Caledonian Mercury*, 4 April, 1, 7 July 1857; *Daily News*, 2, 4, 6, 8, 9 10 July 1857; *Era*, 12 July, 9 August 1857; *Examiner*, 4 April 1857; *Glasgow Herald*, 10, 13 April, 15 June, 1, 3, 6, 8, 10, 13, 15, 17, 31 July, 7 September 1857; *Lloyd's Weekly*, 5 April, 5, 12 July 1857. The journals also covered this case thoroughly: *Dublin Review*, 'A Complete Report on the Trial of Miss Madeleine Smith, for the alleged poisoning of Pierre Emile L'Angelier', 43, September 1857, pp.128–71; [Alexander Forbes Irvine], *Edinburgh Review*, 'Report of the Trial of Madeleine Smith, before the High Court of Justiciary at Edinburgh ...'; *Reynolds's Miscellany of Romance*, 'Madeleine Smith, the Alleged Poisoner', 19, August 1857, p.72; *Tait's Edinburgh Magazine*, 'Circumstantial Evidence', August 1857, pp.163–8; *Illustrated Times*, 'Glasgow Poisoning Case. Extra Number', 11 July 1857 (16 pp.); 'Incidents of the Trial of Madeleine Smith', 18 July 1857, p.61. An unusually high number of trial pamphlets appeared, among them: 'Historicus', *The Story of Minie L'Angelier or Madeleine Hamilton Smith* (Edinburgh, Myles MacPhail, 1857); Alexander Forbes Irvine, *Report of the Trial of Madeleine Smith ... for the Alleged Poisoning of Pierre Emile L'Angelier* (Edinburgh, T. & T. Clark, 1857); John Morison, *A Complete Report on the Trial of Miss Madeleine Smith, for the alleged poisoning of Pierre Emile L'Angelier* (Edinburgh, William P. Nimmo, 1857); Anon., *Glasgow Poisoning Case*.

Unabridged Report of the Evidence in this Extraordinary Trial ... (London, George Vickers, 1857). Modern studies include: Peter Hunt, *The Madeleine Smith Affair* (New York, Collier, 1965); Karin Jacobson, 'Plain Faces, Weird Cases: Domesticating the Law in Collins's *Law and the Lady* and the Trial of Madeleine Smith', *Tennessee Studies in Literature*, 41, 2003, pp.283–312; F. Tennyson Jesse, ed., *Trial of Madeleine Smith* (London, William Hodge & Co., 1949); Douglas MacGowan, *Murder in Victorian Scotland: The Trial of Madeleine Smith* (Westport, CT, Praeger, 1999).

was overwhelming: Letters of Blackwood, Eliot and Lewes, in *The George Eliot Letters*, ed. Gordon S. Haight (London, Oxford University Press/Yale University Press, 1954–78), 7, 12 July 1857, vol. 2, pp.360–63.

aware of this: Mary S. Hartman, *Victorian Murderesses: A True History of Thirteen Respectable French and English Women Accused of Unspeakable Crimes* (London, Robson, 1977), p.82.

287 *deserved commiseration*: James Gray: cited in Roughead, *Burke and Hare*, p.28; the *Caledonian Mercury* fund is cited in a broadside in ibid., pp.402–4; Eliza Chestney and Emily Sandford: *Norfolk Chronicle*, reprinted in *John Bull*, 16 April 1849, p.234; Madeleine Smith: *Berwick Advertiser*, reprinted in *Leeds Mercury*, 25 July 1857, p.4, *Era*, 9 August 1857, p.9; Roughead, *Classic Crimes*, p.151; Wainwright: Walter Wood, *Survivors' Tales of Famous Crimes* (London, Cassell & Co., 1916), p.42.

utility man generally: This description of his job was given by Wardle in his 'Reminiscences of William Morris', British Library, BM Add MS 45350. I am grateful to Fiona MacCarthy for this reference, and for her information on George Wardle's background.

La Femme Sage: *Racing Times*, 20 July 1857, p.229.

288 *lo, it was a Dream*: Anon., *Madeline Smith's Dream in Prison: A Poem* (London, T. Dawson, 1857). Only two copies appear to have survived; no copies appear in WorldCat, a compilation of the catalogues of more than 10,000 libraries worldwide. I suspect that the publisher named on the title page of one copy (the second has none) is false: it appears nowhere else in either the UK's Copac or WorldCat.

worse than death: [Emma Robinson], *Madeleine Graham* (London, John Maxwell & Co., 1864).

289 *White, at that*: Lyn Pykett, 'The Newgate Novel and Sensation Fiction, 1830–1868', in *The Cambridge Companion to Crime Fiction*, ed. Martin Priestman (Cambridge, Cambridge University Press, 2003), p.27.

shall hear it now: Wilkie Collins, *The Woman in White*, p.9.

Yes or No: Clive, *Paul Ferroll*, introduction by Charlotte Mitchell, p.xiii.

290 *concluding number of* Little Dorrit: *Caledonian Mercury*, 'Miss Smith's Trial', 1 July 1857.

resident of Bedlam: These links are discussed by Wynne, *The Sensation Novel*, pp.47ff.

as Miss Smith's had: Wilkie Collins, *The Law and the Lady*, ed. Jenny Bourne Taylor ([1875], Oxford, Oxford University Press, 1999), in particular pp.157–71.

of her inheritance: Maurice-Méjan, *Recueil des Causes célèbres, et des arrêts qui les ont décidées* (Paris, Garnery, 1808–09). The story of the Marquise de Douhault appears in vol. 2, pp.5–344 and vol. 6, pp.5–92.

291 *two years previously*: Clyde K. Hyder, 'Wilkie Collins and the Woman in White', *PMLA*, 54, 1, March 1939, pp.297–303.

his protestations: Wilkie Collins, *Armadale*, ed. John Sutherland ([1864–66], Harmondsworth, Penguin, 1995), p.70.

It was true: Wilkie Collins, *Poor Miss Finch* (London, Richard Bentley & Son, 1872), p.v; Wybert Reeve, *From Life*, p.112. I am grateful to Paul Lewis for directing me to this reference.

292 *close by*: Wynne, *The Sensation Novel*, p.41.

in her honour: Noted by John Sutherland in the introduction to his edition of Wilkie Collins, *Armadale*, p.vii.

294 *vanished after his death*: Sheridan Le Fanu, *Uncle Silas: A Tale of Bartram-Haugh*, ed. Victor Sage ([1864], Harmondsworth, Penguin, 2000), pp.159–63; 'The Murdered Cousin' first published in *Dublin University Magazine*, 1838, in Sheridan Le Fanu, *Ghost Stories and Tales of Mystery* (Dublin, James McGlashan, 1851).

missing the point: [Seymour Hicks and Laurence Irving], 'Uncle Silas', unpublished playscript, for performance at Toole's Theatre, ?Feb [semi-illegible] 1893, Lord Chamberlain's Plays, BL Add MSS 53520 (D).

295 *mansion, long-decayed*: 'The Murders in the Rue Morgue', in *Edgar Allan Poe: Poetry and Tales* (New York, Library of America, 1984), pp.400, 412, 425.

reappropriated by the house: Wilkie Collins, 'A Terribly Strange Bed', in *Mad Monkton and Other Stories*, eds. Norman Page and Kamal Al-Solaylee (Oxford, Oxford University Press, 1994).

a descending ceiling: Anon. *The Poor Boys of London, or, Driven to Crime. A Life Story for the People* ([London, Temple Publishing Co., c.1866]), pp.116–18. Doyle, 'The Engineer's Thumb', in *The Adventures of Sherlock Holmes*.

296 *watchings ... listenings*: Dickens, *Bleak House*, pp.62–3, 260, 410.

watch people: George R. Sims, *Dorcas Dene, Detective* ([1897], London, Greenhill, 1986), p.10.

father's suspicions: Slater, *Two Classic Melodramas*, p.72; James Fitzjames Stephen, 'Detectives in Fiction and Real Life', *Saturday Review*, xvii, June 1864, pp.712–13.

is something terrible: Braddon to Bulwer, cited in introduction to Braddon, *The Trail of the Serpent*. Braddon was discussing the requirements of 'halfpenny readers', from her penny-blood days, but sensation readers seemed to require the same.

297 *happily ever after*: Mary Elizabeth Braddon, *Lady Audley's Secret*, ed. David Skilton ([1861–2], Oxford, Oxford University Press, 1987).

a very heavy door: Dickens, 'Hunted Down', p.47.

298 *not be able to*: Dickens, *Bleak House*, p.796; Edward Ellis, *Ruth the Betrayer; or, The Female Spy* (London, [John Dicks], 1863), pp.1, 3, 68; Collins, *Armadale*, p.484.

299 *paper cigars*: Forrester's *The Female Detective* and the anonymous *The Experiences of a Lady Detective* are riddled with questions. Andrew Forrester's 'G' stories are found in *Revelations of a Private Detective* (London, Ward & Lock, 1863) and *The Female Detective* (London, Ward & Lock, 1864), with *The Private Detective*, and *Tales by a Female Detective* being partial reissues later; the Mrs Paschal stories are found in Anon., *Revelations of a Lady Detective* (London, George Vickers, 1864). *The Experiences of a Lady Detective* (London, Charles Henry Clarke, 1884) is credited to William Stephen Hayward, and is identical to *Revelations* apart from its cover – to the point that even the title page says *Revelations* [not *Experiences*] *of a Lady Detective*.

The 1863 dating of *Revelations of a Private Detective* is generally considered to be suspect, as the trade *Publisher's Weekly Circular* advertised it in 1864, five months before *The Experiences of a Lady Detective*. However the British Library's copy carries an acquisition stamp dated 9 January 1863, which reopens the question. *The Experiences of a Lady Detective* has itself sometimes (almost certainly wrongly) been catalogued as published in 1861. In the discussions of the first female detective, however, *Ruth the Betrayer* appears to have been entirely overlooked, and yet it was issued in parts in 1862, with the British Library's single-volume edition carrying an acquisition stamp dated 28 February 1863.

For a discussion of the dating of the first story to use women detectives: Michele B. Slung, *Crime on her Mind: Fifteen Stories of Female Sleuths, From the Victorian Era to the Forties* (Harmondsworth, Penguin, 1975), p.17; Dagni Bredesen, 'Conformist Subversion: Ambivalent Agency in *Revelations of a Lady Detective*', *Clues: A Journal of Detection*, 25, 1, 2006, 20–32; Dagni Bredesen, in her introduction to *The First Female Detectives*: The Female Detective *(1864)* and Revelations of a Lady Detective *(1864)* (Ann Arbor, MI, Scholars Facsimiles & Reprints, 2010), casts an entirely new light on the reality of women detectives in the nineteenth century, although it appeared too late for me to incorporate her discoveries into my text. I am grateful to Professor Bredesen for sharing her thoughts on Forrester with me.

For 'paper cigars', Isabella F. Romer, *The Rhone, the Darro, and the Guadalquivír: A Summer Ramble in 1842* (London, Richard Bentley, 1843), vol. 1, p.252.

to be bought off: Thomas de Quincey, 'William Godwin', in *The Collected Writings of Thomas de Quincey*, ed. David Masson (Edinburgh, Adam & Charles Black, 1890), vol. 11, pp.329–30; Reynolds, *The Mysteries of London*, vol. 1, p.32; Dickens, *Martin Chuzzlewit*, p.867.

300 *under her bed*: James McLevy, *McLevy, The Edinburgh Detective* (Edinburgh, Mercat, 2001), and *McLevy Returns* (Edinburgh, Mercat, 2002); these collections reprint stories from *Curiosities of Crime in Edinburgh during the Last Thirty Years* (pre-1861) and *The Sliding Scale of Life, or, Thirty years' observations of falling men and women in Edinburgh* (1861); James McGovan's stories can be found in: *Solved Mysteries: or, Revelations of a City Detective* (2nd edn, Edinburgh, John Menzies, 1888), *Brought to Bay, or, Experiences of a City Detective* (1878) and *Hunted Down, Recollections of a City Detective*; *Strange Clues, Traced and Tracked*. Helen Blackwood and her lodgers, Wilson, *Murderess*, p.118.

301 *bloodstains and more*: Ellis, *Ruth the Betrayer*, pp.3–4; Forrester, *The Female Detective*, p.3; Anon., *The Boy Detective*, pp.72, 34–5.

the detective officer: George Roberts, 'Lady Audley's Secret', for performance at the Theatre Royal, St James's, February 1863, Lord Chamberlain's Plays, BL Add Mss 53020 (I). Some sources name the author as Robert Walters, which was a pseudonym used by George Roberts (he is credited thus on a playbill for the 1877 Olympic production); [William Suter], 'Lady Audley's Secret', for performance at the Queen's Theatre, February 1863, Lord Chamberlain's Plays, BL Add Mss 53020 (H); C.H. Hazlewood, 'Lady Audley's Secret', in George Rowell, ed., *19th-Century Plays* (London, Oxford University Press, 1953); John Brougham, 'The Mystery of Audley Court', for performance at Astley's Theatre, August 1866, Lord Chamberlain's Plays, BL Add MSS 53052 (J).

302 *imaginary crime*: Anon., 'Sensation Literature', *English Woman's Domestic Magazine*, 1 May 1863, p.18.

303 *pardoned for the murder*: Collins, *Armadale*, pp.527, 529–31.

304 *man from Scotland Yard*: Ibid., pp.397, 406.

even out of it: Andrew Lansdowne, *A Life's Reminiscences of Scotland Yard* (London, Leadenhall Press, [1890]), p.7.

306 *to detect anything*: Anthony Trollope, *The Eustace Diamonds*, ed. W.J. McCormack ([1871–73], Oxford, Oxford World's Classics, 1998), vol. 2, p.155.

zeal, and judgment: [Charles Dickens and W.H. Wills], 'The Metropolitan Protectives', *Household Words*, 3, April 1851, pp.97–105.

307 *you are overstepping*: Wood, *Mrs Halliburton's Troubles*, pp.315, 323.

310 *never have been hanged*: The details of the crime and trial of Christiana Edmunds have been compiled from: Old Bailey trial transcript, ref. t18720108-185; *Birmingham Daily Post*, 22, 23, 29 August, 1, 8, 9, September 1871, 16, 17 January 1872; *Daily News*, 23, 25 August, 1, 9, September 1871, 16, 17 January 1872; *Illustrated Police News*, 9, 16 September 1871, 20 January, 10 February 1872; *Lloyd's Weekly*, 27 August, 3, 10, 17 September 1871, 21 January 1872; *Pall Mall Gazette*, 25 November, 30 December 1871, 21 January 1872; *Reynolds's Newspaper*, 20, 27 August, 3, 10 September 1871, 21, 28 January, 19 May, 18 August 1872; *The Times*, 1, 8, 9 September 1871, 12 January 1872.

311 *happens to tell him so*: George Eliot, *Middlemarch*, ed. W.J. Harvey ([1871–2], Harmondsworth, Penguin Books, 1985), p.187. For more on the sources Eliot used for her medical and forensic information, see Anna Theresa Kitchel, *Quarry for Middlemarch* (Berkeley, University of California Press, 1950). I am grateful to Michael Wolff for alerting me to this book.

315 *rang through the building*: The case of Adelaide Bartlett has been examined repeatedly. I have compiled my account from: Old Bailey trial transcript, ref. t18860405-466. *Bell's*, 19, 20 April 1886; *County Gentleman*, 27 February 1886; *Illustrated Police News*, 20, 27 February, 1, 6, 8, 13, 20, 27 March, 17, 19, 24 April 1886; *John Bull*, 24 April 1886; *Lloyd's Weekly*, 10 January, 7, 14, 21, 28 February, 7, 14, 21 March, 18 April 1886; *Pall Mall Gazette*, 19, 20 February, 5, 13, 19, 20 April 1886; *Reynolds's Newspaper*, 28 February, 14, 28 March, 18 April 1886; *The Times*, 13, 16, 19 27 February, 1, 8, 13, 20 March, 6, 7, 8, 14, 17, 19, 20 April 1886. Magazine reports include: *Cornhill*, Edward Clarke, 'Leaves from a Lawyer's Casebook: The Pimlico Mystery', 49, 1920; *Lancet*, [editorial], 24 April 1886, 1, pp.794–5, 'Feminine Pruriency', 24 April 1886, 1, p.800, Alfred Leach, 'The Case of Edwin Bartlett: Mercurialism; Death from Liquid Chloroform; Necropsy', 22 May 1886, 2, pp.968–70; 29 May 1886, 2, pp.1017–18. Edward Beale, barrister for the defence, published *The Trial of Adelaide Bartlett for Murder* ... (London, Stevens & Haynes, 1886), and Sir Edward Clarke, *The Story of My Life* (London, John Murray, 1918), has useful detail. There are several modern recountings of the case: Yseult Bridges, *Poison and Adelaide Bartlett: The Pimlico Poisoning Case* (London, Macmillan, 1970); Kate Clarke, *The Pimlico Murder: The Strange Case of Adelaide Bartlett* (London, Souvenir, 1990); and Sir John Hall, *Trial of Adelaide Bartlett* (Edinburgh, William Hodge, 1927).

316 *the same readiness*: Conan Doyle, *A Study in Scarlet* ([1887], Harmondsworth, Penguin, 2007), pp.7–10.

317 *of his audience*: Conan Doyle, 'The Adventure of the Six Napoleons' in *The Return of Sherlock Holmes* ([1905], Harmondsworth, Penguin, 2008), p.241.

318 *man than yourself*: Gould Penn, *The Life of the Reverend George Dyson and his Strange Adventures with Mrs. Bartlett* (London, Williams & Co., [1886]).
Latin verbs: Cited in Whittington-Egan, *William Roughead*, p.203.

319 *goes mad*: Richard Dowling, *Tempest-Driven. A Romance* (London, Tinsley Bros., 1886).
the word 'Forgive': F.C. Philips and C.J. Wills, *The Fatal Phryne* (London, Sonnenschein & Co., 1889).

7: Science, Technology and the Law

321 *trial by combat*: The case of Abraham Thornton is compiled from: *Examiner*, 23 November 1817; *Hull Packet*, 28 April 1818; *Morning Chronicle*, 7, 17, 18, 19, 24 November 1817, 26 January 1818; *The Ladies' Monthly Magazine*, 1 March 1818. Pamphlets include: Anon., *Thornton's Trial!! The Trial of ABRAHAM THORNTON ... for the Murder of Mary Ashford* ... (new edn, Warwick, E. Heathcote, [1817]); Anon., *Wager of Battle. Thornton and Mary Ashford; or, An Antidote to Prejudice* (London, Akerman, 1818); Anon., *An Investigation of the Case of Abraham Thornton, Who was Tried at Warwick, August 8, 1817, for The Wilful Murder, and Afterwards Arraigned for the Rape, of Mary Ashford; (of which charges he was that day acquitted;)* ... 'by an attorney-at-law' (London, James Harper, 1818); Edward Holroyd, *Observations upon the Case of Abraham Thornton ... Shewing the Danger of Pressing Presumptive Evidence Too Far* ... (3rd edn, London, J. Mawman, 1819). A twentieth-century trial transcript can be found in Sir John Hall, ed., *Trial of Abraham Thornton* (Edinburgh, W. Hodge, 1927), and the case has also been examined by the London Feminist History Group, Anna K. Clark, 'Rape or Seduction? A Controversy over Sexual Violence in the Nineteenth Century', in *The Sexual Dynamics of History: Men's Power, Women's Resistance* (London, Pluto Press, 1983), pp.13–42. Daniel J. Ernst, 'The Moribund Appeal of Death: Compensating Survivors and Controlling Jurors in Early Modern England', *The American Journal of Legal History*, 28, April 1984, pp.164–88, explores the legal history of this stratagem. I am grateful to Professor John Langbein for this reference.

322 *portrait of Thornton*: Bell's Life, 'Illustrated Newspapers', 27 December 1884.

Parish of Aston: Revd Luke Booker, *A Moral Review of the Conduct and Case of Mary Ashford, in Refutation of the Arguments Adduced in Defence of her Supposed Violator and Murderer* (Dudley, John Rann, 1818), p.55.

323 *triumphs over evil*: William Barrymore, *Trial By Battle; or, Heaven Defend the Right* (London, J. Duncombe, [1831]).

ever served up: H. Chance Newton, *The Old Vic. and its Associations* (London, Fleetway Press, n.d.]), pp.64–5.

shoots himself: Anon., *The Murdered Maid; or, The Clock Struck Four!!!* (Warwick, 'printed for the author', 1818).

Inordinate Passions: Anon., *The Mysterious Murder; or, What's the Clock, a Melodrama in Three Acts, Founded on a Tale Too True* (Birmingham, 'printed for and sold by the author', [?1818]); the attribution of the authorship to the Birmingham prompter is Richard Altick's, *Studies in Scarlet*, p.87.

324 *contaminating atmosphere*: Scott, *Journals*, 18 November 1826, p.274; Anon., 'The Somnambulist', *Figaro in London*, 22 April 1839, p.12.

326 *just at the crown*: Anon., 'The Murderers of the Round Tower Inn', Lord Chamberlain's Plays.

ready to be produced: The case of Mary Anne Burdock has been compiled from: *Bell's Life*, 19 April 1835; *Bristol Mercury*, 11, 18, 21 April 1835; *The Times*, 13 April 1835. Later reports include: *Glasgow Herald*, 12 March 1856; *Illustrated Police News*, 4 October 1890; the two broadside collections listed below; and a single trial report, Anon., *Trial of Mary Ann Burdock, for the Wilful Murder of Mrs. Clara Ann Smith, by Administering Sulphuret of Arsenic* ... (Bristol, W.H. Somerton, [1835]).

327 *o' their body*: Eliot, *Middlemarch*, p.778.

and execution broadsides: The British Library has a particularly rich cache of Mary Anne Burdock broadsides, shelfmark 74/1880.c.12 ff.1–77; the broadsides cited are all from this collection, and include: 'Further Particulars of the Examination At the Coroner's Inquest and the Verdict returned by the Jury for the WILFUL MURDER of Mrs. Clara Ann Smith, by Mrs. Burdock' (Bonner, Printer, Bristol) [f. 45]; 'The Bristol Assizes, and Learn'd Recorder's Charge to the GRAND JURY' (John Bonner, Printer, Nicholas Steps, Bristol) [f. 50]; 'A Correct ACCOUNT of the TRIAL and PROCEEDINGS in the Case of Mary A. Burdock, FOR FELONY AND MURDER at the Bristol Assizes, April 10th, 1835' (John Davis, Printer, Temple S[remainder of page torn off]) [f. 51]; 'Bristol Assizes. A Correct ACCOUNT of the Trial and Sentence of Mary Ann Burdock' (John Davis, Printer, Temple Street, Bristol) [f. 52]; 'The Correct Confession of MARY ANN BURDOCK, Sworn before the Magistrates by ANN BAYNTON' (T. Watson, St James's Churchyard, [Bristol?]) [f. 53]; 'The Trial of Mrs. BURDOCK this day with the verdict' (Taylor, Redcliff Street, Bristol) [f. no. torn off, but 54]; 'Trial of Mrs. BURDOCK, This Day Five o'Clock' (Taylor, Redcliff Street, Bristol) [f. 55]; 'The TRIAL of Mrs BURDOCK' (J. Bonner, Nicholas Steps, Bristol) [f. 56]; 'The Execution of Mrs. Burdock. Aged 34 Years. convicted at the Bristol Assizes of the Wilful Murder of Clara Ann Smith ... and who was Executed upon the New Drop, this day ... April 15 1835 (John Bonner, Nicholas Steps, Bristol)' [f. 57]; [similar broadsheet, re-laid-out, f.58]; '[page torn]nd Execution of M.A. BURDOCK, Who was Executed at Bristol ... for the MURDER of Clara Ann Smith' (J. Davies [sic], Temple Street, Bristol) [f. 59]; 'Dying Speech, Confession and behaviour of Mary Burdock, Executed at Bristol Gaol ...' (Taylor, Redcliff Street, Bristol) [f. 60]. The second collection is shelfmark 74/1880.c.20, ff.324–67, and includes: 'The Apprehending and Taking of Mrs Burdock ... on the suspicion of the MURDER of Mrs. Clara Smith, With the examination of the Body, which was taken from the Grave on Wednesday ...' (J. Bonner, Bristol) [f.366]; 'The LIFE, CONFESSION and *EXECUTION*, of Mrs. BURDOCK, Who was Executed at the New Drop, Bristol Gaol ... on Wednesday, April 15th, 1835' (John Bonner, Nicholas Steps, Bristol) [f.368].

supply a missing link: *Bristol Mercury*, 25 February 1890, p.8.

330 *paper said, torture*: The case of John Tawell has been compiled from: *Freeman's Journal*, 2 April 1845; *John Bull*, 29 March 1845; *Lloyd's Weekly*, 5, 12, 19 January, 2 February, 16, 23, 30 March 1845; *Morning Chronicle*, 6, 8, 9, 16 January, 14, 15, 17, 21, 22, 29 March 1845; *The Times*, 3, 4, 6, 8, 9, 10, 16, 31 January, 13, 14, 15, 18, 20, 24, 29 March 1845; Thackeray wrote on the case in 'From a Club Arm-Chair', in the *Calcutta Star*, 7 May 1845, reprinted in Henry Summerfield, 'Letters from a Club Arm-Chair: William Makepeace Thackeray', *Nineteenth-century Fiction* 18, December 1963, pp.205–33. A good summary appears in Browne and Stewart, *Trials for Murder by Poisoning*.

331 *returned to England*: Mayhew, *London Labour*, vol. 1, pp.283–4.

332 *to have failed*: *Lloyd's*, 'Clerkenwell Police Court', 30 March 1845; *Era*, classified advertisements, 30 March 1845, p.4; *Punch*, 'Tawell's Clothes', 12 April 1845, p.170.

hung John Tawell: Cited in John Pendleton, *Our Railways* (London, Cassell & Co., 1894), vol. 2, pp.11–12.

did not cause it: For excellent overviews of the garrotting panic, see Jennifer Davis, 'The London Garotting Panic of 1862: A Moral Panic and the Creation of a Criminal Class in Mid-Victorian England', in V.A.C. Gatrell, Bruce Lenman and Geoffrey Parker, eds., *Crime and the Law: The Social History of Crime in Western Europe since 1500* (London, Europa, 1980), pp.190–213; and Rob Sindall, *Street Violence in the Nineteenth Century: Media Panic or Real Danger?* (Leicester, Leicester University Press, 1990). The Newgate chaplain appears in Sindall, *Street Violence*, p.11.

335 *the drop opened*: The case of Franz Müller has been compiled from: *Bell's Life*, 23 July, 10, 24 September, 29 October 1864; *Daily News*, 23 July, 8, 9, 13, 16, 20, 27, September, 25, 28, 29, 31 October, 9, 11, 12, 14, 15 November 1864; *Era*, 14 August, 18 September 1864; *Lloyd's*, 24 July, 14 August, 11, 25 September, 2 October, 6, 13 November 1864; *Reynolds's Newspaper*, 24 July, 11, 18, 24 September, 2 October, 6, 13, 20 November 1864; *The Times*, 11, 12, 13, 14, 15, 16, 18, 19, 20, 21, 26 July, 9, 23 August, 20, 21, 27, September, 22, 26, 28, 29, 31 October, 4, 8, 9, 12, 14, 15, 16, 17 November 1864. Anon., *Proceedings on Extradition of Franz Müller* (New York, n.p., [1864?]), is useful for the return of Müller from New York. Percy Fitzgerald, *Chronicles of Bow Street Police-Office* ... (London, Chapman & Hall, 1888), and G. Belton Cobb, *Critical Years at the Yard: The Career of Frederick Williamson of the Detective Department and the C.I.D.* (London, Faber, 1956), give two views on the case from the police perspective. H.B. Irving, ed., *Trial of Franz Muller* (Edinburgh, William Hodge, 1911) gives a transcript. Cooper, *The Lesson of the Scaffold*, relates to Müller's case insofar as it was treated by the campaign against capital punishment. Forbes, *Surgeons at the Bailey*, has interesting light on the expert testimony.

336 *no longer happen*: 'Verses on the Condemnation of Franz Muller, for the Murder of Mr. Briggs ...' (London, 'at the "Catnach Press" by W.S. Fortey' [1864]); *Glasgow Herald*, 31 July 1865, p.4; Robert Louis Stevenson to his mother, Stevenson, *Letters*, vol. 1, p.115; *Bell's Life*, 'Aquatic Register', 26 August 1865; Pendleton, *Our Railways*, vol. 1, pp.438–9. I am grateful to Christian Wolmar for information on the dates of corridor carriages.

the merest amateur: Edward FitzGerald to Fanny Kemble, November 1875, FitzGerald, *Letters*, vol. 3, p.626; Swinburne, cited in Senelick, 'Prestige of Evil', p.154n.

338 *in a train*: *Lloyd's*, 2 October 1892, p.4.

339 *tinned meat*: John Farmer and William Henley, *Slang and its Analogues, Past and Present* ([London], privately published, 1890–1904).

Dream of Eugene Aram: In, among others, *Freeman's Journal*, 'London Gossip', 21 September 1875; *Leeds Mercury*, 'The Whitechapel Mystery', 21 September 1875; *Pall Mall Gazette*, 31 October 1875, p.15.

thirteen years later: The column count and the comparison to Jack the Ripper's press is in Curtis, *Jack the Ripper and the London Press*, p.104.

practising barrister: H.B. Irving, ed., *Trial of the Wainwrights* (Edinburgh, William Hodge & Co., 1920), p.xxxiv.

341 *penal servitude for seven years*: The case of Henry Wainwright has been compiled from: Old Bailey trial transcript, ref. t18751122-1; *Daily News*, 13, 22, 25 September, 4, 7, 13, October, 23, 24, 25, 26, 29, 30 November, 1, 2 December 1875; *Examiner*, 25 December 1875; *John Bull*, 15 January 1876; *Judy*, 20 October 1875; *Lloyd's*, 19 September, 3, 10, 17, 24 October, 28 November, 4, 12, 26 December 1875; *Pall Mall Gazette*, 21, 24 September, 5, 6, 13, 14 October, 21 December 1875; *The Times*, 13, 14, 15, 16, 17, 18, 20, 22, 23, 24, 25 September, 2, 5, 6, 7, 8, 13, 14, 15, 18, 23, 26, 27, 28, 29 October, 23, 24, 25, 26, 27, 29, 30 November, 1, 6, 7, 10, 21, 22 December 1875. Contemporary memories of the case can be found in Ernest Bowen-Rowlands, *Seventy-Two Years at the Bar: A Memoir* (London, Macmillan, 1924), and in Walter Wood, *Survivors' Tales*. Contemporary forensic information can be found in *British Medical Journal*, 4, 'The Wainwright Case', 4 December 1875, pp.710–11; F.G. Larkin, MRCS, 'The Whitechapel Tragedy: Report of the Post Mortem Examination on the Remains', 11 December 1875, pp.730–31; Thomas Bond, FRCS, 'The Whitechapel Tragedy: Notes of a Report to the Solicitor to the Treasury on the Post Mortem Examination of the Remains', 11 December 1875, p.732; 'The Wainwright Case in its Medico-legal Aspects', 11 December 1875, pp.735–7; 'The Wainwright Case: Dr Meadows on the Post Mortem Diagnosis of a Multiparous Uterus', 11 December 1875, p.744, while a modern analysis is available in Forbes, *Surgeons at the Bailey*. Irving, *Trial of the Wainwrights*, gives a very useful outline.
twenty-five lashes: *Graphic*, 18 December 1875, p.603.
three times: *John Bull*, 15 January 1876, p.45.
weeks of the execution: *Illustrated Police News*, 5 February 1876, p.3.
343 *the real Wainwright*: Royal Clarence Theatre: *The Academy*, 14 October 1876, p.394; Market Harborough: *The Theatre*, 6 November 1877, p.232.
body after death: E.H. Cragg, *Almack, The Detective* (London, [London Literary Society], [1886]), p.25ff.
the latter strongly: The Staunton case has been compiled from: Old Bailey trial transcript, ref. t18770917-672. *Daily News*, 26 April, 21 May, 6, 14 June, 11 July, 9 August, 20, 21, 22, 24, 26, 27, 29 September, 2, 3, 11, 13, 15 October 1877; *Examiner*, 20 October 1877; *Graphic*, 16 June 1877; *Lloyd's Weekly*, 13, 27 May, 3, 10, 17 June, 23, 30 September, 7, 14, 21, 27 October 1877; *Illustrated Police News*, 19 May, 9 June, 6, 13, 20 October 1877; *The Times*, 11, 12, 15, 16, 18, 21, 22, 24, 28 May, 1, 4, 6, 7, 9, 14, 26 June, 11, 24 July, 9 August, 20, 21, 24, 25, 26, 27, 28, 29 September, 1, 2, 3, 4, 5, 6, 8, 9, 10, 11, 12, 13, 15, 16, 18, 31 October 1877; *Penny Illustrated Paper*, October 1877; *Sporting Gazette*, 29 September 1877. Pamphlets include Anon., *The Alleged Murder at Penge. Committal of Four Prisoners for Wilful Murder* ([?Maidstone], n.p., [1877]); Anon., *The Life and Trial of the Four Prisoners connected with THE PENGE MURDER. Summing up! Verdict! Sentence! ...* (London, G. Purkess, 'Police News' Edition, 1877). Clarke's *Story of My Life* has the barrister's memories of the case. Twentieth-century accounts include J.B. Atlay, ed., *Trial of the Stauntons* (Edinburgh, William Hodge, 1911), H.L. Adam, *The Penge Mystery: The Story of the Stauntons* ([1919], London, Mellifont Press, 1936), and Edgar Lustgarten, *The Woman in the Case* (London, André Deutsch, 1955). Burney, *Bodies of Evidence*, and Forbes, *Surgeons at the Bailey* have useful summaries of the medical position.
cause of death: Cited in Forbes, *Surgeons at the Old Bailey*, pp.34–5.
unsupported by the evidence: W.S. Greenwald, 'Some Remarks on the Medical Evidence in the Staunton Case', *Lancet*, 6 October 1877, 2, pp.492–5. Petition cited in Burney, *Bodies of Evidence*, pp.111–12.
348 *Louis' legal responsibility*: *Telegraph*, 'Hang in Haste, Repent at Leisure', 10 October 1877.
people in the dock: Summarized in Conley, *Unwritten Law*, pp.57–8.
349 *brought me great rewards*: Clarke, *Story of My Life*, pp.134–5.
an unmanly way: Anon., 'The Penge Murder. Sentence of Death' ([no printer, place or date of publication]), Bodleian Library, Harding B 12(181), and Anon., *The Alleged Murder at Penge*.

were routinely photographed: *Daily News*, 'The Penge Starvation Case', 2 October 1877; Stefan Petrow, *Policing Morals: The Metropolitan Police and the Home Office, 1870–1914* (Oxford, Clarendon Press, 1994), p.87.

350 *track of human blood*: *City Jackdaw*, October 1877, p.383.

starved for money: Advertised in the *Illustrated Police News*, 19 January 1878 in penny parts, and on 22 February 1879 in a single volume, for 7s.6d.

true actor's reason: My thanks to Matt Demakos and Peter E. Blau for information on Holmes's smoking habits in magazines and onstage.

351 No marks: [William Gillette and Arthur Conan Doyle], 'Sherlock Holmes: Being a hitherto unpublished episode in the career of the great detective and showing his connection with the strange case of Miss Faulkner', unpublished playscript, for performance at the Duke of York's Theatre, London, August 1899, Lord Chamberlain's Plays, BL Add MSS 53686 (N). The authorial attribution is made by the editors in William Gillette, *Plays by William Hooker Gillette*, eds. Rosemary Cullen and Don B. Wilmeth (Cambridge, Cambridge University Press, 1983); no authors' names appear on the Lord Chamberlain's copy.

with the dead servant: Arthur Conan Doyle, 'The Disappearance of Lady Frances Carfax' (1911), in *His Last Bow* and *The Case-Book of Sherlock Holmes* ([1917, 1927], Harmondsworth, Penguin, 2007), pp.181ff.

354 *sent to Broadmoor*: The case of Richard Archer Prince is compiled from: Old Bailey trial transcript, ref. t18980110-113; *Daily News*, 17, 18, 20, 21, 22, 23, 30 December 1897, 14 January 1898; *Era*, 18, 24 December 1897, 1, 15 January 1898; *Illustrated Police News*, 25 December 1897, 1, 8, 22 January 1898; *Lloyd's Weekly*, 19, 26 December 1897, 2, 9 January 1898; *Manchester Guardian*, 17, 18, 21, 23, 30 December 1897, 11 January 1898; *Pall Mall Gazette*, 17, 18 December 1897, 10 January 1898; *The Times*, 17, 18, 20, 21, 22, 23, 30 December 1897, 1, 6, 10, 11, 13, 18, 19 January 1898, 1 February, 17 March, 25 April 1898; *Sporting Mirror and Dramatic and Music Hall Record*, 20 December 1897; *Fun*, 21 December 1897; *Country Life Illustrated*, 1 January 1898. George Rowell, *William Terriss and Richard Price: Two Players in an Adelphi Melodrama* (London, Society for Theatre Research, 1987) covers all the surviving documentation and is an excellent summary of the case and the theatre of the period.

newspaper correspondents: Catling, *My Life's Pilgrimage*, p.248.

saw the first sum: *Manchester Guardian*, 31 March 1898, p.13; Old Bailey trial transcript, ref. t18980620-406.

355 *for identification purposes*: Terriss's understudy: *Daily News*, 17 December p.7; Jessie Millward: *Oxford Dictionary of National Biography*; the dog: *Country Life Illustrated*, 1 January 1898, p.749, and *Horse and Hound*, 1 January 1898, p.3.

BREEZY BILL: Richard Le Gallienne, 'William Terriss: In Memoriam', *Daily News*, 18 December 1897; *Fun*, 21 December 1897, p.200; *Punch*, 'WT', 1 January 1898, p.304.

8: Violence

359 *her no provocation*: The little information on Harriet Parker that is available has been compiled from: Old Bailey trial transcript, ref. t18480131-641; *Bell's Life*, 9 January, 6, 27 February 1848; *Examiner*, 8 January 1848; *Lloyd's Weekly*, 9 January, 6, 27 February 1848; *Morning Chronicle*, 3, 4, 10 January, 14, 21 February 1848; *Observer*, 2, 9 January, 20, 21 February 1848; *The Times*, 3, 4, 10 January, 5 February 1848.

360 *what I was doing*: The very scant information on Elizabeth Martha Brown has been compiled from: *Bell's Life*, 27 July 1856; *Bristol Mercury*, 26 July, 16 August 1856; *Daily News*, 11 August 1856; *Freeman's Journal*, 25 July 1856; *John Bull*, 11 August 1856; *Liverpool Mercury*, 25 July 1856; *Morning Chronicle*, 11 August 1856; *Observer*, 11 August 1856; *The Times*, 23 July, 13, 16, 19, 23 August 1856.

361 *the worst, manslaughter*: *The Times*, 5 February 1847, p.2; *Examiner*, 29 August 1846, p.547; *Daily News*, 10 July 1846, p.2.

killing her husband: Conviction rates for husband murder: Wiener, *Men of Blood*, pp.166, 130; execution rates: Philips, *Crime and Authority*, p.280.

that was extraordinary: Hardy to Lady Hester Pinney, 1926, Thomas Hardy, *The Collected Letters of Thomas Hardy*, eds. Richard L. Purdy and Michael Millgate (Oxford, Clarendon Press, 1980–87), vol. 7, p.5; cited in Michael Millgate, *Thomas Hardy: A Biography* (Oxford, Oxford University Press, 1982), p.63. See also Lady Hester Pinney, 'Thomas Hardy and the Birdsmoorgate Murder', Monographs on the Life, Times and Works of Thomas Hardy, No. 25 (Beaminster, Toucan, 1966).

362 *again, and went on*: Thomas Hardy, *Tess of the d'Urbervilles: A Pure Woman, Faithfully Presented* (New York, Harper & Brothers, 1892) uses the original subtitle. The ending, however, in this American edition, is the one Hardy used in the original serialization, and later replaced: '"Justice" was done, and the Arch-satirist, had had his joke out with Tess,' p.455. For the more familiar ending, see *Tess of the d'Urbervilles: A Pure Woman* (London, Macmillan, 1919), vol. 2, p.277. I am grateful to Audrey Jaffe, and especially to Betty Cortus, who marshalled the resources of the Hardy mailbase to untangle the publication history of these endings for me. My thanks to Richard Nemesvari, Rosemarie Morgan, Carolyn McGrath, Tony Fincham, Peter Lennon and Joanna S. Mink.

create interest: *Blackwood's*, 'Switzerland in Summer and Autumn', p.493; Braddon, *Trail of the Serpent*, p.39.

366 *Watcher of the Defective Force*: *Punch*, 'A Detective's Diary', 21 February 1863, p.180. Compare this mock detective diary with the one that appears in *Punch* during the Jack the Ripper case, p.437 – the similarities of tone and contempt for the police are striking.

disposes of same: Charles Dickens to Wilkie Collins, Dickens, *Letters*, October 1860, vol. 9 p.331.

367 *of a police spy*: The case of Mullins drew a great deal of attention. For an outline, see the Old Bailey trial transcript, ref. 18601022–874, *Daily News*, 18, 21, 25, 27, 28 August, 1, 10, 11, 14, 19, 27 September, 3, 17, 26 October, 3, 20 November 1860; *Lloyd's*, 19, 26 August, 2, 9, 16, 23, 30 September, 7, 21, 28 October, 2 December 1860; *The Times*, 20, 21, 22, 23, 25, 27, 28 August, 1, 3, 8, 10, 11, 18, 19, 24, 27 September, 3, 10, 26, 27, 29 October, 20 November 1860. Conan Doyle wrote a defence of Mullins for the *Strand* magazine: Arthur Conan Doyle, 'Strange Studies from Life. The Debatable Case of Mrs. Emsley', *Strand*, 21, May 1901, pp.481–8. I can't say I find it hugely persuasive.

part of detective-work: Forrester, *The Female Detective*, 'Tenant for Life'.

the room was sleeping: 'The Somersetshire Tragedy' (London, H. Such, [1860]), Bodleian Library, Harding B 14 (261).

speech and confession: The number of broadsides about Constance Kent is from Altick, *Studies in Scarlet*, p.53; the Mannings, from Hindley, *Life of James Catnach*, p.42; Collins, *Armadale*, p.140.

368 *himself with contempt*: *Blackwood's*, 'Judicial puzzles. – Eliza Fenning', 89, February 1861, p.244.

managed to suppress: The case of Constance Kent has been endlessly written about. A small sampling of the works from which the account of the murder and (later in this chapter) confession are drawn can be found in: *Daily News*, 3, 6, 23, 27, 28, 30 July, 13, 14, 23 August, 8 September 1860, p.6; *Lloyd's Weekly Newspaper*, 8, 15, 22, 29 July, 5, 19, 16 August, 19, 16 September 1860, 17 March 1861; p.12; *Reynolds's Newspaper*, 29 July, 19, 26 August, 16 September 1860; *The Times*, 4, 12, 17, 21, 26, 28 July, 6, 14, 16 August, 3, 4, 8, 19, 24 September, 1, 2, 3, 4, 5, 6, 10, 18, 20, 22, 29 October, 6, 7, 10, 26 November, 1, 11 December 1860, 1 February 1861, 20 January 1862, 28 March 1863, 26, 27 April, 5, 6 May, 29 June, 22, 24 July 1865, 24 March, 28 August 1866; *Lancet*, 15 July, 2 September 1865; *London Review*, April, May, July, September 1865; *Reynolds's Miscellany of Romance*, June 1865. Pamphlets include: 'A Barrister-at-Law', *The Road Murder: Being a Complete Report and Analysis of the Various Examinations and Opinions of the Press of This Mysterious*

Tragedy (London, [n.p.],1860); 'A Disciple of Edgar Poe', *Who Committed the Road Murder? or, The Track of Blood Followed* (Manchester, Abel Heywood, [1860]), J.W. Stapleton, *The Great Crime of 1860: Being a Summary of the Facts Relating to the Murder Committed at Road …* (London, E. Marlborough, 1861) [this is by a friend of Samuel Kent]. More contemporary discussions of the case include: John Rhode [pseud. Cecil Street], *The Case of Constance Kent* (London, Geoffrey Bles, 1928); Yseult Bridges, *Saint – with Red Hands?* (London, Jarrolds, 1955); Ian Ousby, 'Wilkie Collins, The Moonstone and the Constance Kent Case', *Notes and Queries*, 21:1, 1974, p.25; Bernard Taylor, *Cruelly Murdered: Constance Kent and the Killing at Road Hill House* (London, Souvenir, 1979). Kate Summerscale, *The Suspicions of Mr Whicher, or, The Murder at Road Hill House* (London, Bloomsbury, 2008) is a return to the archival sources, and is invaluable.
the fatal privy: Summerscale, *Suspicions of Mr Whicher*, pp.88, 70.
369 *must be the truth*: 'A Disciple of Edgar Poe', *Who Committed the Road Murder?*, p.3; Conan Doyle, *The Sign of Four*, p.51.
respectable position: 'Charles Martel' [Thomas Delf], *The Diary of an Ex-Detective* (London, Ward & Lock, 1860), p.106.
taste nor morals: [Margaret Oliphant], 'Sensational Novels', *Blackwood's Edinburgh Magazine*, 91, May 1862, p.568.
370 *revenge, and crime*: Margaret Oliphant, *Salem Chapel* (Edinburgh, William Blackwood & Sons, [1862?]), pp.215ff., 232.
pleasant club-rooms: Charlotte M. Yonge, *The Trial: More Links of the Daisy Chain* ([1864], London, Macmillan, 1888), pp.162, 188–9; Braddon, *Aurora Floyd*, vol. 3, p.287.
371 *in the century*: Mary Elizabeth Braddon, *The Doctor's Wife*, ed. Lyn Pykett ([1864], Oxford, Oxford University Press, 1998), p.12.; Conan Doyle, *A Study in Scarlet*, p.17.
discovering the perpetrator: Henry Mansel, 'Sensation Novels', *Quarterly Review*, 113, April 1863, pp.481–514; [Matilda C. Houstoun], *Such Things Are* (London, Saunders, Otley, and Co., 1863, pp.116–18.
372 *with extreme scepticism*: *London Review*, April 1865, p.451.
373 *of eight pups*: *London Review*, 'Assassins' Cartes-de-Visite', August 1865; *Bell's Life*, 'Greyhound Produce, &c.', 21 January 1871.
guilty of a murder: [Christina Broun Cameron], *Not Proven* (London, Hurst & Blackett, 1865).
she killed her child: John Harwood, *Miss Jane, the Bishop's Daughter* (London, Richard Bentley, 1867).
374 *for the female murderer*: The two versions are: Mrs Henry Wood, 'St Martin's Eve', in *New Monthly Magazine*, 99 (London, Chapman & Hall, 1853), pp.327–42; and *St Martin's Eve* (London, Bentley & Son, 1866).
secret and vengeful: Dickens, *Edwin Drood*, pp.88–90.
murderous monomania: Andrew Forrester, 'A Child Found Dead', *The Female Detective*, pp.194, 183; J. Redding Ware, *The Road Murder. Analysis of this Persistent Mystery …* (London, W. Oliver, 1865).
of English detective-novels: T.S. Eliot, introduction to the Oxford World's Classics edition of *The Moonstone*, 1928, p.xii. For more on the identification of J.R. Ware, see my 'Commentary', *Times Literary Supplement*, 18 June 2010, pp.14–15.
375 *prepared enigma*: 'The Enigma Novel', *Spectator*, 28 December 1861.
376 *run by nuns*: Collins, *Armadale*, pp.522–3, 529.
a rose is: Doyle, 'The Naval Treaty', in *Memoirs of Sherlock Holmes*, p.467.
377 *or somnambulism*: Letter, *The Times*, 2 August 1860, p.10.
378 *without explanation*: Anon., *The Boy Detective*.
or young adults: John Springhall, 'Disseminating Impure Literature: The "Penny Dreadful" Publishing Business since 1860', *Economic History Review*, New Series 47, August 1994, pp.567–84.

hear everything: Braddon, *Trail of the Serpent*, pp.433, 441–2; Hayward, *Revelations of a Lady Detective*, p.101; Collins, *The Moonstone*, pp.441–3; Conan Doyle, *Study in Scarlet*, pp.61–2.

379 *coincidence and providence*: William Travers, 'The Boy Detective', unpublished playscript, for performance at the Effingham Theatre, June 1867 [at the Britannia, 1867], Lord Chamberlain's Plays, BL Add MSS 53059 (P).

roaming the streets: Petrow, *Policing Morals*, p.56.

380 *are upon us*: Ainsworth, *Rookwood*, vol. 1, p.3.

emblematic scene: Ellis and Comer, 'The Red Barn'.

Tableau. Curtain: Tom Taylor, *The Ticket-of-Leave Man*, in Rowell, *19th-Century Plays*.

which fools everyone: C.H. Hazlewood, *The Mother's Dying Child* (London, Thomas Hailes Lacy, [n.d]), vol. 64. The British Library catalogue suggests a date of 1850 for this play, but p.2 says 'first performed at the Britannia ... 1864', and Allardyce Nicoll, *A History of Late Nineteenth Century Drama, 1850–1900* (Cambridge, Cambridge University Press, 1946), also dates the play to 1864. If 1850 were correct, this female detective would predate all other female detectives, and also all male detectives. It seems not only unlikely, but impossible.

tone of voice: Jerome, *Stage Land*, pp.73–4.

381 *nothing to give*: George B. Ellis, 'The Female Detective, or, The Foundling of the Streets', unpublished playscript for production at the Britannia Theatre, June 1865, Lord Chamberlain's Plays, BL Add MSS 53043 (H).

Celebrated Dog Bob: J.F. McArdle, 'The Dog Detective: A Dramatic Sketch', unpublished playscript, for performance at the Surrey Theatre, October 1876, Lord Chamberlain's Plays, BL Add MSS 53225 (E).

383 *only twenty minutes*: The case of Frederick Baker has been compiled from: *Bell's Life*, 31 August, 7 December 1867; *Birmingham Daily Post*, 30 August, 24 December 1867; *Daily News*, 27, 28, 30 August 1867; *Hampshire Telegraph*, 28, 31 August, 4 September, 4, 7, 21, 24 December 1867, 4 January 1868; *Hull Packet*, 30 August 1867; *Illustrated Police News*, 7, 14 September, 14 December 1867; *Leeds Mercury*, 24 September 1867; *Lloyd's Weekly*, 5 April 1868; *Pall Mall Gazette*, 29 August 1867; *The Times*, 6, 7, 24, 27 December 1867, 9 January 1868. The *Illustrated Police News* also published a 'special', *The Alton Murder! The Police News Edition of the Life and Examination of Frederick Baker* (London, Illustrated Police News, [1867]); Anon., *The Hampshire Tragedy: Being a full and true account of the Cruel Murder! of Fanny Adams ...* (Norwich, Upcroft, [1867]), mirrors much of the journalism.

one idea: Tomahawk, 'Merry and Wise', 4 January 1868.

385 *of Eugene Aram*: Tyson, *Eugene Aram*, p.61.

died raving mad: Dickens, *Nicholas Nickleby*, p.238.

of this episode: Davis, *Britannia Diaries*, p.153.

eye looked away: My main sources of information for Dickens' readings are Philip Collins, *Charles Dickens: The Public Readings* (Oxford, Clarendon Press, 1975), and Malcolm Andrews, *Charles Dickens and His Performing Selves: Dickens and the Public Readings* (Oxford, Oxford University Press, 2006). Collins, *Dickens and Crime*, pp.25, 265–71, is also extremely helpful.

386 *advanced in years*: Dickens, *Bleak House*, pp.403–4; the *Bath Chronicle* piece was reprinted in *The Times*, 'A Detective in His Vocation', 17 September 1853; George Thomas Lowth, *High Places* (London, Hertford, 1861), vol. 2, p.207.

387 *no difficulty*: National Archives, PRO, HO 45/9442/66692; Charles Tempest Clarkson and J. Hall Richardson, *Police!* (London, Field & Tuer, 1889), p.274; 'Complete Sensational Library', Anon., *Reaping the Whirlwind: A Detective Story* (No. 7, London, n.p., [1890?]), pp.9–10.

for several hours: The disguises appear in: *The Sign of Four*, 'A Scandal in Bohemia', 'The Man with the Twisted Lip', 'The Final Problem', 'The Disappearance of Lady Frances Carfax' and 'The Empty House'.

NOTES TO PP.387 TO 399

person's incognito: Walter Benjamin, 'The Paris of the Second Empire', *Walter Benjamin: Selected Writings*, ed. Michael W. Jennings (Cambridge MA, Belknap, 2003), vol. 4, p.27.
of the artiste: *The Times*, 28 September 1887, p.3.
393 *slow and painful*: The case of Mary Ann Cotton has been compiled from: *Daily News*, 26 February, 7 March 1873; *Illustrated Police News*, 31 August, 16, 30 November 1872; *Leeds Mercury*, 24 October 1872; *Lloyd's Weekly*, 20 September 1872; *Manchester Guardian*, 26, 28 September, 2, 5, October, 11, 12 December 1872, 22, 26 February, 6, 7, 14, 21, 25 March 1873; *North Wales Chronicle*, 3 August 1872; *Northern Echo*, 24 March 1873; *Observer*, 6 October 1872; *Reynolds's Newspaper*, 30 March 1873; *The Times*, 7 October 1872, 8 March 1873. Arthur Appleton, *Mary Ann Cotton: Her Story and Trial* (London, Michael Joseph, 1973) is invaluable, encompassing much of the local newspaper coverage.
execution accomplished: 'Wholesale Poisoning Case in the County of Durham' (London, [printer illegible], [1873]), Bodleian Library, Firth c.17(99); 'Execution of Mary Ann Cotton, at Auckland, County Durham' (no place of publication, printer, [1873]), Bodleian Library, Firth c.17(98); 'Trial, Sentence, & Condemnation of Mary Ann Cotton, the West Auckland Secret Poisoner' (no place of publication, printer, [1873]), Bodleian Library, Harding B 12(184); 'Execution of Mary Cotton, at Durham, for the West Auckland Poisonings' (no place of publication, printer, [1873]), Bodleian Library, Harding B9/3.217.
a new touring version: Ellis and Comer, 'The Red Barn'.
394 *freak storm*: The advertisements for Mary Ann Cotton in Madame Tussaud's appeared in *Reynolds's*, and in editorial matter in *Lloyd's*, in April and May 1873; advertisements appeared in the *Illustrated Police News* from 3 May through June 1873. For the display history, the catalogues of Madame Tussaud's in the British Library list the model from 1875 through an (undated, but 1890s) catalogue. By 1905, the model no longer appears. The Thornley show: *John Bull*, 31 October 1874, p.745.
after the execution: The title and date of the show are noted in Appleton, *Mary Ann Cotton*, p.134, but not the source of this information.
the following year: *Bell's Life*, 'Coquetdale Meeting', 29 August 1874.
a penny a pair: Cited in Clive Emsley, *Hard Men: Violence in England since 1750* (London, Hambledon, 2005), p.58.
398 *words at night*: Lucy Brown, *Victorian News and Newspapers* (Oxford, Clarendon Press, 1985), p.13.
columns, on Monson: The comparison is made in Curtis, *Jack the Ripper*, p.13.
399 *he was released*: The account of the death of Cecil Hambrough and the trial of Monson, as well as Monson's later history, have been compiled from: *Aberdeen Weekly Journal*, 31 August, 1, 4, 5, 9, 14 September, 3, 14 October, 4, 23 November, 13, 14, 15, 16, 18, 19, 21, 22, 23, 24 December 1893, 24 January 1894; *Birmingham Daily Post*, 31 August, 1 September 1893, 19, 20 January 1894; *Daily News*, 2, 4, 6, 14 September, 6 October, 13, 14, 15, 16, 18, 19, 20, 21, 22, 23 December 1893, 17 January 1894; *Glasgow Herald*, 29, 30, 31 August, 4, 5, 7, 9, 14 September, 2 November, 8, 13, 14, 18, 19, 20, 21, 22, 23 December 1893; *Graphic*, 16 December 1893; *Illustrated Police News*, 9, 16, 23 September, 21 October, 16, 23, 30 December 1893; *Lloyd's Weekly*, 3, 10, 17, 24 September, 1, 8 October, 5 November, 17, 24, 31 December 1893, 3, 17 February 1895; *Pall Mall Gazette*, 19, 29, 30 September, 9 October, 12, 13, 14, 15, 16, 18, 19, 20, 22 December 1893, 6, 7, 9, 10 April 1894, 29 January 1895; *Reynolds's Newspaper*, 3, 10 September, 17, 24 December 1893; *The Times*, 1, 5, 9 September, 5 October, 13, 14, 15, 16, 18, 19, 20, 21, 22, 23, 26, 30 December 1893, 15, 17, 19, 29, 24, 25, 30 January 1894, 29, 30, 31 January 1895. The Monson vs Tussaud case: 1 Q.B. 671 and *National Observer*, 2 February 1895, p.313. Twentieth-century accounts of the trial can be found in William Roughead, *Classic Crimes*; John W. More, *Trial of A.J. Monson* (Edinburgh, William Hodge, [1908]). The Monsons' own take on the events is related in A.J. Monson, *The Ardlamont Mystery Solved, to which is appended Scott's Diary* (London, Marlo & Co., 1894), while Mrs Monson's views appeared in the magazine *To-Day*, 23 July, 6, 13, 20 and 27 August 1898.

on to the floor: *Graphic*, 14 April 1894, p.434.

400 *Hambrough's body*: *Aberdeen Weekly Journal*, p.1, 28 December 1893; *Liverpool Mercury*, p.1, 13 January 1894; *Western Mail*, 'Local Amusements', 27 December 1893.

402 *becoming a tutor*: C.L. Pirkis, *The Experiences of Loveday Brooke, Lady Detective*, pp.48ff. Pirkis published six Loveday Brooke stories in the *Ludgate Monthly* between February and July 1893, with one more following in 1894; she then stopped writing, and founded the Canine Defence League.

408 *agreed: guilty*: The case of Eleanor Pearcey has been compiled from: Old Bailey trial transcript, ref. t18901124-43; *Aberdeen Journal*, 27, 30 October, 12 November, 18 December 1890; *Belfast News-Letter*, 24 December 1890; *Birmingham Daily Post*, 4, 27 November, 22, 25 December 1890; *Bristol Mercury and Daily Post*, 1, 3, 4, November, 4, 6, 22, 27 December 1890; *Daily News*, 4, 10, 12 November, 4, 24 December 1890; *Glasgow Herald*, 2 December 1890; *Hampshire Telegraph*, 21 March 1891; *Illustrated Police News*, 1, 22, 29 November, 6, 13, 20, 27 December 1890; *Ipswich Journal*, 8 November 1890; *Leeds Mercury*, 28 October, 1 November, 30 December 1890; *Liverpool Mercury*, 30 October 1890; *Lloyd's Weekly*, 26 October, 2, 9, 16, 23, 30 November, 7, 14, 21, 28 December 1890, 15 March 1891, 26 December 1897; *Northern Echo*, 28 October 1890; *Observer*, 26 October, 2 November, 14, 21 December 1890; *Pall Mall Gazette*, 27, 28, 29, 30 October, 1 November, 4 December 1890; *Reynolds's Newspaper*, 2, 9, 16 November, 14, 21, 28 December 1890, 4 January 1891; *The Times*, 27, 28, 29, 30 October, 3, 4, 12, 19 November, 2, 3, 4, 24 December 1890; *Western Mail*, 31 October, 24 December 1890, p.5. F. Tennyson Jesse, *Murder and its Motives* (London, William Heinemann, 1924), gives a good overview; Melville L. MacNaghten, *Days of My Years* (London, Edward Arnold, 1914), should be treated with caution.

409 *executed if found guilty*: Figures in Wilson, *Murderess*, pp.315–16.

demand for the paper: Catling, *My Life's Pilgrimage*. Catling mistakenly dates the murder and subsequent reporting to October 1900, not 1890.

411 *to be excluded*: *Evening Standard*, 19 April 1886, cited in Clarke, *Pimlico Murder*, p.206; *Pall Mall Gazette*, 'Occasional Notes', 4 December 1890; *Women's Penny Paper*, 13 December 1890, p.120.

in the Perambulator: The information that Madame Tussaud's purchased all the goods from Mrs Pearcey comes from two documents cited by Chapman, *Mme Tussaud's Chamber of Horrors*, pp.99–100. I have found Chapman unreliable, and indeed the clipping she cites from *Lloyd's* she dates 24 November, although from its content it was written after the verdict, which was handed down on 3 December. Therefore I have made some judgements about who might have sold what, based on who probably owned the goods. *Leeds Mercury*, 30 December 1890, p.4, noted that on display, along with the tableau, were the receipts for the purchase, 'signed by Mrs. PEARCEY herself and the landlord'. Joseph Tussaud's comment can be found in the *Pall Mall Gazette*, 'The Value of Murderers' Relics', 28 October 1892. Hertford Gaol purchase: Pamela Pilbeam, *Mme Tussaud and the History of Waxworks* (London, Hambledon and London, 2003), p.179. Frank Hogg's moustache, and the price of the pram: *Western Mail*, 'Hogg Sold His Beard', 24 December 1890. No other source suggests that Hogg sold his wife and child's clothes, and Madame Tussaud's did not seemingly display a receipt from Hogg, but the clothes are particularly itemized in the advertisements, and it therefore appears likely it was he who would have been entitled to sell them.

the first three days: Pilbeam, *Madame Tussaud*, p.179.

see that, now: *Punch*, 'At the Regent Street Tussaud's', 17 January 1891, p.25.

413 *who go rogue*: Wiener, *Men of Blood*, pp.146–7; *Biographical and Descriptive Sketches of the Distinguished Characters which Compose the Unrivalled Exhibition and Historical Gallery of Madame Tussaud and Sons* (London, M'Corquodale, 1889); Anthea Trodd, *Domestic Crime in the Victorian Novel* (Basingstoke, Macmillan, 1989), pp.158–9. The two Sherlock Holmes stories are 'The Adventure of the Speckled Band' and 'The Adventure of the Copper Beeches', both 1892.

414 *fell swoop*: *Licensed Victualler's Mirror*, 'Between Ourselves', 4 November 1890 and 9 December 1890.

9: Modernity

419 *a guilty verdict*: The case of Israel Lipski is compiled from: Old Bailey trial transcript, ref. t18870725-817; *Illustrated Police News*, 6, 20, 27 August 1887; *Lloyd's Weekly*, 3, 31 July, 7, 14, 21, 28 August 1887; *Pall Mall Gazette*, 29 June, 1 July, 13, 15, 16, 18, 20, 22 August 1887; *Reynolds's Newspaper*, 3, 31 July, 21, 28 August 1887; *The Times*, 29 June, 2, 4, 15, 30 July, 1, 15, 19, 22, 23, 25 August 1887. Martin L. Friedland, *The Trials of Israel Lipski* (London, Macmillan, 1984), is invaluable, and I have relied heavily on it for the account both of the trial and the later campaign in the *Pall Mall Gazette*. Lipski's solicitor, J. Hayward, produced a pamphlet, *The Case of Israel Lipski now Lying under Sentence of Death for the Murder of Miriam Angel* (London, 1887), but I have been unable to locate a copy.

422 *Lipsky's awful fate*: Anon., 'The Whitechapel Tragedy: Condemnation of Lipsky' ([London], Taylor & Smith, [1887]).

anonymous – contribution: The verses are cited by Friedland, *Trials of Israel Lipski*, p.176, but the suggestion that they may have been written by a *Pall Mall Gazette* journalist is my own.

423 *kills himself*: Israel Zangwill, 'The Big Bow Murder', in E.F. Bleiler, ed., *Three Victorian Detective Novels: The Unknown Weapon, by Andrew Forrester; My Lady's Money, by Wilkie Collins; The Big Bow Mystery, by Israel Zangwill* (New York, Dover, 1978).

Jekyll commits suicide: Robert Louis Stevenson, *The Strange Case of Dr Jekyll and Mr Hyde, and Other Stories*, ed. Jenni Calder ([1886] Harmondsworth, Penguin, 1979).

424 *details of a hanging*: *Punch*, 'The Strange Case of Dr. T. and Mr. H.', 6 February 1886; sales figures: July 1886, Stevenson, *Letters*, vol. 5, p.275; sermons: Ibid., 25 May and 18 September 1886, pp.259, 322; *Pall Mall Gazette*, 'The Nightmare at the Lyceum', 7 August 1888.

to improve the world: *Pall Mall Gazette*, October 1888 issues, passim, collated in Christopher Frayling, 'The House that Jack Built: Some Stereotypes of the Rapist in the History of Popular Culture', in Sylvana Tomaselli and Roy Porter, eds., *Rape: An Historical and Cultural Enquiry* (Oxford, Basil Blackwell, 1986), p.191.

Rainhill murderer: Whittington-Egan, *William Roughead*, p.308.

425 *supposed murder in Whitechapel*: This newspaper article, and all others mentioned in the Jack the Ripper case, can be found on the excellent www.casebook.org site, unless noted separately.

newspaper success: Cited in Nicholas Rance, 'Jonathan's Great Knife: Dracula Meets Jack the Ripper', *Victorian Literature and Culture*, 30, 2002, pp.439–53.

426 *Lloyd's 750,000*: Jennifer Ann Bars, 'Defining Murder in Victorian London: An Analysis of Cases 1862–1892' (Oxford, D.Phil, 1994), pp.301–2.

say there were none: Circulation figures in Curtis, *Jack the Ripper and the London Press*, p.59; the round-the-clock printing was reported by H.W. Massingham, assistant editor of the *Star*, cited in Stawell Heard, *Jack the Ripper in the Provinces: The English Provincial Press Reporting of the Whitechapel Murders* (London, self-published, 2005). Curtis's book on the press is invaluable, and I have relied heavily on it for the discussion of the press reporting that follows.

428 *ought not to*: Ousby, *Bloodhounds of Heaven*, pp.128–9.

429 *Birmingham 4.5*: Petrow, *Policing Morals*, pp.59–60.

one Scotland Yard inspector: The information on the restructuring of the Yard, and Anderson's holiday arrangements, Cobb, *Critical Years at the Yard*, pp.107, 181, 225–8.

430 *outraged to death*: Curtis, *Jack the Ripper*, p.93.

intimate bleeding: 'Police Criticized Over G20 Cordon', 6 August 2009, www.bbc.co.uk/1/hi/uk/8187343/stm.

432 *nursed to violence*: *Punch*, 22 September 1888, pp.138–9; 20 September 1888, pp.150–51.

we should smile: *Sporting Times*, 8 September 1888, p.5.

434 *righter-of-wrongs*: *The Times* reported various sightings, including 9 January, 22 February, 3 March 1838. Plays: J.T. Haines, *Spring-Heel'd Jack: The Terror of London* appeared in 1840; Anon., *Spring-Heel'd Jack, or, The Felon's Wrongs* in 1863; W.G. Wills, *Spring-Heel'd Jack* in 1870; penny-dreadfuls, serial versions: Anon., *The Apprehension and Examination of Spring-Heeled Jack, who appeared as a Ghost, Bear, Baboon, Demon, &c.* (no place of publication or printer, ?1840s); Anon., *Spring-Heel'd Jack, the Terror of London* (London, Newsagents' Publishing Co., [1850?]).

upon the tiger: Cited in Martin A. Danahay and Alex Chisholm, *Jekyll and Hyde Dramatized: The 1887 Richard Mansfield Script and the Evolution of the Story on Stage* (Jefferson, NC, McFarland & Co., 2005), p.174.

Murd—: *Punch*, 13 October 1888, p.170.

437 *circulation double*: *Fun*, September 1888, cited in Frayling, 'The House that Jack Built', pp.212–13.

arresting myself: *Punch*, 22 September 1888, p.135.

438 *to catch him*: 'Florence Warden' [Florence Alice Price], *The House on the Marsh*, in *The Family Story-Teller*, 1883.

pipe in his mouth: Wilkie Collins, *My Lady's Money*, in Bleiler, *Three Victorian Detective Novels*, pp.109–10, 112.

439 *Western Morning News*: These appear in Conan Doyle, *A Study in Scarlet*, *The Sign of Four*, 'The Adventure of the Cardboard Box', 'The Adventure of the Dancing Men' and *The Hound of the Baskervilles*.

440 *could print*: Catling, *My Life's Pilgrimage*, pp.183–4.

441 *twenty-four issues*: Curtis, *Jack the Ripper*, pp.201–6.

murderer was a Jew: Friedland, *Trials of Israel Lipski*, p.202.

442 *Maiden Lane*: *Manchester Guardian*, 17 December 1897, p.12.

pieces in Whitechapel: Compton Mackenzie, *My Life and Times, Octave One: 1883–1891* (London, Chatto & Windus, 1963), pp.164–5.

Un penney: Gaston Marot and Louis Péricaud, *Jack l'Éventreur: Drame en cinq actes et sept tableaux* (Paris, Tresse & Stock, 1889), pp.97–8. The translation here and later is my own. The authors' names may be pseudonyms; the names of Xavier Bertrand and Louis Clairian also appear in connection with this play.

444 *the bloodhound Truth*: *Pall Mall Gazette*, 'A Ballad of Bloodhounds', 9 October 1888.

a quiet suburb: Conan Doyle, *The Sign of Four*, p.63.

satisfactory solution: *Punch*, 'Conundrums', 20 October 1888, p.189.

445 *Misery, Jobbery*: *Reynolds's*, 'Pickpockets', 21 October 1888.

under instructions: Anon., *The Whitechapel Murders, or, The Mysteries of the East End* (London, G. Purkess, [1888?]), p.30. The first five issues are in the Bodleian Library, John Johnson Collection, c.435.

446 *& in A Bag*: Danahay and Chisholm, *Jekyll and Hyde Dramatized*, p.38.

in Whitechapel-road: All these cases appear in *The Times*, 9 October 1888, p.3; 10 October 1888, p.3; 15 November 1888, p.21.

in that city: Cited in Curtis, *Jack the Ripper*, p.172.

447 *spot at once*: Jane Beetmoor: *The Times*, 24 September, p.6; 26 September, p.10; Glasgow police: 12 November 1888, p.6.

448 *of his work*: Conan Doyle, 'The Adventure of the Cardboard Box', in *His Last Bow*, pp.49, 53.

449 *ruled by Scotland Yard*: *Fun*, 'Tragedies at the East-End', 24 October 1888.

450 *the police rate*: Charles Warren, 'The Police of the Metropolis', *Murray's Magazine*, 4, 23, November 1888, pp.577–94.

was too late: *Jack the Ripper at Work Again. Another Terrible Murder & Mutilation in Whitechapel* … (4-page pamphlet, no place of publication or printer, [1888]), Bodleian Library, John Johnson Collection, Crime 6 (11).

452 *Chamber of Horrors*: Marie Belloc Lowndes, *The Lodger*, ed. Laura Marcus ([1913],
Oxford, Oxford University Press, 1996), p.195.
too strong: I have found two references to waxworks in the Whitechapel Road in the autumn
of 1888: in the *Daily News*, 10 September 1888, p.6; and in *The Times*, 6 February 1889, p.8
(referring to the events of the previous autumn). There is no way of telling if this was one
and the same exhibition, or whether there were two.
Ripper victims: *Era*, 20 April 1889, p.20; *Era*, 3 December 1892, p.23.
453 *upon Mitre Square*: John Francis Brewer, *The Curse upon Mitre Square A.D. 1530–1888*
(London, Simpkin, Marshall, 1888).
I'm a Gentile: 'John Law' [Margaret Harkness], *Captain Lobe: A Story of the Salvation Army*
([1889], London, Hodder & Stoughton, [1915]). The novel also appeared under the title *In
Darkest London*.
454 *series of murders*: *Thou Art the Man* (London, Simpkin, Marshall, Hamilton, Kent & Co.,
[1894]), pp.75, 95, 153.
impostors, and more: William Westall, *Back to Africa: A Confession* (London, Ward &
Downey, 1891); J.W. Nicholas, *The House of Mystery* (Bristol, J.W. Arrowsmith, [1891]). Yet
another novel, by 'Chas. L'Epine', *The Devil in a Domino: A Realistic Study* (London,
Lawrence Greening & Co., 1897), is so bad I can't even bring myself to summarize it in the
text. It too has a scientist-psychopath murderer.
455 *was in Whitechapel*: Bram Stoker, *Dracula. A Tale* (London, A. Constable & Co., 1897); for
the parallels between *Dracula* and Jack the Ripper I am indebted to Rance, 'Jonathan's Great
Knife'.
dens in London: Oscar Wilde, *The Picture of Dorian Gray*, ed. Robert Mighall ([1891],
Harmondsworth, Penguin Books, 2003), pp.124, 145.
456 *SMITE THEM ALL*: 'Rodissi' [pseud. Jacob Ringgold], *Lord Jacquelin Burkney: The
Whitechapel Terror* (New York, Anton Publishing Co., 1889).
more recent cases: B.G. Johns, 'The Literature of Seven Dials', *National Review*, 2, December
1883, pp.478–9.
founder of the Daily Mail: British Library, shelfmark x200.318.
the Whitechapel Horrors: *The Times*, 1 October 1888, p.3; 'The Whitechapel Blood Book' is
noted in Curtis, *Jack the Ripper*, p.187; *Daily News*, 13 November 1888, p.5.
has survived: Anon., *Two More Horrible Murders in the East-End* (London, n.p., [1888]). The
British Library catalogue gives 1889 as its publication date, but I can see no reason for this
except perhaps the library's acquisition-stamp date. Indeed, there is no way of knowing if
the sheets were ever a single pamphlet – they are now individually mounted – although
they share a format and a typeface. The sheets must have been printed before early
November 1888, as there is no mention of Mary Jane Kelly's murder. The song beginning
'Now ladies all beware' appears again on a ballad sheet held in the Bodleian Library,
Harding B.20(196), this time with the information that it is to be sung to the tune of
'Railway Train'.
458 *comic song above*: Anon., *Jack the Ripper at Work Again. Another Terrible Murder &
Mutilation in Whitechapel* ... (4-page pamphlet, no place of publication or printer, [1888]),
Bodleian Library, John Johnson Collection, Crime 6 (11).
Vitechapel murders: *Daily News*, 10 September 1888, p.6; *Observer*, 11 November 1888,
p.5.
I'm not a butcher ...: Cited in MacNaghten, *Days of My Youth*, p.54.
459 *rest of it*: *Sporting Times*, 'Told by the Pudding Shop Keeper', 6 October 1888.
worthy of remark: The dog that drew condemnation was in the *Belfast News-Letter*, 9
October 1888, p.3; it reappeared on 24 December 1888; three other dogs: *Newcastle Weekly
Courant*, 4 January 1890, *County Gentleman*, 5 July 1890, and *Belfast News-Letter*, 27
January, 30 March 1891 and 2 February 1892; the horses: *Freeman's Journal*, 1 April 1889,
p.7, 25 April 1889, p.7, 11 April 1890, p.7, 15 September 1896, p.7, 31 August 1897, p.7;
Liverpool Mercury, 23 April 1889, p.7, 8 August 1893, p.7; *Ipswich Journal*, 21 June 1889, p.3;

County Gentleman: 29 March 1890, p.435, 23 June 1894, p.816; *Belfast News-Letter*, 26 December 1889, p.3; *Horse and Hound*: 10 May 1890.

best to himself: Filho da Puta, *Sporting Times*, 22 January 1881, p.3; information on names permitted today by Weatherby's, personal communication; *Bell's*, 'Rough Notes on Turf Nomenclature', 31 December 1864.

460 *Zadkiel's Almanac*: *The Times*, 20 October 1888, p.2.

Haynes & Co.: *Myra's Journal of Dress and Fashion*, 1 December 1889, p.637.

heads of families: *Pall Mall Gazette*, 'The Shows in the London Shops', 15 January 1889.

Brooklyn Opera House: *Era*, 'Theatrical Gossip', 10 August 1889; *Pall Mall Gazette*, 'Today's Tittle Tattle', 12 August 1889; *Graphic*, 'Theatres', 17 August 1889. See also *Reynolds's*, 11 August 1889, *Era*, 24 August 1889, *Derby Mercury*, 28 August 1889, *Pall Mall Gazette*, 28 August 1889, *Graphic*, 31 August 1889.

461 *as he did*: Marot and Louis, *Jack l'Éventreur*. I have followed the most frequently used spellings for the names, which appear inconsistently throughout the text. *Era*, 7 September 1889, p.9; *Lloyd's*, 'Jack the Ripper on the Stage', 1 September 1889. The plot summary I give is from the published script. *Lloyd's* description of the evening is substantially different, although whether because the staged performance varied from the script, or because their reporter spoke no French, I cannot say.

462 *conquered this night*: Frank Wedekind, *Die Büchse der Pandora* ([1904], Verlag Jürgen Häusser, Darmstadt, 1990). I am grateful to the late Robin Gibson for his translation. (The English translation by Stephen Spender, *The Lulu Plays and Other Sex Tragedies* (London, Vision, 1952), is slightly abridged and omits much of this Ripperiana.)

gave no particulars: H.A. Saintsbury, 'The Doctor's Shadow', unpublished playscript for performance at the Prince's Theatre, Accrington, January 1896, Lord Chamberlain's Plays, BL Add 53590 (K); death of Mrs Kelly: cited in Gary Coville and Patrick Lucanio, *Jack the Ripper: His Life and Crimes in Popular Entertainment* (Jefferson, NC, McFarland & Co., 1999), p.17; Miss Edith Manley: *Era*, 30 July 1892, p.14.

463 *game's own sake*: 'The Adventure of the Bruce-Partington Plans' (1908) in *His Last Bow and The Case-Book of Sherlock Holmes*, p.108.

take it up: Anon., *Reaping the Whirlwind*, p.32; Arthur Morrison, *Martin Hewitt, Investigator* (London, Ward, Lock & Bowden, 1894), p.121. Arthur Morrison (1863–1945) is of course more famous today for his classic novel of the East End slum, *A Child of the Jago* (1896).

464 *train to Victoria*: 'The Adventure of the Copper Beeches' (1892), in *The Adventures of Sherlock Holmes*, p.260; 'The Adventure of the Greek Interpreter' (1893), in *The Memoirs of Sherlock Holmes*, pp.445–6.

individual's operation: *Lloyd's*, 'Terrible Murder', 26 October 1890.

at work again: *The Times*, 21 January 1890, p.3.

of these missives: Frayling, 'The House that Jack Built', p.186.

compared with the print: *The Times*, 4 October 1888, p.10.

465 *something of the kind*: Doyle, 'The Adventure of the Norwood Builder', in *The Return of Sherlock Holmes*, p.52.

mechanism as they fall: Guy Boothby, *The Lust of Hate* (London, Ward, Lock & Co., 1898).

SOURCES

The following newspapers and magazines have been the most heavily used. Other journals may have the occasional reference, but were not searched systematically:

Newspapers

Aberdeen Journal, Belfast News-Letter, Bell's Life, Birmingham Daily Post, Brighton Patriot, Bristol Mercury, Caledonian Mercury, Champion, Cobbett's Weekly Political Register, Daily News, Derby Mercury, Era, Examiner, Freeman's Journal, Glasgow Herald, Graphic, Hampshire and Portsmouth Telegraph, Hull Packet, Illustrated Police News, Ipswich Journal, Jackson's Oxford Journal, John Bull, Leeds Mercury, Liverpool Mercury, Lloyd's Illustrated Newspaper, London Dispatch, Manchester Guardian, Manchester Times, Morning Chronicle, Newcastle Courant, North Wales Chronicle, Northern Echo, Northern Star, Observer, Pall Mall Gazette, Penny Illustrated Paper, Preston Chronicle, Reynolds's Newspaper, The Times, Trewman's Exeter Flying Post, Western Mail

Magazines and Journals

Age, All the Year Round, Athenaeum, La Belle Assemblée, Bentley's Miscellany, Blackwood's Edinburgh Magazine, Bow Bells, Boys of England, Boy's Own, British Critic, Chambers's Journal, City Jackdaw, Cobbett's Magazine, Connoisseur, Cornhill, Court and Lady's Magazine, Monthly Critic and Museum, Dart, Dramatic Magazine, Dublin Review, Edinburgh Review, Englishwoman's Domestic Magazine, Era Almanack, Examiner, Figaro in London, Fraser's Magazine, Fun, Funny Folks, Gentleman's Magazine, Household Words, Illustrated Chips, Judy, Knight's Penny Magazine, Lady's Cabinet of Fashion, Music and Romance, Licensed Victuallers' Mirror, Literary Gazette, Lloyd's Magazine, London Journal, Mirror of the Stage, Moonshine, Myra's Journal of Dress and Fashion, New Monthly Magazine, New Wonderful Magazine, Once a Week, Owl, Penny Satirist, Pick-Me-Up, Punch, Racing Times, St James's Magazine, Satirist, Sporting Gazette, Sporting Times, Tait's Edinburgh Magazine, Temple Bar, Theatrical Observer, Tomahawk

SELECT BIBLIOGRAPHY

To keep the bibliography within manageable lengths, secondary works and trial transcripts that are cited only once in the text are for the most part not listed below.

Playbills

The main collections of playbills cited in the text can be found in the Victoria and Albert Museum Theatre Collection, where they are catalogued by theatre, and the British Library, in particular shelfmarks 1889.b.10/6, 74/1875.b. (1–9), 840.m.31 (1–5) and Playbills 311–313.

Broadsides

The main collections of broadsides cited can be found in the British Library, in particular shelfmarks 11621.k.4, 74/1880.c.12 and 74/1880.c.20; the Bodleian Library, John Johnson Collection and the Broadsides Collection.

Playscripts

All unpublished playscripts cited come from the manuscripts submitted to the Lord Chamberlain's Office for licensing. The surviving files after 1824 are now in the British Library. Published plays are listed individually in the notes; the bibliography contains only collections of plays.

Penny publications

The British Library holds a large collection of penny-bloods and later penny-publications, which are catalogued as the Barry Ono Collection. See Elizabeth James and Helen R. Smith, *Penny Dreadfuls and Boys' Adventures: The Barry Ono Collection of Victorian Popular Literature in the British Library* (London, British Library, 1998). Many more survive as later, single-volume reprints. Those I have cited that have attributions – or probable attributions – are listed under their authors in the primary sources. The anonymous works I have used are:

The Boy Detective, or, The Crimes of London (London, Newsagents' Publishing Co., [1865–6])
'Complete Sensational Library', *Reaping the Whirlwind: A Detective Story; The Demon Detective; Mat the Marvel: A Detective Story* (Nos. 7, 9 and 14, London, n.p., [1890?])
Maria Martin [sic]; or, The Red Barn Tragedy (London, J. Johnson, n.d.)

The Murderers of the Close: A Tragedy of Real Life (London, Cowie & Strange, 1829)
The New Newgate Calendar, Containing the Remarkable Lives and Trials of Notorious Criminals, Past and Present ([no place of publication, publisher, 1863–5])
Poisoners and Slow Poisoning: A Narrative of the Most Remarkable Cases of Poisoning (London, John Dicks, [1865])
The Poor Boys of London, or, Driven to Crime. A Life Story for the People ([London, Temple Publishing Co., c.1866])
Purkess's Library of Romance, vols. I–III (London, G. Purkess, [?1853])
Purkess's Penny Pictorial Play, nos. 1–32 ([London, G. Purkess, 1858?])

Published primary sources

Alderson, James, 'Deaths from Poison', *Lancet*, 1, 19 January 1856, p.80
All the Year Round, 'Street Terrors', 8, February 1863, pp.533–8; 'Policeman' [poem], 2, 7 May 1859, p.36–7; 'Detectives and Their Work', 36, April 1885, pp.135–9; 'Calamity Mongering', 15, March 1866, pp.187–8
Amos, Sheldon, 'Civilization and Crime', *Fortnightly Review*, 2, September 1865, pp.319–28
Ashton, John, *Modern Street Ballads* (London, Chatto & Windus, 1888)
[Austin, Alfred] 'Our Novels: The Sensation School', *Temple Bar*, 29, June 1870, pp.410–24; 'Our Novels: The Fast School', *Temple Bar*, 29, May 1870, pp.177–94
Austin, Francis E., 'The Medical Evidence of Crime', *Cornhill*, 7, 1863, pp.338–48
[Austin, W. S.], 'Notes on Circumstantial Evidence, *Temple Bar*, 1, December 1860, pp.91–8; 'Some Curious Cases', *Temple Bar*, 2, April 1861, pp.131–40
Baker, H. Barton, 'The Old Melo-drama', *Belgravia*, 50, May 1883, pp.331–9
[Banks, Percival W.], 'William Ainsworth and Jack Sheppard', *Fraser's Magazine*, 21, February 1840, p.227–45
Barham, Revd Richard H., *The Ingoldsby Legends* ([1837–40], London, Richard Edward King, [1893])
Barnard, Richard, *The Life and Travels of Richard Barnard, Marionette Proprietor*, ed. George Speaight (London, Society for Theatre Research, 1981)
Benson, Captain L., ed., *The Book of Remarkable Trials and Notorious Characters. From 'Half-Hanged Smith', 1700 – To Oxford, who Shot at the Queen, 1840* (London, Chatto & Windus, [1871])
Bent, Superintendent [James], *Criminal Life: Reminiscences of Forty-Two Years as a Police Officer* (London, John Heywood, [1891])
Blackwood's Edinburgh Magazine, 'Causes of the Increase of Crime', 56, July 1844, pp.1–14
Blanchard, E. L., 'History of the Princess's Theatre', *Era Almanack*, 1876, pp.1–6; 'History of the Surrey Theatre', *Era Almanack*, 1876, pp.6–10; Vanished Theatres', *Era Almanack*, 1877, pp.88–92
Bleiler, E. G., ed., *Three Victorian Detective Novels* (New York, Dover, 1978)
'Bon Gaultier' [William Edmonstoune Aytoun & Theodore Martin], *Book of Ballads* (New York, Redfield, 1852)
Booth, Charles, ed., *Life and Labour of the People of London* (2nd edn, London, Williams & Norgate, 1889–93)
Booth, Michael R., ed., *English Plays of the Nineteenth Century* (Oxford, Clarendon Press, 1969–76)
—, *Hiss the Villain: Six English and American Melodramas* (Eyre & Spottiswoode, 1964)
—, *The Lights o' London and other Victorian Plays* (Oxford, Oxford University Press, 1995)
Borrow, George, *Celebrated Trials, and Remarkable Cases of Criminal Jurisprudence …* (London, Knight & Lacey, 1825)
—, *Lavengro; The Scholar – the Gypsy – the Priest* ([1851], New York, Dover, 1991)
—, *The Romany Rye* ([1857], Oxford, Oxford University Press, 1984)
—, *The Zincali; or, An Account of the Gypsies of Spain*, (4th edn, London, John Murray, 1846)

SELECT BIBLIOGRAPHY

Braddon, Mary Elizabeth, *Birds of Prey* ([1867], London, Simpkin, Marshall, Hamilton, Kent & Co., n.d.)
—, *Charlotte's Inheritance* ([1868], London, Simpkin, Marshall, Hamilton, Kent & Co., n.d.)
—, *One Life, One Love* (London, Simpkin, Marshall, Hamilton, Kent, 1890)
—, *Thou Art the Man* (London, Simpkin, Marshall, Hamilton, Kent & Co., [1894])
—, *The Trail of the Serpent*, ed. Chris Willis ([1860], New York, Modern Library, 2003)
— [first as 'Lady Caroline Lascelles', later as 'anon.'], *The Black Band, or, The Mysteries of Midnight* ([1861–2], London, George Vickers, 187[6–]7)
Browne, G. Lathom, and C. G. Stewart, *Reports of Trials for Murder by Poisoning ... With Chemical Introduction and Notes on the Poisons Used* (London, Stevens & Sons, 1883)
Bulwer-Lytton, Edward, *Eugene Aram: A Tale* ([1832] London, George Routledge & Sons, [n.d.])
—, *Lucretia, or, The Children of the Night* (Leipzig, Berh. Tauchnitz Jun., 1846)
—, *Paul Clifford* in Juliet, John, ed., *Cult Criminals: The Newgate Novels, 1830–1847* ([1830], Routledge, Thoemmes Press, 1998)
Caminada, Jerome, Chief Det. Insp., *Twenty-Five Years of Detective Life in Victorian Manchester* ([1895], Warrington, Prism Books, 1982–3)
Carlyle, Thomas and Jane, *The Collected Letters of Thomas and Jane Welsh Carlyle*, eds. Charles Richard Sanders, Clyde de L. Ryals, Kenneth J. Fielding et al. (Durham, Duke University Press, 1970–2005)
Catling, Thos., *My Life's Pilgrimage* (London, John Murray, 1911)
Cavanagh, Ex-Chief Inspector, *Scotland Yard Past and Present: Experiences of Thirty-seven Years* (London, Chatto & Windus, 1893)
Chambers's Edinburgh Journal, 'Felon Literature', 515, December 1842, pp.373–4; 'Confessions of an Attorney', 355, October 1850, pp.241–4
Chambers's Journal of Popular Literature, 'Aids of Science in the Detection of Crime', 633, February 1876, pp.101–3; 'Our Detective Police', 1, 22, May 1884, pp.337–9
Clark, Alexander, *Reminiscences of a Police Officer in the Granite City, Thirty Years Since* (facsimile reprint, Aberdeen, Grampian Police Diced Cap Charitable Trust, 1995)
Clarke, Sir Edward, *The Story of My Life* (London, John Murray, 1918)
Clive, Caroline, *Paul Ferroll* ([1855] Oxford, Oxford University Press, 1997)
Cobbett, William, *Rural Rides*, ed. Ian Dyck ([1830], Harmondsworth, Penguin, 2001)
[Collins, Charles Allston], 'Dramatic Grub Street', *Household Words*, 17, 6 1858, pp.265–70; 'Some Wild Ideas', *Household Words*, 1859, pp.505–10; 'The Unknown Public', *Household Words*, 18, 21 1858, pp.217–22
Collins, Wilkie, *Armadale*, ed. John Sutherland ([1864–6], Harmondsworth, Penguin, 1995)
—, 'Curiosities of Literature. I. The Unknown Public'; 'Cases Worth Looking At. II. The Poisoned Meal', in *My Miscellanies* (London, Samson, Low, Son, 1863)
—, *The Law and the Lady*, ed. by Jenny Bourne Taylor ([1875], Oxford, Oxford University Press, 1999)
—, *Mad Monkton and Other Stories*, eds. Norman Page and Kamal Al-Solaylee (Oxford, Oxford University Press, 1994)
—, *Miss or Mrs?, The Haunted Hotel, The Guilty River*, eds. Norman Page and Toru Sasaki ([1871, 1878, 1886], Oxford, Oxford University Press, 1999)
—, *The Moonstone*, ed. Sandra Kemp ([1868], Harmondsworth, Penguin, 1998)
—, *Poor Miss Finch* (London, Richard Bentley & Son, 1872)
—, *The Woman in White*, ed. Matthew Sweet ([1860], Harmondsworth, Penguin, 1999)
Conan Doyle, Arthur, *The Adventures of Sherlock Holmes* and *The Memoirs of Sherlock Holmes*, ed. Ed Glinert ([1892, 1894], Harmondsworth, Penguin, 2001)
—, *His Last Bow* and *The Case-Book of Sherlock Holmes* ([1917, 1927], Harmondsworth, Penguin, 2007)
—, *The Hound of the Baskervilles* ([1902], Harmondsworth, Penguin, 2007)
—, 'My Friend the Murderer' in *London Society*, Christmas Number, 1882

—, *The Return of Sherlock Holmes* ([1905], Harmondsworth, Penguin, 2008)
—, *The Sign of Four* ([1890], Harmondsworth, Penguin, 2007)
—, *A Study in Scarlet* ([1887], Harmondsworth, Penguin, 2007)
Cragg, E. H., *Almack, The Detective* (London, [London Literary Society], [1886])
Cruikshank, Robert, *Cruikshank v. the New Police, Showing the Great Utility of that Military Body, Their Employment, &c.* (London, W. Kidd, [1833?])
[Dallas, E. S.], 'Popular Literature – the Periodical Press', *Blackwood's Edinburgh Magazine*, 85, 1859, pp.96–112, 180–95
Davis, Jim, ed., *The Britannia Diaries, 1863–1875: Selections from the Diaries of Frederick C. Wilton* (London, Society for Theatre Research, 1992)
[Denman, Thomas], 'Report from the Select Committee on the Police of the Metropolis', *Edinburgh Review*, 48, 1828, pp.411–22
De Sola Pinto, Vivian, and Allan Edwin Rodway, eds., *The Common Muse: An Anthology of Popular British Ballad Poetry, XVth – XXth Century* (London, Chatto & Windus, 1957)
Dickens, Charles, *Barnaby Rudge*, ed. Gordon Spence ([1841], Harmondsworth, Penguin, 1986)
—, *Bleak House*, ed. Norman Page ([1852–3], Harmondsworth, Penguin Books, 1985)
—, *Dombey and Son*, ed. Peter Fairclough, intro. by Raymond Williams ([1846–8], Harmondsworth, Penguin, 1970)
—, *Great Expectations*, ed. Charlotte Mitchell, intro. by David Trotter ([1860–61], Harmondsworth, Penguin, 1996)
—, *Hunted Down. A Story, with some account of Thomas Griffiths Wainewright, the Poisoner* (London, John Camden Hotten, [1871?])
—, *The Life and Adventures of Martin Chuzzlewit*, ed. P. N. Furbank ([1843–4], Harmondsworth, Penguin, 1986)
—, *The Life and Adventures of Nicholas Nickleby*, ed. Michael Slater ([1838–9], Harmondsworth, Penguin, 1986)
—, *Little Dorrit*, ed. John Holloway ([1857], Harmondsworth, Penguin, 1985)
—, *The Mystery of Edwin Drood*, ed. Arthur J. Cox, intro. by Angus Wilson ([1870], Harmondsworth, Penguin, 1985)
—, *The Old Curiosity Shop*, ed. Angus Easson, intro. by Malcolm Andrews ([1840–41], Harmondsworth, Penguin, 1985)
—, *Oliver Twist, or, The Parish Boy's Progress*, ed. Philip Horne ([1837–8], Harmondsworth, Penguin, 2002)
—, *Our Mutual Friend*, ed. Adrian Poole ([1865], Harmondsworth, Penguin Books, 1997)
—, *The Posthumous Papers of the Pickwick Club*, ed. Mark Wormald ([1836–7], Harmondsworth, Penguin Books, 1999)
—, *The Dent Uniform Edition of Dickens' Journalism*, ed. Michael Slater and John Drew, vol 1: *Sketches by Boz and Other Early Papers*; vol. 2: *'The Amusements of the People' and Other Papers*, vol. 3: *'Gone Astray' and Other Papers from* Household Words, *1851–59*; vol. 4: *The Uncommercial Traveller and Other Papers* (London, J. M. Dent, 1994–2000)
—, *The Letters of Charles Dickens*, The Pilgrim Edition, eds. Madeline House, Graham Storey, Kathleen Tillotson, et. al. (Oxford, Clarendon, 1969–2002)
—, 'A Detective Police Party', *Household Words*, 1850, pp.409–14; 'Amusements of the People', *Household Words*, 1850, pp.13–15 and 57–60; 'Down with the Tide', *Household Words*, 1853, pp.481–5; 'Lying Awake', *Household Words*, 1852, pp.145–8; 'On Duty with Inspector Field', *Household Words*, 1851, pp.265–70; 'Pet Prisoners', *Household Words*, 1850, pp.97–103; 'Three Detective Anecdotes', *Household Words*, 1850, pp.577–80
[—, and W. H. Wills], 'The Metropolitan Protectives', *Household Words*, 3, 1851, pp.97–105
[Dixon, J. Hepworth], 'The Literature of the Lower Orders', *Daily News*, 26 October 1847, p.3; 2 November, p.3; 9 November, p.2; 25 November, p.3; 29 November, p.3; 16 December, p.3; 27 December, p.3; 30 December, p.3
[Donnelly, Thomas], 'Crime and its Detection', *Dublin Review*, 50, May 1861, pp.150–94

Eden, Emily, *The Semi-Attached Couple* [written c.1830, 1st published 1860] and *The Semi-Detached House* [1859] (London, Virago, 1979)
Eliot, George, 'The Lifted Veil', in *The Lifted Veil, Brother Jacob*, ed. Helen Small ([1859], Oxford, Oxford World's Classics, 1999)
—, *Middlemarch*, ed. W. J. Harvey ([1871–2] Harmondsworth, Penguin Books, 1985)
—, *The George Eliot Letters*, ed. Gordon S. Haight (London, Oxford University Press/Yale University Press, 1954–78)
Ellis, Edward, *Ruth the Betrayer; or, The Female Spy* (London, [John Dicks], 1863)
Englishwoman's Domestic Magazine, '"Sensation" Literature', 1 May 1863, pp.14–20
Era Almanack, 'The Victoria Theatre', 1873, pp.7–12
Fielding, Henry, *An Enquiry into the Causes of the Late Increase of Robbers*, ed. Malvin R. Zirker ([1751], Oxford, Oxford University Press, 1988)
FitzGerald, Edward, *The Letters of Edward FitzGerald*, eds. Alfred McKinley Terhune and Annabelle Burdick Terhune (Princeton, Princeton University Press, 1980)
Fitzgerald, Percy, *Chronicles of Bow Street Police-Office* ... (London, Chapman & Hall, 1888)
Forrester, Andrew, *The Female Detective* (London, Ward & Lock, 1864)
—, *Revelations of a Private Detective* (London, Ward & Lock, 1863)
Fuller, Robert A., *Recollections of a Detective* (London, John Long, 1912)
Funny Folks, 'Precocious Criminals', 5 July 1884, p.212
Fyffe, C. A., 'The Punishment of Infanticide', *Nineteenth Century*, 1, June 1877, pp.583–95
Gaskell, Elizabeth, 'The Crooked Branch', 'A Dark Night's Work', in *The Works of Elizabeth Gaskell*, vol. 4, 'Novellas and Shorter Fiction III', ed. Linda Hughes ([1859], London, Pickering & Chatto, 2006)
—, *Mary Barton: A Tale of Manchester Life*, ed. Stephen Gill ([1848], Harmondsworth, Penguin, 1970)
Godwin, William, *The Adventure of Caleb Williams; Or, Things as They Are* ([1794], rev. edn, London, Richard Bentley, 1849)
Grant, James, *Sketches in London* (London, W. S. Orr, 1838)
Greenwood, James, *The Wilds of London* (London, Chatto & Windus, 1874)
Guy, William A., 'On the Executions for Murder that have Taken Place in England and Wales During the Last Seventy Years', *Journal of the Statistical Society of London*, 38, 1875, pp.463–86
Harwood, John, *Miss Jane, the Bishop's Daughter* (London, Richard Bentley, 1867)
Hawkins, Henry, *The Reminiscences of Sir Henry Hawkins, Baron Brampton*, ed. Richard Harris (London, Edward Arnold, 1904)
[Hayward, William Stephens], *The Experiences of a Lady Detective* (London, Charles Henry Clarke, 1884)
—, *Revelations of a Lady Detective* (London, George Vickers, 1864)
Hazlitt, William, 'The Fight', in *William Hazlitt, Esssayist and Critic: Selections from his Writings*, ed. Alexander Ireland ([1822], London, Frederick Warne, 1889)
—, *The Selected Writings of William Hazlitt*, ed. Duncan Wu; vol. 3: *A View of the English Stage* (London, Pickering & Chatto, 1998)
Hibbert, H. G., *A Playgoer's Memories* (London, Grant Richards, 1920)
[Hindley, Charles], *The Catnach Press: A Collection of the Books and Woodcuts of James Catnach, Late of Seven Dials, Printer, with an account of his life* ... (London, Reeves & Turner, [1869])
—, *Curiosities of Street Literature* ... (London, Reeves & Turner, 1871)
—, *The History of the Catnach Press at Berwick-upon-Tweed ... and Seven Dials* (London, C. Hindley the Younger, 1887)
—, *The Life of J. Catnach, Late of Seven Dials, Ballad Monger* (London, Reeves & Turner, [1878])
Hollingshead, John, *Ragged London in 1861* (London, Smith, Elder, 1861)
Hood, Thomas, 'The Dream of Eugene Aram', in F. Drummond Niblett, *The Henry Irving Dream of Eugene Aram* ([1828], London, Leadenhall Press, [1888])

[Horne, Richard H.], 'Household Crime', *Household Words*, 4, 1851, 277–81
[—, and Charles Dickens], 'Cain in the Fields', *Household Words*, 3, 1851, pp.147–51
Hubbard, Henry W., 'The Poisons of the Day; A New Social Evil', *Macmillan's Magazine*, 46, 1882, pp.238–44
Hunt, Leigh, *Leigh Hunt's Literary Criticism*, eds. Lawrence Huston Houtchens and Carolyn Washburn Houtchens (New York, Columbia University Press, 1956)
Jerome, Jerome K., *On the Stage – and Off: The Brief Career of a Would-be Actor* (London, Field & Tuer, 1885)
—, *Stage Land: Curious Habits and Customs of its Inhabitants* (London, Chatto & Windus, 1889)
Johns, B. G., 'The Literature of Seven Dials', *National Review*, 2, December 1883, pp.478–92
Kent, Charles, *Charles Dickens as a Reader* (London, Chapman & Hall, 1872)
Kilgarriff, Michael, ed., *The Golden Age of Melodrama: Twelve 19th Century Melodramas* (London, Wolfe, 1974)
Lancet, 'Coroners and Magistrates', 17 May 1856, pp.549–50; 'Inquests and Medical Trials. Infants Found Dead in Bed', 24 January 1855, p.103; 'Mrs Wood and Miss Braddon', 18 April 1863, pp.99–103
Lansdowne, Andrew, *A Life's Reminiscences of Scotland Yard* (London, Leadenhall Press, [1890])
Lawrence, W. J., 'Sensation Scenes', *Gentleman's Magazine*, 261, October 1886, pp.400–405
Le Fanu, J. Sheridan, *The Evil Guest* ([1851], London, Downey & Co., [?1895])
—, *A Lost Name* (New York, Arno Press, 1977; facsimile edn of London, Richard Bentley, 1868)
—, 'The Murdered Cousin', *Ghost Stories and Tales of Mystery* ([1838], Dublin, James McGlashan, 1851)
—, *Uncle Silas: A Tale of Bartram-Haugh*, ed. Victor Sage ([1864], Harmondsworth, Penguin, 2000)
London Review, 'The Last Sensaton Novel', 5, 1862, pp.481–2
McGovan, James [pseud. William Crawford Honeyman], *Solved Mysteries: or, Revelations of a City Detective* (2nd edn, Edinburgh, John Menzies, 1888)
Mackenzie, Compton, *My Life and Times, Octave One: 1883–1891* (London, Chatto & Windus, 1963)
McLevy, James, *The Casebook of a Victorian Detective* (Edinburgh, Canongate, 1975)
—, *The Edinburgh Detective* (Edinburgh, Mercat, 2001)
—, *McLevy Returns* (Edinburgh, Mercat, 2002)
MacNaghten, Melville L., *Days of My Years* (London, Edward Arnold, 1914)
[Macnish, Robert], 'The Philosophy of Burking. By a Modern Pythagorean', *Fraser's Magazine*, 25, February 1832, pp.52–65
[Maginn, William] 'Another Caw from Rookwood. – Turpin Out Again', *Fraser's Magazine*, 13, 76, April 1836, pp.488–93
Mansel, Henry, 'Sensation Novels', *Quarterly Review*, 113, 1863, pp.481–514
Marriott, John, and Masaie Matsumura, eds., *The Metropolitan Poor: Semifactual Accounts, 1795–1910* (London, Pickering & Chatto, 1999)
'Martel, Charles', [pseud. Thomas Delf], *The Detective's Notebook* (London, Ward & Lock, 1860)
—, *The Diary of an Ex-Detective* (London, Ward & Lock, 1860)
[Martineau, Harriet], 'A Death-Watch Worth Dreading', *Once a Week*, 2, December 1859, pp.18–22
Maurice-Méjan, Count, *Recueil des Causes Célèbres, et des Arrêts qui les ont décidées* (2nd edn, Paris, n.p., 1808–14)
Mayhew, Henry, *London Labour and the London Poor* ([Griffin, Bohn, & Co., 1861], facsimile reprint, New York, Dover Publications, 1968)
Meason, M. Laing, 'The London Police', *Macmillan's Magazine*, 46, July 1882, pp.192–202

[Morley, Henry], 'A Criminal Trial', *Household Words*, 13, June 1856, pp.529–64; 'Poison Sold Here!', *Household Words*, 2, November 1850, pp.155–7

[O'Brien, W.], 'Criminal Returns. Metropolitan Police', *Edinburgh Review*, 96, July 1852, pp.3–33

Observer, 'Medical Testimony. – What is it Worth?', 17 August 1862, p.5

[Oliphant, Mrs Margaret], 'Novels', *Blackwood's Edinburgh Magazine*, 102, 1867, pp.257–80; 'Sensational Novels', *Blackwood's Edinburgh Magazine*, 91, 1862, pp.564–80

Once a Week, 'Plain-Clothes Men', 9, May 1872, pp.479–82

'by one of the Public', *Major and Minor Theatres. A Concise View of the Question, as Regards the Public, the Patentees, and the Profession* … (London, W. Strange, 1832)

[Paget, John], 'The Philosophy of Murder, *Tait's Edinburgh Magazine*, 18, March 1851, pp.171–6

Pall Mall Gazette, 'Fiction, Cheap and Nasty', 21 July 1890, p.3; 'Madame Tussaud's Flitting: An Interview with Mr. Tussaud', 14 July 1884, pp.11–12; 'Some Relics at Madame Tussaud's', 14 August 1886, p.6; 'The Value of Murderers' Relics: A Chat with Mr. J. T. Tussaud', 28 October 1892, p.7

Parliamentary Papers: PP 627, xiii, 407: 'Report from the Select Committee on the Petition of Frederick Young and Others' [Popay police select committee report], 1833

—, PP 178, xiii, 589, 'Report from the Select Committee on Cold Bath Fields Meeting', 1833

Pelham, Camden, *The Chronicles of Crime, or, The New Newgate Calendar*, 2 vols. (London, Reeves & Turner, 1886)

Pirkis, C. L., *The Experiences of Loveday Brooke, Lady Detective* (London, Hutchinson, 1894)

[?Prest, Thomas Peckett], *Jonathan Bradford; or, The Murder at the Road-side Inn. A Romance of Thrilling Interest* (London, E. Lloyd, [1851])

[Prest, Thomas P., ed. for first 20-odd issues], *The London Singer's Magazine: A Collection of All the Most Celebrated and Popular Songs as Sung at the London Theatres* … (London, John Duncombe, [1839?]),

Quarterly Review, [no title: overview of working-class reading], 171, July 1890, pp.150–70

Quincey, Thomas de, On Murder, ed. Robert Morrison (Oxford, Oxford University Press, 2006)

—, 'William Godwin', in *The Collected Writings of Thomas de Quincey*, ed. David Masson (Edinburgh, Adam & Charles Black, 1890)

Reynolds, G. W. M., *The Mysteries of London*, abridged and ed. Trefor Thomas (Keele, Keele University Press, 1996)

Reynolds's Newspaper, 'London Crime and the London Police', 21 July 1889, p.4

Rice, Charles, *The London Theatres in the Eighteen-thirties*, eds. Arthur Colby Sprague and Bertram Shuttleworth (London, Society for Theatre Research, 1950)

Robinson, F. W. 'An East-End Entertainment', *Belgravia*, 9, October 1869, pp.518–23

Rowell, George, ed., *19th-century Plays* (London, Oxford University Press, 1953)

St James's Magazine, 'The Philosophy of Sensation', 5, October 1862, pp.340–46

Sala, George Augustus, 'The Cant of Modern Criticism', *Belgravia*, 4, November 1867, pp.45–55; 'On the "Sensational" in Literature and Art', *Belgravia*, 4, February 1868, pp.449–58; 'Open-Air Entertainments', *Household Words*, 5, 8 May 1852, pp.165–9

—, *Things I have Seen and People I have Known* (London, Cassell & Co., 1894)

Saturday Review, 'Poisoning in England', 1, 1855, pp.134–5

Scott, Walter, *The Journal of Sir Walter Scott*, ed. W. E. K. Anderson (Edinburgh, Canongate, 1998)

—, *The Letters of Sir Walter Scott, 1828–1831*, ed. H. J. C. Grierson (London, Constable, 1936)

Smith, Alexander, 'A Lark's Flight', in *Dreamthorp* (London, Strahan & Co, 1863)

Stead, W. T., 'Government by Journalism', *Contemporary Review*, 49, January–June 1886, 653–74

[Stephen, James Fitzjames], 'The Criminal Law and the Detection of Crime', *Cornhill*, 2, December 1860, pp.697–708; 'Detectives in Fiction and Real Life', *Saturday Review*, 11 June 1864, xvii, 712ff.

[Stephen, Leslie], 'A Cynic', 'The Decay of Murder', *Cornhill Magazine*, 20, December 1869, pp.722–33

Stevenson, Robert Louis, 'The Body Snatcher', in *The Complete Short Stories: Centenary Edition*, ed. Ian Bell ([1884], Edinburgh, Mainstream, 1993)

—, *The Strange Case of Dr Jekyll and Mr Hyde, and Other Stories*, ed., Jenni Calder ([1886] Harmondsworth, Penguin, 1979)

—, *The Letters of Robert Louis Stevenson*, eds. Bradford A. Booth and Ernest Mehew (New Haven, Yale University Press, 1995)

'A Student at Law', *The Fourth Estate: or, The Moral Influence of the Press* (London, Ridgway, 1839)

Taylor, Alfred S., 'Lectures on Medical Jurisprudence', *London Medical Gazette*, Lecture 12, pp.45–52; Lecture 13, pp.265–71; Lecture 14, pp.661–9, n.s., IV, 1847

—, *Poisoning by Strychnia, with Comments on the Medical Evidence Given at the Trial of William Palmer* ... (London, Longman, Brown, Green, Longmans, & Roberts, 1856)

Thackeray, William Makepeace, 'From a Club Arm-Chair', in the *Calcutta Star*, 7 May 1845, reprinted in Henry Summerfield, 'Letters from a Club Arm-Chair: William Makepeace Thackeray', *Nineteenth-century Fiction*, 18, December 1963, pp.205–33; 'Solitude in September', *National Standard of Literature, Science, Music, Theatricals and the Fine Arts*, 14 September 1833, II, 37, pp.158–9; 'Half-a-crown's Worth of Cheap Knowledge', *Fraser's Magazine*, 17, 99, March 1838, pp.279–90

[—], *Mr. Thackeray's Writings in 'The National Standard' and 'Constitutional'* (London, W. T. Spencer, 1899)

[— and James Churchill], 'High-ways and Low-ways, or, Ainsworth's Dictionary, with Notes by Turpin', *Fraser's Magazine*, 9, 54, June 1834, pp.724–38

Time, 'The Metropolitan Police', 15, 24, December 1886, pp.650–64

'Trim', ed., *The Original, Complete, and Only Authentic Story of 'Old Wild's'* ... (London, G. Vickers, 1888)

Mme Tussaud's catalogues:

—, *Biographical and Descriptive Sketches of the Whole Length Composition Figures, and other Works of Art, Forming the Unrivalled Exhibition of Madame Tussaud* ... and similar catalogues in the British Library, from 1822, 1823, 1835, 1847, 1852, 1869, 1873, 1875; and 1905 catalogue, probably a reprint of the 1892 catalogue written by G. A. Sala

—, *A Visit to Madame Tussaud's* (London, J. E. Hawkins & Co., [n.d.])

[Ward, John], 'Report from the Select Committee on Metropolis Police Offices ...', *Edinburgh Review*, 66, January 1838, pp.358–95

Warren, Charles, 'The Police of the Metropolis', *Murray's Magazine*, 4, 23, November 1888, pp.577–94

'Waters, Thomas' [William Russell], *Recollections of a Policeman* (New York, Cornish, Lamport, 1853)

Waugh, Revd Benjamin, 'Cruelty to Children', *Good Words*, 29, December 1888, pp.818–22; 'Child-Life Insurance', *Contemporary Review*, 58, July–December 1890, 40–63

[Wills, W. H.], 'The Modern Science of Thief-taking', *Household Words*, 1, 1850

Wills, William, 'Essay on the Rationale of Circumstantial Evidence', *Analyst*, 7 June 1837, pp.19–35

Wood, Mrs Henry, *Mrs Halliburton's Troubles* ([1862], London, Richard Bentley, 1888)

—, *St Martin's Eve* (London, Tinsley Brothers, 1866)

[—], 'St Martin's Eve', *New Monthly Magazine*, 99, 1853, pp.327–42

Secondary sources

Allan, Janice M., 'A Lock without a Key: Language and Detection in Collins's *The Law and the Lady*', *Clues: A Journal of Detection*, 25, 1, 2006, pp.45–57

Allen, C. J. W., *The Law of Evidence in Victorian England* (Cambridge, Cambridge University Press, 1997)

Allen, Emily, *Theater Figures: The Production of the Nineteenth-century British Novel* (Columbus, Ohio State University Press, 2003)

Altick, Richard D., *Evil Encounters: Two Victorian Sensations* (London, John Murray, 1987)

—, *The Presence of the Present: Topics of the Day in the Victorian Novel* (Columbus, OH, Ohio State University Press, 1991)

—, *Victorian Studies in Scarlet* (London, J. M. Dent & Sons, 1972)

Anderson, Patricia, *The Printed Image and the Transformation of Popular Culture, 1790–1860* (Oxford, Clarendon Press, 1991)

Andrews, Malcolm, *Charles Dickens and His Performing Selves: Dickens and the Public Readings* (Oxford, Oxford University Press, 2006)

Arnot, Margaret L., 'Gender in focus: infanticide in England, 1840–1880', PhD thesis, University of Essex, 1994

Ascoli, David, *The Queen's Peace: The Origin and Development of the Metropolitan Police, 1829–1979* (London, Hamish Hamilton, 1979)

Ashley, Robert P., 'Wilkie Collins and the Detective Story', *Nineteenth-century Fiction*, 6, 1, 1951, pp.47–60

Aydelotte, William O., 'The Detective Story as a Historical Source', in *The Mystery Writer's Art*, ed. Francis Nevins (Bowling Green, OH, Ohio University Press, 1970)

Babington, Anthony, *A House in Bow Street: Crime and the Magistracy, London, 1740–1881* (London, Macdonald, 1969)

Bailey, Victor, ed., *Policing and Punishment in Nineteenth-century Britain* (London, Croom Helm, 1981)

Bars, Jennifer Ann, 'Defining Murder in Victorian London: An Analysis of Cases 1862–1892' (D.Phil, University of Oxford, 1994)

Bartrip, Peter '"A Pennurth of Arsenic for Rat Poison": The Arsenic Act, 1851, and the Prevention of Secret Poisoning', *Medical History*, 36, 1992, pp.53–69

Bedell, Jeanne F., 'Amateur and Professional Detectives in the Fiction of Mary Elizabeth Braddon', *Clues: A Journal of Detection*, 4, 1983, pp.19–34,

Begg, Paul, and Keith Skinner, *The Scotland Yard Files: 150 Years of the CID* (London, Headline, 1992)

Begg, Paul, Martin Fido and Keith Skinner, *The Jack the Ripper A to Z* (London, Headline, 1991)

Behlmer, George, 'Deadly Motherhood: Infanticide and Medical Opinion in Mid-Victorian Britain', *Journal of the History of Medicine and Allied Science*, October 1979, pp.403–27

—, 'Victorian Medicine, Moral Panic, and the Signs of Death', *Journal of British Studies*, 42, 2, 2003, pp.206–35

Benjamin, Walter, 'Critique of Violence', in *Reflections: Essays, Aphorisms, Autobiographical Writings*, ed. Peter Demetz, trs. Edmund Jephcott (NY, Harcourt, Brace, Jovanovich, 1978)

—, 'The Paris of the Second Empire', *Walter Benjamin: Selected Writings*, ed. Michael W. Jennings and Howard Eiland, trs. Edmund Jephcott et. al (Cambridge MA, Belknap, 2003), vol. 4

Berridge, Kate, *Waxing Mythical: The Life and Legend of Mme Tussaud* (London, John Murray, 2006)

Bolton, H. Philip, *Dickens Dramatized* (London, Mansell, 1987)

Booth, Michael R., *English Melodrama* (London, Herbert Jenkins, 1965)

—, *Theatre in the Victorian Age* (Cambridge, Cambridge University Press, 1991)

—, *Victorian Spectacular Theatre, 1850–1910* (Boston, Routledge & Kegan Paul, 1981)

Boyce, George, James Curran and Pauline Wingate, eds., *Newspaper History: From the Seventeenth Century to the Present Day* (London, Constable, 1978)

Bradby, David, Louis James and Bernard Sharratt, eds., *Performance and Politics in Popular Drama: Aspects of Popular Entertainment in Theatre, Film and Television, 1800–1976* (Cambridge, Cambridge University Press, 1980)

Brake, Laurel, Aled Jones and Lionel Madden, eds., *Investigating Victorian Journalism* (Basingstoke, Macmillan, 1990)

Brantlinger, Patrick, *The Reading Lesson: The Threat of Mass Literacy in Nineteenth-Century British Fiction* (Bloomington, IN, Indiana University Press, 1998)

—, 'What is Sensational about the Sensation Novel?', *Nineteenth-century Fiction*, 37, 1, 1982, pp.1–28

Bratton, J. S., *New Readings in Theatre History* (Cambridge, Cambridge University Press, 2003)

—, *The Victorian Popular Ballad* (London, Macmillan, 1975)

—, Jim Cook and Christine Gledhill, eds., *Melodrama: Stage, Picture, Screen* (London, British Film Institute, 1994)

Bredesen, Dagni, 'Conformist Subversion: Ambivalent Agency in *Revelations of a Lady Detective*', *Clues: A Journal of Detection*, 25, 1, 2006, pp.20–32

—, ed., *The First Female Detectives: The Female Detective (1864) and Revelations of a Lady Detective (1864)* (Ann Arbor, MI, Scholars Facsimilies & Reprints, 2010)

Brice, A. W. C. and K. J. Fielding, 'Dickens and the Tooting Disaster', *Victorian Studies*, 12, 2, December 1968, pp.227–44

—, 'On Murder and Detection: New Articles by Dickens', *Dickens Studies*, 5, 1969, pp.45–61

Brooks, Peter, *The Melodramatic Imagination: Balzac, Henry James, Melodrama, and the Mode of Excess* (New Haven, Yale University Press, 1976)

Brown, Lucy, *Victorian News and Newspapers* (Oxford, Clarendon Press, 1985)

Burney, Ian A., *Bodies of Evidence: Medicine and the Politics of the English Inquest, 1830–1926* (Baltimore, MD, Johns Hopkins University Press, 2000)

—, *Poison, Detection, and the Victorian Imagination* (Manchester, Manchester University Press, 2006)

—, 'A Poisoning of No Substance: The Trials of Medico-Legal Proof in Mid-Victorian England', *Journal of British Studies*, 38, 1, 1999 pp.59–92

Campion, David A., '"Policing the Peelers": Parliament, the Public, and the Metropolitan Police, 1829–33' in Matthew Cragoe and Antony Taylor, eds., *London Politics, 1760–1914* (Basingstoke, Palgrave, 2005)

Carlton, William J., 'Dickens in the Jury Box', *Dickensian*, 52, 1956, pp.65–9

Chapman, Pauline, *Madame Tussaud's Chamber of Horrors: Two Hundred Years of Crime* (London, Constable, 1984)

Chisholm, Alexander, Christopher-Michael diGrazi and Dave Yost, *The News from Whitechapel: Jack the Ripper in* The Daily Telegraph (Jefferson, NC, McFarland, 2002)

Clark, Anna K. 'Rape or Seduction? A Controversy over Sexual Violence in the Nineteenth Century', in London Feminist History Group, *The Sexual Dynamics of History: Men's Power, Women's Resistance* (London, Pluto Press, 1983)

Clark, Michael and Catherine Crawford, eds., *Legal Medicine in History* (Cambridge, Cambridge University Press, 1994)

Cobb, G. Belton, *Critical Years at the Yard: The Career of Frederick Williamson of the Detective Department and the C.I.D.* (London, Faber, 1956)

—, *The First Detectives and the Early Career of Richard Mayne, Commissioner of Police* (London, Faber, 1957)

Cockburn, J. S., 'Patterns of Violence in English Society: Homicide in Kent, 1560–1985', *Past and Present*, 130, 1991, pp.70–106

Cohen, Daniel A., 'The Beautiful Female Murder Victim: Literary Genres and Courtship Practices in the Origins of a Cultural Motif, 1590–1850', *Journal of Social History*, 31, 2, 1997, pp.277–306

Coley, Noel G., 'Alfred Swaine Taylor, MD, FRS (1806–1880): forensic toxicologist', *Medical History*, 35, October 1991, pp.409–27

Collins, Philip, ed., *Charles Dickens: The Public Readings* (Oxford, Clarendon Press, 1975)

—, *Dickens and Crime* (London, Macmillan, 1962)

Conley, Carolyn, *The Unwritten Law: Criminal Justice in Victorian Kent* (New York, Oxford University Press, 1991)

Cooper, David D., *The Lesson of the Scaffold* (London, Allen Lane, 1974)

Coville, Gary and Patrick Lucanio, *Jack the Ripper: His Life and Crimes in Popular Entertainment* (Jefferson, NC, McFarland & Co., 1999)

Critchley, T. A., *A History of Police in England and Wales* (London, Constable, 1978)

Curtis, L. Perry, *Jack the Ripper and the London Press* (New Haven, Yale University Press, 2001)

Daly, Nicholas, 'The Many Lives of the Colleen Bawn: Pastoral Suspense', *Journal of Victorian Culture*, 12, 1, 2007, pp.1–25

Danahay, Martin A., and Alex Chisholm, *Jekyll and Hyde Dramatized: The 1887 Richard Mansfield Script and the Evolution of the Story on Stage* (Jefferson, NC, McFarland & Co., 2005)

Davies, James Atterbury, 'John Forster at the Mannings' Execution', *Dickensian*, 67, 1, 1971, pp.12–15

Davis, Jim, 'The Gospel of Rags: Melodrama at the Britannia, 1863–74', *New Theatre Quarterly*, 7, 28, November 1991, pp.369–89

—, and Victor Emeljanow, *Reflecting the Audience: London Theatregoing, 1840–1880* (Hatfield, University of Hertfordshire Press, 2001)

Davis, Tracy C., *The Economics of the British Stage, 1800–1914* (Cambridge, Cambridge University Press, 2000)

Disher, M. Willson, *Blood and Thunder: Mid-Victorian Melodrama and its Origins* (London, Frederick Muller, 1949)

—, *Melodrama: Plots that Thrilled* (London, Rockliff, 1954)

Donajgrodzki, A. P., ed., *Social Control in Nineteenth-century Britain* (London, Croom Helm, 1977)

Dunae, Patrick A., 'Penny Dreadfuls: Late Nineteenth-century Boys' Literature and Crime', *Victorian Studies*, 22, 2, 1979, pp.133–50

Dzirkalis, Anna M., 'Investigating the Female Detective: Gender Paradoxes in Popular British Mystery Fiction, 1864–1930' (Ph.D thesis, Ohio University, 2007)

Elkins, Charles, 'The Voice of the Poor: The Broadside as a Medium of Popular Culture and Dissent in Victorian Britain', *Journal of Popular Culture*, 14, 1980, pp.262–74

Emmerichs, Mary Beth, 'Getting Away with Murder? Homicides and the Coroners in Nineteenth-century London', *Social Science History*, 25, 2001, pp.93–100

Emsley, Clive, *Crime and Society in England, 1750–1900* (Harlow, Longman, 1987)

—, *Crime, Police, and Penal Policy: European Experiences, 1750–1940* (Oxford, Oxford University Press, 2007)

—, *The English Police: A Political and Social History* (2nd edn, Harlow, Longman, 1996)

—, *Hard Men: Violence in England since 1750* (London, Hambledon, 2005)

—, *Policing and its Context, 1750–1870* (Basingstoke, Macmillan, 1983)

—, and Haia Shpayer-Makov, eds., *Police Detectives in History, 1750–1950* (Aldershot, Ashgate, 2006)

—, and Louis A. Knafla, eds., *Crime History and Histories of Crime: Studies in the Historiography of Crime and Criminal Justice in Modern History* (London, Greenwood Press, 1996)

Forbes, Thomas Rogers, *Surgeons at the Bailey: English Forensic Medicine to 1878* (New Haven, Yale University Press, 1985)

Foucault, Michel, *Discipline and Punish: The Birth of the Prison*, trs. Alan Sheridan (London, Allen Lane, 1977)

Foyster, Elizabeth, 'Introduction: Newspaper Reporting of Crime and Justice', *Continuity and Change*, 1, 22, 2007, pp.9–12

Frayling, Christopher, 'The House that Jack Built: Some Stereotypes of the Rapist in the History of Popular Culture', in *Rape: An Historical and Cultural Enquiry*, Sylvana Tomaselli and Roy Porter, eds. (Oxford, Basil Blackwell, 1986)

Frost, Ginger S., *Living in Sin: Cohabiting as Husband and Wife in Nineteenth-century England* (Manchester, Manchester University Press, 2008)

Gatrell, V. A. C., 'Crime, Authority and the Policeman-State', in F. M. L. Thompson, ed., *The Cambridge Social History of Britain, 1750–1950*, vol. 3 (Cambridge, Cambridge University Press, 1990)

—, *The Hanging Tree: Execution and the English People, 1770–1868* (Oxford, Oxford University Press, 1994)

—, Bruce Lenman and Geoffrey Parker, eds., *Crime and the Law: The Social History of Crime in Western Europe since 1500* (London, Europa, 1980)

Gatrell, V. A. C., and T. B. Hadden, 'Criminal Statistics and their Interpretation', in E. A. Wrigley, ed., *Nineteenth-century Society: Essays in the Use of Quantitative Methods for the Study of Social Data* (Cambridge, Cambridge University Press, 1972)

Hampton, Mark, *Visions of the Press in Britain, 1850–1950* (Urbana, IL, University of Chicago Press, 2004)

Harris, Michael, 'Social Diseases? Crime and Medicine in the Victorian Press', in W. F. Bynum, Stephen Lock and Roy Porter, eds., *Medical Journals and Medical Knowledge: Historical Essays* (London, Routledge, 1992)

Harrop, Josephine, *Victorian Portable Theatres* (London, Society for Theatre Research, 1989)

Hartman, Mary S., 'Crime and the Respectable Woman: Towards a Pattern of Middle-class Female Criminality in Nineteenth-century France and England', *Feminist Studies*, 2, 1974, pp.38–56

—, *Victorian Murderesses: A True History of Thirteen Respectable French and English Women Accused of Unspeakable Crimes* (London, Robson, 1977)

Hay, Douglas, and Francis Snyder, eds., *Policing and Prosecution in Britain, 1750–1850* (Oxford, Clarendon Press, 1989)

Hays, Michael, and Anastasia Nikolopoulou, eds., *Melodrama: The Cultural Emergence of a Genre* (New York, St Martin's, 1996)

Hepworth, M., and B. Turner, 'Confession, Guilt and Responsibility', *British Journal of Law and Society*, 6, 1979, pp.219–34

Hewitt, Martin, ed., *Unrespectable Recreations* (Leeds, Leeds Centre for Victorian Studies, 2001)

Higginbotham, Ann R., '"Sin of the Age": Infanticide and Illegitimacy in Victorian London', *Victorian Studies*, 32, 3, 1989, pp.319–37

Hollingsworth, Keith, *The Newgate Novel, 1830–1847: Bulwer, Ainsworth, Dickens, and Thackeray* (Detroit, Wayne State University Press, 1963)

Howard, Diana, 'The Theatres of the County of London, 1850–1950; A Directory and Bibliography of Theatres, Music Halls and Pleasure Gardens' (Ph.D Thesis, Fellowship of the Library Association, 1966)

Hughes, Winifred, *The Maniac in the Cellar: Sensation Novels of the 1860s* (Princeton, Princeton University Press, 1980)

Jackson, Mark, ed., *Infanticide: Historical Perspectives on Child Murder and Concealment, 1550–2000* (Aldershot, Ashgate, 2002)

James, Louis, ed., *Print and the People, 1819–1851* (London, Allen Lane, 1976)

Jann, Rosemary, *The Adventures of Sherlock Holmes: Detecting Social Order* (New York, Twayne, 1995)

Jones, D. J. V., 'The New Police, Crime and People in England and Wales, 1829–1888', *Transactions of the Royal Historical Society*, 5th ser., 33, 1983, pp.151–68

Jones, David, *Crime, Protest, Community and Police in Nineteenth-century Britain* (London, Routledge & Kegan Paul, 1982)

Joyce, Simon, *Capital Offences: Geographies of Class and Crime in Victorian London* (Charlottesville, University of Virginia Press, 2003)

Kalikoff, Beth, *Murder and Moral Decay in Victorian Popular Literature* (Ann Arbor, MI, UMI Research Press, 1986)

Kestner, Joseph A., *Sherlock's Sisters: The British Female Detective, 1864–1913* (Aldershot, Ashgate, 2003)

King, Joseph F., *The Development of Modern Police History in the United Kingdom and the United States*, Criminology Studies, 19 (Lewiston, NY, Edward Mellen Press, 2004)

Klaus, H. Gustav, and Stephen Knight, eds., *The Art of Murder: New Essays on Detective Fiction* (Tübingen, Stauffenburg-Verl., 1998)

Klein, Kathleen Gregory, *The Woman Detective: Gender and Genre* (Urbana, University of Illinois Press, 1988)

Knafla, Louis A., ed., *Crime, Police and the Courts in British History*, Readings from Criminal Justice History, No. 1 (Westport, CT, Meckler, 1990)

Knelman, Judith, *Twisting in the Wind: The Murderess and the English Press* (Toronto, University of Toronto Press, 1998)

Knight, Stephen, *Crime Fiction, 1800–2000: Detection, Death, Diversity* (Basingstoke, Palgrave, 2004)

—, *Form and Ideology in Crime Fiction* (London and Basingstoke, Macmillan, 1980)

Knight, William, *A Major London 'Minor': The Surrey Theatre, 1805–1865* (London, Society for Theatre Research, 1997)

Krueger, Christine L., 'Literary Defences and Medical Prosecutions: Representing Infanticide in Nineteenth-century Britain', *Victorian Studies*, 40, 2, 1997, pp.271–94

Laqueur, Thomas W., 'Crowds, Carnival and the State in English Executions, 1604–1868', in A. L. Beier, David Cannadine and James M. Rosenheim, eds., *The First Modern Society: Essays in English History in Honour of Lawrence Stone* (Cambridge, Cambridge University Press, 1989)

Leask, Nigel, 'Toward a Universal Aesthetic: De Quincey on Murder as Carnival and Tragedy', in John Beer, ed., *Questioning Romanticism* (Baltimore, Johns Hopkins University Press, 1995)

Lee, Alan J., *The Origins of the Popular Press in England, 1855–1914* (London, Croom Helm, 1976)

Lehman, David, *The Perfect Murder: A Study in Detection* (Ann Arbor, University of Michigan Press, 2000)

Linehan, Katherine, ed., *Robert Louis Stevenson: Strange Case of Dr. Jekyll and Mr. Hyde: An Authoritative Text, Backgrounds and Contexts, Performance Adaptations, Criticism* (New York, W. W. Norton, 2003)

Lyman, J. L., 'The Metropolitan Police Act of 1829: An Analysis of Certain Events Influencing the Passage and Character of the Metropolitan Police Act in England', *Journal of Criminal Law, Criminology and Police Science*, 55, 1, 1964, pp.141–54

McAleer, John J., 'Jemmy Catnach – Catchpenny Czar', *South Atlantic Bulletin*, vol 27, 4, 1962, pp.8–9

McCormick, John and Clodagh, and John Phillips, *The Victorian Marionette Theatre* (Iowa City, University of Iowa Press, 2004)

McDonagh, Josephine, *Child Murder and British Culture, 1720–1900* (Cambridge, Cambridge University Press, 2003)

Mack, Robert L., *The Wonderful and Surprising History of Sweeney Todd: The Life and Times of an Urban Legend* (London, Continuum, 2007)

Mangham, Andrew, 'The Detective Fiction of Female Adolescent Violence', *Clues: A Journal of Detection*, 25, 1, 2006, pp.70–77

—, *Violent Women and Sensation Fiction* (Basingstoke, Palgrave, 2007)

—, ed., *Wilkie Collins: Interdisciplinary Essays* (Newcastle, Cambridge Scholars Publishing, 2007)

Mant, A. Keith, 'Science in the Detection of Crime', *Royal Society for the Encouragement of Arts, Manufactures and Commerce Journal*, 141, 1983, pp.549–55

Marshall, Tim, *Murdering to Dissect: Grave-Robbing, Frankenstein and the Anatomy Literature* (Manchester, Manchester University Press, 1995)

Maunder, Andrew, ed., *Varieties of Women's Sensation Fiction: 1855–1890* (London, Pickering & Chatto, 2004)

—, and Grace Moore, eds., *Victorian Crime, Madness and Sensation* (Aldershot, Ashgate, 2004)

Meisel, Martin, *Realizations: Narrative, Pictorial, and Theatrical Arts in Nineteenth-century England* (Princeton, Princeton University Press, 1983)

Moody, Jane, *Illegitimate Theatre in London, 1770–1840* (Cambridge, Cambridge University Press, 2000)

Morris, Virginia, *Double Jeopardy: Women Who Kill in Victorian Fiction* (Lexington, University Press of Kentucky, 1990)

Murch, A. E., *The Development of the Detective Novel* (London, Peter Owen, 1958)

Nead, Lynda, *Victorian Babylon: People, Streets and Images in Nineteenth-Century London* (London, Yale University Press, 2000)

Nelson, Harland S., 'Dickens's *Our Mutual Friend* and Henry Mayhew's *London Labour and the London Poor*', *Nineteenth-century Fiction*, 20, 3, 1965, pp.207–22

Neuburg, Victor, *Popular Literature: A History and a Guide* (Harmondsworth, Penguin Books, 1977)

Newton, H. Chance, *Crime and the Drama, or, Dark Deeds Dramatized* (London, Stanley Paul, 1927)

Nicoll, Allardyce, *A History of Early Nineteenth Century Drama, 1800–1850* (Cambridge, Cambridge University Press, 1930)

—, *A History of Late Nineteenth Century Drama, 1850–1900* (Cambridge, Cambridge University Press, 1946)

Novak, Maximillian E. ' "Appearances of Truth": The Literature of Crime as a Narrative System (1660–1841)', *Yearbook of English Studies*, II, Literature and its Audience, Special Number, 1981, pp.29–48

O'Brien, Ellen L., '"The Most Beautiful Murder": The Transgressive Aesthetics of Murder in Victorian Street Ballads', *Victorian Literature and Culture*, 28, 1, pp.15–37

Ousby, Ian, *Bloodhounds of Heaven: The Detective in English Fiction from Godwin to Doyle* (Cambridge, MA, Harvard University Press, 1976)

Palmer, Stanley H., *Police and Protest in England and Ireland, 1780–1850* (Cambridge, Cambridge University Press, 1988)

Panek, LeRoy Lad, *An Introduction to the Detective Story* (Bowling Green, OH, Bowling Green State University Popular Press, 1987)

Petrow, Stefan, *Policing Morals: The Metropolitan Police and the Home Office, 1870–1914* (Oxford, Clarendon Press, 1994)

Philips, David, *Crime and Authority in Victorian England: The Black Country, 1835–1860* (London, Croom Helm, 1977)

—, and Robert D. Storch, *Policing Provincial England, 1820–1856: The Politics of Reform* (Leicester, Leicester University Press, 1999)

Phillips, Walter C., *Dickens, Reade and Collins: Sensation Novelists* (New York, Columbia University Press, 1919)

Pilbeam, Pamela, *Madame Tussaud and the History of Waxworks* (London, Hambledon & London, 2003)

Pinney, Lady Hester, 'Thomas Hardy and the Birdsmoorgate Murder, 1856', Monographs on the Life, Times and Works of Thomas Hardy, No. 25 (Beaminster, Toucan, 1966)

Pittard, Christopher, '"Cheap, Healthful Literature": The *Strand Magazine*, Fictions of Crime, and Purified Reading Communities', *Victorian Periodicals Review*, 40, 1, 2007, pp.1–23

Priestman, Martin, *Detective Fiction and Literature: The Figure on the Carpet* (Basingstoke, Macmillan, 1990)

Pykett, Lynn, *The 'Improper' Feminine: The Women's Sensation Novel and the New Woman Writing* (London, Routledge, 1992)

—, *The Sensation Novel: From* The Woman in White *to* The Moonstone (Plymouth, Northcote House, 1994)

Radzinowicz, Leon, *Ideology and Crime: A Study of Crime in its Social and Historical Context* (London, Heinemann Educational, 1966)

—, 'The Ratcliffe Murders', *Cambridge Law Journal*, 1956, pp.39–66

Rance, Nicholas, 'Jonathan's Great Knife: Dracula Meets Jack the Ripper', *Victorian Literature and Culture*, 30, 2, 2002, pp.439–53

—, *Wilkie Collins and Other Sensation Novels: Walking the Moral Hospital* (Basingstoke, Macmillan, 1991)

Reiner, Robert, *The Politics of the Police* (3rd edn, Oxford, Oxford University Press, 2000)

Robb, George, 'Circe in Crinoline: Domestic Poisonings in Victorian England', *Journal of Family History*, 22, 2, 1997, pp.176–190

Robinson, Cyril D., 'Ideology as History: A Look at the Way Some English Police Historians Look at the Police', *Police Studies*, 2, 1979, pp.35–49

Rodrick, Anne Baltz, 'Only a Newspaper Metaphor: Crime Reports, Class Conflict, and Social Criticism in Two Victorian Newspapers', *Victorian Periodicals Review*, 29, 1996, pp.1–18

Rose, Lionel, *The Massacre of the Innocents: Infanticide in Britain, 1800–1939* (London, Routledge & Kegan Paul, 1986)

Roughead, William, ed., *Classic Crimes: A Selection from the Works of William Roughead* (New York, New York Review Books, 2000)

Rowbotham, Judith, and Kim Stevenson, eds., *Criminal Conversations: Victorian Crimes, Social Panic and Moral Outrage* (Columbus, Ohio State University Press, 2005)

Rowell, George, *William Terriss and Richard Price: Two Players in an Adelphi Melodrama* (London, Society for Theatre Research, 1987)

Rudé, George, *Criminal and Victim: Crime and Society in Early Nineteenth-Century England* (Oxford, Clarendon Press, 1985)

Rzepka, Charles J., *Detective Fiction* (Cambridge, Polity Press, 2005)

Schwarzbach, F. S., 'Twelve Ways of Looking at a Staffordshire Figurine: An Essay in Cultural Studies', *Victorian Institute Journal*, 29, 2001, pp.7–60

Seleski, Patty, 'Domesticity in the Streets: Eliza Fenning, Public Opinion and the Politics of Private Life', in Tim Harris, ed., *The Politics of the Excluded, c.1500–1850* (Basingstoke, Palgrave, 2001)

Senelick, Laurence, 'The Prestige of Evil: The Murderer as Romantic Hero from Sade to Lacenaire' (Ph.D thesis, Harvard University, 1972)

Shattock, Joanne and Michael Wolff, eds., *The Victorian Periodical Press: Samplings and Soundings* (Leicester, Leicester University Press, 1982)

Sheridan, Paul, *Penny Theatres of Victorian London* (London, Dennis Dobson, 1981)

Shoemaker, Robert Brink, 'The 'Crime Wave' Revisited: Crime, Law Enforcement and Punishment in Britain, 1650–1900', *Historical Journal*, 34, 1991, pp.763–68

Smith, Helen R., *New Light on Sweeney Todd, Thomas Peckett Prest, James Malcolm Rymer and Elizabeth Caroline Grey* (London, Jarndyce, 2002)

Smith, Keith, 'Stumbling Towards Professionalism: A Post-Revisionist Overview of the Establishment of English Policing in the Ninteenth Century', Cardiff Law School Research Papers (Cardiff, Cardiff University, 2007)

Smith, Philip, 'Executing Executions: Aesthetics, Identity, and the Problematic Narratives of Capital Punishment Ritual', *Theory and Society*, 25, 1996, pp.235–61

Smith, Phillip Thurmond, *Policing Victorian London: Political Policing, Public Order, and the London Metropolitan Police* (Westport, CT, Greenwood Press, 1985)

Smith, Roger, *Trial by Medicine: Insanity and Responsibility in Victorian Trials* (Edinburgh, Edinburgh University Press, 1981)

Snyder, Robert Lance, 'The Artist as Murderer: De Quincey's Essay "On Murder Considered as One of the Fine Arts" ', in A. S. Plumtree, ed., *Thomas de Quincey: Bicentenary Studies* (Norman, University of Oklahoma Press, 1985)

Speaight, George, *Punch and Judy: A History* (London, Studio Vista, 1970),

Srebnick, Amy Gilman, and René Lévy, eds., *Crime and Culture: An Historical Perspective* (Aldershot, Ashgate, 2005),

Steedman, Carolyn, *Policing the Victorian Community: The Formation of the English Provincial Police from 1856–80* (London, Routledge, 1984)

Storch, Robert D., 'The Policeman as Domestic Missionary: Urban Discipline and Popular Culture in Northern England, 1850–1880', *Journal of Social History*, 9, 4, 1976, pp.481–509

Strahan, Linda, 'There's a Hole in the (Inspector) Bucket: The Victorian Police in Fact and Fiction', *Clues: A Journal of Detection*, 23, 3, 2005, pp.57–62

Styles, John, 'The Emergence of the Police: Explaining Police Reform in Eighteenth and Nineteenth Century England', *British Journal of Criminology*, 27, 1987, pp.15–22

Sucksmith, Harvey Peter, 'The Melodramatic Villain in *Little Dorrit*', *Dickensian*, 71, 1975, pp.76–83

Sullivan, Margo Ann, *Murder and Art: Thomas de Quincey and the Ratcliffe Highway Murders* (New York, Garland, 1987)

Sussex, Lucy, 'Edward Bulwer Lytton and the Development of the English Crime Novel', *Clues: A Journal of Detection*, 26, 1, 2007, pp.8–21

Sutherland, John, *Victorian Fiction: Writers, Publishers, Readers* (Basingstoke, Macmillan, 1995)

—, *Victorian Novelists and Publishers* (Chicago, Chicago University Press, 1976)

Swift, Roger, 'Urban Policing in Early Victorian England, 1835–1886: A Reappraisal', *History*, 73, 1988, pp.211–37

Taylor, David, *Crime, Policing and Punishment in England, 1730–1914* (Basingstoke, Macmillan, 1998)

—, *The New Police in Nineteenth-century England: Crime, Conflict and Control* (Manchester, Manchester University Press, 1997)

Thesing, William B., ed., *Executions and the British Experience from the 17th to the 20th Century: A Collection of Essays* (Jefferson, NC, McFarland, 1990)

Thomas, Ronald R., 'Victorian Detective Fiction and Legitimate Literature: Recent Directions in Criticism', *Victorian Literature and Culture*, 24, 1996, pp.367–79

Tobias, J. J., *Crime and Police in England, 1700–1900* (Dublin, Gill & Macmillan, 1979)

—, *Nineteenth-century Crime: Prevention and Punishment* (Newton Abbot, David & Charles, 1972)

—, *Urban Crime in Victorian England* (2nd edn of *Crime and Industrial Society in the Nineteenth Century*; New York, Schocken, 1972)

Trodd, Anthea, *Domestic Crime in the Victorian Novel* (Basingstoke, Macmillan, 1989)

—, 'The Policeman and the Lady: Significant Encounters in Mid-Victorian Fiction', *Victorian Studies*, 27, 4, 1984, pp.435–60

Tromp, Marlene, Pamela K. Gilbert, and Aeron Haynie, *Beyond Sensation: Mary Elizabeth Braddon in Context* (Albany, State University of New York Press, 2000)

Tyson, Nancy Jane, *Eugene Aram: Literary History and Typology of the Scholar-Criminal* (Hamden, CT, Archon, 1983)

Vicinus, Martha, 'Helpless and Unfriended: Nineteenth-century Domestic Melodrama', *New Literary History*, 13, 1, 1981, pp.127–43

Walkowitz, Judith R., *City of Dreadful Night: Narratives of Sexual Danger in Late-Victorian London* (London, Virago, 1992)

Warwick, Alexandra and Martin Willis, eds., *Jack the Ripper: Media, Culture, History* (Manchester, Manchester University Press, 2007)

Weaver, Michael, 'The New Science of Policing: Crime and the Birmingham Police Force, 1839–1842', *Albion*, 26, 2, 1994, pp.289–308

Whittington-Egan, Richard, *William Roughead's Chronicles of Murder* (Moffat, Lochar, 1991)

Wiener, Martin J., 'Alice Arden to Bill Sikes: Changing Nightmares of Intimate Violence in England, 1558–1869', *Journal of British Studies*, 40, 2, 2001, 184–212

—, 'Judges v. Jurors: Courtroom Tensions in Murder Trials and the Law of Criminal Responsibility in Nineteenth-century England', *Law and History Review*, 17, 3, 1999, 467–506

—, *Men of Blood: Violence, Manliness and Criminal Justice in Victorian England* (Cambridge, Cambridge University Press, 2004)

—, 'Murder and the Modern British Historian', *Albion*, 36, 1, 2004, 1–11

—, *Reconstructing the Criminal: Culture, Law and Policy in England, 1830–1914* (Cambridge, Cambridge University Press, 1990)

Wilson, Patrick, *Murderess: A Study of Women Executed in Britain since 1843* (London, Michael Joseph, 1971)

Wynne, Deborah, *The Sensation Novel and the Victorian Family Magazine* (Basingstoke, Palgrave, 2001)

Zedner, Lucia, *Women, Crime and Custody in Victorian England* (Oxford, Clarendon Press, 1991)

INDEX

Abercromby, Helen, 249–51, 256, 258
Abercromby, Mrs (Wainewright's
  mother-in-law), 249
Aberdeen Evening Express, 398
Aberdeen Journal, 67, 68–9
Aberdeen Weekly, 397, 398–9
Adams, Fanny, 339n, 381–4, 430
Adelphi Theatre, London, 130, 352–3
Affecting Case of Eliza Fenning, The, 194,
  196
Age (journal), 95
Ainsworth, William Harrison: *Jack
  Sheppard*, 111, 114, 117, 127, 208n;
  Rookwood, 108, 110–11, 379
All the Year Round (magazine), 10, 256,
  281, 290, 292, 385
Allsop's (of Liverpool), 271
Almack, the Detective (penny-blood),
  342
Amy Paul (anonymous novel), 118
anatomization: of felons, 41, 55, 62, 68
Anatomy Act (1832), 227
Anderson, Robert, 429, 439, 444
Angel, Isaac, 415–16
Angel, Miriam, 415–16, 418, 421, 430,
  441
Angel, Mrs (Isaac's mother), 416
Annals of Crime, 112
Annual Register, 233
anti-Semitism, 419, 421, 441
appeal of murder (law), 321
Aram, Anna, 100, 101, 106

Aram, Eugene, 42, 99–108, 110, 113,
  117–23, 130, 255
Archer, Mrs (Richard Prince's mother),
  354
Archer, Mrs (Richard Prince's sister),
  353
Archer, Richard *see* Prince, Richard
Ardlamont House, Scotland, 395–6,
  397–9, 402
Argosy (magazine), 281
Arnold, Samuel James: *The Maid and
  the Magpye* (stage show), 196–7, 199
arsenic: detection of, 184–5, 253, 275 &
  n, 325–7, 391; availability and use,
  232–4, 236, 238–42, 275; products
  advertised, 234, 284n; sale restricted
  by law, 245–6; and death of
  L'Angelier, 283–5; in Mary Ann
  Cotton case, 389, 391–2; *see also*
  Taylor, Alfred Swaine
Ashford, Mary, 320–22
Ashford, William, 321
Ashton, Thomas, 84–5, 87n, 88, 115,
  425
Astley's Amphitheatre, London, 31, 111,
  129, 301
Athenaeum (magazine), 119

babies *see* children; infanticide
baby-farms, 217–18
Bailey, Richard, 204 & n
Baker, Frederick, 339n, 381–4

Clarke, Edward, 313–15, 317, 345–6,
349
Clarke, John, 15
class (social): and public interest in
crime, 357; *see also* middle classes;
working classes
Clements (Alton attorney), 381
Clive, Caroline: *Paul Ferroll*, 118, 255,
289, 319n
Cobbett, Richard, 43
Cobbett, William, 43
Coburg Theatre, London (*later* the
Royal Victoria, *then* the Old Vic), 30
& n, 31–2, 42, 115, 137, 199, 322–3
Cold Bath Field riot (1833), 79–81, 140
Cole, Mrs (of Brighton), 307
*Colleen Bawn, The, or, The Collegian's
Wife* (anon. play), 137; *see also*
Boucicault, Dion
Collins, C.J., 269
Collins, Wilkie, 366n, 375, 438;
Armadale, 291, 298, 302–4, 367, 375;
'The Diary of Anne Rodway', 298; *The
Haunted Hotel*, 256; *The Law and the
Lady*, 290, 297; *The Moonstone*, 256,
289, 294n, 304–5, 374–9, 385; *My
Lady's Money*, 438; 'The Poisoned
Meal', 199–200; *Poor Miss Finch*, 291;
'A Terribly Strange Bed', 295; *The
Woman in White*, 132, 181, 200, 232,
289–93, 296–7
Colquhoun, Patrick, 13–14, 42; *The
Police of London*, 14–15
Combe, George, 68
confessions, 237–8
Cook, John, 259–60, 262–3, 265–6, 269,
271
copyright: on novels, 108n
Corder, William: and murder of Maria
Marten, 45–54; body displayed and
anatomized, 55–6; popular literature
and melodramas on, 60–61, 166; and
policing, 77; in Tussaud's Chamber of
Horrors, 173; newspaper reaction to,
187

Corn Laws, 192
Cornhill (magazine), 281
coroners: qualifications, 195
Coroners' Society, 234 corpses: stolen
from cemeteries, 62; *see also*
resurrection men
Cotton, Charles Edward, 388–9
Cotton, Frederick, 388–9
Cotton, Mary Ann, 315, 387–94, 415
Country Life Illustrated, 355
Courtney, Sir William *see* Thom, John
Courvoisier, Benjamin-François:
execution, 172n, 205, 207–9; murders
Lord William Russell, 200–202; trial
and conviction, 202–3; mementoes,
350
Creighton (or Crighton), Mr, 405
crime-writing *see* detective fiction;
sensation-fiction
Cruikshank, Robert, 79, 111
Culley, Police Constable Robert, 79
Cushla Ma Chree (anon. play), 137

Daily Chronicle, 441
Daily News: on cholera at Drouet's, 107;
on renaming London streets, 107; on
execution of Sarah Thomas, 213; on
Palmer and insurance transactions,
269n; on trips to Rugeley, 271; on
Smethurst verdict, 276–8, 289; Le
Gallienne writes on Richard Price in,
355; on wife-murders, 361; crime
reporting, 391; on Hambrough, 397;
on Monson, 399; ignores Lipski case,
419; on Jack the Ripper, 425, 458
Daily Telegraph: price and circulation,
262, 426; questions Smethurst verdict,
276; on Christiana Edmunds, 310; on
Wainwright, 339; campaign against
Mrs Staunton verdict, 348; campaign
against Lipski sentence, 420;
euphemism on rape, 430; on Jack the
Ripper, 440–41, 451; opposes stage
horrors, 446
Dalton, S., 55

INDEX

fingerprinting, 464–5
Fitzball, Edward: *Jonathan Bradford, or,
The Murder at the Roadside Inn,*
125–9, 131
FitzGerald, Edward, 292n, 336n
'Forrester, Andrew': identity, 374n;
writings, 463; 'A Child Found Dead',
374, 377; 'The Judgment of
Conscience', 87n; *Revelations of a
Female Detective,* 298, 300, 367, 374
Forrester, Daniel, 2n, 251
Forster, John, 153, 170–71, 252
Fouché, Joseph, 17 & n, 76
Foxall, Eliza, 247
Foxall, Henry, 247
Foxen, John, 205
France: police in, 17 & n, 75–6
Freeman, Sarah, 226, 237
'Frieake, Teddy', 339–40
Friendly Societies: and burial society
murders, 227–8, 232
Fun (magazine), 355, 436, 448
funerals: of murder victims, 5–6

Gadsdell, Roger, 184, 186, 191, 197
Gaiety Theatre, London, 115
Gale, Sarah, 92–6
Gallery of Illustration, Regent Street,
London, 121
Gallop, Mary, 238
Galton, Francis, 465
Gamblers, The (play), 32 & n, 33–6, 42
garrotting, 332
Garside, William (or James), 84–5, 115
Gaskell, Elizabeth: 'A Dark Night's
Work', 128n; *Mary Barton,* 86–9;
North and South, 304
Gay, William, 92
Geering, Mary Anne, 234n, 236
Gentleman Jack (penny-blood), 59
Gentleman's Magazine, 9, 15, 27
George IV, King (*formerly* Prince
Regent), 45
Gilbert, (Sir) William Schwenck, 339n;
Ruddigore (with Sullivan), 122n

Gillette, William: *Secret Service* (play),
351; *Sherlock Holmes* (play), 350–51,
462
Gill's Hill, Hertfordshire, 20–21, 25–6,
35–6
Gipsey of Edgware, The (play), 44
Glasgow Herald (newspaper), 283, 286,
336, 397
Globe (newspaper), 435, 441, 451
Godwin, William: *Caleb Williams,*
102–103, 299
Good, Daniel, 140–47, 158, 166
Good, Molly, 145
Gough, Elizabeth, 362, 366, 369, 376
Gould, R., 205 & n
Graphic, 399
Gray, Mr and Mrs (of Edinburgh),
64–5, 287
Great Exhibition (London, 1851), 306
Green Row Rooms, Portsmouth, 144n
Greenacre, James: Huish writes on, 53;
murders Hannah Brown, 92–6;
popular accounts of, 94–7, 166, 288;
executed, 98
Greenhow (lawyer), 390
Griffin, Gerald: *The Collegians,* 136–7,
139
Grossmith, George: *The Real Case of
Hyde and Seekyll,* 425

Haines, J.T.: *Eily O'Connor, or, The
Foster Brothers* (play), 137
Ham, Thomas, 243–4
Hambrough, Cecil, 395–8, 402–3
Hambrough, Major Dudley, 394–7
Hamilton, Sir William, 68
*Hampshire Telegraph and Sussex
Chronicle,* 29, 106, 127
hangmen *see* executioners
Hanley, Ellen ('the Colleen Bawn'),
133–6, 139
Hardie, Keir, 462
Hardy, Thomas, 361; *Tess of the
D'Urbervilles,* 171, 362
Hare, Margaret, 62, 65

Humble, Revd Henry, 226
Hunt, Joseph, 21, 23–7, 29, 37, 40, 44
Hunt, Leigh, 36, 106
Hyatt, Revd Charles, 52

Illustrated Life and Career of William Palmer of Rugeley, The, 264
Illustrated London News, 147, 161, 234, 447
Illustrated Police News, 341–2, 384, 390–91, 435
Illustrated Times, 262 & n, 263
Imperial Insurance Company, 249
infanticide, 223–32; *see also* burial societies; children
Ipswich Journal, 36, 124, 154–5
Ireland: constables in, 15n
Irving, (Sir) Henry, 99, 121–2, 257, 351, 385, 413, 454

Jack the Ripper: press coverage, 339, 427–8, 430–32, 435–7, 440–52; notoriety, 415; unknown identity and suspects, 424–5, 441–2, 446–7, 451, 465–6; victims, 425–6, 431, 439, 450; police handling, 429, 437–8, 442–4, 448–50; bodies mutilated, 430–33, 436, 440, 448, 450–51; in foreign languages, 442n; in theatre, 442, 460–62; bloodhounds employed, 443–5; Vigilance Committees established, 447–8; fiction based on, 452–6, 463; waxworks of victims, 452; ballads and songs on, 456–9; dogs and racehorses named for, 459; mementoes, 460; legacy, 462, 464–6; and later knife-crimes, 464
Jack the Ripper at Work Again (ballad compilation), 458
Jackson, Harry, 465
Jackson's Oxford Journal, 239
James, Henry, 283
Jefferies, Elizabeth, 209–11
Jermy, Isaac (*formerly* Preston), 149–51
Jermy, Thomas, 150–51

Jerningham (in Monson case), 395, 397
Jerome, Jerome K., 198n, 380n
Jerrold, Blanchard, 48n
Jerrold, Douglas, 48n, 125; *Vidocq! the French Police Spy* (play), 15; *Wives by Advertisement*, 48
Jewell, Margaret, 2–3
Jews: suspected of Jack the Ripper murders, 441–2; *see also* anti-Semitism
John Bull (journal), 97, 118, 222, 239, 316, 330
Jones, Hannah Maria: *The Gamblers; or, The Treacherous Friends*, 42, 43n
Jones, Jane (of Daniel Good case), 141–3, 145–6
Jones, Jane (of Robert Blake case), 357–8
Joseph, Samuel, 68
Journal of Medical Science, 268
Joy, Revd F.W., 120n
Joyce, Eliza, 244–5

Kaleidoscope (magazine), 56
Kean, Charles, 130
Kean, Edward, 205
Kelly, Mary Jane (or Mary Anne), 450–52, 460, 462
Kent, Constance: and killing of half-brother Francis, 44, 258n, 306, 364–71, 377, 425; confesses, 371–2, 374n; fiction based on, 373–6, 378
Kent, Francis Savile, 362–3, 370
Kent, Mary (*née* Pratt), 363–4, 366n, 367–8
Kent, Samuel Savile, 306, 363–5, 367–9, 372
King, Jessie, 398
King, Mrs Percy *see* Lane, Harriet
Kippis, Andrew, 102
Kirby's Wonderful Magazine, 124
Kirk, Wilkison, 332
Knaresborough, Yorkshire, 99–101, 117
Knight, Bernard, 184n
Knox, Dr Robert, 62–5, 69, 71, 287

INDEX

Smith, G.E., 389–90
Smith, Henry, 253, 255–7
Smith, John (executioner), 272
Smith, Madeleine: Emma Robinson
  writes on, 180n; trial, 195, 283–5; as
  middle-class criminal, 258n, 281–2;
  affair with L'Angelier, 281–3, 285–6;
  subscription raised, 286–7; later life
  and marriages, 287n; in literature,
  288, 318, 373
Smith, O. (actor), 280
Smith, William, MP, 12, 17
Snow, John, 226n
Southey, Robert, 17
Southgate, Hannah, 243–4, 315
Southgate, John, 243
souvenirs and relics: of executed
  murderers and victims, 55–6, 67–8,
  173, 350
Spectator (magazine), 375, 422
spiritualism, 350
Sporting Gazette, 347
Sporting Times, 272, 432, 458
Spring Heel'd Jack, 435 & n
Springthorpe, J., 172
'Spy' see Ward, Leslie
Staffordshire Advertiser, 268
Stamford Mercury, 170n
Standard Theatre, Shoreditch, 199
Stanfield, Clarkson, 129–30
Stanfield Hall estate, Norfolk, 149–51
Stapleton, J.W.: The Great Crime of
  1860, 374
Star (London newspaper), 422–3,
  426–7, 432–3, 440–41
Staunton, Elizabeth (née Rhodes), 343,
  345–6, 348–9
Staunton, Harriet (née Richardson),
  343–50
Staunton, Louis, 343–9, 368
Staunton, Patrick, 343–6, 348–9
Stead, William Thomas, 419 & n, 420–21
Stephen, Sir James Fitzjames, 223, 224n,
  418 & n, 419–20; 'Detectives in
  Fiction and Real Life', 296

Stevens, Mr (John Cook's stepfather),
  259–60, 266
Stevenson, Robert Louis, 73–4, 336; The
  Strange Case of Dr Jekyll and Mr Hyde,
  423–5, 427, 435, 445–6, 455
Stockport Advertiser, 85
Stoker, Bram: Dracula, 454–5
Stokes, Alfred, 337, 339, 341
Stone, Elizabeth: William Langshawe,
  the Cotton Lord, 86
Story of Minie L'Angelier (anon.),
  288–9
Stride, Elizabeth, 426, 439, 441, 458
strychnine, 259–60, 264–8, 270
Sue, Eugène: The Mysteries of Paris, 59,
  153
Sullivan, (Sir) Arthur, 339; see also
  Gilbert, (Sir) William Schwenck
Sullivan, Steven, 133–5
Sullivan, T.R., 424
Sunday Times, 47
Surrey Theatre, London, 15, 30–31,
  33–5, 42, 107, 114, 125, 138
Surtees, Robert Smith, 75; Ask Mamma,
  255; Plain or Ringlets?, 181
Sutherland, Harriet Leveson-Gower,
  Duchess of, 158
Sweeney, Edward ('Scott'), 396–7, 400
Sweeney Todd (penny-blood), 128
Swinburne, Algernon Charles, 336n
Sylvester Sound, the Somnambulist
  (penny-blood), 270

Tabram, Martha, 415, 424–6, 429–30
Tait's Edinburgh Magazine, 276
Talfourd, Thomas Noon, 252, 255
Tanner, Inspector (of Stepney), 334
Tawell, John, 329–32
Taylor, Alfred Swaine: on Palmer,
  160–61; declines to analyze
  O'Connor's viscera, 163; testifies in
  arsenic poisoning cases, 232–3 & n,
  241–3, 275n, 276, 278; on Bulwer-
  Lytton's Lucretia, 254; appearance,
  261, 383; on Cook's strychnine

553